READER'S DIGEST
Treasury of
Wit & Humor

READER'S DIGEST

Treasury of

Wit & Humor

Selected by the Editors of the Reader's Digest

THE READER'S DIGEST ASSOCIATION, INC.

Pleasantville, N. Y.

First Edition

PRINTED IN THE UNITED STATES OF AMERICA

By Way of Introduction . . .

The human race has one really effective weapon and that is laughter. —Mark Twain

A GENTLEMAN never heard a story before (Austin O'Malley) . . . *On the other hand:* When someone says, "Stop me if you've heard this one," we are always tempted to ask, "How?" (Olin Miller) . . . Mixed company is what you are in when you think of a story you can't tell there (Richard Armour in *The American Legion Magazine*) . . . When a fellow says, "Well, to make a long story short," it's too late (Don Herold) . . . If you can't remember them, don't dismember them (Anthony J. Pettito)

"WELL, what *is* funny?" Ed Wynn's straight man used to ask (in a famous vaudeville skit) after vainly trying for a laugh on his own. "Darned if I know," Wynn would say. Then, as the comedian himself describes it, "I walk over and take his new straw hat off his head and say admiringly, 'Nice hat, do you like it?' and he says, 'Certainly, very expensive.' And while I'm talking to him I take a knife out of my pocket and slowly cut huge slices off the hat until there is nothing left but the crown, which I gravely put back on his head.

" 'Do you think that's funny?' I ask him, and he shouts indignantly, 'No!' Then I point to the audience which greeted each slice with a roar of laughter and say, 'Look! *They* think it's funny.' "

—J. P. McEvoy

IN A LECTURE to a group of native officers during the Korean War, Lt. Gen. Bruce C. Clarke took two or three minutes to tell his favorite joke. His interpreter then translated the joke, using only seven or eight words. Everyone immediately burst into hearty laughter, however, and General Clarke later asked the interpreter how he had been able to retell such a long joke so quickly.

"Well, sir," he replied, "I didn't think everyone would get the point, so I said, 'The General has just told a joke. Everyone will please laugh.' "

—Lt. Robert H. Selleck

A GUEST at a gag writers' luncheon was startled when one writer yelled "60," and everybody snickered. Another cried "42," and a ripple of laughter ensued. Then a third cried "94"—and a stout party in the corner practically went into convulsions.

"What on earth is all this laughing at numbers?" the visitor asked.

"These jokesters," explained the host, "know every gag in the world. They've given a number to each joke. When anybody calls out a number, they all laugh just as hard as if he had told the actual story."

"But what about that fat fellow who is still choking with laughter because somebody yelled '94'?" asked the guest.

"Oh, him," came the answer. "I guess he never heard that gag before."

—Bennett Cerf

SEVERAL OF US were doing some shopping at a crossroads store in New Hampshire when the elderly storekeeper made a quaint remark which struck us as funny. It was immediately suggested that I write it up for The Reader's Digest.

I was the last one out of the store and, as I left, the old fellow put his hand on my arm. "Miss, don't waste your postage on that," he said. "I been usin' it fer years—and I got it out of the Digest in the fust place!"

—Montanye Perry

Has Anybody Heard Me Lately?

By Corey Ford

YOU DON'T have to say, "Stop me if you've heard this one"—your friends will do it every time. At least *I* never can finish a story, because just as I get to the point somebody upsets a glass, or the doorbell rings, or my wife smells smoke. I'm forever halting an anecdote until the grandfather clock stops striking, and by the time I can make myself heard again, the person I'm talking to has started talking to me.

There must be something about my voice that always starts the baby crying. Either that, or Junior begins to tug at his father's sleeve in the middle of my story, and they engage in an intent whispered conversation in which I catch the insistent phrase: "But I got to go *now!*" As often as not the host has to get up and let the cat out, or the dog in, or else there is a screech of brakes outside and everyone glances expectantly toward the window, waiting for the crash. (This only happens in the case of a story I *want* people to hear. If I try telling a friend a slightly off-color story, the room goes deathly quiet and everyone listens intently while I flounder around trying to think of some way to clean up the tag line.)

Everything I say seems to remind people of something *they* want to say. Last night at dinner I started to tell about the funniest thing that happened the time we drove to Maine, and the lady across the table interrupted to say that she was in Maine last summer and did we stop at Ogunquit? There's a little place in Ogunquit where you can get the best lobsters. This reminded the lady on my right of a place in Boston where you can get the best fried clams, and the lady on my left said that speaking of clams you can get the best shore dinner at a place on Long Island, and along about this time the hostess said that if everybody was through we might as well move into the living room.

Women are born story-stoppers. For example, there's the well-meaning interrupter who kills a point with kindness. She's always breaking in on what I'm saying to ask if I'm *sure* I'm comfortable in that chair, and how about an ash tray, and wouldn't I like my drink sweetened? Her eye keeps roving around the room and just as I reach the climax of my narrative, her face lights up and she waves to some guests who have just arrived. "Well, if it isn't Mr. and Mrs. Alvord; you folks are just in time; George has been telling me the *funniest* thing that happened the time he drove to Maine, and I know you'll want to hear it, too. Start again, George."

Then there is the nervous interrupter who keeps hearing Things. She is sure that somebody is moving around upstairs, or she can hear water running, and she stops your best story in its tracks by holding up her hand suddenly and saying in a melodramatic whisper: "Listen!"

A practiced point-killer doesn't even have to speak in order to stop a story. He tiptoes into the room when you are halfway through and joins the group with an apologetic smile and a silent wave of his hand for you to go right ahead. You wait until his chair has stopped creaking, and start the story over. He listens with rapt interest, never taking his eyes from your face as he fishes out his pipe, raps it against the ash tray and blows through it a couple of times with an unpleasant gargling sound. Needless to say, your story is ruined.

Then there is the story-stopper who corrects you as you go along. Take, for instance, the funniest thing that happened the time we drove to Maine. My wife is very fond of this story, and she's always after me to tell it when we're invited out. "Tell about the time we drove to Maine, George," she insists, "and everybody listen, because you'll die laughing."

"Well," I begin, "last year we were driving up to Maine—"

"It wasn't last year, George," my wife says. "It was the year before, because last summer we spent at the Cape."

"So, anyway," I begin again, "we were trying to get to some place called Simsbury—"

"Sudbury," my wife interrupts. "I'm positive, because we were going to visit the Twitchells."

"I used to know some people named Twitchell," the host remarks, "but they lived in Pennsylvania."

"It was New Jersey," his wife corrects him, "and their name was Twigger."

"Go on with your story, George," my wife urges. "Don't keep stopping all the time."

"So it seems we must have gotten off on the wrong road," I continue, "and we knocked on the door of this farmhouse—"

"We didn't exactly knock," my wife points out. "We blew the horn, because the farmer was working in the yard. Don't you remember, George? That's the whole point of the story."

"Well, as I was saying—"

I am suddenly conscious of the fact that nobody is looking at me; they're all gazing toward the door. The maid nods her head and the hostess rises with alacrity. "Dinner's ready," she announces. "I bet you're all starved."

You Can't Win

A HUSBAND said to his wife, "Have you heard the story about the dirty window?"

"No," she replied.

"Well," he said, "you couldn't see through it anyway."

His wife asked a friend later, "Have you heard the story about the window you couldn't see through?"

"No," said her friend.

"Oh, well," said the wife, "it's too dirty to tell anyway."

—Chuck Acree, MBS

FOR 25 YEARS Morris, a cutter in an East Side garment factory, had never been late for work. One morning, however, instead of checking in at nine, he arrived at ten. His face was crisscrossed with court plaster and his right arm was in a sling. When Mr. Schlepperman, his boss, demanded to know why he was late, Morris explained, "I leaned out a window after breakfast and fell three stories."

Mr. Schlepperman shrugged. "That takes an *hour?"* —Billy Rose

OUR SMALL daughter Poppy was having an argument with Freddy, the eight-year-old son of a neighbor, over which one of the two was going to ride her new bicycle. Said Poppy, by way of terminating the argument, "I tell you what we're going to do. You have it today and I have it tomorrow."

"Okay," Freddy said happily, preparing to take off on the bike.

"Wait!" said Poppy. "Now we're playing it's tomorrow."

—Joseph Wechsberg

A HARASSED HUSBAND never seemed to be able to please his complaining wife. On their wedding anniversary she bought him two ties, one green, the other yellow. He thanked her profusely, but she sighed. "Well, I guess you don't like my gift."

"But, darling, I do. I'm mad about them. I'll prove it to you." He removed the tie he was wearing, put on the yellow tie and beamed: "There." His wife looked at him sadly and sighed: "Don't like green, eh?" —Leonard Lyons

I WAS ON the bus that services a rural area in the Blue Ridge Mountains when a woman got on and handed the driver her ticket.

"This ticket's no good," he said. "It's *from,* not *to.*"

"What difference does it make whether I'm goin' or comin'?" the woman protested. "The fare's the same, ain't it?"

"Yessum, the fare's the same, but I can't take your ticket *from* when you're goin' *to,*" he insisted.

The woman looked exasperated for a second, and then flashed him a triumphant smile. "Well, suppose I ride backward," she said. "Will that satisfy you?"

The driver, with an air of defeat, accepted the ticket.

—Mrs. M. S. Doyle

A TEACHER, making a trip with a group of children, stopped for lunch at a restaurant where one youngster noticed a slot machine and asked what it was. The teacher launched into a lecture on the evils of gambling. To emphasize the futility of trying to get something for nothing, she said she'd show them what she meant. She marched up to the machine, put in a nickel, pulled the handle and hit the jackpot. —Herman M. Patton

Gambler's Odds

IT'S CUSTOMARY for the winner of our office World Series pool to buy us all a round of drinks. But one fall the only girl in the office, a shapely young thing, was the winner. She protested that the pool was so small she wouldn't have any money left for herself after the drinks and suggested instead that she surprise us the next day by bringing in a treat, something we'd all enjoy.

The next morning she came in wearing the surprise—a form-fitting sweater she'd bought with her winnings. —L. Simonaitis

FOR SOME TIME I had dated two Air Force sergeants, Mike and George. Then, for no apparent reason, Mike suddenly dropped me. Later I ran into him in the service club and asked what had happened.

"Oh," he replied, "I can't call you any more or even dance with you. You see, I lost you to George in a poker game."

—Mrs. D. D. McNeese

IN DENVER a government tax expert received a call from a woman who asked, "How much tax is due on a $75,000 income?" About $41,180, not counting deductions, she was told. "Well, what about $150,000?" she asked. The bill jumped to $101,980.

"Thanks for your help," said the caller. "I'm just deciding whether to buy one or two tickets on the Irish Sweepstakes." —AP

At a Florida casino a husband gave his wife, who had never played roulette, $200 to gamble. When she asked what number she should play, a friend suggested she choose her age number. She placed $100 on 28; the pill rolled around and landed on 32.

The gal promptly fainted. —Neal O'Hara, McNaught Syndicate

Warren Saunders, who played poker on Saturday nights and faithfully attended church each Sunday, inadvertently dropped a poker chip in the collection plate one morning. Hastening to the vestry after the services, he found vestryman Mark Linkers counting out the money.

"Mark," said the troubled contributor, "I guess I put some sort of button in the plate by mistake this morning. See if you can find it, please."

Linkers poked around until he found the chip.

"Oh, thank you," said Saunders. "I'm glad to get it back. It's a sort of keepsake—here's a half dollar instead."

"Oh, no, you don't," snapped the vestryman. "I know your game. That's a blue chip, and it will cost you five dollars."

—*The Wall Street Journal*

Stenographer showing huge electronic machine to co-worker: "The darned thing won the office football pool!"

—Daniel Alain cartoon in *Look*

A Scotsman had just won a new car in a raffle but, far from being elated, he seemed decidedly glum. "What's the matter, Jock?" asked a friend.

"Mon," he answered, " 'tis this other ticket. Why I ever bought it, I canna imagine." —W. N. Mackey in Louisville *Courier-Journal*

Scotch and Wry

SANDY AND MAC were having dinner together when, to Mac's disgust, Sandy calmly helped himself to the larger fish on the platter. "Fine manners ye've got, Sandy," Mac admonished. "If I'd been in your place I'd have taken the smaller fish."

"Well," replied Sandy with his mouth full, "ye've got it!"

—*The Outspan*

ANGUS WAS helping at the accouchement of his wife by holding the kerosene lamp. When the doctor had produced not one but *two* fine babies, Angus disappeared with the lamp.

"Here, come back with the lamp. I think there's another!" called the doctor.

"I will no!" called back Angus. "It's the licht that attracts them!"

—L. R. Ingersoll

A SCOTTISH helper on a western ranch was invited to dinner by his employer. He ate a large piece of apple pie with such relish that his hostess offered him a second helping. "No more, thank you kindly, ma'am," he replied. "I would na wish to become an addict."

—N. B. Miller

WHEN MY grandmother, a delightful Scotswoman, and I were sewing on my wedding dress, I said, "Tell me about your wedding dress, Granny. Did you make it yourself?"

"Aye," she replied, "that I did. Blue taffeta it was—with a bustle and a low-cut neck."

"How nice," I murmured. "Tiny as you are and with your blond hair, you must have looked lovely in blue."

"I didn't," was her surprising reply. "It rained on me wedding day and I wore me old Scotch plaid."

—Beryl T. Yocum

Pardon, Your Slip Is Showing®

FROM THE Lamar, Mo., *Daily Democrat:* "The bride was entrancingly gowned in a sheer, soft blue net gown which fell to the floor as she swept down the aisle."

FROM THE Martinsburg, W. Va., *Journal:* "With 23½ pints, the two ladies were high players in four tables of duplicate bridge."

FROM THE Calcutta *Hindusthan Standard:* "Mr. Khrushchev delivered the speech in Russian in a token manner, reading the first few lies only."

FROM A North Carolina state publicity booklet: "Famous mid-south resorts, including Pinehurst and Southern Pines, where it is said that there are more golf curses per square mile than anywhere else in the world. . . ."

FROM THE Vancouver *Sun:* "During the storm on Saturday, Mrs. Timothy McPherson slipped on the ice and hurt her somewhat."

FROM THE New York *Times:* "Walter P. Reuther said today that the next major bargaining goal of the Automobile Workers Union was a shorter work week with no reduction in say."

FROM A society note in the Warren, Ohio, *Tribune Chronicle:* "The party, which was to have been held on the spacious lawn at the Kroehle home, was hell indoors because of rain. . . ."

FROM THE Tulsa, Okla., *Daily World:* "The author of *Forever Amber,* Kathleen Winsor, has written another book, *Star Money,* that is called a '20th-century Amber,' and is supposed to outsmell the two million copies of the first book."

LEAP-YEAR advice to girls in the San Antonio *News:* "Young men are doing their own choosing these days, and a good way to scare them away, they admit, is to look expectant."

AD IN the Springfield, Mass., *Daily News:* "ARE YOU HANDY? A little pain and papering and you will have a good four-bedroom home."

FROM THE Greensboro, N. C., *Record:* "The slightly built general, with four rows of robbins on his chest, took the witness chair."

FROM THE Los Angeles, Calif., *News:* "Fog and smog rolled over Los Angeles today, closing two airports and slowing snails to a traffic pace."

IN AN Irish newspaper, a dance hall announced a new ventilating system: "Chance of air every seven minutes."

FROM A government report: "This report is made impossible through the cooperative efforts of three agencies in the Department of Agriculture." —Quoted by UP

SOCIETY NOTE in the Athens, Ga., *Banner-Herald:* "The nuptial music was furnished by Mrs. Harris Parham who sang 'The Loviest Night of the Year.' "

Wedding Announcements

USHER passing collection plate at church wedding: "Yes, ma'am, it *is* unusual, but the father of the bride requested it."

—Al Kaufman cartoon in *The Saturday Evening Post*

TWO FRIENDS, one 50 and the other 60, were arguing about the forthcoming marriage of the latter to a young lady in her 20's. "I don't believe in these May-December marriages," disapproved the 50-year-old. "After all, December is going to find in May the freshness and beauty of springtime, but whatever is May going to find in December?"

The bridegroom-to-be replied, "Christmas!"

—*Young Man,* quoted in Ventura County, Calif., *Star-Free Press*

MARION HOWLAND, a postal clerk in Arkansas City, Kan., thought he was doing the young man a favor when he sold him 200 special-issue three-cent stamps in a new conservation series, whooping cranes with their young. However, the customer returned a short time later, thrust the stamps through the window and asked for the regular kind. "These just won't do," he said. "We're sending out wedding invitations and my girl says the cranes look too much like storks!"

—Kansas City *Star*

ONE MALE wedding guest to another as they watch bride and groom leave church: "There, but for some fast thinking on a moonlit lake last July, go I."

—Robert Day cartoon in *This Week Magazine*

A COUPLE wanted to get married in a hurry. The man, a soldier on a 48-hour pass, took his blushing bride to see the vicar. "Impossible," said the latter. "Even a special license would take too long."

The would-be bride and groom exchanged a look of misery, then a smile spread across the soldier's face. "Well," he suggested brightly, "couldn't you say a few words just to tide us over the weekend?" —*Indian Horizon*

PEOPLE seldom think alike—until it comes to buying wedding presents. —*The Wall Street Journal*

MY HUSBAND is the absent-minded kind who has to write notes to himself. Shortly after our wedding I happened to find a list he'd made out just before our honeymoon. There were such items as "take blue suit, white shirt, brown sports coat, have car checked."

The last item read: "Pick up Sally." —Mrs. Sally Bebak

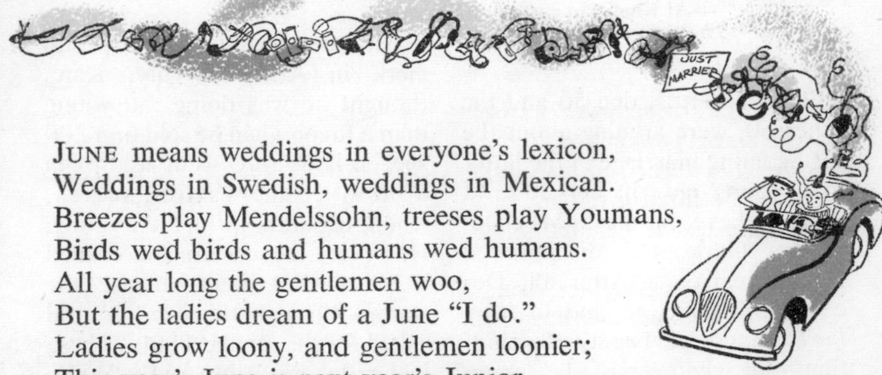

JUNE means weddings in everyone's lexicon,
Weddings in Swedish, weddings in Mexican.
Breezes play Mendelssohn, treeses play Youmans,
Birds wed birds and humans wed humans.
All year long the gentlemen woo,
But the ladies dream of a June "I do."
Ladies grow loony, and gentlemen loonier;
This year's June is next year's Junior.

—Ogden Nash in *Cosmopolitan*

YOUNGSTERS are really getting married early nowadays. Reminds me of a family I know. The son is 17, and he'd been threatening to elope if they didn't okay his marriage to a 16-year-old. So finally they gave in. At the wedding, when they got to the part of the ceremony where the boy repeats after the minister, "With all my worldly goods, I thee endow," the mother turned to the father and whispered, "There goes Junior's bicycle!" —Jack Sterling, CBS

MINISTER to bride at wedding: "Do you, Gladys . . . let me finish . . . Do you, Gladys, take this . . . *Please* let me finish, Gladys . . ."
—Norm Ent cartoon in *True*

ONE YOUNG woman to another during wedding ceremony: "Gosh, I wish *I'd* said that."
—von Riegen cartoon, King Features

LIKE ALL brides she looked heartbreakingly sweet and tremulous. As they turned to march up the aisle she lifted a radiant face to the man beside her and whispered:

"Stand a little straighter, dear."
—"Personal and Otherwise" in *Harper's Magazine*

Now Hear This!

DAN DURYEA advises star-struck young ladies who want to break into show business: "Change your hair style, learn how to walk, buy a sexy wardrobe and before you know it you'll be married, have six kids and forget about all this nonsense." —Gene Sherman in Los Angeles *Times*

I BOUGHT an English-made automobile and after careful computation over a month concluded that I was not getting the phenomenally high mileage so often credited to such cars. So I took it to a local mechanic who, after checking it thoroughly, pronounced it in perfect condition.

"I love the car," I confessed, "but isn't there *something* I can do to increase its mileage?"

"Well, yes," he said. "You can do the same as most foreign-car owners do."

"What's that?" I asked.

"Lie about it."

—Kenneth Britton

THE INSTRUCTOR in a YWCA charm course was urging her students to give their escorts every chance to be gallant.

"Remain seated in the car until he has had time to open the door for you," she said. Then, bowing to reality, she added, "But if he's already in the restaurant and starting to order, don't wait any longer!" —Lynne Davis

ONE Cub Scout to another: "The best way to make a fire with two sticks is to be sure one of them is a match."

—Reamer Keller cartoon, King Features

WILL ROGERS: Don't gamble. Take all your savings and buy some good stock and hold it till it goes up, then sell it. If it don't go up, don't buy it.

CYD CHARISSE, on how to handle men: Treat as any pet. Three meals a day, plenty of affection, a loose leash. Do not disturb while eating.

—Look

SATCHEL PAIGE, former major-league baseball pitcher of indeterminate age, has six rules for staying young:

1. Avoid fried meats which angry up the blood.
2. If your stomach disputes you, lie down and pacify it with cool thoughts.
3. Keep the juices flowing by jangling around gently as you move.
4. Go very light on the vices, such as carrying on in society. The social ramble ain't restful.
5. Avoid running at all times.
6. Don't look back. Something might be gaining on you.

—Collier's

Sports Roundup

ON AN October Sunday, an eastern newspaper made the following listing in its radio schedule: "1:00—Back to God. (If no World Series game.)" *—This Week Magazine*

AT A TRACK in England some years ago a mounted policeman was helping to get the race horses into starting position. At the cry, "They're off!" the policeman's horse broke with the field and the astonished bobby found himself desperately trying to pull in his mount. The best he could do, however, was to slow him down to third place. On the stretch the horse began to fight it out with one of the official entries and, despite the policeman's efforts to pull out of the race, he came in second, a scant neck behind a horse ridden by Freddy Archer, one of England's greatest jockeys. —Dee Eckman in *Collier's*

GLEEFUL PATIENT with foot in traction, to visitor: "The doctor says I'm a natural skier—I have the kind of bones that knit fast."
—Reamer Keller cartoon, Chicago Tribune-New York News Syndicate

IN HIS BOOK, *The Herman Hickman Reader,* Hickman writes: We always had a lot of trouble with Princeton when I was coaching at Yale. One game everything went wrong. Yale would fumble, and Princeton would recover. Princeton would fumble, and Princeton would recover. We would make ten yards on an off-tackle play, then be penalized 15 yards for illegal use of the hands. Nothing that we could do was right. Finally I became so disgusted that I shouted to Jim Ryan, our quarterback, "Go ahead and kick the ball, Jim. They aren't going to give us anything anyway."

The referee heard me and walked over to where I was sitting. "That is going to cost you, Hickman," he said. "Coaching from the sidelines." He took the ball and walked off ten yards.

I jumped up and ran out on the field and said, "Why you dumb so-and-so, you don't even know that coaching from the sidelines is a 15-yard penalty!"

"Listen, Hickman," he said, "for the kind of coaching you're doing, it's only ten yards!" —Published by Simon and Schuster

ON THE ski slope at a New Hampshire winter resort I watched an instructor show a group of novices the proper technique in executing turns. Most of his pupils, attempting to imitate him, failed miserably—their skis spread out and they slid along in a sitting position for a few feet. After one middle-aged woman did this, the instructor lifted her to her feet and with masterly tact remarked, "Very good, madam. Now all you must do is eliminate the middle track." —Clifford C. Cooper, Jr.

AN NBC EXECUTIVE decided to try a little experiment one day. He was watching the fights on NBC television when, as is customary at these affrays, the announcer sternly told him to go to the icebox for that ice-cold bottle of beer. Gulping furiously he managed to stay abreast of the announcer, getting a new bottle every time he was told to. Result: the losing fighter was kayoed in the tenth; the executive was flat on his back at the end of the ninth.

—John Crosby in New York *Herald Tribune*

A TRACK MEET is where a lot of young men, suddenly discovering themselves caught outdoors in their underwear, start running like hell.

—Richard Armour

WHEN LEO DUROCHER was unable to identify the popular song, "Sympathy," on a CBS-TV quiz program, MC Bill Cullen offered clues. "Leo," said Bill, "suppose with the bases loaded the batter for the Giants hits what appears to be a sure triple. The umpire calls it foul by inches. Fifty thousand fans are booing. Now, Leo, what does that ump need starting with the letter 's'?"

"Seein'-eye dog," replied Durocher.

—William E. Woods

Winged Victory. In Upper Darby, Pa., golfer Parker Jerrell missed a 15-foot putt by a hair, then watched a butterfly land on the ball, knock it into the cup.

—*Time*

ONE OF THE questions students entering Ohio State University were asked was to list their places of residence since birth and the number of years spent in each spot. One freshman had lived in 12 different places, and I asked if her father was a minister or an Army officer. "Oh, no," she replied. "He's a football coach."

—William T. Palchanis, M.D.

WOMAN, watching football game in pouring rain, to husband: "This is probably another one of my silly questions. Why don't we go home?"

—Lichty cartoon, Chicago Sun-Times Syndicate

Aside Lines

THE FOOTBALL team had done nothing but fumble all afternoon. So when a substitute, warming up in front of the bench, dropped a ball someone flipped to him, it was too much for a leather-lunged fan. "Send him in, coach," he yelled from the stands. "He's ready!"

—Harold Helfer

ONE WOMAN to another during a performance of *Hamlet:* "I wish they'd turn up the lights. I can't hear so well when it's dark."

"I know what you mean. I can't hear over the telephone without my glasses."

—Mildred Weiler

AT OUR Thule, Greenland, air base, the chaplain was lecturing us on how we could improve ourselves by improving our thinking. After pointing out how great men like Lincoln, Edison and Eisenhower had worked their way to the top by thinking out what they wanted to do, he concluded with a ringing, "Remember, men, what you are is determined by what you think about all the time!"

My buddy turned to me and said, "If that's the case, I'm either a pin-up girl or a Cadillac convertible!"

—A1/c Charles C. Voorhees, Jr., in *True*

THE WOMAN with the bulging shopping bag panted to her seat in the movies just as the feature was reaching its most exciting point. Once settled she ignored the screen in order to dig through her bag, obviously in search of some special parcel.

One by one she removed the packages, unwrapped them and explored their contents, while her neighbors strained to hear the dialogue above the crackling of paper. This persistent, rustling search continued until the man directly in front of her turned and fixed the woman with an infuriated stare. "Lady," he asked, "what are you doing back there—building a nest?"

—Katharine K. Carr in *The Saturday Evening Post*

PROBABLY Robert Benchley's most famous exit from a theater was at the opening of a play called *The Squall,* which dealt with the peasants in the hills around Granada—peasants who all, it seemed, spoke in sultry pidgin English. After there had been a certain amount of to-do in this comic-strip dialect, Robert turned to his wife. "If one more of these wonderful natives shows up speaking pidgin, I leave," he whispered.

Just then a half-clad, wild-eyed gypsy girl staggered onto the stage. Benchley tensed himself as the girl crawled to the feet of the mother of the household and kissed the hem of her garment. "Me Nubi," the gypsy said. "Nubi good girl. Nubi stay here."

"Okay," Benchley whispered, rising. "Me Bobby. Me bad boy. Me go."

—*Robert Benchley, A Biography,* © 1955 by Nathaniel Benchley (McGraw-Hill)

THE MOVIE was *Gone With the Wind,* and the scene was the one in which, late at night, Scarlett waits angrily for Rhett to return home. When he finally arrives, he is very high and forestalls her rebukes by sweeping her into his arms. During the long and passionate kiss that ensues, the audience was completely silent. Then, from the row behind us, a whisper broke the stillness: *"There,* George, *that's* what I mean!" —Mrs. Donald Taylor

Cartoon Quips

WIFE leaving movie, to husband: "I wish just once they'd have as good a picture this week as they're going to have next week!"

—Cathy Joachim in Chicago *Tribune*

ONE GIRL to another: "We had an awful time. I had on my new Angora sweater, and he was wearing a blue serge suit."

—Cavalli in *The Saturday Evening Post*

WOMAN buying olives in supermarket to friend: "I never liked these things until someone showed me how to fix them with gin and vermouth." —Chon Day in *DAC News*

ONE MAN to another at dance: "I have my eye on a strapless gown that can't possibly survive another samba."
—Chon Day in *The Saturday Evening Post*

HUSBAND pointing out motioning traffic cop to off-in-the-clouds wife at steering wheel: "You can go now—or are you waiting for him to turn green?" —Wetterberg in *True's Automobile Year Book*

ONE SWEET young thing to another: "It's the little things about him that I like—he owns a small mansion, a small yacht and a small racing stable!" —George Wolfe in *Collier's*

ROYAL MESSENGER to two cannibals about to heave a luscious blonde into the kettle: "Hold it! The chief wants his breakfast in bed." —Holden in *The Harvard Lampoon*

WOMAN handing package to postal clerk: "It's fragile—so throw it underhand, please." —Bob Barnes in *The Saturday Evening Post*

FATHER TO small boy dragging top half of bikini bathing suit along beach: "Now show Daddy *exactly* where you found it. . . ."
—Bob Barnes in *Collier's*

CLERK IN pawnshop to customer buying a typewriter: "Now here's a bargain—owned by an elderly lady who never went over 30 words a minute." —Bob Schroeter, King Features

SAILOR TO civilian showing him model of a ship in a bottle: "If you think that's hard, you should try to get a bottle inside a battleship." —John Dempsey in *Collier's*

Joe Fyffe vs. The Navy

Condensed from
"All the Ships at Sea"

William Lederer

As THE liner *Coolidge* steamed slowly up the Whangpoo River at Shanghai, Ensign Hymie O'Toole was my official welcoming party. Hymie had arrived in Shanghai a month before and was the communications officer on the U.S.S. *Dale*.

None of the passengers could disembark for two hours; Hymie and I sat in the bar talking. "You know," said Hymie, looking over the *Coolidge's* luxurious lounge, "it's pretty damned marvelous that the Navy sends you out this way. And all for free."

"It's nice, all right."

Hymie said, "It didn't used to be this way. Formerly, if you came by commercial, you paid your own way—and tried to collect later."

"This cost the Navy about $600; I never could have scraped up that much cash."

"Think of the old days though," said Hymie dreamily. "Every time an officer had orders, especially if he had a family, he put out a couple of thousand bucks. That's why officers were always in debt. A distant relative of mine, Commodore Joe Fyffe, was the first one to fight that system. In fact it was through his efforts that legislation finally got passed. He was always fighting with stuffed shirts."

Hymie's eyes misted with sentiment and he ordered a couple of neat whiskies. "To Commodore Joe Fyffe," he toasted, "the Paul Bunyan of all the oceans!" Then Hymie told me about Commodore Fyffe.

When, in August 1870, Lt. Comdr. Joseph P. Fyffe received orders to the Orient via San Francisco, he was a happy guy. It meant independent command of a fine frigate. The only leak in the bilges was that traveling to San Francisco cost money and Joe Fyffe didn't have any.

"The Navy should pay for my transportation," he said, and

forthwith wrote to the paymaster at New London, Conn. The paymaster endorsed the request: "Custom and regulations have determined that the officer pay his own way and submit an expense account upon reaching his destination."

So Joe communicated with the Secretary of the Navy, requesting that the Navy either lay out the money or supply him with railroad tickets or transportation via naval vessel. The reply came from the Chief of the Bureau of Navigation:

To: LIEUTENANT COMMANDER J. P. FYFFE.

IN REPLY TO YOUR LETTER OF THE 18TH. YOUR REQUEST IS CONTRARY TO NAVY REGULATIONS. CARRY OUT YOUR ORDERS.

Joe Fyffe cursed. Then he carefully studied his orders. They terminated with the normal paragraph, WHILE CARRYING OUT THESE ORDERS YOU WILL KEEP THE BUREAU OF NAVIGATION INFORMED OF YOUR WHEREABOUTS. There was nothing which stated when he was supposed to arrive in San Francisco or by what means.

Joe donned his best uniform and strapped his sword to his small handbag. At sunrise on the 25th of August he walked out of New London and headed westward for San Francisco. By sundown he reached East Haddam, where he sent the following telegram to the Chief of the Bureau in Washington:

25 AUGUST 1870

COMPLIANCE ORDERS NUMBER 1998 LT. COMDR. FYFFE EN ROUTE NEW LONDON TO SAN FRANCISCO X ON FOOT X THIS TELEGRAM TO KEEP BUREAU INFORMED MY WHEREABOUTS X MADE GOOD 22 MILES THIS DATE X SPENDING EVENING IN HAYLOFT IN MT. PARNASSUS X VERY RESPECTFULLY FYFFE.

Every evening for the next few days he sent a telegram.

26 AUGUST 1870

EN ROUTE X ON FOOT X MADE GOOD 31 MILES THIS DATE X BY GRACIOUS CONSENT MAYOR OF BRISTOL AM SPENDING NIGHT MAYOR'S STABLES X HAVE NOTICED HE HAS HYBRID MULES SPECIALLY BRED FOR TROPICS X SUGGEST NAVY INVESTIGATE.

27 AUGUST 1870

EN ROUTE X ON FOOT X MADE GOOD ONLY 15 MILES THIS DATE X RAINED ALL DAY X STAYING OVERNIGHT AT LITCHFIELD WITH MY FATHER'S FRIEND GENERAL HOLMES X I FIND STANDARD

BOOTS WORN BY NAVAL OFFICERS INADEQUATE FOR PROLONGED WALKING X SUGGEST SURGEON GENERAL INVESTIGATE.

28 AUGUST 1870

EN ROUTE X ON FOOT X SPENDING NIGHT LAKEVILLE X LOVELY COUNTRY EXPECT BUY HOME HERE SOON AS GET REIMBURSED TRAVEL VOUCHER SUBMITTED BY ME TO NAVY THREE YEARS AGO X TOMORROW I ENTER NEW YORK STATE.

29 AUGUST 1870

EN ROUTE X ON FOOT X MADE 28 MILES THIS DATE DESPITE BADLY WORN SHOES X PEOPLE NOT FAMILIAR NAVY UNIFORMS THIS AREA X GREAT CROWD WALKED PART WAY WITH ME X I SANG THEM SEA CHANTIES X POPULACE THINKS IT GREAT SIGN DEMOCRACY FOR COMMANDING OFFICER OF SHIP TO WALK 3000 MILES TO NEW STATION X POLICE CHIEF HUDSON NEW YORK HAS GIVEN ME BEST CELL IN JAIL FOR OVERNIGHT.

30 AUGUST 1870

EN ROUTE X ON FOOT X ARRIVED ALBANY X REQUESTED RECRUITING OFFICER BE AUTHORIZED ISSUE ME NEW SHOES X SHOES FELL APART NOON TODAY X ENTERED ALBANY BAREFOOTED X WILL REMAIN SEWARD HOTEL TWO DAYS AWAITING ANSWER X EARNING MY KEEP AS BARTENDER X LOCAL RUM FAR SUPERIOR THAT SERVED IN NAVY X AM SENDING SAMPLE X VERY RESPECTFULLY FYFFE.

The next evening the recruiting officer sent a messenger requesting Lt. Comdr. Joe Fyffe's presence. In full uniform, wearing borrowed shoes, Joe went to the recruiting station.

"I have a telegram for you, sir," said the recruiting officer. "Here it is."

PASS FOLLOWING MESSAGE TO LT. COMDR. J. P. FYFFE USN NOW AT SEWARD HOTEL BAR QUOTE I STRIKE MY COLORS X SECRETARY OF NAVY AUTHORIZES RECRUITING OFFICER ALBANY ISSUE YOU SHOES AND PROVIDE YOU QUICKEST TRANSPORTATION FROM ALBANY TO SAN FRANCISCO X EVEN CHIEF BUREAU NAVIGATION CAN LAUGH WHEN OUTSMARTED X UNQUOTE X RESPECTFULLY BUREAU NAVIGATION X

Between hiccups Hymie O'-Toole concluded, "And that's how it is that guys like you have their first-class passage on the *Coolidge* prepaid by the Navy."

The Rank and File

OURS WAS a medium field-artillery battalion that had been on MP duty in Korea before hostilities broke out. We were hurriedly training and girding ourselves for action, meanwhile requisitioning many items of equipment. But in spite of repeated requests, we did not receive essential radios and telephones. Finally our battalion commander, thoroughly annoyed, made out a requisition for 5000 blankets. The commanding general quickly had him on the carpet, demanding why on earth he had submitted a requisition for 5000 blankets.

"Sir," retorted our commander, "I've been requisitioning the radios and telephones that I need for weeks and I still don't have them. I thought if I got these blankets I could at least send smoke signals." —Capt. Gunnar E. Andersson

ON PATROL off Formosa, the officer of the deck of the U.S.S. *Brownson* asked the starboard lookout what he would do if a man fell overboard. "I would yell, 'Man overboard!' "

The officer then asked what he would do if an officer fell overboard. The lookout was silent for a moment, then asked, "Which one, sir?" —Richard A. Sutton

AS THE Chinese Reds unleashed a sudden artillery barrage that rocked the hills in its fury, the young Marine dived into a nearby slit trench. Immediately another form came hurtling in on top of him. The Marine yelled above the din, "You a man?"

"Stop being funny," came the booming reply. "I'm the platoon sergeant."

"It's real comfortin' to hear your voice, Sarge," said the youngster. "I was waitin' for you to explode." —*The Wall Street Journal*

A GI WHO returned to camp in a drunken state after a 24-hour pass was ordered to report to his captain. "There's no need for you to drink like this," the officer lectured. "If you could stay sober you might become a corporal. In fact you might even become a sergeant. Wouldn't you like that?"

"Captain," the soldier replied, "the fact is that when I get a few drops in me I feel like a colonel!"

—Burnett Hershey, quoted by Leonard Lyons

A NAVY recruit lost his rifle on the firing range. When told that he'd have to pay for it, he protested: "Suppose I was driving a Navy jeep and somebody stole it. Would I have to pay for that, too?" He was informed that he would have to pay for all government property he lost.

"Now," the recruit said, "I know why the captain always goes down with his ship." —Julie Coxford

FROM A draftee's first letter home: "About that straw that broke the camel's back: I'm sleeping on it." —H. V. Wade, NANA

WE WAVES were standing stiff at attention for inspection while a male officer looked us up and down, walking back and forth, his face getting redder all the time as he tried to line us up. We were all feeling rather self-conscious when a junior officer piped up, "Sir, I've found the best way to line women up is to sight along the backs of their necks!" —Sharon R. Hubner

A CENSOR in World War I in France told me about coming upon a letter written by one of the men to his wife back home:

"Stop those nagging letters! You are 3000 miles away and it don't do no good. Do let me enjoy this war in peace!"

—Harry Emerson Fosdick, *The Living of These Days* (Harper)

IN KOREA all that one sergeant's outfit did morning, noon and night was discuss the rotation plan. Fed up, the sergeant called them together. "Attenshun! Left face, left face, left face, left face!" he commanded in rapid succession. "Now every last one of you has been rotated," he barked, "and I don't want to hear the word again!"

—R. C. Miller

OUR GROUP of recruits arrived at the Farragut Naval Training Station before dawn of a January morning. First came the regulation haircut. Then, stripping completely, we started through a gantlet of doctors, corpsmen and fault finders, getting a shot in one arm, two shots in the other arm, physical examination, dental check, vaccination, blood test. . . . Finally we started receiving our gear. The first issue was a long white bag in which we put each succeeding article. Dragging this bundle through the supply line we came—still naked, with arms aching, head spinning—to a counter where we each filled out a questionnaire. Reaching the question, "Have you ever contemplated suicide?" I happened to glance at the paper of the youth beside me and saw his answer: "NEVER BEFORE."

—George W. Lee

Blank Expressions

A FAMED film beauty applying for a visa came to the blank: "Single_____Married_____Divorced_____." She hesitated a moment, then wrote, "Everything."

—E. E. Kenyon in *The American Weekly*

APPLICANTS for jobs on Kentucky Dam, when the project was starting, had to take a written examination. One chap read the first question: "What does hydrodynamics mean?" hesitated, then wrote, "It means I don't get the job!"

—Joe Creason in Louisville *Courier-Journal Magazine*

INSURANCE salesman to customer: "You've filled in this application all right except for one thing, Mr. Perkins—where it asks the relationship of Mrs. Perkins to yourself, you should have put down 'wife,' not 'strained.' "

—Follette cartoon in *The Saturday Evening Post*

AFTER winding up his hitch in the Navy with a cruise to Pearl Harbor and back on the aircraft carrier U. S. S. *Boxer*, a young relative of mine entered an Ivy League college. Before long he was invited to join a fraternity. One of the questions in the extensive questionnaire he was required to fill out before initiation was: "Where did you spend the past summer?"

His reply: "Cruising to Hawaii on my Uncle's yacht."

—Nancy Allen

IN MAKING out a report on a wreck involving a pie-company truck and an ice-cream truck, Galveston insurance investigator Oscar Dugey came to a blank labeled, "Results of Accident," wrote, "Pie à la mode."

—George Fuermann, *Houston: Land of the Big Rich* (Doubleday)

A NEW YORK hotel whose clientele includes many salesmen and buyers keeps a record of the companies represented by the guests. A breezy woman buyer from the West, after putting her name and address on the registration card, seemed to be brought up short by the query, "Firm?" She nibbled the end of her pen for a moment, then wrote, "Not very!" —Dan Bennett

A JOB applicant wrote "No" to the query, "Have you ever been arrested?" To the following question, which was "Why?," he answered, "Never got caught." —Dick Wright

AN ATLANTA businessman reports that his wife took some of her presents back to a department store after Christmas for exchange. On the credit slip he found this explanation as the *Reason for Return:* "Gift from husband."

—Hugh Park in Atlanta *Journal*

IN FILLING out a form for the Brooklyn Dodgers, one outfielder, on the line asking, "Length of residence in home town," wrote: "About 40 feet." —Collie Small in *The Saturday Evening Post*

A DRIVER for a Los Angeles firm had a collision. In filling out the required form he stated the accident was unavoidable. Under remarks he wrote: "The woman in front of me signaled a left turn and made a left turn."

—Matt Weinstock in Los Angeles *Daily News*

Enough to Drive You Crazy

The sneakiest thing about "women drivers" is the way they turn out to be men, right after you've criticized their driving to your wife.

—Harold Coffin in *The Saturday Evening Post*

A FEMALE motorist came tootling merrily down the wrong lane of a crowded thoroughfare and ran smack into Mr. Jordan's brand-new convertible. While they were untangling bumpers the lady said grudgingly, "I'm afraid this was largely my fault."

"Nonsense," said Mr. Jordan with a gallant bow. "I assure you the blame rests entirely with me. I saw you fully three blocks away and had ample time to dart down a side street." —Bennett Cerf, *Good for a Laugh* (Hanover House)

IN HEAVY traffic I was edging past a woman driver who was trying to reverse into a parking space that was clearly too small. Suddenly her car swung out and bumped into mine. Flushed with exasperation she leaned out of her window. "You could see I was going to do something stupid," she said. "Why didn't you wait to see what it was?" —Northerner II in *Yorkshire Post and Leeds Mercury*

OUT FOR a drive one Sunday afternoon with my wife I pulled to a stop at an intersection and, unable to see to the right, asked her if any cars were coming.

"No," she replied and, as I proceeded into the highway, added, "Just a truck."

—Donald Morrell

ONE DAY as I was driving into New York the woman in front of me turned right without putting her arm out to signal. In doing so she fouled up a huge trailer truck. The truck driver leaned out and shouted, "Who da ya tink ya are? Venus de Milo?" —Susan Seymour

WOMAN DRIVER to garage mechanic: "My husband tells me there's a screw loose in the driver —wherever that is!"

—George Wolfe cartoon in *Collier's*

"HAVE YOU ever driven a car?" the lady applicant for a license was asked.

"One hundred and twenty thousand miles," put in her husband, "and never had a hand on the wheel." —*Quote*

SEEN IN Los Angeles: A pert blonde driving a sleek new yellow convertible with a dent in the fender over which was boldly painted, "HIS." —Fran Carr

WOMAN DRIVER to friend: "The part I don't like about parking is that noisy crash."

—Fred Balk cartoon in *True*

IN MILWAUKEE a man spotted a young woman futilely edging in and out of a tiny parking space. Ten minutes later, thanks to his directions, the car was neatly parked in the space.

"Thank you very much," the woman said. "This is very nice, but I was trying to get out."

—*The Woman,* quoted in *The Christian Science Monitor*

A SMALL New England college was observing its 150th anniversary, and the heads of institutions of higher learning across the country came to the party with their gowns and bright hoods. The academic procession was almost ready to begin its march to the chapel when the president of the college, who headed the line, thought of the three hours he would have to sit on the platform. So, turning to the two famous educators behind him, he mumbled something about being right back and ducked out of line.

The two college presidents misunderstood him, however. They, and the entire academic procession, followed the president downstairs to the gentlemen's room. —Joe Harrington, quoted by Bennett Cerf in *The Saturday Review*

A FRENCH officer who could not speak German was having lunch in an officers' mess in the French Zone in Germany. The German waitress, who knew no French, brought him a chicken leg. The officer waved it away and asked for white meat instead—trying to show what he wanted by putting both hands on his chest.

The girl smiled, nodded her head and went out to the kitchen. In an instant she was back—with two glasses of milk.

—*UNRRA Team News*

OUR APPLIANCE store in Minneapolis serves a fast-growing suburban development in which whole blocks of houses are almost identical. One morning a customer phoned and said excitedly, "You'll have to send someone out to move our range. It was installed at the wrong address."

"But you were there yourself," protested the manager, "and your family was there."

"Yes, yes, I know," replied the customer. "We moved into the wrong house." —Florence Eng

A PROFESSOR at an eastern university driving to the West Coast one summer had been invited to stop en route at the homes of half a dozen of his former students. A methodically efficient man, he wrote all his thank-you notes beforehand. He sealed, addressed and stamped the letters, bundled them up with a rubber band and put them in his suitcase.

His first stop was in Buffalo. Next night, unpacking in a hotel room about 300 miles farther west, he discovered the thank-you notes were missing. Telephoning his Buffalo host, he asked with studied casualness, "Did you by any chance find a bundle of letters in the guest room?"

"Why, yes," said his friend. "I mailed them for you this very morning." —Regina Schirmer

Dog Tales

For 25 days Pal, a mongrel pup, maintained a lonely vigil above an abandoned mine shaft near Joplin, Mo. Romanticists, fearing that his master had fallen down the 135-foot shaft, insisted that the water in it be drained. Thousands of curious persons looked on as the seven-day, $700 pumping job was completed. "Rescuers" found an ancient, four-inch bone. —*Newsweek*

Man leaving pet shop with new puppy: "C'mon, little feller. You're going to change someone's mind about wall-to-wall carpeting." —Taber cartoon in *True*

Stretched out before the living-room fireplace as I sat in another room was Jimmy, our female mongrel. She didn't see me as I watched her wake up, yawn and look around absently. Her eyes fell on a plate of chocolates on a low table.

Jimmy is very fond of candy, but she has been taught never to help herself. She sauntered over to the low table, picked up a piece and flopped down on the hearth rug with it between her paws. There she nuzzled it a while and then gave a long, sad sigh of resignation. Taking the candy in her mouth again, she returned to the table and dropped it back into the dish. —H. C. Merrill

We don't feed Rover
At the table.
We don't feed—that is,
If we're able
To keep our eyes
From meeting his,
We don't feed Rover . . . .
Well, that is . . . .

—Ethel Jacobson in *The Atlantic Monthly*

Little Mary arrived home one day with a mongrel female dog. Mary, of course, thought the animal was beautiful, but try as she might she could not convince her mother that they should keep the dog. The climax of the debate came one day about a week later when Mary arrived home from school and found her dog running about the yard followed closely by a pack of male dogs.

Mary, her eyes shining with pride and conviction, burst into the house. "Mommy," she called. "Come to the window! Our dog is just a natural-born leader!" —Louis Mertins

THE HIGHLIGHT of our cocker spaniel's day is when we pile into the car in the morning to drive my husband to work. Taffy loves riding more than anything else, and unless I hide the car keys she brings them to me at all hours, begging for a ride.

One morning we didn't want to take Taffy and told her that she must stay home. Head hanging, she left the room. My husband and I were headed for the car when suddenly we both realized that neither of us had the car keys. I turned back—and encountered Taffy. Stretched out at the front door she looked so infinitely pathetic that I just couldn't hold out.

"Oh, all right," I said. "Come along for your ride."

With tail thumping, eyes sparkling, Taffy jumped up. She paused only to pick up the keys—on which she had been lying.

—Nora Bailey

Success Stories

The long & sport of it

1917—Stock Room Clerk

1926—Salesman

1933—Office Manager

1939—Junior Vice President

1949—President

1958—Chairman of the Board

—Irwin Caplan, *This Week Magazine*

IN THE DAYS before he was kissed by fame,
Mortimer Boodle signed his name;

Mortimer Boodle

But he's famous now, we may be sure,
For look at Mortimer's signature:

—Georgie Starbuck Galbraith in *The Saturday Evening Post*

Life With Christopher

Condensed from Vogue

Jean Kerr

WE ARE BEING very careful with our children. They'll never have to pay a psychiatrist $25 an hour to find out why we rejected them. We'll tell them why we rejected them. Because they're impossible, that's why.

From the kitchen window I watch Christopher, our eight-year-old. With a garden rake in one hand he scampers up a tree, out across a long branch and down over the stone wall. But he is unable to get from the living room into the front hall without bumping into at least two pieces of furniture. He has another trick which defies analysis. He can walk into the middle of a perfectly empty kitchen and trip on the linoleum.

Christopher is interested in the precise value of words. I say, "Christopher, you take a bath and put all your things in the wash," and he says, "Okay, but it will break the Bendix."

"Why will it break the Bendix?" I inquire.

So he explains, "Well, if I put all my things in the wash, I'll have to put my shoes in and they will certainly break the machinery."

"Very well," I say, all sweetness and control, "put everything but the shoes in the wash." He picks up my agreeable tone at once, announcing cheerily, "Then do you want me to put my belt in the wash?" I don't know what I say at this point but my husband says, "Honey, you mustn't scream at him that way."

My real problem with children is that I haven't any imagination. I'm always warning them against the commonplace defections while they are planning the bizarre. Christopher gets up ahead of the rest of us on Sunday mornings and he has long since been given a list of clear directives: "Don't wake the baby," "Don't go outside in your pajamas," "Don't eat cookies before breakfast."

But I never told him, "Don't make flour paste and glue together all the pages of the magazine section of the Sunday *Times*." Now I tell him.

Before a dinner party I told the twins and Christopher not to go in the living room, not to use the guest towels in the bathroom and not to leave the bicycles on the front steps. However, I neglected to tell them not to eat the daisies on the dining-room table. This was a serious omission, as I discovered when I came upon my centerpiece—a charming three-point arrangement of green stems.

Soon after Jean Kerr brought out "Please Don't Eat the Daisies" one of her young sons had to write a book report for school. Naturally, he chose his mother's new book, and his report closed with this terse comment: "Mrs. Kerr has written a very funny book, although the parts about her children are greatly exaggerated and in some instances are downright lies."

—Publishers' Weekly

Remarkable Explanations

MY DAUGHTER is rarely surprised at anything she finds in her little boys' pockets, but she was curious when she discovered a wad of grass in the four-year-old's pocket and asked why it was there. "Well," he said, "that worm in there had to eat, didn't he?".

—Mrs. C. W. Haggard in Atlanta *Journal and Constitution Magazine*

ARMED WITH my husband's blank check, I marched into a bank in Ottawa and asked the teller to close out his account. I was directed to a pleasant gentleman at the front desk who asked how much I wished to withdraw. "All of it," I answered.

"Do you have his bank book and some means of personal identification?" he asked.

Eagerly I searched my purse but could produce only my pilot's license bearing my maiden name. Suddenly I became conscious that the banker was staring at the bare third finger of my left hand. Hopelessly embarrassed, I blurted out, "I'm allergic to gold so I don't always wear my rings. We've lost the bank book. You can't write my husband as we live in a tent in northern Manitoba. The ice isn't melted in our lake yet so there's no mail delivery. I've only been married five months so my pilot's license hasn't my married name on it. I need all the money because I'm going to buy an airplane to fly home. We need the aircraft because we're so isolated; I don't see another white woman for months at a time."

"Madam," the official interrupted, "I'll cash your check. No one could invent a story like that!" —Mrs. A. M. Nichols

MARY, a widow who used to preside over our kitchen in Nashville, Tenn., constantly beat her children over the head with their father's halo. "Stop that shufflin' when you walk," she would command. "Pick up your feet and lift up your head like your Pa always done." When they started to school she urged them to make their time count so they might "grow up to amount to something like your Pa did." And when the girls began to have beaux they were cautioned to remember their Pa and not "come traipsin' in at daylight with some no-'count loafer."

After years of this I finally asked Mary what Pa did in this life.

"Do!" Mary laughed scornfully. "That man never worked nothin' but his jaws. But when he up and left me back in Atlanta, I made up my mind he wasn't goin' to skip out free. *He was goin' to help me raise these young'uns somehow. And he did.*"

—Mrs. F. J. Lopez

ARTUR RUBINSTEIN, in order to practice for a concert, told his butler, François, to tell any callers that he was not at home. When the telephone rang, a woman's voice asked for the maestro. With the crashing chords of Rubinstein's rehearsal thundering in from the next room, the butler suavely informed the woman his master was out. "Out?" she protested. "But I can hear him playing!"

"Not at all, madam," the resourceful François told her imperturbably. "It is merely I, dusting the keys."

—Jack Lait, Jr., in Brooklyn *Eagle*

As THE bus was filling up in the terminal, an elderly gentleman got on and was about to sit down next to my friend when he asked her if she was a grandmother.

"Yes," she replied proudly. "Twice."

With that the man moved on to another seat, where he asked the same question, and then moved on again. Upon receiving a negative answer from the third lady he sat down with a sigh of relief.

"I'm a grandfather," he explained, "and if you sit next to these grandmothers you never get a word in—and I like to talk!"

—Mrs. Irving Thorley, Jr.

WHEN MY husband and I, city born and bred, first moved to an isolated part of Wyoming, a neighboring rancher gave generously of his time and experience in helping us get started. We noticed that he invariably hopped on his horse to do even the shortest errand. One day, when he mounted to ride no more than 30 feet, my husband said, "Don't you *ever* walk?"

"Son," the rancher replied seriously, "if the good Lord had wanted me to walk, He'd have given me four legs." —M. B. L.

"I SIMPLY can't stand my husband's nasty disposition," wept the young bride. "Why, he's made me so jittery that I'm losing weight."

"Then why don't you leave him?" asked her aunt.

"Oh, I'm going to," the bride assured her. "I'm just waiting until he gets me down to 120 pounds." —Orlando, Fla., *Morning Sentinel*

Calorie Counters

Diet is a short period of starvation preceding a gain of five pounds.
—John R. McHenry

A COMELY young matron stepped on the drugstore scales after devouring a giant sundae and was shocked at what she beheld. Promptly she slipped off her coat and tried it again. The results were still unflattering, so she slid off her shoes. But then she discovered she was out of pennies. Without a moment's hesitation the lad behind the soda fountain stepped forward.

"Don't stop now," he volunteered. "I've got a handful of pennies and they're all yours."
—Pete Brett

ROAST-CARVING host to rotund guest: "Would you care for another 50 or 60 calories, Mrs. Smith?"
—Currier cartoon, King Features

WHILE DRIVING home from a dinner party, a buxom matron who tries womanfully to stick to her reducing diet had an accident. She saw a big truck coming toward her car, skidding and out of control, and she knew that a crash was inevitable. And what thoughts do you suppose went through her head in those terrifying seconds, with serious injury, perhaps even death in the offing?

"I'm ashamed to confess it," she told me, "but what went through my head was merely this: If I'm going to get killed, what a fool I was to pass up the dessert!"
—Eleanor Clarage in Cleveland *Plain Dealer*

ACTRESS Eve Arden accidentally sat on a piano keyboard. Listening to the awful noise, she exclaimed, "H'm, two octaves! I'll have to reduce."
—*London Opinion*

In my work with the Department of Internal Revenue I came across this example of feminine logic. Under deductions a fashion model listed: "Property improvements—Reducing treatments $200."

—Steve Kormanik

Round Figures. The 20th reunion of the Princeton class of '36 showed that the class had gained 3½ tons since graduation.

—Chicago *Tribune*

A woman stepped off the penny scales and turned to her husband. He eyed her appraisingly and asked, "Well, what's the verdict? A little overweight?"

"Oh, no," said his wife, "I wouldn't say that. But according to that height table on the scale I should be about six inches taller!"

—*New Jersey Bell Telephone News*

Small girl showing bathroom scales to playmate: "All I know is, you stand on it and it makes you mad."

—Franklin Folger cartoon, Chicago Sun-Times Syndicate

In a New York apartment house where many doctors have offices, the plump elevator girl posted this sign at Christmastime: "Please Don't Feed Any Candy to Mabel. Doctor's Orders!"

—Edgar E. Casparius

A Hollywood producer who had been telling everyone about his diet was discovered in a restaurant eating a tremendous steak.

"What's the idea?" demanded a friend. "I thought you were on a diet."

"I am," said the producer. "This is just to give me the strength to continue it!"

—Don Wilson, quoted in *Best*

Symptoms of Being 35

Condensed from the book

Ring Lardner

THE OTHER night one of my friends whose name is Legion got me on the telephone and wanted I should come over and call. But I said no, I was busy on a book which I had promised my publisher I would write it. "What is it about" says Legion. So I told him "How it feels to be 35."

"That guy must think you got a good memory" says Legion.

Well friends 35 is how young I am no matter how old I look, but I am so use to haveing smart Alex make wise cracks when I tell them my age that it don't have no more effect on me now than the 6 day bicycle race. Only I can't figure why they think I would lie about it like I was trying to pose as a boy chess marvel or something. When a man has got a legal wife and 4 and no one hundredths children what does he care if he is 35 or double that amt.

And don't judge a person by their hair gents. Many a man that can remember the first Ford has got more foliage on their egg than myself. Personly I am not sensitive about my plummage. When my features got to the decision that one of them would half to retract all I done was thank God they picked the forehead and not the chin. The only hardship connected with pyorrhea of the scalp is trying to act surprised when the barber says you are looseing your hair.

But at the present writeing, I can at lease state that being 35 don't feel nothing like being under 30. For inst. when the telephone rings now days I am scared to death that its somebody asking us to go somewheres for dinner. Six yrs. ago I was afraid it wasn't. At 29 home was like they used to say on the vaudeville stage, a place to go when all the other joints was closed up. At 35 its a place you never leave without a loud squawk. Its where you can take off your shoes. Its where you can have more soup. Its where you don't half to say nothing when they's nothing to say. Its where you don't half to listen.

When you was 29 you didn't care for the band to play Home sweet Home. It was old stuff and a rotten tune any way. Now you hope they won't play it neither. Its a pretty tune but it makes you bust out crying.

Well it was 5 or 6 years ago when I realized that I was past my nonages as they say. It come to me all of a sudden that the only compliments I had for a long wile was what a pretty tie you got or something. Like for inst. a few wks. back I was up in Boston where I got a young and beautiful sister in law. When it come time to part she kissed me 6 times which was suppose to be once for me and once apiece for the Mrs. and 4 kiddies. Well I thought it was pretty nice and got kind of excited about it till I looked at her husband to see how he took it. He took it without batting an eye. When I had left, instead of lepping at her throat with a terrible curse he probably says "Janey, you're a good game gal," and she gave him a kiss that meant something.

Now an incidence like this would of spoilt my whole trip if I didn't look at it in a sensible way which is to say to yourself, "Well if I wasn't in the Sears and yellow I wouldn't of got them 6 kisses. And 6 kisses is ½ a dozen kisses in any language."

All in all when you get hardened to it they's many advantages in reaching your dottage.

When the Mrs. thinks it would be nice to have a fire in the fire place, you ain't the one that has got to ruin his clothes. Or when one of my young brother in laws is around the house and I come in the rm. and they are setting in the easy chair, why they jump up like food shot from guns and say "Here take this chair."

As for the gen. symptoms of 35 the following may interest science:

1. The patient sometimes finds himself and one lady the only people left at the table and all the others is danceing. They seems to be nothing for it but to get up and dance. You start and the music stops and the young buddies on the flr. claps their hands for a encore. The patient claps his hands too but not very loud and hopes to high heaven the leader will take it in a jokeing way.

2. In going through an old trunk the patient runs acrost a bunch of keep sakes like a note a gal wrote him in high school, a picture of himself in a dirty football suit, a program of an old May festival in South Bend and etc. "Why keep this junk" he says and dumps them all in the waste basket.

3. The invalid goes to a ball game and along comes the last ½ of the 14th. innings and the score is 1 and 1 and the 1st guy up makes a base hit. The patient

looks at his watch and if he leaves the park right away he can make the 6:27 home where as if he waits a few min. he will half to take the 6:54. Without no hesitation he leaves the park right away.

4. The subject is woke up at 3 a.m. by the fire whistle. He sniffes but can't smell no smoke. He thinks well it ain't our house and goes back to sleep.

5. He sets down after breakfast and starts to read the paper. The mail man comes and brings him 3 letters. One of them looks like it was a gal's writeing. He reads the paper.

6. He buys a magazine in April and reads the first instalment of a misery serial. The instalment winds up with the servants finding their master's body in bed and his head in the ash tray. Everything pts to the young wife. Our patient forgets to buy the May number.

In conclusion its customary in these intimate capital I talks to throw in a paragraph of blurb about the little woman. What ever success a man has had he has got to pretend he owes it to Her. So if they's any glory to be gleaned out of my success in reaching 35 and looking even older why she can have it.

Cut Down to Size

HENRY BEAN, who is 40 years old and sound of wind and limb, was feeling pretty chipper. But that was before he was driving his car near Memphis, Tenn. There he got into a right-of-way argument with a couple of teen-agers in another car. The teen-agers, about 18 and brawny, got out and advanced upon him menacingly. Bean doesn't know what might have happened had not a girl in the other car shouted, "Don't you boys dare hit that poor old man!" —Walter Davenport in *Collier's*

WHEN Katharine Hepburn was assigned to her first role at MGM opposite Spencer Tracy, she was frightened over acting with a star who had already won two Academy Awards. But Katie wasn't going to let anyone know it — particularly Mr. Tracy.

Breezing onto the set with her mind made up that she'd get in the first word, she stared at Tracy for a moment, then brashly trilled, "Oh, Mr. Tracy, I'm really afraid I'm too tall for you."

Spencer measured the upstart with a face devoid of all expression. Then he said calmly, "That's all right, dear. I'll soon cut you down to my size!" —*Motion Picture Magazine*

A WELL-KNOWN radio writer, recalled by his draft board, was being interviewed by a bored sergeant who asked, "Did you go to grammar school?"

"Yes. Also high school," said the writer. "And I have an M.S. from Columbia, graduate courses at Cornell, back to Columbia for journalism, a degree from the University of Mexico and . . . "

The interviewer nodded, picked up a rubber stamp and, after flourishing it in midair, slammed it on the questionnaire, imprinting one word: "Literate." —Leonard Lyons

REPRESENTATIVE Brooks Hays had just made his first speech on the House floor. "I worked long and hard on that maiden address," he said, "and really put everything into it when I delivered it. The next day I eagerly opened the *Congressional Record* and there was my speech, word for word, just as I had given it. There was just one thing wrong. The *Record* had given Representative Oren Harris credit.

"I stormed down to the *Record* office and gave them a good talking to. When they apologized I felt ashamed and told them I was sorry for blowing my top.

" 'Oh, that's all right, Mr. Hays,' one said. 'It's really nothing. You should have heard what Mr. Harris said!' "

—J. J. in Little Rock *Arkansas Gazette*

ON A TRAIN in Texas a soldier, homesick for the bustle of New York City, turned to his seat mate and exclaimed disgustedly, "Texas! You can have it."

A rabid Texan she promptly told him at great length about the beauty of the plains, the wild flowers, the rivers and lakes. To clinch her case she pointed to the beautiful scenery outside the window.

"I'll admit it's laid out pretty," he said. "How long's it been dead?" —Doris Kesinger

NOT LONG AGO I was hospitalized by a severe case of hepatitis, a liver ailment which often turns one's skin a jaundiced yellow. (And I am a girl who never did look well in yellow.) Feeling a bit more chipper one morning I decided to go down to the hospital newsstand for the morning paper. I spruced myself with a little powder and lipstick and made my way to the elevator. The sole other occupant was a fine-looking intern—tall, dark and handsome — and my heart fluttered as I noticed him looking at me with interest. Modestly I glanced away. But as the elevator descended and I became more and more aware that he was gazing at me, I wished I'd applied my make-up more carefully. Then he inched closer, and I just knew he was going to speak to me. Pleased, I waited. He leaned forward, looked deep in my eyes and said triumphantly, "Liver?" —Jane Porter

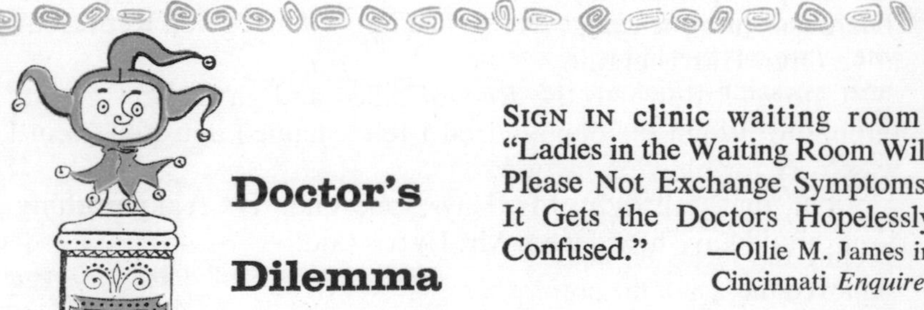

Doctor's Dilemma

SIGN IN clinic waiting room: "Ladies in the Waiting Room Will Please Not Exchange Symptoms. It Gets the Doctors Hopelessly Confused." —Ollie M. James in Cincinnati *Enquirer*

WHILE IN the hospital for the birth of our son, I shared a room with a young mother whose obstetrician was reserved and businesslike. On one of his visits, trying to make conversation, she said, "Doctor, they certainly keep you busy, don't they?"

"Yes," he said quietly, without looking up from his notes. "I have too many men working for me."

—Mrs. Ralph P. Stilphen

"IT WAS about 2 a.m. and I wakes up feeling awful," tells Jimmy Durante, "so I calls my doctor ta come right over. It's a terrible night out so I apologizes ta him when he comes.

" 'Dat's all right,' says the doc. 'I got another patient in the neighborhood—so I can kill two boids with one stone.' "

A FRIEND of mine was going into surgery. They wheeled him in all wrapped up in sheets and lifted him onto the operating table. In the glare of the lights, surgeons and assistant surgeons, anesthetists and surgical nurses in their gauze masks crowded around. Sterilizers were hissing. Oxygen tanks stood ready. They began peeling the sheets off and as they removed the last of the presurgical preparations and got down to his bare torso they found a piece of adhesive tape pasted to his skin. Written on it was the reminder, "Think." —Braven Dyer, quoted by Art Ryon in Los Angeles *Times*

WHEN I was taken to the hospital after an auto accident the doctor, after examining me and putting my leg in a cast, said that I could go home the next day. In the morning, however, he announced, "I think you'd better stay another day to see if something new turns up. I didn't know how bad you were banged up until I read about the accident in the newspaper." —Harlow Landphair

THE PROPRIETOR of an art gallery in London, showing pictures to a customer who didn't know what he liked, tried out a landscape, a still life, a portrait and a floral piece, all without results. "Would you be interested in a nude?" he finally asked.

"Good heavens, no," said the visitor. "I'm a physician."

—*The English Digest*

NURSE comforting a patient: "Don't let the doctors frighten you. Doctors are like politicians —they view with alarm so they can point with pride!"

—From the motion picture *With a Song in My Heart* (20th Century-Fox)

Political Science

Manufacturers' Record: Government should be like your stomach — if it's working right you don't know you have it.

Boston *Globe:* Every little American boy has a chance to be President when he grows up—it's just one of the risks he has to take.

James S. Duncan, Canadian industrialist: You cannot have just a little state planning, any more than you can be just a little bit pregnant.

Ed Ford: Trouble is there are too many Democratic and Republican Senators and not enough United States Senators.

—Quoted by Earl Wilson, Hall Syndicate

Anonymous: Many a person seems to think it isn't enough for the government to guarantee him the pursuit of happiness. He insists it also run interference for him.

—Quoted in Asheville, N. C., *Times*

J. B. Priestley: We should behave toward our country as women behave toward the men they love. A loving wife will do anything for her husband except stop criticizing and trying to improve him.

Frank in the Heart of Texas

Condensed from Holiday

Frank Sullivan

I HAD HEARD so much about Texas that I finally decided to visit our great sister republic and see its wonders for myself. I traveled light—a spare ten-gallon hat, two pairs of chaps, one for business and one for formal evening wear, a lariat and Rhode Island, which I brought along to check on the claim advanced by Texas friends that it would fit 220 times into their great state.

On a typical sparkling Texas morning I debarked at Houston. Two glorious suns were shining, the regular one and the special Texas sun. Above the hum of the traffic rose the gurgle of gushers gushing in the gusheries scattered about the city. Anon, the crack of rifle fire and the sight of a fleeing cattle rustler told that Texas could still dispense frontier justice.

Houston is the chief city of the Texas republic, although I add instantly that Dallas, San Antonio, Galveston, Waco, Fort Worth, Austin and El Paso are

Holiday (December, '48), © 1948 by The Curtis Pub. Co., Independence Square, Philadelphia 5, Pa. Reprinted in "The Night the Old Nostalgia Burned Down," © 1948 by The Curtis Pub. Co. and published by Little, Brown & Co., 34 Beacon St., Boston 6, Mass.

also the chief cities of Texas. Other chief cities may have sprung up since I left. If so, I beg their pardon for not mentioning them. Houston is growing at the rate of 10,000 inhabitants a day, 5000 of them oil millionaires. At its present rate of growth it will outstrip New York in a decade. Perhaps sooner, since Texans are twice as big as New Yorkers.

Before lunch I had time to measure Rhode Island into Houston. It goes seven times.

I shall never forget lunch. We had steak. Steak is the state flower. I set to with a will and soon polished off the last shred of tenderloin. Just then a waiter put a steak in front of me twice as big as the one I had eaten. "What's that thar, pardner?" says I.

"That thar's yore steak, pardner," says he.

"What was that thar I just et?" says I.

"That thar was jest yore hors d'oeuvre," says he.

I tried to tell my hosts how overjoyed I was to be having my first glimpse of their great republic. "No other planet in the universe has contributed as many notable figures to history as Texas," I enthused. "Ma Ferguson, Sam Houston, Abraham Lincoln, George Washington, Queen Victoria, Amon G. Carter, Charlemagne, the Twelve Apostles..."

"Excuse me, pardner," interrupted a Texan, "only nine of the Twelve Apostles was from Texas."

After lunch my hosts asked me if there was anything in particular I wished to see. "Before I leave Houston," I said, "I want to see a new gusher come in."

"Easiest thing in the world. Step this way." We went to a vacant lot back of the post office, and the chairman of the Houston Gusher Commission took a folding divining rod from his pocket and dangled it over a cactus plant. Within seconds there was a heaving under the surface, then a geyser of high-octane black gold shot 92 feet into the air.

"Golly!" I exclaimed in awesome admiration. "I'll wager this will bring you fellows a pretty penny in royalties."

"Why, she's yours," cried the chairman jovially. "Your luncheon favor. Compliments of the Chamber of Commerce." Accounts of the legendary hospitality of Houston are definitely not exaggerated.

I shall never forget my first sight of Fort Worth. As I neared the city it was enveloped in a shimmering halo; golds, crimsons, purples, oranges, bananas, a thousand hues intermingled in a riot of color. I thought I had never seen so gorgeous a sunset. Later I learned that it was not a sunset at all but the day's output of the great Fort Worth Cowboy Shirt Plant hung out to air.

Another Fort Worth industrial giant is its great Cowboy Lament Works. There 20,000 musicians work in three shifts composing the dirges that have made the name of Texas so—what shall I say?—throughout the world.

I shall not name, for I would not dignify him by doing so, a certain viper whom I encountered at a luncheon given for me by the Chamber of Commerce. Chatting casually with this person who had been introduced to me as a Texan, I said, "You've got a mighty fine state down here, pardner."

"Oh, it's all right," he said, in a tone of diffidence which I did not quite like. "It's the biggest state in the Union," I said, bridling.

"Size isn't everything," he remarked. I was now pretty nettled. "Texas has won every war for the United States, including the Revolutionary, the Civil and both World Wars."

"Pooh!"

"You pooh Texas!" I cried.

"Yes, and I re-pooh it!" said he. "Where do you come from?"

"Round Lake, New York."

"I thought so. You foreigners who become enamored of Texas brag worse than our Chamber of Commerce. Texas is just another state."

I know I acted hastily. But I couldn't help it. I shot him.

A week passed and my visit to the Lonesome Star State was coming to a close. I hadn't seen all of Texas. It would take at least another week to do that. But I had completed my research with Rhode Island. It really does go 220 times into Texas. In fact, I had Deaf Smith County left over.

Case Histories

There's nothing wrong with the average person that a good psychiatrist can't exaggerate.

—Toronto *Star*

HAVE YOU heard the story of the middle-aged Texan who went to the psychiatrist? "Doc," he began, "I shore need yore help. I'm in a bad way. I been a Texan all my life and suddenly I just don't give a damn!"

—Inez Robb, United Feature Syndicate

RUTH HUSSEY tells about the actress who phoned a friend and wept, "I just heard my husband wants a divorce."

"So what?" asked her unsympathetic pal.

"Well," said the actress, "my psychiatrist is out of town and I just don't know what to *think!*" —Erskine Johnson, NEA

A FRIEND of mine, threatened with a nervous breakdown, was persuaded to consult a psychiatrist. After their first session he gave her a list of things to do and made a weekly appointment for her. Two weeks later he telephoned her and asked why she had failed to keep her appointments.

"But, Doctor," she explained, "you said for me to stay away from people who irritate me, and I don't know anyone who irritates me more than you do." —Ethel Fischer

PSYCHIATRIST to patient: "Maybe you don't have a complex—maybe you *are* inferior." —Cartoon in a doctor's office, quoted by Herb Stein in *The Hollywood Reporter*

A PATIENT was brought to a psychiatrist by friends, who informed the doctor that the man was suffering from delusions that a huge fortune was awaiting him. He was expecting two letters which would give him details involving deeds to a rubber plantation in Sumatra and titles to some mines in South America.

"It was a difficult case and I worked hard on it," the psychiatrist told some colleagues. "And just when I had the man cured—the two letters arrived!" —*This Week Magazine*

A YOUNG psychoanalyst was telling an older colleague about his troubles in getting intelligent responses from his patients. "Suppose you ask me some of your questions," the old analyst suggested.

"Well, my first question is: What is it that wears a skirt and from whose lips comes pleasure?"

"A Scot blowing a bagpipe," the veteran answered.

"Right," said the younger one. "Now, what is it that has smooth curves and at unexpected moments becomes uncontrollable?"

"Herb Score's pitching."

"Right! What do you think of when two arms slip around your shoulder?"

"Why, a football tackle," replied the veteran.

"Right," said the young doctor. "All your answers were amazingly correct. But you'd be surprised at the silly answers I keep getting!"

—*The Yale Record*

A NEW YORK psychiatrist ran into one of his patients at a restaurant. "Doctor," the woman said, introducing her spouse, "this is my husband—one of the men I've been telling you about."

—Hy Gardner in New York *Herald Tribune*

MOTHER OF small boy to child psychiatrist: "Well, I don't know whether or not *he* feels insecure, but everybody else in the neighborhood certainly does!" —Dick Turner cartoon, NEA

NEW YORKERS tell about the Columbia University professor who decided he needed to consult a psychiatrist. Resolved to get a good man, he picked out one on Park Avenue and entered his reception room. The room was beautifully appointed, but there was no receptionist—only two doors labeled "Men" and "Women." Pushing open the door marked "Men" the professor found himself in a second room. Here were two more doors lettered "Introverts" and "Extroverts." He hesitated a moment, then entered the door marked "Introverts" and found himself in still another room with two doors. These were designated, "Those Making Under $10,000" and "Those Making $10,000 and Over."

There was no question that the professor's was the under-$10,000 door. So he walked through it—and found himself right back on Park Avenue.

—Dr. William L. Pressly, quoted by Hugh Park in Atlanta *Journal*

Foot-in-Mouth Disease

WARNING posted in an office at a southern air base: CAUTION—*Be Sure Brain Is Engaged Before Putting Mouth in Gear!*

—John M. Dowling

AT COLLEGE we had a biology club sponsored by one of the professors—a dignified spinster. A farmer whose place was noted for its wide variety of flowers spoke at one of our meetings. More at home in his garden than on the rostrum, he made a brave start: "I can assure you that it is a pleasure for me to be with you today. I have known your teacher a good many years and during that time we have been intimate . . . "

There was a slight titter and he hurriedly continued: "That is, in a biological way, of course." —George A. Nichols

CLARE BOOTHE LUCE, our former ambassador to Italy, tells about a big reception when the handshaking line suddenly stopped, leaving a flustered American girl standing in front of the ambassador. "Oh, Mrs. Luce," she said, "it's so wonderful to be over here in Rome seeing all these old, romantic ruins—and you, too."

—Ray Josephs in *The American Weekly*

AT FAIRLEIGH-DICKINSON College in New Jersey a shapely coed who wore her sweaters much tighter than necessary was called up to the front of the room to give a report. But the uproarious males in the class never gave her a chance to get beyond her opening words: "Now there are just two points I'd like to bring out . . . "

—Peggy McEvoy

THE VICTIM, a woman in her early 30's, told this one on herself. It had been several weeks since a prosperous farmer had been in the bank where she worked. "Miss Lee," he greeted her, "you seem to be getting a little stouter."

"Don't you know you mustn't ever tell a woman she is getting fat?" she chided.

"Oh," he said with surprise, "I didn't think a woman your age would mind." —Ethel Wiede in *True*

WHEN SAXE COMMINS first lectured on writing at Columbia he wondered if his audience had understood him. A buxom lady in the class reassured him quickly. "Oh, Mr. Commins," she gushed, "your criticisms were as welcome as water to a drowning man."

—Bennett Cerf in *The Saturday Review*

ONE MORNING a Cleveland businessman's secretary was showing off a stunning new tailored suit, her birthday present from her family. Her boss stopped to admire it, then went on into his private office to greet a client who was waiting to see him.

"Sorry to keep you waiting," he told his startled caller, "but I was just admiring my secretary in her birthday suit."

—Eleanor Clarage in Cleveland *Plain Dealer*

The Stenographic Pool

G. K. Chesterton on the emancipation of women: *Twenty million young women rose to their feet with the cry, "We will not be dictated to," and proceeded to become stenographers.*

AN EXECUTIVE dictated some difficult letters to a new stenographer. When the girl brought back the copies for his signature, the official read a garbled version of his carefully thought-out remarks. Returning the letters to the stenographer he barked, "Don't you read these letters before putting them on my desk?"

"Oh, no," she replied. "I thought they were confidential."

OFFICE GIRL to good-looking new girl: "Mr. Hartnig? Keep going until a red-haired man winks at you, then turn right and go all the way back to a hoarse voice that says, 'WOW'—turn left until you run into a low whistle, and you're there."

—Herb Williams cartoon in *Look*

ONE SUPERVISOR was telling another: "When I walk by the

typists I feel like a piece of uranium approaching a battery of Geiger counters."

"What do you mean?"

"The closer I get, the faster they click!" —C. V. Mathis

ONE OF the single girls in our office came in one morning and began passing out cigars and candy, both with blue ribbons. Puzzled and more than a little surprised, we asked the occasion. Proudly she displayed the solitaire on her left hand and announced: "It's a boy—six feet tall and 185 pounds." —Mrs. Tom Heno

SMART YOUNG thing to personnel manager: "If you must know, my last boss fired me because of a mistake I wouldn't make!" —Talbert cartoon in *Men Only and London Opinion*

ONE BUSINESSMAN to another as they admire new electronic computer: "Another big advantage. It will never come prancing in starry-eyed one morning and announce it is leaving to get married." —B. Tobey cartoon in *The Saturday Evening Post*

GIRL PASSING hat to fellow worker: "We're taking up a collection for one of the girls in the office who is not going to get married or leave, but feels that she is stuck here for the rest of her life." —Schulz cartoon in *The Saturday Evening Post*

Memo sent by a secretary at an advertising agency asking for a raise:

The Secretary You Save May Be Your Own.

One Secretary in the Hand Is Worth Two in the Bush.

Damn the Personnel Department, Full Speed Ahead.

They Also Serve Who Sit and Type.

Help Stamp Out Small Wages.

Give Us This Day Our Yearly Raise.

Money Is the Root of All Secretaries.

My Boss Is My Shepherd, I Shall Not Want.

Your Obedient Servant, Ilean M. Clarke

—Dick Neff in *Advertising Agency Magazine*

Ad Ventures

IN SEATTLE an advertisement in the *Times* offered a "good opportunity for an inefficient stenographer to work until we can secure an efficient one."

—*Time*

FROM THE Edinburgh *Scotsman:* "Ship-In-Bottle-Makers! Free Service! Young man accepts full bottles of Duff Gordon Sherry; returns them empty, ready for insertion of ship. Prompt conscientious work guaranteed."

AD ON bulletin board of the Ship Service Store, Naval Base, Norfolk: "For Sale. One 1949 Harley-Davidson motorcycle, in good condition. Contact Geo. Smith 1/c. Fracture Ward, U. S. Naval Hospital, Portsmouth, Va."

FROM A Los Angeles paper: "For Rent: 2-bedroom house in smog-free Burbank. Fireplace, knotty-pine dining room, etc. Near schools, shopping center, transportation. EXTRA! Friendly family next door is just completing an 18 x 24 foot swimming pool."

—Art Ryon in Los Angeles *Times*

WANT AD in Dansville, N. Y., *Breeze:* "Farmer, age 38, wishes to meet woman around 30 who owns tractor. Please enclose picture of tractor."

AD IN the New York *Times:* "Will sell one Opera Seat, subscription, second row orchestra. Monday evenings; very accessible to exit."

—*The Woman*

CLASSIFIED ad: "Man wanted to work in dynamite factory; must be willing to travel." —Hy Gardner in New York *Herald Tribune*

AD IN *Billboard:* "Lion tamer wants tamer lion."

—Gene Sherman in Los Angeles *Times*

Zanies All

A BIG-GAME hunter in Africa was on his way back to camp one night when an enormous lion walked out of the jungle not 20 feet away. As the lion was about to spring the hunter fired his last cartridge and missed. The lion sprang too far and landed 15 feet beyond the hunter, who then ran for camp and made it safely.

The next day the hunter went back of the camp to practice a little shooting at close range. He heard a strange noise in the brush and investigated. It was the lion—practicing short leaps!

—Webster cartoon in New York *Herald Tribune*

"TERRIFIC date last night," Fred told Bill at the office one morning: "Blonde. Really gorgeous. After the dance we went out and parked by the lake. I asked her for a kiss. She said she would if I'd put the top down so we could enjoy the moonlight. So I went to work and got the top down in about an hour and—"

"An hour!" Bill exclaimed. "I get mine down in two minutes."

"Sure," replied Fred, "but *you* have a convertible!"

—R. W. Tupper

AN AFRICAN chieftain flew to London for a visit and was met at the airport by newsmen. "Good morning, Chief," one said. "Did you have a comfortable flight?"

The chief made a series of raucous noises—honk, oink, screech, whistle, z-z-z-z—then added in perfect English, "Yes, very pleasant indeed."

"And how long do you plan to stay?" asked the reporter.

Prefacing his remarks with the same noises the chief answered, "About three weeks I think."

"Tell me, Chief," inquired the baffled reporter, "where did you learn to speak such flawless English?"

After the now standard honk, oink, screech, whistle and z-z-z-z, the chief said, "Short-wave radio."

—Terry Harman

A RAILROAD engineer got up on the wrong side of the bed one morning. The water for his shower was cold. His shoelace broke. At breakfast his toast was burned. His car wouldn't start and he had to taxi to the yards. He was late, so when he started his train he speeded it up to 90 miles an hour. . . . Just as he swung around a curve he saw another train coming straight at him—on the *same* track. He heaved a big sigh and, turning to the fireman, said, "Did you ever have one of those days when just everything goes wrong?"

—Edith Gwynne, John F. Dille Syndicate

HARRY HERSHFIELD tells about the dictator in an oxygen tent who was sinking fast. By his bedside was his second in command, tears streaming down his face. The dictator feebly patted his aide's hand. "Do not grieve so, comrade," he whispered. "I want you to know that because of your loyalty I am leaving you my money, my cars, my plane, my country estate, my yacht—everything!"

"Thank you, thank you," cried his successor. "You're much too good to me. If there was only something I could do for *you!*"

The dying man boosted himself up a bit. "There is," he gasped. "Just take your foot off the oxygen tube!"

—John Wheeler, quoted by E. E. Kenyon in *The American Weekly*

IN ENGLAND Bill McGowran told me the yarn about the rural letter carrier who covered his route on foot and always cut through the fields from one village to the next. One day he climbed a fence and started across a large field when an enormous bull charged toward him. By the time he reached the fence on the far side the bull was at his heels. The mail carrier hurled his pouch across the fence, then threw himself over and landed in a heap, out of reach of the animal. He lay still for a few moments, trembling in every limb, cold sweat on his brow, a few groans escaping from his lips. Then a stranger who had witnessed the excitement said, " 'E almost got you that time!"

Said the letter carrier, " 'E almost gets me *every* time!"

—H. Allen Smith, *Smith's London Journal* (Doubleday)

With a British Accent

AT A MUSICALE at the British Embassy an Englishman brought along his eight-year-old son, a lad who had been living in Washington for the past three years. Nothing untoward happened until the finale when the musicians struck up "God Save the Queen."

At the first note the young Englishman started singing, *not* the British words but a loud, penetrating "My Country 'Tis of Thee!" He continued, letter perfect, right to the end. As the music stopped a shocked British drawl pierced the sudden silence:

"My word! The boy's been brain-washed!"

—Mary Van Rensselaer Thayer in Washington *Post and Times Herald*

BRITAIN'S famous Black Watch Regiment was to put on an exhibition in our Illinois town, and the captain serving as their advance man was being interviewed on TV. After various questions he was asked if the group had performed before in this country. "Yes, sir," replied the captain, "in 1776." —Lauraine B. Ham

VISITORS TO London are familiar with the soapbox orators who congregate in Hyde Park to harangue the public upon the vital, and not so vital, questions of the day. One morning a crowd was gathered around a speaker who was loudly proclaiming the guilt of the ruling classes for the lamentable state of the nation. "They're to blame for all our troubles!" he shouted. "What we should do is to burn down the 'Ouse of Commons—burn down Buckin'am Palace."

When the crowd began to interfere with traffic a bobby stepped up and ordered firmly but politely: "Here, you people, move on and make way for traffic to pass. Them in favor of burnin' the House of Commons step to the right, them in favor of burnin' Buckingham Palace go to the left. Make way, now; make way."

The crowd burst into good-natured laughter and quickly dispersed. —*The Wall Street Journal*

WHAT HOSTESS isn't worried about seating arrangements for her guests? Fortunately, English hostesses can call for assistance in this etiquette-laden matter by writing to the "Heralds of the College of Arms" and hope for an answer as superb as the one received by the anxious hostess of the Aga Khan.

"The Aga Khan," wrote the experts, "is held by his followers to be the direct descendant of God. An English Duke takes precedence."

—*Woman's Day*

WHEN CHARLES LAUGHTON was preparing for the filming of *Mutiny on the Bounty,* he went to a famous court tailor on London's Bond Street and said to a clerk, "I believe you made up a uniform for one Captain Bligh. I should like to have duplicates made to my measure."

"Captain Bligh, sir?"

Laughton nodded.

"And what year would that be?" the clerk asked.

"1789."

Not in the least ruffled the clerk replied, "I'll see, sir."

"And do you know," Laughton said later, "the clerk was back in a few minutes with the complete record and measurements. I had the duplicates made and wore them in the picture."

—Kurt Singer, *The Laughton Story* (John C. Winston)

Abbreviated Speech

EXCERPTS from a series of "Letters to the Editor" in the *Sunday Times,* London:

From Douglas Falby: "Few customers probably see their tailors' private markings on the measurement card, and this spares one from shocks like the one I received when I visited my tailor and—while he was absent—glanced at his card. Under the heading Special Peculiarities was this cryptic note: 'prom tum.' "

From J. B. Freedman: "We tailors can, if necessary, abbreviate still further. For the man with a long neck, sloping shoulders, round back, head forward and 'prom tum' we use a composite description—S.L.B.C.H. Translation: 'Stands Like a Blooming Cab Horse!' "

From R. L. Johnson: "Forced to buy a suit in a hurry I visited one of the top shops in London's West End. My figure made a correct fitting difficult, and the salesman was reluctant to sell the suit I chose. But I overrode him.

"As the suit was being packed I noticed the initials S.A.O.B.J. on the sales slip. When I asked one of the other clerks what they meant, he replied, 'Sold Against Our Better Judgment!' "

THERE'S AN income-tax payer in Winnipeg whose bitterest suspicions about the government's attitude toward its victims have been confirmed. Shortly after his tax had been remitted this citizen received the usual printed acknowledgment, including the request that in case of further correspondence reference should be made to the taxpayer's serial number—SAP 7088. —*Maclean's Magazine*

ONE MAN to another: "He's a boss spelled backward—you know: *double* s.o.b." —Al Deeming

MY FRIEND R. B. Jones doesn't have a first or middle name—only the initials R. B. This unusual arrangement was never a problem until he went to work for a government agency. The government is not accustomed to initialed employes, so R. B. had a lot of explaining to do. On the official forms for the payroll and personnel departments, his name was carefully entered as R (Only) B (Only) Jones.

Sure enough, when R. B. got his pay check, it was made out to Ronly Bonly Jones. —Stephen A. Bomer in *True*

DAVE HOFF, editor of U.S.S. *Appalachian's* newspaper, received a letter from a friend staying at the Hotel Savoy in London.

When he asked for a room the clerk presented him with a big old-fashioned register whose page listing read like this:

Gen. Lord Wilfred I. J. Innis-Kerr, K.C.B., K.B.E., D.S.O., M.C.

Lt. Col. Humphrey Willis Hollister, O.B.E., D.S.O., M.C.
Col. Sir James Illingsworth, V.C., K.C.M.G., O.L.
Cmdr. Paul P. Pottlesworth, D.S.C., S.M., R.N.
WT 2/c. Joe Butts, USN, AWOL.

—Chaplain George E. Thomas, USN

WHEN H. L. Mencken was city editor of the Baltimore *Herald* a young man applied for a job on the paper. Citing his qualifications the applicant told him he had a B. A. degree. Mencken's reply: "Believe Anything, eh!" —Baltimore *Sun*

Personal Glimpses

HEYWOOD BROUN, one of the kindest newspapermen ever, was not blessed with much executive ability. When he was running the *Connecticut Nutmeg* its managing board empowered him to start new hands at $35 a week minimum to $50 maximum. Broun accordingly asked every job-seeker: "Which would you prefer—$35 a week or $50?"

—Bennett Cerf

THE LATE Haakon VII of Norway, as king of a constitutional democratic monarchy, had only very limited authority. Once, during a cabinet meeting, he accidentally dropped his handkerchief. A cabinet member picked it up and handed it to him. "Thank you very much," said the King taking the handkerchief. Then he added with a smile, "This is the only thing into which I dare put my nose." —N. Salvesen

OLIVER HERFORD, famous author, artist and wit, once kept a bear in his New York hotel rooms. He had endless trouble with this pet and finally had to give it away to a zoo. A friend asked Herford why he had gotten the bear in the first place. "It was like this," said Herford. "I received an unexpected sum of money and was so afraid I would spend it foolishly that I bought the bear."

—Arthur Maurice, *The Players Book*

WHEN GEN. Walter Bedell Smith left the State Department to go into private business after 40 years of government service, he told friends the story he liked best about himself: That he was the most even-tempered man in government—always mad.

—"Washington Weather Vane" in New York *Herald Tribune*

RING LARDNER was once requested by a girl reporter to contribute to a symposium about the virtues of wives. The idea was to show that, without their helpmeets, most gents would be in the gutter. Mr. Lardner surprised the lady by replying as follows:

"I was never one to keep a diary, and so must depend on an unsteady, Volsteady memory for the things my wife has done for me. In 1914, I think it was July, she cleaned my white shoes. In 1918 she told the draft board that she and three kiddies were dependent on me for support.

"In 1921 and again in 1923 she brought in some ice, White Rock and glasses. Late one night in 1924 we got home from somewhere and I said I was hungry and she gave me a verbal picture of the location of the pantry. Once a man named Morris called me up and she told him I was out of town. The time our car stalled she suggested it must be out of gas. Another time I quit cigarettes and she felt sorry for me.

"Once, on an overnight train trip, just as I was nearly crazy trying to guess whether I should take the lower or upper berth she solved the problem by crawling into the lower. And once when a waiter was going to put two lumps of sugar in my coffee, my wife stopped him. She didn't touch him or call him a name; she just said, 'Only one lump!' And he did not put the other lump in."

—John Wheeler, NANA

"DURING ONE of my first sessions in the Senate," writes former President Harry S. Truman in *Year of Decisions,* "J. Hamilton Lewis came over and sat down by me. He was from Illinois and was the whip in the Senate at that time. 'Don't start out with an inferiority complex,' he told me. 'For the first six months you'll wonder how you got here—and after that you'll wonder how the rest of us got here.' "

—Published by Doubleday

AT AMHERST Robert Frost's method of teaching his course in English literature was to give informal talks at his home. The poet detested semester exams, but since they were compulsory he obeyed. "But I made them as simple as I could," he told a group of us. "Once I asked only one question: 'What good did my course do you?' and requested brief replies. The answer I liked best was 'Not a damn bit!' "

"Did you pass him?"

"Yes, I gave him a 90."

"Why not 100?" we asked.

"He left the 'n' off damn."

—N. S. Olds in Greenwich Village, N. Y., *Villager*

LYNN FONTANNE, hurrying to keep an appointment after a performance of *I Know My Love,* said to the stage manager, "Please ask Mr. Lunt to come down the stairs in the last scene a little more quickly, as he holds up my line."

The message was relayed to Mr. Lunt. "Please tell Miss Fontanne," he replied, "that if she wants me to come downstairs faster, she should have married a younger man."

—Philadelphia *Inquirer*

JACKIE ROBINSON, the first Negro to play in big-league baseball, entered the majors with a wry, if subdued, sense of humor. On the day of his first appearance he kissed his wife good-by at their hotel and said, "Honey, if you come out to Ebbets Field today you won't have any trouble recognizing me." He paused with the skill of a Frank Fay. "My number is 42." —Bob Considine, INS

Clergymen at Large

ONE DAY the New York Giants' football scout Jack Lavalle bumped into his friend Bishop Fulton J. Sheen in Pennsylvania Station. As Lavalle tells it: "He asked where I was going, and I told him Pittsburgh to scout the Steelers. This was the same time that evangelist Billy Graham was holding revival meetings in Pittsburgh and Bishop Sheen, with a grin, said, 'While you're down there, Jack, how about scouting Billy Graham for me?' "

—Art McGinley, quoted by Kenneth Speer in Pittsburgh *Sun-Telegraph*

A MINISTER who conducts a gospel program on a Detroit TV station read excerpts from viewers' letters, taking care to display the donations clipped to each one. Then he looked straight into the camera and said earnestly, "And now, my dear funds . . ."

—Doris A. Paul

ONE OF my father's favorite stories concerns Father Fitzpatrick, a beloved priest in his home town. As the cleric walked down the street one day he met The Rev.

"Why I Do Not Attend the Movies"

MULLING over the timeworn excuses people give for not going to church, The Rev. Grant H. Elford of Lake Crystal, Minn., and Dr. Ronald Meredith of Fresno, Calif., on a trip together, compiled this list of reasons:

1. The manager of the theater never called on me.
2. I did go a few times, but no one spoke to me. Those who go there aren't very friendly.
3. Every time I go they ask me for money.
4. Not all folks live up to the high moral standards of the films.
5. I went so much as a child I've decided I've had all the entertainment I need.
6. The performance lasts too long; I can't sit still for an hour and three quarters.
7. I don't always agree with what I hear and see.
8. I don't think they have very good music.
9. The shows are held in the evenings, and that's the only time I am able to be at home with the family.

—*Newsweek*

Mr. Whittemore, who was supervising the building of his new Congregational church. The priest inquired politely how the church was coming along and how well the contributions were coming in.

"Everything is fine, Father," the reverend assured him, then added, "Perhaps you'd like to make a contribution yourself."

"I'd certainly like to," answered the priest, "but my bishop would never allow me to contribute to a Protestant church."

The next morning, however, when opening his mail, Mr. Whittemore found a check for $50 with this note from Father Fitzpatrick: "Although my bishop would never consent to a contribution for the erection of a Protestant church, there must be some expense involved in the tearing down of the old church, and I'm sure he would never object to my contributing to that."

—V. A. Barnet

A CANADIAN priest tells of hearing the confession of a rough-and-ready fellow who said it had been two years since he last confessed. He explained that he was a trapper in a remote part of Canada; that it took him the better part of two weeks to get to confession, traveling on foot, by canoe and then by train and bus; and that usually he could not afford to leave his trap lines untended for that long.

"You're way behind the times," the priest said. "You could fly to the city, go to confession and communion and be back home in 36 hours. Why not take a plane next time?"

"I've thought of that," the man said. "But for venial sins, it's too expensive—and for mortal sins, it's too risky." —Ed Anderson

SHE IS rich, opinionated and completely devoted to her friends. I am her friend and also her pastor. One day she confided to me: "You know, Mr. Bagby, I no longer listen to Dr. Sockman and Dr. Peale on Sunday mornings before I come to church. It just isn't fair to you."

—The Rev. Steadman Bagby

A BOYISH-LOOKING Presbyterian minister who was serving his first mission in the hills of Kentucky noticed that one of his faithful parishioners had been absent from services several Sundays in a row, so he decided to go see her and ask why.

She shook her head and looked at him pityingly. "Son," she said, "you ain't old enough to have sinned enough to have repented enough to be able to preach about it." —Mrs. Fred Oehlman

A HOUSTON rabbi received this thank-you letter from a bridegroom he'd married: "Dear Rabbi, I want to thank you for the beautiful way you brought my happiness to a conclusion."

—Earl Wilson, Hall Syndicate

Marry-Go-Round

Something else every couple should save for their old age is their marriage. —Imogene Fey in *Life Today*

THE HONEYMOON is over when he phones that he'll be late for supper—and she has already left a note that it's in the refrigerator.

—Bill Lawrence

A YOUNG MAN whose household was far from placid asked a friend how he and his wife managed to avoid arguments. "When Betty and I were married," he said, "I laid down the law. I told her that I would make all major decisions and that she could make all the minor decisions."

"What's your definition of a minor decision?"

"Well, what school are our kids going to, should I look for a better job, shall we take our savings and buy stocks, shall we buy a new house . . . those are the decisions that Betty handles."

"Then what are major decisions?"

"Oh, something like should we admit Red China to the United Nations." —Mario Lazo, Jr.

HUSBAND TO wife: "I'll tell you whether I still love you when I find out what you're leading up to."

—Goldstein cartoon in *The Saturday Evening Post*

DID a look from your spouse
Ever make you conclude
That if anyone present
Had talked too much, you'd?

—C. C. in *The Christian Science Monitor*

TOGGED OUT in gay gypsy rags I was the fortune-teller at our church bazaar. Business was brisk as people I knew came in to hear the outlandish things I predicted for them. My last customer, a man, was a stranger to me. Trying to sound particularly mysterious and convincing, I intoned in a deep voice, "I see a buried treasure."

"Oh, I know all about that," the man interrupted testily. "My wife's first husband!" —Mrs. D. B. Hairston

TOURNAMENT bridge is a fiercely competitive game that sometimes results in a flare-up of temper between partners, and the outburst is none the less violent when the two partners happen to be husband and wife. At a national tournament in Dallas one of these hassles ended with the man abruptly walking away from the table. An opponent turned to the man's partner and asked, "Is that your husband?" and received the instantaneous reply: "Of course it is—you don't think I'd be living *in sin* with a man like that, do you?"

—Madeline Anderson in *The Bulletin* (American Contract Bridge League)

LIKE MOST women she was perpetually asking her husband to help her rearrange the furniture. Finally, when she went on a visit, he saw his chance to put an end to all this foolishness. He had all the rooms repapered—according to his special instructions.

She was delighted with the redecorating, but almost immediately asked him to help her move the sofa. As they tugged the bulky piece from the wall, she gasped. The wall behind the sofa had not been repapered—and neither had the spots behind the other furniture!

—Eugene Salmi

FOR-SALE ad in the Wayne, Pa., *Suburban and Wayne Times:* "Complete 30-volume set Encyclopedia Americana. Latest edition. Never used—my wife knows everything."

WE HAD BEEN attending a work-simplification class at our plant and were eager to try out the new-found techniques. "But don't try them at home!" our instructor warned us. And he told about the study he made of his wife's getting breakfast. She made innumerable trips between cupboards, stove and table, he said, often carrying only one item. He urged her to save time by taking, for instance, the silver *and* plates together instead of separately.

"When I started the study," he said, "it took her 20 minutes to get breakfast. I reduced the time by saving a minute here and a minute there until now—I can do the whole job in seven minutes!"

—H. D. Langham

WOMAN TO bank teller: "I want to make this withdrawal from my husband's half of our joint account."

—J. Monahan, McNaught Syndicate

My Banking Daze

Condensed from Emily Kimbrough's introduction to Edgar Scott's "How to Lay a Nest Egg"

WHEN I went from Chicago to boarding school in Bryn Mawr, Pa., my parents accompanied me. Anticipating the unhappy moment of parting, my father had provided a surprise. It was not a bag of popcorn, which had up to that time been the panacea of my emotional crises. It was a long, narrow, cardboard-covered checkbook. My father told me that I now had a bank account, and that the Bryn Mawr Trust Company had given me this book so that I could take out money. I admitted, sniffling, that I thought it very kind of the institution.

We sat down on the steps of the school, and Father showed me how to write a check and how to record the amount each time on the "stub." In my emotional and generally stopped-up condition I thought he said "stump." For a long time thereafter I referred with pride to my check stumps.

I was overwhelmed by the importance of having a bank account, but during the weeks that followed I had very little occasion to write checks. When, one Saturday morning, I had a check from my mother to deposit, I persuaded several of my friends to come with me. I did not propose to let pass unnoticed the benefaction I was about to bestow on the Bryn Mawr Trust Company. At the teller's window, nearly bursting with nonchalance, I slid the check to the gentleman on the other side of the grating. He read the check and then turned it over, immediately incurring my distrust. I was not sure that I wanted to place my money in the hands of a man who didn't realize that there was printing only on one side of the check. He increased my displeasure by pushing the check back to me.

"You haven't endorsed it," he said, and added with what seemed to me obnoxious patronage: "That's to identify it. Every check has to be identified."

I took the check and wrote my

identification. Once more I handed it through the window and indicated, with scathing boredom, my writing on the back. The nauseating little pipsqueak read it aloud: " 'Birthday present from my mother.'

"That's not the identification I mean," he said. "All we want is the signature, right there"—he pointed with his finger—"across the back. And would you like me to help you make out a deposit slip?"

I put my hand out for the check. "I have decided not to deposit at all today," I told him, and my voice was as sharp and as cold as an ice skate. "I'm thinking of looking at another bank."

Acute necessity, some months later, forced me to deposit the check at the same bank. I made several trips until I hit upon a time when another teller was at the window.

By the time I reached college I had outwitted the young man to such an extent that my roommate's father went to my father one day with a letter from his daughter.

"I didn't want to talk about this over the telephone," he said, and my father reported the conversation to me later, "but as far as I can make out, our daughters are engaged in a system of juggling checks. They think they've invented it. In lower circles their invention would be called 'kiting' checks, and you or I had better get down there fast to keep them out of jail."

The teller's temperate attitude about this advancement in our banking knowledge broke down considerably my antagonism to him, and his assertion to my father that he saw no need of informing the college authorities made him, at that instant, dear to me.

A few days before my graduation I went to say good-by to him. He opened the grill, and I felt that this was a symbol of the rapprochement we had reached at the end of six years. As we shook hands he said, "I'm sorry you're leaving, Miss Kimbrough. We'll miss you. Would you mind if I asked you one personal question? I feel that I can't let you go before finding it out."

I felt that the rapprochement had gone further than I had realized. The revelation put me all atremble, so that I could only nod my assent.

"Why is it," he said, "that over the years, every so often, you've made out checks to cash or to self for the most peculiar amounts—$1.89, $2.13—sums like that?"

I answered sharply, the old antagonism in my voice again:

"Why, I don't see anything peculiar in that. I write them when my balance gets into odd numbers which are hard to subtract, especially nines. I do one check that brings my balance to zeros and round numbers again so that I can make a fresh start."

"Thank you," he said. "That's something I hadn't thought of. Good-by, Miss Kimbrough. We'll remember you here at the bank."

I thought, as I went out of the building, that that was very generous of him, considering how many customers they had.

Night-Club Highlights

THE BANKERS Trust Company was never quite the same after Robert Benchley bestowed his checking account on it. I understand the bank preserved some of his more uproarious checks, among them surely the one dated 3 a.m. at an uptown hot spot, made out to Cash, and endorsed: "Dear Bank, having a wonderful time. Wish you were here. Love to all. Bob."

—Frank Sullivan in foreword to *Chips Off the Old Benchley* (Harper)

A WOMAN visiting in Florida one winter was taken by friends to one of the plush resort night clubs. When she entered the rest room she discovered a large mural of Adam, wearing only a fig leaf. A sign warned customers: "Do Not Lift the Fig Leaf." But the visitor's feminine curiosity got the better of her, and she upped the leaf.

Bells began to ring, sirens sounded, plaster fell and bedlam set in. She turned and ran out the rest-room door—only to be blinded by a giant spotlight, while the orchestra blared fanfares.

—Bob Walling, quoted by Ronald Furse in Plattsmouth, Neb., *Journal*

I WAS really embarrassed one night. Visiting a Detroit night club I miscalculated the amount of money I'd spent and wound up with just enough to pay the large check, but not enough left over for a tip. There seemed to be no way out of the predicament, so I decided I'd just have to talk to the waiter. I called him over and apprehensively explained the fix I was in. The waiter, the typical suave but tough night-club type, listened to my story without a change of expression.

"Don't let a thing like that bother you," he murmured as he picked up the bill. "I'll just add this thing up again."

—Clarence Roeser in *True*

WHILE ATTENDING a night club with a favorite escort, a young woman had gone to the powder room where she met several friends she hadn't visited with in ages. The conversation was gay and gossipy, and time went on . . . and on . . . and on . . . . Then the maid handed her a note. It was from her obviously weary escort. In a bold, male hand were the words: "Can't understand why you haven't written."

—Betty Jane Balch in *Your Life*

IN A NIGHT club one evening a very pretty girl was wearing, around her neck, a thin chain from which hung a tiny golden airplane. One of the young men in the party stared at it so that the girl finally asked him, "Do you like my little airplane?"

"As a matter of fact," he replied, "I wasn't looking at it. I was really admiring the landing field."

—Athos Cadilhe Abilhoâ

A SAN DIEGO chap took his 13-year-old daughter up to Los Angeles for a big night out. Came the floor show and the father gulped—the chorus girls were wearing just a dab of gold-and-black satin. He stole a couple of sidelong glances at his daughter. Finally she leaned over and whispered, "Do you see what I see?" As the father swallowed uneasily, she said enthusiastically, "They are wearing my school colors!"

—Neil Morgan, quoted by Art Ryon in Los Angeles *Times*

Classroom Classics

School days are the happiest of your life—provided, of course, your youngsters are old enough to go. —*California Grocers Advocate*

PRINCIPAL TO small boy: "It's very generous of you, Russell, but I don't believe your resignation would help our crowded school situation." —Harry Mace cartoon in *The Saturday Evening Post*

A HUSKY Marine sergeant walked into a high-school principal's office in Boston. He wore two rows of ribbons among which was the D.S.C. The principal greeted him warmly and, after some talk of the former pupil's experiences at Iwo Jima and Okinawa, asked if there was anything he could do for him. "Yes, sir," said the sergeant. "I plan to go to college. Could I have a copy of my record here?"

"Certainly," said the principal. "Go to Room 211 and ask for Miss Jones. She takes care of such records."

The Marine hesitated. "Gee whiz, sir," he blurted, "couldn't you send somebody for it? I'm afraid of her." —Charles M. Shapp

A YOUNG Texas grade-school teacher was filling out a health questionnaire for the coming term. Weary after a difficult first semester, she was ready for the query, "Have you ever had a nervous breakdown?"

In big letters she wrote: "NOT YET, BUT WATCH THIS SPACE FOR DEVELOPMENTS." —Arvil Davis

OUR SIX-YEAR-OLD daughter proudly went off to school, looking very grown-up in a new blouse and skirt. When she came home I asked if anyone had liked her outfit. "Yes, the teacher did," said Jackie.

"Oh, she did not!" teased her father.

"She did, too!" retorted Jackie. "She said as long as I was dressed like a lady, why didn't I act like one." —Mrs. John Pregent

WHEN UMPQUA, Ore., pupils were told classes would be dismissed because of teachers' institute, Lonnie Leonard, eight, startled his parents with: "No school tomorrow. The teachers are going on an innocent toot." —AP

MY 14-YEAR-OLD grandson told me that his class was studying Churchill's *History of the English-Speaking Peoples*. "Some of us are going to write him a letter," he said.

"I'm sure Sir Winston will be pleased," I commented.

"Well, I don't know," he replied. "We're going to ask him not to write any more books." —Mary Marsh

TOLD TO come directly home from school my neighbor's first-grader was arriving at a different time each day, the difference sometimes amounting to as much as a half hour. When she scolded him about it he told her it wasn't his fault.

"We get out of school the same time each day," he said, "but the school-patrol boy at the highway who takes us across always makes us wait until a car comes along for him to stop."

—Mrs. J. Campbell

A FIRST-GRADE teacher struggled with the last pair of stubborn galoshes. Three times already that day—once in the morning and twice at noon—she had helped 35 youngsters pull their tight-fitting overshoes on or off, as the hour demanded. As she gave the final tug to Freddy's galoshes, he remarked thoughtfully, "These aren't mine."

His harassed teacher counted to ten, then extracted Freddy's feet. He watched the process in silence. When it was all over he volunteered, "They're my sister's, but Mommy says I have to wear them today!" —T. M. Stinnett in *NEA Journal*

Babe in the Woods

"Topics of The Times" in New York Times

THE SMALL BOY agreed willingly enough last September to a change of schools, from a private school for boys to a small-town public school. Secretly he probably hoped that he might move to a school where they did not bother to teach reading, arithmetic or social studies—those subjects that get in the way of a really good time at school. He went off happily enough the first day, but on his return he howled, "You know something awful about that new school? It has Girls!"

This was about the only thing in school that impressed the small boy for some weeks. All his reporting concerned these incredible intruders into a man's world—girls. One of them—the names were never remembered—cried when she got an ink blot on a map of Vermont. Another actually told the teacher she liked school and homework. Another one—this was reported with what could be called gusto—fell off a swing and sprained her wrist.

It was some weeks before this sort of impersonal reporting on what might have been a recently discovered barbarian tribe stopped. It stopped because there was football at the noon recess, and shop work, and Cub Scouts. There was also the discovery, made almost daily, that anyone who spelled Connecticut with more than two "t's" had to stay after school until he had written that teasing word 50 times. In all these activities there was no mention of girls. They had at last been put in their proper place, where many adult males have often found it hard to keep them—accepted, then ignored.

Then at dinner one night the small boy said, "You want to know something? I think girls are useful. You take a boy—he knows about football and ten-ton trucks and cowboy shooting, but what does a girl know? Nothing!" He added that he had spent his noon recess teaching a girl named Joyce to throw a football and that she seemed eager to learn and told him how well he threw it. The small boy continued, "And that's why girls are useful. You can teach 'em things, that's what you can do with girls."

A small boy has so very, very much to learn.

Toward More Picturesque Speech

THE AVERAGE boy uses soap as though it came out of his allowance (Marcelene Cox) . . . The time to start worrying about a boy is when he leaves the house *without* slamming the door *(Changing Times, The Kiplinger Magazine)*

Love and Marriage: Men who kiss and tell are not half as bad as those who kiss and exaggerate . . . The answer to a maiden's prayer is usually a man's question (James Garis) . . . Matrimony was probably the first union to defy management (Charles Ruffing in *The Saturday Evening Post)*

SKIING's a kind of dementia I prefer to enjoy in absentia (Ethel Jacobson in *Look)*

Winter Scenes: The frosty air has everyone talking in smoke signals (Vesta M. Kelly in *Farm Journal)* . . . Parked cars under their white meringues (Louise Andrews Kent) . . . Children upholstered in snowsuits (Elizabeth Enright in *Harper's Magazine)* . . . The thermometer registered a low opinion of the weather (Coral Hockaday)

Observations: Forbidden fruit is responsible for many a bad jam *(Town Journal)* . . . The reason history repeats itself is that most people weren't listening the first time (Dan Bennett) . . . A camel looks like something put together by a committee (T. R. Quaife) . . . Nothing takes weight off a man faster than a wife who's reducing (Franklin P. Jones in *American Family)*

Draft board—the world's largest travel agency *(Electricity on the Farm)* . . . *Peace*—a short pause between wars for enemy identification (Clemens Kirchner)

Pen Portraits: When opportunity knocked he complained of the noise (R. W. Jones) . . . He's a man of a few ill-chosen words (Budd Schulberg) . . . A southern belle, free and teasy on the drawl (Cy N. Peace) . . . If there's an idea in his head it's in solitary confinement (Tom Pease) . . . A woman with a very low bawling point (Mrs. John Coppersmith) . . . A meek little man with family circles under his eyes (E. Taylor in *Farm Journal)*

NOTHING damages a car more than attempting to trade it in *(Town Journal)* . . . There are few thrills as big as parking on what's left of the other fellow's nickel (Wilf Bennett in Vancouver *Province)*

Thrift With a Capital T

THE NOTION that, when children grow up and get married, parents can relax was blasted again when a Los Angeles woman received a phone call—collect—from her daughter in Chicago asking for a recipe. The mother gave it to her, then asked, "Why don't you buy a cook book?"

"Don't be silly," said the daughter. "That costs $3."

—Matt Weinstock in Los Angeles *Mirror-News*

OUT ON the Philadelphia Main Line a dignified woman took a jacket and sweater to her cleaners. Noticing a sign offering three garments cleaned for the price of one, she promptly slipped off her skirt, handed it to the startled clerk, wrapped her coat tightly about her and marched out.

—Earl Selby in Philadelphia *Evening Bulletin*

A CHICAGO friend of mine who decided to brighten up the weathered exterior of the cottage he had rented at Provincetown, Mass., went to the local hardware store for paint. The proprietor said he knew the place. "Four gallons will be enough for the whole job," he declared.

But my friend was inexperienced and ran out of paint with one wall still to be done. When he returned to the store for another gallon the proprietor regarded him with frank suspicion. "You used up four gallons for three walls?" he demanded.

The Chicagoan admitted that this was so. The Cape Codder shook his head. "Can't see my way to let you have it. It ain't never taken but four gallons to paint that house long as I remember. You must have wasted it. And the way I feel about waste—well, I just can't see my way to sell you five gallons for a four-gallon house."

My friend had to drive 50 miles up-Cape for the extra gallon.

—Kermit Rolland

TO TEACH our son the value of money and to try to curtail unnecessary purchases, we had him start keeping a detailed account of how he spent his allowance. One day as he was laboriously writing down his accounts he said, "You know, Mother, since I've had to write down everything, I really stop and think before I buy something." I was congratulating myself on the lesson he had learned, when he continued, "Nope, I just *never* buy anything that's hard to spell!"

—Mrs. C. L. Duerre

A FRIEND of mine settling a relative's estate had to go through all her belongings. She had been a thrifty soul who had saved everything, labeling each package. My friend thought he had hit a high of some sort when he discovered a package marked "Dress snaps that do not match." But shortly afterward he found a box labeled "String too short to use."

—Carroll Smith

I HAPPENED to be in a service station down on Maryland's eastern shore one day when a dilapidated, antique Ford pulled in for gas. The ancient character driving the relic asked for a dollar's worth of gas. The attendant smiled and said, "Dave, why don't you fill 'er up?"

"Wa-al," drawled the old fellow, "she might not run that fur."

—Gilbert E. Baldwin

LONDON tax officials thought they had Bill Hughes dead to rights when they charged him with bookmaking and failing to pay taxes on the proceeds. The 50-year-old shipyard worker admitted having saved $16,800 on his $56-a-week salary, but said he had done it this way:

Never ate candy, never smoked, never drank, never went out with women, shaved with his brother's razor blades, charged his grandmother 12 percent interest on money she borrowed, worked a night shift and borrowed his father's shoes while the latter slept to save shoe leather, went 13 years without buying a new suit, limited his lifelong movie-going to one picture, ate everything on the table even if he didn't want it, patched everything, including his underwear, never took a holiday trip that cost more than 56 cents.

—UP

High Cost of Living

WHEN SAM was asked how he budgeted his income he replied, "Oh, about 40 percent for food, 30 percent for shelter, 30 percent for clothing and 20 percent for amusement and incidentals."

"But, Sam, that makes 120 percent!"

"Lord, don't I know it!" Sam agreed.

—*Liberty*

MAN AT payroll window to worker: "Sorry, but with the deductions for the Sunshine Fund, social security, withholding tax, hospitalization, savings bonds, union dues, life insurance and gift fund, you owe us $6.80!"

—Hershberger cartoon, NEA

YOUNG WIFE to husband on streetcar: "If we miss two payments on the washing machine and one on the refrigerator, we'll have enough for a down payment on a television set."

—"Over the Teacups" in Toronto *Star*

WIFE POINTING out clerk in supermarket to husband: "Get ahead of him! He's marking up the prices again!" —Pearson cartoon in New York *Herald Tribune*

A MAN had posted himself in front of an office building with a tray of shoelaces. One executive made it a daily habit to give the unfortunate a dime, but he never took the laces. One day the peddler, on receiving the dime, tapped his departing benefactor on the back: "I don't like to complain, sir, but the laces are now 15 cents." —Jack Herbert in *The American Legion Magazine*

HOUSEWIFE TO friend: "We always have too much month left at the end of our money."

—Ottawa *Citizen*

IN INDIANAPOLIS lifer Walter Seward, paroled from the Indiana State Prison after a total of 22 years, was so shocked at the high cost of living that he persuaded the Division of Correction to send him back to jail. —*Time*

Larceny on a Lark

A MAN entered a shop in Jacksonville, Fla., picked up a suitcase and fled with it. The manager pursued, calling a policeman. They soon ran down the culprit. "I don't know what made me do it," the man cried. "If only you won't arrest me I'll be glad to pay for it."

The manager agreed, so they returned to the shop to complete the transaction. There the customer grew cautious. "As a matter of fact," he said, "this bag is a little better than I had in mind. I wonder if you could show me something cheaper?"

—Thomas B. Logue

WHEN A coal-mine operator in Canon City, Colo., found that the combination on his office safe had jammed, he telephoned the warden of Colorado State Prison and asked whether any of his inmates would know how to open it. Twenty minutes later a convict and a prison guard showed up. The inmate twiddled the dials a few moments, then calmly opened the door. "What do you figure I owe you?" asked the mine operator.

"Well," said the convict, "last time I opened a safe I got $1800."

—W. T. Little

A MAN called up the New York office of the FBI and reported that he had stolen a suitcase in Grand Central Station. "It's full of blueprints and other stuff that looks like secret military information," he said. "I've checked it in one of the public lockers and I'm mailing you the key. I'm a thief. But I'm a loyal American thief."

—George Dixon, King Features

IN A SPEECH on honesty Mark Twain said that as a boy he saw a cart of melons which sorely tempted him: "I sneaked up to the cart and stole a melon. I went into the alley to devour it, but I no sooner set my teeth into it than I paused, a strange feeling came over me. I came to a quick conclusion. Firmly I walked up to that cart, replaced that melon—and took a ripe one."

—*Edison Voice Writing*

IN LOS ANGELES police looked for the thief who walked up to a movie house, poked a pistol at theater cashier Kay Lee Stafford, said: "I didn't like the movie. Give me everybody's money back," and walked off with $212.

—*Time*

Living With Murder

Condensed from "Last Leaves"

Stephen Leacock

I AM A great reader of detective fiction. But I may have to give it up. It begins to affect one's daily life too much. I find myself perpetually "timing" everything, as they do in the stories, so as to have it ready for the evidence.

For instance, I went to dine several days ago with my old friend Jimmy Douglas. He lives alone. This, by itself, would make any reader of crime fiction time him. I paused a moment at the door before ringing the bell and noted that my watch said 7:00 p.m. A street clock, however, said 7:02½. I was thus able to place the time fairly accurately as at 7:01¼.

I rang the bell, and a Chinese servant showed me noiselessly into the *apparently* empty sitting room. I say *apparently,* because in the stories you never know. There might be a body lying in a corner. There was an ormolu clock on the mantel (there always is) which I was checking over when Douglas came in.

I could only describe his manner as quiet. Certainly he was free from any exhilaration. Whether this was a first effect of arsenic poisoning, or just from seeing me, I can't say. We had a cocktail. Douglas left two distinct fingerprints on his glass. I held mine by the rim. We sat down to dinner at 7:30. Of this I am practically certain because I remember that Douglas said, "Well, it's half-past," and as he said it the ormolu clock chimed the half-hour.

I noticed that at dinner Douglas took no soup. I took care on my part to take no fish. This, in the event of arsenic poison, would by elimination give indication of how the poison had been administered.

I got to talking and Douglas, I noticed, seemed unable to listen without signs of drowsiness. This might be due to arsenic poisoning. I left at nine, having noticed that Douglas roused slightly as the ormolu clock struck, and said, "Nine! I thought it was ten."

I drove home in a taxi and can easily identify the taxi, even if abandoned in a stone quarry, by a mark I made in the leather.

That was three days ago. I open the paper every morning with a nervous hand, looking for the finding of Douglas's body. They don't seem to have found it yet. I am all ready if they do. I have the taxi, the fingerprints, the ormolu clock—that's all you need usually.

Quotable Quotes

Earl Wilson: Somebody figured it out—we have 35 million laws trying to enforce ten commandments. —*Look*

Brockton, Mass., *Enterprise-Times*: The human being is an incurable optimist. He believes he has a pretty good chance to win a lottery prize, but that there is scarcely the slightest chance of his getting killed in a traffic accident.

Franklin P. Jones: Nothing's more responsible for the good old days than a bad memory. —*Your Life*

Sir Herbert Beerbohm Tree: A committee should consist of three men, two of whom are absent.

Don Marquis: Do not pass a temptation lightly by; it may never come again.

Sylvia Bremer: When somebody says, "I hope you won't mind my telling you this," it's pretty certain that you will. —Davenport, Iowa, *Times*

Lin Yutang: All women's dresses are merely compromises between the admitted desire to dress and the unadmitted desire to undress.

Bill Vaughan: It wouldn't be so bad if civilization were only at the crossroads, but this is one of those cloverleaf jobs. —Bell Syndicate

Tulsa, Okla., *World*: Men really understand women—they just make believe they don't because it's cheaper that way.

Francis O. Walsh: Among those things which are so simple that even a child can operate them are parents. —*The American Legion Magazine*

Dewey F. Barich: A chairman of a meeting is like the minor official at a bullfight whose main function is to open and close the gates to let the bull in and out.

Franklin P. Jones: The trouble with being punctual is that nobody's there to appreciate it. —*The Saturday Evening Post*

Madena R. Wallingford: What is intended as a little white lie often ends up as a double feature in Technicolor.

***The Sign*:** Thrift is a wonderful virtue—especially in ancestors.

Ancestor Worship

IN AN antique shop in Maine I spotted a pair of early American portraits and questioned the proprietor about them.

"Them's ancestors," he said.

"*Whose* ancestors?" I pursued.

"Anyone's a mind to have 'em," replied the enterprising Yankee. —F. P. Whitbeck

A BOSTONIAN from way back met a Mr. Pincus at a lifted-pinky party and bragged that one of his forebears had signed the Declaration of Independence. "Very interesting," said Mr. Pincus. "One of mine signed the Ten Commandments!" —Billy Rose

WE WERE boarding at an old farmhouse in Milford, Conn., whose owner gloried in still having her family's original colonial grants to the land. On the morning of July 4 we heard the sounds of martial music from the village. I asked our landlady if she weren't going down to the parade.

"Oh, no!" she replied. "I'd love to, but I've never felt *privileged* to go to the Fourth of July celebrations. You see, my family were Tories!" —Mildred Wells

A GROUP OF soil conservationists was making a tour through a badly eroded, rocky section of the hill country. At one stop a farmer told the visitors, "My forefathers fought for this here land." Then, looking out across his gullied fields, he added wryly, "They wuz the hotheaded type, I guess." —*The Furrow*

A HARVARD professor, lecturing in Charleston on "The Medes and the Persians," was approached by a gushing lady. "I'm particularly interested in your subject," she said. "You see, my mother was a Meade." —*Southern Literary Messenger*

A NIEMAN Fellow at Harvard, upon first entering the Adams House gallery of portraits where every important Adams since the Revolution is portrayed, said, "What this house needs is a good portrait of Eve!" —Charles A. Wagner

ONE OF THE men in a group going through Appomattox Court House was a loud-mouthed midwesterner who was monopolizing the guide's time, and ours, by showing off how much history he knew. In great detail he named the regiment and company in which his great-grandfather had served on this historic occasion and then said to the guide, "Now tell me exactly where he would have been located during the battle."

"Well, suh," came the answer in soft accents, "thet particulah company drove the ambulance wagons; in those days they nevah came up until the shooting was ovah. It's my pussonal opinion thet youah ancestor was located about ten miles back ovah thet hill yondah."

We heard no more from the blowhard. —Laura Crump

Flag Wavers

THE ALWAYS unpredictable Tallulah Bankhead has been known to introduce devastating ad libs into plays in which she was starring. One Christmas week she was playing *Private Lives* in Birmingham, Ala., practically her home town. In the midst of the amorous second act, while she and Donald Cook were lounging on a couch, she suddenly exclaimed, "Get away from me, you Damyankee!" And reaching into her bosom she hauled out a tiny Confederate flag—which she proceeded to wave enthusiastically.

The audience shook the theater to its foundations.

—Ernie Schier in Washington *Times-Herald*

ONE SPRING Abercrombie & Fitch, the New York emporium for sportsmen, was approached by the owner of a yacht. The customer, for reasons best known to himself, wanted a flag which would signal that his wife was aboard. Abercrombie & Fitch asked no questions, designed one for him. It showed a red battle-ax on a blue field, and sold like crazy. —*Sports Illustrated*

DURING A ship's dance a young Royal Marine couldn't keep his eyes off a pin worn by his partner, which depicted a cluster of Naval signaling flags. "I see you're admiring my brooch," she said. "It was a present from my husband and the flags mean 'I Love You.' "

Knowing that the word "love" wasn't in the Naval signal manual, the Royal Marine turned to his manual as soon as he got back to his quarters. What the flags actually signaled, he discovered, was: "Permission to lay alongside."

—*The Globe and Laurel* (Royal Marines, Eastney Barracks)

AT THE first performance of George Antheil's ultra-modernistic *Ballet Mécanique*, the orchestra contained ten grand pianos, six xylophones, a fire-alarm siren, an airplane propeller and several automobile horns. As the music mounted in volume the audience became fidgety and continued to grow more restless and excitable. Finally after eight minutes of the composition, a man in one of the front rows raised a white handkerchief tied to his cane and the entire audience burst into laughter.

—Deems Taylor, quoted by Irving Hoffman in *The Hollywood Reporter*

A NEIGHBOR of mine has four small children. One summer morning she hung out her usual daily washing. But that day clothes weren't the only things waving in the breeze. Old Glory proudly waved in front of the house.

"Carol, why the flag?" I asked. "Today's not a legal holiday."

"Maybe it's not a legal holiday," laughed Carol, "but it's certainly a red-letter day for me. Take a look at that clothesyard. It's the first time in eight years there hasn't been a diaper on my line!"

—Lois R. Austin

Mother's Day

EXHAUSTED mother whose house is a shambles to homecoming husband: "What do you mean didn't I get anything done today? I got *everything* done at least *twelve* times!"

—Herb Williams cartoon in *Ladies' Home Journal*

AS OUR 17-year-old started out in the family car for a Saturday night date, I gave him the usual caution about the dangers of weekend traffic. "Don't worry, Mom," he said reassuringly. "We'll park."

—Helen J. Tanner

MY FRIEND Susan, who has three active children, was playing "Cowboys and Indians" with them one afternoon when I stopped in for a visit. As the boy leveled his gun at his mother and hollered

TO MAKE A CAKE

Light oven; get out utensils and ingredients. Remove blocks and toy autos from table. Grease pan, crack nuts.

Measure 2 cups of flour; remove Johnny's hands from flour; wash flour off him. Remeasure flour.

Put flour, baking powder and salt in sifter. Get dustpan and brush up pieces of bowl Johnny knocked on floor. Get another bowl. Answer doorbell.

Return to kitchen. Remove Johnny's hands from bowl. Wash Johnny. Answer phone. Return. Remove ¼ inch salt from greased pan. Look for Johnny. Grease another pan. Answer telephone.

Return to kitchen and find Johnny. Remove his hands from bowl. Take up greased pan and find layer of nutshells in it. Head for Johnny, who flees, knocking bowl off table.

Wash kitchen floor, table, walls, dishes. Call baker. Lie down.

—D. L. Winkler in *Today's Woman*

"Bang!" she slumped to the floor and lay collapsed in a heap. When she didn't get up I hurried to her to see if she was all right. As I bent over anxiously she opened one eye and sighed, "Sh-h-h. I always do this. It's the only chance I get to rest!"

—Mrs. James Thompson

My neighbor was telling me how worried she was about the late hours her teen-agers often kept. As we talked her son breezed by and called out, "Don't wait up for me, Mom—I probably won't get in until about three o'clock."

She shook her head irritably and repeated, "Three o'clock! Why, when I was his age . . . " She paused and then looked at me amazed. "When I was his age he was six months old." —Mrs. H. E. Good

A five-year-old showed up at kindergarten one day dressed in faded blue jeans under a frilly petticoat and a beautiful ruffled party dress. Pinned to the dress was this note from her mother: "I hope you don't think this was *my* idea!"

—Katy P. Collins, Bell Syndicate

Mother sorting laundry explains to father: "He sent his college roommate's laundry, too. Says it's the only way he can pay off a loan."

—George Clark cartoon, Chicago Tribune-New York News Syndicate

When I was managing a rooming house for students near the campus of a large university, the mother of one of the new boys telephoned me.

"Please keep an eye on Alvin for me," she begged. "See that he gets plenty of sleep and doesn't drink or run around too much. You see," she added wistfully, "this is the first time he's been away from home—except for two years in the Navy."

—Alice Ryder Landgren

A woman applying for renewal of her driver's license was amused when a special deputy who was interrogating her changed one of the questions slightly, asking: "Have you ever been adjudged insane or feeble-minded—that is, by anyone other than your own children?"

—Lexington, Ky., *Leader,* quoted in Asheville, N. C., *Citizen*

SMALL BOY to mother scolding him for muddy fingerprints on door: "Those marks ain't from me, Mom! I always kick open the door!" —Lichty cartoon, Chicago Sun-Times Syndicate

Joy of motherhood: What a woman experiences when all the kids are in bed. —*Changing Times, The Kiplinger Magazine*

It's Only a Game

Condensed from Harper's Magazine

Shirley Jackson

THE LITTLE LEAGUE was new in our town, which may be why my friend Dot and I were so ill-prepared on the day of the first game. We established ourselves on a little hill near the third-base line and looked complacently down on the neat little field our husbands had helped build. Dot asked me if I remembered the rules of baseball and I said well, I knew both our boys were on the team with dark-blue hats named the Braves, and my son Laurie had been coaching me.

"It's so good for the boys to get in on something like this," I said.

"Learning sportsmanship and all," Dot said.

"I was telling Laurie last night," I said, "that it doesn't matter *who* wins, so long as the game is well played."

"It's only a game, after all," Dot said.

"That's what Laurie told me," I said. ("It's only a game," he had said. "Try to remember, for heaven's sake, it's only a game.")

Presently Marian, a friend of ours whose boy Art was first baseman for the opposing Giants, came along and we offered her part of our blanket. Then suddenly we heard the high-school band playing and everyone stood up to watch it come onto the field. The ballplayers were marching behind the band, tall and proud. The sky was blue, the sun was bright and the boys lined up in their new uniforms, holding their caps while the band played "The Star-Spangled Banner" and the flag was raised. "If you cry, I'll tell Laurie," Dot said.

"Same to you," I said blinking. After a minute I was able to make out that Laurie was playing second base. I told Marian that I was relieved that Laurie was not pitching, since he had been so nervous anyway, and Marian said that the Giants' manager had insisted on putting Artie at first base because he was dependable. "I'm sure he'll do very nicely," I said.

It turned out that Billy was playing first base for the Braves, and Marian leaned past me to tell Dot that first base was a *very* responsible position, but she was certain Billy would play as well as he could. She smiled in what I thought was a nasty kind of way and said she hoped the best team would win. Dot and I smiled back and said we hoped so too. Then the umpire shouted, "Play Ball!"

The first Giant batter hit a triple, although, as my husband explained later, it would actually have been an easy infield out if the shortstop had been looking, and if he had thrown the ball anywhere near Billy at first. By the time Billy got the ball back into the infield the batter—Jimmie Hill, who had once borrowed Laurie's bike and brought it back with a flat tire—was on third. I could see Laurie out there banging his hands together, and he looked so pale I was worried.

The Giants made six runs in the first inning, and each time they scored Marian looked sympathetic and told us that really the boys were being quite good sports about it, weren't they? When Laurie bobbled an easy fly she said to me that Artie had told her Laurie was really quite a good ballplayer and I mustn't blame him for an occasional error.

By the time the Giants were finally retired, Marian had told everyone sitting near us that it was her boy who had slid home for the sixth run, and she had explained with great kindness that Dot and I had sons on the other team—the first baseman, who had missed that long throw, and the second baseman, who had dropped the fly ball.

Then the Braves came to bat. Little Ernie Harrow, who lunched frequently at our house, hit the first pitched ball for a fast grounder. It went right through the legs of the Giant center fielder, and when Ernie came dancing into second Dot remarked to Marian that if Artie had been playing closer to first the way Billy did he might have been ready for the throw. Now Billy came up and smashed a long fly over the left fielder's head, and Dot and I stood up howling, "Run, run, run!" Billy rounded the bases and two runs were in.

Andy Robinson put a surprise bunt down the first-base line which Artie never even saw. Laurie got a nice hit and slid into second. Whereupon the Giants took out their pitcher and put in Buddy Williams, whom Laurie once beat up on the way to school.

Next thing we knew, the score was tied, and Dot and I were both yelling when Ernie Harrow came up for the second time and hit a home run. We were leading 8-6 when the inning ended.

Little League games are six innings, so we had five more to go. The play tightened up as the boys got over their stage fright, and by the middle of the fifth the Braves were leading 9-8. Then in the bottom of the fifth Artie missed a throw at first, and the Braves scored another run. Neither Dot nor I said a word, but Marian excused herself and went to sit on the other side of the field. "Marian's gotten very touchy lately, don't you think?" I remarked.

In the top of the sixth George Harper, who had been pitching well for the Braves, began to tire and walked the first two batters. The third Giant hit a little fly which fell in short center field, and one run came in, making the score 10-9. Then Georgie walked the next batter, filling the bases.

"Oh, no," Dot said suddenly, "you can't *do* it." I stood up and began to wail, "No, no, no." The manager was motioning toward Laurie and Billy to come in as a new battery. Dot said, "He *can't* do it. Don't let him."

"That's my little boy," she explained to a man sitting on the other side of her.

"It's too much to ask of the children," I said. But Laurie was warming up now, throwing slowly and carefully, with a windup he could only have learned from television. I said to Dot, "He doesn't look very nervous," but then my voice failed and I finished, "does he?" in a sort of gasp.

The batter was Jimmie Hill, who already had three hits. Laurie's first pitch hit the dust at Billy's feet, and Billy sprawled full-length to stop it and the crowd laughed. I said to Dot that I thought I would be getting on home. Laurie's second pitch sent Billy rolling again, and a man behind us said maybe the kids thought they were playing football, and Dot turned and said, "Sir, that catcher is my son."

"I beg your pardon, ma'am, I'm sure," the man said.

The umpire called Laurie's next pitch ball three, although it was clearly a strike, and I was yelling, "You're blind, you're blind!" The man behind us said that *this* pitcher wasn't going to last long, and I clenched my fist and turned around and said, "Sir, that pitcher is *my* son. If there are any more personal remarks . . ."

"Strike," the umpire said.

The man behind us announced with some humility that he hoped *both* teams would win, and subsided into silence.

Laurie then pitched two more strikes, his nice fast ball. At this point Dot and I moved down next to the fence. "Come on, Billy boy," Dot was saying, and I was telling Laurie, "Only two more outs and we win, only two more outs . . ."

"He can't hit it, Laurie," Dot yelled, "this guy can't hit," which of course was not true. The batter was Bob Weaver, and he was standing there swinging his bat and sneering. "Strike," the umpire said, and I leaned my forehead against the cool wire and said in a weak voice, "Just two more strikes. Just two more strikes."

Laurie looked at Billy and grinned, and I could see that behind the mask Billy was grinning too. Laurie pitched, and Bob Weaver swung wildly. "Strike two," the umpire said. Dot and I held hands. Then Laurie threw the fast ball for strike three.

One out to go, and Laurie and Billy and the shortstop stood together on the mound for a minute. I hung onto the wire and promised myself that if Laurie struck out this batter I would never, never say another word to him about the mess in his room, I would never . . . "Ball one," the umpire said, and I found that I had my voice back. "Crook!" I yelled. "Blind crook!"

Laurie pitched, the batter swung and connected in a high foul back of the plate. Billy threw off his mask and tottered, staring up. The batter, the boys on the field, the umpire waited—and Dot spoke into the silence. "William," she said, *"you catch that ball."*

Then everyone was shouting wildly, and Laurie and Billy were slapping and hugging each other. The Giants gathered around their manager and gave a cheer for the Braves, and the Braves gathered around *their* manager and gave a cheer for the Giants, and then Laurie and Billy came pacing together toward the dugout, past Dot and me.

I said, "Laurie?" and Dot said, "Billy?" and they stared at us without recognition for a minute. Then they smiled and Billy said, "Hi, Ma," and Laurie said, "You see the game?"

Chain Reactions

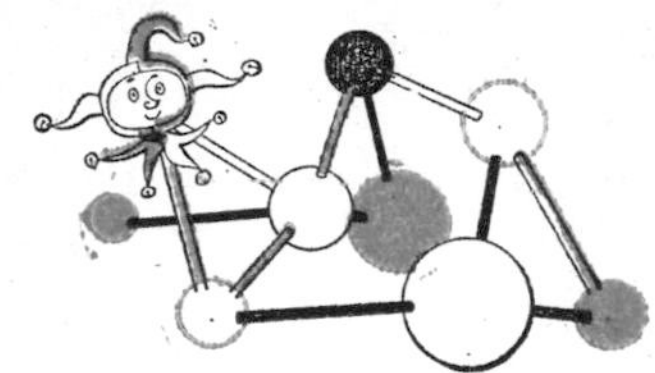

ONE DAY A fifth-grader came home from school bubbling with excitement. She had been voted "prettiest girl in the class." But she was even more excited when she came home the next day. The class had voted her "most popular girl." Several days later, however, when she announced she had won a *third* contest, she was somewhat subdued.

"What were you voted this time?" her mother asked.

"Most stuck-up," the little girl said. —Sylvia Altman Levitt

POPULAR BACHELOR diplomat posted in London, on being asked how he got on during a weekend in a stately country home:

"If the soup had been as warm as the wine, and the wine as old as the chicken, and the chicken as tender as the housemaid, and the housemaid as willing as the duchess, I would have had a wonderful time." —Frances Swinton

A FIRM IN Unadilla, Ga., stamps this on their statements: "Pay us so we can pay them and they can pay him and he can pay you."
—Unadilla *Observer,* quoted in *Pure Oil News*

ON THE TRAIN to Philadelphia a young man asked an elderly passenger for the time.

"Find out from the conductor," snapped the old man.

"Is that a way to talk to a fellow Jew?"

"Look," said the elderly passenger. "If I answer you politely, next thing we'll get to talking, and when I tell you I live in Germantown you'll say you've never been there and I'll ask you home for dinner. At my house you'll meet my daughter, fall in love and ask for her hand in marriage. Let me tell you right now, you no-good, I ain't letting my daughter marry a man who don't even own a watch!" —Billy Rose

DRUGGIST TO customer: "Take the yellow pills if the pink ones make you feel bad. . . . The pink ones are to be taken if you get a reaction from the red ones. . . . The red ones are for your cold. . . ."
—John Dempsey cartoon in *Collier's*

FROM A Ciro ad in the Los Angeles *Times:* "Ciro's four most-wanted fragrances: Danger, New Horizons, Surrender and Reflexions."

A POPULAR bachelor decided to reform. The first day he cut out cigarettes. The second day he cut out liquor. The third day he cut out women. The fourth day he cut out paper dolls.
—Mary Holmes, quoted by Austine in Washington *Times-Herald*

JUST AFTER the *President Cleveland* sailed one blowy afternoon, she ran into a full gale. The dozen Very Important Persons who had been assigned to the captain's table appeared for dinner amidst signs of distress. "I hope the 12 of you will enjoy your trip," the captain greeted them. "It is a pleasure to look into your 11 faces and realize that the eight of us will be dining together for the next few evenings. If any of the four of you would like a rubber of bridge, I'll be glad to see you both in my cabin. Waiter, I dislike dining alone, so I will dispense with the rest of my dinner."
—Bennett Cerf, *Shake Well Before Using* (Simon and Schuster)

All at Sea

DURING AN Atlantic crossing Erskine Caldwell told the captain of the *Queen Mary* this yarn: Youth goes to sea as cabin boy. Works his way up by degrees until he becomes captain of a great liner, most respected man in his field. Second-in-command, anxious to emulate his success, observes that his chief has one invariable habit. At the start of each day, he goes to cabin, opens desk drawer, takes out slip of paper, reads what is on it with earnest intensity, then replaces paper, locks desk. When captain dies, at ripe old age, first act of successor is to open desk, find slip of paper, eagerly read. Contains one sentence only:

"Left side of the ship is port; right side of the ship is starboard."

—Maurice Dolbier in New York *Herald Tribune Book Review*

ALICE ROOSEVELT LONGWORTH tells about a merchant seaman who was being investigated under the McCarran Act. "Do you," asked the interrogator, "have any pornographic literature?"

"Pornographic literature!" the sailor burst out indignantly. "I don't even have a pornograph!" —Deena Clark in *The Diplomat*

THE FIRST public duty of a rear admiral who had just made his broad stripe was to officiate at the commissioning of one of the Navy's largest capital ships. The ceremony went off without a hitch, and as he and his wife were about to leave the ship the side boys began to pipe him over the side. Suddenly his wife grabbed his coat-tails and whispered frantically, "Al, not yet! Hold still! They're piping somebody *important* over the side! *Wait!*"

With a lunge the admiral freed himself from the grasp of his worried spouse, and proceeded once more in dignified fashion, but not before the delighted crowd had heard his indignant answer, "Emmy! Let go my coat-tails! That's *me!*"

—Lt. Comdr. John H. Allen in *U. S. Naval Institute Proceedings*

RAYMOND'S father, skipper of a battleship anchored in Hampton Roads, arranged to take the small boy aboard for an overnight visit after several years' separation. From the moment they stepped aboard the captain's gig, everything was excitement for Raymond—the formal salutes as they came aboard, the ramrod attention that marked their progress about deck, the speed with which doors were opened at their approach. Grinning sailors showered him with attention, mess boys produced an endless supply of Cokes and ice-cream cones. Dinner in the captain's quarters was served with a dazzling show of snowy linen, sparkling glassware and gleaming silver.

Home again in the modest suburban cottage where he and his mother lived, he gave her an enthusiastic report, but looked a little subdued when he finished. "Is something bothering you?" his mother asked.

"What I can't understand," confessed the little boy, "is how Father is so rich and we are so poor." —Robert C. Hempel

A U. S. NAVY officer passionately fond of skin diving was anxious to pursue the sport on a Virginia Beach vacation, but a skin rash on his face made the salt water painful. His dermatologist solved the problem: wear a full-face Halloween mask under regular skin-diving goggles. The officer picked himself out a nice one, close-fitting, if evilly Martian.

That, no doubt, was why a sun-bathing girl on a quiet stretch of beach roused from her doze and—involuntarily—let out a choked scream as she saw the Thing almost leaning over her.

The Navy officer doesn't know why he then said what he did. It was almost involuntary, too. "Take me," he said slowly and carefully, "to your President." —*Sports Illustrated*

HOSTESS seating Navy officer at dinner party: "Will you sit on Mrs. Dilling's starboard beam?"

—Don Tobin cartoon in *This Week Magazine*

The Loves of Goggle

Condensed from Harper's Magazine

Bentz Plagemann

I FIRST BEGAN to be aware of my son's dawning maturity, if I may so dignify an essentially messy process, when he caught me reading the Kinsey Report. I had bought it on the transparent grounds that no writer should be without a copy for reference. When Goggle (the childhood nickname we use among ourselves) asked me what I was reading I replied, blushing, "A book which says that young people know more about sex than we think they do."

"That," Goggle said with the terrible patience he sometimes employs, "is what I keep trying to tell you."

Actually Goggle has been in and out of love constantly ever since he gave up zwieback, and by now I can usually recognize the symptoms of an approaching seizure. Take the evening, for instance, when I first knew that he was in love with Alice.

I was relaxing in a chair before dinner when Goggle came in from play. He was then a magnificent

Harper's Magazine (December, '52), © 1952 by Harper & Brothers, 49 E. 33 St., New York 16, N. Y.

13, and as he entered the living room, pictures trembled on the walls. "How are you, Goggle?" I asked.

He looked at me blankly. "Huh?" he said.

"Never mind," I said. "What happened at school today?"

He had begun to circle the room in a vague, tormented way, whistling through his teeth in the way I had asked him 10,000 times not to do. "Goggle," I said, "would you hand me the evening paper?"

"Huh?"

"The evening paper," I said patiently. "On the table."

"What about it?"

"Would you please hand it to me?"

"Well, why didn't you say so in the first place?" he demanded.

"Dinner won't be for half an hour or so," I said. "Why don't you go outside and break a few windows or something."

"Ha!" he said. "When I'm out you call me in. When I'm in you throw me out. A man can't do anything in his own house." When he slammed the front door on his way out the doorknob fell off. He had been making it burglarproof in some new way.

"It's Alice," my wife said, coming in from the kitchen. "I hear her on the phone. I can hear her asinine giggle two rooms away."

"Is there any chance they may run away and get married, or anything?" I asked hopefully.

"I don't know about the running away," my wife said. "It's the *anything* I'm worried about." She gave me a long, thoughtful look, and went back to the kitchen.

But I am getting ahead of my story. Let us go back to little Mary, the siren of the fifth grade.

We lived in the city then, the city where mothers of little girls prowl with a restless eye, organizing dancing classes and making lists of little boys from which the little boys can never hope to escape until they are transferred to the inactive or married file.

In this steamy milieu of dotted swiss and white gloves, Mary was like a breath of fresh air. She had pigtails and a sweet right uppercut, and every boy in the class was her slave. Mary was the bottleneck as far as the dancing class was concerned, but at last she was thrown and hobbled and enrolled in it, and all the little boys followed. I remember the first session well. We were waiting for Goggle when he got home. It was a very warm afternoon and he rushed into the apartment, peeling his clothes off as he ran. He sank into an upholstered chair and gasped, "Mary chose me."

They had lined the girls up on one side and the boys on the other. When "the lady at the piano" announced that the boys would choose partners, little Mary was almost trampled in the rush, so the forces were redeployed and the girls chose partners. And Mary had chosen our Goggle.

We were all speechless with pride, but we hardly knew what to expect next. What happened shouldn't have happened to a dog, because it was braces on Mary's teeth, and overnight she became a hopeless bag. Goggle buried himself in basketball, and the apartment was littered with scraps of paper on which brilliant plays were diagramed. I threw one in the fire by mistake, a loss to the world comparable with the burning of the library at Alexandria.

Alice appeared on the scene after we moved to the country. She wore her hair down to her shoulders, and it was *such* a nuisance, you know, that she had to keep tossing it back, like this, with her hand. She giggled all the time, and fluttered her eyelashes. When she imparted to Goggle her profound discovery that she really didn't like girls—boys were much more interesting—I knew that Goggle was a gone goose.

Alice gave Goggle a picture of herself, which he carried in his wallet along with his Confederate dollar and his membership card in the Junior Magicians of America. When they walked together she held his hand, and if he said anything even remotely funny she threw her head back with laughter and crinkled her eyes.

Goggle was reduced to a state of absolute idiocy. He became a sort of pint-size Neanderthal man whose only communication with us was "ugh," and he ate his way moodily through about $500 worth of assorted groceries. I don't know where it all would have ended if Goggle hadn't discovered that Alice had also given her picture to Butch Butcher, who was bigger than Goggle and who could stand on his head and drink a glass of water at the same time.

That ended that, and Goggle concentrated on taking apart everything in sight, including the electric mixer, his bicycle and the odd carburetors and clocks which always seemed to find their way to his room. (Our repair bills were rather high at this time.) But not long afterward Goggle got mixed up with a real witch, one of the most beautiful I have ever seen. Little Helen of the chestnut hair, the tawny skin and the warm, slow voice could sit on the edge of a swimming pool in her red bathing suit, and in less than five minutes spin the prettiest web in which ever a man found himself entangled.

I consoled myself by thinking that it was just a summer romance. But when her parents took her away in the fall she wrote letters to Goggle. They were in pale-blue envelopes and had a mysteriously exciting scent, like strawberry jam. Goggle went away to school and the letters stopped coming to us. It was a great relief to think of him safely stashed away in the hills, far from the siren's call, where the teachers might get a few fast algebraic equations into his head while his glands were in abeyance.

When we went up the following spring to bring him home I had to help him pack his things. His room looked like one of the minor stalls in the Augean stables. I stood in the middle, with his foot locker open on one side and a wastebasket on the other, while Goggle directed the disposition of each object as I held it aloft from the shambles. Pack that, he would say, or "toss" that.

It was with agreeable surprise that I discovered all the letters I had written to him neatly stacked on one of the bookshelves. Saved for publication, I decided. "What about these?" I asked.

Goggle looked carelessly over his shoulder. "Oh, toss 'em," he said. "No use saving those."

I tossed them with a sigh. Then I came to a cigar box which, in the moment before Goggle snatched it from me, I discovered to be full of those blue envelopes smelling of strawberry jam. "Might as well start down to the car with a few things," he said gruffly, tucking the box under one arm and grabbing up a load of books in the other.

He went downstairs and I sat on the bed. For the first time it really dawned on me that someday one of these girls was going to get Goggle and take him away for her own. And there just wasn't anything I could do about it, no matter what she was like.

Man-Traps

A little flattery now and then makes husbands out of single men.
—*Basharat*

"TOMMY," said his Uncle John, "do you have a girl?"

"Gosh, no," shouted the ten-year-old and ran off to his baseball game. The little girl next door smiled wisely at Uncle John and said, "They're always the last ones to know." —*The Union*

ONE YOUNG thing to another: "If you left it up to men, they'd *never* think of marriage."

—Herb Williams cartoon in *Ladies' Home Journal*

ONE GIRL to another: "If I could combine their qualities I'd be the happiest girl in the world. Ronald is gay, debonair, rich, handsome, witty, and Clarence wants to marry me."

—Irwin Caplan cartoon in *Collier's*

GAL making up for date to roommate: "He says he likes me just the way I am—so I have to be careful to be just the way I am every time." —Tom Hudson cartoon in *Collier's*

BLONDE beaming at escort across menu: "I'll have *pâté de foie gras* followed by pheasant under glass—provided you're not saving up to buy a ring or something." —Richter cartoon, King Features

ONE SWEET young thing to another: "I could go with him until something better comes along—but what if something better comes along and sees me going with him?"

—J. Monahan cartoon in *The Saturday Evening Post*

BRIDE: "Well, I finally landed a man, and what a chase! I made it my career and prepared plans the way a general gets ready for his biggest battle. I joined a chess club and took to hanging around airfields. At the same time I practiced skeet-shooting and began making numerous calls for information about public questions at the headquarters of my favorite political organization. I played bit roles in an amateur theatrical group and joined a Sunday-morning party to read aloud to veterans in a government hospital. I sold Red Cross memberships, concentrating on athletic clubs, university clubs and the Chamber of Commerce. I became secretary of the lecture forum of the church and saw to it that there was occasion for a brief announcement at the opening of each meeting. People thought I was public-spirited, patriotic, knowledge-hungry, self-sacrificing and progressive, when all along I had just one thing on my mind—how to cop a husband."

—*American Freeman,* quoted in *The William Feather Magazine*

SIGN posted beside a marriage-license window: "When a fellow needs a friend, he sometimes makes the mistake of getting a wife." —Earl Wilson, Hall Syndicate

ON A Maine farmhouse: "LOOK DADDY! Puppies for sale."

—Ruth D. Walch

ON A Los Angeles body-and-fender repairshop: "May We Have the Next Dents?"

SEEN NEAR North Augusta, S. C.: "Try Our Easy Payment Plan. 100% DOWN. No Future Worries About Payment."

—*Nash Air-Flyte Magazine*

NEATLY printed card in the back window of a conservative limousine: "Help Stamp Out Sport Cars."

—Meyer Berger in New York *Times*

OUTSIDE London burlesque theater: "HERE THE BELLES PEEL."

PAINTED on the yachts moored in Key Biscayne, Fla., are the usual romantic names—*Sea Sprite, Moonbeam, Wanderer.* But the one that catches everyone's eye is a small, neat craft named simply: *$18,500.*

—E. E. Kenyon in *The American Weekly*

ON A movie theater: "Extra Added Attraction—No Popcorn."

—E. E. Kenyon in *The American Weekly*

FOUR OUT OF five cottages in a row in a small Cornish village boast large television antennas on their roofs. In the window of the one with the bare roof is a small sign: "INDOOR AERIAL."

—Peter Tipthorp

PLACARD hanging in the office of the Farrell Lines steamship company: "THINK—or thwim."

A METAL plaque on the crest of California's 12-million-ton Shasta Dam reads: "U. S. government property. Do not remove."

—*Pathfinder*

Capital Stories

FELLOW OF our acquaintance was interviewed by an FBI agent about a friend of his who was applying for a government post. Winding up a long interrogation the agent asked, "And do you consider him well qualified for the job?"

"Depends. What's the job?"

"Sorry," said the G-man. "I'm not at liberty to reveal that. Confidential, you know." —*Pathfinder*

ACCOUNTANT TO fellow worker: "For a minute this deficit had me worried . . . I forgot I was working for the government."

—Roland Coe cartoon in *The Saturday Evening Post*

IT WAS TIME for the annual physical exams, and I was waiting at the Naval Medical Center for the doctor. A young intern who was arranging some instruments struck up a conversation, asking me what my job was, how long I had been in Washington, how I liked it and so on. I launched into a highly unflattering report on postwar Washington, its climate, housing and prices, and on the Navy Department and my duties there. He heard me out, then scribbled something on a paper.

A bit apprehensive, I asked, "Did I say something wrong?"

"Oh, no. You just passed the psychiatric part of the exam."

"But what if I'd said everything was just peachy, that I loved my job?"

"Then," he said, "I would have had to ask you a few more questions." —Bruce McCandless

NEAR A big government building a Washington bureaucrat's car was parked in a lot in which a sign read: "All day parking 35 cents." At lunchtime the official asked the boy at the gate if he could drive his car away to lunch, bring it back after an hour and not pay a second time. The attendant's reply was wholly Washington: "Suh, each car comes in has to pay 35 cents, and don' argue with me. I'se not on the policy-making level."—Barbara C. McNamee

A FEDERAL agency received a letter from a taxpayer inquiring about a pending case. He added this postscript: "I haven't made up my mind on this issue, but when I do I'll be very bitter." —AP

A DOOR in a government building in Washington, D. C., is labeled: "4156; General Services Administration; Region 3; Public Buildings Service; Buildings Management Division; Utility Room; Custodial." What's behind the door? A broom closet.

—Rep. Lester Johnson, quoted in Rice Lake, Wis., *Chronotype*

A NEWS ITEM in the Washington *Daily News* reported: "Congress was asked to write a check for $823.48 to pay for replacing steel plates in the Capitol dome. They were buckled by hot air."

A GIRL working at the Orlando Air Force Base Headquarters asked a young lieutenant who was being sent to Washington for a few days if he would mind delivering a message to her girl friend in the Pentagon. She gave him her phone number and the message which read, "Tell Irene I'll answer her letter Sunday."

The lieutenant thought the message rather slight, but he faithfully followed through. Irene, when he called, asked him if he could stop by her office and pick up a gift to go back to the girl in Orlando. It wasn't until after he had picked up the tiny gift box and was dining with Irene at a swanky restaurant that it dawned on him how desperate the man shortage was in Washington.

—William R. Shelton

IN A HOTEL grill room in Washington a man was complaining bitterly—and loudly—about the state of affairs in this country. He became so vehement that a gent at the next table suggested, "Why don't you register your protests with your Congressman?"

"What good would *that* do?" roared the table-thumper. *"I'm* my Congressman!" —Bennett Cerf in *This Week Magazine*

Illustrative Anecdotes

A SOMEWHAT bewildered new official in Washington described his position as being like that of the young Eastern potentate whose father presented him with 100 concubines on his coming of age. "It's not that I don't know what to do," he said. "The question is where to begin!"
—M. C. W.

AFTER A fulsome introduction by an effusive lady, Alfred Hooper, the mathematician, wooed his audience back to good humor with this story: An Italian farmer, bringing a calf to market, was stymied by the animal's refusal to cross a bridge. Cajoling and prodding made no impression whatever. Finally a motorist drove up and let out a loud blast with his horn. The panic-stricken calf made a wild leap over the bridge's railing and was promptly drowned in the whirling current below. The philosophical farmer summed up the situation in one sentence: "Too bigga da honk for so smalla da calf!"
—Bennett Cerf

AN OLD Springfield friend of Lincoln, after an evening at the White House, asked, "How does it feel to be President?"

"You have heard," said Lincoln, "about the man tarred and feathered and ridden out of town on a rail? A man in the crowd asked him how he liked it, and his reply was that, if it wasn't for the honor of the thing, he would rather walk."
—Carl Sandburg, *Abraham Lincoln: The War Years* (Harcourt, Brace)

ADDRESSING A group of New York hotel executives Park Commissioner Robert Moses remarked that he had little advice to offer them: "As a matter of fact I get around to your hostelries only with architects, engineers and other professional advisers. It reminds me of the handsome tomcat who was taken to the vet and returned home somewhat subdued. His owner explained that he now went out only two or three nights a week as a consultant."
—Francis Sugrue in New York *Herald Tribune*

Plane Talk

Air travel—seeing less and less of more and more.

—Raymond Haggars

DURING A long wait at the Jacksonville airport I noticed a disreputable-looking tomcat which sat watching the planes. Suddenly he arose, stretched and headed for a plane that had just landed, halting about ten feet away. The departing passengers ignored him, but the pilot stopped to pat him. Then as the reloading of luggage began Mr. Cat moved closer, occasionally flaunting his tail and, when the compartment was filled, hopped in. This was too much for me. I hailed the pilot as he prepared to go aboard. "Tell me, do you know the cat that just boarded your plane?"

"Him? Again?" The pilot laughed. "That cat certainly is a Lothario. He's got a girl friend in Miami and every so often he just naturally has to see her." —Philip R. Traver

SMALL boy in space helmet to mother as they leave airliner: "A crummy 20,000 feet!"

—Bo Brown cartoon in *The Christian Science Monitor*

ONE OF THE big transatlantic airliners took a group of writers and radio artists—all women—to Europe, and the women, being the only passengers, made themselves completely at home. Several hours out from New York, with the flying perfectly smooth, the loud-speaker intoned: "Everyone please return to your seats and fasten seat belts."

The women rushed to their places, followed instructions and sat tensely waiting developments. In a moment the door of the control room opened and the pilot emerged, surveyed them and smiled. "Now, I suppose, the men's room is clear." —Bob Brugger

A FELLOW aviation cadet and I were having equal difficulty trying to master primary flight training. One day I confided to him that I'd begun to wonder if subconsciously I wasn't actually afraid to fly. "Don't you believe it," he assured me. "I've seen you fly, and you fly like I do. And to fly that way—and still fly—that takes guts!"

—Cecil J. Wright

NOTE TO an airline pilot from his daughter, who had a ski accident near Lake Tahoe: "I'm at 6000 feet with both legs feathered!"

—Herb Caen in San Francisco *Examiner*

ON A Miami-Chicago flight was a lively youngster who nearly drove everyone crazy. He was running up and down the aisle when the stewardess started serving coffee, and ran smack into her, knocking the paper-cupped coffee to the floor. As he stood by watching her clean up the mess, she glanced up at the boy and said, "Look, why don't you go and play *outside?*"

—Eugene Carroll, quoted by Robert Sylvester,
Chicago Tribune-New York News Syndicate

MY BRIDE of only a few months was at the airport to meet me when I returned from Naval duty in the Pacific. We were waiting for my luggage when I pointed out our good-looking stewardess from the plane, Miss Tracy.

"How do you happen to know her name?" she asked.

I explained that it was listed, along with names of the pilot and co-pilot, on the door of the cockpit. My wife's next question was a classic—which I could not answer. "Dear," she asked, "what was the pilot's name?"

—R. L. McEvoy

OUR PLANE, flying at about 16,000 feet, suddenly began to descend rapidly. A Canadian soldier sitting next to me turned and said, "I beg your pardon—does the ringing in my ears annoy you?"

—Larry Adler in *Variety*

THE MIDDLE EAST is a spawning ground for small, short-lived airlines. In Bagdad an American salesman bound for an out-of-the-way desert spot was just getting settled on a plane when the pilot walked through the cabin and announced that he would not fly the ship without an engine change. All the passengers disembarked. An hour later they were again told to get aboard. "Do we have another plane?" the American asked the steward.

"Oh, no," the man replied.

"Did they change the engine?"

"Oh, no," came the reply. "We changed the pilot."

—Florence Teets

International Newsreel

As CONSULTANT to the Royal State Highway Department in Thailand my husband often found himself in wild and remote country. On one such occasion—when he and a young Thai engineer were preparing to leave their village headquarters for a distant construction site—the Thai suddenly grabbed my husband's hand and scrutinized it carefully. "Long life line," he said. "Let's go."

As my husband settled himself beside the Thai in the seat of the dilapidated truck, he asked curiously, "What's all this business about my life line?"

The Thai had the truck well on its zigzag course down the precarious road before he answered cheerfully, "No brakes!"

—Mrs. H. G. Quedens

WHEN THE military government moved into the Izu Peninsula in Japan shortly after V-J Day, the staid New England captain in charge of the American team was shocked to learn that it was common practice for the Japanese to enjoy mixed nude bathing in many of the famous hot springs pools. He immediately notified the local authorities that such bathing was forbidden; that, henceforth, men and women were to bathe separately.

The Japanese obliged at once—by stretching a rope across the center of each pool.

—Theodore Hatlen

MY HUSBAND had to see an official in Madrid and so went around to the man's office about five o'clock in the afternoon. The place was closed and deserted-looking. My husband spoke to a doorman in the patio: "Don't they work in the afternoon?"

"Señor," the doorman an-

swered, "it is in the mornings that they don't work. In the afternoons they don't come."

—Mrs. Cori E. Pessina

On a ferry I boarded in the Sudan scores of people stumbled over the squatting form of a small boy who persisted in sitting in the bottom despite oaths and kicks. I asked the captain to move the boy somewhere to keep him from being hurt.

"Very good, your excellency," he replied. "But it is only fair to warn you that if the boy gets up the boat will sink."

—H. C. Jackson, *Sudan Days and Ways* (St. Martin's Press)

Missionaries are often accused of forcing native peoples to hide their naked loveliness under ugly Mother Hubbards, but a member of one of the more conservative missions to the Dinka people in the Sudan told me quite another story. The Dinka, who had always gone around attired in the clothes they were born with, became too clothes-conscious as soon as they acquired enough education to earn a little money. Sundays, instead of listening to the service, they spent the time comparing clothes. So the church elders met to consider how to deal with such preoccupation with the things of this world. Solemnly they passed a new rule: at communion service, at least, nobody could wear clothes.

—Lawrence Robinson (Methodist Mission of Southern Congo)

In early 1944 a group of 14th Air Force Flying Tigers was billeted in a small Chinese hostel near Kweilin. The houseboy, Cha, awakening us for the pre-dawn briefing for a combat mission, would whisper hoarsely, "Wake up, sir. Your time has come!"

—Capt. John M. Overstreet

One afternoon a rickety old car drew up to a café on Madrid's Gran Via. Its canvas top hung in flounces, its metal was rusty and a heavy cloud of steam issued from the radiator where the cap was missing.

The driver stepped up to a man lounging nearby and asked, "Will you keep an eye on my car while I make a phone call?" The other agreed. When the driver returned he asked the man how much he owed. "Fifty *pesetas,*" was the reply.

"But that's robbery! I was only gone five minutes."

"I know," the man answered. "But it wasn't the time—it was the embarrassment. Everyone thought the car was mine."

—C. M. Monasterio

Embarrassing Moments

A COUPLE OF sailors laying over for a day or two in Sweden decided to go to church. Knowing no Swedish they figured to play safe by doing whatever a dignified-looking gentleman sitting in front of them did.

During the service the pastor made a special announcement of some kind, and the man in front of them rose. The two sailors quickly got to their feet, too—only to be met by roars of laughter from the whole congregation.

When the service was over and they were greeted by the pastor at the door, they discovered he spoke English and naturally asked what the cause of the merriment had been. "Oh," said the pastor, "I was announcing a baptism and asked the father of the child to stand." —Angie Cordero

A YOUNG Los Angeles couple still blush over an experience at a garden party. The hostess came over to where they were seated and said how sorry she was that the husband had been too ill to come to her last party. As he started to blurt that he hadn't been ill and ask what party she was talking about, his wife poked him under the table. Then she looked down—following the hostess' gaze—and realized in horror that her frantic signals were plainly visible through the glass-topped table. —Matt Weinstock in Los Angeles *Mirror-News*

WE WERE anxious not to be recognized as newlyweds, so before we went into the hotel my wife took off the corsage and we carefully shook off the last bits of rice. Then, sure that no one would ever suspect we had just been married that afternoon, I walked up to the desk and said with studied casualness, "I'd like a double bed with room, please."

—Morris Weinberg

AT A FORMAL dinner the hostess, who was seated at the far end of the table from Leonora Corbett, wrote a note to the actress and had the butler deliver it. Miss Corbett can't read without her glasses, so she asked the man at her left to read it to her. "It says," he began, " 'Leonora, dear, do me a favor and please don't neglect the man at your left. I know he's a bore, but talk to him.' "

—Leonard Lyons

WHEN MY Great Dane puppy first came he howled the moment I was out of sight, so when a friend asked me to go to the movies I explained I couldn't. "He's more care in some ways than a baby—at least a baby could be taken along."

"Wait," said my friend. A few minutes later she appeared with an armful of baby clothes. We dressed the passive puppy—dress, bonnet and pink socks. Wrapping him in a blanket I took him to the theater, where he snoozed contentedly through a double feature. Indeed, so perfect was his deportment that he won favorable comment from two ladies behind us as "just the best baby."

But on my way out I suddenly found myself the target of all eyes. People stared, nudging each other, and burst into peals of laughter. I glanced down at my bundle and couldn't understand—until I caught a rear view in a mirror. From the folds of infant swaddling hung a puppy tail, wagging happily. —Reina M. Hulit

STOPPING FOR lunch at a New Jersey Howard Johnson's one summer, I realized that the people at the next table were Harold Stassen and his family. My husband showed no sign of recognition and, knowing he would be disappointed later if I did not call it to his attention, I reached in my purse for a piece of paper and wrote:

"Harold Stassen
is sitting
beside us,
but don't
look now!"

I didn't want to be too obvious about it, so as I passed the note across the table I said casually, "Can you think of anyone else we should send post cards to?"

After only a glance at the note my husband boomed out in a puzzled voice, *"Harold Stassen? Harold Stassen?* Why would we be sending *him* a post card?"

—Polly O'Neil

A NEON sign partially blinked out in front of a "We Never Close" gambling palace in Las Vegas. For several embarrassing hours it read: "We Never lose."

—Erskine Johnson, NEA

A MOTHER I know had spent the whole summer in the company of her children, thinking only of their needs. On her return to New York in the fall she went for the first time in months to an adult dinner party. To her horror she discovered that, to start conversation with the distinguished man next to her, she said automatically, "I bet I can finish my soup sooner than you can."

—John Mason Brown in *McCall's*

Aunt Jean's Marshmallow Fudge Diet

Condensed from "Please Don't Eat the Daisies"

Jean Kerr

FRED ALLEN used to talk about a man who was so thin he could be dropped through a piccolo without striking a single note. Well, I'm glad I never met *him;* I'd hate to have to hear about *his* diet.

When I was a girl—way back in Truman's Administration—it was fun to go to parties. The conversation used to crackle with wit and intelligence because we talked about *ideas*—Gary Cooper in western movies, the superiority of beer over lotion as a wave-set. Go to a party now and the couple next to you won't talk about anything except their diets—the one they've just come off, the one they're on now or the one they're going to have to start if they keep lapping it up like this.

I blame science for the whole business. Years ago when a man began to notice that if he stood up on the subway he was immediately replaced by *two* people, he figured he was getting too fat. So he went to his doctor and the doctor said, "Quit stuffing yourself, Joe." And Joe either stopped or he didn't stop, but at least he kept his big mouth shut. What was there to talk about?

Today, with the science of nutrition advancing so rapidly, there is plenty of food for conversation, if for nothing else. We have the Rockefeller diet, the Mayo diet, high-protein diets, low-protein diets, "blitz" diets which feature cottage cheese and something that tastes like thin sandpaper, and so on and on.

Where do people get all these diets? Obviously not from the newspapers. For one thing, you can never catch the newspaper diet when it *starts*. It's always the fourth day of Ada May's Wonder Diet and, after a brief description of a simple slimming exercise that could be performed by anybody who has had five years' training with the ballet, Ada May gives you the menu for the day. One glass of skim milk, eight prunes and three lamb kidneys. This settles the matter for most people.

If you have formed the habit of checking on every new diet that comes along, you will find that, mercifully, they all blur together, leaving you with one definite piece of information: French-fried potatoes are out. But once in a while a diet will stick in your mind.

The best diet I've heard about lately is the simplest. It was perfected by the actor Walter Slezak after years of careful experimentation. You eat as much as you want of everything you don't like. And if you should be in a hurry for any reason (let's say you're still wearing maternity clothes and the baby is eight months old), then you should confine yourself to food that you just plain hate.

Why is the American woman being hounded into starvation in order to duplicate an ideal figure which is neither practical nor possible for a person her age? I'll tell you.

First, it is presumed that when you're thinner you live longer. (In any case, when you live on a diet, it *seems* longer.) Second, it is felt that when you are skin and bones you have so much extra energy that you can climb up and shingle the roof. Third—and this is what the Beauty Editors are really getting at—when you're thin you are so tasty and desirable that strange men will pinch you at the A & P and your husband will not only follow you around the kitchen breathing heavily but will stop and smother you with kisses as you try to put the butter back in the icebox. This—and I hope those in the back of the room are listening—is hogwash.

Think of the happy marriages you know about. How many of the ladies are still wearing size 12? I've been giving this a lot of thought in the last 20 minutes, and what I have discovered is that the women who are being ditched in my own troubled circle are one and all willowy and slim as a blade. In fact, six of them require rather extensive padding even to look flat-chested.

The reason, I believe, that men hang onto their well-endowed spouses is because they're comfy and nice to have around the house. In a marriage there is nothing that stales so fast as physical beauty—as we readers of the movie magazines have observed. What actually holds a husband through thick and thick is a girl who is fun to be with. And any girl who has had nothing to eat since nine o'clock this morning but three hard-boiled eggs will be about as jolly and companionable as an income-tax inspector.

So I say, ladies, find out why

women everywhere are switching from old-fashioned diets to the *modern* way: no exercise, no dangerous drugs, no weight loss. For that tired, run-down feeling, try eating three full meals a day with a candy bar after dinner and pizza at 11 o'clock. Don't be intimidated by pictures of Audrey Hepburn. Just sit there smiling on that size-20 backside and say, "Guess what we're having for dinner, dear? Your favorite—stuffed breast of veal and corn fritters."

The Men Who Came to Dinner

HEYWOOD BROUN, the columnist, was one of Manhattan's most notable trenchermen; he could put away more food than a blacksmith at a barbecue. One day at a favorite restaurant the waiter handed Broun a lengthy menu and waited for his order. The big columnist perused with care the countless items listed; then, handing the bill of fare back to the waiter, he said genially, "I see nothing to object to." —*The Christian Science Monitor*

WIFE OF departing couple to dinner hostess: "We hate to eat and run, but Herbert is still hungry."
—Don Tobin cartoon, King Features

SOME YEARS ago the American ambassador in a European capital, asked to a formal dinner by a most conservative hostess, told her that he would come with pleasure. The afternoon of the party a Paris couturier put on a fashion show. The elderly ambassador, who was a bachelor with quite an eye for the ladies, attended the showing—and that night turned up at the dinner with the youngest and prettiest of the models on his arm. The hostess, her seating arrangements completely thrown out by the unexpected guest, remarked icily, "But you didn't tell me you were coming with anyone."

"Ah, but I did tell you, madame," replied the ambassador with a flourish "—this is Pleasure!" —Andre Visson

A PLUMP gentleman ate a fine meal at the Waldorf with obvious relish, topped it off with some rare Napoleon brandy, then summoned the headwaiter. "Do you recall," he asked pleasantly, "how a year ago I ate just such a repast in your excellent hotel and then, because I couldn't pay for it, you had me thrown into the gutter like a veritable bum?"

"I'm very sorry," began the contrite headwaiter.

"It's quite all right," said the guest soothingly, "but I'm afraid I'll have to trouble you again."

—Bennett Cerf, *The Life of the Party* (Hanover House)

ONE NIGHT at a large formal dinner in Washington I wore a black satin gown. Almost as soon as we sat down my napkin slid off my slippery lap. My dinner partner, an engaging-looking Englishman, retrieved it for me. A moment later I felt a hand on my knee. I pulled away, but the handling continued. Finally I turned to the Englishman and demanded in a low voice, "Just what are you doing?"

"Madam," he replied unperturbedly, "I dislike diving under the table every few minutes for a napkin. Therefore I am trying to pin the corner of your napkin to the corner of mine. Then I shall wedge mine into my waistcoat and hope to eat the remainder of this meal in comfort. I always carry a pin for this purpose."

—Beth Holden

A RETIRED British admiral had been going on at length about seals at a dinner party. After the retreat of the ladies he told how after the long winter night in the North the bull seals come out of the water and crawl up onto the ice, bellowing for their mates. "Their bellow is really something to hear," he said, "an extr'odin'ry noise that can be heard for miles. I think that I can imitate it for you."

He let forth a terrific bellow—and almost immediately the dining room door opened and the admiral's little wife stood there gently asking, "Were you calling me, Sir Henry?"

—Joseph Cummings Chase, *My Friends Look Better Than Ever* (Longmans, Green)

Animal Crackers

ONE BIRD perched on telephone wire to another: "Did'ja ever notice the way some people's voices make your feet feel funny?"
—John Norment cartoon in *The American Magazine*

THE NEIGHBORHOOD dogs were romping together one day when Scottie came along. "Heavens, Scottie, what's wrong with you?" asked the little Peke. "You look simply awful!"

"I feel awful. I'm nervous, can't sleep, have no appetite."

"You ought to see a good vet."

"Oh, I've seen them all, and they all say the same thing: 'Nothing wrong organically.'"

"Maybe what you need is to see a good psychiatrist."

"Oh, I couldn't—you see, I'm not allowed on couches!"
—J. C. Furnas

ONE KANGAROO mother to another on rainy day: "I dread these days when they can't play outside."
—Larry Harris cartoon in *Laugh Book*

A MICROBE swimming along a vein came face to face with another microbe who looked extremely ill. "What's the matter with you, my poor friend?" he asked.

"Oh! Don't come near me!" the other replied. "I'm afraid I've caught a little penicillin!" —*Revue de la Pensée Française*

GROANED one moth to another: "I'll have to stop eating overcoats—I'm getting ulsters of the stomach."

BEAR standing at the door of his cave reminds a bird: "Remember now—call us about half past April." —Ed Nofziger in *PM*

First Call for Spring

Condensed from "Over the Footlights"

Stephen Leacock

I GATHER that spring is approaching. I am not an observant man, but as the days go by the signs begin to multiply, and among these signs I may mention that the snow has gone. Spring then is upon us, and I should like to suggest that this year we meet it firmly and quietly and with none of the hysterical outburst that it usually provokes in people of a certain temperament. I refer to those unfortunate beings called "Lovers of Nature."

I have an acquaintance who is a Lover of Nature. All through the winter he is an agreeable, quiet fellow, quite fit for general society. I notice him, it is true, occasionally grubbing under the snow. On one occasion, last winter, he was temporarily unmanned by seeing a blackbird sitting on a bough. But for the most part his conduct during the colder weather is entirely normal.

Spring, however, at once occasions in my Nature friend a distressing disturbance. He seems suddenly to desire, at our every meeting, to make himself a channel of information as between the animate world and me. From the moment that the snow begins to melt, he keeps me posted as to what the plants and the birds and the bees are doing. This is a class of information which I do not want, and which I cannot use. But I have to bear it.

"I noticed a scarlet tanager this afternoon," says my friend. "You don't say so!" I reply. What a tanager is I have never known; I hope I never shall. In point of ornithology I only know two birds: the crow and the hen. I can tell them at once either by their plumage or by their song. I can carry on a nature conversation up to the limit of the crow and the hen; beyond that, not.

So for the first day or so in spring, I am able to say, "I saw a crow yesterday," or "I noticed a hen out walking this morning." But somehow my crow and hen seem to get out of date awfully quickly. My friend, on the contrary, keeps up his information for weeks, running through a whole gamut of animals. "I saw a gopher the other day," he says. "Guess what the little fellow was doing?" If only he knew it I'd like to break out and answer, "I don't care what the Hades the little fellow was doing."

My particular anger with these Nature Men springs from the singularly irritating kind of language that they use: a sort of ingratiating wee-wee way in which they amalgamate themselves, as it were, with Nature. They really seem to feel so cute about it. If a wee hepatica peeps above the snow they think they've done it. They describe it to you in a peculiar line of talk almost like baby language. "What do you think I saw?" says the Nature Man. "Just the tiniest little shoot of green peeping from the red-brown of the willow!" He imitates it with his thumb and finger to show how the little shoot shoots.

And notice, too, the way in which they refer to colors; never plain and simple ones like red or black or blue; always stuff like "red-brown" or "blue-green." My friend asks me if I have noticed the peculiar soft "yellow-brown" that the water fowl puts on in the spring. Answer: No, I haven't; I don't know where you look for water fowl and I didn't know that they put anything on. I have seen a blue-black crow and a burnt-indigo-sepia hen; but beyond that I have not seen anything doing.

And I wish furthermore to give this simple notice: If any other of my friends has noticed a snow-drop just peeping above the edge of the turf, will he mind not telling me? If any of them has noticed that the inner bark of the oak is beginning to blush a faint blue-red, would he mind keeping it to himself? If there is any man who has seen two orioles starting to build a nest behind his garage, and if he has stood rooted to the ground and watched the dear little feathered pair fluttering to and fro, would he object to staying rooted and saying nothing?

There are signs of spring that every sensible man respects. He sees the oysters disappear from the bill-of-fare, and knows that winter is passing. He notes the first timid appearance of the asparagus just peeping out of its melted butter, and he sees the first soft blush on the edge of the Carolina strawberry. These are the signs of spring that any man can appreciate. They speak for themselves.

Viewed thus, I am as sensitive to the first call for spring as any of my fellows. But for the kind of spring that needs a text-book of biology to interpret it, I have neither use nor sympathy.

Spring Songs

The best thing about spring—it comes when it is most needed.

—New York *Times Magazine*

MY GRANDMOTHER used to tell of a neighbor woman she knew when they were both young women homesteading on the middle western prairies. "I am always so glad," the neighbor told my grandmother one April day, "when the house is clean, the garden planted and the baby born. Then I know that spring has come."

—Jean Z. Owen, *Widows Can Be Happy* (Greenberg)

AMONG THE first signs of spring are the blooming idiots along the highways. —*Newsette*

"If Winter comes,"
The old-time lyric ran,
"Can Spring be far behind?"
You bet it can!

—Reginald Arkell, *Green Fingers* (Harcourt, Brace)

IN THE cold days of February a girl informed her sweetheart that she couldn't think of marrying him until he had saved a thousand dollars. However, with the arrival of spring and the world in bloom, she asked him how much he had saved.

"Oh, about $35."

"Well," she said with a blush and a sigh, "I guess that's near enough." —*Your Weekly Guide to Boston*

ON A drive-in theater near Coatesville, Pa.: "When spring is sprung and grass is riz, this is where the movies is."

SPRING IS wonderful. Yesterday I saw a farmer and a golfer begin their plowing together. —David Condon in Chicago *Tribune*

ONE MAY afternoon when my neighbor had opened her living-room window to let in the first warm spring breezes, a herd of dairy cattle that was being driven by her house suddenly started across her lawn.

Picturing greedy bovine mouths snatching at her perennials she grabbed a broom and rushed to the door—and stopped in amazement. The cows were standing outside her living-room window, listening intently to the soap opera she had on the radio.

The herdsman came hurrying up to shoo them away and to apologize. "It's your radio," he explained. "That's the program we been following on the barn radio all winter—and I guess they didn't want to miss none of it." —Mrs. T. M. Makin

IT WAS the first warm day after one of the coldest winters Idaho had ever experienced, and in the grocery store a man was enjoying a cola drink and staring out at the beautiful sunshine. Turning to the clerk he remarked, "Sure makes a fellow glad he didn't winter-kill." —Myrtle Williamson

Verdant Vernacular

IN PHOENIX, ARIZ., on business, Sheriff B. O. Dalton of Piggott, Ark., entertained the local deputy sheriff, John Kimmis, and Mrs. Kimmis in high style one evening. They went to the best restaurant, had steak and all the trimmings. The lavish meal over, Dalton called for the check. When it arrived he glanced at the staggering total, replaced it with great dignity on the table and murmured quietly, "Suh, in our country, we *winter* on that kind of money." —Margaret Savoy in Phoenix *Gazette*

ON MY WAY into the men's gymnasium at Northwestern State College of Louisiana one day I encountered the well-loved janitor. "Good morning, Ike," I said. "Working hard?"

"No, suh," Ike replied, "not ha'd—but so mis'able reg'lah."

—Huey P. Hinckley

TWO GRIZZLED "ridge runners" from the hills stopped on a street in Kingston, N. Y., to exchange the time of day. "How's things to home?" inquired one.

"Wal," said the other, "the ole woman ain't talkin' to me this mornin' and I ain't in a mood to interrupt her." —Paul W. Kearney

IN A SOUTH Georgia town a group of men discussing tobacco on a street corner were joined by a South Carolinian who owned one of the local warehouses. "Abel," one of the men asked a farmer, "you know Bob Morgan, don't you?"

"Well," replied Abel extending a hand, "we've howdied but we ain't shook."

—Anna Pomeroy

A CARPENTER once said to me, "Best rule I know for talkin' is the same as the one for carpenterin': measure twice and saw once."

—Virginia Baldwin

DURING OUR vacation on Cape Cod we were talking with a native one day when a group of strangers passed. We asked if they were local people. "Well, two of them are," he replied, "but the others are just summer complaints."

—I. D. F.

IN THE crowded bus a lanky Kentuckian sat opposite a young woman whose skimpy skirt kept creeping up over her knees. She fought a constant battle with it, pulling it down, but as soon as she released her hold, up it crept. After one hard yank she looked up and met the gaze of her traveling companion.

"Don't stretch your calico, sister," he advised her. "My weakness is liquor."

—Mabel Osborne

You Bet Travel Is Broadening

By Ogden Nash

DOCTORS tell me that some people wonder who they are,
They don't know if they are Peter Pumpkin-eater or Priam,
But I know who I am.
My identity is no mystery to unravel,
Because I know who I am, especially when I travel.
I am he who lies either over or under the inevitable snores,
I am he who the air conditioning is in conflict with whose pores,
I am he whom the dear little old ladies who have left their pocketbooks on the bureau at home invariably approach,
And he whom the argumentative tippler oozes in beside though there are thirty empty seats in the coach.
I am he who finds himself reading comics to somebody else's children while the harassed mother attends to the youngest's needs,
Ending up with candy bar on the lapel of whose previously faultless tweeds.
I am he in the car full of students celebrating victory with instruments saxophonic and ukulelean,
And he who, speaking only English, is turned to for aid by the non-English-speaking alien.
I am he who, finding himself the occupant of one Pullman space that has been sold twice, next finds himself playing Santa,
Because it was sold the second time to an elderly invalid, so there is no question about who is going to sit in the washroom from Philadelphia to Atlanta.
I guess I am he who if he had his own private car
Would be jockeyed into sharing the master bedroom with a man with a five-cent cigar.

—From Ogden Nash's *Versus* (Little, Brown)

Self-Appraisals

THE COMMITTEE for a charity drive in Newport one summer was counting on a hefty contribution from the resort's richest resident, August Belmont, until the prominent Boston minister serving as chief speaker at a rally launched into a scathing denunciation of horse racing. "If people would contribute to charity," he concluded, "one tenth of what they squander on horse races, drives like this would be unnecessary."

"You've probably offended August Belmont," the distracted chairman told the minister. "He not only loves horse racing but has a track named after him! He won't give us a cent now."

The contrite minister hastened to Belmont's side and assured him, "If I touched on one of your weaknesses, sir, I'm sure you realize it was unintentional."

Unperturbed, Mr. Belmont replied, "Don't let it worry you. Any minister who could talk five minutes without hitting one of my weaknesses wouldn't be worth a plugged nickel!" —Bennett Cerf

GROUCHO MARX: "I'm an ordinary sort of fellow—42 around the chest, 42 around the waist, 96 around the golf course and a nuisance around the house."

A NEW CHILD was getting acquainted with some of the early settlers in our neighborhood. "I'm not very well adjusted," I heard her say, "so if I say anything you don't like, why, I probably don't mean it. Okay?"

—Margaret Lee Runbeck, *Miss Boo Is Sixteen* (Houghton Mifflin)

GEORGE JESSEL had been telling Moss Hart about the inefficiency of a certain movie magnate, and concluded, "I told him how to run his studio, all right."

"Then what happened?" asked Hart.

"Oh, nothing," said George. "We parted good friends. He boarded his yacht and I took the subway home."

—William J. Reilly, *How to Improve Your Human Relations by Straight Thinking* (Harper)

WE WERE on a steaming coral island astride the equator during World War II. Thousands of ammunition cases were lying on the beach, and our platoon had the job of hauling them inland. Hour after hour we plodded through the beach sand, our sweaty bodies bent into button hooks with the weight of the ammunition. A group of Polynesians lolling in the shade of a coconut palm were watching us. Each time we passed the grinning natives the dough-foot in front of me would mutter, "Stupid, ignorant savages!" About the sixth time I said to him, "You shouldn't talk about those people like that."

"Those people!" he exploded. "Who's talking about *those* people? I mean us!"

—D. Mitchell

OSCAR LEVANT: "Once I make up my mind I'm full of indecision."

WALLY COX: "I've got the kind of face that looks as though I've already been waited on."

—NBC-TV

WHEN A critic raved about Charles Laughton's reading "act" but added, "Laughton appeared on the stage in a blue, baggy suit," the actor retorted, "The suit was brand-new. It was me that was baggy."

—Erskine Johnson, NEA

AFTER THE war I walked into a famous New York advertising firm to apply for a job and was handed a long, complicated form to fill out. I answered each question with care until I came to this one: "Please describe the type of work for which your military training has especially prepared you."

I tried to think of an acceptable answer, but two years of cloak-and-dagger operations with OSS had conditioned me to brutally honest reporting. So I wrote: "Burglary, train-wrecking, arson, murder and assassination."

Several months after I was hired my secretary happened on my employment folder in the company files and brought it to my desk, her eyes twinkling. On the margin of my application someone had penciled: "He's one of us, obviously. Recommend that we hire him."

—Cy Coggins

DOWN-AND-OUTER as he watches successful man whirl by in a Cadillac: "There but for me go I."

—T. V. Smith cartoon in *The Saturday Review*

AFTER HIS election as mayor of New York City Fiorello La Guardia promptly disposed of the problem of office-seekers. He called his entire campaign force together and said in a very few sentences that a cause, not a man, had succeeded. "My first qualification for this great office," he wound up, "is my monumental personal ingratitude!" —Ernest Cuneo, *Life With Fiorello* (Macmillan)

HOME-COMING husband to wife: "Whew! I took an aptitude test this afternoon. Thank goodness I own the company!"

—Sylvia Strum Bremer in Davenport, Iowa, *Daily Times*

The Business Whirl

COMPANY EXECUTIVE to junior executives: ". . . and when Mr. Biglee's son starts working here tomorrow he'll have no special privileges or authority. Treat him just as you would anyone else who was due to take over the whole business in a year or two."

—Marcus cartoon in *The Saturday Evening Post*

THE MANAGER and one of his salesmen stood before a map on which colored pins indicated the representative in each area. "I'm not going to fire you, Cartwright," the manager said, "but just to emphasize the insecurity of your position I'm loosening your pin a little."

AT A WASHINGTON party some years ago two well-known reformed lobbyists were comparing notes on how the five-percent business had fallen off. One asked the other, "How's business?"

"Well, you know how it is," said the other. "This business is like sex. When it's good, it's wonderful. When it's bad—it's pretty good." —"Austine" in St. Louis *Globe-Democrat*

TWO BUSINESSMEN at lunch in luxurious restaurant: "No, Harry, let's go Dutch—you use your expense account and I'll use mine." —Cartoon in *Punch*

AS UNIT MANAGER of a camera crew filming local color on New York's 42nd Street I noticed two stores across from each other, both displaying banners announcing big going-out-of-business sales. I asked the proprietor of one about it.

"That fellow across the street," he said, "is just going into the going-out-of-business business. In a month he *will* be going out of business! But we've been in the going-out-of-business business for ten years. We're successful because we have established a dependable going-out-of-business business reputation."

—Jack Dlugatch

"ONE OF THE most tactful men I ever knew," says a California manufacturer, "was the man who fired me from my very first job. He called me in and said, 'Son, I don't know how we're ever going to get along without you, but starting Monday we're going to try.' "

—Gene Sherman in Los Angeles *Times*

ONE MAN TO another: "We're a nonprofit organization. We didn't mean to be—but we are."

—Mike Connolly in *The Hollywood Reporter*

WHEN A MAN wrote to the B. F. Goodrich Co. asking for some information he added a warning note: "I don't want any advertising material—and no salesman." It was difficult to put the information into a letter, so the company ignored the warning and sent a salesman around to see him. The fellow didn't wait for an explanation. "I told them," he said to the Goodrich man, "no salesman."

The caller—a youngster just out of the rubber company's training school—sighed and replied, "Mister, I'm as close to a no-salesman as they've got." —Kenneth Nichols in Akron *Beacon Journal*

Memo posted at the Pappas Refrigeration Co. in Houston: TO ALL EMPLOYES. Due to increased competition and a desire to stay in business, we find it necessary to institute a new policy. We are asking that somewhere between starting and quitting time, and without infringing too much on the time usually devoted to Lunch Periods, Coffee Breaks, Rest Periods, Story Telling, Ticket Selling, Vacation Planning and the rehashing of yesterday's TV programs, each employe endeavor to find some time that can be set aside and known as the "Work Break."

—George Fuermann in Houston *Post*

Office Mottoes

SIGN under an office clock: "It's earlier than you think."

—*Efficiency Magazine,* London

IN THE research and development group of the Navy's Bureau of Air: "If it works, it's obsolete."

—Frederick C. Othman, United Feature Syndicate

IN A Navy office in the Pentagon: "If you can keep your head when all about you are losing theirs, maybe you just don't understand the situation!" —Capt. B. H. Shupper

IN ANOTHER Pentagon office: "Look alive. Remember, you can be replaced by a button."

—Ventura County, Calif., *Star-Free Press*

SIGN IN Senator Lyndon Johnson's office: "You ain't learnin' nothin' when you're talkin'." —New York *Times*

NORMAN C. MOORE, assistant to the Dean of Students at Princeton, has this sign on his desk: "There's no damn reason for it; it's just our policy."

—*The Princeton Tiger*

Definitions With a Difference

Efficiency expert: A guy smart enough to tell you how to run your business and too smart to start his own.

—Rochester, N. Y., *Times-Union*

London clubman's definition of the country: A damp sort of place where all sorts of birds fly about uncooked. —Joseph Wood Krutch, *The Twelve Seasons* (Sloane)

Tourists: People who travel thousands of miles to get a picture of themselves standing by the car.

Sweater: A garment worn by a child when his mother feels chilly.

—Alma Denny

Platonic friendship: One that half the town says isn't.

—Raymond Duncan in Ellaville, Ga., *Sun*

Wife: A person who can look in the top drawer of a dresser and find a man's handkerchief that isn't there.

—Lorimor, Iowa, *Lorimorian*

Genius: The infinite capacity not only for taking pains but for giving them. —Richard Armour in *The Saturday Evening Post*

Worry: Putting today's sun under tomorrow's cloud.

Confusion is one woman plus one left turn; excitement is two women plus one secret; bedlam is three women plus one bargain; chaos is four women plus one luncheon check.

—*Changing Times, The Kiplinger Magazine*

Actor: A guy who, if you ain't talking about him, he ain't listening. —Marlon Brando, quoted in London *Observer*

Psychology: The science that tells you what you already know in words you can't understand.

—"The Beulah Show," CBS

Petition: A list of people who didn't have the nerve to say "no."

—*The Sign*

Autobiography: Fiction written by someone who knows the facts.

—Clyde Moore in Columbus *Ohio State Journal*

Hospital room: A place where friends of the patient go to talk to other friends of the patient.

—Francis O. Walsh in *The Saturday Evening Post*

The Maine Line

Excerpts from the book "And One to Grow On"

John Gould

Doctor Pillsbury: One of the doctors in our town was known all over the state and wasn't really a small-town doctor at all. We were lucky to have him, but he was ahead of his time in lots of things, and almost got run out of town a couple of times for pooh-poohing time-honored necessities like mustard plasters and fumigations.

As I look back now, I can see that he actually knew altogether too much. He was too good a doctor. And there must have been something he lacked, because it was Dr. Pillsbury who had the fuller life, and the greater esteem, and I suppose a bigger practice—because he took care of a lot of people that other doctors wouldn't agree were sick. Dr. Pillsbury did keep up-to-date in many ways, but he would always approve a mustard plaster if you thought that was what you needed, and he would fumigate clear out into the back woodlot if you asked him to.

The truth of the matter is that some doctors treat patients and some doctors treat people. Dr. Pillsbury treated people. There were families in our town that thought he was greater than God, and a good deal more available during perplexities. He had practiced there for over 50 years, and the town had few people he couldn't prescribe for with his eyes shut.

Dr. Pillsbury was one of those rare people who know something about everything to some degree. He even went to a veterinarian college long enough to pick up some pointers on animal troubles. When he went to take care of somebody, there would often be a dog or a cow in distress, and he wanted to be able to help. Most doctors feel that animals are beneath their dignity. But Dr. Pillsbury was perfectly willing to sew up a barbwire gash or make a hound dog comfortable, and that is a fine thing. A dog can be wept for too, and some farmers are a good deal more wrapped up in their livestock than they are in their wives—not too many, but some. A doctor should know about these things, and Dr. Pillsbury did.

His office was little more than a study. There were no murderous-looking cases of instruments about. He had a library of medical books, but he also had some law books, the classics and anything else that appealed to him. He was always reading when somebody came in. And sometimes he would read you a little of it before he put the book down—depending on the occasion. I wouldn't wonder if sometimes some patients forgot what they came for before he decided to look at their tongues.

Like country doctors in a thousand other places, he made shift under all kinds of circumstances and did all the storied things—appendectomies on kitchen tables and many an operation while somebody held a lamp and somebody else held the patient. But Dr. Pillsbury was a philosopher first. He actually quoted Aristotle in town meeting—and everybody listened. He applied the humanities to about everything he did. And he could play upon the people in our town as if they were a piano.

Once he came to see Dan Thurlow, who was one of these hearty people who never had a sick day and consequently was scared silly when he got took down. He really was sick, as it turned out, but Dr. Pillsbury wasn't going to admit it while the man's fears were the strongest. So when the doctor came into the sickroom he saw a newspaper on the bed, and said, "Oh, the paper—I haven't seen a paper in two days," and he sat down and began to read.

"But, Doc," Dan said. "I'm sick."

"Yes, I been notified. You'll get well."

"But dammit, Doc, don't just set there and read. I feel awful."

"You may feel worse before you're better. This paper prints the silliest editorials. Here's one here trying to figure out how Europe feels. What does an editor in Portland know about Europe? Why don't he write about things here in Maine, things he has a fair chance to know about? I think I'll write him a letter and say so."

"For God's sake, Doc Pillsbury, will you put that damn paper down and give me a pill, or something?"

"I suppose that is what I came for, after all. What seems to be the trouble, now? Something sore?"

"I just feel awful. I think I may die."

"Well, what of it? People do. Don't mean a thing to anybody else. If you die, you'll be surprised how soon the general grief will pass away. It won't bother you any, either. So what of it? Been eating something you shouldn't, like green corn or scallops?"

Dan got well, and he used to tell all round about the conversation he had that morning. "Damned old coot knew just what he was doing, too—got me so mad I forgot how sick I was, and first thing I knew I felt better. I could have killed him though. I found out afterward he'd seen that same paper in at least ten other bedrooms, and took it at home himself besides."

Frank Blaisdell's Pasture: One of the points that ran out into our little harbor used to be the back pasture of Frank Blaisdell's farm. It was just an ordinary Maine pasture, consisting of rocks, juniper bushes, wild roses and sweet fern. But it was covered with blackcap raspberries, too, and there isn't anything nicer for jam. We had blueberries and island cranberries, and everything else, but those blackcaps had something special about them and became a town tradition. Every summer we'd go down by the dozens and pick them. Some of us took a skiff and rowed across the harbor to spend a day, picnic and all, filling our milk pails. Frank Blaisdell used to come down and pick with us, too. He never said anything about picking his blackcaps. We knew they were in the public domain, and so did Frank.

So what happened? One day a rich New Yorker came to our town and bought the whole point. Paid a good price, Frank said, and then he put a fence around it. Woven wire with metal posts. Cost a fortune. Our people didn't mind, because, having always been land-poor, we understood how it is with people who never had ownership of land in their backgrounds. The poor man had a deep sense of possession. He'd slaved a whole lifetime at something he hated so he could retire to Maine and own some land, and when he got it he naturally put up a fence so he could walk around and see just what was his.

The fence didn't bother us much at first. When the blackcaps were ripe, we went down and climbed over the fence and picked them. There was a big oak tree in one corner, with a limb that hung just so, and we could swing over the fence, pails and all. But after a few days the New Yorker put up a No Trespassing sign, cut off the limb and threatened those of us who climbed the fence with arrest. We were greatly puzzled, for we felt we were being evicted from an inalienable right. After that we only picked blackcaps when he wasn't around. Otherwise, the blackcaps ripened in the sun as before, but they dropped off the bushes when they were ripe, and the New Yorker walked about his woven wire fence and basked in the importance of ownership.

A few years later this New Yorker felt the road out to his place wasn't just what he'd like. At just about the time public indignation over the blackcaps was highest, he met Arthur Mercennes, our road commissioner, and said it would be nice to have a new road out to the point. Art said it was a splendid idea, and that a six-lane job with solid-gold paving blocks would be a great improvement. One word led to another, and Art finally punched the New Yorker in the nose.

The New Yorker brought suit, but when he found out so many people were clamoring to be on the jury, he dropped it. Then he made a political issue of it and tried to get Art beaten at the next town meeting. He also put an article in the Town Warrant asking for $5000 to construct a passable road to his point. Art said the proposed road could only serve two possible purposes—either to take people out to the point to see the New Yorker, which nobody would want to do, or bring the New Yorker to town, which he thought was entirely unnecessary. The project was dismissed, and Art was re-elected by the biggest majority he ever got.

And it's funny how those things hold over. In late years a lot of people have built cottages and homes down along the Blaisdell Point road, and some of them are nice people. But the road has never been repaired, and as long as that fence stands around the blackcap raspberries, I doubt if it ever will be.

Independent Spirits

In John Gould's town they like to tell about the time the minister asked all in the congregation to rise who wanted to go to heaven. All but one man rose. Then the minister asked those to stand who wanted to go to hell. Nobody rose. The puzzled parson stared down at the non-coöperator and asked where he wanted to go. "Nowhere," said this stalwart son of Maine. "I like it here."

—From Lewis Gannett's review of *And One to Grow On* by John Gould, in New York *Herald Tribune*

I HAD BEEN listening to the energetic but unsuccessful efforts of a young Salt Lake City bus driver to drum up trade for his sightseeing trip when my attention was diverted to a quaint figure walking toward us. The elderly lady, tall and graceful, wore a black lace dress that almost touched the ground and barely revealed her old-fashioned button shoes. A crocheted cape hung over her shoulders, and a large black hat with a single rose bobbed up and down with each step.

The bus driver's eyes brightened. "See the sights of Salt Lake City, madam?" he said hopefully.

The lady drew herself up. "Young man," she said with dignity, "I *am* one of the sights of Salt Lake City." —Mary Craig

WHEN SOUND MOVIES first came into being there was a mad scramble for directors who could handle dialogue and the Hollywood moguls turned to Broadway. One man in particular was in demand—John Golden—and one studio after another tried to seduce him, but Golden said no. Finally the biggest, most affluent of them all sent its super-mogul east. "We've got to have you," the Big Mogul pleaded. "You can have anything you want; write your own ticket."

Golden thought it all over and said, "Let me ask you just one question: Who pushes the button? Do I push it and you come in, or do you push it and I come in?"

The Hollywood bigwig hesitated. "Well," he said, "we have an enormous studio and there are a lot of problems and making movies is new to you, and there'll be times when . . . "

"That's all I want to know," said Golden. "Here I push the button—and here I stay!" —J. P. McEvoy, McNaught Syndicate

AN ELDERLY WOMAN was shopping for a hat and the salesgirl kept showing her new types of headgear which didn't suit the old lady at all. Finally she said, "Listen, I wear a corset and I wear drawers, and I want a hat to match."

—Cedric Adams in Minneapolis *Tribune*

AN UTTER LACK of show—and of modern conveniences—characterizes a certain Cape Cod hotel. Its owner, a retired sea captain, steadfastly refuses to paint the old building on the theory that it would "attract the wrong kind of people." However, its fine food, good sailing and swimming draw customers who devotedly return each year. One summer a banker from Philadelphia reserved one of the outlying cottages and offered to install, at his own expense, a modern bathroom. "Go ahead," replied the captain, "but if you put her in you must rip her out in the fall."

And that's just what happened. The hotel still has no conveniences to attract "the wrong kind of people." —Gordon L. Hough

Telephone Lines

SHORTLY AFTER one Vermonter had had a telephone installed, a neighbor dropped in and found him immersed in the business of filling out a form from a mail-order catalogue. The telephone was ringing persistently, but its possessor took no heed whatever.

"Alex," the caller ventured, "ain't that your number?"

"Ehyah, 'tis."

"Wal, ain'tcha goin' to answer it for gossakes?"

"William," said the other, looking up, "I'm busy and I had that durn thing installed for *my* convenience."

—Frederic F. Van de Water, *The Circling Year* (John Day)

IN LOS ANGELES a chap who happened to be loitering in the lobby of the Biltmore reports that a woman arrived, slightly out of breath, snatched one of the house phones and gave the operator a room number on the sixth floor, apparently that of an out-of-town friend who had recently checked in. After the usual greetings the woman settled down to a conversation that went on and on, all about their aunts and uncles and mutual friends and how everything was back in Illinois. After 20 minutes of this she paused. "Good-by, Alice," she said. "I'll be right up."

—Gene Sherman in Los Angeles *Times*

MAN DESCRIBING summer cottage: "Just a little shack near a lake, with no conveniences to speak of, except that it doesn't have a telephone." —Bill Gold in Washington *Post and Times Herald*

AFTER REPEATED telephone calls I finally pinned Harpo Marx down to a promise to appear in a benefit performance at one of the hospitals. To make sure he kept the appointment I went to his apartment to fetch him. As he closed the door the phone rang. Should he go back to see who it was? "No," said Harpo, "I'm not going back. It's probably you again."
—Myra Thompson, quoted by Bennett Cerf in *The Saturday Review*

ONE SATURDAY morning in a crowded bus terminal I watched a young soldier change a dollar and range the dimes in rows on the shelf in a telephone booth along with a cup of coffee. His first call was lengthy, consisting on his side mainly of repetition of "Gee, honey," and "Sure thing, honey."

A middle-aged man waiting for a booth listened, looked over the array of coins and finally went over to the lunch counter. He came back with a plate of spaghetti, opened the door of the booth and said kindly, "Here, sonny, you'll be needing dinner in here if all your girls are as big talkers as this one." —Florence C. Bowles

A SALESMAN called a prospective customer and the phone was answered by what was obviously a small boy. "Is your mother or father home?" the salesman asked. The child said no. "Well, is there anyone else there I can speak to?"

"My sister," the youngster piped. There was a rather long period of silence, then the salesman heard the boy's voice again.

"I can't lift her out of the play pen," he said.
—Dick Friendlich in San Francisco *Chronicle*

ONE MORNING, on coming into his office, a Montgomery, Ala., businessman was surprised to see his secretary holding her nose while talking on the phone to a customer in New England. Her explanation: "On long-distance calls these Yankees can't understand a thing I say—unless I hold my nose!" —Mrs. R. A. Dennis

Southern Exposure

I WAS with a group of Boy Scouts visiting West Point and our guide was a friendly cadet from the South. Pointing to one impressive monument he said it was a memorial to the northern men who died in the War Between the States. "Of co'se," he added, "Ah call it a tribute to s'uthun marksmanship." —Andrew R. De Mar

WHEN Cecil B. de Mille, the movie producer, was a guest at a luncheon in Atlanta, he was introduced as a southerner. "Actually," he confessed, "I am a Yankee imposter. I was supposed to have been born in the old family home in North Carolina, but my mother was visiting in Massachusetts and I—impetuous as always—couldn't wait for the proper time and arrived early.

"My father was a stanch southerner and just couldn't have a Yankee boy, so he smuggled my mother and me back to North Carolina. There my mother went to bed and I was tucked in beside her. After all the worried relatives and friends had assembled, after they had stood in the hall whispering for an hour or more, my grandmother flung open the door, stalked out and announced, 'It's a boy!' "

—James Saxon Childers in Atlanta *Journal and Constitution Magazine*

CASEY STENGEL, manager of the New York Yankees, is quite a one for spinning tall tales. One concerns the pitching prodigy from deepest Alabamy who failed to show up at the spring training base. Inquiry brought this reply from his irate pappy: "Forget that scoundrel son of mine, suh. When he boasted he was going off to put on a Yankee uniform, I shot him." —Bennett Cerf in *This Week Magazine*

A NEW YORKER had always heard that the South was a romantic place, but her first house party in Mississippi so far surpassed her expectations that she became a little worried. "I've got a problem and I don't know what to do," she said to her hostess one day. "All the boys are *proposing.*"

"My dear, don't let that give you a moment's concern," the older woman reassured her. "On a Mississippi house party that's just common courtesy."

—John D. McCready

TWO OHIO boys driving through Tennessee found themselves lost in the hills with evening coming on. The road was deserted, but finally a figure appeared trudging toward them. Relieved, they stopped and asked, "Which way to Chattanooga?"

The man stared at them a moment without replying, then asked, "Whar you boys from?"

"Ohio."

"I thought so," he said. "Wal, you found it in 1863. Let's see you find it again."

—Wendell P. Long

AS I APPROACHED the dairy case in a neighborhood supermarket in Memphis, Tenn., I noticed a woman studying the labels on various containers. Then she turned to a woman waiting behind her and said, "Excuse me, please, but could you tell me which kind of buttermilk I should buy to make cornbread?" The other woman shook her head pityingly and replied, "It wouldn't make no difference, honey—you ain't gonna make no cornbread fit to eat anyway with that accent."

—Mrs. William Cooper

Supermarket Specials

SIGN ON the cash register of a pretty checker in an Atlanta supermarket: "Just Married; Count Your Change Twice."

—Greensboro, N. C., *Daily News*

HUSBAND TO wife shopping in supermarket: "Never mind the large economy size . . . get the small, expensive box we can afford."

—Chon Day cartoon in *The Saturday Evening Post*

HOUSEWIFE IN supermarket: "I'm sorry, I can't remember the brand—but I can hum a few bars of the commercial."

—E. E. Kenyon in *The American Weekly*

ONE CART-PUSHING husband to another: "I estimate the cost per mile to operate one of these things is around $300!"

—Jack Markow cartoon in *Collier's*

IRATE GENTLEMAN to check-out clerk: "I know they're empty. I ate the stuff while I was waiting in line."

—Harry Mace cartoon in *The American Legion Magazine*

Wee Moderns

As I waited outside a supermarket a boy about eight, in the car parked alongside ours, was wildly twisting the steering wheel and uttering motorlike sounds. I watched him a while, then leaned over and said, "Hey, bud, you better stick your arm out when you go round a curve or you'll get a ticket."

He regarded me scornfully. "Look, bub," he said, "you stick your arm out of a space ship and you'll have it ripped off."

—Stanley H. Brile

Small boy to chum: "So *that's* it. I always figured the stork had too short a wingspread to carry an eight- to ten-pound load."

—Corka cartoon in *Today's Health*

Mrs. Charles A. Lindbergh told friends about taking the flier's 11-year-old daughter to see *The Spirit of St. Louis*. In the middle of the movie the youngster turned to her mother and whispered anxiously, "Mummy, does he make it?"

—Leo Aikman in Atlanta *Constitution*

Two small girls brought home a box full of dirt one day and warned their mother to be very careful of it. "All right," she promised. "But tell me, why is it so special?"

"Instant Mud Pies," they answered. —Walter Carss, quoted by George Fuermann in Houston *Post*

Our four-year-old son, who has become an avid viewer of ballet on TV, spotted a large dog one afternoon in the usual pose at a fire hydrant. "Look, Daddy," he shouted. "Ballet!"

—George H. East

DURING A bad electrical storm a mother in Virginia thought her young son would be frightened, so she tiptoed into his room to comfort him. The boy opened his eyes and murmured, "What's Daddy doing with the television set now?"
—Marjorie Truitt in *The Progressive Farmer*

A NURSERY-SCHOOL teacher handed one of her charges a magazine and suggested he cut out a picture of something he thought his father would like. The four-year-old flipped the pages, then without hesitation jabbed the scissors into a page and clipped out a picture of a bottle of gin. —AP

The Cocktail Party

Cocktail party: where they cut sandwiches and friends into little pieces.
—Chuck Norman

THE COCKTAIL party was in full swing when the host's small daughter pulled at her father's sleeve. "Daddy," asked the puzzled youngster, "haven't we had this party before?"
—Bob Considine, King Features

FRANK MORGAN was at a cocktail party one afternoon, holding a Scotch and soda, when the hostess suddenly appeared with a tray of silly-frilly canapés. She insisted on serving him. "No, thanks," grunted Frank, taking a firmer grip on his glass. "I belong to Hors d'Oeuvres Anonymous."
—Sidney Skolsky, United Feature Syndicate

A NEW ORLEANS woman planning a cocktail party thought the invitations ought to read "from six to eight," but her husband objected that this would appear to be telling the guests when to go home. So the invitations merely stated "cocktails at six," with the inevitable result. Long after midnight the party was still going strong.

Shortly after one the police arrived. Somebody in the neighborhood had complained, and the racket would have to stop. The host was outraged, said he couldn't imagine one of his neighbors making a complaint. But the sergeant was adamant—a complaint had been received. That broke up the party, and as the last guest filed out, the hostess turned to her husband, "I wonder who called the police?"

Replied her weary husband, "I did."

—Thomas Griffin in New Orleans *Item,* quoted by Bill Gold in Washington *Post*

WIFE TO husband after several rounds of drinks at a cocktail party: "Henry, don't take another cocktail. Your face is already getting blurred."

—Perrin C. Galpin

AT A RECEPTION in Paris where there were many titled guests, the wife of an American general stepped up to the cocktail table. "Looking for something?" asked another guest.

"Yes, a bourbon."

With a courtly bow he asked, "Would a Hapsburg do?"

—Maggi Nolan in New York *Herald Tribune,* European edition

MY MOTHER has long had a summer cottage in a fishing village, living alone except for weekends when my brother and I usually go there. One Fourth of July we had a big cocktail party and I forgot to throw the empty bottles into the rubbish bin. I was surprised to find seven of them standing primly beneath the pantry sink when I came out the following Friday. "What's the idea?" I asked Mother.

"Bill," she said severely, "you know very well that Charlie Burns has been picking up my rubbish for 20 years. I wouldn't want him to think we drank all that whiskey in one weekend. So I've been putting out one bottle each morning."

—Bill Russel

ONE MAN to another at cocktail party: "I'm bushed. I think I'll flirt with some good-looking dame so my wife will take me home."

—Leo Garel cartoon in *Collier's*

RHODE ISLAND'S Senator Theodore F. Green, 90 and a bachelor, is one of the most popular men in Washington society and goes regularly to more parties than anyone else in town. At one cocktail party he was asked how many he was attending that day. "Six," he said, looking up from a small notebook.

"What are you doing, seeing where you are to go next?"

"No," replied the energetic Senator, "I'm trying to find out where I am now!"

—Les and Liz Carpenter in *Quote*

Young in Heart

THE YOUNG coed brought a friend home from college, an extremely attractive and curvaceous honey blonde. Introducing her friend to her grandfather the girl added, "And just think, Marilyn, he's in his 90's."

"Early 90's, that is," the old gent amended with a gleam in his eye. —*Navy News Magazine*

MY GRANDMOTHER, a demure lady of 70-plus, has always professed disdain for the wrestling which is so popular on television. Yet every night she sits through the matches, saying she can't sleep if she retires too early. Then one night a young hoodlum climbed into the house via Grandma's window, but tripped over a footstool and fell. Before he could move Grandma had grabbed his leg, twisted it around the bedpost and held it firmly while she called for help. Afterward she explained airily, "Oh, I just took him with a step-over toe hold." —W. F. Abata

A PRETTY young Richmond matron, walking through a sparsely settled district toward the bus line one morning, realized that she was being followed. Not wishing to turn and look she increased her pace. The footsteps accelerated, too. Reaching a thickly populated area she slowed down. The unknown did likewise.

At the bus stop she turned to face the offender; to her amazement it was the courtly old gentleman from next door. "Why, Colonel Ashby," she exclaimed, "you frightened me. Why in the world didn't you speak or catch up with me?"

The colonel doffed his hat and bowed. "Well, ma'am, I was kinda havin' a debate with mahself as to whether to catch up with you and enjoy the conversation, or stay behind and enjoy the view."

—S. K. Joynes, Jr.

OUR USUAL Saturday-afternoon routine was upset: for the first time in years Grandpa was not at his usual place beside the radio listening to the opera. We spent an anxious afternoon asking about him at every conceivable place and were about ready to try the police when the door opened and Grandpa walked in. "Where have you been?" we demanded frantically.

"Oh, I got tired of just *listening* to opera," he replied nonchalantly. "So I went downtown and applied at the Met. I not only carried a spear across the stage—I even hummed a bit."

—L. Weiss

THREE OLD men were passing the time of day discussing the ideal way of leaving the world. The first, aged 75, remarked he'd like to go quickly, and suggested a crash in a speeding car. The second, aged 85, agreed on a speedy end, but thought he'd prefer a jet-propelled plane.

"I've got a better idea," mused the third, aged 95. "I'd rather be shot by a jealous husband."

—*Variety*

A TEXAN who was visiting New England had been boasting about the healthful qualities of the Texas climate and as proof mentioned that his father, who was 75, still rode horseback. One of his listeners allowed that that was pretty good, but that it couldn't come up to a neighboring Yankee the same age who had spent ten hours every day the past week plowing—except Saturday afternoon, when he had to knock off to go to his father's wedding.

"How old was his father?" asked the Texan.

"Ninety-nine."

"What did he want to get married for at that age?"

"Want to? He *had* to!"

—G. E. G.

MY 75-YEAR-OLD mother and a young matron, on a trip to New Orleans, went on a conducted tour of the French Quarter one night. Around 11 o'clock they came to a theater on Bourbon Street where, as the chorus girls walked up the aisle, pinching by the male customers seemed to be part of the act. As the show proceeded my mother's young friend became quite perturbed. "Mrs. Criddle," she said finally, "this is more than we bargained for. We had better leave."

"Don't be a fool, honey," replied my mother. *"I'm* not going up that aisle."

—Edward S. Criddle

Audience Participation

Temptation: In Burbank, Calif., William C. Kiele was arrested on suspicion of assault with a deadly weapon; he was caught in the eighth row of a burlesque theater armed with a slingshot and an evening's supply of metal staples. —*Time*

AN ATTORNEY for the local gas and electric company was addressing a town meeting in Roxbury, Mass. "Think of the good this company has done for all the people of Boston," he exhorted the audience. "If you would permit a pun, I would say in the words of the immortal poet Lord Tennyson, 'Honor the Light Brigade.' "

From the rear of the hall came a clear small voice, "Oh, what a charge they made!" —E. Butera

HOMER LIVINGSTON, president of the American Bankers Association, tells about the time he was addressing a large group of bankers in Louisville when the microphone ceased to function. Raising his voice he asked a man in the back row if he could hear.

"No," said the man, whereupon a man in the front row stood up.

"I can hear," he shouted to the gent in back. "And I'll change places with you." —Chicago *Tribune*

CHARLES LAMB loved the theater and managed to get one of his plays produced. It was a howling failure. On the fatal first, and only, night the audience hissed it heartily and Lamb joined in the hissing. He explained that he did so because he was damnably afraid of being taken for the author.

—*The Selected Letters of Charles Lamb,* edited by T. S. Matthews (Farrar, Straus and Cudahy)

DURING THE British election campaign Tony Leavey, Conservative candidate in Blackburn East, was addressing a meeting when a Socialist heckler shouted, "Why have we the finest generation of children ever known in this country?"

Immediately from the hall came the reply, "Because they were produced by private enterprise." —London *Daily Telegraph*

Private Enterprise

ONE HUNDRED and eighty babies born on October 15, 1953, to families of General Electric employes received five shares of GE stock apiece. That was the company's way of celebrating its 75th anniversary. GE stock celebrated, too, by jumping three points that day, so each infant got stock worth nearly $400, at a total cost of some $71,000 for the company.

GE, which had been thinking in terms of perhaps a dozen births figured on the average number of births in the general population, had announced the plan almost exactly nine months before. —*Business Week;* AP

WHEN AIRLINES were young and people were wary of flying, a promotion man suggested to one of the lines that they permit wives of businessmen to accompany their husbands free, just to prove that flying was safe. The idea was quickly adopted, and a record kept of the names of those who accepted the proposition. In due time the airline sent a letter to those wives, asking how they enjoyed the trip. From 90 percent of them came back a baffled reply: *"What* airplane trip?" —Marguerite Lyon, *And So to Bedlam,* © 1943 by The Bobbs-Merrill Co., Inc.

Monkeys Out on the Town

Condensed from "They Never Talk Back"

Henry Trefflich
As told to Baynard Kendrick

About 10:15 Saturday morning, May 11, 1946, lights began to flash and telephones to jangle at the Old Slip police station in New York City. A moment later came the riot call. Nearby Fulton, Vesey and Church streets were jammed with people. Downtown New York was being taken over by monkeys!

At 9:45 that morning Gus Hildebrand, an employe in my pet shop at 215 Fulton Street, had noted a monkey entangled in the wire mesh of his cage. Gus opened the door of the cage and untangled the little fellow, who promptly raced out. Before Gus could make a move, 19 other monkeys, gibbering with glee, followed the leader.

The monkeys held a quick consultation and apparently decided that it would be unfair to leave their fellow primates behind bars. In an instant they had opened the other four cages and 80 more monkeys poured into the room. Then, while Gus was frantically trying to trap some of them, one bright little fellow opened the door and discovered, there in the hallway, a ladder leading to an open skylight! Immediately the 99 other monkeys followed him up the ladder to the roof—and to freedom.

... CHESTER GORDON, employe of a Vesey Street grocery store, was in the third-floor storeroom showing a customer a new stock of coffee when a cloud of 40 monkeys entered noisily through an open window behind him. Mr. Gordon turned his attention to the half of the visitors who were opening sacks of coffee and aromatic spices. The customer made his way to the ground floor, accompanied by the other half, non-coffee drinkers who meant to investigate the bananas in the fruit department.

Though a little green, the bananas proved edible, and since clerks and customers had obligingly left, everything was quite convivial until some dogs tried to chisel in. These strays were greeted with a barrage of banana skins, pop bottles and cans from the shelves. The dogs beat a strategic retreat.

Exhibiting remarkable presence of mind, Mr. Gordon slammed the upstairs window shut, then dashed downstairs and shut all the other windows and doors. Twenty minutes later the 40 monkeys (netted by SPCA agents) and Mr. Gordon were removed from the store —alive and unharmed.

... EVERYTHING was quiet at the three-story firehouse on Fulton Street. A handball game was underway on the roof, and on the second floor two firemen were engaged in a game of checkers.

"It's your move," one player said impatiently. "Why are you sitting there staring at the wall?"

The other man shook his head as if to clear his brain. "Five monkeys just slid down the pole," he said. "One was holding a handball."

Everything broke loose at once.

Two irate firemen burst into the room yelling, "Who stole our handball?" Just then all the showers in the adjoining locker room were turned on full force. The locker-room door flew open and five more monkeys ran gleefully to the shiny brass pole and disappeared to the floor below. A fireman dashed into the locker room and gazed in stunned disbelief at ten monkeys taking showers.

For 35 minutes every member of the fire company chased monkeys over and under the hook-and-ladder truck, up the stairs and down the brass pole. Then the gong sounded.

When the hook-and-ladder started to roll, ten monkeys were left taking showers, while the other ten clung to the truck. The firemen didn't have far to go: it was just a call from down the street where a ladder was needed to get some monkeys off a building. But when the hook-and-ladder rolled to a stop, a policeman looked and shook his head. "It ain't possible," he said. "They're bringing *more!*"

. . . THE Trinity Church choirmaster was starting a practice session at the Fulton Street mission house. When he got the choirboys quieted down, he struck his tuning fork, raised his finger to give the beat—and then one of the boys giggled.

"I'm sorry, sir," the giggler said, "but there's a monkey on the piano. Another just came in the window."

A moment later there were four boys on top of the piano, but now the monkey was hanging from a chandelier. The second monkey was swinging gaily from a curtain rod.

The choirmaster calmly closed the window. He had been dealing with choirboys for a number of years—what were a couple of monkeys? With military precision he broke the choir up into squads of four, arming each squad with a slip cover stripped from a chair. The monkeys proved no match for the boys. The two were bagged in seven minutes flat and deposited in the corner to wait for their owner.

. . . A BARREL-CHESTED longshoreman, Pete by name, was just winding up a three-week binge. That Saturday morning he drifted into the White Rose Tavern on Fulton Street, ordered a drink and looked around.

He reached for his drink. It wasn't there. Pete grinned sheepishly and pretended he'd been reaching for a cigarette. He wasn't going to tell the bartender that a half dozen monkeys had just come along and one of them had drunk his whiskey and thrown the glass back of the bar! But then he saw the bartender had hold of a monkey who was trying to get out through the ventilating fan.

Pete turned to the customer next to him—the customer wasn't there! Suddenly Pete felt sick. The bar was deserted except for himself and the barkeep. But no, it wasn't deserted—that was the trouble.

Pete had heard about pink elephants. But monkeys! There were three—no, four—running around in front of the mirror sampling bottles. And when Pete looked in back of him there were a lot of others hopping from table to table, eating pretzels.

Pete reached out to snatch a drink some customer had left, but a monkey beat him to it. That did it. A few minutes later a patrolman at the Old Slip police station answered a phone call.

"This is the bartender at the White Rose Tavern," a voice said. "You'd better send the booby-hatch wagon, four men and a jacket. There's a guy here screaming, *'There are no monkeys in here! There are no monkeys in here!'* "

"Oh, DT's," the officer said.

"No, not that," the bartender said. "He's crazy. The damn place is full of them!"

IT WAS three months before all the monkeys were rounded up. One elusive little female retreated at last into the sanctuary of the drums and cables that operate the elevator in Callanan's Grocery Store. A newsman photographed her there, squatting on the cable drum. The picture appeared on the front page of the New York *Daily Mirror* the next morning, captioned: WE'VE BEEN WAITING YEARS TO USE THIS GAG—A MONKEY WENCH IN THE WORKS.

Press Releases

A FAIR YOUNG graduate of the School of Journalism got a job as cub reporter on a Long Island daily. Her first story won the editor's approval, but he pointed out a few minor inaccuracies.

"Remember," he concluded, "it was Joseph Pulitzer, founder of the School of Journalism, who declared that accuracy is to a newspaper what virtue is to a woman."

"That in itself is not entirely accurate," said the girl triumphantly. "A newspaper can always print a retraction!"

—Bennett Cerf, *Shake Well Before Using* (Simon and Schuster)

THE WARM SPRINGS, Calif., *Courier* once announced: "The combined circulation of the *Courier* and *The Saturday Evening Post* now has reached 4,600,500." —Ventura, Calif., *Star-Free Press*

YEARS AGO an assignment in the Far North led author Gene Fowler to compose an expense account that has survived as a classic in American newspaper literature.

Mr. Fowler had discovered that the cost of inside straights and antifreeze compound could be prohibitive, and the first draft of his expense sheet left him short of his goal by several hundred dollars. Pouring himself three fingers of truth serum, he tried again.

This time he included a substantial rental for a dog team and sledge. Even that was insufficient for his needs. Sadly he added a notation that the lead dog had succumbed to the rigors of the journey, and he listed an item of $100 recompense for the noble beast's owner. Still having failed to meet his goal, he dashed off the line that will live forever: "Flowers for bereaved bitch, $50."

—Red Smith in New York *Herald Tribune*

FOR YEARS the Dayton, Ohio, *Journal-Herald* had run on its women's page a favorite recipe. But one day, in the customary space, a picture showed a woman dumping the contents of a pan into a garbage pail. Instead of the recipe was this editor's note: "Today's recipe for Tomato Surprise Supreme will not be printed."

—Neal O'Hara, McNaught Syndicate

Newsweek quoted the Savannah, Ga., *Morning News* in the throes of grammar trouble: "The investigators theorized that the two must have lain down on the two must have laid down on the two must have layed down on the tracks and fell asleep."

IN GARBER, Okla., the editors of the *Free Press*, who had moved to a new office, apologized for a rash of misspellings in recent editions of the newspaper: "Please excuse. Most of the words we use frequently and cannot spell are written correctly on the wall in our old location."

—*Time*

DURING A Washington *Post* open house for newspaper people, a gray-haired little lady came into the lobby, went down the receiving line of distinguished editorial hosts. Then, swept along with the other guests, she was steered through all the departments, welcomed officially in each.

It wasn't until she had completed the tour that the breathless little lady exclaimed, "Gracious! I certainly didn't expect you to make all this fuss over somebody who just stopped by to leave a classified ad for tomorrow's paper." —Bill Gold in Washington *Post*

AFTER NOTING that "the following letter is printed in its entirety," the Providence, R. I., *Sunday Journal* published this note: "Editor: I am so damn mad I forgot what I was going to say. Jim Payne."

A NOTE FROM the editor in the McLean County, Ky., *News:* "This is another of those weeks when we didn't publish nearly all we knew. For which many may be thankful."

—Walter Davenport in *Collier's*

WHEN THE Prestonburg, Ky., *Floyd County Times* was late one week, editor Norman Allen explained in his front-page column: "The *Times* is late this week. The trouble started in a cornfield, maybe years ago. From there it reached our linotype. Yet the trouble lies not with the machine. You see, the corn grew, fermented, aged in the wood and finally reached our operator."

Rye Humor

ONE MORNING my father met Frank Thompson, an engaging inebriate. "Frank, why don't you cut out the booze?" he asked.

"Well, Lou," Frank answered, "sometimes I do get to feelin' mighty mean, and my stomach goes back on me, and I decide to swear off. I go for two or three days without touchin' a drop, and then one morning I wake up, and the sky is blue and the birds are singin' and the sun is all bright and warm—and then, by God, Lou, I rally!" —Claude M. Fuess, *Independent Schoolmaster* (Little, Brown)

AT A PARTY: "I can stand the smell of liquor, but I sure hate to listen to it" (Frank D. Felt) . . . Young lady after the fifth martini: "I certainly feel a lot more like I do now than I did when I came in!" (John R. Clark)

AN AMERICAN tourist went into a dimly lit bar in South Africa. When his eyes adjusted to the darkness he saw on a stool beside him a perfectly formed human being in military uniform—only six inches high. Incredulous, the tourist stared until the bartender spoke up in broad cockney accents. "Don't you know the Myjor, sir?" he asked, reaching across the bar, picking the little fellow up and placing him on the bar. The tourist shook his head.

"Speak up, Myjor," the bartender said. "Tell the Yank about the time you called the witch doctor a bloody damned fool."

—J. D. Ratcliff

A MAN telephoned a Montreal police station one night and excitedly reported that the steering wheel, brake pedal, accelerator, clutch pedal and dashboard had been stolen from his car. A sergeant promised to investigate. But soon the telephone rang again. "Don't bother," said the same voice—this time with a hiccup. "I got into the back seat by mistake." —CP

IDLY TURNING the pages of the Gideon Bible on the bedside table of my hotel room, I was amazed to find a crisp 20-dollar bill tucked between the pages. Clipped to the bill was a note which read: "If you opened this book because you're discouraged, read the 14th Chapter of John. If you're broke and this would help, take it. If you had a fight with your wife, buy her a present. If you don't need it, leave it for the next fellow." The note was signed: "Just a Wayfaring Stranger."

But the punch came with the P. S. "On second thought, maybe you ought to take it down to the Mirror Room and try their martinis. That's the way I got this idea anyway!"

—Mrs. J. F. Leonhard

AMONG FORMER Vice President Alben Barkley's favorite stories was one about a fellow—already feeling his liquor—who returned to the barroom for another drink but couldn't remember the name of it. "All I can remember," he told the barkeep, "is that it's tall, cold and full of gin."

Another fellow leaning over the bar turned on him and snarled, "Sir! You are speaking of the woman I love!" —Peggy McEvoy

EUGENE FIELD once ran up a bill of $140 at a Kansas City bar. Unable to pay the bill he stopped coming to the saloon. This distressed the proprietor, since Field's presence had attracted other customers. The proprietor summoned Field one day and presented him with the bill marked "Paid in full." Field folded the bill into his pocket and leaned solemnly across the bar. "Now isn't it customary," he asked quietly, "for the bartender to set 'em up when a man pays his bill?" —Debs Myers in *Holiday*

Collectors' Items

THE CREDIT department of the Hudson's Bay Co. received this letter from a Canadian farmer: "I got your letter about what I owe. Now be pachant. I ain't forgot you. When I have the money I will pay you. If this was the Judgment Day and you was no more prepared to meet your maker than I am to meet your account you sure would go to hell. Trusting you will do this."

—Tom Mahoney, *The Great Merchants* (Harper)

ASKED WHERE he got the persuasive dunning letters he sent to customers whose accounts were long overdue, the head of a company replied, a bit ruefully, "I use the best bits out of my son's letters when he's away at college." —Margaret Helms

AFTER A WEEKEND at a de luxe resort hotel in Palm Beach the tourist expected a large bill, but he wasn't prepared for a three-page, itemized account. He managed to identify every item but the very last, and smallest one—for a dollar. He was told it was for stationery.

"But," he protested, "I didn't *use* any stationery."

"The stationery referred to," explained the cashier loftily, "is the paper on which this bill is made out!" —Bennett Cerf

WHILE LOOKING UP my family lineage I discovered in newspaper files an obituary of my great-grandfather who died in 1867. The undertakers who had arranged the funeral were one of the oldest firms in the city and I wrote them asking if their records showed the name of the father of John Hopper, buried in 1867.

The reply was prompt. "Our records reflect that we buried John C. Hopper, but do not show his birthplace or the names of his parents. We find in Ledger B, which contains all unpaid accounts, that the funeral expenses were $140 with a payment of $25, leaving a balance of $115. If it is convenient for you to make this payment, we would be grateful." —Millard Hopper

IN GRAND RAPIDS, Mich., a businessman who took after a delinquent customer with a sarcastic dunning note inquiring, "Are your assets frozen?" promptly got back a check frozen into the center of a cake of ice. —Arthur Lansing in *The American Magazine*

"MY GOOD MAN," said Mr. Benningham to the grocery-store owner, "how is it you have not called on me for my account?"

"Oh, I never ask a gentleman for money."

"Indeed! But what do you do if he doesn't pay?"

"Why, after a certain time," said he, "I conclude he is not a gentleman, and then I ask him." —*The London Prison Farmer*

A CALIFORNIA bank received the following brief note with a final payment on an auto contract: "Dear Sir: This should make us even. Sincerely, but no longer yours." —*The Bankamerican*

A NEBRASKA newspaper declares the following collection letter produces excellent results:

"Dear Sir: A glance at the date of our original invoice will soon prove we've done more for you than even your own mother—we've carried you for 12 months."

—Robert Phipps in Omaha *World Herald*

Ways and Means

A FRIEND lamented to John D. Rockefeller that he had not been able to collect a $50,000 loan made to a business acquaintance.

"Why don't you sue him?" asked Rockefeller.

"I neglected to have him acknowledge the loan in writing."

"Well," said the oil tycoon, "just drop him a letter demanding the $100,000 he owes you."

"But he owes me only $50,000."

"Precisely," said Rockefeller. "He will let you know that by return mail—and you will have your acknowledgment."

—E. E. Edgar

ONE RAINY spring a Washington State taxpayer living on a neglected muddy road put up this sign: "THESE ROAD CONDITIONS WERE CAUSED BY AN ACT OF GOD. SOMEBODY OUGHT TO TELL THE COUNTY THAT HE DON'T INTEND TO FIX THEM." It brought results.

—Pat Kelly

ONE OF THE girls in the senior class had received an engagement ring the night before, but to her chagrin no one at high school noticed it. Finally in the afternoon, when her friends were sitting around talking, she stood up suddenly. "My, it's hot in here," she announced. "I think I'll take off my ring." —Steve Bennson

A SHIPLOAD of Marines had just arrived from overseas at San Diego. It was late afternoon by the time 5000 sea bags had been hauled to the Marine base and dumped in a hopeless jumble on the parade ground. Long after dark Marines armed with flashlights were going from one bag to another, trying to find their gear.

About 10 p.m. one Marine wandered into the maze of sea bags, stood quietly with his head cocked to one side. Soon there was the faint but unmistakable ringing of an alarm clock. The Marine confidently followed the sound, picked up his own sea bag and strode off. —Harold R. Dickman

OFFICE WORKER having cocktails at his desk to boss: "I trust you don't mind, sir? Just a little celebration on the tenth anniversary of my last raise." —Gardner Rea cartoon in *Look*

A MANUFACTURING plant in the Panama Canal Zone employed 20 local women. After a few months they all quit their jobs. Offers of shorter hours and more pay failed to entice them back—they had earned enough money to satisfy their wants.

The problem was solved when the manager wired a mail-order house to send each woman a catalogue showing its products. All 20 women returned to their jobs. —Cecilia H. Burnham

THE MOTHER of three teen-agers solved one of her problems successfully when she ruled that the last one in on Saturday night had to get Sunday morning breakfast for the family.

—*This Week Magazine*

WHEN "RICII," who graduated from West Point, reluctantly agreed to postpone his marriage until he returned from foreign duty, he proceeded to devote considerable time and effort to reducing the calculated risk of the agreement. I saw the result when I attended his girl's graduation exercises at a Massachusetts college. His present to Ann was a parakeet whose cage bore the inscription: *"My Ambassador for the Duration. Love, Rich."*

Ambassador took but a moment to smooth his feathers, then, in a remarkable imitation of Rich's voice, began chanting, "Remember Rich! Remember Rich! Remember Rich!" —Tay Cook

EACH TIME I put our two-year-old on the closed front porch to play, he objected violently when I locked his gate to make sure he stayed there. Then one day my husband put the youngster in his "playroom" and locked the gate, and for once he didn't scream, but played happily by himself. My husband's explanation was simple: "I just told him I was locking the gate so that you couldn't get in and bother him." —Lil Oswald Olsen

THE PLEASANT old gentleman being served in the liquor store seemed undecided. "How much is that?" he asked, indicating a quality Scotch.

"That sells for $6.35."

"Let's see, that would be . . . $12.70," the customer mused. "Have you something a little less expensive?"

The clerk studied him a moment, then said courteously, "Here's one for $5.75."

The old man pondered. "That would mean $11.50," he muttered hesitantly. He asked for other prices and finally made his choice.

"Sir," the clerk said, "would you mind telling me why you always doubled the figure I quoted you? Were you thinking of two bottles?"

"Not at all. You see, the way I look at it, the Lord is entitled to just as much as the devil. Every time I make an investment in some sort of vice, I match it dollar for dollar with a donation to my church. That way the Lord gets an even break, and it makes sinning so expensive I can't afford much of it."

—Wendall L. Clevinger

"The Lord Helps Those . . ."

Condensed from "Mark Twain in Eruption"

Mark Twain

ONCE WHEN William Swinton and I were poor young cub reporters, a frightful financial shortage occurred. We had to have three dollars that very day. Swinton maintained with simple confidence, "The Lord will provide." I wandered into a hotel lobby, trying to think of some way to get the money. Presently a handsome dog came along and rested his jaw on my knee. General Miles passed by and stopped to pat him.

"He is a wonder. Would you sell him?"

I was greatly moved; it was marvelous the way Swinton's prediction had come true. "Yes," I said, "his price is three dollars."

The general was surprised. "Only three dollars? Why, I wouldn't take $100 for him. You must reconsider."

"No, three dollars," I said firmly. The general led the dog away.

In a few minutes a sad-faced man came along, looking anxiously about. I asked, "Are you looking for a dog?"

His face lit up. "Yes. Have you seen him?"

"Yes, I think I could find him for you."

I have seldom seen a person look so grateful. I said I hoped he would not mind paying me three dollars for my trouble.

"Dear me! That is nothing! I will pay you $10 willingly!"

I said, "No, three is the price," and started off. Swinton had said that that was the amount the Lord would provide; it would be sacrilege to ask more. I went up to the general's room and explained I was sorry but I had to take the dog again; that I had only sold him in the spirit of accommodation. I gave him back his three dollars and returned the dog to his owner.

I went away then with good conscience, because I had acted honorably. I never could have used the three that I had sold the dog for; it was not rightly my own, but the three I got for restoring him was properly mine. That man might never have gotten that dog back at all if it hadn't been for me.

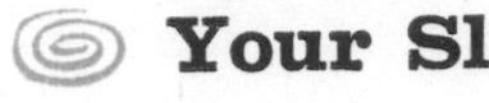

Pardon, Your Slip Is Showing®

Classified ad: "Wanted: Position by young woman, to hell with housework."

—Quoted by Olin Miller, Chicago Sun-Times Syndicate

From the Tulsa, Okla., *World:* "Try to be a happy person. Think happy, talk happy, practice being happy, get the sappiness habit."

From the birth announcements in the Santa Ana, Calif., *Register:* "To Mr. and Mrs. Ben Mendez, a son, 7 lbs. 12 oz. more t kum more more more mor."

From the Victor, N. Y., *Herald:* "Mrs. Homer Cotton discovered a berry bush bearing both purple and red raspberries. And Mr. Stanley Palmer—to mention another freak of nature—has an apple tree with apples and also blossoms and buds."

From the Las Vegas *Sun:* "Ever add anchovy fillets and green olives to potato salad? God!"

From the Burlington, Vt., *Daily News:* "Thirty-seven persons suffered seat exhaustion during a parade at Pittsfield, Mass."

From the Payson, Calif., *Star:* "Miss Rogers was winking for the third time when the life guard seized her and dragged her ashore."

—Quoted in *Capper's Weekly*

From the Galveston *News:* "The government unveiled its new income-tax forms, including a simple 15-lie card for wage earners."

The Bakersfield *Californian,* reporting on British comedienne Lynne Bretonn's "breath-grabbing 39 bust," commented: "Over in London Lynne claimed she never thought much of it, but the way Americans react has made her very shelf-conscious."

—Quoted in *Editor & Publisher*

From the University of Washington *Daily:* "A white bridal gown signifies purity. Light pastel shades are becoming quite popular, however."

From an ad in *Westchester Life:* "The rave notices about Chequit Inn are understatements! As for the service, guests agree . . . it's tips!"

Tip-Offs

After a week of tipping doormen, bell boys, waiters, hat-check girls, ad infinitum, a hotel guest was completely fed up with the whole system. Then came a knock on his door. "Who is it?" he called.

"The bell boy, sir. Telegram for you."

A crafty gleam came into the eyes of the tip-tortured guest. "Just slip it under the door," he directed.

Barely a moment's hesitation, then, "I can't, sir."

"And why not?" snarled the unhappy guest.

"Because, sir," answered the determined bell boy, "it's on a tray." —Leo W. Beckstrom

When the parents of a nine-year-old threw a party they allowed her to stay up, provided she took care of the guests' hats and coats. Unobserved she slipped into the kitchen for a saucer, placed a lone dime in it and left it on a table near the coat closet. When the first guest arrived, he noticed the dime, put a quarter in the saucer.

After the party the astonished host and hostess discovered their daughter counting up her profits for the evening—a neat $6.70.

—"All Things Considered" in Milwaukee *Journal*

My husband's boss, at a very exclusive resort in West Virginia, noticed a porter bring down some bags for a nicely dressed old gentleman and put them in his super-duper Cadillac. The old gentleman obviously wanted to give the porter a tip and asked if he could change a dollar.

"Around here, suh," said the porter, "a dollar *is* change."

—Evelyn Hively

She was a very young and obviously inexperienced waitress, and during the course of dinner she committed every crime in the book. She placed my soup in front of me with her dainty thumb immersed, brought lamb chops instead of veal cutlets, forgot to bring the rolls and butter I had ordered. Growing more flustered she murmured something about "my first day here"—and spilled coffee on my sleeve. I managed to keep a smile on my face, though toward the end it became somewhat forced. As I prepared to give her a tip she blushingly shook her head and handed *me* 50 cents. "You earned it more than I did," she said. —Herbert L. Brown

THE LATE Robert Benchley was known to tip handsomely whenever services were rendered him. During a brief stay at a fashionable resort hotel, however, he found the simple courtesies lacking and decided not to tip at all. On his departure he thought he had gotten by all those who might expect tips when he encountered a doorman holding open the door of his waiting car.

"You're not going to forget me, sir?" the doorman inquired anxiously, thrusting out his palm.

Benchley grasped the outstretched hand and shook it. "No," he said in a voice charged with emotion, "I'll write to you."

WHEN WE lived in Paris there was always a steady procession of visitors to our apartment the week between Christmas and New Year's. Every person who had served us in any way would ring our bell and hold out his palm for his "gift." There was the man who swept the gutter, the woman who sold flowers, the delivery boys, the postman. We doled out francs to them all. One year, just when we thought there couldn't possibly be anyone else left to tip, I opened the door to a man I'd never laid eyes on before. But he used the set formula: *"Bonjour,* monsieur, a Happy New Year to you. A little present, if you please."

"Pardon me," I said, "but I can't remember ever having had the pleasure of seeing you."

"No," said the little man, "you have never viewed me, but I have looked after monsieur's and madame's safety all through the year. *I,* monsieur," he said dramatically, "am the person who greases the elevator." —Ben K. Raleigh

MAN TO waiter: "Take your time. I'm not much of a tipper anyway." —Henry Boltinoff cartoon in *The Saturday Evening Post*

ON MARTHA RAYE'S first visit to Chicago's famous Pump Room she was a member of a party hosted by Jimmy Durante. When a waiter hurried by with a portion of shishkebab—lamb held aloft on a flaming sword—Miss Raye was startled and exclaimed, "What the heck was that?"

"A customer who only left a ten-dollar tip," Durante explained. —Dick Eastham, quoted by Bennett Cerf in *The Saturday Review*

IN A SMALL restaurant in Colorado there is a sign on the wall: "Please do not insult our waitresses by tipping them." But on our table was a small white box, with a slit across the top, labeled: "Insults." —Marjorie Major

ONE DAY during the rush hour in Cleveland I picked up an elderly lady in my cab. As she settled back for the ride to her hotel she said pleasantly, "Would you like a piece of candy?"

I said I would, so she passed a pound box over my shoulder. I took a piece and, after eating it, told her I'd enjoyed it very much.

"I'm so glad you did," she replied. There was a pause, then she added, "—because you've just eaten your tip." —A. J. Womack

Traffic Snarls

All we need now is drive-in streets.

—Luke Neely in *The Saturday Evening Post*

TWO TAXIS crashed outside the Senate Office Building in Washington. "Wattzamatter?" hollered the driver of one. "Ya blind?"

"Blind?" the other countered. "I hit ya, didn't I?"

—George Allen, quoted by Bennett Cerf in *This Week Magazine*

Wherever the place,
Whatever the time,
Every lane moves
But the one where I'm.

—Ethel Barnett De Vito in
The Saturday Evening Post

A PROVIDENCE, R. I., motorist trapped in a four-hour traffic jam swears this happened:

Motorist A signaled Motorist B, who rolled down his car window and asked, "What can I do for you?"

"Nothing," said A, "but we're not going anywhere. Let's talk."

—UP

A BROOKLYN man drove his wife to the Newark, N. J., airport and put her on a plane for Buffalo. After fighting his way through

Detroit, Spare That Wheel!

By Ogden Nash

THEY WHO make automobiles,
They hate wheels.
They look on wheels as limbs were looked on by Victorian aunts,
They conceal them in skirts and pants.
Wheels are as hard to descry as bluebirds in lower Slobovia,
The only way you can see a wheel complete nowadays is to look up at it while it is running ovia.
They who make automobiles,
They are ashamed of wheels,
Their minds are on higher things,
Their minds are on wings.
The concept of earthly vision is one that their designers stray from;
Currently, a successful parking operation is one that you can walk away from.
Unremittingly the manufacturers strive
To provide point-heads with cars that will do a hundred and twenty miles an hour where the speed limit is fifty-five.
The station wagon that shuttles the children between home and school is hopelessly kaput
Unless two hundred and thirty horses are tugging at the accelerator under Mummy's foot.
I don't like wings, I like wheels;
I like automobiles.
I don't want to ride to the station or the office in jet-propelled planes,
All I want is a windshield wiper that really wipes the windshield, and some simple method of putting on chains.

—*You Can't Get There from Here,* © 1957 by Ogden Nash (Little, Brown) the traffic, he finally arrived back in Brooklyn and, wearily ascending the steps to his home, found this telegram in his mailbox: ARRIVED SAFELY LOVE LULU. —*Sunshine Magazine*

CONGRESSMAN Richard H. Poff of Virginia says Washington, D.C., traffic gives him three choices:

1. Leave home between 6:30 and 7 a.m. and join the rush to beat the rush.
2. Leave between 7 and 8:30 a.m. and join the rush itself.
3. Leave after 8:30 and join the rush that waited to miss the rush. —Washington *Star*

IT WAS LATE afternoon in a large, crowded shopping center near Oak Park, Mich., when a distraught-looking young housewife dashed into a phone booth. Then she stood outside until a taxi drove up. "Where to, lady?" the driver asked.

"Just drive around the parking lot," she answered. "I've lost my car!" —Barbara Zohott

TICKET-WRITING motorcycle policeman to sports-car driver: "Perhaps you weren't doing a hundred. However, I'm going to reward you for trying." —Blakley cartoon in *D.A.C. News*

HOUSTONIANS, who insist their drivers are the world's worst, tell of a policeman who asked an injured pedestrian if he had noticed the license number of the driver who struck him.

"No," was the reply, "but I'd remember his laugh anywhere."
—George Fuermann, *Houston: Land of the Big Rich* (Doubleday)

AN UPROOTED palm tree suspended on chains from a boom truck suddenly swung around into the street and hit a parked car. The driver jumped out and looked over the damage. "You've got to come with me and explain this to my husband," she said to one of the men. He assured her that his company would pay for having the dent taken out, but the woman was adamant. "It isn't the money," she explained. "I want a witness along when I tell my husband I was hit by a tree." —Margaret Farris

THE NUMBER of blasts that come from auto horns in a traffic jam is equal to the sum of the squares at the wheel.

—*Phoenix Flame*

WHEN HIS engine conked out, the pilot of a light plane glided to a landing on the New York State Thruway. The pilot jumped out and walked back to the only car in sight, which had pulled off the road out of his way, to ask for a lift to the closest interchange. As he neared the car the woman sitting beside the driver stuck her head out the window and said excitedly, "We'll get out of the way, mister, if you'll just show us where to go. This clown here is the only driver in the country who could start out on the thruway and wind up in the middle of an airport!"

—*The Wall Street Journal*

Lonely Hearts Club

FROM THE San Angelo, Texas, *Standard-Times:* "LOST, ONE WIFE, somewhere between wedding day and 15th anniversary, in vicinity of kitchen sink, PTA meetings, WSCS, Cub Scout den meetings, Dollar Day, pre-school clinic, Community League, church socials, Brownie troop meetings, Little League Baseball transportation, music school, grocery store, cooking school, bridge club and spring house cleaning. Has kind disposition, bites only when tired. Lonesome husband will be glad to get her back."

HELP-WANTED ad in the Ardmore, Pa., *Main Line Times:* "Wanted—Gentleman to escort Mrs. T. R. Roberts to the Wayne PTA dance Saturday night. Preferably Mr. Roberts."

How Johnny Ate His Way to Fame

Condensed from "Love Story"

Ruth McKenney

WHILE WE were living in Washington our son John, aged five, became the hero of a government pamphlet on child feeding and sold 312,000 copies in his first edition: a great deal better, I might say, than Mommy or Daddy ever did. Of course, Johnny only sold for ten cents and postage, but even so, it gave the old folks pause.

This best-seller originated in Johnny's nursery school, where feeding problems were acute. Children are cunning creatures; once they have discovered that Mama is horrified by a failure to consume strained carrots or liver soup all is lost. Convinced that her angel will develop rickets, low-grade respiratory infections, night blindness, feeble-mindedness, or heaven knows what other horrors, the poor mother goes all to pieces. It is not true that a child won't let himself go hungry; some children will go whole days without food, reducing their wild-eyed parents to utter despair.

Johnny's alma mater was a veritable hotbed of the self-starved. Out of 203 registered scholars, aged one to five, 187 were officially labeled "feeding problems," running the gamut from Incipient to Habitual to Aggravated. Of course, the feeding problems at the Washington Child Study Demonstration Center were well above the all-American average. In this government-patronized school visiting pundits from Columbia and other universities peered at your child from behind screens, took his mental pulse with colored blocks and recorded his various habits on elaborate charts.

Now all this is not as cockeyed as it sounds. Manufacturers used to come around and ask the Department of Commerce what color to paint kiddy cars or electric trains; the department sent the inquiry around to the Washington Child Study Center, *et voilà!* The WCSDC had all the latest dope on whether yellow was repulsive to the four-year-old or green fascinating to the "early fives." And millions of American babies are raised on the government pamphlets it produced.

It was in the winter of 1942 that the harassed teaching staff at the Study Center began to crack up under the high prevalence of children who threw their LOVELY dinners right smack on the floor. Distracted mothers produced their limp offspring at 8:30 a.m. with the discouraging report that Sally hadn't had a mouthful of breakfast, and ditto for last night's supper, and they did hope Sally was going to have a FINE lunch.

"Won't," Sally would say, narrowing her eyes dangerously.

"Now, Sally dear, we just love to eat out of our DEAR little plates, don't we? With the TEDDY BEARS on them?"

"No," Sally said.

The Study Center had tried everything, especially with the fours and the fives. The threes, twos and ones were dopes; the moment Mama was out of sight, they actually *would* eat—some, anyway. But the fours rejected the Teddy-Bear-on-the-bottom-of-the-plate dodge; they all helped play house and set their dear little tables and carry around the dishes like big people. Then when Miss Strang said happily, "And NOW, one, two, THREE, we sit down and ALL GOBBLE UP OUR DINNER!"—they wouldn't gobble. There was the sit-until-we-finish approach; duck soup for the fives. They'd been sitting in front of untouched food since the age of nine months; they could outlast any adult in recorded history. There was the famous occasion when mothers arriving at four o'clock found Miss Strang's entire class, minus three, seated at the lunch tables, staring into space.

Finally Miss Strang felt she had to Take Steps. Pawing through the back records she noticed something very odd—all the children sat at tables for three and at one of these tables Jennie Benwether, little Artie North and our Johnny all ate. They ate a lot. They often ate up what the other tables didn't eat. But look! Miss Strang's hair stood on end; last year, in the fours, Jennie and Artie had been Aggravateds. In fact, Artie was marked VERY Aggravated (throws things).

"Heavens!" Miss Strang said to herself. "Why, I've missed the OBVIOUS."

The next day Johnny (rather to his annoyance) was removed from his old pals Jennie and Artie and installed at a table with Sally and Freddie, two *severe* Aggravateds. Johnny regarded the three serving dishes lined up on the table. He was, he knew, supposed to help himself from these dishes.

(Another feeding dodge—the child helps himself, feels personally involved in eating. A simple trick, scorned by the Aggravateds. They just didn't help themselves.) Now Johnny had a cunning thought. He looked around. Miss Strang was carefully staring into space. Johnny put out a tentative paw and took the serving dish of chopped meat meant for three. He rapidly ate it all up. He glanced around again—Miss Strang was bending over Betty Jo-Anne, telling her how NICE the carrots were.

"Ha," Johnny said, and he reached out like lightning, got the dish of potatoes and ate THAT all up. No comment from Miss Strang. No comment from anybody. The carrots followed next, then the three slices of bread, then *his* glass of milk.

"You want your milk?" Johnny inquired of Sally.

Sally and Freddie had been sitting through this exhibition of low, vulgar greed, watching Johnny in a dazed, appalled sort of way. Thus openly challenged on the milk question, Sally hesitated; and to hesitate with my five-year-old son was to be forever lost. He reached out a hand, seized Sally's milk and drank it.

"MISS STRANG!" Freddie yelled. "JOHNNY'S GOING TO DRINK MY MILK."

"Well," Miss Strang said, "you'd better drink it up before HE does."

Freddie seized his glass and drained it. When the chocolate pudding arrived, he hunched over his dish with both arms to protect it from the locust across the table.

It took Johnny three days of serious eating to cure Sally of a life-long feeding problem; Freddie broke completely on the second day and even shed tears because Johnny grabbed his raisin cookie.

Sally's mother reported, dazed, "She eats her scrambled EGGS; and she HIT her little brother because he wanted her banana."

Of course, it was slow work. There were 19 children in the fives group and 22 in the fours. Johnny pigged his way through one set of Aggravateds after another; then he was transferred to Habituals. So far as Johnny was concerned it was Christmas every day in the week. I think he grasped the general idea in a dim way, but he didn't care; he was single-minded about his food. For that matter I believe the Aggravateds soon knew what was up. The twins, for instance, were evidently determined not to be affected by Johnny's undainty feeding habits; they watched him for two whole days in perfect blank silence. Then something in Johnny's aggressive manner must have acted like a gauntlet flung down, for one twin, George, leaned over and without a word grabbed the serving dish of that day's meat. Johnny was surprised at this sudden attack; he hung on and George hung on in a deathly tug of war, until Miss Strang came over and dispensed justice—meat all around for three.

Miss Strang's report on how to solve the feeding problem at nursery schools concentrated its full fire on her energetic stalking-horse, and Johnny ended up in a government pamphlet, famous.

He graduated from kindergarten, a *succès fou* in feeding problems, pre-reading, visual perception and clay modeling, although he was a total failure in hopping. It was a considerable, if not unique, record for a five-year-old.

Relatively Speaking

SMALL NANCY arrived at nursery school one morning with the assured air of one bearing important information. She had hardly taken off her coat when she demanded, "Guess what my mummy has hanging around her neck!" The teacher made several guesses, but each try brought a shake of Nancy's head. "I give up," said the teacher. "What *does* your mummy have hanging around her neck?"

"All of Daddy's relatives!" was the triumphant reply.

—Harriet Hayes

GRACIE ALLEN looking at a new photograph of her husband: "It's wonderful—looks enough like George to be his brother."

—Sidney Skolsky in New York *Post*

"I DON'T MIND being a grandfather," the late Senator Arthur H. Vandenberg remarked to his wife when informed of the birth of his first grandchild, "but I'm a little dubious about being married to a grandmother." —Harlan Miller in Washington *Post*

MY BROTHER, John Barrymore, was awed by only one person in the world—our sister, Ethel. John and Ethel were sitting outside one of MGM's sound stages one day, resting after the completion of a scene, when a studio press agent spied them. Seeing a chance for a publicity shot he addressed John: "Show some animation, Mr. Barrymore. Tell Miss Barrymore something."

"*Tell* her something!" John said. "I should say not. But I will *ask* her something." —Lionel Barrymore, as told to Cameron Shipp, *We Barrymores* (Appleton-Century-Crofts)

MEN SPEAK OF their in-laws as if their wives didn't have any.
—Anthony J. Pettito in *The Saturday Evening Post*

A LITTLE OLD lady entered a suburban bungalow and found a lad of four in sole possession, playing with his toy train.

"You don't know me," said the old lady, "but I'm your grandmother—on your father's side."

Without looking up from his train, the lad replied, "I'll tell you right now you're on the wrong side."

—Bennett Cerf, *Good for a Laugh* (Hanover)

SMALL BOY on telephone as teen-age sister rushes to grab it: "You must have the wrong number. I don't have a beautiful sister." —Hank Ketcham cartoon in *Woman's Home Companion*

DURING THE royal tour of Australia in 1954 a long stream of people were being presented to the Duke of Edinburgh at a university function. When a young married couple were presented as "Mr. and Dr. Robinson," the Duke raised his eyebrows. Mr. Robinson explained that his wife was a doctor of philosophy and "very much more important than I."

To this the Duke replied, "Ah, yes, we have that trouble in my family, too."

—H. U. Willink, quoted in London *Daily Telegraph and Morning Post*

Great Ladies

WHILE IN South Africa some years ago, England's Queen Mother quickly won the hearts of the stern Dutch Calvinist republicans, although many of them had declared in advance their intention to boycott the royal tour. One particularly dour mayor, indeed, had announced that he would tell the Queen exactly what he thought of the iniquities of the imperialistic English at the expense of the simple Afrikaner. And he did, for 20 minutes on end at the luncheon table. At the conclusion of his discourse the Queen said sweetly, "Oh, I do understand so well. That's just how we feel about them in Scotland."

—Dermot Morrah in New York *Times Magazine*

PHILADELPHIA'S hotels were filled for the opening game of the 1950 World Series when a gray-haired woman came looking for a room. She finally found one across the river in Camden. "Are you a baseball fan?" asked the clerk, looking at her curiously.

"Oh, yes, indeed," she answered eagerly. "My husband pitched the first ball in the 1924 World Series."

The clerk looked down at the register and read: "Mrs. Calvin Coolidge, Northampton, Mass." —Charles F. McCarthy, NBC

MAMIE EISENHOWER has a facility for the merciful remark, the joke that attracts attention while someone else removes his foot from his mouth. At a Washington banquet for Gen. George Marshall, ex-Ambassador Joseph C. Grew, serving as toastmaster, said in a loud voice that Marshall wanted nothing more than to retire to Leesburg with Mrs. Eisenhower. While the guests roared Grew squirmed unhappily and murmured, "My apologies to the General."

Mamie smiled at him and asked, "Which General?"

—Robert Wallace in *Life*

THE LATE Queen Mary visited a hospital ward one day and paused for a moment at the bed of a little girl. She asked the child where she lived and the child said in Battersea, a poor district in London. "Where do *you* live?" the girl asked, unaware of the rank of her visitor.

"Oh, just behind Gorringe's Department Store," Queen Mary replied. —New York *Herald Tribune*

WHEN WINSTON CHURCHILL assumed the burden of war leadership in 1940, Mrs. Churchill took with her to No. 10 Downing Street years of experience as a hostess, a serene charm, a sharp wit and the cool courage which enabled her to remark to a friend when German bombs were falling on London, "I have made up my mind to ignore all this completely." —Reuters

A FEW YEARS ago freshmen at the Citadel, famous Charleston, S. C., military college, thought up a novel time-killer. They mailed a batch of post cards to eastern colleges for girls, addressed to the same letter-box numbers they themselves had, and sat back to see what would happen. Replies started rolling in from Vassar, Skidmore, Wheaton, Sweet Briar and Mary Baldwin colleges.

One freshman sauntered up to his box, No. 408, wondering if it contained a reply from No. 408 at Sweet Briar, to whom he had written:

> Dear Box 408: I was wondering what the holder of my box number at Sweet Briar looks like. As for me, I am tall, dark and drive a Ford V-8. I am a freshman. What do you like? Where are you from and what class are you in?

There was a reply in the box, and it read:

> I am tall, too, and not so thin as I once was. My hair is white and I drive a Buick. I was a freshman in 1896. Maybe you will get to Sweet Briar in your Ford V-8 some day. If so, come in and see me.

The letter was signed Dr. Meta Glass, president of Sweet Briar.

A FRIEND of mine who lives in Washington, D. C., believes in buying good clothes and wearing them season after season. Attending a social function in a five-year-old suit, she was somewhat self-conscious to notice that a woman near her was wearing its identical "twin." The woman turned and took in the humor of the situation.

"They've worn well, haven't they?" remarked Mrs. Franklin D. Roosevelt, with casual friendliness. —Eva L. Dunbar

ASKED ONE DAY whether she understood her husband's theory of relativity, Mrs. Albert Einstein hesitated a moment, then replied with a slow smile, "No, I do not understand it. But, what is more important to me, I understand Dr. Einstein."

—Harry Emerson Fosdick, *Successful Christian Living* (Harper)

Distinctions

A COLLEGE freshman met one of his instructors and asked, "What's your guess about Saturday's game? You don't think we'll do too bad, do you?"

"Don't you mean 'badly'?" inquired the professor.

"What's the difference?" said the frosh. "You know what I mean."

"An 'l-y' can make quite a difference," persisted the professor. Pointing to a shapely coed he explained, "For instance, it makes a difference whether you look at her sternly—or at her stern."

—Cliff Walters in *Pageant*

WOMAN TO friend: "George and I like the same things, only he likes to save it and I like to spend it."

—Sidney Hoff cartoon in *Collier's*

GEORGE E. ALLEN, on a CBS-TV program told about a political convention down in Mississippi where one of the delegates got somewhat intoxicated. During a discussion on appointing the temporary and permanent officers, the drunk got up and tried to make a motion. A crony pulled his coattail and hissed, "Keep quiet!

You're drunk and you don't know what you're talking about. You don't even know the difference between permanent and temporary."

"Oh, yes, I do," he retorted. "I'm drunk, and that's temporary. But you're a darned fool, and that's permanent."

EVERY TIME a woman leaves off something she looks better, but every time a man leaves off something he looks worse.

—Will Rogers

AT CHICAGO'S Presbyterian McCormick Theological Seminary—so named because of the generous endowments of farm-machinery maker Cyrus H. McCormick—a theology professor was showing a visitor around. "By the way," he remarked, "we never refer to the Grim Reaper around here. It's always the International Harvester."

—*Time*

ITALIAN COMPOSER Rossini, who enjoyed the gay life, was once told by his doctor: "Your trouble stems from wine, women and song."

"I can get along without the songs," volunteered Rossini, "since I compose my own."

"Which of the other two are you prepared to give up?" asked the doctor.

"That," replied Rossini, "depends entirely on the vintage."

—E. E. Edgar

A MOTORIST traveling through New England stopped for gasoline in a tiny village. "What's this place called?" he asked the station attendant.

The native shifted from one foot to the other. "All depends," he drawled. "Do you mean by them that has to live in this dad-blamed, moth-eaten, dust-coated, one-hoss dump, or by them that's merely enjoyin' its quaint and picturesque rustic charms fer a short spell?"

—Dan Bennett

The New England Character

MY SLIM-SHANKED, salt-wind-tanned neighbor, Jabel Hitchcock, who stands as straight as a New England church steeple and has a similar attitude toward life, is 99 years old. I brought a friend to meet him one morning, by way of showing the sights of a Down East town.

"I guess you've seen some changes in your day!" my friend said.

"Yep, young man," Jabel answered, "and I've been agin every one of 'em!" —Florence Southard

MORE THAN mildly perturbed over her Vermont neighbors' lack of acceptance of herself and her husband, a friend of mine confided in the crossroads grocer.

"I wouldn't worry none, ma'am," he reassured her. "First, we got to add and subtract you, then multiply and divide you. What's left, we accept."

—Donald B. Bice

A PRACTICAL note runs through New England humor. A respected citizen of Freedom, N. H., passed away, and his friends followed him out to the cemetery, a mile from the village. Among the mourners was a palsied patriarch tottering on a cane. A neighbor inquired, "How old are you, Gramp?"

"Eighty-seven," the old man croaked.

The neighbor shook his head thoughtfully. "Don't hardly pay you to go back to town."

—Corey Ford

A TOURIST spending the night in a small Vermont town joined several men sitting on the porch of the general store. They were a taciturn bunch and, after several vain attempts to start a conversation, he finally asked, "Is there a law against talking in this town?"

"No law against it," answered one of the men, "but there's an understanding no one's to speak unless he's sure he can improve on silence." —Margaret Schooley

A MAN whose business occasionally takes him to Maine reports that at the end of his last trip he went into a small railroad station to get a train back home. "Is the New York train on time?" he asked the ticket agent.

"Yep," said the agent.

The man waited. Ten minutes passed . . . 15 minutes . . . half an hour. Finally the train pulled in a full hour late. "I thought you told me the train was on time," he said accusingly.

"Son," said the ticket agent, "I ain't paid to sit here and knock the railroad." —Jack Sterling Show, CBS

ONE BITTER wintry morning in Maine a farmer driving to town noticed his neighbor out chopping wood. Nothing strange about that except that the neighbor was clad in a long flannel nightshirt.

"Jed!" called the farmer. "What in blue blazes are you choppin' wood in your nightshirt for?"

"Well," Jed replied, "I allus have dressed beside a fire in the mawnin' and, b'gad, I ain't goin' to stop now!" —Joyce Ingalls

TWO NEW HAMPSHIRE natives were arguing about the merits of their respective towns. One man said, "I druther be the meanest man in my town than the best man in yours."

"Wal," the other drawled, "yer got your druther."

—Mrs. F. H. Van Blarcom

Caustic Comments

LORD BEAVERBROOK'S servants, it appears, do not refer to him as "his Lordship" or "Lord Beaverbrook," but as "the Lord." When Randolph Churchill called at Arlington House he was told by the butler, "I am sorry, sir, but the Lord is walking in the park."

"Oh," said Randolph. "On the lake, I presume?"

—"Pharos" in *The Spectator*

WHEN THE late editor Harold Ross founded *The New Yorker* his original office was modest and almost bare of equipment. One of the earlier members of the staff was writer Dorothy Parker. One day during working hours Ross met her in a restaurant downstairs. "What are you doing here?" he demanded. "Why aren't you upstairs working?"

"Someone was using the pencil," she explained. —E. E. Edgar

ONE AFTERNOON during World War II, W. C. Fields, Lionel and John Barrymore and Gene Fowler were discussing the course of events. Their hatred of the foe inspired quite a few drinks, which increased their hatred of the foe. Finally, in full battle humor they drove down to enlist, taking Lionel Barrymore's wheel chair along in case they got an immediate overseas assignment.

The girl at the recruiting center, after her first shock, had them fill out several forms, upon which she noted many doubtful entries. John Barrymore gave his age as 19, Fowler outlined somewhat more military experience than General Pershing's, and Fields requested duty as a commando. The girl looked them over carefully, then came up with what all of them cherished as a topping example of spot wit. "Who sent you?" she asked. "The enemy?"

—Robert Lewis Taylor, *W. C. Fields: His Follies and Fortunes* (Doubleday)

VISITING A newly rich friend in the country, Wolcott Gibbs refused to be impressed by tennis courts, swimming pools, stables and other forms of luxury. Finally, returning to the house, the owner pointed to a magnificent elm growing just outside the library window and boasted, "That tree stood for 50 years on top of the hill. I had it moved down here so on pleasant mornings I can do my work in its shade." Said Gibbs, "That just goes to show what God could do if He had money." —Frank Case, *Do Not Disturb* (Lippincott)

THE FAMILY was discussing a domineering and extremely self-centered maiden aunt. Mother, exasperated by Aunt Ella's latest demand, said, "What Ella needs is to experience some *real* trouble, such as losing someone she loves very much."

Grandma, who had been listening, remarked quietly, "True, child, true. But you can't cry at your own funeral."

—B. A. Rummelhart in *True*

INVITED TO spend the weekend at Alexander Woollcott's house in Vermont, Harpo Marx arrived in a dilapidated Model-T Ford with shredded side curtains and flapping fenders. Staring down at the spectacle, Woollcott demanded, "What in the world is that?"

"Oh," replied Harpo loftily, "this is my town car."

"What town?" demanded his outraged host. "Pompeii?"

—*The Wall Street Journal*

IN *The Vicious Circle* Margaret Case Harriman writes about her father, Frank Case: "He could not abide the grimy horrors of William Faulkner's books. Meeting Faulkner in the lobby of the Algonquin Hotel one day, he said, 'Hello, how are you?' and Faulkner replied that he wasn't feeling so well, he'd had kind of an upset stomach lately. 'Ah,' said Father, 'something you wrote, no doubt.' "

—Published by Rinehart

Cartoon Quips

ONE GUEST to another at literary cocktail party: "The movie they just made from his book has given him an idea for a new novel."
—Corka in *The Saturday Review*

GLAMOUR GIRL to perfume clerk: "Do you have something that will bring out the mink in a man without disturbing the wolf?"
—J. Monahan, McNaught Syndicate

REAL-ESTATE agent showing couple house about to fall down: "You can do a lot with this place if you're handy with money."
—Bill King in Chicago *Tribune*

WOMAN DRIVER to friend: "Will you look how close that maniac is driving ahead of me!" —Charles Rodrigues in *Collier's*

ONE GIRL to another: "Their beautiful friendship ripened into another office collection." —Lichty, Chicago Sun-Times Syndicate

WIFE TO husband: "If we continue to save at our present rate . . . at retirement we will owe two million dollars."
—Bill Warden in *The Saturday Evening Post*

NURSE TO anxious father-to-be in waiting room: "You have a possible future President of the United States—if we ever get the good sense to elect a woman." —John Dempsey in *Look*

LUSCIOUS YOUNG thing to Sultan on the make: "Don't *any* of your wives understand you?" —Gene Carr in *The American Magazine*

YOUNG MAN to draft board: "But you *can't* turn me down—I've proposed to three girls, told my boss what I think of him and sold my car!" —George Wolfe in *The American Magazine*

Popping the Question

When a girl says no to a proposal, she usually expects to be held for further questioning. —D. O. Flynn in Durham, N. C., *Sun*

"WHY WON'T you marry me?" he demanded. "There isn't anyone else, is there?"

"Oh, Edgar," she sighed. "There *must* be!"

—John Carpenter in London *Evening News*

FRIENDS OF a man who was known for his inability to think of anything to say to women were amazed when, the morning after the shy one met a girl at a dance, it was announced that he had become engaged. One inquired as to how it happened. "Well," said the bashful man, "I danced with her three times, and I couldn't think of anything else to say." —Dan Bennett

IT WAS the end of a wonderful and exhausting day—a family reunion to celebrate our grandparents' 50th wedding anniversary. On the porch steps two great-grandchildren fought loudly over a pair of roller skates; around the corner two "cowboys" chased an "Indian" relative; my sister's little girl was bewailing a skinned knee; from the kitchen came laughter of children and grandchildren washing the dishes.

As I hurried past the two guests of honor, who sat rocking on the porch, I overheard Grandfather say to Grandmother, "Crim-iny, Mame, I sure wasn't aimin' to start all *this* that night I asked you to ride home with me in my buggy after the ice-cream social!"

—Mrs. E. D. Barrett

BOLD BLONDE to bashful beau: "I really don't think it's proper for me to continue going out with an unmarried man."

—Jane King cartoon in *Collier's*

A YOUNG MAN of a scientific bent spent a summer at Harvard and became intensely interested in a summer-school girl. The only trouble was he couldn't get near her; always too much competition. But summer came and went, and he remembered her address and phone number. Then one autumn day he called her up and took her to a football game. After that there were movies and dinners and flowers.

Unfortunately, the poor fellow couldn't seem to find out how well he was doing. On one of their dates they were sitting together on the couch, and he was wondering just what he should say or do. She looked so pretty, but not a flicker of anything special in her face and eyes. Suddenly the young man looked at the pulse in her neck and mentally counted the beats. It was so far above the female average he took the chance and grabbed her. Of course, they were married and lived happily ever after.

—Primus II in *Harvard Alumni Bulletin*

A HILLBILLY had been courting a mountain gal. At last her father spoke up: "You've been seeing Nellie for nigh onto a year. What are your intentions—honorable or dishonorable?"

The startled young blood replied, "You mean I got a choice?"

—Harry Hershfield

AD IN a Rome newspaper: "Will the gentleman who kissed me and proposed to me on the Spanish Steps last Saturday evening kindly get in touch with me at once. Otherwise I shall be forced to marry my present fiancé."

—*Munich Illustrated,* quoted in *Everybody's,* London

REJECTED SUITOR departing in a huff: "If I *had* all the qualities you want in a man, I'd propose to somebody else."

—Martha Blanchard cartoon in *Look*

A Dash of Bitters

MAN TO psychiatrist: "I have neither illusions nor delusions, Doctor. My problem is that I exist day after day in a world of grim reality." —Leo Garel cartoon in *Medical Economics*

WIFE, reading newspaper, to husband: "This just seems to be one of those centuries when everything goes wrong."

—Chon Day cartoon in *The Saturday Evening Post*

ONE DAY I heard a prophecy that the end of the world was coming the next weekend. I repeated this to a friend with three children under seven, whose maid had just left, and her only answer was, "Good!" —*The Outpost*

THEY told him it couldn't be
done.
With a smile, he went right
to it.
He tackled the thing that
couldn't be done—
And couldn't do it.

—From an ad for *Editor & Publisher*

PAUNCHY middle-aged man, perspiring profusely, to other man in businessmen's gym: "The trouble is I'm not in shape to keep fit." —Jeff Keate cartoon in *Collier's*

TOYSHOP clerk: "It's an educational toy designed to adjust a child to live in the world of today . . . any way he puts it together is wrong." —Lichty cartoon, Chicago Sun-Times Syndicate

H. L. MENCKEN: There is always an easy solution to every human problem—neat, plausible and wrong.

—*A Mencken Chrestomathy* (Knopf)

WOULD-BE borrower to man in bank's loan department: "I'd like to combine all my little obligations into one backbreaking load."

—Goldstein cartoon in *The Saturday Evening Post*

A LETTER from my 13-year-old daughter at summer camp contained this noteworthy paragraph:

"The first day I didn't have hardly any friends. The second day I had a few friends. The third day I had friends and enemies."

—Janet L. Richardson in *Coronet*

DURING A convention of atom scientists at Las Vegas, one of the professors spent all his free time at the gambling tables. A couple of his colleagues were discussing their friend's weakness.

"Hotchkiss gambles as if there were no tomorrow," said one.

"Maybe," commented the other, "he *knows* something!"

—E. E. Kenyon in *The American Weekly*

"Why Didn't Somebody Tell Me?"

By H. Allen Smith

ONE OF THE reasons I don't like big parties is that I'm seldom at ease with strangers; I get nervous. I get nervous because I have a long and sordid history of embarrassments growing out of a positive talent for saying the wrong thing. The fault lies, I think, in the way people are introduced to one another: "Mr. Blodgett, meet Mr. Caraway." "Hodjado." "Mrs. Williams, this is Mr. Caraway." "Hodjado." "Mr. Cleewhorts, Mr. Caraway." "Happy to meet you." And so on to the end of the line. The brain swims, the senses blur and the confusion is not unlike that which prevailed at the Battle of Hastings.

After that comes clumping. We get off in little clumps, and sometimes there are only two persons in a clump. Mr. Blodgett, perhaps, and Mrs. Williams. "Isn't Dolly a marvelous hostess?" says Mrs. Williams. "Utterly charming," agrees Mr. Blodgett. "Have you ever tasted her wonderful stuffed pork chops?" Mrs. Williams asks—and suddenly a deep-freeze chill settles over the conversation. How was Mrs. Williams to know that Mr. Blodgett is a vegetarian, that he considers the mere act of stuffing a pork chop to be a barbaric crime against nature?

Years ago I attended a party at which a foreign correspondent, just back from Europe, was holding the center of attention with his analysis of The Situation. All the women were hanging on his every word, and nobody was paying a bit of heed to *my* opinions. So, finding myself standing next to a handsome stranger, I began telling him, in fairly vigorous tones, about the *true* state of affairs in Europe as well as the Far East. He listened intently, nodding and smiling and occasionally saying, "Very interesting," and even "Quite sound." At length, after I had made a particularly wild observation about the secret schemings of the Cambodians, he murmured, "An extremely provocative thought. Mind if I repeat it to my class tomorrow?"

"Your class?" I said. "You mean you *teach?*"

"Yes," he said. "At Columbia."

I swallowed a couple of times, then asked, "What's your subject?"

"Political science," he said. It turned out that he was one of the nation's foremost authorities on international affairs, a man who would soon have an important role in the United Nations, and who later became president of Columbia University. His name was Dr. Grayson Kirk.

There have been other times, equally embarrassing. At a party in Arizona I met another handsome man who expressed some curiosity about my work as a writer, so I told him *all* about it: about first drafts and revisions, how to put a publisher in his place, the use of the colon, and so on. *He* turned out to be Erskine Caldwell, one of the most widely read of American authors.

All such gaucheries could be avoided if introductions were a trifle more specific. The plain fact is that Mrs. Williams, in her pork-chop conversation with Mr. Blodgett, was not to blame; the etiquette books were. Those books ordain that guests should never be billboarded, that a hostess "who exploits her friends as though she were the barker at a side show is a bore no less than a pest."

Emily Post, for example, allows only one category of information to be conveyed in party introductions—that of family relationship. It is perfectly genteel for the hostess to say, "I'd like you to meet Mr. Blodgett, my second cousin," or "This is Mrs. Whitter, my sister-in-law." I can only assume that this is a sort of warning against making any unseemly cracks about the hostess to her kinfolk. If that be true, I think it's even more important that Mrs. Williams be told where Mr. Blodgett stands on the matter of meat; a vegetarian might be much more sensitive about pork chops than about his second cousin.

Some social arbiters recommend that the efficient hostess keep a card index on all past and prospective guests, listing their likes and dislikes. Let us assume that Mr. Cleewhorts is about to spend a weekend at the Whitter house. Mrs. Whitter digs out his card: "Troy Cleewhorts. Bachelor. Doesn't like to be called 'Troy,' prefers 'Piggie.' Won't eat kidneys. Favors Old Noggin-Throb Bourbon. Hates tiny ash trays. At best when talking about his immunity from poison ivy."

Such a dossier is quite sensible, but I would like to recommend that it be expanded and put to its maximum use. Note should be made of Piggie's political and religious beliefs, employment, state in which he was born (especially if it's Texas), any physical defects, hobbies and any such other pertinent information. Then, when the party hour arrives, the cards of all guests should be spread on a table in the foyer for everyone to inspect. There's only one drawback to this: the hostess would have trouble getting her guests out of the foyer.

Mrs. Post, I'm sure, would never agree to the card scheme. Yet I think she might unbend a little and permit a hostess to identify her guests graciously without making the information offensive. Once at a small party in my own home I introduced an English lady to Mrs. Donald Briggs. Somewhat later I heard the English lady giving Mrs. Briggs a lecture on the state of the American theater, and delving at length into the various techniques in dramaturgy.

I have never seen a person as embarrassed as that English lady when she found out that Mrs. Donald Briggs is Audrey Christie, who has been active in the theater since she was 15 years old. And it was all my fault. During the introduction I could have said, "Surely you remember Audrey Christie in *The Voice of the Turtle*"—and, just in case the English lady might think that was the name of a London pub, I could have added, "Great li'l ole actress, Audrey!"

If the rules for introductions aren't changed, then I've got to find another solution or quit going to parties. One way out would be to take matters into your own hands. Confront the stranger boldly and give him a fill-in on yourself. Say: "I'm Carl Clinkinfuss. I happen to be a tree surgeon. Of all the trees in the world, I like the sugar maple best. That's my wife over there—you might not notice it but she's got a wooden leg. It's ash." If you could say that much, before long your companion surely would be telling you a few things about himself, as well as about *his* wife.

Some years ago I read that Clare Boothe Luce has a nice gambit for getting a conversation going at a party. Finding herself seated next to a stranger, she says, "Now tell me all about that fascinating job of yours!"—and soon Mrs. Luce learns everything she needs to know about her companion. I decided that this simple device was exactly what I was seeking. But, as I've suggested, the breaks seem to go against me. The very next time I found myself involved with a stranger at a party, I switched on my smile and said, "Now tell me all about that fascinating job of yours."

The stranger gave me a long, quizzical look. Then he said, "I'm an undertaker."

What Next!

THE TRADING-STAMP craze hit a new peak when a Greensboro funeral home advertised: "We Give Top Value Stamps."

—Greensboro, N. C., *Daily News*

IN A NEW super-drugstore in Washington, D. C., among the items of merchandise on the floor near the aspirin, was a white Jaguar sports car "specially priced" at $3495. —AP

AD IN *Your Weekly Guide to Cape Cod:* "ATTENTION all skiers! When you break an arm or leg, have your friends write their names on your cast. When removed, send cast to me. I will transform it into a beautiful, indestructible vase, lamp or umbrella rack. A treasured heirloom possession."

HELP-WANTED ad in the New York *Times:* "GIRLS WITH DOCTORATES. Fabulous Flamingo Hotel in Las Vegas staging lavish productions built around 16 girls with doctorates from accredited universities. Not to be confused with chorus girls. These productions all in excellent taste. Built around girls to be known as the Hi Phi Betas. Slight dancing ability necessary and good looks too. Already have 2 Ph.D.'s, 1 Dr. of Anthropology, 1 Dr. of Physics and 2 Dr.'s of Home Economics. Girls with only Master's degrees not acceptable."

AN UNDERWATER billboard now hugs the ocean floor off Key Largo, Fla. The sign, painted on concrete, urges submerged skin-divers to purchase additional gear from a shop near Miami.

—Howard Cohn in *Collier's*

IN MILWAUKEE a liquor store offered a "Mother's Day Special —Straight Kentucky Bourbon at $3.98 a fifth." —AP

Father's Day

SMALL BOY'S definition of Father's Day: "It's just like Mother's Day, only you don't spend as much on the present." —Toronto *Star*

A FATHER and his small son were out walking one afternoon when the youngster asked how the electricity went through the lighting wires.

"Don't know," said the father. "Never knew much about electricity."

A few blocks farther on the boy asked what caused lightning and thunder.

"To tell the truth," said the father, "I never exactly understood that myself."

"Say, Pop," began the lad after a while. "Oh, well, never mind."

"Go ahead," said the father. "Ask questions. Ask a lot of questions. How else are you going to learn?" —Mrs. Steven M. Siesel

THE CHILDREN were in the midst of a free-for-all. "Richard, who started this?" asked the father as he came into the room.

"Well, it all started when David hit me back."

—Martin Agronsky, ABC

RIGHT BEHIND us at the movies sat a father with his small daughter. The picture was *This Woman Is Dangerous,* and several times the child's voice piped up: "Daddy, where is the dangerous woman?" He shushed her but she was persistent. "Which one is the dangerous woman?" she wanted to know. Finally he reached the end of his patience. "For heaven's sakes, be quiet," he snapped. "They're *all* dangerous."

—Muriel M. Lovinggood

LITTLE BOY to mother: "Mom, can Freddie and I go out and listen to Daddy put the tire chains on?" —Jerry Marcus cartoon in *Look*

AS A YOUNG Frenchman pushed his son's carriage down the street, the youngster howled with rage. "Please, Bernard, control yourself," the father said quietly. "Easy there, Bernard, keep calm!"

"Congratulations, monsieur," said a woman who had been watching. "You know just how to speak to infants—calmly and gently." Then, leaning over the carriage, she said, "So the little fellow's named Bernard?"

"No, madame," corrected the father. "He's named André. *I'm* Bernard." —Jean Pierre Vaillard in *L'Anneau d'Or*

A YOUNG father reached the ultimate one night when he overheard himself yelling up the stairs: "Okay. This is the last time I'm going to tell you kids for the last time!"—Bill Vaughan, Bell Syndicate

THE PARENTS of children who attend the Sunset School, San Francisco, gathered one night to hear a talk by a specialist in child psychiatry. After he finished he called for questions and patiently handed out advice on behavior problems. The pleasant evening broke up as a grim-faced father in a back seat arose and asked seriously, "Doctor, how do you feel about capital punishment?"

—Herb Caen in San Francisco *Chronicle,* quoted in *Coronet*

MY POP'S TOPS

EACH JUNE hundreds of Wisconsin youngsters send in letters for "My Pop's Tops," the Father's Day contest sponsored by the Milwaukee *Sentinel*. Here are excerpts from past entries:

"My pop's tops because he is not got a bad tempir. He dont get mad easy, but when he does he allus has a good reasin—me."

"My pop's tops because he lets me help him work in the garden even if I don't want to."

"He lets me take acordine lessons. He lets me practice outside. When I practice outside he goes inside. He can tell better from a distance."

"He is very considert. Our family which has five kids always wanted a cockie spanial dog. Pop said no cockie spanial, then he came home one day with a dash hound. A dash hound is better because we can all pat him at once, and no fights."

"He is never to tired to sit strawled out in his easy chair telling stories while we children wash up the dishes."

"Every child should love their father because if it was not for their father where would they be? Nowhere, that's where they'd be. If it was not for fathers you wouldn't see hardly no children around Milwaukee." —Charles House

TV Guides

HUSBAND TO wife: "I'll say this for television—the more unsuitable the program, the quieter it keeps the children!"

—Lichty cartoon, Chicago Sun-Times Syndicate

ANNOUNCER: "We have just received a bulletin of a catastrophe, the like of which has never been known to mankind—but first, a word from our sponsor."

—L. Dove cartoon in *True*

THE PLATOON was drilling raggedly, and the disgusted sergeant finally brought the men to a halt.

"You should all be ashamed of yourselves," he growled. "I've seen better drilling by little cans of beer on my television set!"

—*The Wall Street Journal*

HEADLINE from *Variety:* "Winnie's 'Finest Hour' Cut to 30 Mins. on TV." —Joseph Kaselow in New York *Herald Tribune*

ALTHOUGH they are usually composed of stupid husbands, smug wives and ill-mannered children, there is one thing you have to admire about the families in the TV serials—they don't waste their time watching TV. —Denver *Post*

WALT SMITH, of Walter Harrison Smith Productions, offers this vignette of the TV business: On his way to lunch he noted idly that the water level in the bottled-water fountain was very low. When he came back, there was a sign attached to it reading: "Get coffee and drinking water in rest rooms. Until the next delivery of water is made, let's reserve for taking of pills." —Joseph Kaselow in New York *Herald Tribune*

SIGN above a TV executive's desk: "In this office flattery will get you nowhere, but to the top."

—*Vogue*

PREPARING his TV audience for the inevitable commercial, Alfred Hitchcock said, "When I was a young man I had an uncle who frequently took me out to dinner. He always accompanied these dinners with minutely detailed stories about himself. But I listened—because he was paying for the dinner. I don't know why

I am reminded of this but we are about to have one of our commercials."
—*Newsweek*

HUSBAND TO wife as they watch television: "Sometimes I wish I had a lower IQ."
—B. Tobey cartoon in *This Week Magazine*

WHEN Garry Moore received a television award for his spontaneity, he turned right around and paid tribute to "the four guys responsible for my spontaneity—my writers." Bishop Fulton Sheen, the next to receive an award, said, "I also want to pay tribute to my four writers—Matthew, Mark, Luke and John." —Faye Emerson, United Feature Syndicate

WHEN I asked Goodman Ace about the state of television one summer, he reported, "We've enjoyed television very much this summer. We've got a six-foot screen now, you know."

"A six-foot screen!" I exclaimed.

"Yes, it's a Japanese screen," he explained. "We have it in front of the television set."
—John Crosby in New York *Herald Tribune*

AS GRANDMA Mapes approached the century mark her friends made plans for a gala celebration. "How would you like a ride in an airplane?" suggested one publicity-conscious relative. "I could arrange the flight."

"I ain't a-goin' to ride in no flyin' machine," said the determined old lady, who had crossed the plains in a covered wagon. "I'll just sit here and watch television, like the Lord intended I should."

TV, I Love You

I FIRST glimpsed the glories of TV's commercials during a hymn of praise to cigarette lighters. The announcer chanted a hypnotic ritual, holding the lighter of destiny before me in his hand. He turned confident eyes upon me. "Flick," he intoned, "and it's lit." He pressed the lighter and continued to look at me for a sublime second, then glanced sidelong at the lighter. It was unlit. Flick, flick, flick, he pressed madly on the lever. When the lighter recovered, his magic was gone and I was prostrate with laughter.

Two nights later a cream-voiced announcer beamed at me from a Washington station. "Deep-down smoking enjoyment with never a scratch of the throat," he sang. He inhaled deeply on a cigarette and exhaled. "Never an irritation," he said—then broke into an apoplectic cough. The camera, its operator probably frozen with fright, remained steadfastly upon him while he struggled and choked.

The blight also touched a hawker of beer, one of those whose duty it is to hold a beaded glass of the brew close to his lips, grinning lustfully as he eyes its goodness. I knew the routine. He would sigh at his beer and the camera would switch for an instant, to return as he held the empty glass before him, still sighing in ecstasy while the announcer sang of malten glories. But this time the camera did not switch. The drinker held his smile a moment, then turned and sloshed the beer into a pail at his side.

So long as we can actually *see* the participants at their work, we shall now and again catch them in a moment of frustration. And that is the interlude that refreshes in life as lived on the air waves.

—Evangeline Davis in *The Atlantic Monthly*

The Repairman Cometh

SIGN IN a California shop: "TV Sold, Installed and Serviced Here. Not Responsible for Summer Programs." —Joe Plicke, quoted by Walter Davenport in *Collier's*

THE PLUMBER knocked on the back door. "Is this the place where there's a leak in the boiler?"

"So you've come at last," snapped the housewife. "I phoned you two days ago, on the tenth."

"Sorry," said the plumber, shutting his bag. "Wrong house. The party I'm looking for phoned on the ninth." —Frances Rodman

THE BEAUTY of the old-fashioned blacksmith was that when you brought him your horse to be shod he didn't think of 40 other things that ought to be done to it.

—*Sunshine Magazine*

FROM THE *TV Technician's Handbook on Customer Relations:* "There will be occasions when in order to make time you may inadvertently have a few small screws left over after repairing a television set. Solution: Either put them in your pocket when the customer is not looking or mingle them with other items of the same type you may have in your tool kit." —*Time*

PLUMBER'S helper to plumber: "I don't like the way she keeps referring to me as your accomplice." —La Mendola cartoon in *The Saturday Evening Post*

GARAGE mechanic to car owner: "My advice is to keep the oil and change the car." —Hickey cartoon in *The Saturday Evening Post*

ONE DAY while waiting for my car I watched a mechanic pick up a piece of paper from the seat of another automobile. He glanced at it and began to chuckle. Then he handed me the paper. It was a long list of repairs the owner wanted done. Penciled across the bottom was: "Please stop when you reach $15." —David Wing

More Truth Than Poetry

AN ANNOUNCER reading a commercial on a Massachusetts radio station came up with: "No matter how small the matter is with your car you can depend on Blank's Garage making a major repair." —Martha Meadows

OUR OFFICE cleaning woman once said, "I haven't always lived in London, sir. I used to live in the shruburbs." —Lewis Barton, *Considered Trifles* (Werner Laurie)

A RHODE ISLAND teacher discovered that one of her youngsters was singing with great seriousness: "My country 'tis of thee, sweet land of liberty, of thee I sing; land where my fathers died; land of the pills inside." —*NEA Journal*

BRAGGING about his uncle's promotion, a small boy said, "The longer he stays in the Army the ranker he gets!" —Mrs. Sam Wengrow in Columbia, S. C., *State*

LITTLE GIRL when asked what her father was doing, replied, "He's listening to the ignited nations." —James L. Frisbie

WOMAN talking about a friend in the hospital: "She was so ill that they had to feed her inconveniently." —Eleanor Clarage in Cleveland *Plain Dealer*

A SMALL boy repeating the Lord's Prayer ended by asking, ". . . and deliver us from people." —Katherine Sullivan in Columbus, Ohio, *Citizen*, quoted in *Ohio Penitentiary News*

IN DALLAS a woman asked a court clerk for a copy of the papers the judge wrote in her divorce case. "I guess what I want," she said, "is the order of disillusion." —AP

WHEN MY neighbor's maid came to work one muggy hot morning she announced, "I always feel so tired on these sulky days." —Shirley D. Cain

A CITY GIRL telling friends about her brother-in-law's farm said, "It's one of those experimental farms where the cows have calves without any bulls around—they call it artificial inspiration." —Kathryn Donnelly

WHEN I questioned the price of a porch glider at a furniture store, the young salesman explained earnestly, "Our prices are a little higher since nearly everything we sell is on the extortion plan." —George Sparger

The Preposterous Overestimate

$$$$$$$$$$$$$$$$$$$$$$

Parke Cummings
in *This Week Magazine*

THEY USED to call me Old Goggle-Eyes. When my friends boasted about the amount they paid for things or spun assorted tall tales, they were sure to get an astonished gasp from me coupled with a "Gosh! No kidding? As much as all that?"

Now all this is changed. A year or so ago I decided to strike back at the braggarts and the know-it-all boys. It started one evening when I got myself surrounded by foreign sports-car enthusiasts (the car I drive is at least 108 percent American). One of them boasted of a new acquisition—I think it was called a Leopard or an Ocelot —and added smugly, "They don't give those things away, you know."

I don't know what made me do it, but I promptly replied, "I imagine that buggy set you back $50,000, eh?"

From his frown of annoyance I knew I'd scored a victory. "Well, no," he said, "not as much as that, but it ran over $10,000."

I quickly followed up my advantage with, "As little as that? I'd no idea."

I've been deflating people with the Preposterous Overestimate ever since.

The reverse of this gambit, the Preposterous Underestimate, is a deadly weapon against a different class of extroverts—those who like to boast of their shrewdness at picking up fantastic bargains. Such a man was Higgins, who informed me the other day that he'd made a wonderful buy on a custom-built deep-freeze unit. "What do you think I got it for?" he inquired eagerly.

"About $20?" I asked. It was with some reluctance that he admitted (at my insistent urging) that he paid $150.

But you don't have to confine my system solely to money figures. The field is virtually limitless. Take people who like to brag about their children. Hathaway, for instance, seems convinced he has fathered a brood of giants and Amazons. Speaking of his 11-year-old son, Tim, he remarked, "It's unbelievable how that boy's growing. How tall would you guess he is?"

Peering up at Hathaway, who is six-four, I estimated, "Why, I bet he's taller than you are by now."

He glared, shrank about two inches and replied, "Well, no. But he's darn near up to my chin, and that's pretty tall for a boy of his age." Hathaway was silenced for the evening.

Yep, I'm a tough customer now, and you'd better think twice before tackling me. I may not fight clean, but I fight darn effectively.

Where Do You Look?

By Cornelia Otis Skinner

MAYBE IT'S a sign of neurosis (and if it is, I hope nobody lets me know), but I am becoming more and more acutely sensitive about those moments when one doesn't know where to look.

Consider the elevator situation. The act of waiting for an elevator brings out a suspicious streak in people. You arrive and push a button. Another person comes along, and after a glance of mutual appraisal you both look quickly away. The new arrival suspects you of not having pushed the button; and you wonder if he is going to be mistrustful and give the button a second shove—a tension broken by his walking over and doing just that. Then back to waiting and the problem of Where To Look.

Shoes are convenient articles for scrutiny—your own and those of the other person—but only for a short time. Hotels, of course, often provide framed reading matter nearby. But you can study such items as "Dance tonight in our Avocado Room to the Conga rhythms of Pepe Alvarez and his Poncho Gauchos" just so long—after that you're taken for a retarded adult with a reading deficiency.

When there's no reading matter, the arrow of the indicator comes in for a lot of absorbed attention. But, like the watched pot, the watched arrow is reluctant to do its duty. It seems either to go into the slow motion of Big Ben's hour hand or to stop fixed at a distant upper floor for so long you begin to think the operator is up to no good. Failing an arrow, some people wait for the delivering glow of the Down light with the devotion of religious zealots waiting for the fiery chariot. When the light does go on, the where-to-look problem continues.

Inside the elevator—especially in these modern, crowded, claustrophobic boxes—any mutual exchange of glances on the part of the occupants would add almost a touch of lewdness to such already over-cozy sardine formation. Some people gaze at the back of the operator's neck; others stare trancelike at those little lights which flash the floors.

A rather similar situation arises in a Pullman diner when one is obliged to sit opposite an unknown at a table for two. How to fill in the awkward wait between writing out "Luncheon No. 4 with coffee" and its arrival? If you are not the type who, given the slightest provocation, bursts into friendly chit-chat with a stranger, you run the risk of getting involved with someone who is.

Two strangers sitting opposite each other at a distance of a foot and a half, and determined to avoid each other's eye, go in for a fascinating little game. They reread the menu, fool with the cutlery, inspect their fingernails. Comes the inevitable moment when glances meet; but they meet only to shoot instantly out the window for a view of the passing scene. Sometimes the scene isn't passing, being a station-stop close-up of a motionless freight car. Then there is again some interesting reading matter, such as A. T. & S. F. or Route of the Zephyrs.

Another looking problem *à deux* is when your dentist is bending over you and coming closer and closer with the intensity of Rudolph Valentino. What he's after is not your soul but your cavity. To look back with responding intensity doesn't seem just right, and anyway who could, with a mouth wide open and wadded with a lot of little cotton bolsters? Moreover, by the time this sheik of the bicuspid is going with light and pickax into the depths of the molar cavern, his face is at such immediate proximity that if you look directly into his eyes your own will become crossed. It means closing them—which might be considered affected—or rolling them heavenward.

The oculist settles that question by his specific command of "Look straight at me." With him it's a question not of where to look but of where to breathe, for after plunging the room into darkness he advances with lowered head as if to play "owl's eyes" and remains with you, brow to brow, for long moments of meditation. This weird session always rouses in me a girlish impulse to giggle, or to see what he'd do if I were to purse my lips and kiss him. (I have up to now managed to keep such manic urges under control.)

I am fond of music, but not when it is played *at* me, like an individually addressed oration. I remember having a business luncheon with a TV agent in a restaurant where the violinist strolled about the room, playing soulfully before various tables. When I observed him coming in our direction, I lowered my head to the angle where my hat brim became a sheltering umbrella and conferred earnestly with the agent—a subterfuge which didn't in the least discourage the violinist. Having finished his selection, he stood waiting for recognition, smiling and bowing eagerly.

I bowed back in a manner I hoped implied gracious dismissal, but, as I feared, he asked me to name my favorite tune. A sudden question like that has a paralyzing effect on the mind and I can never think of anything but "Star Dust," which is actually not particularly a favorite. Feeling slightly idiotic I named it. The ambulant maestro's bow swept out the opening bars with the mechanical ennui of a performer who is constantly receiving requests for the same old piece from the same old country bumpkins.

I tried to pick up the business conversation, but I felt obliged to glance up occasionally at the virtuoso, who gazed at us with fatuous knowingness. Apparently in his fantasy, the agent and I must surely be recalling how long ago we danced to these magic strains on our Bermuda honeymoon, or had listened to it coming over the radio of our clandestine love nest. In a horrified effort to correct such possible impressions, I sat up straight and fixed him with a matter-of-fact look. But it was impossible to keep it fixed, for by now his gaze of ecstasy gave the further horrifying impression that it was he rather than the agent with whom I shared the love nest.

What does one do under such

circumstances? Gaze back? And if so, with what expression? A way out would have been the closed-eye coma of the music devotee, but "Star Dust" doesn't rate it. The unsatisfactory solution was to continue my conversation with the agent and to glance up at the persistent minstrel from time to time with bright little nods of approval—until he went away.

If all this implies that I am one of those unpleasant shifties who can't look a fellow man in the eye, I have been grossly misleading. For no one is to me more irritating than the person who keeps glancing off as though looking for someone more interesting to come along, or possibly communing with some unseen spirit. And that in itself offers yet another where-to-look puzzler. Does one glance off to see what he's looking at, or continue talking to the side of his face?

This supersensitivity may indeed be a sign of neurosis. If it is, and if it gets bad enough for me to have to do something about it, there's comfort in the thought that the where-to-look problem won't arise on the analyst's couch. Maybe that's what the couches are there for. Maybe—and it's a cheery supposition—analysts themselves suffer from the same complaint.

Ladies' Daze

A FLABBERGASTED mistress of ceremonies who had lost her notes once introduced Cornelia Otis Skinner thus: "Because of the exorbitant price of Rear Admiral Byrd, we have with us this evening Cornelia Otis Skinner."

—Emily Kimbrough, quoted in Philadelphia *Record*

FOR A GOOD 15 minutes the three women at the next table had gone after a mutual acquaintance hammer and tongs. Finally came a brief silence, then one of them sighed, "I tell you, she's a real menace. You don't know that woman like I do."

"Oh, yes I do," countered another. "I know her every bit as well as you do."

"Piffle," snorted the first woman. "How could you possibly know her as well as I do? I'm her best friend."

—Bill Gold in Washington *Post and Times-Herald*

A FLORIDA woman was so incensed when her favorite cure-all could no longer be purchased without a doctor's prescription that she went to Washington to lodge a protest with Senator George A. Smathers. He checked with the Food and Drug Administration, found that the remedy had been banned because it is habit-forming. "It is not habit-forming!" she cried indignantly. "I know it's not, because I've been taking it every day for 25 years!"

—George Dixon, King Features

MAKING HER debut at a League of Women Voters' gathering, a young matron sat silently through a two-hour discussion of international trade. Afterward she thanked the women to whose spirited pros and cons she had listened. "I'm awfully glad I came," she said, "because I was so terribly confused about international trade. Of course," she confessed, "I'm still confused, but on a much higher plane." —Warner Olivier in *The Saturday Evening Post*

YOUNG MRS. SCOTT attending her first ball game listened patiently to her husband's brief explanations. But when he sprang from his seat and waved his hat madly, Mrs. Scott exclaimed, "What on earth's the matter, John?"

"Why," he answered, "didn't you see the fielder catch the ball?"

"Of course," said Mrs. Scott quietly. "I thought that was what he was out there for." —Chatham, Ont., *Daily News*

THE LUGGAGE-LADEN husband stared miserably down the platform at the departing train. "If you hadn't taken so long getting ready," he admonished his wife, "we would have caught it."

"Yes," the little woman rejoined, "and if you hadn't hurried me so, we wouldn't have so long to wait for the next one!"

—*The Wall Street Journal*

ON THE PROMENADE of the famous health resort at Vichy, France, two women listened intently to an orchestral rendition of Haydn's Farewell Symphony. In this piece one player after another lays down his instrument and tiptoes away. The ladies watched in astonishment as the last musician disappeared and the conductor stood alone before the empty chairs. Suddenly one of the ladies whispered to her friend. "I don't wonder," she said compassionately. "It's the effect of all that Vichy water."

AN ERRATIC lady driver ignored a red light and smacked a brand-new sedan amidships. Before the echo of the crash had died away, she was out of her car with fire in her eye. "Why don't you keep your eyes open?" she demanded. "You're the fourth car I've hit this morning." —Bennett Cerf in *This Week Magazine*

AS THEY rode up together in the elevator one morning, one Dallas businessman was telling another about a bad day which his secretary had recently. Her mistakes got so frequent and blatant that he finally demanded, "What's the matter with you? Are you in love?"

"Goodness, no," she replied. "I'm married."

—Paul Crume in Dallas *Morning News*

Ups and Downs

THE WIFE of a middle-aged business executive met him at his office late one afternoon. As they were going down in the elevator, it stopped and a high-octane secretary got on. Poking the executive in the ribs she said gaily, "Hello, cutie pie!"

Unperturbed, the executive's wife leaned over with a smile and announced, "I'm Mrs. Pie."

—Matt Weinstock in Los Angeles *Mirror-News*

JOE LAGORE of Paducah, Ky., tells about the fellow who swaggered into a hotel elevator and, as it moved upward, started trying to impress the pretty young operator. But she wasn't having any, thank you. Finally, moving a little closer, he cooed, "I'll bet all these stops and starts make you mighty tired."

"No, I really don't mind the stops and starts," she said icily. "But I sure do get tired of all the jerks!"

—Joe Creason in Louisville *Courier-Journal Magazine*

WANT AD in a Pennsylvania paper: "Woman, 21, would like job running elevator in office building. Has no experience and would like to begin in low building." —Fred Sparks in *Parade*

SIGHT-SEEING at Hoover Dam in Nevada, we got into the elevator that was to take us to the bottom of the dam. Because it seemed as though we were plunging miles down into the center of the earth, I felt skittish and asked the operator if the cable had ever broken. "Lady," he said, "these elevators don't run on cables, they run on government red tape—and that never breaks!"

—Wanda Peacock

TV COMIC George DeWitt says he met a fellow with the world's greatest inferiority complex. Whenever he tells an elevator operator what floor he wants to stop at, he adds apologetically—"if it isn't out of your way." —Hy Gardner in New York *Herald Tribune*

THE DAY our son was born, my husband and I stepped into the hospital elevator to go to the maternity ward on the fifth floor. As we slowly rose, the operator, a grizzled little man, murmured, "Second floor—broken bones, ingrown toenails, pretty nurses."

A couple of passengers stepped out with an amused glance at the operator, who just looked straight ahead. Everyone was listening closely now. The third floor brought a low recitation of "Operations, plain and fancy, clean beds, costly doctors," and the fourth, "Bandages, sprains, rheumatism and lumbago."

We strained our ears to hear how our destination was announced. It was simple: "Fifth floor—American Production Company." —Mrs. James P. Bradshaw

Stork Quotations

FATHER going over obstetrical bills to mother weighing baby: "Comes to $48.37 a pound!"

—Aubrey L. Cox cartoon in *The American Magazine*

JUST BEFORE I was married I called the Associated Hospital Service to let them know that I wanted to change my subscription to the family plan. The representative told me that I would be eligible for maternity benefits "only if the contract has been in effect for ten consecutive months preceding the hospital admission." Then, looking at my record, she said, "Oh, I see you've been a subscriber for quite a number of years. In that case you can have a baby seven months after you are married and have nothing to worry about." —Gloria Liebowitz

HUGH WALPOLE had such an instinctive knowledge of how to break bad or startling news gently that he was always being called upon. "But," the author admitted, "there was a nurse in the maternity ward of a London hospital who had me beaten. One evening, for instance, I saw an excited father stop her in the hall and quaver, 'End my suspense, Nurse. Is it a boy?' Calm as a cucumber, she answered him, 'Well, the one in the middle is.' "

—Bennett Cerf in *The Saturday Review*

IN MEXICO, N. Y., encouraged by teacher Lucy Salley to discuss local news, a second-grader stood up before the class, reported: "Last night my mother had a baby, and now I think my aunt's coming down with it." —*Time*

WHEN BEATRICE AYER married George Patton, Jr., and began her career as an Army wife, her mother gave her this advice: "Make friends with everyone; confide in no one." The young bride took the maxim so to heart that she became the enigma of

Fort Sheridan. After she had been there for perhaps six months, the wife of an elderly major paid her a call, chatted casually, then said, "I'm the oldest wife on the post, and the others have delegated me to ask you a rather delicate question."

"I'll be glad to answer if I can," said Mrs. Patton.

"You have confided in no one," said her caller, blushing, "and we wondered if you know you are going to have a baby."

—Alden Hatch, *George Patton, General in Spurs* (Julian Messner)

MY FRIEND Sally went with her conspicuously expectant daughter-in-law to visit a neighboring rancher. As they were departing the rancher asked Sally if she would leave his hunting rifle with a gunsmith in a village along their way. Having parked the automobile in the village, the two women were strolling leisurely along, Sally with the rifle under her arm.

Suddenly she turned to her daughter-in-law. "Eloise," she said, "would you mind walking on the other side of the street?"

—Helen W. Bromfield

WIFE knitting tiny garment to husband: "Oh, I meant to tell you—it wasn't psychosomatic after all."

—Alan Dunn cartoon in *Ever Since Adam and Eve* (McGraw-Hill)

OUR TWO little girls, ten and eight, have had all their questions about the facts of life answered frankly and honestly. Thus, after a recent TV showing of a movie in which the stork story was repeated several times in an excited, hush-hush manner, our eight-year-old asked what on earth a stork had to do with having babies. Realizing then that the youngsters had probably never heard the stork story, we burst out laughing.

"That's what's the matter with this family!" exclaimed the ten-year-old. "No one ever tells us *anything!*" —E. M. Birch

WHEN JANE DAVIES, pilot in the British Air Transport Auxiliary during World War II, discovered she was going to have a baby, the medical officer told her she would have to stop flying. Jane asked pertly if there was anything in the regulations about pilots not having babies—and continued ferrying aircraft. Finally, however, an ultimatum appeared in daily orders. "Third Officer Jane Davies relieved of flying duties as of this date," and specifying chapter and paragraph of the regulations on which the order was based. Indignant, Jane rushed to the nearest set of regulations to find the exact words which had struck her down. There they were, brief, definite, final: "Third Officer pilots are not allowed to carry passengers." —H. R. Paterson in *Coronet*

WHEN OUR first baby was born my husband gave me a pair of baby shoes for my charm bracelet. For the second baby the next year he added a tiny bassinet to the bracelet. A year later, when our third baby arrived, the charm was a sterling silver stop sign!

—Lorraine Bailey

Home Truths

ANY SUBURBAN mother can state her role sardonically enough in a sentence: it is to deliver children —obstetrically once and by car forever after.

—Peter De Vries in *Life*

NOBODY WHO can read is ever successful at cleaning out the attic. —Franklin P. Jones in *The Saturday Evening Post*

THE SUCCESSFUL housewife is one who makes no mistakes she can't either pour mushroom soup on or slip-cover.

—Bill Vaughan, Bell Syndicate

A LOT of suburban dwellers have discovered that trees grow on money. —Fred Houston in *Look*

MY KIDS can forget school assignments, forget to bathe, wash dishes, empty garbage, sweep, dust, sleep, even forget to eat. But they can remember any careless promise I might have made them five months or five years ago.

—Oren Arnold in *Better Homes & Gardens*

DISGUSTED husband to clerk in paint store: "She wants 'just the right shade of green, a *good* green, but not *too* green . . . and definitely not that horrid sickening green.' " —Mort Walker cartoon in *The Saturday Evening Post*

IT'S NICE for children to have pets until the pets start having children. —*The Wildrooter*

THE BEST way for a housewife to have a few minutes to herself at the end of the day is to start doing the dishes. —Arthur Godfrey

NOTHING widens a narrow driveway quite as much as looking at it with a snow shovel in your hands. —David O. Flynn in *The Saturday Evening Post*

AS EVERY parent knows—out of the mouths of babes come words we shouldn't have said in the first place. —Ruth E. Renkel

AD IN the Mishawaka, Ind., *Enterprise:* "YOU too can have ulcers! Buy our good upright piano for $30 and try to get your child to practice."

BY THE time a couple can really afford to have children, they're having grandchildren. —Ashely Robey in *Look*

REAL-ESTATE salesman to couple: "This is truly a restricted development. No one is allowed to build a house they can afford!" —Lichty cartoon, Chicago Sun-Times Syndicate

Collier's — Jo Spier

The Dog That Wouldn't Come Home

Condensed from
The New York Times
Magazine

James Thurber

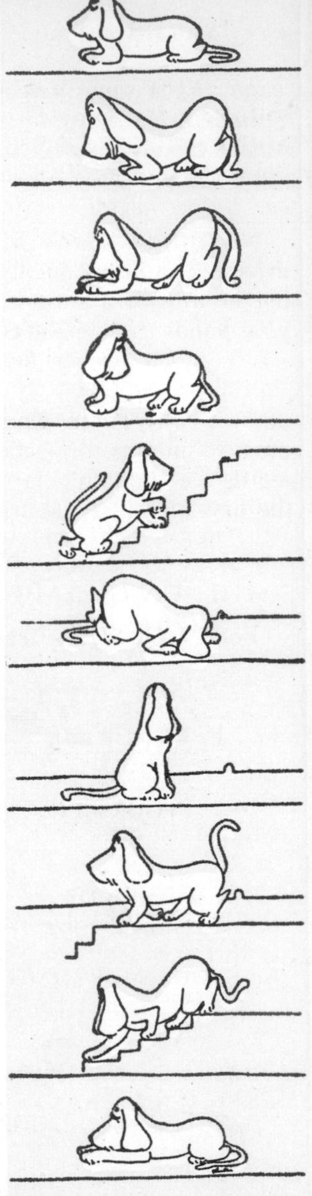

JEANNIE WAS a small Scottish terrier. Her jaw was skimpy, her haunches frail, her forelegs slightly bowed. She thought dimly and her coordination was only fair. Even in repose she had the strained, uncomfortable appearance of a woman on a bicycle.

Jeannie did everything the hard way, digging with one paw at a time, shoving out of screen doors sideways, delivering pups on the floor of a closet completely covered with shoes. She developed a persistent troubled frown which gave her the expression of someone trying to repair a watch with gloves on.

Jeannie spent her first two years in the city. When she was taken to the country to live, she clung to the hearth for weeks, poking her nose out now and then for a dismaying glimpse of what she conceived to be God's great Scottie trap. But finally the scent of moles in the lawn and the scurry of squirrels brought her out for tentative explorations.

Within a few months Jeannie took to leaving the house when the sun came up and returning when it began to get dark. She began to look sleek, fat, smug

The New York Times Magazine (February 8, '48), published by The New York Times Co., Times Square, New York 18, N. Y. The drawings on this page are copyrighted by James Thurber and were originally published in The New Yorker.

and at the same time pleasantly puzzled, like a woman who finds more money in her handbag than she thought was there. I decided to follow her discreetly one day, and she led me a difficult four-mile chase to a group of summer cottages. Jeannie, it came out, was the camp mascot. She had muzzled in, and was shaking down the cottagers for hamburgers, fried potatoes, cake and marshmallows. Jeannie had won them over with her only trick. She could sit up, not easily but with amusing effort, placing her right forefoot on a log or stone, and pushing. Her sitting-up stance was precarious, but if she fell over, she was rewarded just the same. She couldn't lose. The camp was a pushover.

Little old One Trick gradually figured out that the long trip home after her orgies was a waste of time. There all she got was a plain wholesome meal once a day—no pay-off for a terrier who had struck it rich over the hills. She took to staying away for days at a time. I would have to go and bring her back in the car.

One day the summer people brought her home themselves, and Jeannie realized the game was up. The next time I drove to the camp to get her she wasn't there. I found out finally from the mailman where she was. "Your little dog is stayin' with a schoolteacher on the other side of the lake," he said.

The schoolteacher, I found out, had opened her door one morning to discover a small Scottie sitting up in the front yard, begging. The cute little visitor had proceeded to take her new hostess for three meals a day, topped off now and then with chocolates. But I had located Jeannie's hiding place, so she moved on to fresh fields. "Your little dog's stayin' with some folks over near Danbury," the mailman told me a week later.

I found her, and opened the door of the car. She climbed slowly up onto the seat beside me. We both stared straight ahead all the way home.

Jeannie was a lost dog. There wasn't anything to do about it. After all, I had my own life to live. Before long I would have had to follow her as far as Stamford or Darien or wherever the gravy happened to be thickest. "Your little dog —" the mailman began a few days later. "I know," I said, "thanks," and went back into the house. She came home of her own accord about three weeks later and I think she actually made an effort to adjust herself to her real home. It was too late, though.

When Jeannie died, at the age of nine, possibly of a surfeit of chocolates, I got a very nice letter from the people she was living with at the time.

On the Shy Side

AS I LEFT the house to go to a luncheon party, one of my husband's students from the fraternity house up the street came running toward me.

"Come quickly!" he shouted.

Fearing that one of the boys was in trouble, I took off after him, hanging on desperately to my fancy hat. We dashed into the house and upstairs, and there in the middle of a bed the fraternity cat was having kittens. The boys were all standing around solicitously, and a pre-medical student appeared to have the situation well in hand. "What do you want me to do, John?" I asked after I caught my breath.

"Why, we don't want you to *do* anything, ma'am," he said, looking surprised. "We just thought there ought to be a lady present."

IN *Medical Economics* a Georgia doctor writes: "Short-handed during the war, I gave hip injections in my office without benefit of draping. Most patients took it in good spirit, but a little spinster well into her 60's was hesitant about lifting her skirt. When she blushed and stammered a request to 'put it in my arm' I complied. By her next visit I had completely forgotten the incident, and again asked her to get ready for the hip injection. She turned pink, but dutifully raised her skirt. To my amazement there was a round opening, two inches across, neatly buttonholed in her knitted pants."

A TIGHT-LIPPED maiden lady complained to the sheriff one summer because small boys were bathing nude in a nearby stream, in plain view of her porch. The sheriff told the boys to move up the stream a bit. A few days later the lady spoke to the sheriff again. "Haven't the kids moved?" he asked.

"They have," snapped the lady, "but if I go upstairs I can still see them from the window." So the sheriff asked the boys to go still farther away. They said they would.

In a week the lady was back in the sheriff's office. "They've gone upstream," she said, "but I can still see them from the attic window with spyglasses."

—Morris L. Ernst & Alexander Lindey in *The Censor Marches On* (Doubleday)

HERB SHELDON had a gimmick on his TV show in which he phoned people at home and gave them a contest quiz. One day he got a woman in Connecticut who just wouldn't believe that Herb was talking to her while actually on the air.

"I'm on the air, all right," said Herb. "Just go into your living room, turn on the set and I'll wave to you."

"Oh, I couldn't do that," said the gal. "I'm not dressed."

—Robert Sylvester, Chicago Tribune-New York News Syndicate

Airbreaks

DURING A station break over Station WABC in New York, opera narrator Milton Cross, advising his audience of the news program that was to follow immediately, said, "And now, stay stewed for the nudes."

—Kenneth Sneider

SOME YEARS ago an announcer asked Billy Southworth, then with the St. Louis Cards, whether he had shaved with a Gillette razor that morning (Gillette was sponsoring the World Series broadcast). Southworth's startling reply was: "You know bloody well I did!"

—Lawrence H. Singer in *Promenade*

MAYOR George W. Freyermuth of South Bend, Ind., speaking at the 84th birthday of the Studebaker Company, told a coast-to-coast audience, "Studebaker, I congratulate you! For 84 years you have been turning out a product equal to few and superior to none."

—J. Bryan, III, in *The Saturday Evening Post*

AN ANNOUNCER on a Gainesville, Fla., radio station delighted his audience with the following launderette commercial: "Ladies who care to drive by and drop off their clothes will receive prompt and individual attention." —Mrs. H. B. Black

BE SURE to listen next week when the sermon will be "Cast Thy Bread Upon the Waters." This is the National Breadcasting Company . . . Stay tuned to Phil Spitoolny and his all-ghoul orchestra. —Kermit Schafer, "Pardon My Blooper" (Jay-Gee Record Co.)

AT THE END of a program in the Famous Romances series, the Wedding March throbbed and faded, and MC Jimmy Wallington spoke through happy tears, "So ends another virgin . . . ."
—J. Bryan, III, in *The Saturday Evening Post*

A CONTESTANT on a quiz show in St. Paul mentioned that the population of her home town had remained the same for a number of years. "Every time a baby is born, someone leaves town," she explained. —William B. Koenen, Jr.

ANNOUNCER Westbrook Van Voorhees had a coughing fit on a cigarette program, excused himself with, "Guess I've been smoking too much!" —Richard L. Tobin in program for New York *Herald Tribune* Fresh Air Fund football game

Smoke Signals

Smoke and the world smokes with you; swear off and you smoke alone.
—*Changing Times, The Kiplinger Magazine*

SIGN in the lobby of the New York theater showing Cecil B. de Mille's *The Ten Commandments:* "Thou Shalt Not Smoke."
—Leonard Lyons

IN A London paper a want ad pleaded: "Can anyone recommend a cure for smoking for a gentleman being impoverished by the cost of tobacco? No suggestions calling for will power, please." —*Time*

SECRETARY of State John Foster Dulles, an inveterate pipe smoker for 30 years, gave it up on being told it was bad for his blood pressure. But he left orders with his physician to cable him, anywhere, the minute medical science proves he can safely go back to his pipe. —*Newsweek*

A FRIEND of mine who commutes to New York always avoids the smoking car—can't stand smoking himself and doesn't like other people to smoke. One day he took a seat as usual in a nonsmoking car, but to his dismay a man came in, sat down facing him and lighted a cigar. Not wanting to make a scene, my friend waited till the conductor came around to punch his 26-trip ticket. As he handed it to the conductor, he nudged him and nodded at the brazen smoker. The conductor nodded back, punched the ticket again and went on.

—Irving Hoffman

OVERHEARD in the elevator of a New York office building: "I just finished that article on cigarette smoking in The Reader's Digest, and I've decided to give up reading!" —Willis Wing

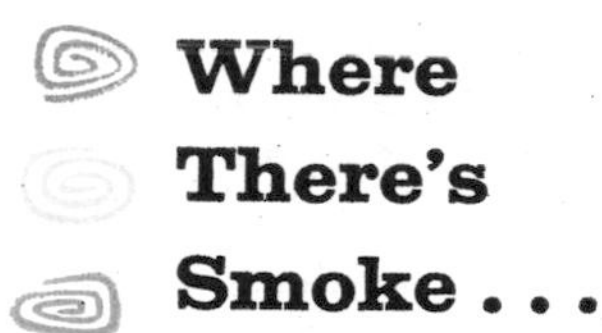

Where There's Smoke . . .

An excerpt from the book, "Warm Bodies," in which the author, Donald R. Morris, gives landlubbers an uproarious picture of life in the peacetime Navy aboard an LST:

THE CIGARETTE incident occurred on our trip to Thule. As we worked our way well up the western coast of Greenland it got a little colder, which was just as well, because on the bridge we had to wear the new foul-weather gear issued in New York. The new outfits started with long johns and worked their way up through bizarre layers of odd textiles to a final hooded parka, firmly strapped and zippered over everything that went below. There was a face mask with goggles and buttoned flaps for the mouth and nose, and boots that were laced, zippered and belted. I held the ship's record for answering a call of nature from a fully buttoned condition—four minutes and 18 seconds. Until the trouble with the cigarette, I felt myself one with Peary.

The incident occurred on the morning I reached the bridge and suddenly realized that both tobacco and lighter were in my shirt pocket, about seven stops down the line. It was the first really cold day, and the ship was headed into the teeth of a strong, moist breeze. I pulled off the heavy outer mittens and the gloves, unbuttoned the mouth flap and held the mittens and gloves in my teeth. Then I pushed aside my slung binoculars, unbelted, unbuttoned and unzipped the parka, and unzipped the windbreaker. I undid the front of the overalls, lowered them far enough to get at the bottom edge of my sweater, raised that and unbuttoned the vest, undid my shirt pocket, got the cigarettes and lighter out, put them on the gyro repeater, buttoned my shirt pocket and vest, pulled down the sweater, pulled up the overalls and fastened them, zipped up the windbreaker, zipped, buttoned and belted the parka, and replaced the gloves, mittens, face mask, parka hood and binoculars.

By this time I needed the cigarette badly. I unbuttoned the mouth flap, pushed a cigarette through, and poked until I found my mouth. I lit it, and then replaced the goggles and hood.

When I started to exhale, the smoke caught inside the face mask and I started to cough. I reached up to pull the cigarette out, but what with the mittens and all it caught inside the mouth flap and slipped down to my chin. I tried to pull the face mask off, but the goggles and the parka hood and the binocular strap were all in the way. I pulled off the gloves and mittens again, pushed the parka hood back, pulled off my watch cap and started to work on the straps at the back of my head. I couldn't tell the binocular strap from the goggle strap from the face-mask strap, and my hands were getting cold.

While I was fumbling with the straps I suddenly realized that something (it later turned out to be the turtle-neck sweater) was on fire. I started to yell "Fire!" but since I was still coughing and had a number of things over my face, no one understood me over the voice tube. The helmsman, the man at the engine-order telegraph and the messenger disagreed on what I was saying so they finally compromised on sounding General Quarters.

When the captain got to the pilothouse, the messenger insisted there was a fire somewhere, so the captain sounded the fire alarm, too. All stations were manned but nobody could find the fire.

The captain then climbed up to

the conning tower and saw me thrashing around in a dense cloud of smoke near the voice tubes. He ran over and at once decided that all the smoke was coming out of the new voice tube from the engine room, so he sent the fire party down there. One officer was sitting at the log-room desk bringing his logs up to date when the fire party burst in and started to spray him with chemical fog. By this time I had gotten some of the gear out of the way and I started to yell for help. One of the quartermasters finally spotted the difficulty and put the fire out with a cup of coffee. I had to be led below and unpacked. It took quite some time for the excitement to die down.

Theatrical Moments

WHEN Henry Miller opened in *The Great Divide,* one of the first tryouts was in Pittsburgh, and Henry got plenty sore when the critics panned the play and accused him of hamming it up. In New York, however, the play was a smash and ran for two seasons. When the show went on tour, the first stand was a repeat in Pittsburgh. This time the critics reversed themselves and said both Miller and the play were fine.

One night, in the middle of his big love scene with Margaret Anglin, Henry noticed that several customers were sneaking up the aisle and making for the exit. "Get back to your seats," he yelled. "The last time I played this oversized smudge pot I was insulted, and I don't propose to let it happen again!"

The people went back to their seats and the play went on, but a few seconds later another bunch got up and began to leave. This time Miller almost threw a fit.

"Knaves and varlets," he screamed, "back to your seats!"

Margaret Anglin grabbed him by the sleeve. "Stop acting like a jackass, Henry," she said. "The theater's on fire." —Billy Rose

A NICE BIT of radio ad-libbing is attributed to Juano Hernandez, who played De Lawd in *Green Pastures* for "Theater Guild on the Air." When a fellow actor forgot his lines and froze, Hernandez came to the rescue. "Son," he said reassuringly, "you is nervous before me and I can understand that. But I is de Lord, and I knows what is on your mind." Whereupon he supplied the missing lines. —Louis Berg in *This Week Magazine*

CHARLES COBURN, the actor, tells this story: As a boy, I fell in love with the theater and started seeing plays whenever possible. "One thing, Son, you must never do," my father warned. "Don't go to burlesque houses."

I, of course, asked why.

"Because you would see things you shouldn't," Father replied.

That settled it. The next time I managed to get the price of admission, I went straight to a burlesque house.

Father was right. I saw something I shouldn't have seen—my father. —Louis Azrael in Baltimore *News-Post*

TIME after time concerts and plays at our San Jose Civic Auditorium have been interrupted by latecomers traipsing down the aisle. One of the worst offenders was a local dowager who was always 10 to 15 minutes late. She obviously enjoyed every minute of her march to her first row seat.

Oscar Levant was in the middle of a number one evening when this socialite and her entourage arrived. As usual she was resplendent in jewels and furs—and all eyes turned to watch the glitter. As she started down the aisle the pianist stopped his performance of a Chopin concerto and began mimicking her walk by playing in time with her steps. She hesitated and slowed down—Levant slowed down. She stopped—Levant stopped. She hurried—Levant hurried. By the time she reached her seat the audience was in hysterics and the grande dame was in a state of wild confusion.

The next time there was a performance at the auditorium she arrived a good ten minutes before curtain time, and she hasn't been late since. —Philip Ethier

JESSIE ROYCE LANDIS has had some odd turns during her years as an actress, but few have caused such mirth as an episode during a warm-up of Guy Bolton and Somerset Maugham's *Theater*. In the scene a call boy knocks on her door with the warning: "The stage is waiting." Miss Landis, preoccupied with her lines, had forgotten to put on her skirt. But faithful to her cue she rushed to the door, flung it open, strode out on stage and declared, "Well, Captain Brown, there are some things I've kept hidden from you long enough." —Frank Farrell in New York *World-Telegram*

It All Started With Europa

Condensed from the book

Richard Armour

Brief excerpts from a slyly distorted history of Europe which the author, a professor of English and writer of light verse, dedicated "to history students and teachers who for generations have made each other equally unhappy."

EUROPE, like the rest of the world, was originally too hot to handle. Its beginnings are shrouded in impenetrable myths. According to one of these, it was named after Europa, a girl who rode around on a bull named Jupiter. The fact that Jupiter was actually not a bull but a god gives us some indication of the uncertainty of those early days.

IMPROBABLE as it may sound, the cradle of European civilization was the Mediterranean basin. The most important country of this region was Egypt, which was ruled for centuries by Pharaohs who had an obsession for building pyramids. These pyramids served no useful purpose except for burying Pharaohs, but to Egyptians who had been held down for years by a Pharaoh, there was some satisfaction in knowing that the Pharaoh was held down by a pyramid. These ancient structures provide interesting backgrounds for middle-aged tourists, whom they make look younger.

GREEK ART reached its peak under Pericles. All the artists were classical and every work of art was a classic. It was called the Golden Age for prestige purposes, although everything was actually made of marble. The men in Greek statues are invariably clad in the simple, severely classical fig leaf. The art of wearing a fig leaf without suspenders was lost with the Greeks.

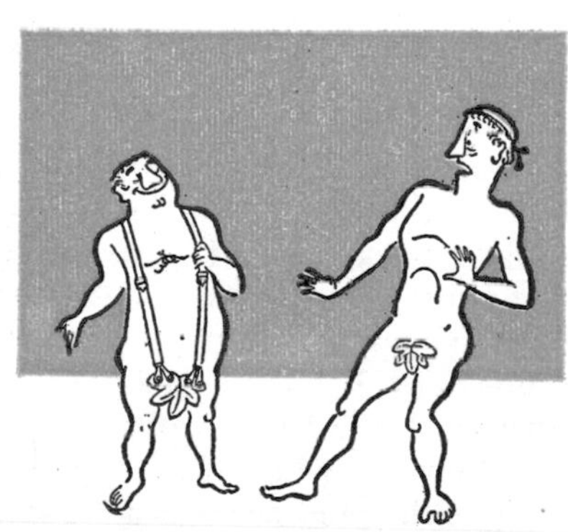

THE GREATEST of the Roman emperors was Julius Caesar, who led his legions all over Europe. He especially enjoyed conquering Gaul, which he divided into three parts: Veni, Vidi and Vici. Caesar was the first general to write his memoirs, thus setting a precedent that too many have followed.

After Julius Caesar there came Mark Antony. He went to his downfall with Cleopatra, which must have been better than going there alone.

BUT FOR the Norsemen we would probably not have Norway, Sweden, Denmark, Wisconsin or *smorgasbord*. The more adventurous were known as Vikings, who roamed the seas in quaint sailing vessels called *sagas*. One extremist who sailed as far as Russia and settled there became known as Eric the Red. When they died, the Vikings often went to Valhalla, which was popular despite the presence of Valkyries, overweight ladies with flaxen braids and huge lungs chock-full of Wagner arias.

TO UNDERSTAND the Middle Ages it is necessary to understand chivalry, a system whereby a man, after he was knighted, went out looking for a damsel to distress. Other favorite occupations were tilting and making love to the queen. Tilting was done in tournaments, where there were long lists of knights who were horsed, unhorsed or just horsing around. Making love was done in the king's absence.

DURING THE Dark Ages everyone was ignorant. Toward the end someone threw a switch and there was a revival of learning. People began to know more and more and to correct each other on names and dates and the source of familiar quotations. Universities opened their doors; those that taught chemistry opened their windows. The first university was named Bologna, probably by the students.

MODERN times in Europe were ushered in by wars and rumors of wars, most of the latter being well-founded. It was now that Napoleon rose rapidly, despite his appearance; he became a general while people were still calling him "the little corporal." (What they may have meant was that he was "a little corpulent.") He was so short that he would have had trouble seeing parades if he hadn't always been in them. From the beginning he put his hat on sideways, and no one ever dared tell him.

SOON THE steam engine replaced the stagecoach, and the steam whistle replaced the whinny. Steam was in turn superseded by electricity, which was invented by three dwarfs named

Amp, Ohm and Erg. Nevertheless, steam continued to have its uses, being better than electricity for pressing pants, opening envelopes and inhaling when your nose is stopped up.

WORLD WAR I was the first war to be numbered. It is not known why this convenient device was not employed earlier. If it had, this might have been World War CXVIII. World War II, also called the War to End Wars to End Wars, having come to one end in Europe, came to another in Asia. Whatever else is said about World War II, it is the only war with two ends.

JOSEPH STALIN was born Joseph Vissarionovich Dzhugashvili, which he did away with because it was too long to get on the ballot. Later, just to play safe, he did away with the ballot. Officials who wanted to stay out of trouble busied themselves changing the names of cities and streets to Stalingrad, Stalino, Stalinabad and Stalinagood. A collectivist, Stalin soon acquired all the neighboring countries.

TWO COLD wars followed World War II, one against the Common Cold and the other between the East and West. (Since the North and South had already fought it out, this was all that was left.) Neither war has yet come to a conclusion, though experiments continue with explosives—and antihistamines.

Some credit must be given to the United Nations. Despite some long speeches, this organization has proved that wars are better heard than fought.

The Grand Tour

VETERAN Federal Judge Frank A. Picard, of Michigan's Eastern District, who had just returned from a trip to Paris, told me, "It was a wonderful trip. Paris is a grand place. But I wish I had made the trip 20 years ago."

"You mean when Paris was Paris?" I asked.

"No," said the Judge. "I mean when Picard was Picard."

—Charley Manos

A WOMAN I know was at long last making her first trip to Europe. She was delighted with everything about the plush liner except that, in the dining salon, she was seated at a table with women only. On the second day out, meeting the captain, she murmured, "Everything about your ship is lovely, except that I'm at a table with nothing but women. Would it be possible for you to put me with some nice bachelors?"

"Certainly, madam," the captain replied gravely.

That evening, looking her prettiest, she swept into dinner to find that the captain had been true to his word: at her new table she was greeted by seven smiling priests! —Isabella S. Kelly

HOST TO visiting couple: "We took one of those 'all-expense tours'—and that's just what it was." —Hoifjeld cartoon in *Banking*

A CUSTOMS official was examining a suitcase in which a socialite returning from Europe had hidden an undeclared bottle of perfume. As his hand roamed to the danger zone, the woman's small daughter clapped her hands in great excitement and squealed, "Oh, Mummy, he's getting warm, isn't he?"

—Elaine Cutler in *Pageant*

SNATCH OF overheard dialogue: "—and the third day out the weather was so awful George had to be lashed to the bar!"

—E. E. Kenyon in *The American Weekly*

TWO AMERICAN women stopping at the Hotel Tivoli in Lisbon wanted another chair in their room. The steward who answered their ring could not understand English. One of the women pointed to the only chair in the room, then to herself and her companion. When the steward looked blank, she tried pantomime, seating herself in an imaginary chair. With a knowing smile the steward bowed and motioned for her to follow him.

At the end of the corridor he stopped, smiled, bowed again and pointed triumphantly to the door of the Ladies' Room.

—Marie Freligh

THE AMERICAN couple was in Paris doing the Louvre on a Cook's tour. "What time is it?" the wife asked. "What's the name of that painting?" the husband answered.

The woman walked up and examined the picture's title. "Mona Lisa," she replied. Her husband scanned his Cook's itinerary. "Then it's quarter past two if we're on time," he told her.

—T. H. in *The Christian Science Monitor*

Not According to Plan

A WEALTHY American art collector came across a newly discovered Old Master in Italy and secretly bought it. Knowing that the Italian government would not allow a picture of this value to be taken out of the country, he thought up an ingenious way of smuggling it out. He hired a run-of-the-mill Italian painter to paint a modern landscape over the Old Master, knowing that this could be removed by a new process when the canvas arrived in New York. The plan worked successfully, and the collector took the painting to a well-known restorer to have the superimposed painting removed. A week later he received the following wire from the restorer:

"Have removed landscape, also Old Master, and am now down to portrait of Mussolini. When do you want me to stop?"

—Alexander Barmine

AN ANNAPOLIS midshipman, irked at having to attend chapel services every Sunday, finally hit upon a plan of escape. He announced that he had been converted to Mohammedanism and asked to be excused from chapel and allowed to worship in his own way.

The commandant agreed. But at dawn the next morning the midshipman was awakened from a sound sleep by the officer of the day and told to face Mecca to perform the rites of his new religion. The midshipman was shortly reconverted to Christianity.

—Comdr. A. Talerico, Jr.

THE NATIONAL sales manager for an inflatable bra—created for the girls nature short-changed—was flying from Los Angeles to San Francisco with his No. 1 model. She was, of course, loyally wearing one of the boss's products. It turned out that the plane had a nonpressurized cabin, and the higher they flew the more outstanding the model became. It was so nerve-racking for the other passengers that she finally had to retreat to the pilot's compartment. She finished the flight there, gradually deflating.

—Herb Caen in San Francisco *Examiner*

BECAUSE I enjoy bird watching, my son gave me an Audubon birdcall. I promptly took it out in the yard and, twisting the little screw, made a series of chirps and twitters. My call was quickly answered—by two hungry cats! —Anona McConaghy

AT A MEETING of Dale Carnegie fans, one man testified how he had applied the prophet's teachings to an encounter with a business prospect. "I did everything in the rule book. I started off by greeting him warmly, then I smiled at him and asked him about himself. I paid very close attention while he told me. I went out of my way to agree with his views on how wonderful he was. He talked for nearly an hour and when we finally parted company I knew I'd made a friend for life." The man paused for breath. "But, boy!" he concluded, "what an enemy *he* made."

—*Maclean's Magazine*

THE PATRONS at a Tampa drive-in theater were settled back in their cars enjoying the feature, when suddenly the projector was turned off and a voice came through the speakers. "This is the manager," said Bill Hamer. "I'm sorry to have to interrupt the show, but there is a man here at the box office who says he is certain his wife is in the theater in a car with another man. He insists that he is going from car to car until he finds her. So I'm keeping the screen dark and the lights off for one minute. And I'm going to ask the woman, if she is in the theater, to leave, please. I don't want any trouble."

It was all a joke, and Hamer had arranged for two cars to roar away during the minute of darkness—to give his patrons a laugh. But to his amazement four cars sped off.

—John Perry in Tampa *Morning Tribune*

AN OXFORD medical student dug up an ancient University regulation that said he was entitled to a pint of beer as refreshment while cramming for final exams. He was so persistent that the authorities finally gave in and provided him with his pint.

They also searched the regulations, and slapped on him a fine of £5 for not wearing a sword. —*The Lancet,* quoted by UP

College Humor

ONE DAY in the course of explaining a point of grammar to her remedial English course for freshmen, a colleague of mine was interrupted by a brawny football player who disagreed. He was so insistent that she exclaimed in exasperation, "I've been teaching this course for several years, and I think I know a little more about it than you do."

"I'm sorry, ma'am," he replied, "but this is the third time I've taken it, and I think I know something about it, too."

—Mary Jane Cook

A NEW Georgia Tech graduate, applying for a job, listed his extra-curricular school activities in one word: "Married."

—Hugh Park in Atlanta *Journal-Constitution*

Girls at college
Are of two strata:
Those with dates
And those with data.

—Richard Armour in *Collier's*

AN ALUMNUS, shown a list of current examination questions by his old economics professor, exclaimed, "Why, those are the same questions you asked when I was in school!"

"Yes," said the professor, "we ask the same questions every year."

"But don't you know that students hand the questions along from one year to the next?"

"Sure," said the professor. "But in economics we change the answers."

—Minneapolis *Tribune*

COLLEGE glamour girl to suitor: "By 'secret engagement' I suppose you mean no ring." —Mary Gibson cartoon in *This Week Magazine*

PRESIDENT A. Whitney Griswold of Yale told about a student who was asked by his dean whether he was in the top half of his class. "Oh, no, sir," responded the student. "I'm one of those who make the top half possible."

—Edgartown, Martha's Vineyard, Mass., *Vineyard Gazette*

GIRL GRADUATE: "Four years of college! And whom has it got me?"

—General Features Corp.

WHEN A student at the University of Tennessee received a report card with four F's and one D, he was called before the dean and asked if there could be any explanation for *four* failing grades. "I guess I just spent too much time on the other subject," was the blithe reply.

—Knoxville, Tenn., *Journal*

A YOUNG college student remarked to his date, "That's 'Pink Lightning' lipstick you're wearing, isn't it?"

Flattered that he should notice the color of her lipstick, the girl replied, "Why, yes, but how did you know?"

"Oh," he quipped, "I've been struck by it before!"

—Mrs. W. N. Lawton

What's in a Name?

W. C. FIELDS once set some kind of record for embarrassing a sponsor, while appearing on the Lucky Strike program. All through the broadcast he talked about an imaginary son named Chester. Everyone attached to the program laughed heartily at the stories—until they put the first and last names of Fields' son together.

—Blanche Manor in Raleigh, N. C., *News and Observer*

THE NEW young butcher prided himself on remembering names, but for some reason Dressler seemed to give him trouble, and I always had to tell him my name before he could write out the slip. One day I told him just to remember "Dress" and add "ler" to it. Because I'm a large person and take a good-sized dress, I said jokingly, "Just remember that it's the biggest thing about me." After all this, I was sure that he'd remember my name. The next day when I stepped up to the counter he greeted me cheerily with: "Good afternoon, Mrs. Butler!" —Elizabeth Dressler

FROM THE Essex, England, *Chronicle:* "Women in the Essex village of Ugley have changed the name of their organization from The Ugley Women's Institute to The Women's Institute (Ugley Branch)."

DURING World War II Joseph "Ducky" Medwick, former St. Louis Cardinal outfielder, visited the Vatican with a group of servicemen who had been granted an audience. As each man approached him the Pope asked the visitor his vocation in civilian life. When Medwick's turn came he stepped forward and said, "Your Holiness, I'm Joseph Medwick. I, too, used to be a Cardinal." —*The Holy Name Journal,* quoted in *The Catholic Digest*

SOCIETY NOTE in an Ohio weekly: "Mr. and Mrs. Pratt drew the first blush at the Aurora volunteer firemen's ball when they skidded on a slippery spot and fell flat on their last name."

—Cedric Adams in Minneapolis *Star*

AT A Washington party photographers were busy snapping pictures of Dame Edith Sitwell, the English poetess. During the workout one cameraman was seen shaking his head and muttering to himself. "What's the matter?" asked a pal.

"I just don't like it," he said. "People shouldn't call a dignified broad like that a dame." —Andrew Tully, Scripps-Howard Newspapers

THE CHICAGO *Tribune* made a study and came up with these facts: Foreigners call all Americans Yankees. Southerners say that Yankees are northerners. Northerners say that Yankees are from the New England states. People in New England say it is the Vermonters who are Yankees. Vermonters reply that a Yankee is just someone who eats pie for breakfast. —*Woolery Digest*

SUDDENLY called out of town, Paul Harvey, the Chicago news commentator, told a new secretary, "Write Allis-Chalmers in Milwaukee. Say that I can't keep that appointment Friday. I'm off for Texas. I'll telephone when I get back. Sign my name." Upon his return, Harvey found this carbon waiting:

Alice Chalmers
Milwaukee, Wisconsin
Dear Alice:
I'm off for Texas and can't keep that date . . .

Harvey promptly phoned the tractor division and said, "I hope you haven't received a certain letter."

"Received it!" came the reply. "It's been on the bulletin board for three days!"

They Tell It on Themselves

MAJOR GENERAL A. C. McAuliffe tells this story about himself: "When I returned to the States I found that my contribution to four campaigns of World War II had been boiled down to one dreg—my 'Nuts!' reply to the German demand that I surrender the 101st Airborne Division at Bastogne.

"Wherever I went the word 'nuts' was whispered or shouted. I couldn't talk with anyone two minutes without being questioned about it. Soon I began to hate the word with a passion. Then, while stationed at Camp Mackall, N. C., I went to a dinner party one evening at a dear old southern lady's home. I waited and waited, but 'nuts' never entered the conversation! All evening the detested word wasn't even hinted. But as I bid good night to my considerate hostess she said graciously, 'Good night, General McNuts.' "

—Bart Hodges, Hall Syndicate

IN *Variety* the late Gertrude Lawrence wrote of the day she went before the cameras for the movie *The Glass Menagerie:* "I didn't look as impeccable as I have, say, in some of my more sophisticated roles. I had my hair in curlers and wore a faded, ragged old bathrobe. To top it off I was padded in the places a woman does not like to be padded.

"Costumed like this I was introduced to a visitor on the set. 'Well,' he boomed, scanning my hair curlers, sloppy robe and padded figure, 'Gertrude Lawrence! I'd know you anywhere!' "

ROBERT MOSES, New York State's peppery Park Commissioner, told this story on himself in the New York *Herald Tribune:* "Not long ago a prominent gentleman whom I seem to have offended, hearing that his college was giving me a doctorate of Humane Letters, grumbled audibly, 'That guy never wrote a humane letter in his life!' "

IN REVIEWING his long career, actor Ernest Thesiger said that the saddest moment for him was when he was approached by a lady who had last seen him as a handsome young matinee idol, and she asked: "Weren't you Ernest Thesiger?" —Leonard Lyons

SINCLAIR LEWIS told me about the time, crossing the Atlantic, he saw an old lady on deck reading his latest book, about which there had been some hot discussion. By the number of pages she had read, he judged that she was approaching the shocking passage which had caused the most trouble; and he kept an eye on her to see how it would affect her. Presently the old lady rose up, walked firmly to the rail and flung the book far into the ocean.

—A. P. Herbert, *Independent Member* (Methuen)

WHEN SHE delivered a Founder's Day speech at Pratt Institute, Mildred McAfee Horton, former president of Wellesley College, was given an unusually glowing introduction. "Whenever my ego is inflated," she began, "I'm reminded of a visit I made to my sister's home in Ohio. The children welcomed me eagerly, and everything seemed fine until they were being put to bed. Then I heard a small but piping voice say, 'Mommy, why was it we were so glad Aunt Milly was coming?' " —Evalena King

How We Kept Mother's Day

Condensed from "The Leacock Roundabout"

Stephen Leacock

One year our family decided to have a special celebration of Mother's Day, as a token of appreciation for all the sacrifices that Mother had made for us. After breakfast we had arranged, as a surprise, to hire a car and take her for a beautiful drive in the country. Mother was rarely able to have a treat like that, because she was busy in the house nearly all the time.

But on the very morning of the day, we changed the plan a little, because it occurred to Father that it would be even better to take Mother fishing. As the car was hired and paid for, we might just as well use it to drive up into the hills where the streams are. As Father said, if you just go out driving, you have a sense of aimlessness, but if you are going to fish, there is a definite purpose that heightens the enjoyment.

So we all felt it would be nicer for Mother to have a definite purpose; and anyway, Father had just got a new rod the day before, which he said Mother could use if she wanted to; only Mother said she would much rather watch him fish than try to fish herself.

So we got her to make up a sandwich lunch in case we got hungry, though of course we were to come home again to a big festive dinner.

Well, when the car came to the door, it turned out that there wasn't as much room in it as we had supposed, because we hadn't reckoned on Father's fishing gear and the lunch, and it was plain that we couldn't all get in.

Father said not to mind him, that he could just as well stay home and put in the time working in the garden. He said that we were not to let the fact that he had not had a real holiday for three years stand in our way; he wanted us to go right ahead and have a big day and not to mind him.

But of course we all felt that it would never do to let Father stay home, especially as we knew he would make trouble if he did. The two girls, Anna and Mary, would have stayed and gotten dinner, only it seemed such a pity to, on a lovely day like this, having their new hats. But they said that Mother had only to say the word and they'd gladly stay home and work. Will and I would have dropped out, but we wouldn't have been any use in getting the dinner.

So in the end it was decided that Mother would stay home and just have a lovely restful day around the house, and get the dinner. Also it turned out to be just a bit raw out-of-doors, and Father said he would never forgive himself if he dragged Mother round the country and let her take a severe cold. He said it was our duty to let Mother get all the rest and quiet she could, after all she had done for all of us, and that young people seldom realize how much quiet means to people who are getting old. He could still stand the racket, but he was glad to shelter Mother from it.

Well, we had the loveliest day up among the hills, and Father caught such big specimens that he felt sure that Mother couldn't have landed them anyway, if she had been fishing for them. Will and I fished, too, and the two girls met some young men friends along the stream, and so we all had a splendid time.

It was quite late when we got back, but Mother had guessed that we would be late, so she had kept back the dinner to have it hot for us.

We sat down to a big roast turkey. Mother had to get up and down a good bit during the meal fetching things, but at the end Father noticed it and said she simply mustn't do it, that he wanted her to spare herself, and he got up and fetched the walnuts from the sideboard himself.

The dinner was great fun, and when it was over all of us wanted to help clear the things up and wash the dishes, only Mother said that she would really much rather do it, and so we let her, because we wanted to humor her.

It was late when it was all over, and when we kissed Mother before going to bed, she said it had been the most wonderful day in her life, and I think there were tears in her eyes.

"The Compleat Angler"

I would rather fish than eat, particularly eat fish. —Corey Ford

ONE DAY on a fishing trip my wife and I had several bites, but my mother-in-law seemed to be having no luck at all. Finally, in disgust, she pulled in her line, held it up to me and said, "Please put another worm on my hook."

"But you have a good bait on your line now," I protested.

"But this one," she said, pointing scornfully at the worm, "isn't *trying.*" —P.D.

FROM A news item in *Sunset Magazine:* "They will visit Martinez Lake for catfish and bass fishing. There will be a beef barbecue after the fishing."

A TRAVELER strolled up to a fisherman. "Having any luck?"

"Pretty good," replied the angler. "I haven't had a bite in three hours."

"What's so good about that?" asked the amazed traveler.

"You see that guy over there? Well, he hasn't had a bite in six hours." —*Victorian Magazine*

ON A raw, windy day in Maine one summer I decided to wait in the car while my husband went sailing. On the pier was a fisherman whose luck seemed to be as bad as the weather. For over an hour I watched him try one lure after another on his line—a big rusty door key, the top of his tin bait can and several other objects he dug out of his pockets which I couldn't identify. None interested the fish.

Finally, after due meditation, he took something from the front of his clothing, tied it to the line, and I saw a glint of yellow as it disappeared into the water. Almost at once the pole bent and he pulled in a fish, then another and another in quick succession. I got out of the car and walked over to him. "What charm did you use?" I asked.

He held up his line. Tied to the hook was a Phi Beta Kappa key.

—Julia T. Ramsey

A CONSCIENCE-smitten Sunday fisherman stuffed a dollar bill under the door of a Halifax church one Sabbath, shortly after dawn, pinned to a scribbled note that read: "I feel bad but I'm still going fishing. Please put in collection plate." —*Maclean's Magazine*

We'd had no bites in an entire evening of fishing. As darkness fell and we pulled toward shore we passed a couple in another rowboat.

"Did you have any luck?" we called.

"No," said the young man gloomily.

"What kind of bait were you using?"

For a moment the young man was silent. Then he said, "I wasn't fishing." —Kenneth E. Pollard

—*Weirton Steel Employees Bulletin*

How to Ketch Trouts

Condensed from

"Best Sports Stories of 1944"

George W. Heinold

My objective was trout. But all forenoon I had waded over the slippery rocks of a Connecticut stream, whipping early-season bucktails and wet flies in vain. Weary and disgruntled I leaned against the rails of a rustic old river bridge. Working downstream I had reached tidal water, below which conditions were considered hopeless. A noisy old farm truck approached and the driver, a gray-bearded patriarch, brought his ancient conveyance to a stop. "Ketch any trouts, young fella?" he asked.

"Nope!" I answered. "Not even a rise."

The farmer regarded me with humorous blue eyes. "You know, young fella," he said, "people these days don't know how to fish this here crick. Shucks, there's plenty of trouts left in it. Big fellas thet'll go two pounds, mebbe three!"

"You're not kidding, are you?" I replied.

"Course I ain't," he snorted. "Thet's the whole dern trouble with you young'uns: you think everybody's kiddin' you. Why, I've told a dozen of you fellas how to ketch trouts in this here crick, but I ain't heard of any of you tryin' it!"

"Tell me how it's done," I requested, humoring him.

"Sure!" he said eagerly. "Fust of all, you hike down the crick a piece—mebbe a mile or so on an incomin' tide—"

"Now listen," I interrupted, "that's tidewater. No trout live down there."

"Is thet so?" the old gentleman flared. "Now you listen to me, sonny! You'll never ketch trouts down there if you go stompin' along the bank swishin' flies and plunkin' worms. Them trouts only feed on the incomin' tide, an' their feedin' grounds change with flood water. 'Tis a matter of locatin' where they're feedin' and ketchin' them without 'rousin' their suspicions."

"But how can you locate them?" I asked.

He chuckled. "My grandpappy told me how. But supposin' I tell you?" he inquired suspiciously. "Are you goin' to laugh an' say, 'Sure, sure,' like them other fellas I told?"

"No," I promised, "I won't laugh."

"Wal now, one thing more! Will you promise to try it out?"

My willing promise delighted the old man. "Thet's the spirit!" he beamed. "You c'mon to the farm with me. I'll tell you on the way." As he unveiled his secret, it became increasingly apparent that I was one of those people Barnum referred to.

It seems that the old-time fishermen merely tossed bamboo poles six or eight feet long into the current and let them drift upstream with the incoming tide. To each pole was fastened about ten feet of twine with a baited hook. Sooner or later the bait drifted over the feeding grounds, and the fish would grab it. After the tide had reached its peak the fishermen would row upstream to retrieve the poles, plus a fine mess of fish.

"Trouble is," I stalled, "I haven't suitable gear with me."

"Don't let thet worry you none, sonny!" my host said reassuringly. "I've got at least a dozen rigs all ready."

"But I haven't any bait."

"Jest you take thet spade out to the manure pile. You'll find a can out there, too!"

When he had driven me back to my car, he issued final instructions: "Throw these poles from thet old boat landin'—one at a time and a couple minutes apart —an' then keep your eye on 'em till full tide. Then use thet rowboat tied up near there to fetch 'em back in. And let me know how you've fared when you bring back the gear."

A short time later I stood on the boat landing and watched the tide flood upstream. Several times I glanced furtively about to make certain there were no witnesses, for I felt like a senior deacon who had been asked to jitterbug.

I had decided against following one instruction: I wouldn't attach any hooks to the twine on my floating poles; instead, I'd just tie the worms on. Should I see the rigs bobble (though I doubted they would), I'd crawl within range and use my trout rod. I wasn't too sure that the state laws permitted this unorthodox method of angling; but since I wasn't using hooks, the worst they could do was to hale me before a psychiatrist.

I threw three of the rigs into the stream, which at that point was about 35 feet wide. I hid the ones I didn't use, and following on the bank watched the poles voyage serenely upstream. When the leading rig came to a sharp bend in the stream, it began to tilt up and down violently. "Probably a big eel playing with it," I said to myself, determined not to entertain false hopes. But I had my trout rod ready, for hope springs eternal.

I approached the bend cautiously; hiding behind a big boulder I managed my first cast. I allowed the bucktail to sink almost to the bottom when *wham!* a big fish struck. In an instant my rod bent to a half circle and my line cut through the water like a knife. From then on it seemed more like a tug of war with a young sand shark than a battle with a trout, for this fellow was determined and powerful.

But in due time I led him to the bank. When he was netted I kneeled over him in awe-struck wonder. He was a genuine speckled brookie all of 18 inches long. "These old-time farmers," I murmured penitently, "sure know what it is all about!"

Even with this proof in my creel, I scarcely dared to hope for a repeat performance, but I put three more poles to floating. And in the next hour, by employing all the rigs, I annexed five beautiful brookies running from 16 to 19 inches.

When it came time to call it a day, and a very fruitful day at that, I retrieved the poles with the rowboat. As I wound the lines around them tenderly, I thought how much I owed to their kindly and wise owner. How to express my appreciation? How to make amends for my doubts?

He was sitting in the doorway of his corncrib when I returned.

"Look!" I cried elatedly, and I opened the creel and displayed the five big trout. "That method of yours certainly produces results!" He gazed at the fish for a long time, like a man who can't believe his own eyes. Finally he scratched his head. "Wal—by gosh!" he exclaimed. "So it actually does work. Grandpa was right!"

"Do you mean to tell me," I demanded, "that you've never tried it yourself?"

The old man took another sheepish look at the fish, sighed and shook his head. "Wal, no!" he said. "You see, Grandpa used to spin such yarns about fishin' thet I wasn't exactly sure it would work. But now I guess I'll have to try it myself tomorrow!"

Comic Relief

A MAN WHO had discovered the joys of fishing became even more insistent than most fishermen upon recounting his triumphs to skeptical acquaintances. Disgruntled by their thinly veiled hints that he was a liar, he bought a pair of scales, installed them in his library and had his friends watch while he weighed his fish.

One evening a neighbor burst in excitedly to borrow the scales. He was back in ten minutes, his face flushed with delight. "Congratulate me," he cried. "I'm the father of a 24-pound baby boy!"

—*First Federal's Home Life Magazine,* quoted in *Coronet*

THE TEACHER had asked her pupils to list, in their opinions, the 11 greatest Americans. As they were writing, she stopped at one desk. "Have you finished your list, Bobby?" she asked.

"Not quite," answered the boy. "I can't decide on the fullback."

—Dan Bennett

AMONG THE old mother-in-law jokes is this one Alben Barkley used to tell about the farmer's wife who died—and somehow on the day of the funeral there was a shortage of cars. The funeral director asked the husband of the deceased if he would mind very much riding in the same car with his mother-in-law.

"All right," he muttered, "but it'll ruin my whole day."

—Peggy McEvoy

THE TEEN-AGER wanted to borrow the family car on a foggy night to take his girl to a drive-in theater. "In this fog?" his father exclaimed. "Oh," explained the son, "we've already seen the movie."
—*Motor Service*

NUNNALLY JOHNSON, Hollywood screenwriter-producer, is fascinated with unusual names. Some time ago when someone referred to an actress named Giselle Werbischek Pfiffle, he insisted on looking up her name in the telephone book and calling her himself. The ensuing dialogue went like this:

"Is this Miss Giselle Werbischek Pfiffle?"

"Yes . . . ?"

"This is Nunnally Johnson."

"Who?"

"Nunnally Johnson. You don't remember me?"

"No, I don't believe I do."

"I'm sorry. I must have the wrong Giselle Werbischek Pfiffle."
—Peggy McEvoy

IN A JOKE that has wriggled through the Iron Curtain an escaped Russian, newly arrived in Britain, watches newsreels, comedy skits and drama over television with great boredom. Then he switches to a different program and his eyes light up. "Now I feel at home," he exults. *"Puppets!"*
—Irving Hoffman in *Collier's*

THE SUN-BAKED cowboy swaggered into the saloon and through parched lips ordered the bartender to give his horse a bucket of his best whiskey.

"And what'll you have, stranger?" asked the bartender.

"Nothin'," shot back the dusty cowboy. "I'm drivin'!"
—J. C. Salak in *Laugh Book Magazine*

SAM LEVENSON tells of a large-scale real-estate enterprise whose president received an emergency phone call from his superintendent.

"A dreadful thing has happened," the superintendent reported.

"We sold our model house yesterday, took away the scaffolding —and the whole house collapsed."

"How many times do I have to tell you?" shouted the president. "Don't take away the scaffolding until you've put up the wallpaper!"

—Leonard Lyons

"I THOUGHT you were going to your lodge meeting?"

"It was postponed. The wife of the Grand Exalted Invincible Supreme Potentate wouldn't let him out tonight."

—General Features Corp.

TRYING TO eclipse his brother's gift of a Cadillac, a Hollywood producer paid $10,000 for an amazing mynah bird to give his mother on her birthday. The bird spoke 11 languages and sang grand opera. On the night of her birthday he called her long distance. "What did you think of the bird, Mama?" he asked.

"Delicious!" she said.

—Reginald Gardiner, quoted by Earl Wilson, Hall Syndicate

Happy Birthday!

A YOUNG executive in a New York advertising agency had a well-deserved reputation as a wolf, and for several months a new secretary firmly refused all his invitations. So he was surprised when she agreed to a dinner date on his birthday. He was even more amazed when, after dinner, she invited him up to her apartment for a "birthday drink," soon excused herself to change into something more comfortable. When she called through the closed door, "Why don't you come in here, John?" he walked in.

He was greeted by a chorus singing, "Happy Birthday to You" —and there stood the entire office staff.

DISTRAUGHT mother to group of wild children at birthday party: "There will be a special prize for the one who goes home first!"

—Bill Yates cartoon in *Ladies' Home Journal*

AT BERGDORF Goodman's a staff member was amazed to see a customer trying on a blouse with a blindfold on.

"But of course," a clerk explained matter-of-factly. "She's getting it for her husband to give to her for her birthday. It's going to be a surprise." —Booton Herndon, *Bergdorf's on the Plaza* (Knopf)

WHEN MY Jonnie got around to thanking his Uncle Herbert for a Christmas gift along about March 25, he wrote, "I'm sorry I didn't thank you for my present, and it would serve me right if you forgot about my birthday next Thursday . . . ."

—Bennett Cerf in *This Week Magazine*

ON MY BIRTHDAY I received a lovely gift from a friend; an empty envelope attached bore this message:

"Dear Fran, Would you mind, next time you're in Dale's Department Store, stopping by their greeting-card section. Under 'Birthdays—General,' second rack from left, second row down, third card in, you will find *your* card. I couldn't get anyone to wait on me! Love, Betty." —Frances M. Short

ONE DAY at Corona Naval Hospital, where I was stationed as an X-ray technician, a young seaman timidly asked for an X ray of his chest. I asked the boy for his doctor's consultation slip.

"I don't have one," he said. "I wanted the X rays for myself."

Swallowing my exasperation I asked what he wanted to do with radiographs of his chest.

"Well," he said, "next week's my pop's birthday, and I just want to show him my heart's in the right place." —R. J. Gonzalez

WEEPING WIFE to husband: "For weeks I've been telling you not to buy me anything for my birthday—and *still* you forgot to get me something!" —Ed Reed cartoon, The Register and Tribune Syndicate

New Americans

PAUL KOZLOFF and his wife, who left Communist Russia to come to the United States, live in San Francisco, where Paul had been ruling the roost as master-of-the-house in traditional European style—until the day, that is, when he took his citizenship exams and returned home to announce proudly: "At last I am an American citizen."

"Fine," beamed his wife, draping her apron around his middle. "And now—wash the dishes!" —Herb Caen in San Francisco *Examiner*

WITH THREE other men from our office, I usually spent my "coffee break" in a nearby luncheonette. Often this period developed into a gripe session: national issues, wages, prices. During all these discussions John, the Greek proprietor, had maintained a smiling neutrality, but one day, during an attack on the city's transportation facilities, he entered the fray. In somewhat broken oratory but with meaning clear, John blasted transportation from bus to subway. We all sat stunned, until I finally asked, "How come you suddenly start putting your two cents' worth in, John?"

Pointing to a newly framed certificate on the wall, he proudly said, "Yesterday I become citizen." —Thomas F. Flynn

WHEN I WAS living in the Lower Rio Grande Valley of Texas, near the Mexican border, I was surprised one day to see my neighbor García mowing his lawn. García had done well since he came to this country and I knew that he had a yardman, José, who has only to whisper to plants to make them bloom luxuriantly.

"Buenos días," I greeted García in my faltering Spanish. "Why do you cut your own grass? Is it perhaps a fiesta day?"

"Compadre," García replied, taking advantage of the interruption to mop his brow, "we do indeed live in strange times. I mow the lawn so that José may do the dishes, so that my wife may attend the Girl Scout Training Course—where she will learn how to live in the outdoors like the humblest peon in Old Mexico." —V. Cain

Toward More Picturesque Speech

AMERICA is no longer a melting pot—it's a pressure cooker (Luigi Basco) . . . This is the country where people in all walks of life prefer to ride (Carey Williams)

Defined Points: Hot dog—the only animal that feeds the hand that bites it (*Farm Journal and Country Gentleman*) . . . Balanced diet—what you eat at buffet suppers (Richard Armour) . . . Maternity dress—space suit (Lewis E. Sullivan) . . . Hangover—something to occupy a head that wasn't used the night before (Howard W. Newton) . . . Grandfather—a grandchild's press agent (Cedric Adams in Minneapolis *Star*) . . . Patience—the ability to idle your motor when you feel like stripping your gears (Howard W. Newton)

A LOT of wolves hang around a woman with a past, hoping that history will repeat itself (Dick Stone in Asheboro, N. C., *Courier-Tribune*)

A Word to the Wise: One way to save face is to keep the lower half shut (Toronto *Commercial News and Building Record*) . . . It's better to give than to receive—and it's deductible (Stephanie Martino) . . . The best place for your bathroom scales is in front of your refrigerator (Imogene Fey in *The Saturday Evening Post*)

Earmarked: He's got a lot of depth on the surface, but deep down he's shallow (Peter De Vries) . . . On what do you bias your opinion? (John Kersey) . . . If I had it all to do over again, I wouldn't have the strength (Joe E. Lewis, quoted by Walter Winchell)

THE ESKIMO term for summer is "season of inferior sledding" (Bernardine Kielty) . . . In the Orient the pidgin English expression for piano is "big fellow box, you fight 'im teeth, he cry" (Freling Foster in *Collier's*)

A TOASTMASTER is a man who eats a meal he doesn't want so he can get up and tell a lot of stories he doesn't remember to people who've already heard them (George Jessel, quoted by Earl Wilson in *Esquire*)

Street Scenes: Soldiers armed with pretty girls (Lucy Freeman) . . . A squadron of ladies entered the restaurant in tea-formation (Robert Bruce) . . . Men carrying brief cases, faking work home (C.W.F.) . . . Buses, like huge vacuum cleaners, sucked up the people waiting on the street corners (Alice B. Bovard)

us Lines

HE CITY bus drivers in Charlotte, . C., are noted for their courtesy, ough it is sometimes severely rained. Our bus was halfway be- veen stops when it was hailed by n old man struggling with an verload of bundles. The driver ot only stopped but helped the ld man on and settled his par- els. He had hardly started, how- ver, when the new passenger iped, "This is the Elizabeth bus, in't it?"

"No," said the driver, "this is ne Queens Road bus."

"Lemme out, please, suh. I'm n the wrong bus," the old man aid agitatedly. Patiently our river stopped, helped the flurried assenger off and handed him his undles. But as he took his seat gain I heard him murmur to him- elf, "Danged if I'm not a *nice* uy!"

—Polly Lufler

OUR CROWDED bus stopped in South Carolina town and the river addressed the passengers s follows:

"Folks, this is a half-hour meal top. My employer does not per- nit me to recommend one eating lace as being superior to another. ut if I can be of service to you vithin the next half hour, you will find me at the Elite Café, four doors down the street on the right."

—Inez Tucker

APPARENTLY lost, a small dog was running about on a bus I boarded one day. When a little boy and his mother got on he immediately adopted the boy, who was soon begging to take the puppy home, but his mother explained that he already belonged to someone. "No, he doesn't, lady," said the driver. "He was left here and I'm afraid I'll have to take him to the pound." It was a happy boy and dog that got off the bus.

A few days afterward on a bus I again saw a puppy, this time making friends with an elderly gentleman. I patted the dog and asked what kind he was. "I don't know," said the man, "but I wish I had one like him."

At once the bus driver spoke up —the same driver. "If you want him, you can have him. Somebody left him."

As the man got off with the puppy, I questioned the driver. "My dog, Bessie, had pups," he explained. "I'm helping her find good homes for them."

—Mrs. R. Finlay

As OUR bus pulled out of the Boston terminal, heading for Portsmouth, N. H., the driver called over his shoulder, "Well, folks, it's hot, I know, but it won't be long now. I'll soon have you out of this state and into real country—New Hampshire! We've got sweet, clean, cool air in *our* state."

The next 30-odd miles were hotter than the city, and after a few ineffective struggles to open windows we settled back to wilt in silence. Then our driver again called out, "We'll be in New Hampshire in another mile." As we flashed by the state marker the bus cooled off suddenly and refreshingly. The passengers were amazed. I was the only one who noticed that the driver had surreptitiously pushed a knob on the instrument panel as we passed into the promised land. By leaning forward I could make out its label: "Cooling System."

—Carl L. Beggs

AT A BUS stop on the West Coast a beautiful young girl was leaving amid the fond farewells of a group of boys and girls. Since she was embracing and kissing them all around, our departure was considerably held up.

Finally our handsome young bus driver heaved himself out of his seat and got in line with the affectionate youngsters. When it came his turn he gave the girl an enthusiastic kiss and hug, then picked her up and put her aboard the bus—and we were off.

—Mrs. A. M. Stevens

Out Where the West Begins

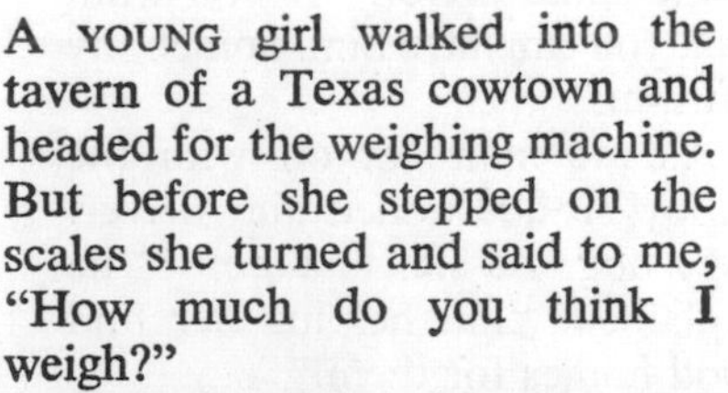

A YOUNG girl walked into the tavern of a Texas cowtown and headed for the weighing machine. But before she stepped on the scales she turned and said to me, "How much do you think I weigh?"

She was slight of build and I guessed 116 pounds. Turning to a man at another table, she repeated her question. "Well, I reckon about 131 pounds." The scales balanced at 132.

"How in the world did you guess so close?" I asked incredulously.

"Shucks, feller," he replied, 'I've bought and sold a lot of attle in my day. And I always udge 'em by the hindquarters irst."

—Jack DuBois

AT A national cattle growers' onvention a group of us went to famous Phoenix steak house for linner. We each asked for our avorite cut of beef until the last nan spoke up—he ordered a louble portion of lamb chops.

Amazed by such heresy from a 'eteran Arizona cattleman and trong booster of beef, we asked im how come. Straight-faced he xplained: "Eat the durn things p and get rid of 'em—that's my heory!"

—H. W. Jackson

WHEN I WAS transferred to the Marine Corps Training Center at Twenty-nine Palms, Calif., located in the middle of the Mojave Desert, my wife and I started ooking for a place to live. Finally ve found a house, owned by an old-timer of the desert, that ooked as if it would meet our eeds. Before committing ourelves, however, my wife looked p at the roof and asked, "Are 'ou sure the roof doesn't leak?"

A puzzled expression crossed he old-timer's face. Then he rinned and asked, "Leak *what?*"

—S/Sgt. L. K. White

AT THE Frontier Days rodeo at Cheyenne, Wyo., some soldiers from the Warren Air Force Base were discussing cowboys and westerners in general. "Man, these people out here are crazy," said one of them, shaking his head. "They pay $20 for a cowboy hat, $40 for a pair of boots—and $1.98 for a pair of pants!"

—D. S. Stoval

ON THE outskirts of an Oklahoma town are six service stations in a row. Posted in front of the first is a large sign: "Last Chance to Buy Gas—the Next Five Stations Are Mirages."

—Mrs. Clyde Herndon

IT WAS Saturday night in Dodge City, Kan., and the town was full of cowhands from the surrounding ranches. One of the cowboys came into a stationer's shop where I was looking for post cards. He was in full dress—wide, cream-colored sombrero, beautifully tooled high-heeled boots, silver spurs—movie version to the last detail. To my surprise he carefully looked over the large assortment of wild-West magazines, then selected eight with the most dramatic covers and departed.

"Do cowboys read this wild-West stuff?" I exclaimed.

"Sure," said the storekeeper. "They gotta know how to act."

—Geneva Seybold

Book Marks

PUBLISHER to author: "Your novel is excellent, but right now I'm looking for trash."

—John W. Frost cartoon in *Collier's*

GYPSY Rose Lee flew to Seattle with her son Eric to help exploit her autobiography, *Gypsy*. A skeptic asked Miss Lee if she ever used ghost writers. "Listen, you," Gypsy replied indignantly, "I write my own books, catch my own fish, and Eric here isn't an adopted child." —Leonard Lyons

IN AN American bookshop in the Argentine a middle-aged woman, trying to master the English language, approached a clerk and said haltingly, "Your Señor Gunther—I have read his books *Inside Asia* and *Inside Europe*. Please, I would like to know—are any more of Señor Gunther's Insides out?" —Winifred Barton

SOMEONE once remarked to William Allen White that he must be getting a great deal of praise for a newly published book. "Not a damned bit more than I need," he replied.

—Maxwell Droke, *The Speaker's Handbook of Humor* (Harper)

AUTHOR Lloyd Lewis's never-ending research in Lincolniana prompted a classic remark by his wife, former newspaperwoman Kathryn Dougherty. Attending a clubwomen's tea she was asked by a welcoming member, "And what does your husband do for a living, Mrs. Lewis?"

"I lost my husband," replied Mrs. Lewis, "in the Civil War."

—Savage in Chicago *Tribune*

"I ALWAYS wonder," said a friend to Anita Loos, "how you could write *Gentlemen Prefer Blondes* when you are a brunette."

"That's how I know," sighed Anita. —Walter Winchell

FROM THE Mankato, Minn., *Free Press:* "The Book-Lovers Club had a get-together with the husbands of members Thursday evening. Following dinner the group went to the home of a member to watch television."

HELEN HOKINSON-type woman to author at party: "I've read your book, and I must say I've had some very interesting arguments with people who liked it."

—Doris Matthews cartoon in *The Saturday Evening Post*

AT A book-and-author luncheon somebody asked, "I wonder where the dime novel has gone?"

"It's gone," answered Quentin Reynolds, "to $3.95."

—Bennett Cerf in *The Saturday Review*

LETTER FROM a reader in Keokuk, Iowa, to *Collier's* editors: "Dear Sirs: It may interest you to know that I was going to write a story for your magazine. But I find stories easier to read than write."

WHEN Edna Ferber and George S. Kaufman collaborated on their play *The Royal Family,* they wrote a good part of it in Miss Ferber's suite at the Hotel Algonquin, often working through the day and into the night. One midnight a new and overzealous clerk telephoned the apartment and inquired, "I beg your pardon, Miss Ferber, but is there a gentleman in your room?"

"I don't know," Miss Ferber replied. "Wait a minute, and I'll ask him."

—Margaret Case Harriman, *The Vicious Circle* (Rinehart)

TITLE to render obsolete that champion formula title of all time, *Lincoln's Doctor's Dog*, is Charlie W. Shedd's *Pray Your Weight Away.* —Harvey Breit in New York *Times Book Review*

IN A publisher's mail one morning was a bulky package marked in heavy pencil: "Do not destroy. Not a manuscript." —Bennett Cerf in *The Saturday Review*

WRITER autographing books to stunning female customer: "Care to curl up with the author?"

—Wenzel cartoon in *Cavalier*

"Where There's a Will . . ."

THE FRENCH novelist Honoré de Balzac loved the good things of life. So when an uncle, who was old and stingy, left him a sizable sum, Balzac wrote friends the good news in these words:

"Yesterday, at five in the morning, my uncle and I passed on to a better life."

—Eddo Galassi, quoted in *Storia*

BLUNT, gruff Harold L. Ickes stepped on many toes, official and otherwise, when he was Secretary of the Interior. As a result he made a lot of people happy in their pure, unblemished hatred of him. One day the wife of former Democratic National Committeeman Lawrence Robert phoned her lawyer to change her will.

"What change do you want to make?" her lawyer asked.

"I don't want to leave anything to Harold Ickes," she said.

"But you *aren't* leaving anything to Harold Ickes," the attorney protested.

"I know," she said happily, "but I want to *say* so."

—Robert M. Yoder in
The Saturday Evening Post

SIX PROMINENT Berkeley men were named as pallbearers in the will of a man who died penniless and owing them considerable sums. "They have been wonderful creditors," the will said, "and I would like to have them carry me to the end." —Glen King in
Berkeley, Calif., *Daily Gazette*

THEN there's the story about the Hollywood writer who left instructions that he be cremated and ten percent of his ashes thrown in his agent's face.

FROM THE Lansing, Mich., *Christian Banner:* "A new loudspeaker system has been installed in the church. It was given by one of the members in memory of his wife."

THE LAWYER I was working for was summoned to the bedside of an octogenarian who had only a few days to live and wanted to make his will. I went along as a witness.

"To my son Jim, in fatherly love," the old man began, "I bequeath $10,000. To my son John the same, and to my daughter Mary, ditto. And to each of my eight grandchildren, $1000 . . ."

The lawyer interrupted. "Hold on there, Mr. Roberts," he said. "Your estate isn't worth more than $3000—just how do you suppose these beneficiaries are going to get the money?"

Mr. Roberts reared up indignantly on his bed. "Git it?" he shouted. "Let 'em work for it, same as I had to do!"

—Edward H. Waples

Father Wasn't Excitable

By Hamilton Cromie

MY FATHER, a lawyer in a small city in Illinois, was in one particular unlike most lawyers: as a rule, he didn't have much to say. It wasn't that he was surly or aloof—he was just a wonderful man for keeping his mouth shut.

One summer, for instance, we were vacationing in a big old house in Michigan, and in the middle of the night my mother woke the household screaming, "There's a bat in this bedroom! Robert, get up!"

Father made some sleepy response which we couldn't catch; then my mother's voice, excited and mad, carried clear across the hall, "Well, if you aren't going to do anything about it, I'm going to spend the rest of the night on the divan downstairs!"

We were all asleep when she screamed again, "There's another one down here!" This time my father's answer was loud enough to be understood. "I could have told you *that,*" he called out. "I saw it before I came up to bed."

But what happened one evening the next summer may give you a better idea. Father had just come home from work and opened the paper when Mother asked if he'd mind running down to Armstrong's delicatessen for a loaf of rye bread. I was tired of playing catch with my kid brother so I tagged along.

Just as we walked into the store a nervous-looking fellow with a dirty handkerchief over his face poked a gun at my father and said, "This is a stickup!"

Maybe Father misunderstood. In any event he turned toward the bread rack, saying, "All I came in for is a loaf of rye bread." With that the man jabbed his gun into Father's ribs and cried, "Stick 'em up, or I'll let you have it!" Then he slapped me across the face and told me to put my hands up, too.

At this point my father grabbed the gun, belted the stranger behind the ear with it and threw him right through Armstrong's screen door.

"Thank you," said Armstrong, reaching for the phone. He looked as if he hadn't really waked up from a bad dream yet.

"That's all right," my father said. "Better get that screen fixed right away. Lots of flies this time of year. Where do you keep the rye bread?"

"We're sold out," Armstrong said. So we went on.

In the next block we stopped at Prell's grocery, but their rye bread had caraway seeds in it and my mother hadn't mentioned anything about caraway seeds, so we went on again. My father was sure we could find what was wanted at the Consolidated Market on Main Street. Halfway there, though, he crawled under some broken latticework to get a kitten for a little girl who was crying and eating an orange at the same time. Then he stopped to change a tire for two women.

By the time we got to the Consolidated it was closed, and my father decided we might as well go on downtown. I believe we might have made it to the State bakery on time, but there was a man with a microphone running a curbstone quiz show in front of the Empire theater. My father identified Chester A. Arthur, spelled Byzantium correctly and recalled Ty Cobb's 1921 batting average (.389). The man handed him $25 and we went on.

Father seemed rather jubilant about the windfall and said we might as well get two loaves while we were at it. The bakery was closed, though.

By this time the street lights were on, and Father admitted it was getting late. "Your mother may have to bake herself some bread," he said.

We started home, walking fast, and as we went by Armstrong's the proprietor came running out with a package. "Found this mixed in with the white after you left," he said. "Take it with my compliments."

"That's all right," Father said, counting out 23 cents. "This saves a lot of bother. Glad to pay you for it."

When we got home dinner was cold and Mother looked hot and out of sorts. Father sat down in his favorite chair, slipped off his shoes and reached for the paper again. Mother stood there with the package under her arm and demanded to know how anybody in God's Green World could take three hours to buy a loaf of rye bread.

"Listen, Martha," Father said finally, as she kept after him, "the rye was mixed in with the white—took Armstrong a little while to locate it."

Then he snapped the paper open in a way that meant the discussion period was over.

Brief Encounters

OUR HANDYMAN came in one day and reported that, while walking down the main street, he had suddenly discovered he was side-by-side with movie actor Alan Ladd.

"Did you talk to him?" we asked.

"Well, it was like this," he said slowly. "I knew who he was and he knew who he was—and it just didn't make sense us discussing it."

—Herm Hines

LORADO TAFT, the great Chicago sculptor, used to tell this story on himself. One blustery, rainy day as he came out of the Art Institute he saw two nuns across the street. The wind was whipping their robes around them, and, as a sculptor, he was fascinated by the line they made. At the time he was working on a piece of sculpture of a mythological figure with robes blown by the wind, so he was delighted to have this example to study. Completely absorbed he walked along on the opposite side of the street watching them.

Suddenly he saw that a man was deliberately following the nuns. Profoundly shocked at such an outrageous thing, the moment he could get through traffic Mr. Taft flew across the street, caught up with the man, grabbed him by the shoulder, whirled him around and said, "How dare you!"

To his amazement Taft found himself looking into the face of a fellow sculptor—Daniel Chester French.

—Emily Kimbrough, WCBS, New York

JOHN DREW had shaved off his mustache to play a part which greatly changed his appearance. Shortly afterward he met Max Beerbohm in the lobby of a London theater and could not recall who Beerbohm was. Beerbohm's memory was better.

"Oh, Mr. Drew," he said, "I'm afraid you don't know me without your mustache." —*Everybody's Magazine*

A SMALL BOY was taken to have tea at Sir Winston Churchill's country house. On the way his nanny impressed upon him the honor of the occasion. "Don't forget," she said, "that you are going to see the Greatest Man in the Whole World."

But alas, when they arrived Sir Winston was resting in bed. So they had to have tea alone, and the little boy had to be content with playing by himself while his nanny enjoyed a quiet gossip with the staff.

"It is a great pity," said the nanny on the drive home, "that you did not see Sir Winston."

"Oh, but I did see him!" said the boy.

While the nanny's back was turned the boy had followed the butler with a tea tray into a bedroom, where he saw an old gentleman in bed studying a mass of papers. The boy approached nearer and said, "Excuse me, sir, but are you the Greatest Man in the Whole World?" The old gentleman glared at him through his glasses. "Certainly!" he replied. "And now, buzz off!"

—Beverley Nichols in *Saturday Night*

A GENTLEMAN with an unwieldy box of flowers under his arm was about to board a Madison Avenue bus one day when Mignon

Eberhart, the mystery writer, hailed him. She was sure she recognized him, but for the life of her couldn't recall his name. He looked equally puzzled, but let the bus go by and shook her hand warmly. There followed one of those animated, supercordial exchanges of amenities that always feature the meeting of two people who aren't sure of each other's identity. Finally the gentleman said, "It's been fine seeing you again, but I really must run."

Just as he stepped on the bus Miss Eberhart remembered, in a frightening flash, one, why his face was familiar, and two, that she never had met him in her life. It was ex-President Hoover.

—Bennett Cerf, *Shake Well Before Using* (Simon and Schuster)

BACK IN the days when William Allan Neilson was president of Smith College, a freshman returning from a date one dark night found herself locked out of her dormitory at an hour when all students were supposed to be in bed. She succeeded in opening a window on the lower floor and was hoisting herself up, struggling to get through it, when a hand was placed on her posterior and she was boosted on through. She turned in time to see President Neilson, who smiled, tipped his hat and walked away. —H. Allen Smith, *People Named Smith* (Doubleday)

THE DUCHESS of Windsor was standing in the lobby of the Waldorf-Astoria in New York one day, waiting for an elevator to take her to her tower suite. A guest spied her and exclaimed, "Why, you look just like the Duchess of Windsor!"

"Oh, no," the Duchess replied. "I know her well, and she's a *much* younger woman." —Conrad Hilton in *The American Magazine*

FORMER Secretary of State Dean Acheson got into a taxicab in front of his office. The cab driver slewed around and subjected him to a long look absolutely devoid of expression. Finally the driver said, "Aren't you Dean Acheson?"

"Yes," replied the gentleman whose term in office was not marked by complete unanimity. "Do you want me to get out?"

—George Dixon, King Features

Taxi Gabs

WHEN A MAN who wears a hearing aid got into a Washington taxi the driver displayed great interest in the gadget. "Those things any good?" he asked. The man replied he would be lost without it.

"Must be tough to be hard of hearing," sympathized the hackie. "Aw, well," he added philosophically, "nearly all of us have something the matter, one way or another. Take me, for instance. I can hardly see."
—George Dixon, King Features

IRATE TAXI driver to fare: "There'll be no charge, lady; you did most of the driving."
—Charles Williams cartoon in *The American Magazine*

A TAXI driver, weaving in and out of Atlanta traffic at a practiced clip, burst out laughing. "What's so amusing?" asked his fare.

"Aw," he said, "I was thinking of the two preachers and the cab driver who went up to heaven at the same time. St. Peter asked the first minister, 'Who are you and what have you done?'

" 'I'm a Baptist minister and I've preached for 25 years.'

" 'Well, stand over to one side there,' ordered St. Peter. He then put the question to the second clergyman.

" 'I've been a Methodist pastor for 25 years.'

" 'Stand to one side,' said St. Peter. 'What about you?' he asked the last man.

" 'I'm a taxi driver,' the cabbie answered. 'Been one for about 15 years.'

" 'Pass through the gates,' intoned St. Peter.

" 'Why have you allowed that man to go before us?' the preachers protested.

" 'Because,' said St. Peter, 'in 15 years he has scared more hell out of people than you both have in half a century.' "
—Hugh Park in Atlanta *Journal*

A WINSTON-SALEM woman was riding in a taxi in New York City when the driver slowed up a little to miss a pedestrian. Apparently figuring that such unusual courtesy called for an explanation, he turned to her and said, "If you hit 'em, you've gotta fill out a report."

—Roy Thompson in Winston-Salem, N. C., *Journal and Sentinel*

ON THE WAY to his hotel from the airport, a London publisher visiting New York decided to pick up a couple of American shirts, so he told his taxi driver to stop at the first haberdashery.

"Yassuh," said the driver. But at the first red light he inquired, "What was dat you said, boss?"

"A haberdashery," the publisher repeated.

"Yassuh," he agreed again, "a haberdashery it is."

They rattled along a couple of blocks and then he stopped once more. "Lissen, boss," the driver assured the publisher, "wid me dey is no use beatin' round de bush. What is it you wants—liquor or women?"

—Bennett Cerf in *The Saturday Review*

Word Trouble

A MIDDLE-AGED woman wandered into the Senate Interstate and Foreign Commerce Committee one day and asked if a Mr. Sexauer worked there. A helpful employe thought she might be looking for the Banking and Currency Committee, offered to check by telephone. When a feminine voice answered his ring he inquired politely, "Do you have a Sexauer over there?"

"Listen," she snapped, "we don't even have a ten-minute coffee break any more."

—Ruth Montgomery, Chicago Tribune-New York News Syndicate

DIZZY DEAN has been a huge success as a television broadcaster of baseball games, partly because of the innovations he has made in our language. "He slud into third" was the first much-publicized departure. Later he varied "slud" with "slood" and then one afternoon came up with, "The trouble with them boys is they ain't got enough spart." Pressed for an explanation of this, he obliged: "Spart is pretty much the same as fight or pep or gumption. Like the *Spart of St. Louis,* that plane Lindbergh flowed to Europe in."

—Allen Churchill in New York *Times Magazine*

THE INSURANCE man had his prospect on the hook and was proceeding briskly to the kill. "Now that amounts to a premium of $6.90 per month on a straight life," he said. "That's what you wanted, wasn't it?"

"Well," said the customer wistfully, "I *would* like to fool around a bit on Saturday nights." —*Pure Oil News*

ONE DAY I overheard my small grandson doing his arithmetic homework. "Three plus one, the son of a bitch is four," he was saying. "Three plus two, the son of a bitch is five. Three plus three, the son of a bitch is six." And so on. Horrified, I asked him where on earth he had picked up that language. "Oh, that's the way they teach us at school," he replied. The following day I went to see his teacher and asked her about it. At first she was equally horrified, then her face broke into a grin. "I get it!" she cried. "We teach the children to say, 'Three plus one, the sum of which is four. Three plus two, the sum of which is five.' " —F. H.

TEXAS COLUMNIST George Fuermann tells of a Houston music lover who inquired in a music store for a record of a certain Bach chorale. The clerk said they didn't have any song about a back corral, but how would Frankie Laine's "Mule Train" do?

—Matt Weinstock in Los Angeles *Daily News*

A MAN WHO stuttered badly went to a specialist and after ten difficult weeks learned to say quite distinctly: "Peter Piper picked a peck of pickled peppers." His friends congratulated him on his achievement. "Yes," said the man doubtfully, "b-but it's s-s-such a d-difficult remark to w-w-work into an ordinary c-c-conversation, d-don't y'know!" —*The Log*

A GROUP of foreign students I was teaching were discussing the things they wanted to do and see while in America. When it came the turn of a pretty young graduate student from France, she said, "Always I have wanted to go to Texas and find a cowboy and ride away wiz heem into ze mountains on a bum steer."

—Virginia Carroll

WHILE I was visiting my aunt, who prides herself on her tact in dealing with young people, my date and I lingered on the front doorstep longer than she considered proper. Finally she slipped from her warm bed and called gently to us, "If you two knew how pleasant it is in bed, you wouldn't be standing out there in the cold."

—K. A. Larsen

AT A school-board meeting in a Pittsburgh suburb an elderly member, a bit confused by the discussion of merit raises, cut in with: "Merit or single—what's the difference? Pay 'em the same!"

—Charles F. Danver in Pittsburgh *Post-Gazette*

A FRIEND of mine had eight children in 11 years, and I believe the first moment she had to center her full attention on one of them came the night 12-year-old Sally tried on her Confirmation dress. "Sally, honey," her mother said, after a long, loving look, "I think you're beautiful!" The youngster's face lit up. Then her mother added teasingly, "Of course, I'm prejudiced."

Sally's face fell. "Oh, Mother," she wailed, "not *again!*"

—Katharine Lawrence

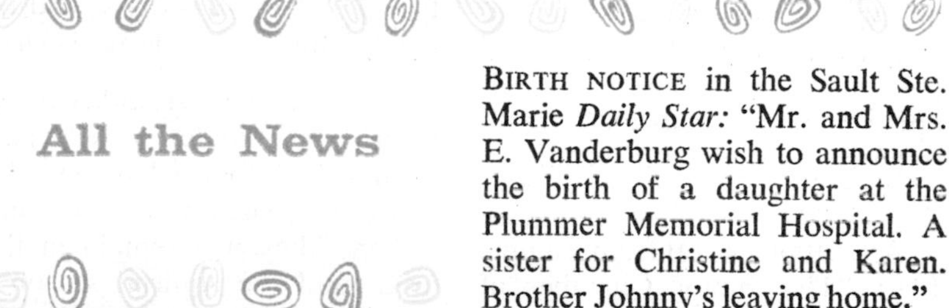

All the News

BIRTH NOTICE in the Sault Ste. Marie *Daily Star:* "Mr. and Mrs. E. Vanderburg wish to announce the birth of a daughter at the Plummer Memorial Hospital. A sister for Christine and Karen. Brother Johnny's leaving home."

FROM THE Escondido, Calif., *Daily Times-Advocate:* "Mrs. Bernice Cimino has informed us that the title of her poem listed in the *Times-Advocate* as 'There Ain't Gonna Be No War' is 'There Ain't Gonna Be Any War.' "

FROM THE Springfield, Ill., *Public Schools Bulletin:* "Mr. and Mrs. Calvin Rippel are recovering from auto-accident injuries. Mr. Rippel will teach high school industrial arts this fall instead of driver training."

SOCIAL NOTES from the Corning, N. Y., *Leader:* "Mrs. Freddie Preston entertained a group of children Saturday in honor of her little daughter's third birthday. About 20 children were present.

"Mrs. Freddie Preston entered the Wellsboro Hospital late Sunday afternoon for observation."

FROM THE Montrose, Calif., *Ledger:* "Ysidro E. Reyes of California Ambulance Service told Montrose Chamber of Commerce directors there must be enough business to support the service before it can be installed. He asked the chamber for support in developing the 100 calls per month required to make the venture a paying proposition."

AN AP DISPATCH from Tampa, Fla.: "The Junior Chamber of Commerce decided to cancel its December 27 meeting. The program chairman observed that this could be done conveniently, since the scheduled speaker had quit his job. His topic was to have been 'My Job and What It Does for Me.' "

FROM A North Carolina paper: "Dr. Briggs is once more among us for a brief season. He says and does exactly as he thinks right, without regard to the opinion and belief of others. His wife is not with him." —Quoted in Burlington, N. C., *Times-News*

FROM A church bulletin in Detroit, Mich.: "The next meeting of the Men's Club promises to be a good one. We don't know what the menu will be but there will be a different cook."

FROM AN American Marketing Association *Newsletter:* "It has been brought to our attention that last month we labeled a picture 'Herb Breseman,' while the photograph was of Bob Fernald. However, since the article was about Ed MacDonald—disregard the whole thing." —Quoted in *Quote*

FROM THE Culver, Ind., *Citizen:* "Carl and Stokley Brock have been called to Harlan, Ky., because of the death of their grandfather. They will remain in that area until the squirrel season is over."

FROM THE Huntington, Ind., *Herald-Press:* "Mrs. Florence Sunderman, president, presided and opened the meeting with a poem, and the Lord's Prayer was read and approved."

FROM AN annual report for the Bury and Rossendale Hospital Management Committee: "The Committee understands that at some time in the not too far distant future the Hospital will be supplied with a new Operating Theater suite, and this in turn will probably involve a new Mortuary and Post Mortem Room."

—The Rev. J. Norman Beard

FROM THE Le Center, Minn., *Leader:* "The Young Matrons Bridge Club met Saturday night at the home of Mrs. T. J. Lloyd. No prizes were given because none of the members knew how to keep score. It is hoped that this situation will soon be corrected."

—Quoted in Santa Barbara, Calif., *News-Press*

Informative Double

A WOMAN who lives on an estate up near Katonah, N. Y., is a great bridge player, and one day she drew what she considered to be a remarkable hand. She thought she played it perfectly, but she wasn't sure. So she wrote a letter to a noted bridge expert. She described the hand, told how she had played it and asked if he could detect any flaw in her strategy. A few days later she got a reply. The expert said it was truly a remarkable hand, that she had played it exactly right. And he enclosed a bill for $100. She was pretty indignant about it and decided she would refuse to pay it. She'd let him sue her first. But she was quite disturbed.

A week later on a train to the city she found herself sitting next to a neighbor who is a New York lawyer. They chatted for a while, then she told him about the bill. She said she thought it was an outrage; after all, he hadn't given her any advice, he only told her that she had played the hand correctly. She wanted to know what the lawyer thought about it.

"You knew he was an expert," he replied. "You knew that he makes his living as a bridge expert. I don't see that you've got an out. I think you'd better pay him." And the following day's mail brought a bill for $100 from the lawyer.

—H. Allen Smith in *The Saturday Evening Post*

Court Jesters

"WHEN I was a boy," reminisced a famous lawyer, "my highest ambition was to be a pirate."

"That so?" said his client. "Congratulations." —*Basic Blast*

SAID THE law professor, "If you have the facts on your side, hammer them into the jury, and if you have the law on your side, hammer it into the judge."

"But if you have neither the facts nor the law?" asked a student.

"Then hammer on the table," answered the professor.

—W. Somerset Maugham, *A Writer's Notebook* (Doubleday)

A WOMAN on trial for murdering her husband was acquitted because of the efforts of one little old lady on the jury. After the trial the latter explained her attitude: "I guess I just felt sorry for her. After all, she was a widow."

—*Townsend National Weekly*

THUG IN witness chair: "Then everything went blank comma pause and wipe eyes with handkerchief." —Burr Shafer cartoon in *The Saturday Evening Post*

AN OLD-TIME judge in the Northwest had a great fondness for assessing fines. Once he sat both as judge and coroner over the body of a stranger found dead in the woods with $40 in gold and a six-shooter in his pockets. The judge fined the corpse $40 for carrying a concealed weapon.

—"A Philadelphia Lawyer" in Philadelphia *Bulletin*

"WHAT IS your age?" asked the judge. "Remember, you're under oath."

"Twenty-one years and some months," the woman answered.

"How many months?" the judge persisted.

"One hundred and eight."

—General Features Corp.

ABRAHAM LINCOLN, as a young lawyer, was pleading two cases the same day before the same judge. Both cases involved the same principle of law, but in one he appeared for the defendant, in the other he spoke for the plaintiff. In the morning he made an eloquent plea and won his case. In the afternoon he took the opposite side and was arguing with the same earnestness. The judge, with a half-smile, inquired the cause of his change in attitude.

"Your honor," said Lincoln, "I may have been wrong this morning, but I *know* I am right this afternoon!" —Nellie Revell, *Right Off the Chest* (Doubleday)

IT WAS the first case for most members of the jury in a little New England town, and they debated for hours. At last they came back, and the foreman solemnly voiced the verdict:

"The jury don't think that he done it, for we allow he wasn't there; but we think he would have done it if he'd had the chanst!"

—Dan Bennett

IN COURTROOMS where smoking was permitted, the great trial lawyer, Clarence Darrow, sometimes lit a cigar when the prosecution began its argument and sat, leaning forward in rapt attention, while the cigar ash grew longer, longer. Soon the jury's attention became so fixed upon that ash, awaiting its fall, that the prosecution argument went largely unheeded. Some claimed that Darrow had cigars especially made, with a wire running through them to hold up the ash—and his intimates knew him to be capable of that. —Kenneth S. Davis in New York *Times Magazine*

Historical Allusions

CLARENCE DARROW once addressed a woman's club on the civilization of the ancient Phoenicians. When he had run down, the beaming chairlady said, "Oh, how *can* we thank Mr. Darrow for the *fascinating* lecture he has given us tonight?" Darrow returned to the lectern and added the following postscript: "I entirely forgot to tell you that it was the Phoenicians who first invented money."

—Frank Crowninshield in *Vogue*

IN MARCH 1944, in Germany near the Rhine, our 69th Division had just taken a small town south of the Remagen bridgehead. A priest came out of his church and began talking with us. He pointed out that one of the twin steeples of his church was badly damaged. "And we had just completed the war repairs on the other steeple," he sighed.

"What damaged the first steeple?" I asked. "An air raid?"

"Oh, no," he replied, "It was artillery."

Since the American artillery had only that day moved up within range, I was puzzled and asked, "Whose artillery?"

"Napoleon's," he answered.

—Maj. Nels A. Parson

A Washington correspondent riding a campaign train through a lush valley of California sat beside a British writer on his first tour of the U. S. The Englishman, after silently observing mile after mile of fertile, prosperous land, finally spoke: "Damn George III!"

—*Quote*

The two chorus girls were great friends, although one was a live wire, the other quiet and reserved. One day the vivacious Phyllis said, "Look, Ruth, I don't mind digging up dates for us, but you just sit around like a zombie and never open your mouth. Why don't you read up and get something to talk about?" Ruth promised to try.

Next town they hit, Phyllis had two local Lotharios waiting for them at the stage door. Later in the evening one of those painful silences occurred. Ruth fidgeted, gulped, then let them have it. "Isn't it too bad," she inquired, "what happened to Marie Antoinette?"

—Kay Painton

A Bostonian visited San Antonio and asked a native, "What is that dilapidated-looking ruin over there?"

"That, suh, is the Alamo. In that building, suh, 136 immortal Texans held off an army of 15,000 of Santa Anna's regulars for four days."

"Um-m-m," said the Bostonian, "and who was that man on horseback on that hill over there?"

"That, suh, is a statue of a Texas Ranger. He killed 46 Apaches in singlehanded combat and broke up 27 riots in his lifetime. Where you from, stranger?"

"I'm from Boston. We have our heroes there, too. Paul Revere, for instance—"

"Paul Revere!" snorted the Texan. "You mean that man who had to ride for help?"

—Leonard Lyons

A woman tourist visiting the Holy Land went to a tourist office for information on roads. Told that it was now possible to go by car all the way from Dan to Beersheba, she confessed, "Do you know, I never knew that Dan and Beersheba were places. I always thought they were husband and wife, like Sodom and Gomorrah."

—Paul Steiner, *Israel Laughs* (Bloch)

Punch Lines

Changing Times, The Kiplinger Magazine: After you've heard two eye-witness accounts of an auto accident, you begin to worry about history.

Grace Williams: We learn from experience. A man never wakes up his second baby just to see it smile.

—Frances Rodman in New York *Times Magazine*

George Jessel: The human brain is a wonderful thing. It starts working the moment you are born, and never stops until you stand up to speak in public.

—Irving Hoffman in *The Hollywood Reporter*

Phoenix Flame: A mistake at least proves somebody stopped talking long enough to do something. —General Features Corp.

St. Paul *Pioneer Press*: What this country needs is more free speech that's worth listening to.

Pacific Northwest Coöperator: Probably nothing in the world arouses more false hopes than one good cantaloupe.

G. Norman Collie: The surest way to get a job done is to give it to the busiest man you know—he'll have his secretary do it.

Anonymous: One humiliating thing about science is that it is gradually filling our homes with appliances smarter than we are.

Mark Twain: I have been complimented many times and they always embarrass me—I always feel that they have not said enough.

—Quoted by Donald Day

Times of Brazil: Love is like a mushroom. You never know whether it's the real thing until it's too late.

Robert Benchley: In America there are two classes of travel: first class and with children. —Quoted in *Ladies' Home Journal*

The Tortures of Weekend Visiting

Condensed from "Of All Things"

Robert C. Benchley

My title might well be, "The Need for a Clearer Definition of Relations between Host and Guest." For who has not wished that his host would come out frankly at the beginning of the visit and state the rules and preferences of the household in such matters as the breakfast hour? And who has not sounded his guest to find out what he likes in the regulation of his diet and mode of living?

Take the matter of arising in the morning. Of course, where there is a large house party the problem is a simple one, for you can always hear the others pattering about and brushing their teeth and so can regulate your own arising. But if you are the only guest, there is apt to be a frightful misunderstanding. "At what time is breakfast?" you ask.

"Oh, any old time on Sundays," replies the hostess. "Sleep as late as you like. This is 'Liberty Hall.' "

This sentiment seems perfectly bully at the time, but in the morning there is a vagueness about it that is simply terrifying.

Let us say that you awake at eight. You listen and hear no one stirring. Then, over on the cool pillow again until 8:20. Again up on the elbow, with head cocked. There is a creak in the direction of the stairs. They may all be up and going down to breakfast! You bound out of bed and listen at the door. Deathlike silence, broken only by the ticking of the hall clock. Probably they are late sleepers. Maybe 11 o'clock is their Sunday rising hour.

Shut the door and sit on the edge of the bed. More sleep is out of the question. Let's take a look at the pictures in the guest room. Here's a group showing your host in evening clothes, holding a mandolin. Probably his college glee club. Rather unkempt-looking bunch, you *must* say.

Back to the door to listen again. Tick-tock-tick-tock. Probably, if you started your tub, you'd wake the whole house. Hello, here are some books on the table. *Fifty*

Famous Sonnets, illustrated by Maxfield Parrish. Never touch a sonnet before breakfast. *My Experiences in the Alps,* by a woman mountain climber who has written on the flyleaf, "To my good friends the Elbridges, in memory of many happy days together at Chamonix." That settles *that.*

It must be nearly noon now! Ten past nine, only! Well, the only thing to do is to get dressed and walk about the grounds. And so, very cautiously, almost clandestinely, you proceed to dress.

And now, just to reverse the process. Suppose you are the host. You have arisen at eight and listened at the guest's door. You have crammed flannel bears into the infant's mouth to keep him quiet. "Bill looked tired last night. Better let him sleep," you whisper to your wife. And so, downstairs on your hands and knees. A bracing walk on the porch, resulting in a terrific appetite.

A glance at the watch shows nine o'clock. Sunday breakfast is usually at 8:30. You feel starved. You sneak into the dining room and steal one of the property oranges from the sideboard, but little Edgar sees you and sets up such a howl that you have to give it to him. Your wife suggests that your friend may have sleeping sickness. Weakened by hunger, you hotly resent this, and snarl, "Oh, very well, I'll go up and rout him out."

You creep upstairs and pause, in listening attitude, just in front of the guest's door. Slowly the door opens, inch by inch, and finally his head is edged cautiously out toward yours. "Hello, Bill," you say flatly. "What are you getting up at this time for? Thought I told you to sleep late."

"Morning, Ed," he says, equally flatly. "Hope I haven't kept you all waiting." Then you both lie and eat breakfast.

Such a misunderstanding is apt to go to almost any length. I once knew of a man on a weekend visit who spent an entire Sunday in his room, listening at his door to see if the family were astir, while in the meantime the family were, one by one, tiptoeing to his door to see if they could detect any signs of life from him.

Don't think, just because I have taken all this space to deal with the rising-hour problem that there are no other points to be made. Oh, not at all. There is, for instance, the question of exercise. After dinner the host says to himself, "Something must be done. I wonder if he likes to walk." Aloud, he says, "Well, Bill, how about a little hike in the country?"

A hike in the country being the last thing in the world Bill wants, he says, "Right-o!" And so, although the host has weak ankles, he bundles up with a great show of heartiness and grabs his stick as if this were the one thing he lived for. After about a mile of hobbling along the road the host says hopefully, "Don't let me tire you out, old man. Any time you want to turn back, just say the word."

The guest, thinking longingly of the fireside, scoffs at the idea of turning back. So on they jog, each wishing that it would rain so that they could go home. Here again the thing may go to almost tragic lengths.

I once visited a man who had an outdoor swimming pool. It was in April, long before spring really understood what was expected of her. My first night there my host said, "Are you a morning plunger?"

Thinking he referred to a tub plunge in a warm bathroom, I glowed and said, "You bet."

"I'll call for you at seven in the morning, then," he said, "and we'll go out to the pool."

It was evidently his morning custom, and I wasn't going to have it said of me that a middle-aged man could outdo me in virility. So, at seven in the morning, in a dense fog (with now and then a slash of cold rain), we picked our way out to the pool and staged a vivid Siberian moving picture scene, showing naked peasants bathing in the Nevsky. My visit lasted five days, and I afterward learned that my host now has chronic joint trouble as a result of those plunges. "But I couldn't be outdone by a mere stripling," he confided to a friend, "and the boy certainly enjoyed it."

All of this might have been avoided by the posting of a sign in my bedroom reading: "Personally, I dislike swimming in the pool at this time of year. Guests wishing to do so may obtain towels at the desk." How very simple and practical!

The sign system is the only solution I can offer. It is crude and brutal, but it admits of no misunderstanding. A sign in each guest room, giving the hours of meals, political and religious preferences of the family, general views on exercise, etc., etc., with a blank for the guest to fill out, stating his own views, would make it possible to visit (or entertain) with a sense of security thus far unknown upon our planet.

Sampler hanging over bed in guest room: "There's No Place Like Home."

—Schroeter cartoon, King Features

Quick Recoveries

ROBERT BENCHLEY was staying at the estate of a very boring elderly maiden aunt. She had planned to go strolling with him one afternoon, but he excused himself on account of bad weather. Shortly afterward she saw him sneaking out alone. "Oh, Robert," she cried, "has it cleared up?"

"Just partly," said Benchley. "Enough for one, but not enough for two." —Boston *Globe*

FOR A dinner party the first Mrs. John D. Rockefeller, Jr., asked orchestra leader Meyer Davis to provide a string orchestra with ten violins. Davis scrambled about and got the required men, but at the last moment one of them became ill. When hurried phone calls failed to produce a substitute, Davis said to a top pianist who always accompanied him on his jobs, "Mrs. Rockefeller wants ten violins—and ten she'll get. Tonight you play the violin!"

"But I can't play the violin!" sputtered the pianist.

"Well, sit there and make like a violinist," said Davis, taking his own fiddle from the case and soaping the bow. What Davis hadn't counted on was that, although no violinist, the musician was a terrific actor. He sat there dreamily drawing his bow back and forth—making not a sound, but looking like a dedicated Heifetz. Before long Mrs. Rockefeller beckoned to Davis. "That violinist!" she beamed. "He's an artist! Can you ask him to play a solo for us?"

Davis thought fast. "Mrs. Rockefeller," he replied grandly, "he is not only a fine artist, but versatile. Did you know he is an even better pianist?" The piano was rolled out and the "violinist" gave the performance of his life. —Peggy McEvoy

AFTER SIGNING a batch of personal letters his secretary had typed for him, a White House staff member asked her to add a postscript to one saying, "Congratulations on the new arrival." The secretary inadvertently added it to the wrong letter, and the puzzled recipient wrote back to set his friend straight.

The secretary redeemed herself by drafting this reply for her boss's signature: "Sorry about the mix-up over the new baby. I must have been laboring under a misconception." —Elton Hailey

Rising to the Occasion

DURING World War II Steve Trumbull, a salty, old-time newspaperman, was commissioned in the Navy only to find himself in Indoctrination School among students and instructors many years his junior. Thoroughly bored, he was dozing through a class in Navy correspondence when he was startled into wakefulness by the instructor saying, "Lieutenant Trumbull, you are to imagine you must report on the following incident: Yesterday, a mine-layer was refueling at a pier when a mine somehow went off. The ship exploded and set fire to the pier and all other ships tied up there. In addition, an ammunition shed blew up. A great amount of damage was incurred. To whom would you address your report?"

Not knowing the correct answer, Lieutenant Trumbull hedged. "This seems important enough to send directly to Frank Knox, Secretary of the Navy."

The instructor replied that, although it wasn't the answer he had in mind, perhaps the incident justified his course. "Very well, Lieutenant. Now how would you begin your report?"

Trumbull started dictating, "My God, Frank, you should have been here last Sunday!"

—Dorothy Billheimer in *The Saturday Evening Post*

JIMMY WALKER, the former mayor of New York City, was gifted with a rare and spontaneous sense of humor. One night at a banquet Walker had been introduced and had just started to speak when the speakers' platform gave way. In the confusion and even as the platform was collapsing, Jimmy quipped, "Reminds me of some of the platforms I've run on."

—James A. Esser

AIRPLANE pioneers Wilbur and Orville Wright were extremely taciturn. Above all they hated to make speeches. One day at a luncheon attended by a group of inventors, Wilbur was called on by the toastmaster. "There must be some mistake," stammered Wilbur. "Orville is the one who does the talking." The toastmaster turned to Orville. The latter stood up and said, "Wilbur just made the speech." —E. E. Edgar

WHEN Carter L. Burgess resigned as Assistant Secretary of Defense to become president of Trans World Airlines, he was awarded an exceptional civilian service medal by the Army. After listening to the long and glowing tribute paid him by Army Secretary Brucker, Burgess said, "I am sorry my mother is not here. She not only would have enjoyed this ceremony, but she would have believed every word of it."

—Walter Trohan, Chicago Tribune-New York News Syndicate

UPON BEING introduced as the toast of radio, the toast of movies and the toast of television, Dinah Shore responded with, "I love the way you buttered that toast!"

WHEN COLUMNIST Merryle Stanley Rukeyser got up to speak at a luncheon of the Pittsburgh Advertising Club, he asked president Carl Dozer, "How long shall I speak?"

Carl told him cheerfully, "Take as long as you like—we all leave at 1:30." —Charles F. Danver in Pittsburgh *Post-Gazette*

ASKED AT a gathering what sort of speech he intended to make, Gen. Carlos Romulo, United Nations delegate, said, "I have two types. My Mother Hubbard speech is like the garment—it covers everything and touches nothing. Then there's my French-bathing-suit speech—it covers only the essential points."

—Malvina Stephenson

AT A LITERARY luncheon held shortly after the publication of her memoirs, Gypsy Rose Lee was preceded by author Walter Lord. At the conclusion of his talk he remarked that just before the luncheon Gypsy had said to him: "Walter, your speech will be a hard act to follow, so to insure close attention to my speech, I've decided to take all my clothes off!"

Gypsy rose from her seat, smiled demurely at the audience and said, "Why, Mr. Lord, you know that isn't true. You know I'd never end a sentence with a preposition!" —Richard G. Sheehan

PAUL-HENRI Spaak of Belgium was on a lecture tour in the United States. "Oh, Mr. Spaak," exclaimed a lady after his lecture in Houston, Texas, "you have been wonderful! You look like Winston Churchill and speak like Charles Boyer."

"Madam," retorted Spaak, "I would prefer to look like Charles Boyer and speak like Winston Churchill!" —Andre Visson

Sir Winston Churchill

"I am always ready to learn, although I do not always like being taught." —*The Eloquence of Winston Churchill* (New American Library)

IN A SPEECH to a group of journalists in London, the famed British cartoonist, David Low, stated that every time he had to make a speech he felt as if he had a block of ice, nine inches by nine inches, right in the pit of his stomach.

After his speech he was approached by one of the audience, a Mr. Winston Churchill. "Mr. Low," asked Churchill, "how large did you say that block of ice is?"

"Nine inches by nine inches," replied Low.

"What an amazing coincidence," replied Churchill. "Exactly the same size as mine." —Jeff Keate

CHURCHILL'S HUMOR is not the polished variety; it smacks much more of the music hall. In 1939 when he was serving as First Lord of the Admiralty he told with relish how a destroyer had dropped a depth charge, but instead of finding a submarine, bits of an old wreck had come to the surface. "And would you believe it," he added with a grin, "there was a door bobbing around with my initials on it! I wanted to recount this important occurrence in a speech, but Mr. Chamberlain cut it out—he thinks my taste is questionable."

—Virginia Cowles, *Winston Churchill: the Era and the Man* (Harper)

DURING World War II Churchill once submitted a draft of an important wartime speech to the British Foreign Office for comment which was returned to him with no comment whatever on content. But where he had ended a sentence with a preposition a Foreign Office purist had careted the preposition into its stiffly grammatical position.

At this the Prime Minister flew into a lather. To the offending purist he dispatched a note: "This is the type of arrant pedantry up with which I will not put!"

WINSTON CHURCHILL was lecturing in Toronto when the amplifying system broke down. Angry cries of "Louder! louder!" began at once. Churchill raised his hands for quiet. Grasping the portable microphone which hung from his lapel, he held it aloft for all to see, and with a dramatic gesture flung it to the ground where it smashed in pieces. Then he thundered, "Now that we have exhausted the resources of science, we shall fall back upon Mother Nature!"

—Louis J. Alber with Charles J. Rolo in *Current History and Forum*

A CHURCHILLISM recalled by friends on the eve of his 75th birthday: "I am ready to meet my Maker. Whether my Maker is prepared for the great ordeal of meeting me is another matter."

—*Time*

The Political Game

SIR WINSTON CHURCHILL was once asked what qualifications he thought the most essential for a politician. Without hesitation he answered, "It's the ability to foretell what will happen tomorrow, next month and next year—and to explain afterward why it did not happen."

A SOUTHERN Congressman stumping for re-election opened his rally to questions. "Congressman, how do you stand on this here Taft-Hartley law?" asked an overalled man.

The young Representative bethought himself of his sharply divided audience, but he didn't hesitate.

"I'm *all right* on that one," he shot back.

The crowd cheered.

—*Ladies' Home Journal*

REPUBLICAN Senator John Sherman Cooper tells about the time he was campaigning in a fiercely Democratic area of Kentucky and, as usual, was shaking every hand in sight. One old fellow, though, seemed reluctant.

"I'm John Cooper," the Senator said.

"You're a Republican, ain't you?" the man countered guardedly.

"Yes."

"Well," drawled the man extending a limp paw, "just press it light."

—Paul F. Healy in *The Saturday Evening Post*

COED ON her way to political rally: "I'm going with an open mind, a complete lack of prejudice and a cool, rational approach to listen to what I'm convinced is pure rubbish."

—*Ram Buller,* quoted by Bruce Patterson, King Features

SENATOR Styles Bridges of New Hampshire tells the story about one of his predecessors, Senator George H. Moses, who came storming into the White House during the Coolidge administration to complain that a man under consideration for a Republican Senatorial nomination was "an out-and-out s.o.b."

"That could be," Coolidge conceded. "But there's a lot of them in the country and I think they are entitled to representation in the Senate."

—Walter Trohan, Chicago Tribune Press Service

THE MISTAKE a lot of politicians make is in forgetting they've been appointed and thinking they've been anointed.

—Mrs. Claude Pepper, quoted by Leonard Lyons

A MAN we know ran into an old civil-servant friend in Washington and found him looking better than he had in years. The friend, who had held many controversial posts, said that right now he was with the Department of the Interior working on the national rat-extermination campaign. "It's just wonderful," he said, heaving a satisfied sigh. "*Everybody's* against rats."

—Jean and Robert Boardman in New York *Herald Tribune*

THE LATE Alben Barkley invariably bridled all over again whenever he told the classic True Story of the Ungrateful Constituent: "He's a farmer down home," Alben would begin. "During the First World War, I got his allotment fixed and his government insurance. Then he was wounded in Belleau Wood and I went to see him in the hospital over in France. After the Armistice I wrote a personal letter to General Pershing to get him back home. I got him a loan for his farm. A couple of years later a big flood nearly washed his farm away—so I got him a Disaster Loan and a job for his wife as postmistress.

"In 1938 when Happy Chandler ran against me for the Senate nomination, I heard this farmer was 'agin' me. I went around to see him and asked him, 'Is it true that you're not going to vote for me?' He just nodded."

Choking with rage, Barkley ticked off all the favors he'd performed for his constituent, ending, "Surely you must remember all these things I've done for you?"

"Yeah," admitted the farmer grudgingly, "but what in hell have you done for me *lately?*" —Peggy McEvoy

THEY WERE talking about political differences between husbands and wives. A young bride, who was a Democrat, was asked how she and her Republican husband handled the problem.

"Oh, it hasn't been any problem," she said. "We've been too busy launching a third party." —Dean O. Mumy

A DELEGATION from Kansas calling upon Theodore Roosevelt at Oyster Bay was met by the President with coat and collar off. "Ah, gentlemen," he said, mopping his brow, "I'm delighted to see you, but I'm very busy putting in my hay just now. Come down to the barn and we'll talk things over while I work." When they reached the barn there was no hay waiting to be thrown into the mow. "James!" shouted the President to his hired man in the loft. "Where's that hay?"

"I'm sorry, sir," admitted James, "but I just ain't had time to throw it back since you forked it up for yesterday's delegation." —*The Christian Science Monitor*

A STANCH old Republican invariably managed to show up at all the Democratic rallies. A friend suggested that perhaps he was thinking of swapping sides. The die-hard snorted indignantly. "Change parties? Never!" he snapped. "I just go to their meetings so's to keep my disgust fresh." —Senator Leverett Saltonstall in *Quote*

Pride and Prejudice

A CHICAGO mother has raised her six sons to be stanch "straight ticket" Democrats. So when one lad announced that he might vote Republican his mother was most upset. "Mom," the son counterattacked, "if the Good Lord Himself were running on the Republican ticket I don't think you'd vote for Him!"

"Of course I wouldn't," she replied quickly. "He'd have no business to change now." —Albert T. White, Jr.

LIKE MANY another exclusive men's store, Brooks Brothers long ago surrendered to an invasion by women. I discovered, however, that within its walls there is still a bastion untouched. For some time I had been eying the Scottish kilts displayed in their window and I finally decided to buy one.

"I'd like to order a kilt," I told the dignified clerk in charge of the department.

"Certainly, madam," he replied. "Have the gentleman come in and our tailor will take his measurements."

"It's not for a gentleman. It's for me," I explained.

The clerk shook his head. "I'm sorry," he said. "We don't sell kilts to ladies."

"That's perfectly ridiculous," I said crossly. "After all, Queen Elizabeth has one."

"Perhaps, madam," he replied, "but she did not purchase it at Brooks Brothers." —Nardi Reeder Campion

SIGN IN a California market: "ORANGES—GIANT, MEDIUM, SMALL, Florida."

TWO WELL-DRESSED women were chatting by the swimming pool at the Huntington-Sheraton Hotel in Pasadena. One of them, obviously showing the other around, pointed out that it wasn't necessary to be a guest at the hotel to use the pool—anyone could go in for a small fee. "But how do they keep out the riffraff?" the visitor asked.

"My dear," the woman answered, "in California the riffraff have their own pools." —Everett B. Clary

OLD CAPTAIN Mel Grant's schooner had sunk off the Maine coast, and friends were helping him beach it for repair.

"Too bad she had to sink, Cap'n," remarked one of them.

"She didn't sink," the old sea dog rejoined tartly. "She just didn't rise up with the tide." —C. B.

THE DEEP-SEATED rivalry between California's two largest cities crops out in unexpected places. One day in Los Angeles I wanted to buy a small pocket compass, but neither a department store nor a five-and-dime had one. I went into a stationer's and explained my difficulty.

"I doubt whether you'll find one in Los Angeles," said the clerk. "What use could we have down here for a little gadget that doesn't do anything but point to San Francisco?" —Vera Roden

City Scapes

Los Angeles: Six suburbs in search of a city.
—Quoted by Leo Rosten in *Look*

Hollywood: A place where you live happily and get married forever afterward.
—Nancy Craig, quoted by Hy Gardner in New York *Herald Tribune*

Las Vegas: The land of the spree and the home of the knave. —Quoted by K. M. Coggeshall

Reno: Largest inland seaport in America with the tied running in and the untied running out. —John O. Moseley

Barbed Wires

AFTER SOME years of marriage the wife of a successful writer divorced him. Writers were too temperamental and unpredictable, she complained, and she no longer could put up with this one's quirks and peccadilloes. What did she do next, however, but fall in love with *another* famous author.

The ex-husband read of the wedding and sent his former bride this cable: "Heartiest congratulations and best wishes. (Signed) Frying Pan." —Bennett Cerf in *This Week Magazine*

WHEN HIS son was born humorist Bugs Baer sent this telegram to his wife: "I hear you had a boy in your room last night." —Charles Samuels in *True*

AFTER A week of minor marital discord over money matters, my friend and his wife, who are the parents of two small boys, David, age seven, and Lewis, age five, decided to separate. His wife moved to a hotel and took Lewis with her.

No word passed between the couple for ten days. The deadlock was broken, hilariously, when the wife received this telegram: "Will trade David for Lewis and throw in $500." —R. Stevenson

PUBLISHER Richard Simon decided to include a half dozen adhesives in a juvenile called *Dr. Dan the Bandage Man,* and wired to a friend at the Johnson & Johnson Co., "Please ship two million Band-Aids immediately."

Back came a telegram reading, "Band-Aids on the way. What the hell happened to you?" —Bennett Cerf, *Good for a Laugh* (Hanover)

A CRUSTY old newspaperman who has worked all over the world has one pet hate. It is editors who don't bother to check handy reference sources but instead wire last-minute queries to far-flung reporters. Some years ago he was covering a Florida speedboat race in which Gar Wood was participating. Our boy had already filed his story, but late at night he got a telegram from his editor that read: "How old Gar Wood?"

The reporter wired back: "Old Gar Wood fine. How you?" —"Almanac" in Minneapolis *Tribune*

Classified Classics

AD IN Cape Cod guidebook: "Specially treated logs. Will burn for at least six hours at your beach party. If they go out after that, it's time you went home yourself."
—Boston *Daily Traveler*

IN A Seattle, Wash., paper: "Position wanted about December 1; at present employed at City Hall, but will work if I have to."
—*Successful Farming*

AN ADVERTISEMENT in the St. Louis *Post-Dispatch* for a "Tournament of Thrills," promising a bullfight exhibition with vicious fighting bulls from Mexico, had this footnote: "Due to a Humane Society ruling, no bulls will be allowed in exhibition. A demonstration of capework only will be presented. As an added stunt two cars will crash head-on at 60 m.p.h. while drivers remain at wheel."

FOR-SALE ad in the Sacramento *Bee:* "Pink Diamond about ¼ K, $150. Microscope, $30."

FROM THE New York *Times:* "Author-psychologist wants secretary, college graduate who has majored in any subject but psychology."

AD IN THE Walla Walla, Wash., *Union-Bulletin:* "ATTRACTIVE, ethical, employed brunette widow wishes single, cleancut, reliable outdoor type escort 40-50. Mutual expense. Object: Companionship, not marriage. Write Box 697."

Three days later this "personal" appeared in the same column: "MEN not meeting Box 697's qualifications, please write Box 702. 'Two Desperate Secretaries.' "

REAL-ESTATE ad in program of The Barn Playhouse, New London, N. H.: "For Sale. Business site in large city. Busy intersection with traffic light out of order. Just the right spot for doctor or lawyer."

FROM THE San Diego *Evening Tribune:* "Lost or Strayed: Tan leather wallet . . . contained pictures, personal papers and $350 currency. Finder may keep the pictures, the personal papers and the wallet, but I have a sentimental attachment to the money."

CLASSIFIED ad in the Dallas *Times-Herald:* "My husband's $50 puppies for sale for a lot less. If he answers, hang up." —AP

No Escape

Excerpt from "How to Protect Yourself Against Women"

Charles W. Morton

CONSIDER the Narrow-Escape Technique: The husband has vowed never again to set foot in the house of George and Ethel Grudge, because he detests them.

The husband is in his office. He has just finished an exhausting phone call with the bank about the company's needing a bigger loan. His wife telephones: "Oh, Jack, I'm *so* glad to find you. I've been *simply terrified* that you'd be out to lunch. The most *awful* thing has happened. *I don't know what to do.*"

"What is it? What's wrong?"

"Well, I took the children and got out the car and started off to the Wilsons'—you know they asked the children over to play—"

"Yes, yes. Yes, yes."

"Well, I was on my way down Elm Street—you know that bad corner by Hayworths' place—when *fortunately* I remembered I hadn't brought along the books I was going to give to Henrietta" —harrowing pause—"so I had to go back to the house, *and when I got there . . .*"

By this time the husband has imagined in fast succession (a) terrible accident to wife; (b) terrible accident to children; (c) total destruction of house by fire. He is responding normally. "Yes-yes-yes. *What is it?*"

"Well, while I was in the house the phone rang, and it was that awful Ethel Grudge, and-she-asked-us-for-dinner-tomorrow-night-and-I-didn't-have-the-energy-to-say-no-and-I-said-we'd-come-and-I-know-you-won't"—wail—"What shall I do?"

"Don't worry about it. I'll do whatever you want—g'by." H-m-m, his subconscious tells him as he puts down the phone, not so bad as it sounded for a while.

But as the husband mounts the Grudges' steps the next evening he is tormented with self-doubt. What madness brought him here again? Has he lost his mind?

Any astute observer could enlighten the husband: he has gone to the Grudges' not because he is a mental defective but in perfectly natural response to the Narrow-Escape Technique. He never had a chance.

Terse Verse

Oh wad some power the giftie gie
us
To see some people before they
see us. —Ethel Watts Mumford in
Family Circle

Girls on summer holiday,
'Ware the handsome wolves of
prey:
Be discreet, and only mingle
With the obviously single;
Men are a deceptive lot:
Summer bachelors—some are not.
—Norman Jaffray in
New York *Times Magazine*

A pair can live—
And often do,
On what it costs
For one to woo.
—D. O. Flynn in *Capper's Farmer*

The Perfect Husband

He tells you when you've got on
too much lipstick,
And helps you with your girdle
When your hips stick.
—Ogden Nash, *Versus* (Little, Brown)

Sometimes with secret pride I sigh
To think how tolerant am I;
Then wonder which is really mine:
Tolerance or a rubber spine?
—Ogden Nash in
The Saturday Evening Post

Broccoli
While not exoccoli,
Is within an inach
Of being spinach.
—Rod Maclean in *Collier's*

Bather, bather, burning bright,
Seeking for new sides to fry on,
How you're gonna wish tonight
You had saved a side to lie on!
—Georgie Starbuck Galbraith
in *The Saturday Evening Post*

Experience is a fine teacher, it's
true,
But here's what makes me burn:
Experience is always teaching me
Things I'd rather not learn!
—Ethel M. Wegert in
The Saturday Evening Post

The Bedchamber Mystery

Condensed from Cosmopolitan

C. S. Forester

NOW THAT more than a century has passed, one of the scandals in my family can be safely revealed.

It is doubtful if, in 1843, the Forester sisters—Eulalie, Emily and Eunice—ever foresaw a world in which their story could be told blatantly in public print. At that time it could only be hinted at in feminine drawing rooms; but it was whispered about enough to reach the ears of my grandfather, who told it to me.

Miss Eulalie, Miss Emily and Miss Eunice Forester were maiden ladies of a certain age. They lived a modestly retired life; they went to church, visited those of the sick whom it was proper for maiden ladies to visit, read the more colorless current novels and sometimes entertained other ladies at tea.

And once a week they entertained a man.

Old Dr. Acheson was a widower and a keen whist player. For years now the ladies had looked forward eagerly to their weekly evening of cards—all the ritual of setting out the green table, the two hours of silent play and the final few minutes of conversation as Dr. Acheson drank a glass of Madeira before bidding them good night.

For 13 years they had played their weekly game before the terrible thing happened. To this day we do not know whether it happened to Eulalie, Emily or Eunice.

Each had retired to her room and had progressed far toward the final stage of getting into bed. They were not dried-up old spinsters, but women of substance, with buxom contours. It was this weight which was the undoing of one of them, Eulalie, Emily or Eunice.

Suddenly, through the quiet house sounded the crash of china and a cry of pain. Two of the sisters hurried to the bedroom of the third—her identity is uncertain—to find her bleeding profusely from severe cuts in the lower part of the back. The jagged china fragments had inflicted severe wounds, unfortunately just in those spots where the injured sister could not attend to them herself. Under the urgings of the other two, she fought down her modesty sufficiently to let them attempt to deal with the wounds, but the blood of the Foresters streamed from the figure lying face downward on the bed in terrifying quantity.

"We shall have to send for the doctor," said one of the ministering sisters. It was a shocking thing to contemplate.

"Oh, but we cannot!" said the second sister. "Think of the disgrace! We might even have to explain to him how it happened!"

"But she's bleeding to death," the first sister protested.

"I'd rather die!" said the injured one, joining the conversation. Then a fresh appalling thought struck her. "I could never face him again. And what would happen to our whist?"

That was a new aspect of the case, and it was enough to make them blench. But they were of stern stuff.

We do not know which one thought of a way out of the difficulty, and we shall never know. We do know that it was Miss Eulalie, as befitted her rank as eldest sister, who called to Deborah, the maid, to fetch Dr. Acheson. But that does not mean that it was not Miss Eulalie who was injured.

Deborah conducted Dr. Acheson to Miss Eunice's bedroom, but that, of course, is no indication that it was Miss Eunice who was in there. Dr. Acheson had no means of knowing; all he saw was a recumbent form covered by a sheet. In the center of the sheet a round hole a foot in diameter had been cut, exposing the seat of the injury.

Dr. Acheson needed no explanations. He sewed up the worst of the cuts and attended to the minor ones.

Finally he straightened up. "I shall have to take those stitches out," he explained to the silent figure, which had borne the stitching without a murmur. "I shall come next Wednesday."

Until Wednesday the three Misses Forester kept to their rooms. Then Deborah conducted Dr. Acheson once more to the same bedroom. There was the recumbent form; there was the sheet with the hole in it. Dr. Acheson took out the stitches. "It has healed nicely," he said. "I don't think any further attention from me will be necessary."

The figure under the sheet said nothing. Dr. Acheson gave some concluding advice and went his way. Later, he was glad to receive a note penned in Miss Eulalie's hand:

Dear Dr. Acheson,

We will all be delighted if you will come to whist this week as usual.

When Dr. Acheson arrived he found a slight but subtle change in the furnishings of the drawing room. The stiff high-backed chairs on which the three Misses Forester sat bore, each of them, a comfortable cushion upon the seat.

There was no knowing which of the sisters needed a cushion.

Whodunits

AS I ENTERED the police station one evening to pay a parking fine I noticed that an old lady just ahead of me was trembling all over. I paid my $3 and was about to leave when I saw the lady sitting on a bench in the corner absorbed in a book. "What's the trouble?" I asked. "Is there anything I can do?"

"No, thank you," she replied sedately. "You see, I was at home all alone reading this mystery, and I got so scared that I came down here to finish it under police protection." —Wayne Gray

A PROSPECTIVE guest from Erie, Pa., wrote the manager of New York's Hotel Taft: "Dear Sir, I regret to inform you that due to an untimely murder in our family, I must cancel our reservations." —Hy Gardner in New York *Herald Tribune*

THE PUBLISHERS of Mary Roberts Rinehart's books asked her to check her first three mystery novels, written some 50 years ago, for reissue. Mrs. Rinehart, who never rereads her books once they're published, was reading one of these early novels when her publisher stopped in to discuss them. "I'm having the most wonderful time," she said. "I'm reading *The Man in Lower Ten,* and I can't figure out who committed the murder!"

—Stanley M. Rinehart, Jr., in *Parade*

AFTER A visit to dancing school, one mother advised her daughter that she should not just dance silently like a totem pole; talking to her partner was also a part of the social picture.

On a later visit the mother saw that each time the music started the same little boy tore across the floor, bowed to her daughter and swept her away to the music. Later the mother asked about this boy. "Oh, him!" the daughter explained. "I'm telling him a continued murder mystery." —Des Moines *Tribune*

ALFRED HITCHCOCK, director of movie mystery thrillers, stepped into a New York hotel elevator with a friend and immediately began talking as though continuing a conversation:

"So I turned on the light, and there was this girl in the middle of the floor. Her throat was slit and there was a great puddle of blood. Beside the body was a knife. I was in a spot. If I called the police, there'd be a nasty row, and if I didn't somebody would find me there. So I took out my handkerchief and carefully . . . "

At this point the elevator stopped at Hitchcock's floor and he quietly stepped off with his companion, leaving everybody in the car goggle-eyed. —Chicago *Tribune*

FINNISH CONDUCTOR Boris Sirpo and his wife, soon after arriving in America, moved into a house that was supposed to be haunted. Sure enough, they were awakened the first night by ghostly sounds. Mrs. Sirpo suggested that Boris investigate. "No, my love," he said. "You go. Your English is better." —*Time*

A QUESTION that set Agriculture Department employes wondering came from a woman who wrote: "Could you possibly send me a booklet explaining the use of different poisons for vegetables in the garden? I have lost my husband and have a lot of poisons on hand." —Patricia Wiggins, UP

RAIN LASHED the windows of the old castle and the wind howled mournfully as the timid guest was escorted to his room under the castle eaves. "Has anything unusual ever happened in this room?" he asked the sinister-looking butler.

"Not for 40 years."

Heaving a sigh of relief, the guest asked, "What happened then?"

The butler's eyes glittered ominously as he hissed, "A man who stayed here all night showed up in the morning."

—Irving Hoffman in *The Hollywood Reporter*

A BUSINESSMAN in love with a night-club entertainer employed a detective agency to check up on her. He received the following report: "The young lady has an excellent reputation. Her past is without a blemish. She has many friends of good social standing. The only scandal associated with her is that she has often been seen lately with a businessman of questionable character."

—*Phoenix Flame*

They Asked for It

MY FRATERNITY brothers and I spent a good deal of time ogling the girls in the sorority house next door. So one night when a girl started to get ready for bed without pulling the blind, the news traveled through our house like wildfire. She was particularly deliberate in all her motions. Then just as she reached the critical point, the side of our frat house was completely covered with floodlights which the other girls had placed in their darkened rooms. The spotlights revealed fully two thirds of our membership squeezed into all available space on a fire escape, and the rest hanging out of the windows. —Dean Dunnicliff

DRIVING ALONG a California highway, my husband and I slowed down when we approached a MEN AT WORK sign. Just then a car dashed by us. A worker painting a white line down the center of the road ahead looked up just in time to see the car bearing down on him. Jumping out of the way, he held his brush out stiffly in front of him and painted a wide stripe the full length of the car.

—Mrs. J. H. F.

AN EXECUTIVE of a large company maintains on his farm in the Brandywine Valley a purebred dairy herd whose milk is sold locally at a few cents over the regular price. His cows have the latest word in living quarters, are given vitamin-enriched feed, and when the milk is periodically examined the bacteria count is always low and the butter-fat content high. A lady who lives nearby visited the farm one day and after admiring everything said to the owner, "I have only one complaint: I don't like having to pay a special price for my milk. As a neighbor, I feel I ought to receive it at cost."

"Why, I'll be glad to arrange that," said the gentleman-farmer.

At the end of the month the lady got her bill: each quart of milk cost 75 cents.

—Hanna N. Barrows

JOHN D. ROCKEFELLER, JR., now in his 80's, still insists upon the "Jr." after his name. When despite his protest the editors of the Social Register dropped the "Jr." from his listing, he sent them a subscription check signed exactly as he was listed. The check bounced.

—Leonard Lyons

ARTHUR SCHNABEL, the late pianist, took a firm stand against playing encores after a concert appearance. But the stubborn applause of one Cleveland audience recalled him time after time. Finally Schnabel surrendered. He seated himself at the keyboard —and played a sonata that lasted 45 minutes.

—Will Leonard in Chicago *Tribune*

INEZ ROBB writes: It is a mystery to me why so many women are hollering for the equal-rights amendment. They don't seem to understand that, if it passes, some men are just mean enough to enforce it. I learned about it the hard way during the 1944 Democratic National Convention in Chicago. About 2 a.m. I was with a bunch of the boys—including Paul Gallico and Jesse Jones—in the ballroom of the Blackstone. There was a little desultory talk about an equal-rights proposal and, just as the waiter arrived with the check, I opened my big mouth and said, "But what *is* equal rights?"

Mr. Gallico picked the check right out of the air, handed it to me and said, "This is it, honey!" And they let me pay it! —INS

THE OWNER of a $10,000 limousine, pulling up at a light beside a small car driven by a friend, couldn't resist the chance to heckle. "Gosh sakes, man," he said, "what is that dreadful rattling sound in your car?"

"Oh, that?" said the small-car driver. "That's just $9000 jingling around in my pocket!" —Bob Barnes, quoted in Toledo *Blade*

LORD PONSONBY, a 19th-century English diplomat, was famed for his imperturbable manners, tact and quick wit. Once when the Sultan of Turkey felt that the diplomatic corps in which Ponsonby served did not show sufficient humility when entering the royal presence, he had a very low door built so that the diplomats would have to crawl in. But Lord Ponsonby, confronted with the new door, was up to the obstacle. He simply turned and crawled through the door backward—presenting a splendid expanse of white satin breeches to the waiting Sultan. —*Time*

SENATOR Theodore F. Green of Rhode Island, the oldest member ever to serve in the Senate, says that one of his valuable lessons came after his valedictory address at college. A woman complimented him on the speech, and Green said modestly, "Oh, madam, you couldn't mean that. The talk really wasn't that good."

"Of course I didn't mean it," she retorted. "Your speech wasn't good at all. You must learn when you receive a compliment to accept it in the spirit in which it was given." —Leonard Lyons

Complimentary Angles

WE WERE all dejected to learn that the most attractive secretary in our office was leaving. Far from being jealous of her good looks and style, the other girls often sought her advice on their own clothes problems. And needless to say, the men in the company were her devoted slaves.

As she was making the rounds saying good-by, one of the junior executives said firmly, "We're all striking for a raise when you go."

"But," she asked, puzzled, "what's my going got to do with your salary?"

"Well," he explained, "we've always considered you one of our fringe benefits." —Grace K. Reinhardt

WHILE THE doctor bandaged his hand, a tall, lanky farmer talked about how wonderful his bride was. The doctor asked him why he hadn't brought his new wife along to be introduced. "Why, Doc," he said earnestly, "you'd 'a been dissatisfied for life."

—Kay Lawson

IT WAS A beautiful evening and Aunt Louisa, looking very lovely in her long white dress and little fur cape, her white hair piled high, strolled outside to wait for the taxi she had called to take her to the concert. A noisy jalopy rattled by, full of students from the nearby college. Then a piercing wolf whistle split the air and one of the boys leaned out. "Wish we were 40 years older, ma'am!" he called. —Dorothy B. Layman

THE MAYOR of Cumberland, Md., welcoming a group of men from Pittsburgh: "I shall always remember Pittsburgh; I spent the first ten years of my honeymoon there." —J. L. Richards

A SMALL BOY invaded the lingerie section of a big California department store and shyly presented his problem to a woman clerk. "I want to buy my mom a present of a slip," he said, "but I don't know what size she wears."

"Is she tall or short, fat or skinny?" asked the clerk.

"She's just perfect," beamed the small boy. So the clerk wrapped up a size 34 for him.

Two days later Mom came to the store herself—and changed it for a 52. —Bennett Cerf in *The Saturday Review*

Growing Pains

A GIRL about 12 years old was walking back and forth in front of a counter in the lingerie department of a large Manhattan store, evidently trying to reach some sort of decision. Finally a salesgirl asked if she could help.

The girl blushed, then pointed to the brassiered mannequin on the counter and blurted, "Do you have anything like that for beginners?" —Gary Belkin in *True*

SMALL BOY to playmate as pretty little girl passes by: "Boy! If I ever stop hating girls, she's the one I'll stop hating first!"
—George Clark cartoon, Chicago Tribune-New York News Syndicate

A TEEN-AGER sent his girl her first orchid with this note: "With all of my love and most of my allowance."
—Mrs. Phil Roos in *Dixie Roto Magazine*

LIKE so many little girls of the machine age, Barbara was crazy over horses. Her heroes were gallant steeds out of books. Her dolls were jockeys. Her blocks built stables. Her world trotted past on a diet of oats.

But Barbara could not always stay young. As she turned nine she was being polite and kind beyond any consequence of parental training. She said, "Thank you," ever so sincerely to elevator operators. She held doors open for strangers. She was maturely courteous to saleswomen.

At last the explanation emerged. "Mother," Barbara confided, "I believe that people have feelings just the way horses do."

—Franklin Courtney Ellis

ONE TEEN-AGER to another: "He hasn't actually kissed me yet, but he steamed my glasses a couple of times."

—Paris cartoon in *The Saturday Evening Post*

IN HOLLYWOOD about half past ten one evening Michael Arlen called his wife in New York, only to be told by a strange masculine voice that Mrs. Arlen was in bed. Telling me the story he said, "I broke into the damnedest cold sweat. I asked to speak to her just the same, and this man said, 'I'm afraid you can't. I don't like to waken her.' 'But look here,' I shouted, 'I'm her husband! Who are you?' At that there was an alarmed squeak at the other end of the wire. 'Why, Daddy, don't you know me?' "

It was Arlen, Jr., and his voice was changing.

—Ilka Chase, *Free Admission* (Doubleday)

MY TEEN-AGE daughter was trying to decide what to give her best friend for a birthday present. "Maybe I'll get a bracelet," she told me, "but it will have to be silver. Beth wears only silver jewelry now, because it goes with her braces." —Mrs. N. L. Rothman

BEFORE chauffeuring my son on his first date I explained that he must help the girl on with her wraps, take her arm when walking, open the car door and see that she got in first. The big night arrived and my son's manners were above reproach. He held the girl's coat for her, took her arm when they came down the front steps and, with a fine courtly gesture, flung open the back door of the car. I was just congratulating myself on the success of my etiquette lesson when I heard the car door slam and my son tumbled into the front seat. "What on earth are you doing up here?" I asked under my breath.

"Well, gee whiz, Mom," he said, "you didn't tell me I'd have to sit with her, too!" —Sylvia Cohen

I ONCE asked my 12-year-old daughter how she could be demolishing a large plate of cookies when we had just finished dinner. "Eating," she replied quietly, "makes me hungry."

—Dick Ashbaugh in *This Week Magazine*

ONE TEEN-AGER to another: "I don't see how you can call it true love if your family approves of him."

—John Cook cartoon in *Ladies' Home Journal*

Betty MacDonald on Adolescents

THE TRICKY thing to remember about adolescents is that they are going to be miserable no matter what they are doing, but they would rather be miserable doing the things *they* choose. This is all so easy for me to understand now that Anne and Joan are 24 and 25, charming, intelligent, companionable, married. It was harder to remember when they were 14 and 15, and bolted themselves in the bathroom for hours at a stretch and wore lipstick to bed.

Frankly I do not know any answer to adolescence. About the only thing to do is to try to hang on to your sanity and pray. While you are hanging on I will reach down into the black pit of my experience and give you a few things to think about:

1. Adolescents do not hate their parents. They merely feel contempt, occasionally coated with condescending pity for them. They all refer to their father as "oh him" and their mother as "she": *"She* won't let me go, naturally." "Who was that on the phone? *Oh him."*

2. All adolescents "go steady"—daughters with boys who appear weak-chinned and untrustworthy; sons with girls

DURING THE preliminary inspection at a Boy Scout camp near Hazleton, Pa., the director found a large umbrella hidden in the bedroll of a tiny scout. Obviously not one of the items of equipment listed, the director asked the lad to explain. The tenderfoot did so neatly by countering with this question: "Sir, did you ever have a mother?"

—Joe Falatko

WIFE TO husband about teen-age daughter: "Her new boy friend is coming to dinner Sunday, dear . . . she wants us to paint the house, redecorate the living room and buy a new car."

—Lichty cartoon, Chicago Sun-Times Syndicate

A PUBLISHER friend of mine had his troubles with a ten-year-old daughter who was so obsessed with clothes she could think of

who appear hard-eyed and brazen. No parent gets anywhere combating these romances. How can anyone as stupid as "oh him" or "she" evaluate a big wheel like Billy—who, it "just so happens is on the football team and president of SqueeGees, *the* high-school fraternity?"

3. All adolescents telephone. This is part of the cohesive quality that makes them all eat in the same beanery, walk in bunches, keep in constant touch. (You will not solve anything by having two telephones. "Wow, *two* phones!" Anne and Joan's friends said, and kept them both busy.)

4. All adolescents intend to have the family car all of the time. To accomplish this they resort to the gentle nag or water-dripping-on-stone method, the smooth lie or the cold tearful silence.

5. Adolescents are not careful of their own possessions, but are absolutely reckless with anything belonging to their parents.

6. All adolescent girls would prefer to live in a bathroom.

7. All adolescent boys would prefer to live in a car.

—Excerpt from *Onions in the Stew*, © 1954, 1955 by Betty MacDonald and published by J. B. Lippincott Co.

little else. One day her mother decided the time had come to tell her about the bees and the flowers. The daughter listened attentively, and finally her mother said, "Well, that's it. Any questions?"

"Just one thing isn't clear, Mother. What does a girl wear for things like that?"
—Bennett Cerf in *This Week Magazine*

Clothes Line

SWEET YOUNG thing to clerk in bathing-suit department: "I want something that will look all right to my mother until I put it on at the beach."
—John Dempsey cartoon in *Collier's*

"I DON'T KNOW the style or color of shoes, but I want low heels," the tall blonde told the clerk.

"To wear with what?"

"A short, fat, elderly executive."
—Jennie Anderson in Louisville *Courier-Journal Magazine*

HOST INTRODUCING man to woman wearing a strapless gown: "This is Professor Schmertz, authority on structural engineering. He wants to ask you something."
—Ben Roth cartoon in *The Saturday Evening Post*

Let us not bandy hilarious
cracks
Concerning milady dressed in
slacks.
For to make the world it takes
all sorts
As proof, I give you milord in
shorts!
—Georgie Starbuck Galbraith in *The Saturday Evening Post*

OVERHEARD: "I'm in the girdle-and-brassiere business—what we on the inside call the Meat Packing Industry."
—*The American Freeman*

CLERK TO wife of man who is trying on suit: "How does he like it?"
—Lyons cartoon in *The Saturday Evening Post*

HOST TO guest as wife shows off new dress: "Oh, it's just something Edith made out of an old 50-dollar bill."
—Brad Anderson cartoon in *The Saturday Evening Post*

SHE HAS A passion for hats, none of which return her affection.
—Storm Jameson, *The Intruder* (Macmillan)

WOMAN trying on fur coat to salesgirl: "I wish it were called something besides broadtail. My husband fancies himself a comedian." —Ketcham cartoon in *True*

WIFE TO husband picking out tie to go with loud sports jacket: "Well, *I'll* tell you something that won't go with that jacket—*me!*"
—Brad Anderson cartoon in *Ladies' Home Journal*

LYNN BARI, describing a glamour girl's gown at a Hollywood party: "It was one of those black numbers that pick up everything —including men."
—Erskine Johnson in *Photoplay*

JAZZ TRUMPETER Bobby Hackett on why he doesn't believe women dress to please their husbands: If they did, they'd wear last year's clothes.
—Irv Kupcinet, quoted in *Look*

Strip Tease

Condensed from The Quill

Richard L. Neuberger

I BELIEVE it was Mark Twain who said, "The average American would rather see Lillian Russell naked than General Grant in full uniform." A substantial number of U. S. newspaper and magazine editors seem to have become aware of this great truth. I learned it when an editor advised me that a photographer was en route to Oregon to illustrate a piece I had written.

"It would be very helpful," he said, "if you could put our photographer in touch with a pretty girl with attractive legs who might appear in one of the pictures."

Hastily I thumbed through a carbon of my manuscript. Had I forgotten some exotic reference? Perhaps, in a moment of fantasy, I had departed from the subject at hand to make mention of a wood nymph or bathing beauty. But, alas, my copy was as humdrum as usual. Just power dams, lumberjacks, Chinook salmon, etc. Where, then, did the luscious damsel fit?

The photographer arrived and explained: "She doesn't have to work right in with the copy exactly —only just approximately."

"How do you mean, approximately?"

"Oh," said the photographer, "your article is about the Pacific Northwest. This girl lives in the

The Quill (February, '52), published by Sigma Delta Chi, 35 E. Wacker Drive, Chicago 1, Ill.

Pacific Northwest. See?" And so the pattern was set.

For instance, I wrote a piece about Oregon's anachronistic state constitution—four times the length of the U.S. Constitution. Where did a modern Lillian Russell fit into the picture?

Well, after all, Oregon has art schools and art schools have models. Why shouldn't a model, resting between poses, be studying a copy of Oregon's anachronistic state constitution? And if she became so engrossed that she forgot to drape her creamy shoulders and bosom—well, was there anything in the anachronistic state constitution outlawing that?

I write a good deal about Alaska, and I have learned the type of picture which illustrates appropriately any Alaskan scene. In the dead of winter, with the thermometer standing at 65° below zero and only sled dogs and polar bears astir, a photo of a brave young woman in a bathing suit beside a snowdrift will demonstrate the Spartan quality of the females of America—a grim warning to the Iron Curtain countries not to underestimate the hardihood of the 77 million American females.

A few skeptics think that some periodicals occasionally stretch a point to include a photograph of a skimpily clad girl. I challenge this. If a girl has won the national skiing championship, she obviously must be photographed in a bathing suit to reveal the legs which carried her to this glorious victory.

I'll admit, though, that we sometimes encounter difficulties—like the time I wrote a piece about cougar hunting. The photographer and I scratched our heads over that one. After all, you can't go cougar hunting in a bathing suit, what with brambles on the trail and the sharpness of the rimrock, and perhaps even the talons of the 250-pound kitty.

Yet finally the hunt was over, and the dreaded cat run to earth and skinned. It was a nice soft pelt, measuring ten feet from whiskers to tip of twitching tail. Why shouldn't someone wrap up in front of the fire in that velvety hide? Someone of the opposite sex? And did you ever hear of anyone needing even a bathing suit when she was all nicely enveloped in a cougar pelt?

Well, not *completely* enveloped!

My Career in Sports

Condensed from Journal of Lifetime Living

H. Allen Smith

In my boyhood people talked a lot about their dreams, and the weirder their narratives the more laughter they provoked. Then came Freud and a long period of self-conscious silence on the subject. During all those years I dreamed some dandies, but I kept my mouth shut about them. Nobody was going to find out about me *that* way.

For some reason, though, people are once again telling what happened in their sleep last night, and nothing is said about anxieties and emotional conflicts and suppressed wantonness. I'm glad the change has come, for the strain of keeping my dreams to myself has been nerve-racking. Now I can unload some of my best ones.

Mostly they're concerned with my athletic exploits. I am five feet nine and weigh 150, but remember it's us little guys who furnish the real thrills in sports. I have scored more touchdowns against Notre Dame than all the people who ever played for Army. I play halfback with Defiance College—

Journal of Lifetime Living (August, '57), © 1957 by Lifetime Living, Inc., 1625 Bay Rd., Miami Beach, Fla.

the team I used to watch in action when I was a child—and we have never lost to the Irish, largely owing to my brilliant running and passing.

In recent years, since I passed the age of 45, I have had to let up a little, and have become a place kicker. One night recently I was sent onto the field to try a long placement, and when the ball came back from center, it hit my thumbs and fell to the ground. A chorus of groans arose from the Defiance stands—Flawless Smith had fumbled.

Notre Dame players were swarming toward me. I snatched up the ball, eluded two tacklers, swished my hips gracefully, straight-armed a 280-pound guard and then raced like an antelope through the confusion, running 45 yards to score the winning touchdown.

I have pitched many a major-league ball game. My contract always specified that I was not to be bothered with signals, even from my catcher. In one game I deliberately walked three men to get at Mantle, and my manager, in the dugout, remarked nervously, "Well, I s'pose he knows what he's doin'." I did.

Usually, however, I'm celebrated for my hitting. I'm not a long-ball hitter; I have the knack of whacking them just over the heads of the infielders. Sometimes they try a special Smith Shift, moving the infielders out and the outfielders in so that they are all congregated where my hits usually fall. When they do that I smile and rap one on the ground just out of reach of the pitcher—plenty good for a single, and there's always a man on third. I have never been at bat without a man on third and two out.

Once I won the Kentucky Derby. The owners of a horse named Gallant Rabbit called me in secretly after announcing that Arcaro would be their rider. Nobody knew I would be up on Gallant Rabbit until the horses came on the track. Thirty thousand gasps arose from the immense throng. "Who is it?" they cried. "Who's that on th' Rabbit?" Then a sports writer recognized me and cried, "My God, it's Smith! Have the Wheedlers took leave of their senses?"

Little did he know! I let the Rabbit lay back in 17th place, swung wide at the head of the stretch and then began talking to him, using that marvelously resonant voice of mine, coaxing him on. We nipped the favorite at the wire. Paid $76.20 for a $2 ticket, and while I was pleased with my performance, my thighs ached something awful for I had never ridden a horse before.

I well remember the night I broke the four-minute mile, long before Roger Bannister. It was in the Garden and I was a late entry, having got into the thing on a dare flung at me by Rita Hayworth. The crowd tittered when I came on the track for my warmup. I suppose I did look awkward, being pigeon-toed, but that night I had Mohawk Indian blood in me and it is well known that the fleet-footed Mohawks were pigeon-toed.

In the early stages of the race there was nothing in my performance to suggest what was coming. I made my move, or kick, in the last quarter mile and was actually sprinting in the final lap, passing everything in sight. At the finish line, with other runners flailing their arms and collapsing all around me, I calmly took a deep breath, lit a cigarette and smiled disdainfully toward the box where Miss Hayworth was sitting.

In golf my specialty is putting. I drive accurately but my tee shots are not as long as those of the other stars, such as Hogan and Snead and Middlecoff. Yet I'm always on the green in two or three and I've never been known to miss a putt once I'm up there. I made an "impossible" shot one night to win the Masters Tournament at Augusta. It was one of the great moments of my nighttime sporting career. My ball lay close to the 18th green, but squarely between the ball and the cup stood an oak tree 150 feet high.

A hush fell over the gallery as I walked onto the green to examine the situation. Then I walked back and spoke to my caddie, Joan Crawford. "My sizzerfiss, please," I said. She handed me my sizzerfiss—a club I designed for shooting straight up in the air. I addressed the ball, glanced up at the top of the tree and swung. The ball soared over the topmost branches, came down a foot and a half on the far side of the hole, then hopped backward into the cup. President Eisenhower, who was in the gallery, applauded until his hands were raw.

What I consider my most thrilling exploit came as a consequence of an interesting wager. I was dining with Eleanor Holm in a small, intimate Manhattan restaurant when she said, "It's a shame that you've never gone in for aquatic sports."

"My dear," I said, "how would you like to see me dive off the George Washington Bridge, 250 feet above mean high water, with my shoes on?"

"Pshaw!" exclaimed Eleanor. "I'll bet you a month's alimony you can't do it."

I gave her my world-weary smile, summoned the waiter and

said in a soft, untroubled voice, "Please call a taxi."

At the bridge I mounted the rail. Eleanor, alarmed now, begged me to forget the whole thing. I pretended not to hear her and suddenly I leaped outward in a graceful arc and then shot down through the darkling crepuscular void. About 100 feet above the water I gave my body the secret Acapulco twist. It is a trick I perfected one evening at Acapulco when, to please Dolores Del Rio, I dove off the Quebrada cliffs at El Mirador with a small pig under each arm. The twist starts my body spinning like a bullet fired from a rifle and I continue spinning until I cleave the water.

That was a good one. There have been many other good ones. I want to emphasize the fact that in these adventures I am always sensible, always logical. Therefore I don't want any psychoanalysts examining these paragraphs and telling me that I need help.

Bedtime Stories

Insomnia is what a person has when he lies awake all night for an hour. —Paul H. Gilbert, General Features Corp.

A FRIEND of mine burst into my house one morning and stormed indignantly, "I'm so mad at Jim I don't know what to do!"

"Why?"

"Last night I dreamed that some blonde hussy was flirting with him, and he was purring like a kitten."

"Oh, Helen," I said, "it was only a dream."

"Well," she exploded, "if he acts like that in *my* dreams, what in the world do you suppose he does in his?" —Joyce J. Christy

DURING "Sharing Period" at school Johnny was telling about refurnishing their house. "We've been having arguments—most every day—about our new furniture, but I guess it's all settled now," he said. "Mommy got her way about the living room, but Daddy won on the bedroom deal."

"Yes?" said the teacher, encouragingly.

"Yes," replied Johnny. "Mommy wanted twin beds, but Daddy said that he commuted every day and he'd be darned if he was going to commute at night." —Mrs. S. Holley

LAWRENCE LAURENT, radio and television editor of the Washington *Post and Times Herald,* received a call from a woman who said breathlessly, "I've just got to know how 'Big Town' came out last night. It was one of the most exciting programs I've seen in a long time. But I didn't get to see the end." Laurent promised to check, then asked curiously, "Why did you miss the end of the program?"

"Well," she said, "I fell asleep."

A MAN who has his initials on his pajamas must be uncertain of himself. Surely you should know who you are by bedtime.
—Christopher Morley, *The Man Who Made Friends With Himself* (Doubleday)

IRVING BERLIN, an expert insomniac who claims he hasn't slept well for 32 years, was vacationing in Bermuda with columnist Irving Hoffman. One morning Hoffman, noticing that the composer looked even more finely drawn than usual, asked if he got any sleep at all. "Yes, I slept," Berlin said bitterly, "but I *dreamed* that I didn't." —Walter Ross in *Esquire*

I WAS DOZING in the lounge on a night flight from Atlanta to New York when a stunning girl came in carrying a pillow under her arm. She made herself comfortable by stretching out on two seats. Conscious that other passengers were staring at her, she smiled and said, "I've got to get some sleep—I have a busy day ahead of me in New York."

She pulled her skirt modestly down around her knees, adjusted her pillow and soon fell asleep. However, as she restlessly tossed and turned, her skirt kept going higher and higher. I squirmed nervously, wondering if I should wake her. Just then a young man got up, went out and returned with a blanket which he draped over our sleeping beauty. She awakened and turned a pair of questioning eyes upon him. "Begging your pardon, ma'am," he said, "I also have a busy day in New York tomorrow—I've got to get some sleep, too!" —Helene H. Beasley

"MY WIFE had a funny dream last night," confided a man to his companion. "She dreamed she had married a multimillionaire."

"You're lucky," sighed the companion. "My wife dreams that in the daytime." —Bennett Cerf, *Laughter Incorporated* (Garden City)

A MINISTER friend of mine records his sermons on wire, then listens to them on Saturday evening in order to fix them in his mind for Sunday. One evening while listening to his sermon, he fell asleep and did not awaken until the silence which followed the recording. —Adiel J. Moncrief, D.D.

TELLING HER child a bedtime story, a movie actress began: "There was a mama bear, a papa bear and a baby bear by a previous marriage."

—Lenny Sherman, quoted by Sidney Skolsky in New York *Post*

Hollywood Roundup

SPEAKING of a certain movie actor: "He'd divorce his wife—but he doesn't need the publicity just now." —Earl Wilson, Hall Syndicate

THE DAUGHTER of a wealthy producer was asked at school to write a story about a poor family. Her essay began: "Once upon a time there was a poor family. The mother was poor. The daddy was poor. The children were poor. The butler was poor. The chauffeur was poor. The maid was poor. The gardener was poor. Everybody was poor." —Carleton Young, quoted by Erskine Johnson, NEA

THE FORMER chorus girl obviously knew nothing about acting, and the Hollywood director was frantic. Finally he roared, "Can't you show me *any* emotion?"

"Well, I don't see how," she pouted, "when all you've been photographing is my face!"

—Wade Havens

A YOUNG actor was telling how he met a big producer: "He just put out his hand and I went right up and shook it."

"Shook it!" gasped a Hollywood veteran. "You're finished. You should have licked it!"

—Ted Cannon in Salt Lake City *Deseret News*

HOLLYWOOD producer to writer: "I want you to find out if Abe Lincoln ever knew any dame that might have remotely resembled Marilyn Monroe."

—John Ruge cartoon in *Collier's*

HEDY LAMARR, noted in Hollywood for her "temperament," was reported to have said in an interview, "I sincerely respect anyone who tells me, straight from the shoulder, that I'm wrong."

On which a publicist who has worked with her commented, "Okay, so I tell her she's wrong, and she respects me—but where would I find another job?"

—Jimmie Fidler

Double Features

On a Jamestown, N. Y., movie marquee:

ONE RECKLESS MOMENT
BABY MAKES THREE

In Los Angeles:

GO FOR BROKE
LAS VEGAS STORY

In Fayetteville, Tenn.

I AM A CAMERA
OVEREXPOSED

In Edinburgh:

THE GENTLE SERGEANT
THE UNKNOWN MAN

A MOVIE director was trying to impress a young actress with the importance of her entrance in a scene.

"When you enter the room," he told her, "I want every man in the audience to drop his popcorn!"

—Philadelphia *Inquirer Magazine*

TWO HOLLYWOOD children of oft-divorced parents got into an argument. As it became more heated, one said, "My father can lick your father."

"Are you kidding?" cried the other. "Your father *is* my father!"

—Jack Gilford, quoted in Akron *Beacon Journal*

Spotlight on Today

ON A VISIT to Hollywood, CBS news correspondent David Schoenbrun went to a drugstore and asked for a small tube of toothpaste. He was handed a tube marked "large." When Schoenbrun objected the clerk explained, " 'Large' is the smallest size we have. The next size is 'giant' and then comes 'super.' If you want the small size, you have to ask for 'large.' " —Guyon Madison, CBS

OVERHEARD in a Connecticut bus: "But, my dear, it *isn't* automatic. You have to turn a switch."

—Harold G. Newsham

AFTER LUNCH one day a jet pilot landed at a Nevada air base to have his radio repaired. He said he was in a hurry to make a dinner date. My friend, who was working on the radio, misunderstood his destination. "It'll be finished in plenty of time," he said, "for you to make California."

"California, hell," replied the pilot, "my date is in South Carolina." —Annamae Robinson

SHOPPING AT a supermarket, I was standing near a mother and her young son when he picked up a box of something from a shelf and brought it over to her. "Oh, no, honey!" she exclaimed. "Put it back. You have to *cook* that!"

—Tecla Vandermade

ANYONE who doubts that this is the age of specialization is referred to the case of a woman who moved from Manhattan to Long Island. When her dog came down with a case of pip the very next day, she quickly phoned the nearest vet. A soft-voiced female answered, listened sympathetically to a recounting of the canine symptoms, then politely asked the breed of the dog. "Toby's a cocker spaniel," she was told.

"Oh, I'm *so* sorry," the vet's receptionist said sadly. "You see, Dr. X specializes in French poodles!"

—Dorothy Kilgallen, King Features

WHEN MY granddaughter was married I sent her a sewing basket fully equipped with scissors, thimble, needles, thread, buttons and the rest.

"But Grandmother," she wrote back, "where are the directions?"

—Mrs. D. Eugene Callender

A FATHER was telling a neighbor how he stopped his son from being late to high school. "I bought him a car," he said.

"How did that stop him from being late?" the neighbor asked.

"Why, he's got to get there early to find a parking place."

—*Concrete Citizen,* quoted in *Scholastic Teacher*

HUSBAND examining can wife has just opened for dinner: "Ah, yum, *yum!* Certified coloring, artificial flavors, potassium nitrate, benzoate of soda and monosodium glutamate!"

—Stan Hunt cartoon in *True*

American city: A place where, by the time you've finished paying for your home in the suburbs, the suburbs have moved 20 miles farther out.

—Ottawa, Kan., *Herald,* quoted by Earl Wilson, Hall Syndicate

WOMAN to friend: "But, my dear, their house is one of those Early American places where one has to go outdoors to the garage."

—Cincinnati *Enquirer*

GORDON BROWNING, former governor of Tennessee, asked what he thought was the greatest progress in agriculture in the past 35 years, replied: "Well, nowadays you can't tell a farmer's daughter from a city girl."

—Walter Davenport in *Collier's*

THIS MODERN electro-mechanical age is getting to the point where it's just too complicated. Take the man in Eldorado, Ill., who had a new air conditioner installed in his home, turned it on and blissfully retired for a comfortable night's sleep.

But when the conditioner brought the temperature down to a delightful 68 degrees, his furnace automatically switched on.

—St. Louis *Globe-Democrat*

Weather Reports

One of the most annoying things about weather forecasts is that they're not wrong all the time, either. —*Farm Journal*

WEATHER forecast in the Pasadena *Independent:* "Clear today except for early fog, followed by smog, followed by evening fog."

May

May be chill, may be mild,
May pour, may snow,
May be still, may be wild,
May lower, may glow,
May freeze, may burn,
May be gold, may be gray,
May do all these in turn—
May May.

—Justin Richardson in *The Countryman,* quoted in New York *Herald Tribune*

SOON AFTER drenching rains ended the Texas drought this ad appeared in the Stanton *Times:* "J. H. Hones withdraws his candidacy for Treasurer of Martin County. It has rained sufficiently for Mr. Hones to return to farming." —George F. Taubeneck in *Air Conditioning & Refrigeration News*

JUNE FORECAST: Plenty of showers, followed by brides.

—Mike Connolly in *The Hollywood Reporter*

ABOUT the first of August every year an Arizona church puts this sign on its bulletin board: "You think it's hot here?"

—General Features Corp.

FROM THE Portland *Oregonian:* "Tomorrow we may expect strong northwest winds reaching a gal in exposed places."

—Quoted in *Better Farming*

THE WEATHER in the Southwest was so bad one winter that when the sun finally shone for a few hours the El Paso, Texas, *Herald-Post* splattered the front page with this headline: "PRODIGAL SUN RETURNS."

—Neal O'Hara, McNaught Syndicate

SIGN on an outdoor theater near Bethlehem, Pa.: "Closed for the season. Reason: Freezin'."

—Bethlehem, Pa., *Globe-Times*

IRASCIBLE Sir William Eden, father of Sir Anthony, is said to have wrenched from the wall a barometer showing "Fair" and to have flung it through a window into the rain, shouting, "There, you damned fool, see for yourself!"

—Lewis Barton, *Considered Trifles* (Werner Laurie)

I Demand Worse Weather!

Parke Cummings in This Week Magazine

THE WEATHER around my place isn't bad enough. I wish it would get worse, like on my neighbors' land where the elements constantly go berserk. Recently, for example, during a rugged cold snap, our thermometer registered ten below zero one morning. On the train I cited this figure to Thompson, my neighbor. "That all?" he asked. "You got off lucky. Fourteen below at my place."

"We had 19 below," chimed in Jameson, who, curiously, lives across the street from us. "Was up all night with an electric heater to keep our pipes from freezing."

It's always like that. If we get snowdrifts five feet high in our driveway, the man next door gets them eight feet high. Wind that blows my hat off blows people's coats off when it leaves our property.

Occasionally, of course, an erratic cloud wets us as much as it does the neighbors—above ground, that is. But not in our cellar. We're continually being humiliated by the puny floods we get there. If the water's up to our ankles, it's up to Jameson's knees. If mice are swimming around in ours, the Thompsons have beavers.

I'm beginning to suspect the trouble. We've got a leak somewhere that lets the water out. I'm going to locate that leak and plug it up with the best cement. Then, for the next cloudburst, I'm going to install a giant blower in the cellar.

Waves? Brother, we're going to have whitecaps!

Cartoon Quips

HOMEOWNER fishing in flooded basement to friend: "We gave up trying to keep it dry and had it stocked."
—Lyons in *The Saturday Evening Post*

LONG-WHISKERED man to fellow commuter: "It all started about ten years ago—you see, I have three daughters and only one bathroom." —Dave Gerard in *The Saturday Evening Post*

ONE FRENCH Foreign Legion soldier to another: "I joined the Legion two or three weeks ago to try to forget a girl called Elsie or something." —*Punch*

SMALL BOY at dinner table to parents: "I've chewed the mouthful of carrots ten times. Now what do I do with them?" —Chon Day in *Ladies' Home Journal*

WOMAN DRIVER who has just backed into a tree to companion: "I'm getting so I just despise reverse!" —Jeff Keate in *The American Magazine*

PERFUME SALESGIRL showing newest brand to customer: "To be frank, I consider it unsportsmanlike—in the same class with dynamiting fish!" —Von Riegen in *Collier's*

HUSBAND doing dishes to wife: "There are some peas left over. Shall I throw them away now or put them in the icebox and let you throw them away next week?"
—Don Tobin, King Features

BOSS to employe: "Yes, Dawson, I know you can't get married on the money I'm paying you, and someday you'll thank me for it." —George Reckas in *The Saturday Evening Post*

TEEN-AGER to chum: "My father used to help me with math, but since I started geometry he says I'll get a lot more out of it if I do it myself." —Kate Osann, NEA

LONG-FACED doctor to patient: "Let me know if this prescription works—I'm having the same trouble myself." —Sivic in *The Saturday Evening Post*

COLLEGE GIRL to roommate: "Bill is intelligent, sensible, thoughtful and the finest character I ever met—while Jack is a welcome relief!" —Tom Hudson in *Collier's*

WIFE at breakfast table to grumpy husband: "Look on the bright side. In 16 hours you'll be back in bed." —John Dempsey in *The Saturday Evening Post*

Slightly Clock-Eyed

HE'D STAYED around much too long with the boys, as usual, *and* he'd got himself pie-eyed—as usual. Here it was nearly 3 a.m., when he'd promised to be home by 11. What a row he was in for! He fumbled with the key, tiptoed unsteadily across the hall and started up the stairs. It was here that his chance came. As he reached the half-landing the cuckoo clock cuckooed three times. For a precious moment the mental overcast seemed to clear and inspiration came: when the cuckoo stopped he went right on cuckooing himself, up to 11. That would fox her. He undressed on the landing, moved gingerly into the room, slipped into bed—and she never even stirred. He was home!

Next morning at breakfast she said, "We're going to have to do something about that cuckoo clock, Henry."

"Why," he asked, "it's keeping perfect time, isn't it?"

"I don't know what it's doing," she said, "but it's certainly behaving very funnily. Imagine what happened last night as I was lying in bed waiting for you! It cuckooed three times, then it hiccoughed, then it said 'damn,' and then it cuckooed 14 times more."

—Terry Hargreave

POP HAS an uncontrollable passion for taking things apart and putting them together again. The Sunday afternoon he set to work on the new cuckoo clock we all gathered about to watch. Taking it apart was easy. Pop laid out first the bird, then each screw, each nut, bolt, spring, pin and wheel. Then came the reconstruction project. His fingers were nimble; nuts joined bolts happily; springs glided into place. Every last screw was accounted for and the cuckoo back in its cage by 3:45.

The minutes ticked off slowly. At one minute to four the witnesses stopped breathing. Four o'clock. Silence. All eyes on the little door waiting for the bird. Finally she came out—backward—turned about, glared at the crowd and shrieked, "Does anybody around here know what time it is?"

—Sam Levenson

Problem Solvers

EARLY IN his career Henry Ford, in granting a subcontract for engine parts, specified that these parts were to be delivered in wooden boxes of a certain size, held together by screws, not nails. He even indicated the exact size and location of the screws.

In order to receive this lucrative order the subcontractors willingly accepted the conditions, although they privately agreed that "this guy Ford is slightly batty." Many of his own employes felt that the "old man" was being unnecessarily dogmatic about the shipping cases, too, but they chalked it up to erratic genius.

Came delivery day—and revelation. Henry Ford's "whimsy" had been the work of genius all right, but hardly erratic. The sides of those precisely measured wooden shipping boxes were exactly the size of the floorboards of Henry's Fords. With each screw hole correctly spaced and drilled, the boards were ready to be slipped into place. —George Relf, quoted by Helen Houston Boileau

ONE QUESTION on an examination given to Royal Australian Air Force National Service trainees posed this problem: "What is the first thing you would do if you were piloting an aircraft and the Queen of England fell out of the back seat?"

The answers varied a good deal. "I'd swoop down and try to catch her," said one hopeful.

"Commit suicide," said another.

"Disappear," said a third.

The approved solution? "Adjust tabs to compensate for reduced weight in the rear section." —Reuters

THE ATLANTIC FLEET was holding maneuvers. On a destroyer the call to general quarters had the whole crew hastening to their stations, while already reports of simulated damage were being recorded by damage control. On deck an officer, crayon in hand, surveyed the hurrying men, then stooped and traced out a rough circle several feet in diameter, extending from rail to superstructure, and scrawled in the middle of the area, "Bomb hit. Deck gone." Then he stood by to watch.

A belated seaman, running to his post, reached the artificial wound and stopped. He gazed wistfully at the far side of the circle, then his face lighted. Plucking the crayon from the hand of the astounded officer he quickly drew two straight lines through the center of the circle, scribbled in the middle, "Six-inch plank"—and hastened on his way.

—James P. Marshall

"WHAT STEPS would you take," a question in a college exam read, "in determining the height of a building, using an aneroid barometer?"

One student, short on knowledge but long on ingenuity, replied, "I would lower the barometer on a string and measure the string."

—*The Wall Street Journal*

I WAS STANDING on a highway cloverleaf, one of those mazes of overpasses and underpasses, trying to hitchhike a ride back to my base, when a flashy car went by. I didn't pay much attention until it came back around again. It came around a third and fourth time. On the fifth time a woman opened the car door and called, "Sailor, my husband said never to pick up hitchhikers, but if you'll just show me how to get off this darn thing, I'll take you anywhere you want to go!"

—Jack H. Hanna

WHEN MY SON, a Marine staff sergeant, was home on leave, he was quite unexpectedly left in charge of his three-month-old niece for an afternoon. All went well at first; then a crisis arose and the sergeant put in a frantic call to his uncle, who took care of the problem in man-to-man fashion.

"First," he said, "place the diaper in position of a baseball diamond, with you at bat. Fold second base over home plate. Place baby on pitcher's mound. Then pin first base and third base to home plate."

It worked.

—Helen A. Ryan

WHEN PRIME MINISTER Harold Macmillan was British Resident Minister in Algeria during World War II, he was called upon to settle a dispute between British and American officers in the Allied mess. The Americans wanted drinks served before meals, the British after. Macmillan's solution was worthy of Solomon: "Henceforth, we will all drink before meals in deference to the Americans, and we will all drink after dinner in deference to the British." —*Newsweek*

MY 13-YEAR-OLD son proudly announced one day: "I was the only one in our class that got 100 in the Social Living test."

"That's fine," I said. "Were the questions hard?"

"Well, the only one I didn't know the answer to was, 'What is the salary of the Chief Justice of the United States?' but I figured it out. I knew that Ted Williams got $100,000 a year from the Red Sox, and I decided that a Chief Justice would probably get about a fourth as much. So I put down $25,000 and it was right." —Ruth Whetstine

Wage Scales

A CHICAGO girl sued for annulment of her marriage on the ground of fraud. She said her husband pretended to be a $40-a-day bricklayer when he was, in reality, only a banker. —*Swing*

WHEN A carpenter working on a Long Island housing development fell off a roof and suffered a severe leg fracture, a call was put in to the nearest metropolitan hospital and a young intern was rushed to the scene. As he worked over the injured man, more and more of the other workers—representing the cream of the construction trades and earning three to four dollars an hour—left their jobs and gathered around to watch, observing his every move with rapt attention. When the young intern finished, he carefully put away his instruments, closed his bag and, as he rose, casually looked at the assembled crowd. Then, looking down at the injured man briefly with the satisfied air of a job well done, he commented, "Not bad for 18 cents an hour." —Harold Levine

IGOR STRAVINSKY was offered $4000 to compose the music for a Hollywood film. "It is not enough," he said.

"It's what we paid your predecessor," replied the producer.

"My predecessor had talent," responded Stravinsky. "I have not. So for me the work is more difficult." —*Paris-Match*

A FEW YEARS ago a $1000-a-week Hollywood writer got in trouble with the front office. His contract had six months to go, but the bosses decided to get even by making him work out his contract as a messenger boy. One day the $1000-a-week messenger boy was asked to take some visitors—stockholders in the studio—on a tour of the lot. He gave them a very fine tour and when it was over one of them offered him a $10 tip.

This was the moment the writer had been waiting for. "Thanks very much," he said sweetly, "but I'm very well paid as a messenger boy. Look—here's one of my checks—$1000 a week."

There was hell to pay in the front office. —Erskine Johnson, NEA

A NAVY Civil Engineer Corps commander attended a top-brass conference on the deplorable service-pay situation. He emphasized his plea to the group responsible for nudging Congress with this personal note: "Comparing my salary with those of all the other engineers in my college graduating class, I find I am the second lowest paid. The only one making less is in San Quentin!" —K.B.E.

MASS OBSERVATION, a British poll organization that feels the public pulse on timely topics, asked members of the middle class, "Given a one-tenth reduction in income, where would you make your cuts?"

Replied one dismal country parson, "Across my throat." —AP

The Perfect Squelch

THE CIVIC CLUB's discussion had hit a snarl on the question of devoting funds to a project which might be operated at a loss. "Gentlemen, no matter how much good it may do, the plan is unbusinesslike," said one member. "Let me warn you that I never remain identified with any organization that operates with a deficit."

There was a long hush—until another member asked, "You're still an American citizen, aren't you?" —George P. Stimson

A LOCAL busybody, unable to contain her curiosity any longer, asked an expectant mother point-blank whether she was going to have a baby. "Oh, goodness, no," the young woman said pleasantly. "I'm just carrying this for a friend."

—Jack Bell in Miami *Herald,* quoted in *Coronet*

ON A TRAIN during a tour of the United States an Englishman fell into conversation with a Texan, who embarked on a long recitation of the wonders of the Lone Star State. "Maybe you didn't realize it while you were going through my state," the Texan wound up, "but all of Great Britain could fit into one corner of it."

"I dare say it could," said the Englishman dryly. "And wouldn't it do wonders for the place!"

—Luke Neely in *The American Legion Magazine*

A MOTHER who wanted to help her ten-year-old with her reading was told flatly by the girl's teacher, "You'll only retard her progress if you teach her yourself."

"Perhaps," replied the mother. "But will it be all right for me to read her diploma to her when she graduates?"

—*American School Board Journal,* quoted in *Nuggets*

BEATRICE LILLIE wrote to the owner of a Bermuda estate with a view to renting it for a vacation. He answered: "My place is on a small island, so you will need my boatman to ferry you to Hamilton and back. The estate rents for $25,000, but with the boatman's services included the price will be $30,000."

"Kindly rush photograph of boatman," Miss Lillie cabled.

—Bennett Cerf in *The Saturday Review*

AT A PARTY one guest completely monopolized the conversation, much to the annoyance of the hostess's elderly mother. By the time he launched into a story of his experiences during the war, she was bored to the point of retaliation. "I was torpedoed in the Pacific," he began. "In fact, I lived for a week on a can of sardines."

"Really!" exclaimed the exasperated old lady. "Weren't you afraid of falling off?"

—Eleanor C. Wood in *Coronet*

DURING A campaign against excessive speed at one of the larger Naval installations in California, a Marine private stopped a military jeep for exceeding the speed limit and politely asked the driver, a Navy commander, for his operator's permit. The Marine proceeded to make out the traffic-violation certificate. "Private," the commander roared, "do you know who I am? I'm the executive officer of this base and I'm en route to a golf engagement with your commanding officer and this will undoubtedly make me late."

"I'm sorry, sir," the Marine replied, "but I'm writing as fast as I can."

—Harry Bullock

AT A DINNER party the hostess, whose kittenish ways were most annoying, produced a family album. "This," she said coyly, holding up a mother-and-child picture, "is myself 28 years ago."

A guest examined the photograph, then asked slyly, "Who is the baby on your lap?"

—*This Week Magazine*

Age is a funny thing
Cherished in a tree,
And cheese
And furniture
And wine—
Most anything
But me.

—Helena K. Beacham, quoted by Marguerite Walton in New Canaan, Conn., *Advertiser*

MRS. YEHUDI MENUHIN, confessing her age: "I'm 38. I always tell the truth—even if it is a little embarrassing to some of my younger girl friends of the same age."

—Herb Caen in San Francisco *Examiner*

MRS. ROSINA SHERWOOD, mother of the late playwright, Robert E. Sherwood, once observed: "It feels good to reach 94, except for seeing your children become depressingly middle-aged."

—Leonard Lyons

WOMAN TO beauty-shop receptionist: "I don't intend to grow old gracefully—I'm fighting every step of the way!"

—Mary Gibson cartoon in *Collier's*

GRACIE ALLEN: "My husband will never chase another woman. He's too fine, too decent, too old."

EVERY TIME a little boy went to a playmate's house he found the friend's grandmother deeply engrossed in her Bible. Finally his curiosity got the better of him. "Why do you suppose your grandmother reads the Bible so much?" he asked.

"I'm not sure," said his friend, "but I think it's because she's cramming for her finals."

—Carl T. Schuneman

AT A PARTY I hardly recognized an old friend, for she was wearing glasses. When I remarked about it she replied, "Oh, I've needed them for a long time, but I've just reached the age where my curiosity is greater than my vanity." —Mrs. Carl I. Aslakson

ONE OF our friends had undergone a serious operation and was still in a coma. Her worried husband stood at the foot of her bed. "Well," said the nurse reassuringly, "at least her age is on her side."

"She's not so young," said the husband. "She's forty-three."

At this point the patient moved slightly, and quietly but firmly murmured, "Forty-two." From then on, she improved steadily.

—Charles J. Butler

ON HIS 70th birthday William Allen White, famous publisher of the Emporia, Kan., *Gazette,* was asked how it felt to be three score and ten. "Well," Mr. White said wistfully, "today the girls come and sit on the side of your chair and pat you on the head and look down at you in reverence, because they're not afraid of you any longer. And that's the hell of it!"

—Cornelius Vanderbilt, Jr., quoted in *California Grocers Advocate*

How to Stay a Bachelor

Condensed from This Week Magazine

Loyd Rosenfield

MORE AND MORE victory-flushed brides are passing on in print the secrets of their success to jittery maidens who are still paying for an occasional meal of their own. I deem it only fair, therefore, to make public my own system for avoiding that bachelor's mirage called marriage. The perfect formula is, of course, don't go out with girls. But I pass over this drastic expedient in favor of more practical advice.

Don't go steady. I know the rotation system is a lot of work,

This Week Magazine (March 18, '51), © 1951 by United Newspapers Magazine Corp., 420 Lexington Ave., New York 17, N. Y.

and sometimes you forget which technique you are working on whom, but the lazy man who gets into the habit of going with one girl already has one foot in the cottage.

Don't be kind to children and dumb animals. I don't mean for you to go out of your way to kick them or tie tin cans to their tails, but don't be overly enthusiastic. If anything evokes a rising tide of tenderness in the female bosom it is the picture of a big strong man fondling a puppy or chucking a baby under the chin.

Issue dreary financial reports. In the presence of her father complain bitterly about how hard you work for a pittance. Cross your legs casually and let him see the hole in the sole of your shoe. Borrow her mother's manicure scissors to trim your frayed shirt collar. Occasionally borrow five dollars from her and forget to pay it back. If she'll let you forget.

Don't be your own lovable self around her mother. The downfall of many an otherwise careful young man has been being too attentive to what he soon discovers is his mother-in-law. Such little courtesies as bringing Mom a corsage every time her daughter gets one, telling Mom what a good cook she is and taking her along to the show once in a while have made many surprised daughters realize they were desperately in love.

Beat her father at games. When the old boy takes you out for a round of golf, try to win every hole, fight for every stroke, even cheat a little if you have to. If this doesn't convince him you are a cad, get him into a card game, play for money and beat him soundly. If he accidentally wins you can laugh, say, "That was fun," and forget about paying him.

Make her friends dislike you. Sooner or later she will have a group of her friends over to pass judgment on you. This is a critical moment, for if even one of them draws her aside and whispers, "He's cute. Where did you ever find him?"—brother, you're cooked! So whenever there's a gang of hers around, and the girl of your dreams goes to the kitchen to fix some goodies, do card tricks for the women, disagree politically with the men and ask if anybody happens to know whether your girl's father has money.

Don't be too generous or overly courteous. I don't mean not to give her a Christmas present if you've failed to get her sore at you around that season. But be sure to leave the price tag on and be sure the amount isn't over five dollars.

Don't be too generous with the little courtesies such as helping her on with her coat or opening the car door for her. When a woman gets the idea she can get this type of service free for the rest of her life merely by coaxing you into a church for a few minutes, she can make herself more attractive than a twilight double-header.

Try to appear unattractive to other women. One thing that will convince a woman that you are the man for her is to let her know some other woman is after you. Therefore, remark about how few young ladies there are in town and how busy they always seem to be. When she says she has a date with another fellow, act horrified at the thought of losing her. If this perks her up, intimate it is because you are too old to start looking around for other women.

If, after obeying the above instructions, she still melts when she looks into your eyes and your heart does nip-ups when you look into hers, and you'd rather be with her than play poker in your regular Tuesday-night game, then stall for time and wait for further advice from me. On second thought, I can't help you much—I'm planning on getting married.

Oblique Angles

CELEBRATING his 100th birthday a man in Arcadia, Calif., declared he owed his longevity to being a bachelor: "Marriage is for women only. A man should have nothing to do with it." —Arthur Lansing in *The American Magazine*

THE FOUR-year-old was busy playing in his yard when a grownup stopped by. "Hi, Mike," she said, "Where's your friend Jason?"

"Away," he replied.

"Don't you miss him?"

"Yes," Mike admitted. Then, meditating darkly on the number of times Jason had beaten him, he added, "But I like missing him."

—This Week Magazine

ONCE A friend of Tallulah Bankhead's was asked by a magazine interviewer, "Tell me, off the record, did you ever have an affair with Tallulah?"

"Well," replied the friend, "she'll consider me a cad for saying so—but I didn't."

—Irving Hoffman in *The Hollywood Reporter*

SNATCH OF overheard dialogue: "You know what they call people who use the rhythm system of birth control?"

"No. What?"

"Parents." —Mary Flink

I WAS a nurse assisting a very competent surgeon during an operation when suddenly the patient started to hemorrhage. Anxiety mounted as we seemed to be unable to locate the source of the bleeding and, to make matters worse, the first assistant panicked and blurted out that maybe we should call in the chief of the surgical staff for help.

The surgeon, without looking up from his work, made a retort that broke the tension—and probably led to a speedier repair of the trouble. "What would I want to call him in for?" he asked quietly. "He never gets into trouble—he wouldn't know how to get us out of it!" —E.S.

IN CONNECTION with a story my friend was reading to her second-graders she asked each one if he thought he lived near the school or far away, and how long it took him to get home. She couldn't help smiling at one little boy's answer. "I must live pretty close," he said seriously, "because when I get home my mother always says, 'Good grief, are you home already?' " —H. Judson Carr

THE OLD doctor had never refused a call, from rich or poor—but now he was tired. "Have you any money?" he asked a midnight caller. Certainly he had money. "Then go to the new doctor. I'm too old a man to get out of bed for anybody who can pay for it."

—Marie Brandt

MY FATHER, the late Frederick Lewis Allen, editor of *Harper's*, was somewhat farsighted. One evening at a friend's house my stepmother, Agnes Rogers Allen, noticed that Dad was spending a great deal of time with a very pretty girl. On the way home Agnes remarked, "Well! That was certainly an attractive girl you were with most of the evening."

"Was she really?" replied my father. "I didn't have my glasses, and I never got far enough away from her to see what she looked like!" —Oliver Allen in *Book-of-the-Month Club News*

IN A SPEECH in Paris, Gen. Alfred Gruenther, President Eisenhower's former Chief of Staff, discussed the large numbers of people who have been experting on the proper way to set up defenses against the Russian threat. "There are two professions in which the amateur is far better than the professional," said Gruenther. "The second of these is military strategy." —Leonard Lyons

Mr. President

DURING THE meeting of the Constitutional Convention in Philadelphia, one of the members moved "that the standing army be restricted to 5000 men at any one time." George Washington, being the chairman, could not offer a motion, but he turned to another member and whispered, "Amend the motion to provide that no foreign enemy shall invade the United States at any time with more than 3000 troops."
—*Patriots off Their Pedestals,* © 1927, 1955 by Paul Wilstach (Bobbs-Merrill)

ONCE WHEN Calvin Coolidge was Vice President and presiding over the Senate, an altercation arose between two Senators. Tempers flared, and one Senator told the other to go straight to hell. The offended Senator stormed from his seat, marched down the aisle and stood before Mr. Coolidge, who was silently leafing through a book. "Mr. President," he said, "did you hear what he said to me?"

Silent Cal looked up from his book and said calmly, "You know, I have been looking through the rule book. You don't have to go."
—Quoted by Lester Buford

LINCOLN'S own favorite story among the many that circulated about him during his lifetime was about two Quakeresses discussing the Civil War leaders, Lincoln and Jefferson Davis. "I think Jefferson will succeed," declared one.

"And why does thee think so?"

"Because Jefferson is a praying man."

"And so is Abraham a praying man."

"Yes, but," countered the first, "the Lord will think Abraham is joking." —Dixon Wecter, *The Hero in America* (Scribners)

PRESIDENT Eisenhower's mother, who disliked hearing her sons Arthur and Edgar addressed as "Art" and "Ed," decided to give her next child a name nobody could shorten. She named him Dwight. "She was right. Nobody could shorten it," says the President. "So I became Ike."

—Morton Downey, quoted by Leonard Lyons

WHEN ex-President Taft was visiting Hampton Institute he was overheard talking to a charming woman who was also to be a speaker at the final convocation. Handing the woman her wrap, Mr. Taft said, "Perhaps you had better carry it yourself. If we should be separated, and I were found with the wrap I might be accused of having stolen it."

"Why, Mr. Taft," she said laughingly, "are you accustomed to such accusations?"

"My dear lady," replied Taft, "I am accustomed to anything. I have been President of these United States." —Dagny Carter

PRESIDENT Franklin D. Roosevelt's favorite story was about the commuter from Westchester County, a Republican stronghold who always walked into his station, handed the newsboy a quarter, picked up the New York *Herald Tribune,* glanced at the front page and then handed it back as he rushed out to catch his train. Finally the newsboy, unable to control his curiosity any longer asked his customer why he only glanced at the front page.

"I'm interested in the obituary notices," said the customer.

"But they're way over on page 24, and you never look at them," the boy objected.

"Boy," said the tycoon, "the ——— ——— I'm interested in will be on page one, all right!"

—*Presidents Who Have Known Me* © 1950 by George E. Allen (Simon and Schuster)

ONE OF Theodore Roosevelt's sons said of him, "Father always wants to be the bride at every wedding and the corpse at every funeral."

—Nicholas Roosevelt, *A Front Row Seat* (University of Oklahoma Press)

WHEN Woodrow Wilson was president of Princeton he was cornered one registration day by a freshman's mother who proceeded to cross-examine him about the university. Both he father and grandfather had attended Harvard, but her husband, a Princeton man, wanted their son to follow in his footsteps. Frankly, she had her doubts. "We want our only child to have the very best education—one that will mold him for great things. Can you assure me that he'll do well here?" she demanded.

"Madam," said Wilson mildly, "we guarantee satisfaction, or we return the boy." —Calvin M. Floyd in *The Saturday Evening Post*

Figuratively Speaking

A COMMENCEMENT speaker was warning the graduates against the pitfalls of statistics. "A survey showed," he said, "that the families of Princeton graduates average 1.8 children, whereas for Smith graduates the figure was 1.4. A faulty conclusion could be drawn from these figures—that men have more children than women."

—*The Atlantic Bulletin*

A FEW YEARS ago when I was living in a town in the Deep South, the local chapter of the Ladies' Aid Society decided to bring a little sunshine into the state prison by writing cheery letters to the inmates. My landlady didn't quite know how to go about addressing a man she knew only by a string of numerals. But finally she achieved what she happily believed to be a measure of friendliness: "Dear 688395," she wrote. "May I call you 688?"

—Charles W. Creighton

SIGN on a Los Angeles movie marquee: "See Jane Russell on our giant screen. Bust 395 inches! Waist 241 inches! Hips 372 inches!" —Mike Connolly in *The Hollywood Reporter*

THE AVERAGE housewife can get Junior ready for outdoor play on a cold winter day in 12 minutes and 29 seconds, or roughly three times the length of time he'll stay outside. —Dick Emmons in *Look*

THE LATE Robert Sherwood, distinguished author-playwright, rose to the spectacular height of six feet, seven inches. Robert Benchley, when asked if he knew Sherwood, immediately leaped onto a chair, extended his hand over an imaginary head and said, "Know him! Why, I've known him since he was this high!"

—Collie Small in *Collier's*

WHEN Mrs. Estes Kefauver arrived home from a political campaign trip and was regaling her children with a description of her various experiences, the big dinners and so forth, one youngster asked, "Mommie, what did you eat?"

"Chicken, mashed potatoes and 6792 peas," she replied.

"Aw, Mommie," protested the youngster, "how do you know *how* many?"

"Child, what do you think I *do* when your daddy's talking?"

—Robert Wallace in *Life*

IN *More Fish to Fry,* an account of summering on Orcas Island in the Pacific Northwest, Beatrice Cook writes:

The afternoon Gramp Anthony, our ever-helpful neighbor, came over to help plant pole beans, he said, "Now, before we put in the poles, I'd better take some measurements."

"What do you have to measure?" I asked.

"You," he said.

"Turn around and lean over," he went on, taking a tape measure from his rear pocket. "No use a-gittin' the poles so close together you can't git between 'em. Forgot to measure my wife one year and *I* had to pick the beans."

—Published by Morrow

MY GRANDFATHER used to tell the story on himself of arriving home from school in New Ipswich, N. H., all out of breath. His mother asked him what was the matter and he replied, "I ran all the way—a thousand dogs were chasing me."

"A thousand dogs, George?"

"Well, five hundred, Mother."

"There aren't that many dogs in the village."

"Well," he said finally, "our dog and another dog."

Nowadays whenever a member of the family exaggerates, he is likely to hear, "Our dog and another dog?"

—Ruth T. Jordan

IN OPELOUSAS, La., a restaurant displays the sign: "We Are Reducing Our Ten-Cent Hamburgers from Twenty Cents to Fifteen Cents."

—Bill Burkett, quoted by Walter Davenport in *Collier's*

Diners' Club

RESTAURANT OWNERS have long been famous for the various little "extra charges" they can dream up "to help meet overhead expenses." And I thought I'd encountered them all, until I stopped at an oceanside drive-in for lunch one day. Accompanying my order for fried chicken was this bill:

1 F. chick 1.25
Well done .10

—Carrie M. Shaw

SIGN IN A Montreal restaurant: "The Early Bird Gets the Worm! Special Shoppers' Luncheon before 11 a.m."

—*Maclean's Magazine*

A LITTLE short man came into a local restaurant and sat down in a booth. The waitress brought him a glass of water and a menu, then left to wait on another customer. It was a busy hour, the little man's head did not show over the back of the booth, and the waitress forgot him. Eventually she realized she had never taken his order. She rushed to the booth. It was empty, but a note was propped neatly against the glass.

It read: "Out for Lunch."

—Virginia Larsen

ON THE MENU of a Fresno, Calif., hotel: "Smörgasbord $2.50. Half price for children who remain seated at their table while parents serve them."

—Gene Sherman in Los Angeles *Times*

WE WERE DINING at a hotel in Cleveland, and just as we got up to dance the waiter brought the soup. He gave us a despairing look as he placed saucers over the soup cups. Then, as we danced into sight again on the edge of the floor, he plucked at my husband's sleeve. "Sir," he pleaded, "dancing is forever—the soup is *now!*"

—Mrs. W. H. McConnell

THE BRIDE and groom came down to the coffee shop of the hotel where they had spent the first night of their honeymoon. "Now be nonchalant and don't act as if we were newlyweds," quietly cautioned the groom.

While he studied the menu, his bride gave her order to the waitress. "Orange juice and black coffee, please." Whereupon he exclaimed in a voice everyone in the place could hear, "Good heavens, is that all you eat for breakfast?" —Edward B. Anderson

ONCE MILTON BERLE played Pittsburgh for a one-week stand. On Monday he picked out a restaurant that looked attractive. "I always eat whole-wheat bread," he told the waitress, but she brought white. On Tuesday he reminded her about the whole-wheat, but was served white again. Wednesday she made the same mistake, not to mention Thursday and Friday. Finally on Saturday when she took his order, Berle said, "Just for the heck of it, I think I'll take white bread today." "That's funny," said the waitress. "Aren't you the party who always orders whole-wheat?"

—Bennett Cerf, *Anything for a Laugh* (Grosset & Dunlap)

DINERS AT A cafeteria in Washington, D. C., were perplexed to find two vegetarian platters offered—one 75 cents, the other 90 cents. "The 90-cent one doesn't have spinach," explained the attendant. —T.R.B. in *The New Republic*

THE WAITRESS took the parents' orders, then turned to their small son. "What will you have?" she asked.

"I want a hot dog . . . " the boy began timidly.

"No hot dog," the mother interrupted. "Give him potatoes and beef . . ." But the waitress ignored her. "Do you want ketchup or mustard on your hot dog?"

"Ketchup," the boy said with a happy smile.

"Coming up," the waitress said, starting for the kitchen. There was a stunned silence. Then the youngster said, "Know what? She thinks I'm real." —Thomas P. Ramirez in *American Mercury*

Report to the Homefront

THAT WE fathers spend too little time with our families was brought home to me one evening in an unexpected and forceful fashion.

I had dashed home from the bank for dinner, announcing that I had to go back right afterward for a night session of work. As my wife placed a delectable-looking dish on the table, one of our three sons started to help himself first. But he didn't get far, for the youngest stopped him—and us—with the remark, "Serve Daddy first—he's our guest." —Gale Norman

A GRADUATE student working on juvenile delinquency reported in a Wisconsin University sociology seminar that he was having difficulty in collecting data. His project was to telephone a dozen homes around 9 p.m. and ask the parents if they knew where their children were at this hour.

"My first five calls," he lamented, "were answered by children who had no idea where their parents were!" —Mrs. Michael Timko

A FRIEND of mine sometimes feels that his wife and two children do not fully appreciate him. While reading an article called, "A Workable Cue to Happiness and Personality" in a Reader's Digest he underlined in red a sentence he thought aptly summed up his position:

"The father, upon his arrival home, is often greeted with greater affection by the dog than by his own children."

Having got this off his mind, he thought no more about it until he happened to thumb through the magazine a week later. Someone had underlined in green the sentence immediately following his red-marked one.

It read: "For that matter, he may greet the dog with more enthusiasm than he greets his family." —Gordon Akers

Mrs. Douglas MacArthur II, daughter of Alben Barkley, tells this story about the former Vice President: When Father was a judge in Kentucky he was also in charge of juvenile delinquency. There were three of us children, and my little brother was a real heller. One day a woman telephoned my father and said, "Judge, I've simply given up on my little boy. I can't do anything with him. He lies, he fights, he disobeys . . . "

The indignant judge broke in to read her the riot act. "Madam," he thundered, "do you mean to tell me that a grown woman can't control a three-year-old boy!"

Then Mother changed back to her natural voice and said sweetly, "No, Alben, and neither can you!"

—Ruth Montgomery, Chicago Tribune-New York News Syndicate

Mamma Spanks Me

Condensed from Ladies' Home Journal

As told to G. M. White

Sometimes my daddy spanks me. Mamma spanks me too. They don't believe in spanking. They do it because they are mad about something. I don't know what.

Today I was making sand pies. I needed a can of water from the sink. I spilled the water on the floor so I needed some more water. Mamma mopped the floor and gave me a half a can of water. This was enough for only one pie. I went in and climbed up on the stool beside the sink. I filled two cans. Mamma said not to let the door slam again going out but how could I help it with both hands full?

Most of the water leaked out of one can so I needed some more water. I went back with my big bucket to get plenty and a thin old glass on the drainboard broke. I set the bucket on the floor to pick up the pieces of glass. Mamma came in and kicked the bucket. That spilled it so I needed some more water. While Mamma went to get the mop I climbed up on the stool again but the stool slipped and I fell. Mamma screamed because I spilled a little water not *nearly* as much as she did and she put me and the bucket outside and said not to dare come in for any more water. She said she had a headache and was going to lie down.

Pretty soon I needed some more water but I remembered what Mamma said so I filled my big bucket full of sand and carried my pans cans tins cups lids boxes ladles shovels and spoons into the kitchen. Not much of the sand spilled on the floor. Then everything was handy and I didn't need to come in for any more water. I rolled the pies out on Mamma's worktable and put sugar on them. I did not waste any sugar. I scraped the extra sugar back into the bowl. I started to put one pie in Mamma's oven. The door flipped up and knocked it out of my hand. This made noise. When I turned around Mamma was looking at me. She looked mad about something.

Mamma spanked me. I don't know why. Daddy says Mamma is pretty hard to figure out sometimes. When Mamma spanks me Daddy says you know that doesn't do any good. When my daddy spanks me Mamma says that doesn't do any good you know. There's two of them and only one of me. I wish they'd get together more.

Daddy was late driving home from work. Mamma said what have you been doing all this time? He said air was getting into my gas line and then I had a flat. Mamma said I don't care how many you have but why don't you phone and tell me? Daddy chewed a while and then he said these fried potatoes don't taste like my mother used to fry. Mamma said then why didn't you stay with her? Daddy said my mother has only one fault she snores in bed.

Mamma choked and said don't make me laugh I've been chasing this boy all day. Daddy said how can that be? *That* boy Mamma said. She pointed at me. Oh Daddy said. How would you like a baby brother? I said I want a baby sister so I can beat her. Mamma stood up and prayed oh Lord forgive me for I know not what I do. Daddy mussed my hair. Well you are going to get a baby brother and like it he said. He went around the table and kissed Mamma so she wouldn't cry. I guess he was tired because he went outside and lay down under the car.

When Daddy fixes things I help him. I took a little hammer to fix the car radiator. I poked it a few times to clean out a bug. Daddy crawled out and said oh that's all right it leaks anyway. But may I borrow your screw driver? He took my hammer and crawled back under the car. He left a big pan of oil so I started to pour the oil on the car's insides. Daddy stuck his head out and it was all black with oil. He said son that oil is too dirty to put back in the car. Why don't you do something for Mother? So I took a few hammers to work on her washing machine.

I had just started on the washer when Mamma came and took the big hammer away from me without saying a word. I said what are you going to do with the hammer because I need it to fix the washer? She said I am going to use it to fix my head pretty soon. Then Daddy came around and said do you have my socket wrench old man? He took my other hammer. He said you haven't been using my electric drill have you? I said no and he found his electric drill and crawled back under the car. The line on the drill caught under a tire. When Daddy jerked it the plug fell out of the wall. He said oh shucks no power. He started to put the wire back on the drill so I put the plug back in the hole on the wall. There was a loud bump as Daddy hit the car with his head. He came out from under that car fast. He jumped up and down and shook his fingers. He yelled *dammitalltohell!* I jumped up and down and shook my fingers. I laughed and said *dammitalltohell!*

Daddy spanked me. I don't know why. What would Daddy do if he *believed* in spanking?

Sitting Pretty

Baby-sitters: Girls you hire to watch your television set *(Consumers Topics)* . . . The baby-sitter was sitting in the living room, ticking like a taximeter (Mary Augusta Rodgers in *Today's Woman)*

SITTER to returning parents: "Everything went fine, Mrs. Evarts. Francie drank all her milk . . . Junior went to bed without a peep . . . and, oh, yes . . . a quiz show called. I won $10,000."

—Larry Harris cartoon in *Collier's*

THE PARENTS of twins a few months old considered the 12-year-old girl next door grown up enough to ask her to baby-sit one night. Her mother wasn't sure whether she was better qualified to sit or to be sat with, but the youngster was so eager that permission was reluctantly granted.

When the big evening arrived, the mother briefed her daughter carefully — especially about how to prepare the formulas, one for the boy and a different one for the girl. "If you have any trouble," she said, "just give me a ring and I'll come right over." An hour ticked slowly by. Then the phone rang, and the mother flew to answer it. "Are you having trouble with the formulas?" she asked.

"No," her daughter replied. "I've got them all fixed. One for the boy and one for the girl."

"Then what's the matter?"

There was a brief silence from the other end. Then: "Mama—which one is the boy?"

—Bill Gold in Washington *Post and Times Herald*

DEPARTING baby-sitter to parents: "By the way, I promised Janie that if she'd go to bed without any fuss you'd buy her a pony in the morning."

—Larry Harris cartoon in *Collier's*

YOU NEVER know what your next trip may be when you drive a taxi. I answered a call one day and a lady came out of the house with three small children, put them in the cab and said, "Pull the meter, please. I'll be back in a few minutes."

So I sat there waiting, and the children bawled and yelled. Fifteen minutes later their mother came back. "How much do I owe you?" she asked.

I asked her if she wasn't going any place. "No," she said. "But I had a long-distance phone call to make and needed peace and quiet. Here's the fare and thanks for waiting."

—Wendall P. Dean

FROM THE Dekalb, Ill., *Daily Chronicle:* "DAY NURSERY — Expert supervision for ages six weeks to five years. By hour or day. Unreasonable rates for unreasonable children."

A FRIEND of mine, who is the father of 12, volunteered to baby-sit one evening so his wife could go to the movies. "Don't let a single one of them come downstairs," his wife instructed him as she went out. He promised to carry out orders to the letter and had just settled down to a book when he heard steps on the stairway. "Get back upstairs and stay there," he commanded sternly.

He read in peace for a few minutes, then again heard soft footsteps. This time he added the threat of a spanking. Soon he again detected stealthy sounds, and dashed out in time to see a small lad disappear up the top steps. He had hardly returned to his book when a neighbor came in distractedly. "Oh, Fred," she wailed, "I can't find my Willie anywhere. Have you seen him?"

"Here I am, Ma," said a tearful voice from the top of the stairs. "He won't let me go home!"

—Ruth McManus

Not So Well Remembered

ADMIRAL Jerauld Wright, Supreme Allied Commander, Atlantic, and Commander in Chief U.S. Atlantic Fleet, prides himself that during a 1941 tour of duty at the United States Naval Academy he learned the names and faces of every firstclassman — over 1000 men—and can still recognize most of them over 15 years later. One day he saw an officer whom he recognized as a member of that group. "You're Martin of the class of '41," he told the pleased, and surprised, officer. After they'd exchanged a few words, Admiral Wright asked, "By the way, what are you doing now?"

"I'm on your staff, sir," Martin replied. —F. Jester

DR. FRANK H. SPARKS, president of Wabash College, tells this story: My memory for names is notably bad, and at public gatherings I always rely on Mrs. Sparks to help me. But on one occasion we became separated, and I beheld a matron bearing down upon me whom I felt that I should recognize. I was greeting her with a warm handclasp when a man I knew rather well came along. Still clasping the lady's hand, I waved my other hand in greeting. "Hello, Fred," I called. "How is your lovely wife these days?"

"You ought to know," replied Fred. "You're holding hands with her!" —*Quote*

LAWRENCE LANGNER, absent-minded impresario, one day boarded a taxicab in front of the Theatre Guild office and announced: "I have only 20 minutes to catch my train. Please get me to Grand Central as quickly as you can," then opened his evening paper. Fifteen minutes and ten pages later he looked up for the first time and noted that he was still in front of the Theatre Guild office.

That's when he discovered that there was no driver in the taxicab.

—Bennett Cerf in *The Saturday Review*

HAVE YOU ever wondered what became of the absent-minded professor of yesteryear? Well, I can tell you: He's the research scientist of today. I found this out while living in California at a secret test center with my husband and 102 other Ph.D.s. One of the brainier ones was seen leaving the laboratory with this sign pinned to his lapel: "Do not give me a ride home. I have the car today."

—Mary Agnes Liddell

OUR ENGINE company was dispatched to an apartment house, but when we arrived there was no sign of a fire. We radioed the dispatcher, and he insisted the woman was on the phone again and was frantic. In a moment he called back and told us that she gasped, "Oh, my God! I've just moved!"

We dashed to her new residence and had quite a fire to work on.

—Arthur Papp

Guardian Angels

A WOMAN who lives most of the year in the city was surprised one spring day to receive a telephone call from a girl who works for her during the summer at her country place. "There is a bad forest fire up here and it is getting near your house," the girl informed her.

"My goodness!" the lady exclaimed. "Is there anything I can do?"

"Well," the caller replied, "I thought maybe you might want to put some more insurance on the house."

—B. H. Mallory

OUR NEIGHBOR'S young son had always wanted a dog, and when a cocker spaniel down the block had a litter, his father got him one of the pups. The boy's mother insisted that the new pet be kept in the basement at night.

The first night, not surprisingly, the puppy howled pitifully until dawn, keeping the entire neighborhood awake. Things were no better the second night. The morning after that our neighbor heard a pawing at his front door and opened it to find the pup's mother standing there. The spaniel walked in, picked up her offspring by the scruff of the neck and, leaving the man in the doorway with mouth agape, marched home.

—Arthur J. Zuckerman

MY HUSBAND stopped at a small-town garage in Georgia. "Whenever I hit 70," he told the mechanic, "there's a knocking in the engine."

After a lengthy examination and much testing of the engine the mechanic wiped the grease from his hands and drawled, "I don't see nothing wrong, mister. It must be the good Lord a-warning you."
—Priscilla H. Berenzweig

THE NEW people next door were scarcely moved in when I found some of their mail pushed through my letter slot. I took it over to them and, in the process, made their acquaintance.

A day or so later I saw another neighbor carrying mail to their house. The following morning I chided the postman for his carelessness. "Did you get to know the people?" he asked, his eyes twinkling.

"Yes," I replied. "They're a nice couple."

"Best way I know for people to get acquainted," he said.
—G. S. Anderson

MY TEEN-AGE daughter visited a pet shop and was entranced by the horned toads it was featuring. She would have come home with one but for the understanding attitude of the store. When she asked the price of the toads the clerk told her, "They are 85 cents —and a note from your parents."
—Jeannette H. Reese

WHEN I had to make an unexpected trip to a city with which I was unfamiliar, I selected a hotel at random from a hotel guide and asked my secretary to wire for a room to be held for me. The title "The Reverend" which she used in the message must have given the receiving operator some concern. For this telegram came back to me:

"DO NOT FEEL HOTEL BLANK DESIRABLE FOR YOU HAVE RESERVED ROOM HOTEL WHITE *(signed)* WESTERN UNION."
—The Rev. Walter J. Lake

How's That Again?

SIGN IN an English hotel: "Please do not wait to be introduced to your fellow guests; we are all one big family. Do not leave valuables in your bedroom." —*Picture Post*

FROM DONALD and Eleanor Laird's book *Sizing Up People:* "There is usually a temporary rise in IQ at the time of puberty. This occurs earlier in girls than in boys, and gives girls more intelligence than boys during their early teen years. But in another year or so the boys catch up with the girls, and from then on it is neck-and-neck."

CHAIRMAN at a Liverpool meeting: "In most associations half the committee does all the work, whilst the other half does nothing. I am pleased to put on record that in this society it is just the reverse."

—Liverpool *Echo,* quoted in *Picture Post*

FROM THE Vermont *Standard:* "Mrs. Sarah Putnam is poorly this spring—her face is much missed in church, it being always there when she is able to be present."

FROM THE Richmond *Times-Dispatch:* "Percy A. Tucker—the Richmonder who built one of the country's largest pen businesses from scratch—"

FROM A report of a speech in the Newcastle, England, *Journal:* "Capital punishment applied to the wrong type of child—the nervous, sensitive type—may do irreparable harm."

—Quoted in Baltimore *Evening Sun*

A "FALSIES" manufacturer running an ad in a Norfolk, Va., paper cautioned: "Beware of imitations."

—Quoted in *Tide*

FROM A report of the American Psychological Association's convention in the San Francisco *Examiner:* "Women who are cooperative and good sports are more likely to have large families . . ."

FROM A report of the Williamsburg, Va., police department: "Eleven patients escaped from Eastern State Hospital. Thirteen patients were returned."

—Quoted in Newport News, Va., *Daily Press*

ITEM IN the London *Times:* "The Clairvoyant Society will not have its usual meeting this week, due to unforeseen circumstances."

—Quoted in Columbia University *Jester*

AT LACKLAND A.F.B. a group of new WAFs were listening to a long lecture on the Standards of the Service Woman. After much advice on what to do and what not to do in uniform, the speaker concluded, "If you're going to do anything that would disgrace your uniform, take it off."

—A/3c Nancy Donaldson

Military Maneuvers

WHEN THE fighting was over in New Guinea, the Army stationed a small contingent of WACs there to take over the paperwork and release men for combat duty. Women were a rarity in the Pacific theater, and the men vied for their attention. A GI who had managed to engage one of the WACs in conversation was trying to impress her with tales of the action he had seen. "Why, one time," he boasted, "our company held off 10,000 Japs for six hours!"

"That's nothing," retorted the WAC. "Our company of girls has been holding off 100,000 Americans for six months." —Joe Ryan

THE OCEAN was rough and visibility poor, and as our ship fell into the convoy column it bumped the stern of another vessel, but without doing any real damage. The weather grew even worse, and ships of the convoy became scattered over a wide area. Finally we received a coded radio message telling us where to rejoin the convoy. We changed our course, and a few minutes later there was a terrific crash. We had rammed the same ship a second time. Frantic, our captain signaled, "CAN YOU STAY AFLOAT?"

"YES," flashed the other skipper. "TRY AGAIN."

—J. A. Rademacher

ATTU, the most western of the Aleutian Islands, is probably best remembered by those who served there because of its mud, snow, perpetual fog and high winds. Heating our Quonset huts was complicated by the fact that the oil stoves were continually being blown out by blasts of wind when the men forgot to close the doors. The carpenters' mates of the Naval Air Facility found a way to lick this problem and still observe military courtesy. On the door of their shop, in large block letters, was the sign:

SHUT THE DOOR, STUPID!
NOT YOU, SIR!

—Lt. Comdr. R. G. Vliet

WHILE SERVING in the Navy Yard at Bremerton, Wash., I was having some much delayed dental work done. On about the sixth trip to the dispensary I was greeted by a Navy dentist who surprised me by saying, "Now if I hurt you, be sure to tell me." All during the appointment he kept asking, "How does that feel?" and "Does this hurt?" Finally I said to him, "I've been coming here for weeks and no one has cared if he hurt me or not. You're the first Navy dentist I've seen who considered the patient's feelings."

"Oh," he replied, "I don't care about your feelings—it's just that I'm getting discharged next week and I'm trying to regain my civilian touch." —Capt. J. R. Luckett

COMEDIAN Red Skelton, serving at Camp Roberts during World War II, brought daily humor into our lives. I remember one night when he got up and went to the drinking fountain. His voice boomed out in the barracks, "My God! Somebody put water in the chlorine." —Al Wakefield

A FEW YEARS ago the senior American naval officer in Europe flew down to the Mediterranean from London to inspect the Sixth Fleet on maneuvers. The trip was to be a short one so the admiral wore his work uniform and carried along his blues for dress. But in port, after maneuvers, he was invited to an official reception and the uniform specified was whites. It wasn't difficult to find an extra white uniform for the admiral, but where could they find a set of shoulder boards? The next senior officer within a thousand miles was still only a vice admiral. As a last resort the flag lieutenant sent a dispatch to all ships asking if anyone had a pair of admiral's shoulder boards. The dispatch was received with snickers in the wardrooms. Who would be that optimistic? But, to everyone's amazement, a spanking new ensign produced a set.

He had received them as a graduation gift from his girl, with this note: "You may be only an Ensign to the Navy, but you will always be an Admiral to me."

ON A BUS crossing the flatlands of Texas I overheard a young GI, evidently en route to Fort Sam Houston, say plaintively to his fellow rookies, "I doan think I'm goin' to like it—you cain't even go AWOL from a Texas post. They can *see you* for five days!" —Marion A. Knight

THE NURSES on Guam had rather primitive bathing facilities—walls but no ceiling. This didn't disturb us until we noticed that a helicopter would hover overhead when the showers were the busiest. Finally our chief nurse made a formal complaint about this aerial Peeping Tom.

The plane disappeared, and we heard that the lieutenant involved had been grounded. But a few days later the plane turned up again and remained glued overhead. Our chief nurse returned to do battle. She learned that the lieutenant had been grounded all right—now the colonel was flying the 'copter. —Ruth Haskell Smith

Toward More Picturesque Speech

Listen: An orchestra whimpering to begin (Herbert Harris in Durban, S. Africa, *Sunday Tribune and Post*) . . . Tomcats exchanging insults on different frequencies (Gilbert R. Payson) . . . A flock of crows holding a caw-cus (John C. A. Kelly in *Farm Journal and Country Gentleman*) . . . Old-fashioned radiators clanking like ghosts rattling their chains (Margaret Millar)

NOTHING is impossible to the man who does not have to do it himself (Earl Wilson)

Man to Man: If you don't think women are explosive, just try dropping one (P. Evans in *Hudson Newsletter*) . . . She was wearing a sweater so tight I could hardly breathe (Donald Zec in London *Daily Mirror*) . . . Girls are always running through his mind—they don't dare walk (Mike Connolly in *The Hollywood Reporter*)

Adverteasements: For frozen foods, "Best Meals You Ever Thaw" . . . For Gossard corset, "If you're thick and tired of it" . . . For tear-jerker at drive-in theater, "Be sure to bring your windshield wiper" (Pittsburgh *Post-Gazette*)

On Pills and Needles: Monty Woolley about his operation, "I feel like an overworked vein of coal" . . . On her first visit to the doctor she gave him a preamble to her constitution (Mrs. W. M. Rowlett) . . . It takes a long time for people to get over an illness if compensation sets in (Margaret Schooley) . . . A doctor with a graveside manner (Eleanor Clarage in Cleveland *Plain Dealer*) . . . Hypodermic needle—sick shooter (Ray Cvikota, quoted by Arch Ward in Chicago *Tribune*)

THE KIND of man who goes through life pushing doors marked pull (John Masters) . . . The kind of housewife who thinks the clothes won't dry unless she hangs them out herself (Ann P. Hodge)

Spring is here;
How do I know?
A little virus told me so.
—*Ohms Newsletter*

IF ALL the people who go to sleep in church were laid end to end they would be a lot more comfortable (Mrs. Robert A. Taft) . . . If all the cars in America were placed end to end on a long hill, some fool would try to pass them (Raymond Duncan) . . . If all the economists were laid end to end, they'd still point in all directions (*Hudson Newsletter*)

South of the Border

THE INCREASING number of North American tourists with little or no knowledge of Spanish visiting Puerto Rico has prompted the Department of Tourism to request a San Juan furniture store to change its window display. The window contained a selection of comfortable-looking beds with a sign: "SIN PRONTO."

Many of the visitors failed to understand that this is a Spanish colloquialism for "no down payment." —Morton Sontheimer

SIMON BOLIVAR, the great South American liberator, was scheduled to pass the night in a small Peruvian town. His aide sent word to the local innkeeper asking that "a room be prepared with special accommodations, food, etc., etc., etc."

Arriving in the village Bolívar was shown the best room in the hotel. After he had expressed approval the great man was conducted into an adjoining room where sat three lovely señoritas. "And who are these young ladies?" Bolívar asked.

"The three et ceteras," replied his host. —*South American Digest*

MY SISTER thought she had mastered Spanish until she went to Panama on a trip. She was returning at midnight from a night spot with her husband in an open taxi. It was pouring rain and the driver was speeding like a madman down a curving road. She called out to him in a loud voice, "Stop! You are ruining my hat! What's the hurry? We have all night. Stop, I say!"

But none of her commands were heeded. When they reached the hotel she popped out and started to give the driver a piece of her mind. When she was through he calmly shrugged his shoulders. "I'm sorry, madam," he said. "I thought you two were making love." —Daisine Smith

ON A fishing trip I was attempting to board a train in Mexico when my interpreter and the Mexican conductor got into a terrific argument. "What's the uproar all about?" I asked.

"He says," explained the interpreter, "that this is yesterday's train. Our tickets are for today's train which isn't due until tomorrow!" —Jack McElroy

WALKING DOWN the streets of Taxco, Pancho spied his friend José, who was smiling broadly. "José, amigo," said Pancho, "why for you so happy?"

"Ees love, amigo," beamed José. "Ees to get married."

"Aha!" responded Pancho. "Ees nice. Who is the lucky señorita?"

"Carmen del Valle." Pancho's face clouded. "You don't want to marry Carmen. Ees no good."

José's eyes were daggers. "Why not?"

"Amigo, she's make love weeth every man in Taxco."

"Sí," replied José with a shrug. "But Taxco is such a *leetle* town."

—Capt. Bruce E. Davis

All in Your Point of View

I GOT LOST in the wild woods of the Cumberland Mountains during a fishing trip one summer, but finally picked up a trail which led to a group of cabins and a small general store. "How peaceful it is in the country," I said to the proprietress; "so different from the mad pace of cities. No people and traffic pushing you around."

"Well," she replied politely, "I wouldn't know whether you're right or not. Fact is, I've never lived in the country—I've always lived right here in town."

—Franklin Escher, Jr.

I WAS on top of Roan Mountain, Tenn., the third Sunday in June—practically the only day of the year when anyone drives up the narrow, twisting road. That weekend hundreds of people came to see the magnificent display of wild rhododendron, acres and acres blooming in a setting of blue spruce and mountains rolling to the horizon. When I returned to the hot, dusty parking area, crowded with cars from many states, I was struck by the rapt expression of a mountain woman. "Beautiful sight, isn't it?" I said.

"Shore is purty," she agreed. "All them beautiful cars. Every year I come up here just to see them."

—Nancy Tanner

WE HAD a fire at our house, not a large one but big enough to bring an engine, hook-and-ladder truck and helmeted firemen clanging to the scene. My main concern, after assuring myself of everyone's safety, was the effect on our youngsters of being snatched out of their beds in the middle of the night and hurried out of doors into the smoke, noise and excitement. A traumatic experience perhaps? One that would leave permanent scars—fright, nightmares? Apparently I needn't have worried. Two days later my eight-year-old was told to write a composition on "The Most Exciting Thing That Has Happened to Me or My Family." He labored arduously on his composition.

The topic? "Our Cub Scout Meeting." —Nancy R. McKelligott

MY FRIEND from the Maine woods was paying his first visit to Florida. He delighted at first in our sunny, mild weather, but after weeks of flawless sunshine he looked out the window one morning and muttered, "Oh, hell, another damned beautiful day."

—Walter A. Pearce

A SALESMAN stranded in a small village asked one of the natives if there was a movie in town. "Nope," was the reply.

"Any poolrooms?"

"Nope."

"What form of amusement do you have?" asked the salesman.

"Wal, come down to the drugstore," said the old man. "Thar's a freshman home from college."

—*Pell-Mell,* quoted in *Stanford Chaparral*

Seeing Cells

Excerpt from "My Life and Hard Times"

James Thurber

I PASSED all the other courses that I took at my university, but I could never pass botany. This was because all botany students had to spend several hours a week looking through a microscope at plant cells, and I could never see through a microscope. This used to enrage my instructor. He would wander around the laboratory, pleased with the progress all the students were making in drawing the involved and, so I am told, interesting structure of flower cells, until he came to me. I would just be standing there. "I can't see anything," I would say. He would begin patiently enough, explaining how anybody can see through a microscope, but he would always end up in a fury, claiming that I could *too* see through a microscope. "Try it just once again," he'd say, and I would put my eye to the microscope and see nothing at all, except now and again a nebulous milky substance. "I see what looks like a lot of milk," I would tell him. This, he claimed, was the result of my not having adjusted the microscope properly, so he would readjust it for me, or rather, for himself. And I would look again and see milk.

I finally took a deferred pass and waited a year and tried again. The professor had come back from vacation brown as a berry, bright-eyed, and eager to explain cell structure again to his classes. "Well," he said to me cheerily, the first laboratory hour, "we're going to see cells this time, aren't we?" "Yes, sir," I said. Students to right of me and to left of me were seeing cells; what's more, they were quietly drawing pictures of them. Of course, I didn't see anything.

"We'll try it," the professor said to me, grimly, "with every adjustment of the microscope known to man. As God is my witness, I'll arrange this glass so that you see cells through it or I'll give up teaching. In 22 years of botany, I —" He cut off abruptly for he was beginning to quiver all over.

So we tried it with every adjustment of the microscope known to man. With only one of them did I see anything and that time I saw, to my pleasure and amazement, a variegated constellation of flecks, specks and dots. These I hastily drew. The instructor, noting my activity, came back, a smile on his lips and his eyebrows high in hope. He looked at my cell drawing. "What's this?" he demanded, with a hint of a squeal in his voice. "That's what I saw," I said. "You didn't, you didn't, you didn't!" he screamed. He bent over and squinted into the microscope. His head snapped up. "That's your eye!" he shouted. "You've fixed the lens so that it reflects! You've drawn your eye!"

Chasing the Wild Motel

Condensed from Woman's Day

Robert M. Yoder

ONE NEGLECTED reason for the great popularity of motels and tourist courts today is that these bedding-down places, ranging from passable to exceptional, have turned the otherwise stodgy business of going to roost into the liveliest feature of a day on the highway. Around 5 p.m. travelers by the hundreds begin passing up spots that would do all right, in the hope of grabbing off something superior. The result is a stirring new game, something like musical chairs at 65 miles an hour.

This nervous roaming in the gloaming is a light variety of gambling, contains elements of bargain hunting and is a dandy form of self-inflicted anxiety. As the sun sinks to rest, and travelers figure on doing the same, the driver in any expedition says, "Keep your eyes peeled, now, for a good place to stop. What about that joint right there?" Nobody says no, but nobody is willing to

Woman's Day, the A&P Magazine (September, '53), © 1953 by Woman's Day, Inc., 19 W. 44 St., New York 36, N. Y.

say yes, either. The crafty decision is to look a little longer. The game is in full swing.

It is generally agreed that to accept the first place, however pleasant, is for weaklings. They submit meekly to their fate, like horses trudging into their appointed stalls. The bold, the venturesome and those who made a bad choice last night forge ahead.

For best results there ought to be two factions in every car, and nature, in her infinite wisdom, usually provides them. The conservatives' policy calls for stopping pretty soon, or we're going to end up in the crummiest joint on Route 202. It is the duty of the conservatives to remark, "That place would have been fine," just after the place is well passed. The progressives, secretly losing confidence as day fades, simply put on speed. The idea is that if there isn't much ahead we can at least get there fast.

The best motels on any route are always located at 1:30 p.m. This is mildly supernatural, but entirely true. At this hour, when Mount Vernon itself at two dollars a night would be no good to you, you run into a belt where there are good ones to the left and better ones to the right. At five o'clock, however, they vanish like taxis in the rain.

You can, of course, go to the extreme of making reservations in advance. This is the prudent thing to do, and in perhaps three cases out of a thousand somebody does it. It accomplishes one thing: it exercises a remarkable effect on weather, road surfaces and traffic. Yesterday you crawled along over pitted highways in dense traffic and spent two hours on detours and alternates. Today, in beautiful weather, you bowl along over superior roads through traffic so light that you reach your reserved stop at precisely 3:30 p.m. Stop, and you will have five or six hours of good driving time in which to bicker about whose idea this was, anyway. Or you can kill time watching the improvident grasshoppers show up at about 6 p.m. and get fine accommodations, on the spur of the moment, at the court across the road, a spot so new it wasn't in your guidebook.

Those who say you can't take it with you never saw a car packed for a vacation trip.

—Howard Haynes in *The Saturday Evening Post*

Young Ideas

A SIX-YEAR-OLD was motoring to the West Coast with his family. The weather had been bad; the traveling had been very rough. After a particularly hard day they stopped in a Texas town, took the only available hotel rooms and sank wearily into their beds. Suddenly the silence was broken by the six-year-old. "Mommy," he wailed, "why don't we just go back home and live happily ever after?" —Claire MacMurray in Cleveland *Plain Dealer*

FOR THE first time little Judy saw a cat carrying one of her kittens by the nape of the neck. "You're not fit to be a mother!" she cried in shocked tones. "Why, you're hardly fit to be a father!"

—*The Kalends*

YOUNGSTER writing home from boarding school: "Send food packages! All they serve here is breakfast, lunch and dinner."

—*The Diners' Club News*

A THIRD-GRADE teacher asked her pupils to draw a picture of what they wanted to be when they grew up. The pictures came in—pictures of nurses, of space cadets, of firemen—but one little girl handed in a blank sheet of paper. "Don't you know what you want to be when you grow up?" asked the teacher.

"Sure I know," retorted the little girl. "I want to be married. But I don't know how to draw it!"

—John Crosby in New York *Herald Tribune*

CHILD explaining why she didn't drink pop at the party, "It has too many 'scuse me's in it."

—J. M. Sheppard

WHEN I looked at the clock I was grateful the school day was over. Although kindergarten had been in session a month, little Alberta still bellowed like a calliope for the first half hour of the morning while I tried to read aloud. Billy caused no end of concern by getting lost on his way to the office with the attendance cards. A parent called and upbraided me for not recognizing a case of measles before the symptoms appeared. Pretty Yvena resented the inattention of a little boy she favored and dumped red tempera paint on his head. It had been a day!

Now it was time for dismissal —that is, after pulling 30 pairs of last year's galoshes over this year's bigger shoes and rounding up mittens, hats and lunchboxes. Finally I returned to my desk just in time to retrieve my pay envelope from a little boy who was playing with it. "What's that?" he asked.

"It's my pay check, Johnny."

"Oh," he shouted, full of interest, "do you work someplace?"

—G. C. A.

DURING observance of Animal Week the fourth-graders told about their kindnesses to pets. Asked what he had done, one little boy said, "I kicked a boy for kicking his dog." —Mary Wright

WATCHING a mother and her small son shopping for shirts in a Phoenix department store, I saw him eying a bright-red one longingly. "But, Mother," he argued, "this one won't show the blood!"

—Marguerite Cameron

THE FIRST-GRADERS were on a field trip to observe the birds beginning their migration. Explaining that they were noisy and excited because they were going on a long journey, the teacher asked the class, "What do you suppose they are saying?"

"I imagine," said one little girl shyly, "that the mother birds are telling their children they'd better go to the bathroom before they start." —Edith Fair

THE YOUNG daughter of William Howard Taft III was asked to write a brief autobiographical sketch when she started a new grade. Her composition read: "My great-grandfather was President of the United States. My grandfather was Senator from Ohio. My father is Ambassador to Ireland. I am a Brownie."

—E. H. L.

SMALL BOY to chum: "I know I'm not adopted because if I was they would have sent me back by now." —Bill King cartoon in *The Saturday Evening Post*

A LITTLE girl stayed for dinner one night at a friend's house. There were buttered parsnips and the mother asked if she liked them. "Oh, yes," replied the child politely. "I love them."

However, when the platter was passed, she refused to take any.

"But, dear," said the hostess, "I thought you said you liked buttered parsnips."

"Oh, I *do,*" explained the child, "but not enough to eat them!"

—E. E. Kenyon in *The American Weekly*

A Hole Is to Dig

From the book of first definitions collected by Ruth Krauss

DR. ARNOLD GESELL once stated, "The child of five is a pragmatist and defines things in terms of use." Intrigued by this statement, Ruth Krauss set about collecting definitions from children in nursery school and kindergarten. Some of her prizes:

Buttons are to keep people warm.

Mashed potatoes are to give everybody enough.
A lap is so you don't get crumbs on the floor.
A dream is to look at the night and see things.
Dishes are to do.
Cats are so you can have kittens.
Rugs are so dogs have napkins.
A nose is to blow.
A hole is to dig.

A rock is when you trip on it you should have watched where you were going.

Tee Time

SMALL GIRL, as golfer in sand trap pauses for breath: "He's stopped beating it, Mummy. I think it must be dead."
—*A Century of Punch Cartoons,* edited by R. E. Williams (Simon and Schuster)

EDITOR Frank Crowninshield was an inveterate golfer, making up in zeal what he lacked in skill. In a golf match he was all square with publisher Condé Nast going down to the green on the 16th hole. He tugged his caddie's sleeve and asked loudly, "Is that my dear friend's ball in the trap or is the son-of-a-so-and-so on the green?" —Bennett Cerf, *Laughter Incorporated* (Garden City)

AS WE WAITED to tee off on the 18th hole, a man in the foursome ahead drove three successive balls into the water. In a fury he picked up his golf bag and hurled it into the lake, then stamped off toward the clubhouse.

We weren't surprised to see him sheepishly return a few minutes later, roll up his pants, take off his shoes and wade in after the clubs. It was what we'd expected.

But to our amazement, he fished out the bag, unzipped the pocket, took out his car keys, flung the clubs into the water again and stalked off. —Louis H. Williams

TWO STRANGERS met in Pro Winny Cole's shop at the Vicksburg Country Club one day, each looking for a game. "What's your average score?" Mr. A asked Mr. B.

"Between 90 and 95," Mr. B replied.

"Fine. That's about what I shoot, so suppose we play a round."

"All right," said Mr. B, "but we ought to have a little bet, just to make it interesting." So they rigged up a stout wager.

After the match Mr. A rushed into Cole's shop and cried, "You know that lying so-and-so I was playing? I had to shoot a 73 to beat him!" —Fred Beck and O. K. Barnes, *73 Years in a Sand Trap* (Wyn)

LIKE MOST beginners he managed to hit one magnificent, long drive during the 18 holes. When the round was over he couldn't stop boasting about that particular shot. "Wasn't that drive marvelous?" he asked a friend for the tenth time.

"Yes," was the bitter reply. "It's a shame you can't have it stuffed!" —Dan Bennett

A Matter of Degree

ONE WOMAN golfer to another: "You're improving, Muriel. You're missing the ball much closer than you used to."

—George Hamilton Green cartoon in *The American Magazine*

QUENTIN ROOSEVELT developed the philosophic mind at an early age. A friend of the family, visiting at Sagamore, came on him at a local drugstore, grasping a nickel in his hand and looking longingly at the soda fountain. The friend, knowing that the boy was supposed to be careful what he ate, remarked, "Quentin, I wouldn't take a soda. It might make you sick."

Quentin looked at the lady with round, solemn eyes. "*How* sick?" he asked.

—Hermann Hagedorn, *The Roosevelt Family of Sagamore Hill* (Macmillan)

A WOMAN who attended a wedding to which she had not been invited explained: "I wasn't so mad that I wasn't invited that I wouldn't come." —Mrs. E. C. Rieth

BOSS TO stenographer: "Congratulations, Miss Simpkins—this is the earliest you've ever been late!" —Hoff cartoon, King Features

A TORONTO homemaker had a set of slip covers made to order —paid a good price for them and they were guaranteed not to shrink. But they did shrink the first time she had them cleaned, and even though this was several years later, back she went to the store to demand a refund, which she got.

Passing through the slip-cover section a few days later, she discovered her former property offered on the bargain counter for $15. She bought the set, later explaining to her mystified husband, "Well, they weren't *that* shrunk." —*Maclean's Magazine*

Counter Attacks

WOMAN shopping for wallpaper to clerk: "Now we're getting somewhere—that's the exact opposite of what I want."

—Ian Peterson cartoon in Barrie, Ont., *Examiner*

WHILE I WAS shopping at Klein's Department Store in Hempstead, Long Island, a booming voice came over the public-address system: "A little lost boy is at the nursery. He says he is two and one half years old and that his name is Two-Gun Goldberg."

—Phil S. Freiberg

THE CHRISTMAS rush at one of our Houston department stores was in full swing. On the crowded escalator I heard one harried store employe say to another, "Hey, Joe, you still workin'? I thought you was gonna quit!"

"I am gonna quit," his friend answered. "I been tryin' all day to quit, but I can't find nobody to quit to."

—Alma Geisenhoff

WHEN I WAS being fitted for a new girdle, the saleswoman asked, "Is madam *quite* comfortable?" Madam was. "Can madam breathe deeply with ease?" Madam could. "Does madam feel she could wear this garment all day without discomfort?" Madam did.

"Then," said the clerk, "madam obviously needs a smaller size."

—Mrs. N. McLennan

AT THE COUNTER of a Fifth Avenue shop a woman with a Pekingese on a leash was standing next to a man waiting to be served. The dog kept hovering around the man's legs and the man kept drawing away from the animal. Finally the woman said, "Don't be afraid. My Pekingese won't bite you."

"Madam, I'm not afraid your dog is going to bite me," said the man, "but, as he kept lifting his leg, I was afraid he was going to kick me." —E. V. Durling, King Features

WOMAN, hurrying into a department store sale, to companion: "I hope they don't have anything I want." —M. Stewart

AN ACQUAINTANCE of mine who worked as a fashion consultant at Neiman-Marcus, Dallas' famous store, was approached one day by a prosperous-looking Texan matron who wanted advice on the proper blouse to wear with a new evening skirt. "I'll be glad to help you," the consultant said. "What kind of skirt is it?"

"It's made outa mink," the lady said. "But I'm having it sheared to look like velvet." —Patricia C. Beaudouin

SIGN IN a women's shoe store in Brooklyn: "Ten percent discount given if you make your purchase within ten minutes of entering store." —Hy Gardner in New York *Herald Tribune*

A BROOKLYN department store made a big fuss over its millionth customer. The store president made her a speech, she was given gifts and had her picture taken. After the ceremonies the customer continued to her original destination—the complaint department. —Robert Sylvester in New York *Sunday News*

Complaint Department

COMPLAINT-DEPARTMENT clerk to carping woman shopper: "Madam, it may interest you to know that 19 of our clerks have turned in complaints about *you!*"

—Henry Boltinoff cartoon in *Nation's Business*

In Sterling, Ill., Albert D. Martin sued two policemen for $10,000, complained that if they had arrested him for drunken driving five minutes sooner he would never have had a smashup.

—*Time*

Just after the late Robert R. Young became chairman of the board of the New York Central System, he got his first complaint from Bristol, Ind. An indignant farmer wrote in to complain that a New York Central train had been late for three Sundays.

"Unless you do something about it I'll take the matter up with the Interstate Commerce Commission in Washington," he wrote. "Our minister times his sermons by the whistle of your train and it has been 20 minutes late three Sundays in a row."

—Walter Trohan, Chicago Tribune Press Service

The parking-lot owner called the three attendants together. "Look, boys," he said, "we haven't had one single complaint about a dented fender all week." He paused to let his words sink in. "Now tell me," he bellowed, "how can we make any money leaving *that* much space?"

—Hal Chadwick

An indignant citizen in Grand Rapids, Mich., complained to the Better Business Bureau that the book which he ordered after being intrigued by the publisher's circular carrying such chapter heads as "Some Girls Know How," "Since Eve Ate Apples" and "Bachelor Bait" turned out to be a cookbook.

—Arthur Lansing in *The American Magazine*

Sweet young thing to man at telephone-company complaint desk: "Nobody ever calls me!"

—Dale McFeatters cartoon, Publishers Syndicate

An angry little man bounced into the postmaster's office. "For some time now," he shouted, "I've been pestered with threatening letters, and I want something done about it!"

"I'm sure we can help," soothed the postmaster. "That's a federal offense. Have you any idea who is sending you these letters?"

"Indeed I have," snapped the little man. "They are all coming from those pesky income-tax people."

—Maurice Bodington, CJBC, Toronto

AN INDIGNANT commuter wrote the New Haven Railroad: "I take your 9:35 a.m. train daily. I cannot get a seat near the front of the train and sometimes have to stand all the way. Several coaches on this train near the rear end carry very few passengers. Will you please advise me why those coaches cannot be put on the front of the train so we won't be so crowded?"

—William W. Kealy

OUTSIDE AN Indianapolis gas station: "To keep from having complaints about our free service, there will be no free service."

—AP

Tit for Tat

I WAS ON duty at the complaint counter of a West Coast store when a woman approached carrying an automatic toaster. "Do you recall persuading me to have this repaired instead of getting a new one in exchange for it?" she asked.

"Yes, madam," I replied.

"Well, I've brought two slices of bread with me and I want you to toast them for me right now," she insisted.

Obligingly I plugged in the toaster, inserted the bread and pushed down the lever. Sudden darkness descended upon the busy noonday rush as every light on the floor level blew out.

"Now do I get a new toaster?" she demanded. —John W. Sheedy

WHEN I STOPPED at a Las Vegas hotel a gangling cowboy, carrying a large leather suitcase, preceded me to the desk. Registering for the room he had reserved, he noticed a discrepancy in the price. "Ma'am," he said hesitantly, "this calls for $14 a day. I only paid $9 for that room before!"

The young lady excused herself and returned in a moment. "The manager asked me to explain," she said, "that this hotel has changed hands."

The cowpoke paused thoughtfully; then, picking up his bag, he drawled, "Please explain to the manager, ma'am, that this hand has changed hotels." —Charles T. Maxwell, Jr.

AN ARDENT fisherman from Dallas made a trip to Bull Shoals Lake in Arkansas. After pulling in a 6½-pound largemouth bass the Texan boasted to his native guide, "Why, heck, in Texas we use that size for bait."

The Arkansan smiled, nodded appreciatively—and dropped the fish back into the lake. —INS

MY GRANDFATHER, Dr. William T. Hornaday, the zoologist, was known for his belligerence as a wildlife conservationist. Consequently, when he came home one day from his director's office in Bronx Park to tell us that he had delivered a crushing blow to one of his bitterest enemies, the family had dire visions.

"Did you attack the man with your fists, William?" asked Grandmother in trepidation. He shook his head.

"Are we open for libel? Will he sue us for slander?"

"Much too roundabout and subtle for any court to understand," said Grandfather with triumph. "On a sudden impulse this afternoon I mailed each of his four children a package of 100 crayons."

—Temple Fielding

A FARMER in a small Virginia community was very proud of his crop—the finest, largest and most delectable watermelons in the entire state. But as the melons ripened, the farmer missed several each morning. Finally he erected a large sign which announced: DANGER! ONE OF THE WATERMELONS IN THIS PATCH IS POISONED!

The following morning the farmer was appalled to find his sign changed. It now read: DANGER! TWO OF THE WATERMELONS IN THIS PATCH ARE POISONED! —Dr. Arthur M. Whitehill, Jr.

"MAY I SPEAK to the person who takes care of jobs for cooks and maids?" requested a man standing at the information desk of the State Employment Service. He was directed to the proper place. There he asked, "Are you the man who sent me a cook yesterday?"

The interviewer checked his records and smiled. "Yes, I am."

"Well," said the visitor, "it would please me immensely if you would have dinner with me tonight." —Clarence Roeser

THE OTHER DAY I heard my five-year-old boy screaming in the playroom, and when I ran in I found the baby pulling his hair. "Never mind," I tried to comfort him, "your baby sister doesn't understand that it hurts you." I hadn't been out of the room for a minute when more shrieks sent me running back. This time the baby was crying. "What's the matter with the baby," I asked the boy.

"Nothing much," he replied calmly. "Only now she knows."

—Amelia Dexter in *Magazine Digest*

ONCE WHEN Eve Arden was appearing in summer stock her co-star decided to spring a practical joke. In a scene where he and Eve spoke to each other across the stage, he had a phone in the actress's corner ring out in the middle of her recital. Eve retained enough stage presence to answer the phone. Thinking quickly, she turned to the prankster and said, "It's for you."

—Sidney Skolsky, United Feature Syndicate

A MEMBER of the Cornell University faculty, noted for his tact, was awakened at 4 a.m. by his telephone. "Your dog is barking and keeping me awake," said an irate woman's voice.

The professor thanked her and hung up. The following morning at four the woman's telephone rang. "Madam," said the professor, "I have no dog." —Norman Michie

Every Dog Should Own a Man

Condensed from This Week Magazine

Corey Ford

EVERY DOG should have a man of his own. There is nothing like a well-behaved person around the house to spread the dog's blanket for him, or bring him his supper when he comes home man-tired at night.

For example, I happen to belong to an English setter who acquired me when he was about six months old and has been training me quite successfully ever since. He has taught me to shake hands with him and fetch his ball. I've learned not to tug at the leash when he takes me for a walk. I am completely housebroken, and I make him a devoted companion.

The first problem a dog faces is to pick out the right man—a gay and affectionate disposition is more important than an expensive pedigree. I do not happen to be registered but my setter is just as fond of me as though I came from a long line of blue bloods. Also, since a dog is judged by the man he leads, it is a good idea to walk the man up and down a couple of times to make sure his action is free and he has springy hindquarters.

The next question is whether the dog and man should share the house together. Some dogs prefer a kennel because it is more sanitary, but my setter decided at the start that he'd move right in the house with me. I can get into any of the chairs I want except the big overstuffed chair in the living room, which is his.

Training a man takes time. Some men are a little slow to respond, but a dog who makes allowances and tries to put himself in the man's place will be rewarded with a loyal pal. Men are apt to be high-strung and sensitive, and a dog who loses his temper will only break the man's spirit.

Punishment should be meted out sparingly—more can be accomplished by a reproachful look than by flying off the handle. My setter has never raised a paw to me, but he has cured me almost entirely of the habit of running away. When he sees me start to pack my suitcase he just lies down on the floor with his chin on his forepaws and gazes at me sadly. Usually I wind up by canceling my train reservations.

The first thing to teach a man is to stay at heel. For this lesson the dog should hook one end of a leash to his collar and loop the other around the man's wrist so he cannot get away. Start down the street slowly, pausing at each telephone pole until the man realizes that he's under control. He may tug and yank at first, but this can be discouraged by slipping deftly between his legs and winding the leash around his ankles. If the man tries to run ahead, brace all four feet and halt suddenly, thus jerking him flat on his back. After a few such experiences the man will follow his dog with docility. Remember, however, that all such efforts at discipline must be treated as sport, and after a man has sprawled on the sidewalk the dog should lick his face to show him it was all in fun.

Every man should learn to retrieve a rubber ball. The way my setter taught me this trick was simple. He would lie in the center of the floor while I carried the ball to the far side of the room and rolled it toward him, uttering the word "Fetch!" He would watch the ball carefully as it rolled past him and under the sofa. I would then get the ball from under the sofa and roll it past him again, giving the same command, "Fetch!"

This lesson would be repeated until the setter was asleep. After I got so I would retrieve the ball every time I said "Fetch!" my dog substituted other articles for me to pick up, such as an old marrow bone or a piece of paper he found in the wastebasket.

The matter of physical conditioning is important. A man whose carriage is faulty, and who slouches and droops his tail, is a reflection on the dog who owns him. The best way to keep him in shape is to work him constantly and never give him a chance to relax. Racing him up and down the street at the end of a leash is a great conditioner. If he attempts to slump into an easy chair when he gets back, the dog should leap into it ahead of him and force him to sit in a straight-backed chair to improve his posture. And be sure to get him up several times a night to go out for a walk, especially if it is raining.

Equally important is diet. Certain liquids such as beer have a tendency to bloat a man, and a dog should teach him restraint by jumping up at him and spilling his drink, or tactfully knocking the glass off the table with a sweep of his tail.

Not every dog who tries to bring up a man is as successful as my setter. The answer lies in understanding. The dog must be patient and not work himself into a tantrum if his man can't learn to chase rabbits or wriggle under fences as well as the dog does. After all, as my setter says, it's hard to teach an old man new tricks.

Conditioned Reflex

A FRIEND of mine with a new cocker-spaniel puppy wanted to train him to "speak" for his meals. He would hold the dog's food just out of reach and then bark a few times before giving it to him. The pup, he hoped, would associate barking with food and begin to "speak" for himself.

After a week or so of this he again held the food just out of reach, and waited for the dog to bark. The puppy failed to take his cue, but the owner put the dish before him anyway. Then my friend got a real shock. The puppy refused to eat—until his master barked. —K. J. Bentley

A MINNEAPOLIS Marine officer, en route home with his family from duty in Hawaii, was on a bus in San Francisco, Calif. He was reading a newspaper, his wife was tending the baby and their rowdy small son was cavorting in the aisle. Just then the earthquake hit.

Without even looking up from his paper, the Marine yelled at the kid, "All right, you, cut that out!"
—"Almanac" in Minneapolis *Tribune*

A GOVERNMENT worker sat at the table after breakfast one morning, engrossed in his newspaper for over an hour. Finally he asked for another cup of coffee. "Coffee!" echoed his wife. "But look at the time. Aren't you going to the office today?"

"Office?" exclaimed the startled man. "Heavens! I thought I *was* at the office." —Dan Bennett

THE HERD instinct in New Yorkers probably shows up most sharply in the subways. A high-school teacher, conducting a class of 30 pupils underground at Times Square one day, stuck his head back inside a front car when his group lagged. He hollered, "Everybody out, now, quickly!" The car emptied right off, not only of his charges, but of all the other passengers. Embarrassed, the teacher walked off with his kids and left the natives standing, bewildered.

—Meyer Berger in New York *Times*

WHEN WE went next door to hear our neighbor's new hi-fi set, he put on a record, sat down squarely in front of the machine and stared at it intently. Finally I asked what in the world he was looking at. Grinning sheepishly he tried to settle back in his armchair. "I'm so doggone used to looking at television," he explained, "I just can't listen any other way!" —Dottie Knight

ON HIS FIRST day out, a rookie policeman in Chicago was having trouble with a bum. He had got him as far as a patrol call box when the derelict swung at him and knocked him down. Another policeman, seeing the commotion from across the street, started over to help. But as he approached the rookie scrambled to his feet and started to run. The other officer finally caught him and demanded, "What's the matter with you anyway?"

"Holy suffering!" panted the new recruit. "I forgot I was a policeman. In the neighborhood where I was brought up we always ran from cops!"

—Lucy Key Miller in Chicago *Tribune*

Police Blotter

BEFORE A Pennsylvania-Columbia game at Baker Field a "happy" group of Penn students were maneuvering a topless jalopy up and down the sidewalks, brandishing a jug and cheering for Penn until a Manhattan policeman stopped them, reached into the car and took out the keys. Too nonplused to protest, the boys obeyed his order to get out, meekly followed him to a nearby stationery store.

"Gotta dime?" he asked. They produced a dime and the officer bought a stamped envelope. "Let's see yer drivers' licenses." The boys handed them over. The policeman put the keys and licenses in the envelope, wrote the owner's name and address on it. Then he walked outside, dropped the whole thing in the mailbox—and went back to directing traffic.

—Tom O'Reilly in *Town & Country*

EMERGING FROM the beauty parlor just in time to see a policeman ready to tag her car for overtime parking, my young friend begged him not to give her a ticket. "The meter time just now expired," she said. "I know because I had it all figured out." The policeman looked her over critically and asked where she had been. Patting her new, smooth boyish haircut, she told him.

"Tell you what I'll do," he said. "I won't give you a ticket if you'll take the fine and go right back there and have them put in some curl." —Peggy Anne Rogers

PATROLMAN, driving police car at head of long line of autos, to officer with him: "Let's see how slow we can go before they get up nerve enough to pass us."

—Gerald Green cartoon in *The American Magazine*

AN EX-GI undergoing an examination for appointment to the New York police force was asked, "If your beat was a lonely path in Central Park, and a beautiful girl rushed up to you and declared that a strange man had grabbed her, hugged and kissed her, what would you do?" The GI replied instantly, "I'd endeavor to reconstruct the crime." —Bennett Cerf

TWO North Carolina state troopers stopped a driver on a routine check and asked to see his operator's permit. After fumbling in his wallet the man finally handed them a printed card bearing not the slightest resemblance to a driver's license. Somewhat baffled, the troopers renewed their request, to which the man replied, "Well, I'm looking for it. I just thought you'd like something to read until I find it."

—*Tarheel Wheels,* quoted in *The State*

MY MOTHER and my wife returned to the car after shopping to find a traffic officer writing out a parking ticket. Miffed when her dissuading tactics failed, my mother snapped, "Young man, what procedure do you use when you catch someone who is *really* guilty?"

"I don't know, ma'am," he replied respectfully, handing her the ticket. "All I ever catch are the innocent ones." —Lester Higby

IT WAS ALMOST midnight following a busy freshman registration day when I noticed a couple enjoying a lingering embrace in the only automobile left in the college parking lot. Thinking that my policeman's uniform would give them a hint to move on, I walked slowly up to the car.

"Sorry, Officer," the man in the driver's seat explained. "We lost all track of time. Just left our youngest son, our baby, there in the dorm. This is the first time Mother and I have been alone for 27 years." —Porter Kemp

Toward More Picturesque Speech

THE SADDEST words of tongue or pen: "We just sold Junior's buggy, then—" (*Basic Blast,* quoted by General Features Corp.)

Word Pictures: A village where time was always Sunday afternoon (Raymond Playfoot) . . . Women running up the code flags of Monday wash (Jim Grady, KCBS, San Francisco) . . . A day so soft you could wrap a baby in it (Marcelene Cox in *Ladies' Home Journal*) . . . A puppy at the gnaw-it-all stage (Elsie Hawes) . . . Wheat fields with crew cuts (Elizabeth Scofield) . . . A smile that could eat a banana sideways (Arthur "Bugs" Baer)

PRIZE-WINNING slogan to explain torn-up streets in Corpus Christi, Texas: "When you gotta grow, you gotta grow!" (*Town Journal*)

An old-timer is one who remembers—when charity was a virtue and not an organization (*Town Journal*) . . . When the only people who paid income taxes were those who could afford them (D. Crown in *The Saturday Evening Post*)

Musical Notes: Nowadays, whatever is not worth saying is sung (Philadelphia *Daily News*) . . . Her singing was mutiny on the high C's (Helen H. Boileau) . . . The trouble with disc jockeys—too much chatter before the platter (James W. Power in *The Saturday Evening Post*)

THE TROUBLE is that the car of tomorrow is being driven on the highway of yesterday by the driver of today (Jim Seals, quoted by Gordon Gammack in Des Moines *Tribune*) . . . Cloverleaf—crossroads puzzle (M. M. Keachie, Jr.) . . . To kindle a quick blaze try rubbing two fenders together (Franklin P. Jones in *Quote*)

Sign Language: In a repair-shop, "Cuckoo Clocks Psychoanalyzed (*Quote*) . . . On a reducing salon, "Thinner Sanctum" (*The Safe Worker*) . . . On a roadside shop, "For sale: Antiques and Junque" (Harry Lang in Los Angeles *Examiner*)

Pen Portraits: He sounds off on world news as if the morning paper printed only one copy—and he had it (Nunnally Johnson) . . . She's the picture of her father and the sound track of her mother (Earl Wilson) . . . Looking as satisfied as if she had just met an old girl friend who had put on weight (Richard Powell) . . . A little gray chap who would get lost in a crowd of two (Philip Wylie) . . . She reminds me of a switchboard —when she walks all her lines are busy *(Delco Radio Broadcaster)* . . . She spends money like it was going out of style (John A. Straley in *Investment Dealers' Digest)*

IF YOU ever feel neglected, think of Whistler's father (Andrew Fisher, quoted in *Technology Review)*

MARK TWAIN, describing an encounter with an opponent: "Thrusting my nose firmly between his teeth, I threw him heavily to the ground on top of me " (Quoted by Donald Day)

My Fight With Jack Dempsey

By Paul Gallico

IT WAS 1923 and I had been movie critic for the New York *Daily News* a scant six months when the publisher demanded that the smart alec who kept denouncing the daily film fare be fired. This might have ended my newspaper career had not a friendly managing editor concealed me in the sports department, without benefit of by-line.

I was assigned to Jack Dempsey's training camp at Saratoga Springs to write some color pieces on his preparations for the defense of his title against the massive Argentinean, Luis Angel Firpo, the "Wild Bull of the Pampas."

There was lots of color at Uncle (Crying) Tom Luther's camp: the rough, tough Dempsey, still no great distance from the hobo jungles of his youth; the scented Beau Brummell, Jack Kearns, his manager; the bland Tex Rickard; famous sports writers; and all the rag, tag and bobtail of the prizefight world. But there was also mystery there, at least for me. It was boxing itself.

I had attended a few fights and watched boys tagged on the chin go rubbery at the knees, eyes glazing over suddenly, or seen them fall down, struggling to rise. What was it like to be on the floor from a punch with nine seconds to rise? What thoughts pass through a man's head when he has bees in his brain, sickness gnawing at his middle and molasses in his legs? How could I write about these things graphically without having experienced them? I felt that I had to find out or I would never be any good at my job.

It was foolhardy for a chap who never boxed in his life to want to climb into the ring with the man-destroyer Dempsey, yet I did just that. If ever a man began a literary career from the reclining position it was myself.

I presented myself to Dempsey one August afternoon on the porch of his cottage at the camp and asked whether he would spar a round with me so I might write a story on how it felt to be hit by an expert. Dempsey, clad in an old sweater, sat on the porch rail. He looked me up and down, then inquired in his high-pitched voice, "What's the matter, son? Don't your editor like you no more?"

I explained that I expected to survive and said my only serious doubt was my ability to take it in the region of the stomach. I asked the great man if perchance he might confine his attentions to a less unhappy target.

Dempsey reflected, then replied, "I think I understand, son. You just want a good punch in the nose." He agreed to stage the affair the next Sunday. We shook hands and I departed well pleased.

Kearns was aghast when he learned what Dempsey had promised. It must be remembered that I was an unknown in the sports world; I was just under six feet three, weighed 190, and was still in superb condition after having captained the varsity crew at Columbia. With my glasses off and stripped down I looked as ugly and capable as any professional pug. Nobody would have guessed that within this menacing monster beat the heart of a rabbit.

Thoughts of the plots and machinations of this profession inflamed the brain of Kearns. I might be what I said I was, or I might be a ringer from the Firpo camp sent to butt, cut or otherwise injure Dempsey before the fight. His verdict to Dempsey was: "Don't take chances with this guy—nail him quick!"

Sunday was gala day at the camp and some 3000 spectators were on hand. Hype Igoe, a leading sports writer of his time, said to me, "I hear you're fighting the champ this afternoon."

"Oh, not fighting," I said. "We're just going to fool around. Dempsey's going to take it easy."

Hype gave me a pitying look and said, "Son, don't you know that man *can't* take it easy?"

I stood near the ring clad in swim trunks, boxing shoes and boxing gloves. Dempsey, wearing a brown leather head-protector, was boxing with a middleweight to develop speed. In a clinch he cuffed the spar mate on the back of the neck with the side of his fist. "What's that tapping on the back of the neck for?" I asked one of Jack's sparring partners.

The fighter replied, "Shakes you up. Here, I'll show you." Thereupon he hit me on the back of the neck with his gloved hand. My eyes glazed, my knees began to give and I nearly collapsed. I came close to being the first man ever to be knocked out *before* climbing into the ring.

Next Farmer Lodge, a huge heavyweight, entered the ring with Dempsey. He shuffled about for a few seconds; then there was a flurry and a hook accompanied by the sound as of a steer being pole-axed. The Farmer sank to the canvas and lay there. Four mates reverently removed him. Kearns came over to me and said, "Okay, Gallico. You're next."

Kearns did up the introductions in style. "In this corner, the heavyweight champion of the world, Jack Dempsey!" The hills echoed the cheers of the spectators. Next: "In the opposite corner, Paul Gallico of the *Daily News.*" From the 3000 came only a clammy silence, except for one voice from the crowd which inquired mockingly, "Who?"

The bell rang. Reluctantly I left my corner. Dempsey danced over and touched my gloves perfunctorily, then went into his crouching weave from which he could explode those lethal hooks. I felt lonely and assumed my own version of "Pose A" from the *Boxer's Manual,* the same being left arm extended fully and all the rest of me removed as far from Jack as possible. Dempsey pursued, weaving and bobbing. Gone was the friendly smile with which he had lulled me on the porch. With the broad leather headband across his brow, baleful eyes and snarling lips, he resembled nothing so much as a tiger stalking his kill. I wasn't angry at him, but he seemed irritated at my presence. I established that there was some room behind me and retreated thither.

Someone in the crowd made a rude noise. Its result was to undo me by arousing the pride of the Gallicos. Tentatively I stuck out my left. Dempsey ran into it with his nose. Wow! A point for Gallico. Overwhelmed by what I had done, I poked out another left, and another, landing them all for the simple reason that Dempsey didn't bother to defend himself. Three jabs landed! Why, this was fun. Fancy Dan Gallico, the Galloping Ghost of the Squared Circle. I'll just try another. I did.

"BOOOOOOOOOOOOM!"

I can remember seeing Dempsey's berry-brown arm flash for

one instant before my eyes. Then there was this awful explosion within the confines of my skull, followed by a bright light, a tearing sensation and then darkness.

Slowly it grew light again. I was sitting on the canvas with one leg folded under me, my mouth bleeding, grinning foolishly. The ring made a clockwise revolution, stopped and then returned counterclockwise. I heard Kearns counting: "Six—seven—eight—"

And, like an idiot, I got up!

I didn't have to. I had proved my point. I had gained the precious secret I had sought. But the posture on the deck was humiliating before all those people. And so with my head swimming and a roaring in my ears I climbed to my feet on legs of soft rubber tubing.

Dempsey rushed over and pulled me into a clinch, dancing me around and at the same time holding me up. He had proved *his* point; namely, that I wasn't any ringer but just a bum fresh out of college who had never had a glove on. Even Kearns was laughing.

Dempsey whispered into my ear, "Hang on and wrestle around until your head clears, son."

Mercy from the killer! I clutched him like a lost brother. We wrestled around a bit. Absently, Dempsey hit me a half dozen of those affectionate taps on the back of my neck, and the next thing I remember was Kearns again counting over me. I would have been there yet except they needed the premises for further exercises. They told me the affair lasted just one minute 37 seconds.

I was assisted from the enclosure and taken someplace else to lie down until my addled wits collected themselves sufficiently for me to get to my typewriter. I had a splitting headache and was grateful to be alive.

My story was printed under my first sports by-line. They say that the publisher of the *News* laughed his head off when he read it and saw the photograph of me stretched out colder than a mackerel. About a year later he made me sports editor.

Prize Remarks

IN YEARS of hobnobbing with fight managers and lesser figures of the pugilistic trade, sports editor Dan Parker of the New York *Daily Mirror* developed a fine ear for Manhattan's ringside speech. On one occasion Parker gave a health report on Armand Weill, manager of former heavyweight champion Rocky Marciano, as told by "Al" himself:

"My blood pressure is poifick. It was 150 vitriolic and 98 diabolic. The doctor said I had a coupla minor ailments and I says, 'That's funny. I never woiked in the mines.' So he told me I had fallen archeries. Since I went on that diet I ain't got no ulsters or no abominable trouble. I had to practickly fast for a coupla days —jest a large cup of demitasse in the mornin' and a little brought at night—lamb brought. He said I didn't have no sign of kodiak trouble around the heart or no coroner's trombone disease. Everythin' was okey dokel wit' my gold bladder too."

Concluded columnist Parker: "As I looked at the healthy specimen I impulsively exclaimed, 'What a built!' " —*Time*

WHEN JOE LOUIS visited the offices of *Life,* office boys lined up looking for an autograph. "You just wait," said Joe in his soft voice. "I'll bet they'll have bad pictures for me to sign."

"What do you consider a good picture of yourself?" one of the staff asked.

"Why, I like them where I'm standing up," he replied gravely.

—Jeanne Perkins Harman, *Such Is Life* (Crowell)

A PRIZE FIGHTER visiting the studio of James Montgomery Flagg asked if the artist thought he had inherited his ability. "I doubt it," said Flagg. "Now you take the Spanish painter Velasquez. Did you ever hear of Velasquez's father?"

"No," the prize fighter said.

"Did you ever hear of Velasquez's mother?"

"No."

"Well," Flagg said, " you see what I mean?"

"Not exactly," the prize fighter said. "I never heard of Velasquez, either." —E. E. Edgar

NEWSPAPERMEN like to tell about the time a sports editor we'll call Bunny McBride was making up the sports page, when a fight manager came in with his fighter to try to sell Bunny a column.

"Bunny," he said, "meet the champion of South Africa."

"Who let you in?" Bunny wanted to know. "Sorry, can't talk now. I'm busy. Some other time."

The manager was persistent. "But, Bunny, really, this is the champion of South Africa. Make you a good story."

McBride still waved him away. "Sorry, too busy."

The manager was insistent. "Bunny, you oughta meet this kid. He's champion of South Africa!"

McBride really got mad. Looking up for the first time he lifted as beautiful a wallop as was ever seen, in or out of the ring, and caught the champion of South Africa smack on the kisser. He went down in a heap without a sound. "Now I'm the champion of South Africa," muttered McBride, and went on with his work.

—Irving T. Marsh in New York *Herald Tribune*

ASKED WHY he decided to retire from the prize ring, Rocky Graziano said, "I looked in the mirror after my last fight and saw my beaten-up face and decided there must be an easier way to meet congenial people of my own age." —George DeWitt

Retirement Policies

IT WAS once remarked of a venerable Oxford don who refused to retire that he had all the Christian virtues except resignation.

—Bliss Perry, *And Gladly Teach* (Houghton Mifflin)

WHEN Dr. Alan Gregg was about to retire from his position as vice-president of the Rockefeller Foundation some of his colleagues were discussing how awful it would be after he was gone. Finally Dr. Gregg spoke up. "Relax, gentlemen," he said. "Nothing succeeds like successors."

—*The Pleasures of Publishing* (Columbia University Press)

OCTOGENARIAN Chancellor Konrad Adenauer, asked by a reporter when he planned to retire from German politics, replied, "I've already had my retirement. Twelve years under the Nazis."
—Bob Considine, INS

NOT LONG after Dr. James Moffatt retired from active service on the faculty of Union Theological Seminary, someone commented on his new title of Professor Emeritus.

"You know what that means?" replied Dr. Moffatt. "It comes from the Latin *e* meaning 'out,' and *meritus* which means 'ought to be.' "
—Luther A. Weigle, Dean Emeritus of Yale University Divinity School

WHEN A man retires and time is no longer a matter of urgent importance, his colleagues generally present him with a watch.
—R. C. Sherriff, quoted by Herbert V. Prochnow

FROM THE Maplewood-South Orange, N.J., *News-Record:* "Available: white-haired office boy. Types, reads blueprints, construction work. Now 'Chairman of the Bored.' "

SAID WRITER Somerset Maugham on his 75th birthday, "When I was 20, I made up my mind to quit at 50 and have a good time. When I was 50 I decided to keep at my work until I was 70."

"And at 70?" asked a newsman.

"At 70," said Maugham, "I realized how right I had been at 20."
—John Cameron Swayze, McNaught Syndicate

PRESIDENT A. Lawrence Lowell of Harvard, then over 70, was asked if he was retiring. "When I'm ready to retire," he replied, "Mrs. Lowell will tell me."
—Quentin Reynolds, quoted by Leonard Lyons

Whose World?

It's a Woman's World

WHEN A MAN is born people ask, "How is the mother?" When he marries they exclaim, "What a lovely bride!" And when he dies they inquire, "How much did he leave her?"

—*Mexican-American Review*

It's a Man's World

JUST LOOK at the difference in these descriptive words and phrases.

If a man doesn't marry he's a "bachelor"—glamorous word. If a woman doesn't marry she's an "old maid."

When it's his night out he's "out with the boys." When it's her night out she's at a "hen party." What he hears at the office is "news." What she hears at a bridge party is "gossip."

If he runs the family he is "head of the house." If she runs it she "wears the pants in that family." If he is overly solicitous of her he is a "devoted husband." If she is overly solicitous of him he is "henpecked." If he keeps his eye on her at a party he is an "attentive husband." If she sticks close to him she is a "possessive wife."

In middle age he is "in the prime of life" or "at the peak of his career." At the same age she's "no spring chicken." If he is an easy spender he "does not deny his family anything." If she doesn't count the pennies she's "extravagant" or a "poor manager."

Gray hair gives him a distinguished look. If she has it, she's an old hag. If he hasn't any small talk he's "the quiet type." If she hasn't any she is "mousy."

It all depends on one thing — whether you're speaking of a man or a woman. —Ruth Millett, NEA

Pert and Pertinent

SHORTLY AFTER Admiral Byrd's notable polar expedition returned from the land of ice, someone asked one of the men what one thing he missed most while away. "Temptation," was the brief answer. —*The Jax Air News*

VICTOR BORGE, who had just bought a chicken farm in Connecticut, was asked if he knew anything about raising chickens.

"No," he answered, "but the chickens do." —*Politiken*

DOROTHY PARKER, when asked for the two most beautiful words in the English language: "Check enclosed."

—Bernardine Kielty in *Book-of-the-Month Club News*

A STARLET remarked about a certain producer: "He may be old, but he's still in there pinching."

—Jimmy Starr in Los Angeles *Evening Herald and Express*

BECAUSE I was having a club meeting at my home I asked Inga, a German refugee woman who comes in to help me, if she could come on Thursday morning instead of her usual day. "I'm going to have 40 women here Thursday afternoon," I explained, "and you know what that means."

"*Ja,*" she said, "—80 eyes!" —Jane Windeler

ON THE maiden voyage of the colossal and luxurious *Queen Elizabeth* one passenger summoned a steward and said, "Would you please direct me to the Atlantic Ocean?"

—Bennett Cerf, *Shake Well Before Using* (Simon and Schuster)

THE OLD FARMER looked at me quizzically while I expounded on the high cost of living. "Lady," he smiled, "look around you! It ain't the high cost of living. It's the cost of folks living too high."

—Margaret T. Longstreth

A FRIEND living in an isolated Montana mining town suspected that she wasn't getting the best dental care. Her first trip to a competent dentist in Butte confirmed her suspicions. After a thorough examination the dentist asked but one question: "Been doing your own work?" —Mrs. Conrad LaSalle

GYPSY ROSE LEE'S succinct biography of another girl: "She is descended from a long line that her mother listened to."

—Katherine Brush

MICHAEL GOODMAN, University of California Professor of Architecture, on being asked what he thought of a speech by Frank Lloyd Wright: "Well, I thought he was more Frank than Wright!" —Herb Caen in San Francisco *Examiner*

Ego Twists

A THEATRICAL figure of a man strode majestically to the witness stand and swore the oath. He wore his white hair long and flowing and was smartly dressed like a 19th-century westerner. The county attorney began the examination. "Your name?"

"Frank Lloyd Wright."

"Your occupation?"

The witness sat up straighter, fixed the silk handkerchief in his suit pocket and rapped his elegant Malacca cane against the floor for emphasis. "I'm the world's greatest living architect!"

An exasperated friend later asked Wright how he could say such a thing. "I had to," Wright answered. "I was under oath."

—Martin L. Gross in *True*

OPERA SINGER Jan Kiepura stormed into his agent's office and complained that another client, Lauritz Melchior, received more publicity. When the agent explained that the press felt the Polish tenor was conceited, Jan muttered unbelievingly, "Conceited? Me? The Great Kiepura?" —David Green in *Cosmopolitan*

AFTER ONE of the Boston Symphony's performances in Symphony Hall an excited dowager swept backstage to conductor Serge Koussevitzky's dressing room. "Maestro!" she cried. "Maestro, you play so magnificently! You—you are God!"

Koussevitzky turned to the woman and, with a perfect deadpan, replied humbly, "Yes, modom—and *soch* a responsibility."

—*Time*

ENGLISH actor-manager Sir Herbert Beerbohm Tree hired a talented young actor whose ego became more inflated with each success. One night after scoring a triumph in a new drama he fairly strutted off the stage. Just as he disappeared into the wings there was a terrific explosion in the street outside. The blast rocked the theater.

"My God," Tree gasped, "his head has burst!" —E. E. Edgar

FROM THE start of his career composer George Gershwin had faith in himself. He used to praise his mother by explaining, "She is so modest about *me*." —Lewis Gannett in New York *Herald Tribune*

VOICE FLOATING out of a Hollywood actor's dressing room: "I'm *not* conceited, although gosh knows I have every reason to be!" —Mike Connolly in *The Hollywood Reporter*

"ALIBI IKE," Ring Lardner's scathing character study of a big-headed ballplayer, was modeled after a famous outfielder. Lardner gave him a copy of the story. Next day the enraged "Ike" stormed into his office yelling, "How could you do this to me? I should sue you!"

"But," butted Ring, "I didn't mention your name."

"That's the trouble," groaned the ham. "Nobody knows it's me!"

—Walter Winchell

Indian Reservations

ON AND OFF the mound, the famous baseball pitcher Chief Bender, a Chippewa and an alumnus of the Carlisle School, was a man of vast dignity and grave amiability. But there was one afternoon when the batters were giving him a bad time of it and part of the crowd burst into barbaric war whoops. The Chief decided he had had as much of it as the rules required him to take. He walked with majestic stride to the first-base line where his tormentors were congregated and addressed them as follows: "You ignorant, ill-bred foreigners! If you don't like the way I'm doing things out there, why don't you just pack up and go back to your own countries?" —From a Washington *Post* editorial

IN WASHINGTON they tell about the Indian who came as a delegate to the White House education conference and signed the registration blotter at the Mayflower Hotel "X X."

"What does that stand for?" the clerk asked.

"The first X," the Indian said, "represents my name, Sitting Bull, Jr."

"And the second?"

"The second stands for Ph.D." —New York *Times*

SIGN AT a Seminole Indian village along Florida's Tamiami Trail: "Genuine hand-woven Seminole Indian blankets. AC or DC." —Caskie Stinnett in *Speaking of Holiday*

AN OLD Blackfoot Indian and I used to patronize the same country store where, over a bottle of soda pop, we often discussed the ways of the world. "Do you like women?" I asked one day.

"My squaw, she good woman."

"She must be for you to have stayed married 31 years," I commented.

There was a long silence and then he said, "First ten years, me and squaw fight, fight, fight. Second ten years, papooses and squaw fight, I shut up. Third ten years, papooses grow up, I grow up, we all shut up." —Glen F. Tarbet

INDIANS living near Sault Ste. Marie take a dim view of the current uranium boom. Asked how it was affecting his tribe, Chief Steve Buzwah said:

"Two or three hundred years ago white man come to north shore of Lake Superior. He take all the fur and give Indian strings of beads. Then a few years later he cut down all big trees; build lumber mills. Soon all big trees gone—he go away. Few years later he come back; build paper mill at Espanola, cut down all small trees. Nothing left on north shore but rock. Now, by gosh, he come back for rock." —Sault Ste. Marie, Ont., *Daily Star*

First Impressions

WHEN URANIUM prospectors armed with Geiger counters first began invading his region, a mystified Kentucky old-timer confided to a visitor: "I don't know what this is all about. Fust thing I knew was when some feller came on the place with a Goober counter and said he was huntin' for geraniums."

—Joe Creason in Louisville *Courier-Journal Magazine*

A LITTLE BOY taken to the ballet for the first time watched curiously as the dancers cavorted about on their toes. "Mummy," he whispered loudly, "why don't they just get taller girls?"

—E. E. Kenyon in *The American Weekly*

AT THE Wright brothers anniversary celebration at Kitty Hawk —just about the fanciest air show ever staged in the United States —a grizzled old-timer who was unaccustomed to such modern air shenanigans watched with open mouth as four Sabrejets thundered toward the Wright Memorial Monument in a diamond formation at several hundred miles per hour. They flew in such a steady pattern that they seemed to be attached to one another. Just as they got over the monument the jets zoomed straight upward, then suddenly went off in four different directions.

At this the old-timer paled and exclaimed, "Dern, I knowed that thing was gonna come apart!"

—Tom Fesperman in Charlotte, N. C., *News*

BRUCE GOULD, *Ladies' Home Journal* editor, after a visit to England: "In England I would rather be a man, a horse, a dog or a woman, in that order. In America I think the order would be reversed."

AFTER SEEING his first American musical a European accustomed to Viennese light opera commented, "Very interesting. Nobody could sing but everybody sang."

—"Off Stage" in *Theatre Arts*

A LITTLE BOY, aged five, was playing with the small daughter of new neighbors. They had been wading at the lake and finally decided the only way to keep their clothes dry was to take them off. As they were going back into the water the little boy looked the little girl over. "Gosh," he remarked, "I didn't know there was *that* much difference between Catholics and Protestants!"

—I. P. Taylor

SOON AFTER his arrival in the United States a Hungarian youth who took part in the 1956 uprising was a panelist on "College News Conference." Afterward moderator Ruth Geri Hagy entertained some of the young people at her home, and a couple of the Democrats among them fell to denouncing the administration.

The startled Hungarian whispered to Miss Hagy, "Is this the American underground?" —Jay Nelson Tuck in New York *Post*

Variations on a Theme

Diplomat

A FELLOW who has to watch his appease and accuse.

—*London Opinion*

A PERSON who can be disarming even though his country isn't. —Sydney Brody in *The Saturday Evening Post*

DIPLOMACY is the art of saying "nice doggie" until you have time to pick up a rock.

—Frances Rodman

Highbrow

A MAN who has found something more interesting than women.

—Edgar Wallace, quoted by Russell Lynes in *Harper's Magazine*

A PERSON who enjoys a thing until it becomes popular.

—*California Public Survey*

Neurotic

A PERSON who has discovered the secret of perpetual emotion. —Dan Bennett

A PERSON who, when you ask how she is, tells you.

—Quoted by Eleanor Clarage in Cleveland *Plain Dealer*

Budget

A MATHEMATICAL confirmation of your suspicions.

—A. A. Lattimer in *The American Legion Magazine*

A PLAN that enables you to pay as you go—if you don't go anywhere.

—Evan Esar, The Register and Tribune Syndicate

ASKED the meaning of the word budget, one little boy replied, "It's a family quarrel."

—Robert Walden in *Coronet*

Education

THE ABILITY to describe a beautiful girl without using your hands.

—Joseph Charles Salak, quoted by Arch Ward in Chicago *Tribune*

THE ABILITY to quote Shakespeare without crediting it to the Bible.

—Evan Esar, The Register and Tribune Syndicate

WHAT'S left over after you've forgotten the facts.

—*Memphis Transit News*

Bachelor

A MAN who has faults he doesn't know about.

—Franklin P. Jones in *The Saturday Evening Post*

THE ONLY species of big game for which the license is taken out after the safari.

—Thomas Lyness

A MAN who never quite gets over the idea that he is a thing of beauty and a boy forever.

Statistics

THERE ARE three kinds of lies: lies, damned lies and statistics. —Benjamin Disraeli

STATISTICS are like a Bikini bathing suit. What they reveal is suggestive, but what they conceal is vital.

—Economist Aaron Levenstein, quoted by Leonard Lyons

STATISTICS can be used to support anything—especially statisticians.

—Franklin P. Jones in *The Saturday Evening Post*

Adolescence

TEEN-AGE is when youngsters aren't bright enough to realize their parents couldn't be that stupid. —*Town Journal*

AN ADOLESCENT is a teen-ager who acts like a baby when you don't treat him like an adult. —S. F. Brandt in *The Saturday Evening Post*

ADOLESCENCE isn't a period; it's a coma.

—Richard Armour in *Look*

Summer

THE SEASON when children slam the doors they left open all winter. —*Changing Times, The Kiplinger Magazine*

WHEN YOU ride bumper to bumper to get to the beach where you sit the same way.

—Herb Shriner, quoted by Earl Wilson, Hall Syndicate

THE KIND of weather when everything that is supposed to stick together comes apart, and everything that is supposed to stay apart sticks together.

—*The Prison Mirror*

Pardon, Your Slip Is Showing ®

FROM A UP dispatch: "Queen Elizabeth arrived to begin a Paris visit that inspired the warmest welcome the French have given any royal figure since they guillotined their own Queen Marie Antoinette."

FROM THE Worcester, Mass., *Sunday Telegram:* "State Senator Ernest A. Johnson, seeking reelection, said, 'I have made no wild promises, except one—honest government.' "

AD IN the Kalispell, Mont., *Inter Lake:* "NEW G.E. Automatic Blanket, Duel control."

FROM THE Newport, Ark., *Daily Independent:* "Following the ceremony there was an informal reaction in the vestibule of the church."

AD IN Clifton Forge, Va., *Daily Review:* ". . . save regularly in our bank. You'll never reget it."

FROM THE Malone, N. Y., *Telegram:* "William Andrews returned home yesterday from the hospital, where his left leg was placed in a cast following a fracture of the right ankle."

FROM THE Grand Rapids, Mich., *Press:* "Mr. ______ visited the school yesterday and lectured on 'Destructive Pests!' A large number were present."

FROM THE Hollywood, Calif., *Citizen-News:* "One can peek in most any evening on this home-loving young actress and find her cuddled up in an easy chair with a good boob before a crackling log fire."

—Quoted in *Capper's Weekly*

FROM AN ad in a New Jersey paper: "Visit our clothing department. We can outwit the whole family."

FROM A book review in the Fairmont *West Virginian:* "The book is nicely printed and contains few typographical errors; however, it is strange that the proo readers should rave permitted 'Lay on MacDuff' to come out 'Law on Macduff.' "

FROM THE Yeovil, England, *Western Gazette:* "The first swallow has arrived at Devizes. It was spotted by Police Constable John Cooke, of Seend, whose hobby is bird watching, sitting wet and bedraggled on telephone wires."

My War With the Ospreys

Condensed from Holiday

John Steinbeck

MY WAR with the ospreys, like most wars, was largely accidental—and it is not over yet. The coming of winter caused an uneasy truce, but hostilities may soon reopen, although I can find it in my heart to wish for peace, even friendship. I hope the ospreys, wherever they may be, will read this.

I shall go back to the beginning and set down my side of the affair, trying to be as fair as possible.

Three years ago I bought a little place on a beautiful point of land near Sag Harbor, which is quite near the eastern tip of Long Island. Sag Harbor is a fishing town, inhabited by people who have been here a long time. Though we are outlanders, still I believe that the people of the village have accepted my wife, my two young sons and me as citizens. With the ospreys, however, I have not only failed to make friends; I have, on the contrary, been insulted, have thrown down the gauntlet and had it accepted.

In the upper branches of a half-dead oak tree on the very tip of our point, there was, when I took possession, a tattered lump of trash which looked like an unmade bed. "That's an osprey's nest," a native told me. "They come back every year. I remember that nest since I was a boy."

"They build a messy nest," I said.

"Messy, yes," he said, "but I doubt if I could design something the winds wouldn't blow out. It's darned good architecture from a staying point of view."

Toward the end of May, to my delight, the ospreys came back from wherever they had been, and from the beginning they fascinated me. They are about the best fishermen in the world. They would coast along, hanging on the breeze perhaps 50 feet above the water; then suddenly their wings raised like the fins of a bomb and they arrowed down and nearly always came up with a fish. I became a habitual osprey watcher.

In time two of my ospreys were nudged by love and began to install new equipment in the great nest on my point. They brought unusual material—pieces of wood, rake handles, strips of cloth, reeds, swatches of seaweed. One of them, so help me, brought a piece of two-by-four pine three feet long to put into the structure. They weren't very careful builders; the ground under the tree was strewn with the excess stuff that fell out.

I mounted a telescope on the sun porch and even trimmed some branches from intervening trees, and from then on those love-driven ospreys didn't have a moment of privacy.

And then one morning the ospreys were gone. I walked out to the point and saw, sticking halfway out of their nest, the shaft and feathers of an arrow. Now Catbird, my younger son (he was eight at the time), is the archer of the family. I ran him down and gave him what-for in spite of his plaintive protests that he had not shot at the nest.

The birds did not come back. They were across the bay. I could see them through the telescope building an uneasy nest on top of a transformer on a telephone pole where they were definitely not wanted.

I got a ladder and climbed up to the nest on our point, and when I came down I apologized to Catbird. For in the nest I had found not only the arrow, but my bamboo garden rake, three T shirts and a Plaza Hotel bath towel. Apparently nothing was too unusual for ospreys to steal for a nest.

Now I must admit I had been pleased and a little proud to have my own osprey nest. I had planned to observe the nestlings when they arrived. The empty nest on the point that summer was a matter of sorrow and perplexity to me. I went to my Audubon, and it told me the following:

"Osprey (fish hawk), length 21 to 24 inches, wingspread 4½ to 6 feet, weight 3½ pounds . . . Provided they are not molested, ospreys will nest wherever there is a reasonably extensive body of clear water and some sort of elevated nest site. The birds are excellent watchdogs, driving off crows and other birds of prey. For this reason platforms on tall poles are often erected to encourage them to nest about homes and farmyards."

It was in February of 1956 that I asked myself: If people put up platforms on poles, why not build a nest so attractive as to win back my own birds? (The power company had meanwhile torn their nest off the transformer.)

In late winter I went to work. Climbing the oak tree, I cleaned away the debris of the old nest. Then I firmly wired in place horizontally a large wagon wheel. I cut dry pampas grass stalks and bound them in long fagots. With the freezing blasts of winter tearing at my clothes, I reascended the tree and wove the reeds into the spokes of the wheel until I had a nest which, if I had any oviparous impulses, I should have found irresistible.

After that I had trouble with the novel I was writing, since I had to rush constantly to the telescope to see whether my prospective tenants had returned. Finally June first came and school was out, and I put my boys on watch.

One morning Catbird charged into my study. "Ospreys!" he shouted. "Come running—ospreys!" I rushed for my telescope. There were the ospreys all right. But they weren't settling into my beautiful nest. They were tearing it to pieces, lifting out the carefully bound reed pads, carrying them across the bay and propping them clumsily on top of the power company's transformer.

Of course my feelings were hurt. Why should I deny it? But on the heels of injury came anger. Those slipshod, larcenous birds, those ingrates, those—those ospreys. My eyes strayed to the shotgun that hangs over my fireplace, but before I could reach for it, a Machiavellian thought came to me.

I wanted to hurt the ospreys, yes. I wanted revenge on them. But with number-four shot? No. I ached to hurt them as they had hurt me—in their feelings, psychologically.

I am an adept at psychological warfare. I declared the garage off limits to everyone. My novel came to a dead stop. Daily I worked in the garage, using pieces of chicken wire and a great deal of plaster of Paris. Then I asked my neighbor, Jack Ramsey, a very good painter, to come to my workshop.

At the end of two days we emerged with our product: a life-size replica of a nesting whooping crane. It is my belief that there are only 37 of these rare and wonderful birds in the world. Well, this was the 38th.

Chuckling evilly I hoisted the plaster bird up in the tree and wired her firmly in the nest. Her white body, black tail and brilliant red mask stood out magnificently against the sky. I went back to the sun porch and turned my telescope on the ospreys, who pretended to go about their nest-building on the transformer as though nothing had happened.

I knew what must be going on over there, though. Mrs. Osprey was saying, "Lord Almighty, George. Look who has moved into the apartment *you* didn't want. Why did I listen to you?"

And I laughed to myself. These are the wounds that never heal. This is psychological warfare as it should be fought.

Two days later my son Thom came running into my study. "The nest!" he cried. "Look at the nest!" I bolted for the door. The ospreys in jealous rage were dive-bombing my whooping crane. But all they could accomplish was the breaking of their talons on the hard surface of the plaster. Finally they gave up and flew away, followed by my shouts of derision.

The ospreys have not attacked any more, but we have had other visitors. One morning I looked out the window to see a rather stout lady in khaki trousers and a turtle-neck sweater creeping across my lawn on her hands and knees. Field glasses dangled from her neck, and she held a camera in front of her. When I went out to question her she angrily waved me away. "Go back," she whispered at me hoarsely. "Do you want her to fly away?"

"But you don't understand—" I began.

"Will you keep your voice down?" she rasped. "Do you know what that is? The club will never believe me. If I don't get a picture of her, I'll kill you."

Yes, we have had bird watchers —lots of them. You see, our whooping crane can be sighted from a long way off. After a time they discovered the nature of the thing, but they would not listen to my explanation of the ruse. In fact, they became angry; not at the ospreys—where the blame surely rests—but at me.

No one can say I am unforgiving, though. I have taken my whooping crane down and restored the nest to its old beauty. It is ready and waiting. Let us see whether this year the ospreys are big enough to let bygones be bygones.

Strictly for the Birds

THERE IS a great satisfaction to us clumsy humans when we see an animal that is supposed to surpass us in skill making a monkey of itself. I am still gloating over a blackbird that I saw, with my own eyes, in as disgraceful a bit of flying as any novice ever put in.

I was sitting in an automobile by the side of the curb when this bird swooped down with some idea evidently of making a two-point landing just to show off. But as his feet hit the sidewalk one of them slipped out from under him, and I was witness to the remarkable sight of a full-grown, adult bird falling on its tail. A vaudeville comic couldn't have taken a neater spill.

The chagrin and humiliation of that blackbird were gratifying to see. He got back his balance immediately and tried to act as if nothing had happened, but he knew that I had seen him and he was furious.

Everyone ought to see a bird fall on its tail at least once. It is a gratifying experience and good for the soul. —Robert Benchley, *Benchley—Or Else!* (Harper)

FROM THE "Lost and Found" column of a Nashville paper: "BIRD OR HAT—Flew in or blew in out of car passing Dannaher's Service Station, Franklin Road. It's sorta round with green and red polka dot quills or feathers in it. If you've lost a hat or a bird, drive by and see it—it's funny."

WHEN I was a child, neighbors had a pet crow that could talk. It fascinated me, but my mother hated the bird and frequently chased it away with a broom. The crow bided its time. One day when a two weeks' washing, spotless white, snapped in a March wind, the crow started at one end of the line and pulled out every clothespin, one by one, until the last bit of wash had fallen to the muddy ground. He squawked until he saw a face at the window, then flew home. —Marc A. Rose

FROM CAPTION of picture in the Milwaukee *Journal* of a woman feeding pigeons: "She declines to give her name, but says she's been something for the birds for more than 40 years."

MOISTURE dripped from the eucalyptus trees, the skies were gray, the ground was damp where 15 college students crouched, their attention focused on a young man who, at regular intervals, was giving the plaintive hoot of an owl. Presently there came a distant answering hoot, and the bird-study class from one of our large western universities moved cautiously, stopped, and their instructor hooted again.

For some 20 minutes the hooting and creeping forward continued while the answering hoots grew louder and louder. Quietly the class rounded a small hill.

Instead of sighting their quarry they came upon a young man, hooting mournfully. Behind him stood another group of cold, damp, eager students.

—Mrs. John H. Sugden, Jr.

THE METAL strips used to band birds are inscribed: "Notify Fish and Wild Life Service, Washington, D.C." They used to read Washington Biological Survey, abbreviated to "Wash. Biol. Surv." This was changed after an Alberta farmer shot a crow and then disgustedly wrote the U. S. government: "Dear Sirs: I shot one of your pet crows the other day and followed instruction attached to it. I washed it and biled it and surved it. It was turrible. You should stop trying to fool the people with things like this . . . ."

—Hugh Newton in *Liberty*

IN STORRS, Conn., a woman asked ornithology professor Jerauld Manter to identify a bird whose strange cry she couldn't place. The professor journeyed to the scene, identified the cry as that of a bulldozer in need of oil.

—*Bluebook*

L. E. WILSON of Syracuse, N. Y., relates that while tramping in Canada one bitterly cold winter day he saw a redheaded woodpecker perched on a large rock, tapping so hard and fast with its beak at the granite that sparks were flying. The bird, skipping nimbly, was stepping on the sparks as fast as they fell, thereby keeping its feet warm.

—Lowell Thomas

WIFE, pointing to husband stretched out in hammock, explains to friend: "Jack's hobby is letting birds watch *him.*"

—Al Kaufman cartoon in *This Week Magazine*

THE Hasselhuhn Williams Co. in Rutherford, N.J., was bothered by 100 pigeons fluttering around a coal pocket. An employe suggested what he called an old family remedy. This was to mix a batch of cracked corn with some hard liquor to get the birds drunk and keep them away from the coal pocket. The mixture was spread around the coalyard—and the next day 300 pigeons showed up.

—UP

FATHER of three baby birds to mother bird: "Just about the time we manage to get a nest egg salted away, more bills accumulate."

—Cartoon in *The Teller*

All in Pun

HOME from Korea, the pilot of a jet bomber showed friends pictures of a beautiful native lass. "Take a look," he suggested, "at one of my near Mrs."

—Bennett Cerf

WHEN John D. Rockefeller, Jr., at the age of 77 married a woman in her 50's, the new Mrs. Rockefeller was jokingly called his child bride. "What did he give her for a wedding present?" a newspaperman asked. "Blocks?"

"Yes," replied a friend. "Forty-ninth and Fiftieth—on Fifth Avenue." —Cleveland Amory, *The Last Resorts* (Harper)

IN A college biology test a young coed defined "inbreeding" as breeding in the same stock; for example, one Holstein cow with another Holstein cow.

The professor's comment: "A no-ble conception."—B. R. Weimer

A SOLDIER from New England stationed in an Army camp in Louisiana was continually singing the praises of the local girls. Asked why he found them so attractive, he thought for a moment, then replied, "I think it must be their southern assent."

—Dan Bennett

AN ARTICLE in *This Week Magazine* described the dress of an Indian Maharanee as a sarong instead of a sari. The copy chief, who allowed the error to slip past him, wrote to the editor: "All I can say is I'm sari I was sarong."

—Florence, Ala., *Herald*

A BOSOMY young pianist in a New York night club attracted much attention from the world of music with her skill at swinging the classics. Pianist Artur Rubinstein went to see her one evening and was much impressed. "I knew you'd like her boogie woogie," said a friend, "but a great pianist like yourself—well, I didn't imagine you'd be so impressed with her Bach."

"It isn't her Bach," exclaimed Rubinstein. "It's her front!"

—Dan Bennett

Concert Pitch

WHILE OSCAR LEVANT was playing an especially brilliant passage of Gershwin's "Piano Concerto in F" in a college auditorium, a telephone began ringing in a nearby office. Levant ignored the persistent ringing, but the audience began squirming. Finally, without interrupting his playing, Levant looked out toward the audience and said, "If that's for me, tell them I'm busy." —Thelma White

SIR MALCOLM SARGENT, the British conductor, once rehearsed the Royal Choral Society in Handel's *Messiah*. Not liking the women's rendition of "For Unto Us a Child Is Born," he rapped sharply for attention and said, "Just a little more reverence, please—and not quite so much astonishment."

—David Ewen, *Listen to the Mocking Words* (Arco)

SIR THOMAS BEECHAM was conducting a rehearsal of Massenet's *Don Quixote* in which Chaliapin, the Russian basso, was starring. At one point in the last act the singer playing Dulcinea persistently failed to come in on the beat. "It's Mr. Chaliapin's fault," she protested at last. "He always dies too soon."

"Fraulein," said Sir Thomas, stroking his beard, "you are grossly in error; no opera singer has ever died half soon enough for me." —Stephen Williams in New York *Times Magazine*

ONE MUSIC publisher to another: "I've never heard such corny lyrics, such simpering sentimentality, such repetitious uninspired melody. Man, we've got a hit on our hands!"

—Brad Anderson cartoon in *The Wall Street Journal*

ARRIVING at the opera with his wife, a man reached inside his coat and exclaimed, "Good grief, I remembered the tickets!"

—Rodney deSarro cartoon in *The Saturday Evening Post*

IN A MIDWESTERN town on a bright June afternoon parents and grandparents assembled in the school auditorium to see their offspring participate in the eighth-grade commencement. The girls, their hair curled as tight as screen-door springs, wore crisp new dresses. The boys, their hair plastered down, made speeches with their legs shaking under knife-sharp creases in their trousers.

The program went off smoothly until a boy launched into an interminable zither solo. At first folks listened attentively, then began to wriggle in their seats. Finally, when everyone was at the breaking point, the principal walked to the edge of the platform and asked in a stage whisper, "Aren't you almost to the end?"

"I've *passed* the end!" the boy groaned. —A. P. Savage in *The Christian Science Monitor*

IRVING BERLIN once urged Victor Borge to stick to the classics.

"But, Irving, every time I play Mozart I hear a little voice that whispers, 'Don't play it. Don't play it.' "

"You recognize the little voice?"

"Yes, Irving. It's Mozart's."

—Victor Borge, as told to Dean Jennings in *The Saturday Evening Post*

Laughing Matter

A CHICAGO show girl swathed in a new mink coat encountered a couple of old friends who complimented her on her luxurious acquisition. "Oh, this," she said coyly, shrugging her shoulders. "I got it for a mere song."

"A song?" echoed one of her pals. "Looks more like an overture to me!"

—"Nestor" in *The Diplomat*

THE YOUNG husband had settled himself in his favorite chair to read the evening paper. His wife of six months sat opposite him. Pulling out her knitting she remarked, "I went to see the doctor today."

He kept on reading. At long last he looked up and absently replied, "Oh, you did? How *is* he?" —Alex Osborn

HERMAN LEVIN, producer of the sellout musical, *My Fair Lady,* tells of the two women who sat in the orchestra, an empty seat between them. At the intermission one said, "I waited eight months for my ticket."

"So did I," said the other.

"What a shame—this empty seat," said the first.

"Oh, that's mine, too," replied the other. "It was my husband's, only he died."

"But couldn't you have brought a friend?"

"No," she said, shaking her head. "They're all at the funeral."

—Leonard Lyons

"IN SKONA var I vas born," said Sven, "vas such fine echo ve could stand on mountaintop and yell, 'Yonson,' and in 20 minutes back comes such strong echo, 'Yonson,' ve nearly fall off mountain."

"You call that fine echo?" countered Ole. "Vy, right here in Minnesota ve can stand on shore of lake and yell, 'Yonson,' and in vun minute back come 10,000 echoes, 'Vich Yonson?' "

—John in *Capper's Weekly*

AN AGITATED young man ran frantically down the ferry slip, leaped across a strip of water and landed with a crash on the deck of the boat. "Well," he gasped, as he picked himself up, "I made it!"

"What's your hurry?" asked a deck hand. "This boat's coming in." —University of Utah *Unique*

"ANY PHYSICAL defects?" asked the draft-board doctor.

"Yes, sir," replied the hopeful inductee. "No guts!"

—*The California Plasterer*

ONE NIGHT at the movies I overheard this exchange between a teen-ager and his date:

"Can you see all right?" he asked.

"Yes."

"Are you in a draft?"

"No."

"Does the man in back of you have his feet on your chair?"

"No."

"Mind trading places?" he asked. —B. L. Lindsay

ON A BUS I overheard two college students discussing an astonishing fact they had just learned: that our bodies are 92 percent water. At that moment an extremely shapely young lady boarded the bus. Conversation ceased for a moment as the boys took her in. Then one remarked, "Boy, she sure did a lot with *her* eight percent!" —Herb Callison

TV DIRECTOR to actors: "Put more feeling into it; it isn't for namby-pambies, it's for bloodthirsty children."

—Glynn cartoon in *Gags*

DID YOU hear about the Texan who just bought his son a cowboy outfit—a 20,000-acre ranch, 1000 head of cattle and 200 horses?

—Bobby Breen, quoted by Frank Farrell in New York *World-Telegram and Sun*

AS A junior-high-school teacher distributed the first report cards of the year, she noticed that one blond teen-ager was scowling. "What's the matter? Aren't you satisfied with your marks?" she asked.

"I certainly am not," said the girl. "You gave me an F in Sex and I didn't even know I was taking it!"

—Mrs. William H. Hamann

Grade-A Reports

SMALL BOY to teacher: "I can't get that report card back for you. You gave me an 'A' in something and they're still mailing it to relatives." —Jeff Keate cartoon in *The American Legion Magazine*

THE ENGLISH writer Francis Toye tells of a schoolmaster he had at Winchester who enjoyed a reputation for short reports to parents. On one occasion he wrote of a certain boy, "Trying," which delighted the boy's parents until the next report came in. This one read, "Very trying."

—Bennett Cerf in *The Saturday Review*

ENTRY on a third-grader's record: "Possible maladjustment—reads books."
—"Almanac" in Minneapolis *Tribune*

AN ENGLISH master, confronted with what to put on a boy's report when he knew the youngster was cheating but couldn't prove it, finally came up with—"Forging his way steadily ahead!" —"Miscellany" in Manchester *Guardian*

TEACHERS in an eastern girls' school were required to comment on what each student had accomplished in class during the semester. On one card the anthropology instructor wrote, "Accomplishments—two Argyle socks, one cardigan sweater." —Jane Bixby

MY SMALL nephew's first report card, one of the informal letter types, was climaxed with the comment: "Stanley contributes very nicely to the group singing by helpful listening."

—Betty Robinson

REMARK on an English schoolboy's report card: "The dawn of legibility in his handwriting reveals his utter incapacity to spell."
—Alec Hay in a letter to the *Times,* London

COMMENTING on a nursery-school report that described her daughter as emotionally immature, a young mother said, "If you can't be immature at three, when *can* you be?"

—Eda J. LeShan in *National Parent-Teacher*

REPORT received by a Montreal father from his young son's teacher: "Dull but steady—would make a good parent."

—Montreal *Gazette,* quoted in Toronto *Star*

Social Notes

At a White House dinner a woman trying to engage taciturn Sherman Adams in small talk asked about his son, who was then at St. Paul's School in Concord.

Well, Adams observed, his son was doing well scholastically and was on the hockey team.

"Oh, tell me all about him," she sang.

"Just did," Adams replied.

—Robert J. Donovan in *Collier's*

From the Princeton, N. J., *Town Topics:* "Dept. of utter confusion! Will the party who invited the Agles for dinner Saturday call again? We don't know where to go."

An El Cajon, Calif., matron, who has a hectic social schedule, hit on the idea of posting a calendar in her bathroom for jotting down social engagements.

One night she and her husband were entertaining a couple to whom they had long been obligated. During the evening the guest visited her hostess' bathroom. Upon her return to the living room her manner was definitely chilly.

After the couple had departed the hostess heard a muffled shout from her husband. It came from her bathroom. The husband had taken a casual glance at his wife's calendar. The entry for that day read: "Have the Peaches for dinner and get it over with."

—Si Casady in El Cajon, Calif., *Valley News*

From the Andrews County, Texas, *News:* "Refreshments of cake squares, iced in pink and glue, were served" . . . From the Amarillo, Texas, *Globe:* "Miss Opal McNary won first prize for the most original costume at the Hi-Jinx masquerade. Needless to say Miss McNary was quite pickled" (Quoted in *Capper's Weekly)*

Producer Harry Kurnitz went to a Hollywood party where, to his horror, there was a scavenger hunt. The guests were given individual lists of dreadful things to get, and Kurnitz, list in hand, started tiptoeing to the door. The hostess asked, "What are you supposed to get?"

"Eight hours' sleep," he told her, and disappeared into the night.

—Leonard Lyons

WOMAN TO friend at a Dallas country-club party: "I'm miserable. I've got on my sitting-down shoes and my standing-up girdle."

—Dallas *News*

AT A New York college the faculty arranged a get-acquainted bridge party at which all those with matching favors started the evening as partners. A new art instructor, fresh from Holland, drew a Kewpie, as did one of the faculty wives. The next evening he found himself being introduced to the same lady at another reception. He electrified all within earshot when he protested, "Oh, no, do not introduce *us*. We haf babies together last efening."

—Mrs. Clough F. Gee

A YOUNG LADY spent a nightmarish evening with a very high-toned, intellectual group. As most of the talk was completely beyond her, she sat the greater part of the time in silence. Finally, however, the party gathered around the piano and someone asked her to suggest a song they might all sing. Distrusting her own taste entirely by now, she played it safe. "Well," she said meekly, "I've always liked the one about the bombs bursting in air."

—*This Week Magazine*

AT A DINNER party a shy young man had been trying to think of something nice to say to his hostess. At last he saw his chance when she turned to him and remarked, "What a small appetite you have, Mr. Jones."

"To sit next to you," he replied gallantly, "would cause any man to lose his appetite."

—*Capper's Weekly*

Party Patter: Certainly, invite him over, but let's dilute him with friends (Weldon W. West) . . . If I've said something I'm sorry for, I'm glad of it *(The Country Guide)* . . . To have him over for an evening is to prove that the night has a thousand I's (Onancock, Va., *Eastern Shore News)* . . . Cocktail party —sort of a subway rush hour with martinis (Bill Conklin in *Today's Living, The Herald Tribune Magazine)* . . . Going to a party with your wife is like going fishing with the game warden (Amos 'n' Andy) . . . Repartee—what a person thinks of after he becomes a departee (Dan Bennett)

OUR guests are about to go—
That is, they're all set to start
To plan to prepare to get ready
To begin to commence to depart.

—Richard Armour, *Light Armour* (McGraw-Hill)

We Don't Need to Leave Yet, Do We? Or, Yes We Do

From Ogden Nash's "Family Reunion"

One kind of person when catching a train always wants to
allow an hour to cover the ten-block trip to the terminus,
And the other kind looks at them as if they were verminous,
And the second kind says that five minutes is plenty and will
even leave one minute over for buying the tickets,
And the first kind looks at them as if they had cerebral rickets.
One kind when theater-bound sups lightly at six and hastens
off to the play,
And indeed I know one such person who is so such that it
frequently arrives in time for the last act of the matinee,
And the other kind sits down at eight to a meal that is
positively sumptuous,
Observing cynically that an eight-thirty curtain never rises
till eight-forty, an observation which is less cynical than
bumptuous.
And what the first kind, sitting uncomfortably in the waiting
room while the train is made up in the yards, can never
understand,
Is the injustice of the second kind's reaching their seat just
as the train moves out, just as they had planned,
And what the second kind cannot understand as they stumble
over the first kind's feet just as the footlights flash on at last
Is that the first kind doesn't feel the least bit foolish at
having entered the theater before the cast.
Oh, the first kind always wants to start now and the second
kind always wants to tarry,
Which wouldn't make any difference, except that each other
is what they always marry.

—Published by Little, Brown. This poem, © 1942 by Curtis Pub. Co.,
originally appeared in *The Saturday Evening Post*

Island Interlude

Condensed from "Mister Roberts"

Thomas Heggen

IT WAS a very hot, sweaty afternoon when the Navy cargo ship *Reluctant* put in at the island. At first it seemed just another Pacific island, so nobody's heart beat very much faster. But the little anchorage bay was really rather lovely. The water off the reef was terribly blue, and instead of the usual flat barren coral, the island's lush green foliage ran up to remote and impressive purple hills.

The crew, lined along the rail, began to feel obscurely good at being here, and one of the seamen was even moved to remark, "This ain't a bad place, you know it?" But the island's intrinsic and most spectacular virtue fell to Sam Insigna to discover. Sam, a little wizened monkey of a man, not quite five feet tall, was up on the flying bridge with the other signalmen, idly scanning the scene through the mounted telescope. Dead ahead, and adjoining a small base hospital, was an amazing thing: an authentic civilian house. It was yellow, long, low and rambling. It was obviously old, bleak and ugly, yet here, in the middle of the Pacific, it seemed a thing of great magnificence. Sam swung the telescope around to have a look at it. For perhaps a full minute nothing happened, and then Sam suddenly jerked upright. "Good God!" Sam said, and there was only reverence in his voice. "She's naked!"

One of the many anomalies of our ponderous Navy is its ability to move fast, to strike the swift, telling blow at the precise moment it is needed. There were accessible in the wheelhouse and charthouse seven pairs of binoculars; on the flying bridge were two spyglasses and two long-glasses, and the ship's telescope; and on a platform above was the range finder, an instrument of powerful magnification. Between 15 and 20 seconds after Sam had sounded the alarm all of these lenses were manned and on the target.

Sam's discovery was basically simple. He had discovered that nurses lived in the long, yellow house; that two large windows in the second story had none but shade curtains, retracted; and that these windows belonged to the bathroom. It is, of course, redundant to say that he had also discovered a nurse in the shower stall. All of this would seem to be reasonable and natural: what could be more logical than that there be nurses attached to this hospital, that their bathroom have windows, and that these nurses bathe? Nothing, you would think. And yet to these signalmen and quartermasters (who had last seen a white woman, probably fat, certainly fully clothed, perhaps 14 months ago) this vision was literally that—a vision, and a miracle. Like Sam, they were stricken with reverence in its presence. Those who could speak at all managed only to breathe, "I'll be damned!"

The word spread fast, although how it is difficult to say; certainly no one left the bridge. The four-to-eight signal watch, Niesen and Canappa, never known to relieve before the stroke of the hour, appeared at 3:30 and met an equally incredible thing: a watch that refused to be relieved. "Get the hell out of here," Sam told the newcomers. "We're staying up here till chow." There was some bitterness and much indignant insistence by Niesen and Canappa of their *right* to relieve the watch, but the old watch, firmly entrenched at the glasses, stayed by them until chow was piped. Sam had scarcely gone below for supper, however, when he was back again, demanding and getting his telescope. He and the rest of the watch stayed on until sunset, when lights went on in the bathroom and the curtains were pulled chastely down for the night.

That first day was chaotic, comparable perhaps to the establishing of a beachhead. It was ill-organized; there was duplication and wasted effort. The next day went much better. A system and a pattern appeared and, it being fatiguing to squint through an eyepiece for long periods, Sam arranged that one man, by turns, keep the lookout during the off hours and give the word when action developed. But he refused to let Mannion take a turn. "That so-and-so watched one strip down yesterday and didn't open his mouth," he accused.

It was possible by this time to establish the routine of the house. After the big early-morning rush there was only an occasional visitor until around ten, when the night watch would begin to get up. From ten to 11 was fairly good, and 11 until noon was very good. From lunch until two was quiet, but from two until 2:45 there was again a rich procession. All glasses, including pathetic little two-power opera glasses, were manned during those periods, and the flying bridge presented a solid wall of variously magnified eyeballs.

Soon the assignment of glasses came to be understood. Three pairs of binoculars belonged down below for the officers of the deck and two quartermasters. The other four pairs of binoculars, the spyglasses and the long-glasses belonged to the signalmen. The range finder, for instance, was recognized as officer property and was almost continually manned by a rotating team of two officers. The big telescope, of course, was a prize. It magnified 32 times. Sam's right to it remained strangely unchallenged, perhaps in recognition of his zeal. But Lieutenant (jg) Billings, who was the communication officer and Sam's boss, began to chance on the bridge frequently, and every time he would relieve Sam briefly on the telescope. Not only that, he had an uncanny talent for arriving at the most propitious moment. Sam got pretty sore over the whole business.

By the third day personalities began to emerge from the amorphous group of bathers. Despite the fact that the light was usually bad up around the face, the boys were able to distinguish one nurse from another with considerable accuracy. The two blondes were the real stars, though at first there was a tendency to confuse them—both young and pretty—until their separate identity was established by evidence of a most distinctive sort.

As Mannion put it, looking up

from his glass, "What the hell is that she's got?" Sam didn't look up from his glass. "You dumb cluck, that's a birthmark."

"Birthmark!" Mannion said scornfully. "Who the hell ever heard of a birthmark down there? That's paint; she's gotten into some paint."

Sam's rebuttal was simple and unanswerable: "Who the hell ever heard of paint down there?"

With the emergence of personalities came the recognition of personal habits. The tall skinny brunette always let the shower run for several minutes before stepping in. The stubby little brunette with the yellow bathrobe always used the bathtub. The girl with high-piled-up hair would fuss for an hour extracting hairpins, and then take a shampoo in the washbasin without removing her robe. "That's a stupid way to take a shampoo," Sam commented.

But by far the most notable idiosyncrasy belonged to the blonde with the birthmark. It was one which endeared her to all the rapturous watchers. It consisted simply of shedding her bathrobe before every bath and standing for several minutes looking out over the glass-smooth bay. Undoubtedly, this was a girl who loved beauty, and certainly the view was a fine one. Fortunately, although the tranquil scene included the ship riding peacefully at anchor, she could not at that distance hear the cranking of the range finder.

There were occasional dull days when few nurses bathed and Sam probably spoke for all when he said, "Hell, and they call themselves nurses! They're nothing but a bunch of filthy pigs." But by and large it could not fairly be said that the nurses were disappointing. In fact, Sam himself was once moved to observe, "This is too good to last." It was one of the most prophetic things Sam ever said.

One morning a few days later, Lieutenant (jg) Langston, the gunnery officer, who had been having a good bit of trouble with his eyes, went over to the base hospital to have them refracted and new glasses prescribed. It took about an hour and a half to find just the right lenses, and while he was waiting for his pupils to contract, Langston talked with the pleasant-faced nurse who helped the doctor. It came out that she was from a town not 20 miles from Youngstown, Ohio, where he lived. On the strength of this bond Langston invited her to dinner on the ship that night. The nurse, whose name was Miss Williamson, accepted readily, adding, however, that she would like to bring a friend, "a terribly cute girl." Langston of course assented, saying he would assign her to Ensign Pulver, an engineering officer.

When the girls came aboard that night, escorted by the two officers, the entire crew was massed along the rail and on the bridges. As the white-stockinged legs tripped up the gangway, one great, composite, heartfelt whistle rose to the heavens. Ensign Pulver's girl, Miss Girard, turned out to be a knockout—soft blond hair which she wore in bangs, wide blue innocent eyes, and the pertest nose there ever was.

After dinner the two officers proposed a tour of the ship, and both girls enthusiastically approved. First they toured the main deck, galley, sick bay and engine room. From there they went up to the bridge, through the radio room and on up to the flying bridge. That was a thoughtless thing for the two officers to do, but fortunately an alert quartermaster had preceded them. The inspection party found the signalmen clustered in an innocent group under the canvas awning, and the telescope trained at an angle 90 degrees from the yellow house. The signalmen presented a curious sight. They were speechless and seemed welded to the deck with awe. The two nurses giggled a little, no doubt over the prospect of these men so obviously dumfounded at seeing a woman that they could only gape.

When the party started to walk around behind the funnel, Ensign Pulver noticed that Sam Insigna was trailing them. He was a little annoyed, but, being a young man of poise, he made a sort of introduction. "This is Sam," he said, "one of our signalmen." Miss Girard smiled at Sam. "How do you do, Sam," she said graciously. Sam was evidently too flustered to speak; he just grinned foolishly. The inspection party took a turn around the funnel, then came forward again and went over to the port wing to look at the 20-millimeters. By this time the signalmen had got their tongues back and were having a bitter and quite vocal argument. It was obvious that they were trying to keep their voices guarded, but the restraint only intensified them. Sam's voice in particular carried well. "Dammit," the party heard him say, "I'll bet you 100 bucks!" Lieutenant (jg) Langston nodded toward the signalmen, smiled superiorly, and said to the nurses, "Seems to be an argument."

Then Sam's voice came to them again. That voice was several things: it was shrill, combative, angry; but most of all it was audible. It traveled in an unfaltering parabola, fell on the ears of the inspection party and broke into words of simple eloquence. "You stupid lunkhead. I tell you, that's her! I got 100 bucks that says that's the one with the birthmark on her fanny! Now put up or shut up!"

Sam may have been right, at that. No one ever knew; no one on the ship ever saw that birthmark again. The curtains of the two middle upstairs windows were not raised next morning, and when the ship sailed three days later they were still down. It was three weeks before a sizable membership of the crew would speak to Sam except to curse him, and it was longer than that before Ensign Pulver would speak to him at all.

Humor in Uniform

MY COUSIN was one of the first to enlist in the Waves. Soon after arrival at boot camp her contingent was herded into a long narrow building that had only two doors—one at each end. The rear door led to the dispensary where a doctor was to give the newcomers their physical examinations. Stripped to the skin, and embarrassed beyond words, the girls waited. Suddenly the dispensary door opened. Through it a seasoned pharmacist's mate thrust his head and, without showing any signs of indecision, sang out, "Close your eyes, girls. I'm coming through!" —George E. Wisner in *The Saturday Evening Post*

I HAPPENED to be in the adjutant's office at an Air Force base when a visiting general arrived to make an inspection. He soon discovered that the adjutant, a first lieutenant, didn't know too much about his job and office. "What were you before you became an officer?" the general asked.

The lieutenant replied, "I was a staff sergeant, sir."

"Well," said the general, "I can understand how you made first lieutenant, but I'll be darned if I know how you ever made staff sergeant!" —Roy T. Simmons

IN 1950 OUR ship was sent to the Mare Island Naval Shipyard for general overhaul and repairs. During our stay there we had "change of command" ceremonies. The crew assembled on the fantail and the old skipper, after a lengthy speech, turned the command over to our new skipper and left the ship. The new captain looked the crew over and said,

"Men, before anything more is said, I would like to clear up one thing. This isn't my ship—this isn't your ship—it's *our* ship!"

A voice from the crew muttered, "Good! Let's *sell* it!"

—Charles S. O'Connor

SITUATIONS-WANTED ad in the St. Louis *Post-Dispatch:* "Young man desires traveling job. Uncle Sam, please do not answer; once was enough."

TO THE Junior Chamber of Commerce in Norfolk fell the job of finding accommodations for the 15,000 visitors expected at the 1957 International Naval Review. With an offer of a room here and a room there, it was an arduous task. So the committee was overjoyed when a letter arrived offering accommodations for 400 young women. But their elation was short-lived.

A check of the address revealed that it was a sailors' barracks at Norfolk Naval Base.

—Lt. J. R. Kint

"WE'LL HAVE to fight like hell, men," said the C.O. in Korea. "We're outnumbered four to one."

A hillbilly soldier who had listened carefully was among the first to get into the fight. Later, however, the commanding officer found him lolling comfortably against a tree. Up forward the rifles cracked and the men were still battling furiously.

"What's the idea, Terwilliger?" barked the officer. "Why aren't you fighting?"

"Ah got mah four," replied Terwilliger. —*The Bluejacket*

OUR SHIP had just received a yard overhaul after 13 months in the South Pacific, and it was the crew's last Stateside liberty. At 1 a.m. I returned aboard just as a very drunk bos'n's mate staggered up the gangway with a fifth of whiskey in each hand. With the left-hand bottle he saluted the quarterdeck, and with the right-hand bottle he saluted the officer of the deck. The OD, trying to keep a straight face, explained that Navy regulations do not permit men to bring whiskey aboard.

"Tell you what," he said. "I'll turn my back and I want to hear two splashes in the water. Then you go below and we'll forget the whole thing."

The officer turned away, heard two splashes and was satisfied. But I was in better position to see the mate, still clutching a bottle in each hand, lurch rapidly out of sight—in his stocking feet.

—John E. Hamilton in *True*

MY BROTHER-IN-LAW in the Sea-Bees was stationed in the Philippines. I was on leave visiting my sister when she received a letter with a snapshot of him with a group of sailors about to go on liberty. I noticed my sister looking over the snapshot with a large magnifying glass. Then she wrote for a few seconds and got up from her desk. "Did you finish your letter to Bob so quickly?" I asked.

"Yes," she said. "Would you like to read it?" I took the magnifying glass, looked at the picture and smiled.

She had written only five words: "WHERE IS YOUR WEDDING RING?"

—Clifton Durgin

A Couple of Fan Letters

Condensed from "Ensign O'Toole and Me"

W. J. Lederer

WHILE ASSIGNED to the *Princeton* in Korean waters I had the good fortune to see an interesting communication addressed to a naval aviator named Ensign Joseph X. Smith, USN.

Ensign Smith was a youthful pilot who had performed heroics against the Communists and received wide publicity throughout the United States. Along with the write-up, the papers used an extremely attractive picture showing Ensign Smith in flight gear, standing beside his jet fighter on the deck of the *Princeton.*

There was something extra charming about the picture. Perhaps it was Smith's boyish grin. Perhaps it was the smudge of grease on his face. Perhaps it was the way he held his wounded arm. Whatever the magic was, readers looked at the picture twice; and bobby-soxers wrote to the Navy Department for copies.

A short time after the photograph was published, Ensign Smith, still attached to the *Princeton,* received a fan letter on perfumed stationery:

Dear Joe Smith,

I am not in the habit of writing strangers. But when I saw your picture in the *Post Dispatch* I said to myself, here's a guy I can go for.

So forgive me if I seem a bit forward in writing you.

But, of course, is there anything wrong with falling for a hero?

I don't know where the *Princeton* is now, so I am sending this letter to your home in California. I hope your mother will forward it to you.

I am 20 years old; I am blond, blue-eyed, five feet two, and weigh 115 pounds. My measurements are the same as those of Marilyn Monroe. Last year the boys at the University of Illinois voted me the girl they'd most like to bundle with.

Don't get the wrong impression. I really am the home-loving type. I am a better-than-average cook. My specialty is charcoal-broiled steak with mushrooms and wine sauce.

I love to play tennis, golf, and ride horses. My special hobbies are tournament bridge and automobile driving. I have a Cadillac convertible.

Now I am going to ask something of you. I would love to meet you when the *Princeton* comes back from Korea. I could drive over and I'd be glad to act as your chauffeur and take you wherever you like. And I mean anyplace!

Affectionately, your fan,
Mary Lou Bookbinder

AT THE bottom was a postscript in another handwriting:

Dear Joe Smith,

Mary Lou Bookbinder's letter was delivered to my house. I opened it in error before I noticed it wasn't for me. Excuse me, please.

But it is an interesting coincidence that I, too, had seen your picture and story in the papers. Believe me, I got a thrill reading of what you had done.

I am 19 years old, redheaded, and have hazel eyes. There's no use deceiving you about my looks; I definitely am no Marilyn Monroe. However, my friends say that I am "wholesome" and have a "good personality."

My cooking is not fancy. Frankfurters and beans and homemade ice cream is what we have for parties at my house.

I don't know how to play bridge.

I love driving a car. I have a darling old beaten-up Ford convertible which, like me, has a "good personality." I hope, however, some day in the next few years, to be able to afford a new car.

I am not much of an athlete. As a matter of fact, I haven't played golf, tennis, or ridden a horse for ages.

My physical measurements really aren't so hot. I weigh 145 pounds and am seven months pregnant.

Will I do?

Your loving wife,
Hilda

P. S. de Resistance

IN MY JOB of announcing for the American Forces Network in Germany, I received many musical requests—most of them from *Fräuleins* to their GI boy friends. Among them was this one:

"Dear Disc-Jockey:

"Please play 'So Long, It's Been Good to Know You,' for my *Schatzie,* Cpl. John B—, who is going back to the States next week. Hilda H—

"P.S. Also, would you play for Pvt. Jerry L—, the song 'Getting to Know You'?" —Cpl. Edw. R. Muscare

A FEW HELPFUL tips for anyone who wants to catch a porcupine were offered by the Lands and Forests Department of Ontario, Canada, in a bulletin reading in part as follows:

"The best way to effect his capture is to wait until he's in the open. Then, watching for his slapping tail, rush in quickly and pop a large washtub over him." The bulletin adds: "Thus you have something to sit on while you figure out the next move." —*Awake!*

A PHILOSOPHICAL New Yorker who gave up all hope of getting perfect letters from his office typist, now sends the letters out as they come from her mill—spelling errors, erasures and all. He evens matters with a rubber stamp that he had specially made. It marks in the lower left-hand corner: "She can't type—but she's beautiful." —Meyer Berger in New York *Times*

TO LET HIS employer know what he thought about his alleged salary, a young New Yorker carefully wrote above his signature, when he cashed his check, "Any resemblance between this and a living wage is purely coincidental." —*Rockefeller Center Magazine*

WHEN I WAS in Paris I tried earnestly to make the messages on the post cards I sent friends back home short and personal. For a sculptress friend I chose a picture of the statue of the Venus de Milo, glorious in her unarmed, unclothed beauty, and on it wrote: "Naturally I thought of you when I saw this."

Some postal employe exercised his traditional right to read post cards, and when it was delivered my message carried this enlivening postscript: "You must be quite a dame, Arline!" —B. C.

AT AN ICE plant in a western town there are a number of slots which take coins of various denominations and dispense ice of various sizes and kinds. Directions are printed over each slot. In the center is a large sign: WHEN ALL ELSE FAILS, TRY READING DIRECTIONS. —Marian W. Parmenter

WHEN THE boy friend of a teen-age friend of mine went to call on his girl, he found the family had been unexpectedly called out of town. The girl had left this note taped to her front door: "Hi, handsome! Have gone to Texas. Will be back Sunday afternoon.

"P.S. Don't tear up this note—you aren't the only one!"

—Dorothy P. Gregory

A CLEVELANDER on vacation received a letter from her mother. On the envelope, in her father's writing, was the notation: "Carried by slow male three days."

—Jean Palmer, quoted by Eleanor Clarage in Cleveland *Plain Dealer*

A VETERAN Air Force major and a shiny new lieutenant, flying cross country, were approaching Lake Michigan when warning came of a thunderstorm ahead. At the controls the confident lieutenant dashed off a note on his knee-pad that they could easily beat the storm across the lake. The weather-wise major shook his head, signaling the lieutenant to go *around* the lake.

Not one to give up easily, the stubborn young pilot wrote: "Have 20 hours over-water flying time. Will go across."

The major promptly scribbled back: "Have two days in-the-water time. Will go around." —T. D. Hoskins in *True*

SIGN ON a country hotel: "Open to Take Tourists." Under the printed words someone had written: "And how!"

—*Talks and Stories of Frank M. Totton* (Association Press)

Road Show

AN ALABAMA filling-station sign read: "Mississippi Dead Ahead. Last Chance for 28¢ Gas." So an Iowa tourist told the man to fill her up. As he paid, the driver asked, "How much *is* gas in Mississippi?" And the fellow answered, "Twenty-four cents."

—Walter Davenport in *Collier's*

HOWARD CHAMBERLAIN of Cincinnati's WLW reports that after driving for miles over endless salt flats in Utah he came on a billboard reading: MONOTONOUS, AIN'T IT?

—Ollie M. James in Cincinnati *Enquirer*

WE WERE HAVING the gas tank filled before braving the Big Horn Mountains when a big sedan drove up. Hoping to get the latest news about the road, I walked over to the car. The driver was pale and seemed agitated but the man sitting beside him seemed calm, even a little smug.

"Yes, it's pretty rugged up there," the driver replied to my question. "I met this fellow"—motioning to his companion—"in a place where we couldn't pass and neither of us dared back. So, after 20 minutes of haggling, I bought his old jalopy and pushed it over the edge." —R. C. Olsen

ON THE BACK of a 1940 model auto seen in Memphis: "Out of date—but out of debt." —UP

As I motored along a California country road, a boy wearing the jacket of a local college hailed me—his car was in a ditch. It was an ancient vehicle that looked as if it were held together with little more than chewing gum and courage. But as he climbed into the seat beside me, he took a long look at it and shook his head sadly. "I can't understand it," he said seriously. "I've owned seven cars and every darned one of them turned out to be accident-prone." —Mary Ann Hedger

Service station: A place where you fill the car and drain the family (Vesta M. Kelly in *Quote*) . . . The long lane that has no turning is now called a turnpike (Clyde Moore in Columbus *Ohio State Journal*)

While my British sports car was being serviced in a small western town I went across the street for a cup of coffee. I came back to find two old-timers inspecting it. "Well, I'll be danged," commented one. "Must be the runt of the litter." —Ann Seaward

Woman to officer making road survey: "Don't count us. We'll be coming back in a few minutes when my husband admits he's going in the wrong direction."

—Marcelene Cox in *Ladies' Home Journal*

Man to wife, on motor trip: "Mind nagging me a little? I'm starting to fall asleep." —Bill Yates cartoon in *Collier's*

Just as I became really irritated over being stuck behind a slow-moving truck on a long, steep hill, the truck driver held out a sign with large black letters reading: PATIENCE AND FORTITUDE!

—Mrs. Newton Rose

Motorist: "Aren't you the fellow who sold me this car two weeks ago?"
Salesman: "Yes, sir."
Motorist: "Well, tell me about it again. I get so discouraged."

—*Times of Brazil*

Banner Boners

WHEN A veteran salesman for B. F. Goodrich in Akron retired, he married again and settled down in his home town —Lansing, Mich. The Lansing newspaper had a nice story about the wedding on the society page, but something went wrong and the headline from a story on another page appeared over the account. It read: OLD POWER PLANT REACTIVATED. —Kenneth Nichols in Akron *Beacon Journal*

HEADLINE in La Grange, Ga., *News:* REV. KEY RESIGNS; ATTENDANCE DOUBLES.

IN Sutton Coldfield, England, *News:* GIRL PASSENGER SAYS SHE WAS NOT BEING KISSED; DRIVER FINED FOR CARELESSNESS. —Quoted in *Punch*

IN Salem, Mass., *Evening News:* DR. ISRAEL KAPLAN ELECTED BOARD OF HEALTH CHAIRMAN. HEARING ON CEMETERY EXPANSION NEXT WEEK.

IN *Idaho State Journal:* POCATELLO MATTRESS FACTORY PLAYS IMPORTANT ROLE IN CITY'S GROWTH.

IN Atlanta *Journal:* HEAVY RAINS ASSURE CITY'S MILK SUPPLY.

IN Caro, Mich., *Tuscola County Advertiser:* MAYVILLE GIRL IS FIRST IN CHICKEN-OF-TOMORROW CONTEST.

IN a Los Angeles paper: COUNTY OFFICIALS TO TALK RUBBISH.

IN Milwaukee *Journal:* WEDDINGS HERE SHOW DROP, ISSUE MORE TRAPPING PERMITS.

IN Vancouver *News-Herald:* FRENCH DAM SITE BETTER OFF WITH U.S. AID FUNDS.

Infernal Revenue

If Patrick Henry thought taxation without representation was bad, he should see it with *representation.* —*Handy News*

WOMAN TO Internal Revenue clerk: "I do hope you'll give my money to some nice country."

—Franklin Folger cartoon, Chicago Sun-Times Syndicate

THE REV. Hilary Zwisler, of St. Sebastian's in Akron, tells about the time an Internal Revenue agent visited him on a personal matter. "While I'm here," the agent said, "I'd like to see your church. I've heard so much about it."

Delighted with the request the priest took him on a tour of the church. "Well," he asked proudly, "what do you think of it?"

"I'm rather disappointed," the agent said, then explained: "From the amount of money your parishioners list as gifts to your church I'd come to believe that the aisles were paved with gold."

—Kenny Nichols, *All About the Town* (Danner Press)

PARKED NEAR the Minneapolis Armory, surrounded by cars bearing such identifications as "Military Dept.—State of Minnesota" and "Official Business—U.S. Air Force," was an automobile displaying a sign: "Official Business—U.S. Taxpayer."

—Roy L. Smith in Asheville, N. C., *Citizen*

AFTER KENT FREELAND, Boyne City, Mich., high-school teacher, filed his income-tax return, the Department of Internal Revenue sent him two refund checks for $60. He deposited one in the bank, anticipating that the government would soon discover its mistake. Sure enough, a letter came asking for the $60 overpayment. He sent his personal check to cover that amount. Then came another letter asking for $2.60 interest on the $60.

"I sent the government the money," he says, "but that wasn't the end of it. They sent me another notice saying I still owed five cents as additional interest between the time they asked for the $2.60 and the time I paid it."

After several exchanges of letters he finally relented and sent in a nickel. Then he received one more letter which read: "Inasmuch as the amount is too small to process and since we consider your account as fully paid, the writer has taken the liberty of sending the five cents to the Salvation Army as a contribution from you. You are entitled to claim this contribution as a personal deduction on your next income-tax return." —UP

OVER THE incoming door at the Los Angeles tax bureau is a sign: "Watch Your Step." Over the outgoing door is: "Watch Your Language." —Jimmy Starr in Los Angeles *Herald and Express*

WIFE TO worried-looking husband working on tax return: "Why don't we turn it all over to the government and let them give us what they think we need?"

—Doris Matthews cartoon in *The Wall Street Journal*

Arthur Godfrey: I'm proud to be paying taxes in the United States. The only thing is—I could be just as proud for half the money.

ONE YOUNG girl to another as they sort tax returns in Internal Revenue office: "Here's another good one, Madeline—bachelor, no dependents, $35,000 a year!" —Irwin Caplan cartoon in *True*

A STRANGER dashing into a house in answer to a woman's screams found a frightened mother who explained that her young son had swallowed a quarter. The stranger grabbed the child by the feet, shook him vigorously until the coin fell from the boy's mouth. "Doctor," the woman gasped, "it certainly was lucky you happened by. You knew just how to get it out of him."

"I'm not a doctor, madam," the stranger explained. "I'm a Deputy Collector of Internal Revenue."

—*National Association of Employes of Collectors of Internal Revenue Bulletin,* quoted in Philadelphia *Inquirer*

Dedications With a Difference

COLUMNIST Earl Wilson dedicated *Let 'Em Eat Cheesecake:* "To one who, by repeated urgings, drove me on, shared with me for richer or for poorer, and to whom I shall always, as long as I live, owe a great deal—the Collector of Internal Revenue."

—Published by Doubleday

THE LATE Senator Arthur Vandenberg presented a Senate secretary with his picture inscribed: "With all the affection that the law allows."

—Jack Pollack, quoted by Leonard Lyons

MARK HELLINGER always had an unflagging zeal to avoid the conventional. The acknowledgments at the end of *The Ten Million* include: "To my wife—for permitting me to work, and for going out to the movies three times a week alone, I hope. To the Bing & Bing Construction Company—for not building anything near my apartment for the past six months. And to Saks & Co.—for underwear that does not bind while seated before a typewriter."

—*The One With the Mustache Is Costello,* © 1947 by George Frazier (Random House)

JEAN DALRYMPLE, the brisk, brittle and beautiful press agent and producer, has an autographed picture from composer Deems Taylor inscribed: "For Jean, whose rough exterior covers a heart of stone."

—H. N. Oliphant

COMEDIAN Joe E. Lewis' inscription on a picture of himself in the window of a New York restaurant reads: "This picture was taken when I was much older."

—Walter Winchell, quoted by E. E. Kenyon in *The American Weekly*

Barbershop Talk

THE FAMOUS French comedian Fernandel went to a new barber. Excited at having such a prominent customer, the barber almost danced around him and could hardly do enough. Finally he was finished, procured a mirror, held it in back of the famous head and whispered, "Is that all right?"

Fernandel looked at him sternly. "Almost. Just a little longer in back, please." —Munich *Revue* (*Quote* translation)

SIGN IN barbershop window: "Four Barbers in Attendance—Panel Discussions." —Serrano cartoon in *Town Journal*

A MAN WHO went to have his thinning hair cut met up with a barber who wanted to singe it instead—at double the price. "Each hair is a tiny tube that sort of bleeds at the cut end," he said, "so it gets weaker every time your hair is cut. But singeing seals the end, and the hair keeps its vigor."

"Then can you explain why the hair on my chin is growing stronger all the time, though each hair has been cut off every morning for 25 years?"

"No trouble at all," answered the barber. "You just ain't the kind of feller that story was made up to tell to." —Ralph Root

CALVIN COOLIDGE was having his hair cut in the one chair of the small Vermont barbershop where they still tell this story. The town doctor entered, sat down to wait and said, "Cal, did you take the pills I gave you?" Minutes went by before Coolidge answered, "Nope!"

Still later the doctor asked, "Are you feeling any better?"

Another long silence, then, "Yup!"

His haircut finished, Coolidge started to walk out when the barber hesitatingly asked, "Aren't you forgetting something, Mr. Coolidge?"

A bit sheepishly Cal replied, "I'm sorry; I forgot to pay you. I was so busy gossiping with the doctor it just slipped my mind."

—William E. Duggan

VIP Sidelights

WHEN WOODROW WILSON was president of Princeton University the mother of one of the students urged him to make it a coeducational institution.

"Why?" he asked.

"To remove the false glamour with which the two sexes see each other," she replied.

"My dear madam," Wilson shot back, "that is the very thing we want to preserve at all costs."

—Quoted by Dr. Raymond B. Fosdick on "Biographies in Sound," NBC

ONE NIGHT after a stage performance, the manager told Ethel Barrymore that two ladies wanted to see her. "They say they went to school with you," he explained.

"Went to school with me!" exclaimed Miss Barrymore. "Well, wheel them in!"

—George Freedley in *The Playbill*

AT ONE TIME the House of Wyoming's state legislature had only one Democratic member, Thurman Arnold. He had a marvelous time being the only Democrat.

As "minority leader" he nominated himself for Speaker of the House. "I have known this fine young man all his life! I would trust him as far as I would trust myself!" he declaimed magnificently. He sat down, then sprang to his feet and seconded the nomination. A third time he jumped up —to withdraw his name. "Some misguided enthusiast," he said humbly, "some impulsive admirer of mine has placed my name before this body!"

—Olga Moore, *I'll Meet You in the Lobby* (Lippincott)

FOR HIS ENTRY in the British *Who's Who,* author Sir Osbert Sitwell wrote that he was educated "during the holidays from Eton."

—*The Christian Science Monitor*

BENJAMIN F. FAIRLESS, speaking at the National Foreign Trade Convention:

A predecessor of mine as president of U. S. Steel was a man of unusually persuasive powers. His name was Charlie Schwab. One incident that illustrates this gift of his concerns a new steel mill. Company officials had collected all but one parcel of a large tract of land they needed. The farmer who owned this parcel stubbornly refused to sell. Vice-presidents, lawyers, the local mayor, everybody took a crack at trying to win him over. They offered him more money, company stock, double the acreage somewhere else. The farmer would not budge.

Then Charlie Schwab went to call on the farmer at his home. They sat down together on the parlor sofa and Charlie put his big, genial arm around the farmer's shoulder. Turning on the full voltage of his electric personality, he started to reason with him. Schwab had talked only a short time when suddenly the farmer jumped up. "Mr. Schwab," he said, "I'll sell you the property, but thank God I'm not a woman."

EDWARD JOHNSON, former general manager of the Metropolitan Opera, was reminiscing about the time he sang at the Rome première of Puccini's *Gianni Schicchi*. Puccini himself conducted, and when the opera was over Johnson tried to get him to come onstage for a bow. The composer-conductor modestly seemed reluctant. But as Johnson held his arms, urging him to come onstage, Puccini whispered, "Pull, pull!"

—Leonard Lyons

ONE DAY in the Mayo Clinic an affluent and obnoxious newcomer spied a white-haired doctor in the lobby. He strode up officiously and said, "Tell me, my good man, are you the head doctor here?"

Dr. Will, elder of the two famous Mayo brothers, bowed courteously: "No, kind sir, it must be my good brother you are seeking. I am the belly doctor."

—Helen Clapesattle, *The Doctors Mayo* (University of Minnesota Press)

TALLULAH BANKHEAD was crowding 17 when she arrived in New York from Alabama, stage-struck and sultry-voiced. Her father, Congressman William Bankhead, was not wild about the idea of Tallulah's going on the stage. But he agreed to finance a limited excursion to New York and Tallu arrived at the Hotel Algonquin chaperoned by her Aunt Louise. After a month or two Aunt Louise was called home. She left reluctantly, first saying to Frank Case, owner of the Algonquin, "You *will* keep an eye on our little girl?"

It was not until several months later that he was heard to murmur, "Either I keep an eye on Tallulah Bankhead or I run this hotel. No man does both."

—Margaret Case Harriman, *The Vicious Circle* (Rinehart)

AT A WASHINGTON banquet, as the toastmaster rose to get the program under way, a Congressman's wife sitting next to Senator Theodore Green of Rhode Island whispered, "May I pour you some coffee, Senator?"

"Good gracious, no," replied

the Senate's oldest member. "It might keep me awake during the speeches." —Andrew Tully, Scripps-Howard Newspapers

ONE TIME when Admiral Byrd was hotelman Ernie Byfield's guest in the Pump Room, he rose to dance with Mrs. Byfield and the host brought down the house by warning him loudly, "Remember now, Admiral, no exploring!"

—Bennett Cerf, *Shake Well Before Using* (Simon and Schuster)

CHARLES LAMB disliked office life and was inclined to be uncertain about his office hours at the India House. One day his chief said to him, "Mr. Lamb, I notice you come very late to the office." "Yes, sir," replied Lamb, "but you will notice that I go early."

The excuse so puzzled his superior that he could think of nothing to say. By the time he had worked it out Lamb was gone.

—Johannesburg *Sunday Times*

Are You a Skid-Talker?

By Corey Ford

"YOU CAN'T blame me for making a mistake," my friend Bunny said the other day. "After all, none of us are human." I was trying to figure that one out when she added thoughtfully, "I may be wrong but I'm not far from it."

Bunny is a skid-talker. Skid-talk is more than a slip of the tongue. It's a slip of the whole mind. In effect it puts one idea on top of another, producing a sort of mental double exposure—and my friend Bunny is a master of the art. When her husband, a prominent Hollywood director, completed a screen epic she told him loyally, "I hope it goes over with a crash." She was very enthusiastic after the preview. "It's a great picture," she assured everyone. "Don't miss it if you can."

That's the insidious thing about skid-talk—you're never quite sure you've heard it. Skid-language is like a time bomb; it ticks away quietly in your subconscious, and suddenly, a few minutes later, your mind explodes with the abrupt realization that something about the remark you just heard was a trifle askew.

"If George Washington were

alive today," Bunny told me once, "he'd turn over in his grave." On another occasion she opened a debate with the challenging sentence: "For your information, let me ask you a question."

The simplest kind of skid-talk consists of mixing words. For example:

"Too many cooks in the soup."

"From time immoral."

"There I was, left holding the jackpot."

"It was so dark you couldn't see your face in front of you."

"I want some hot-water juice and a lemon."

A devoted mother added another gem to my collection: "I'm going to have a bust made of my daughter's head." And a stranger feeding pigeons in Central Park explained to me with quiet dignity, "I believe in being dumb to kind animals."

Sometimes a skid-talker will turn an entire sentence inside out so effectively that the listener can't possibly set it straight again. I keep wondering about a statement I overheard the other day at the station: "He tells me something one morning and out the other." And I have yet to discover what's wrong with Bunny's advice to a young married couple: "Two can live as cheaply as one, but it costs them twice as much."

Bunny is a natural skid-zophrenic. "I'm a split personality all in one," she describes herself happily. She lives in a handsome country place of which she says dreamily, "Isn't it pretty? The lake comes right up to the shore." "I went to a wonderful party," she said of one celebrity-studded banquet. "Everybody in the room was there." She made sure to thank the hostess as she departed. "Darling, that was the best dinner I ever put in my whole mouth."

Bunny's insults are equally bewildering. "I never liked you, and I always will," she told a prominent screen star frankly. And a perennially young starlet is still trying to decipher Bunny's candid appraisal: "You're old enough to be my daughter."

The best skid-talk fuses two thoughts together, creating a new shortcut which speeds up the language. I remember a New Year's Eve party when Bunny became fearful that the sounds of midnight revelry might disturb the neighbors. "Don't make so much noise," she told the celebrants. "Remember, this isn't the only house we're in."

I had an affectionate note from Bunny after a visit. "Come see us again soon," she wrote. "We miss you almost as much as if you were here."

Another Language

A PASADENA girl took a job as a forelady in a shop employing several Mexican women. The first morning she addressed each of them cordially in her high-school Spanish. The women shrank from her. When the same thing happened next day the mystified girl told the boss. He asked her what she had said to them. "Just good morning," she replied.

"But how did you say it?"

"I said *'Buenos Dios, Buenos Dios!'* "

The boss howled. "If you wanted to say good morning you should have said *'Buenas dias.'* You've looked at each of these women the first thing in the morning and said 'Good God, Good God!' "

—Matt Weinstock, *My L.A.* (Current Books)

WHEN I WAS courting a charming young lady of European descent, our devoted maid disapproved heartily of this foreign intrusion. Trying to impress Rosie with my new girl's background, I announced that she was a baroness. "How's dat?" exclaimed Rosie. "You mean she can't have no chillun?" —Robert R. Perry

RED SMITH, the sports columnist, was an honored guest one evening at a banquet tendered by the Don Q Rum Company in Puerto Rico. Smith delivered his speech nobly, but for one detail —he persisted in referring to his hosts as the "makers of that wonderful Bacardi rum."

Every time he mentioned the competing name "Bacardi," a mortified Don Q official would jump up and correct him with, "Don Q, señor, Don Q." And every time Red Smith answered graciously, "You're welcome." —Bennett Cerf in *This Week Magazine*

A PAN AMERICAN World Airways employe in Accra advertised that he wanted a kerosene refrigerator, received this reply: "I have the honour most respectfully to submit this my humble application soliciting for employment as a kerosene refrigerator. I successfully passed the seventh standard at Oboden Methodist Middle School and hold documents testifying my character and ability."

—New York *Herald Tribune*

BRITISH Colonial Secretary Oliver Lyttelton said that differences in the use of the Queen's English can, and sometimes do, cause Anglo-American misunderstandings. To illustrate his point he related this incident:

The vicar of a British church destroyed during World War II wrote an American colonel who had been stationed in the badly bombed town and explained that a fund was being raised to rebuild the ruined church. The American replied in a charming letter and enclosed a check for $5000.

The village was so grateful that they sent the colonel a recording of the consecration ceremonies. The colonel had proudly invited friends in to hear it, but suddenly he took the record from the phonograph and smashed it on the floor.

The vicar had begun to speak and, referring to the colonel's gift, he said, "Now let us all thank God for this timely succor."

—UP

Church Bulletins

OUR MAID asked for an advance on her week's salary. "Our preacher is leaving the church this Sunday," she told us, "and the congregation wants to give him a little momentum."

—Fred G. McKnight in *Coronet*

OWEN WISTER, in a foreword to *The Family Mark Twain*, recounts a yarn that the humorist once told him. "It was on a Sunday up at Hartford some years ago," Mark Twain began, and then continued:

A missionary preached that morning. His voice was beautiful. He told of the sufferings of the natives; he pleaded for help with such moving simplicity that Twain mentally doubled the 50 cents he had intended to put in the plate. As the address proceeded, describing so pitifully the misery of the savages, the dollar in his mind gradually rose to five. A little farther along the missionary had him crying. He felt that all the cash he carried about him would be insufficient and decided to write a large check.

"And then that preacher went on," said Mark Twain, falling into a drawl, "went on about the dreadful state of those natives. I abandoned the idea of the check. And he went on. And I got back to five dollars, four, two, one. But he went on. And when the plate came around—I took ten cents out of it."

—© 1935 by Harper & Brothers

AD IN THE Leslie, Mich., *Local-Republican:* "WANTED—Men, women and children, to sit in slightly used pews Sunday mornings 10 a.m. Leslie Methodist Church."

AT A CEREMONY in the Princeton University Chapel, an old lady buttonholed an usher and commanded, "Be sure you get me a seat up front, young man. I understand they've always had trouble with the agnostics in this chapel!"

—Whitney Darrow, quoted by Bennett Cerf in *The Saturday Review*

WHEN I WAS holding the 9:30 service one Sunday I noticed that one parishioner was very late. To my surprise he was at the 11o'clock service as well. But when the congregation rose to sing the hymn before the sermon he left, murmuring to the usher, "This is where I came in." —The Rev. Charles F. Rehfus

IT STARTED at the end of a Sunday morning service in an Ontario church. The choir began the recessional, singing as they marched in perfect unison up the center aisle to the back of the church. The last young lady in the women's section was wearing a new pair of shoes with needle heels—heels that are so slender they slip through any grating. And in the aisle was a grating that covered the hot-air register.

Without a thought for her fancy heels, the young woman sang

and marched. And the heel of one shoe sank right through a hole in the register grate. Instantly she realized her predicament. She knew she couldn't hold up the whole recessional while she back-stepped to pull out her heel. She did the next best thing in the emergency. Without missing a step she slipped her foot out of her shoe and continued up the aisle. There wasn't a break in the recessional. Everything moved like clockwork.

The first man following that young woman noted the situation and, without losing a beat, reached down and picked up her shoe.

The entire grate came with it. Startled but still singing, the man continued up the aisle bearing in his hand one grate attached to one shoe.

Never a break in the recessional. Everybody singing. Everything moving like clockwork. And then in tune and in time to the beat the next man stepped into the open register.

—Kitchener-Waterloo, Ont., *Record,* quoted in *The Lutheran*

AT A SUNDAY-school club discussion of the purchase of new chairs for the church, one woman got determinedly to her feet. "I am willing to spend *some* of the money in our treasury for the chairs," she said firmly, "but I do not think we should strip ourselves to the bottom." —Mrs. Lee A. Smith

A CONNECTICUT minister, preaching a sermon in a little church in Vermont while on his vacation, received the greatest compliment of his ministry from one of the laconic natives. The Vermonter gripped the pastor's hand, beamed all over, said, "Didn't get my nap today." —Kenneth M. Swezey

TWO LADIES, dressed to the hilt in their Easter finery, were making slow progress in the crowd headed for the entrance to the church. Finally one of them burst out impatiently, "Now wouldn't you think that these people who do nothing but go to church Sunday after Sunday would stay home on Easter and leave room for the rest of us!" —M. C. D.

Faith and Begorra!

It had to be this kind of a world before the Irish could drop out of sight as the most peaceful nation in it. —*Quick*

THE ELOQUENT preacher had just addressed the ladies of the congregation on "The Glory, the Beauty and the Sanctity of Motherhood." Coming out of church Mrs. Riley, the mother of eight, said to Mrs. O'Hara, mother of 13, "Marvelous sermon, wasn't it?"

"It was so, Mrs. Riley, a grand sermon, a movin' address; and would to heaven, Mrs. Riley, I knew as little about the subject as the dear man himself."

—Romeyn Berry, *Dirt Roads to Stoneposts* (Century House)

PATRICK, suffering from toothache, got up enough nerve to visit his dentist, but lost it again when he was about to get into the chair. The dentist told his assistant to give Pat a tot of whiskey. "Got your courage back now?" he asked.

"No," replied Pat. So a second tot was brought, and a third.

"*Now* have you got your courage?" asked the dentist.

Pat squared his shoulders. "I'd like to see the man," he said, "who'd dare to touch me teeth now!"

—Cambridge, England, *Daily News,* quoted in *The Atlantic Log*

WHEN STUYVESANT FISH was president of the Illinois Central Railroad there walked into his office one morning an Irishman, hat on and pipe in mouth, who said, "I want a pass to St. Louis."

"Who are you?" asked President Fish, somewhat startled.

"I'm Pat Casey, one of your switchmen."

Mr. Fish, thinking it was a good chance to impart a lesson in etiquette, said, "Now, Pat, I'm not going to say that I will refuse your request, but there are certain forms a man should observe in asking a favor. You should knock at the door, and when I say, 'Come in,' you should enter and, taking off your hat and removing your pipe from your mouth, you should say, 'Are you President Fish?' I would say, 'I am. Who are you?' Then you should say,

'I am Pat Casey, one of your switchmen.' Then I would say, 'What can I do for you?' Then you would tell me, and the matter would be settled. Now you go out and come in again and see if you can't do better."

So the switchman went out. About two hours later there was a knock on the door and President Fish said, "Come in." In came Pat Casey with his hat off and pipe out of his mouth.

"Good morning," he said, "are you President Fish of the Illinois Central Railroad?"

"I am. Who are you?"

"I am Pat Casey, one of your switchmen."

"Well, Mr. Casey, what can I do for you?"

"You can go to hell. I got a job and a pass on the Wabash."

—Merrill, Iowa, *Record,* quoted in *A Treasury of Railroad Folklore,* edited and © 1953 by B. A. Botkin and Alvin F. Harlow (Crown)

WHEN DENNIS and Murphy drifted into the big city they came to share the same room. Dennis knew that somewhere back home Murphy had a wife, but his friend seldom mentioned her. One day Murphy received a letter and Dennis inquired, "Who's it from?"

"From me wife," Murphy replied.

"But, Murphy," Dennis protested as he watched his friend draw a perfectly blank sheet of paper from the envelope, "there's nothin' written there!"

"Oi know," Murphy replied. "Me and the missus ain't speakin'."

—*The Curtis Courier*

MR. DOOLAN caught the bartender at Moriarty's saloon in an unguarded moment and begged, "Mike, me mother-in-law has gone to her just reward, and it's a ten spot I'm needin' for a wreath to uphold the Doolan standards. Can ye advance me the ten?" The bartender emptied his pockets and the cash register but the total came to $9.30.

"That'll do," said Doolan hastily. "I'll take the other 70 cents in drinks."

—Bennett Cerf in *This Week Magazine*

LOVE OF the land dominates the Irishman's every other urge. As a farmer of 60 outside my home town back in Tipperary put it, "The girl I'm going to marry isn't much to look at, but she has a darlin' bit o' land."

—Mai B. McCarthy

My Luck

By J. P. McEvoy

NOW THAT I peer back through the fog of confusion and recovered fumbles which I call my career, I find I had an asset more precious than Pulitzer Prize prose—I was a farm boy with a conditioned reflex for hard work that was one big callus. Years ago we had a spread-the-work program down on the farm. Instead of concentrating it all in eight hours, we spread it through 16. Before dawn I groped my way to the barn to wake the cows up and forcibly take the milk away from them. That was my first lesson in semantics. Cows do not "give" milk. If you are wily and strong and ruthless, you can have it for the taking.

Come to think of it, there was a lot of loose talk down on the farm in those days. When you plowed "new ground" that had just been cleared and was all full of stumps and roots that jumped right out of the earth and attacked you, they said you "broke" the ground. Actually it was the other way around. All day from dawn to dark you were said to be "spraying the apples" with Paris green and arsenate of lead but most of the time the wind was blowing the other way and you came home looking like an old bronze statue of General Grant, covered with a poisonous green scum that would have killed anybody but a farm boy.

What I'm trying to say is that, when I finally got to the big city and learned that if you worked only 12 hours you had all the rest of the day to yourself, I couldn't believe my luck.

—McNaught Syndicate

Toward More Picturesque Speech

THE KIND of night when the moon halts cars on lonely roads (R. E. Getchius) . . . A cat walking up a dark lane with both of his headlights glowing (Albert Kelley in *Farm Journal*)

Marriage Knots: She worships her husband—places burnt offerings before him three times a day (Don Ameche) . . . He looked like a man being led to the shopping block (Mrs. W. H. Wood) . . . Irate wife to husband: "Are you a man or a mouse? Come on, squeak up!" (Mrs. T. J. Nolan)

Apt Comparisons: Thirsty as a child that has just gone to bed (Richard Kinney) . . . Confident as a Marine from Texas (Earl Wilson) . . . Inseparable as coat hangers (Ethel Clemmer) . . . Overworked as a dog with four children to follow (Marcelene Cox in *Ladies' Home Journal*) . . . Impatient as a kid who has mailed in a boxtop (Lee Priestley)

WHEN a person tells you, "I'll think it over and let you know"—you know (Olin Miller) . . . If you think there ought to be a law, there probably is *(The Re-Saw)*

KISSING a girl is like opening a bottle of olives—if you get one the rest come easy (*Chatham News*)

THINK no evil, see no evil, hear no evil—and you will never write a best-selling novel (Dan Bennett in *Quote*)

Overheard: At a college faculty meeting: "This place is nothing but a hotbed of cold feet" ("Atticus" in *Sunday Times*, London) . . . Such traffic! We drove five hours a mile (Dorothy Nelson) . . . She was born in the year of Our Lord only knows when (Ivan Paul in San Francisco *Examiner*) . . . Such a wonderful day—it makes me feel the way I wish I did (Charles W. Ferguson)

Vacation Notes: Those rainy days for which a man saves usually arrive during his vacation (*Link-Belt News*) . . . Going to the beach is like going to the attic—you are surprised at what you will find in trunks (*The Prison Mirror*) . . . Tourists so thick that they were getting into each other's snapshots (Harlan Miller in Des Moines *Register*) . . . He who believes that where there's smoke there's fire hasn't tried cooking on a camping trip (*Changing Times, The Kiplinger Magazine*)

THERE seems to be plenty of money in the country, but everyone owes it to everyone else (From an English calendar)

Money Matters

Anonymous: Money isn't everything, but it's way ahead of whatever is in second place.

—Gordon Gammack in Des Moines *Tribune*

John Kirk Nelson: More and more these days I find myself pondering on how to reconcile my net income with my gross habits.

Joe E. Lewis: A bank is the thing that will always lend you money if you can prove that you don't need it.

Samuel Butler: All progress is based upon a universal innate desire on the part of every organism to live beyond its income.

The Re-Saw: Another reason you can't take it with you—it goes before you do.

—General Features Corp.

Abe Martin: When a feller says it ain't the money but the principle of the thing, it's the money.

—John F. Dille Syndicate

Buyers Beware

MITCHEL Air Force Base officials received a note from an enterprising Garden City, L.I., homeowner who lives near the end of a certain runway. "Please do not use the runway before noon Saturday," he requested. "I am showing my house to a prospective buyer." —New York *Times*

THE NEW assistant in the optical-goods store was being instructed by the proprietor: "Now, son, we want to get a fair and honest price out of every customer. After you have fitted the glasses and the customer asks, 'What's the charge?' you say, 'The charge is $10.' Then you pause. If the customer doesn't flinch, you say, 'That's for the frames; the lenses will be another $10.'

"Then you pause, and again you wait. And if the customer doesn't flinch, you say, 'Each.' "

—Randolph-Macon Woman's College *Potpourri*

A MAN trying to buy a horse from a Vermont farmer was startled when he named $1000 as his price. Nonetheless the prospective buyer countered with a reasonable $100 offer. "That's a helluva discount," mused the farmer, "but I'll take it."

As the buyer counted out the money he couldn't resist asking why the farmer had accepted $100 after first naming ten times that sum. "Well," he drawled, "I thought mebbe you'd like to own a thousand-dollar hoss."

—*Egan Echoes*

IN FRONT of a house being built in Philadelphia were the customary signs saying the builder was so-and-so, brickwork by somebody else, architect so-and-so. In the middle was a small sign put up by the owner-to-be: "Victim: I. D. Levy." —Earl Selby in Philadelphia *Bulletin,* quoted by Art Ryon in Los Angeles *Times*

ONE NIGHT when my wife and I were having dinner with another American couple in a small French restaurant in Nice, a Moorish peddler approached our table with a tray of exquisite silver bracelets. When he told us the price was 5000 francs per bracelet my wife became discouraged. But the other woman, who had been living in Nice for some time, began a spirited negotiation with the Moor. To our amazement the price kept dropping steadily while the two principals matched wits with obvious enthusiasm. Finally one bracelet was sold for a mere 500 francs.

My wife promptly offered to buy a second bracelet at the same price. The peddler, however, drew back in evident disdain. "But no, madam," he replied. "For you we start over again."

—Lt. Comdr. Patrick Leehey

A NEW YORK man who was looking for a country place found an ad in the paper for an old saltbox house on a couple of acres at Sherman, Conn., near the lake and also near the general store.

The ad was a blind—signed with a box number in care of the newspaper—but the man immediately set out for Sherman. He went to the general store and described the house to the old gentleman behind the counter. "Must be Fred's place," the grocer said, pointing outside helpfully. "You can see it right out the window there."

"That can't be it," the New Yorker protested. "The lake must be four miles from here. And that house isn't like the ad." He handed over the clipping to prove his point. The grocer studied it for a moment, then handed it back. "Nope," he said, "the house ain't like the ad, but, by Godfrey, the ad is like Fred!"

—Herbert A. Thompson

AT THE farm auction bidding was particularly brisk on an old hand-blown whiskey bottle, and finally a collector on my left was the successful taker at $6.75. When his purchase was handed over to him an aged but sharp-eyed farmer standing nearby leaned over and took a good look at the bottle.

"My God," the farmer gasped to his friend, "it's empty!"

—Harriet Y. Clough

Going Around in Circas

An excerpt from "Acres and Pains"
S. J. Perelman

IS ANYBODY looking for a bargain in an Early Pennsylvania washstand in mint condition, circa 1825? It's genuine pumpkin pine, with ball-and-claw feet, the original brasses, and a small smear of blood where I tripped over it last night in the dark. I'm holding it at $16, but not so tightly that I wouldn't let it go to the right party for circa ten cents.

I also have an authentic trestle table which collapses into a small space when you rest your elbows on it, and a patchwork quilt I bought from a very old lady who remembered seeing Lincoln. In fact I'm disposing of my entire collection of antiques to the lowest bidder, and if he doesn't want it I intend to set fire to it as soon as I am able to find an Early American match.

When we left a cozy New York flat to exile ourselves in a primitive farmhouse back in the mid-'30's, we broke clean with the 20th century. We were ready to dip candles and card our own flax. We installed a spinning wheel in every room in case anyone should need some quick homespun, and replaced our luxurious inner-spring bed with a period four-poster. (Our neighbor hesitated to relinquish it, as it had been serving as a roost for his chickens, but finally exchanged it for five acres of prime bottom land.) We even discarded the electric stove and returned to cooking in the fireplace.

In spite of all our efforts, however, the house still seemed bourgeois and prosaic. The lamps gave off too much light and the bureau drawers worked too easily. We lusted for lamps made out of old seltzer bottles or apothecaries' jars, and Victorian dressers that nobody could open.

Then one day on a back-country road we stumbled into a web run by a spider named Jake Meserve. Outwardly Jake was a farmer. He had a long linen duster, steel-bowed spectacles, and a field of papier-maché corn in front of his place as a blind. In his hayloft, however, he kept a few choice heirlooms you could persuade him to sell by dropping your hat. We immediately fell in love with a rare old cobbler's bench, as fine a piece as you would find outside the Metropolitan—that is the Metropolitan Shoe Repair Shop. After a brisk tussle Jake stowed away my $39 and hauled out a rickety sofa.

"You folks ever seen a real old-time Victorian courtin' chair?" he inquired, stroking the plush. "My Uncle Zeb proposed to Aunt Mildew in that chair. I wouldn't part with it if I was starvin'." Suddenly he choked back a sob and turned away. "Take it," he muttered brokenly. "Ninety-three dollars. It's like sellin' my own flesh and blood."

I whittled him down to $60, and drying his eyes he disgorged three more family mementos—a dough tray, a glass bell containing his mother's baby hair, and a little chest of drawers lettered, "Willimantic Spool & Thread Co." He stripped my wallet of everything but the social-security card, and we embarked. As I threw the car into gear he staggered up bearing a table. "Just ran acrost this in my feed bin," he panted. "My grandpa bought it off Nancy Hanks. You can scrape off the paint with a stiff brush."

I threw him my watch and chain, and we whizzed away. I spent the next week hacking at the table with a blowtorch, steel wool and sandpaper. It had six coats of paint, including one like porcelain that had been baked on. When I had finished, I overturned it accidentally and discovered a sticker reading, "R. H. Macy & Co. Reduced to $3.98." And that, children, is how Daddy met his first psychiatrist.

Quotable Quotes

Howard W. Newton: An antique is an object that has made a round trip to the attic.

—*Redbook*

Ellaville, Ga., *Sun*: A woman who is smart enough to ask a man's advice seldom is dumb enough to take it.

Joe E. Wells: Was there ever a grandparent, bushed after a day of minding noisy youngsters, who hasn't felt the Lord knew what He was doing when He gave little children to young people?

—Frances Rodman in New York *Times Magazine*

William James: We all want our friends to tell us of our bad qualities; it is only the particular ass that does so that we can't tolerate.

—Dickinson S. Miller, *William James, The Man and The Thinker* (University of Wisconsin Press)

***Changing Times, The Kiplinger Magazine*:** A lot of mothers in the last generation had their daughters vaccinated in places they wrongly thought would never show.

Tulsa *Star*: So far science has not figured out how a man can tell what a woman is thinking by listening to what she's saying.

Claude Callan: Things are pretty well evened up in this world. Other people's troubles are not so bad as yours, but their children are a lot worse.

—Kansas City *Times*

Anonymous: A sense of humor is what makes you laugh at something which would make you mad if it happened to you.

—Virginia Sullivan Tomlinson, King Features

Ironical, Isn't It?

HAD HE BEEN of a different temperament, David Falk of Hampton, Va., might have been satisfied to stretch the $5000 his father gave him when he entered the University of Wisconsin to cover his four years of college. But instead Falk decided to indulge in a bit of extracurricular tycoonery.

He spent his nest egg as down payment on a rooming house, which he remodeled in his spare time and soon had filled with students. With the profit he made he bought 47 acres of land, cut them up into three plots, sold them individually. Having made more money on the first two lots than he paid for the entire 47 acres, he bought himself another thriving rooming house. Finally he traded his first house for a third, making a profit on the deal. Thus, as he neared the end of his studies for a degree in dairy husbandry, Falk (then 21) figured he had about $30,000 to buy a farm for himself and his bride.

The only sour note in his academic career—the near-failing D he received in a course on real estate. —*Time*

AN INVOLVED employment application form used by a large industrial firm seeking the services of floor sweepers included such queries as, "Are you sexually stable?" "What type of books do you read?" "Do you blush easily?" and so on, and on. But they neglected to ask one significant question: "Have you had any experience handling a broom?"

—Willard P. Bitting in *Printer's Ink*

IN HARTFORD, Conn., Mrs. Anna Katzman got two notices from the city: (1) the tax assessment on her tenement house was raised 20 percent, (2) the building was declared unfit for occupancy. —*Time*

FROM A letter written by our son, who was receiving his basic training at Lackland Air Force Base, Texas: "We were supposed to have survival training today but it was postponed on account of rain." —Mrs. Paul Gregory

THANKS TO the alertness of the sportscasters and the miracles of modern communication, it is often possible to know the score of every major football game in the country—except the one to which you are listening.

—Bill Vaughan, Bell Syndicate

AT THE HEIGHT of the Pearl Harbor attack several men refused to open up the ammunition supplies without receipt of a proper written order. Walter Lord, doing his research for *Day of Infamy,* found one of them still insisting that he had been right. Lord asked him under what circumstances he would have felt justified in operating without such an order. "Only," the man said stanchly, "in case of an emergency."

—Maurice Dolbier in New York *Herald Tribune Book Review*

EXPORT-IMPORT situations in Europe have caused some strange upheavals. Some years ago, for instance, when Gunnar Myrdal, Swedish economic expert, was dining at the home of Jean Monnet in Paris, his host apologized because he was unable to offer any of France's celebrated Camembert cheese. But he did have some genuine English Stilton. Next day Mr. Myrdal had lunch in London with Sir David Waley, who expressed regret that he could serve no Stilton cheese. "However," he said, "I can give you some real French Camembert."

—London *Sunday Times,* quoted by *Worldover Press*

A FRIEND whose son had just earned his wings as an Air Force jet pilot said, "It seems incredible. They didn't think anything of handing him a $900,000 airplane to fly—and just a couple of years ago I was very cautious about letting him drive our Buick."

—Kenneth Nichols in Akron *Beacon Journal*

AT THE ROME meeting of the International Police Commission they were discussing sex crimes. One by one delegates from the major Western powers reeled off their grisly statistics. Finally the Burmese delegate diffidently climbed to the rostrum. "I must apologize to the assembly," he said, "for I have no statistics on this subject. We are a backward nation and have no sex crimes. But as our civilization catches up with those of the distinguished delegates who have been speaking I hope we may do better. Next year I will try to bring some good statistics on this matter."

—Ian Fleming in London *Sunday Times*

As Others See Us

An Italian scientist visiting in this country was being shown through a large dairy bottling plant when a pipe sprang a leak and cream spurted in all directions. Immediately one workman calmly turned off the main valve, another mended the leak.

The Italian visitor was dumfounded. "In my country everyone would have run about shouting; nobody would have thought of cutting off the main valve until everything had been covered with cream. They would have had a wonderful time and talked about it the rest of the day." He shook his head. "That's the reason you have so many nervous breakdowns here—you don't let yourselves go." —Bernice B. Cronkhite

A minor Soviet official, after several months' tour of duty in the United States, was asked what his impressions were. "Some things are really magnificent," said the Russian thoughtfully, "but in other respects I am disappointed. The cities, for instance, are so poor in hygienic installations. Now, in the Soviet Union you would find a delousing station for public use in every large railroad station. Here in the United States I've never seen one."

—Donald Patterson

The Shah of Iran, on his visit to the States, startled a reporter who asked what he thought of American women. "I see many of them in the streets," he said in puzzled tones, "but I don't see many pregnant." —*Time*

Near the university in Stockholm I saw a mob of wildly shouting students holding a fair-haired lad high on their shoulders. There was a wreath of green leaves around his shoulders and he was being pelted with roses by the girls, while boys and girls alike shouted, "Rah, rah, Carl! Rah, rah, Carl!"

Football captain, I thought, and then inquired of a good-looking Swede, "Some brilliant athlete, I suppose?"

"No, madame. He is graduating and is the honor student of the year."

"Well, it's the first time I ever saw such wild excitement over scholarship," I commented.

There was a politely veiled glint of amusement in the man's eyes as he asked, "For what purpose, then, does your country build schools?" —Montanye Perry

Higher Learning

AN EASTERN professor visiting the University of California at Los Angeles was impressed by the beautiful buildings, the miles of eucalyptus-lined lawns, the athletic fields. "Wonderful," he said to his guide, a dean. "And just how many students do you have here?"

"Let me see," the dean replied thoughtfully. "I'd say about one in a hundred." —*Script*

A COLLEGE education is one of the few things a person is willing to pay for and not get.

—William Lowe Bryan, President Emeritus of Indiana University

I EARLY learned that a Ph.D. thesis consists of transferring bones from one graveyard to another. —J. Frank Dobie

A LAFAYETTE College professor's explanation of why undergraduates were compelled to take so many English courses: "In order to teach them a language other than their own."

—*Indiana Teacher*

PRESIDENT George L. Cross of the University of Oklahoma, asking the state legislature for more appropriations: "We're working to develop a university the football team can be proud of."—*Time*

A DEBATABLE forward step in higher education occurred at Texas A & M when the registrar's office—at the insistence of a number of old grads—passed a rule prohibiting sons of alumni from looking up their fathers' grades.

—E. E. McQuillen, quoted by George Fuermann in Houston *Post*

PRESIDENT Lowell of Harvard, explaining why universities have so much learning: "The freshmen bring a little in and the seniors take none out, so it accumulates through the years."

—Brooks Atkinson in New York *Times*

Public Notices

A NOTICE spotted by a summer-school student on the office door of the university president: "This office closed for the summer. For anything important see the janitor." —Marguerite M. McConnell

MY NEIGHBOR'S two youngsters built a clubhouse in their yard. On the wall in childish lettering was a list of club rules. No. 1 reads: "Nobody act big, nobody act small, everybody act medium."

—Jack Denham

FROM THE London *Economist:* "We regret that, owing to a misunderstanding about a last-minute correction in proof, the paragraphs of our lead article last week were printed out of their intended order. We apologize to those of our readers who thought our views even less coherent than usual; those who noticed nothing wrong possibly owe us an apology."

FROM THE Salt Lake City *Tribune:* "Notice to our friends, to bill collectors, radio and TV poll takers, *et al:* due to our daughter's return from college for the holidays we expect a 30-minute to three-hour delay on all telephone calls to our residence. Mr. and Mrs. H. H. Fisher."

IN FRYBURG, Ohio, Pusheta Township trustees posted a notice: "Effective immediately, there will be no parking at the No Parking signs."

—*Time*

NOTICE ON a community bulletin board in San Francisco: "Ten-year-old boy would like garden work and odd jobs after school and on Saturdays to help support a dependent who eats like a horse. P.S. It *is* a horse."

—Lilli Stockenberg

FROM THE Ontario, N. Y., *Wayne County Mail:* "West Walworth Volunteer Fire Department will blow the siren 15 minutes before the start of each fire."

FROM THE Elmwood Park, Ill., *Mont Clare News-West Suburban Times:* "To our friends and neighbors. The inconvenient half hour of interrupted electric service in our neighborhood last Friday was caused by equipment failure or an act of God and not by either of our sons. We know and we can prove that both boys were home in bed at the time, so please do not knock on our door with complaints. Alfred A. Pellegrini."

NOTICE IN the Red Lake Falls, Minn., *Gazette:* "St. Joseph's and Oak Grove cemeteries will be closed November 15 for the winter. Residents of the area should take due notice and govern themselves accordingly."

Grammaw Didn't Like Funerals

Condensed from "Gone Are the Days"

W. Bruce Bell

THE TELEPHONE jangled our number that morning about nine o'clock—one long and two short—as Mother and Grammaw were making sickle-pear preserves. Mother took down the receiver from the wall phone. At first she used her everyday tone of voice in greeting Miss Delia, the operator. But soon a sharp change of key told us that Miss Delia was reporting bad news. In the kitchen Grammaw sliced a pear and listened, trying to find a clue as to what had happened.

"What was the matter with her, Miss Delia?" Mother cried. "What? Speak up, I can't hear you! You don't say! Yes, of course I will. I'll have to hurry. Thanks for calling."

Mother hung up. "Aunt Hettie Wade is dead," she said. "Her funeral is to be at the church at ten and they want me to help with the singing. They tried to reach us yesterday but the phone was out of order."

Grammaw was so surprised she hardly knew what to say. "How *could* Hettie be dead? Why, I saw her just last Sunday after church and she was pert as a jay bird. What did she die of?"

"Miss Delia tried to tell me, but there was so much frying on the line I couldn't hear her." Mother looked at the clock. "Goodness! It's already 20 past nine. I must hurry."

She paused briefly. "Ma," she said, "don't you think you ought to go with me? Aunt Hettie was almost the same as kinsfolk."

Grammaw studied a moment because she was in a quandary. On Huckleberry Knob in our little Indiana farming community everybody dressed up and turned out for a funeral as a sign of respect. That is, everyone except Grammaw. She didn't want to be unsociable, but she differed in one way from other elderly women in our community. She just didn't enjoy funerals. Country people of the early 1900's did not always embalm their dead, and Grammaw once knew a woman, she said, who had fallen into a deep coma and had suffered the terrible fate of being buried alive. So ever since then Grammaw had balked at funerals. She had the creepy notion that the main character might rouse up during the services.

But now Grammaw said, "I reckon I'll put-near have to go. People will talk if I don't. I didn't have a chance to wait on poor Hettie before she died. But I do hope"—Grammaw hesitated—"I do hope that Hettie is really dead." Grammaw set her crock of sickle pears on the table and spread a towel over them.

Mother and Grammaw rushed across the churchyard just as the bell clanged the first note of its slow, measured tolling. Mother went up and joined the choir, and Grammaw dropped into the first empty seat she found. She peered out at the hearse when it pulled up just outside the open door. Through the tassels and plush draperies she could see one end of its black, silver-handled freight with the bouquets of pink and white carnations on top. Inside the church here and there a muffled sob broke the silence.

As the flower-covered coffin moved down the aisle the choir sang softly the sad, comforting words of "What a Friend We Have in Jesus." Sniffles broke out all over the meetinghouse, and Grammaw held a black-bordered handkerchief to her face. The preacher mounted the platform and delivered a brief prayer, then put on his glasses and spread the obituary out on the pulpit. Just as the congregation settled down to hear the reading a small woman tiptoed in and sat down in the back row not far from Grammaw. Grammaw blinked through her tears, wiped her eyes and took another unbelieving look. The woman was Aunt Hettie Wade!

Aunt Hettie nodded to Grammaw and gave her a brisk smile. Grammaw wanted to stand up and holler, "Stop the funeral! Aunt Hettie's not dead. There she is on the back seat!" But she hesitated to make a spectacle of herself, so she decided to wait and see what happened when it came time to view the remains.

At last the preacher finished the closing prayer, and the undertaker shuffled down the aisle and opened the coffin lid. He didn't jump when he looked inside, Grammaw noticed, so at least it wasn't *empty*.

The choir began to sing "When the Roll Is Called Up Yonder," and now, pew by pew, the people rose and filed past the coffin. Finally it was Grammaw's turn. She joined the line, hesitated a moment, then peeped in—at a middle-aged woman she had never laid eyes on before.

After the service Grammaw

was swept along with the congregation into the cemetery, and there she saw Mother with Aunt Hettie. They could hardly keep from laughing at the look on Grammaw's face. Mother had learned right away from someone in the choir that the woman who died was Annetta Wade, a distant relative who didn't live in the neighborhood any more. In Miss Delia's excited phone call the name Annetta Wade had come over the noisy wire as Aunt Hettie Wade.

Grammaw was happy to see Aunt Hettie alive, but it made her mad that she had left her pear preserves to go and cry her eyes out over a stranger.

PERT though Aunt Hettie looked, she took down with pneumonia the following winter and died. She lingered long enough, however, for Grammaw to be of some service in caring for her. The morning she was to be buried, Mother asked, "Ma, are you going with me to Aunt Hettie's funeral?"

"No, I'm not," Grammaw stated flatly. "I've already been."

Cadillacitis

A MAN IN anticipation of death bought the finest casket available for delivery at the appropriate time. He told a friend what he had done, describing the gold fittings, teakwood carvings and other features, and mentioning the cost of the casket. His friend expressed horror and urged him to cancel the deal.

"Do you realize that for only a few hundred dollars more you could be buried in a Cadillac?"

—Samuel Pace

HAVE YOU heard the story about the man in the market for a car who saw an ad in a Long Island paper offering a new Cadillac for sale for $50? The first day he passed it up as a joke, but when it appeared for the third time he went to look at the car. The address given turned out to be a beautiful estate. The owner, an attractive middle-aged woman, showed him the car and let him drive it. It was in perfect condition, and he promptly clinched the deal. After the bill of sale was in his hand he couldn't suppress his curiosity any longer. "Would you mind," he asked the woman, "telling me why you're selling such a beautiful car for $50 when you could have gotten at least $4000?"

"Not at all," she replied. "In my husband's will he left instructions to deliver the proceeds from the sale of his Cadillac to his secretary, who had been so kind to him."

AT A NIGHT spot in a northern New York resort we were watching a group of college boys, each trying to pick up a pert, shapely blonde. She was playing the field, keeping them impartially at bay. Then, during an intermission the orchestra leader announced, "Will the owner of the yellow Cadillac convertible please move his car as it is blocking the driveway."

We looked to see who the owner was. One of the boys detached himself from the group and strolled out the door with dignity. A few minutes after his return the girl was seated at a table with him, giving him her undivided attention.

We happened to leave at the same time they did and saw them climb gaily into the yellow car—to our surprise a much-decorated, ancient Model A Ford roadster. —Flag Herrick

GORDON GAMMACK, the Des Moines columnist, relays the story of the Iowa farmer who made a lot of fast dough. Among his early spending splurges was the purchase of a custom-made Cadillac. One day a friend who hadn't seen him for a long time came on a visit, and the farmer met him at the airport. The friend was amazed at the custom job with its leopard-skin upholstery, its sliding panels, its silver-embossed steering wheel and solid gold instrument panel.

As they started off the friend was surprised to see the farmer, a very nearsighted fellow, take off his glasses and stick them in his pocket.

"Hey," said the friend, "I'm not going to ride with you until you put your glasses back on. You're blind as a bat without them."

"Relax," said the farmer. "I had the prescription built into the windshield." —Cedric Adams in Minneapolis *Star*

A FAMOUS author was autographing copies of his new novel in a Cleveland department store. One gentleman pleased him by bringing up not only his new book for signature, but reprint editions of his two previous ones as well. "My wife likes your stuff," he remarked rather apologetically, "so I thought I'd give her these signed copies for a birthday present."

"A surprise, eh?" hazarded the author.

"I'll say," agreed the customer. "She's expecting a Cadillac."

—Bennett Cerf, *Anything for a Laugh* (Grosset and Dunlap)

Family Album

A NEIGHBOR admonished his wife one morning to beware of a local speed trap. "A friend of mine," he told her, "got a ticket yesterday for doing 30 in a 25-mile zone."

Later that day, as his wife was going through the pockets of her husband's suit before sending it to the cleaner, she found a receipt for a traffic ticket. It stated that the driver had paid a fine for disobeying the speed limit in a 25 m.p.h. zone. She put the receipt in an envelope marked "For Future Reference" where she kept clippings of household hints. One morning some weeks later she had reason to remember the receipt.

Pouring her husband's coffee she said sweetly, "Remember that friend of yours who got a ticket for doing 30 on Ridgewood Avenue? Well, guess what? Yesterday his wife got a ticket for the same reason!"

—Mrs. Ralph W. Seeger

AFTER A hard day at the office Dad landed on Junior for something he had been warned against several times. "Don't punish him this time," Mother pleaded. "Wait 'til he does it again."

"Yeah," challenged the father, "but what if he doesn't do it again?" —Ralph Paul, quoted by Larry Wolters, Chicago Tribune-New York News Syndicate

WIFE reading evening paper to half-asleep husband: "Here's an interesting item about a married couple—they went to a dance." —Bob Barnes cartoon in *Ladies' Home Journal*

THE FAMILY were objecting to their son's girl, insisting that he ought to be a little more particular about the company he kept. "I'm sorry, Dad," said the boy, "but that's the best girl I can get with the car we've got." —Mrs. Ernest T. Fehlings

A WIFE whose husband arrived home after a few drinks too many was more than a little irritated. "If it were the first time, Max," she said, "I could forgive you. But you came home like this in November 1916." —General Features Corp.

FATHER TO son: "Jimmy, you'd better go do your homework now so that your mother will stop nagging you and I won't have to remind you again."

—Carla R. Haines, quoted by Bill Gold in Washington *Post and Times Herald*

SMALL GIRL showing her older sister's bedroom to playmate: "My sister's 19. I thought I'd have her room someday, but she never married."

—George Clark cartoon, Chicago Tribune-New York News Syndicate

MOTHER TO daughter: "You had two callers—one was a loud rasping honk-honk, the other was a shrill toot-toot."

—Stamaty cartoon in *The Saturday Evening Post*

SMALL BOY to father absorbed in newspaper: "Wanna know what you said 'uh-huh' to?"

—Charles Skiles cartoon in *The Saturday Review*

A PROUD 16-year-old turned into the family driveway at the wheel of the family car. His father sat beside him. Several younger brothers converged on the scene.

"I passed my driving test," shouted the happy driver. "You guys can all move up one bike." —*The Wall Street Journal*

PERPLEXED WIFE at dinner table to angry husband: "Monday you liked beans; Tuesday you liked beans; Wednesday you liked beans. Now all of a sudden on Thursday you *don't* like beans!"

—Don Tobin cartoon in *Collier's*

DISTRESSED teen-ager: "Mom! Dad! What happened to my new record—the one I played all day yesterday?"

—George Clark cartoon, Chicago Tribune-New York News Syndicate

A HIGH-SCHOOL freshman was telling her family about making biscuits in home economics. "Do they let you eat what you cook?" her mother asked.

"Let us?" she roared. "They *make* us!"

—Lydel Sims in Memphis *Commercial Appeal*

WHEN A Philadelphia eight-year-old retires to his room in injured dignity he has a sign he hangs outside his door: "Do Not Enter Without Knocking. Do Not Even Knock."

—Alberte Wright, quoted in *Ladies' Home Journal*

TEEN-AGERS and telephones are inseparable, as any parent knows. The solution I decided was to have a second phone installed for my daughter's exclusive use. But one afternoon soon after the phone was connected I came home and found her using mine. When I asked why, she said, "But Mother, I may get an important call, and I wouldn't want my phone to be busy!"

—Lanna Folena

FATHER TO son asking for money: "Junior, have you ever thought of being a professional fund raiser?"

—Lichty cartoon, Chicago Sun-Times Syndicate

Baby Talk: A perfect example of minority rule is a baby in the house (Milwaukee *Journal*) . . . A baby clouding up for a squall (Marjorie Hitchcock) . . . People who say they sleep like a baby usually don't have one (Leo J. Burke in *The Saturday Evening Post*)

ARRIVING home and finding himself locked out, a neighbor of ours settled himself on the steps to wait for his wife's return. Considerable time passed and another neighbor, seeing his plight, invited him to come eat dinner with them. He thanked her politely, but refused. "If I get comfortable and fed," he explained, "I'll get all smoothed down—and I want to be good and mad when she gets here."

—Mrs. L. R. Dale

IT WAS THE teen-aged daughter's first dance, and she desperately wanted a strapless frock. Her mother felt she wasn't old enough to wear anything so sophisticated. There was a heated family discussion, and it was the father who finally settled the problem. "Well," he proposed, "let her try on one. If it stays up—she's old enough to wear it."

—Margaret Helms

Strong Medicine for Careless Guests

Condensed from This Week Magazine

Parke Cummings

WHEN FRIENDS visit us in our house in the country they're apt to leave various articles behind when they depart, after which they write and ask me to mail them back to them. None of them ever repeats this offense, however. I am allergic to wrapping up stuff and lugging it to the post office, and I have devised a system to break them of this careless and irritating habit.

What I do is cheerfully coöperate. Let me illustrate with how I handled Ed Hamilton, who left a pair of shoes after a weekend last October. The minute I received his request to mail them I answered.

October 18

Dear Ed: Got your letter. I was wondering how you could have left your shoes behind. Did you go home barefoot? I hadn't noticed. Parke

This Week Magazine (April 11, '54), © 1954 by United Newspapers Magazine Corp., 420 Lexington Ave., New York 17, N. Y.

Ed replied that he hadn't gone home barefoot. He had taken an extra pair of shoes, and he wanted me to mail them to him. Again I coöperated.

November 7

Dear Ed: I'm all set to send those shoes back to you, but first I've got to know which pair you left here, the ones you were wearing when you arrived or the extra pair you brought along? Parke

Ed wrote back demanding, for Pete's sake, what difference did it make whether he left the pair he was wearing or the spare pair? He wanted those shoes. My own reply was considerably more courteous.

November 23

Dear Ed: The reason I asked was because I wanted to know what color the shoes were. Please let me know because I want to return them to you *at once*. Hope your family is feeling fit. Parke

The next letter from Ed struck me as a bit abrupt. It just said "Brown."

After I recovered from a cold that had laid me up I promptly wrote him another letter.

December 17

Dear Ed: Now we're getting somewhere! I figured they were either brown or black, and it's good to know definitely. The shoes are as good as yours. Just tell me where you left them and I'll send them without delay. Best wishes to you and the family for Christmas.

Parke

Soon afterward I received another letter: "In the guest room, stupid! Where else?" Not a word of Christmas greeting from him. However, I ignored this rudeness when I next wrote.

January 11

Dear Ed: Great news! I found your shoes. Size 10½,

eh? Don't bother to confirm this, as I want to get them off to you without a moment's unnecessary delay. Unfortunately I mislaid your earlier letters and I forget whether you want me to send them by railway express or parcel post.
Parke

In his reply Ed said he didn't give a damn how I sent them just as long as I got those shoes off in a hurry.

As soon as I could, I wrote him back.

February 18

Dear Ed: It sure looks as though you'd be receiving those shoes any day now. I've decided on parcel post. Do you want me to mark the package "Fragile"? Please give me this information so I can get them off promptly. Warmest regards to you and all your lovely family.
Parke

Shortly afterward I got a wire from Ed saying, "Quit stalling and send those shoes."

A few days later I actually mailed them. My guess is that Ed will be less apt to leave his property behind when he makes future visits, and the same holds true of other guests with whom I have coöperated. And it's highly gratifying to know that I've never once addressed a single unkind word to any of them.

Jokers Wild

WRITING ABOUT Douglas Fairbanks, Sr., in *Woman's Home Companion,* Joan Crawford reports that he loved practical jokes. There were always wired chairs at Pickfair, and even guests like Lord and Lady Mountbatten got the "hot seat." One time as Fairbanks approached a guest he gave a signal to the butler to turn on the juice. The visitor gave no evidence of shock. Her host gave the signal again. Still the lady sat her ground. "Would you stand for just a moment?" he asked.

Fairbanks took the chair and promptly jumped. "Didn't *you* feel anything?" he asked.

"Well, yes," admitted his guest. "But I thought that's just how you felt at meeting a movie star!"

WHEN NEW YORK restaurateur Toots Shor made his first visit to California, his friend Pat O'Brien sent east for a handful of Toots' own menus. O'Brien then steered Toots into a famous Beverly Hills establishment and thrust one of the menus into his hands. Toots didn't recognize it for a moment. He glanced over the list of dishes and murmured in a shocked voice, "Holy mackerel! What prices!" —Bennett Cerf

A SLIGHTLY pompous young ranger of the National Park Service was lecturing an enthralled audience, preparing for the eruption of Yellowstone's famous geyser, Old Faithful. Unseen by him but in full view of the crowd, two "greenhorn" college boys, summer employes, were setting themselves to avenge weeks of ridicule at his hands. The boy farthest from the geyser had driven the post of an old automobile steering wheel into the ground and squatted attentively over it; his partner wigwagged elaborate directions with all the aplomb of a hydraulics engineer. At each preliminary spurt of the geyser the kids pretended to be opening and closing the valve of some underground water system.

As the act progressed the crowd began to giggle, then to laugh. The ranger plowed on through his speech, red-faced and stiff, not deigning to look behind him but pitching his voice higher and higher as time for the big eruption approached.

"Okay, Charlie, let 'er go!" yelled the boy near the geyser. Charlie swung madly at the wheel and—to the horror of the ranger, who looked as if he had been betrayed—sure enough, up Old Faithful went, over 150 feet. —Brian Duff

DURING World War II Hugh Troy, artist, writer and accomplished practical joker, was sent to a southern Army camp where he was soon in rebellion against paperwork. Reports, reports and more reports on the most trivial details went to the Pentagon. One day Troy devised a special report blank and had it mimeographed —re the number of flies trapped during each 24-hour period on the 20 flypaper ribbons that hung in the mess hall. The report included a map of the mess hall, showing the location of each ribbon, each of which was identified by code number. Troy's first flypaper report showed that during a 24-hour period Flypaper Ribbon X-5 trapped and retained 49 flies. Ribbon Y-2 did even better—63 flies. And so on. He sent the report off to Washington. Every day he sent in a report.

About a week after he sent in the first one, two fellow officers called on him. "You been catching any hell from Washington," they asked, "about some kind of goofy flypaper reports?"

"Why, no," said Hugh.

"It's about a daily report on flypaper in the mess halls. We've been getting Pentagon queries asking why we haven't been sending them in."

"Oh," said Troy. "I send *mine* in every day."

They protested that nobody had told *them* about any flypaper reports, so Troy gave them copies of the mimeographed blank. After that every bundle that went in to Washington included a census of dead flies. Troy thinks it's possible that the daily flypaper report became standard Army procedure.

—H. Allen Smith, *The Compleat Practical Joker* (Doubleday)

AT A New England fair there were rumblings of discontent among the handicraft workers because some craftsmen placed a nominal value on their pieces, whereas others valued their quickly made modernistic carvings at seemingly fantastic prices. Then one morning an exhibitor brought in a striking example of modern sculpture. No one was quite sure what it represented, but there was no doubt about the price: $50. A visitor who admired the work remarked that the price seemed high. The exhibitor replied, "Not a bit. And you won't think so when I tell you that the lady who sculptured this rarity did it all with her tongue, and it took her 'most a year to finish it."

The judges, knowing its origin, gave the sculpture first prize. It turned out to have been made from a block of stable salt. And the sculptress who had fluted it so neatly with soft curves was the exhibitor's family cow! —Edmund Mulcahy, Jr.

AN M.I.T. STUDENT went home for a vacation and left his car parked behind his dormitory. Some of the young engineers who remained at school that vacation took it apart, lugged it piece by piece into the dormitory.

When the owner came back to school he found his car assembled and parked in his room. —Joe Harrington in Boston *Post*

Oh, Doctor!

If you still have your tonsils and appendix at 30, chances are you're the doctor.

ROBERT BENCHLEY, who always had a sneaking suspicion that doctors were only one step ahead of the public as far as knowledge went, and that they could be thrown off balance by anything completely unexpected, had a chance to test this theory in 1940. He came down with pneumonia and his doctor gave him one of the new "miracle" sulfa drugs. He took the pills as directed and then, one afternoon before the doctor was due to call, he and Charles Butterworth broke open a pillow and, with library paste, glued the feathers all over him, from the waist down.

When the doctor arrived he examined Benchley's chest, asked him how he was feeling and if the pills had done any good. Benchley said he thought they had, then added, as he threw back the bedclothes, "But I don't know quite what to make of this. Is *this* all right?"

—*Robert Benchley, A Biography,* © 1955 by Nathaniel Benchley (McGraw-Hill)

THE MORNING after my operation, though I was barely conscious of what was going on, my nurse insisted on changing me from the hospital gown to one of my own, brushed my hair carefully, powdered my face and added a touch of lipstick. Stepping back, she surveyed her handiwork with evident satisfaction.

"There!" she said, and added confidentially, "Dr. Culpepper simply *hates* to see his patients look sick." —Mrs. Milton W. Edwards

TWO SISTERS who have a tearoom in a small Virginia town depend greatly on Mary, an old family retainer, and when she failed to show up for several days they went to investigate.

"My sister's in the hospital," Mary explained. "They operated on her and she's mighty sick."

The sisters expressed their sympathy and asked what the trouble was.

"I don't know, ma'am. The doctah just cut her open and help himself."

—Mrs. William M. Lewis

WITH FIVE children in rapid succession, I'd been a regular caller at the obstetrician's office. Then came a gap of three years before I again pushed open his waiting-room door and greeted his nurse. She looked startled.

"Why, Mrs. Clifford," she exclaimed, "I'd put you on our inactive list."

—Mrs. Paul C. Clifford

A COUNTRY DOCTOR in northern Ontario left his ancient Model-T Ford in front of the village drugstore and on his return found several of the youths who customarily loitered there making merry at the old car's expense. As he climbed up into the well-worn driver's seat the doctor inspected the group carefully, then leaned out and said, "The car's all right, boys—it's paid for. You"—and the doctor looked deliberately from one boy to another—"are not."

—Joan Morris

CHATTING WITH the proprietor of a curio shop in San Francisco's Chinatown, a tourist asked if China had good doctors. "We got plenty good doctors in China," the saffron sage replied. "Hang Chang is best. He save my life."

"How was that?" asked the tourist.

"Me velly sick, call Dr. Hang Kin. He give medicine make me sicker. Call Dr. San Sing. Give more medicine make me more sick. I feel I gonna die. Bimeby call Dr. Hang Chang. He gone somewhere else. No come. Save my life." —*The Wall Street Journal*

OUR NEW medical officer, young and very green, was doing his best to ignore the baby-blue eyes of his patient, the prettiest civil service employe in headquarters. With great dignity he prepared to give her a routine checkup and in the process dropped his stethoscope.

"Is anything the matter, sir?" she asked sweetly, enjoying his discomfiture.

"Of course not," he replied, collecting himself and his equipment. "Now then," he ordered in his most professional tone, "deep breathely!" —W. W. Wright

THE DOCTOR had finished the examination and was ready to give his professional advice. "Quit smoking and drinking, go to bed early every night and get up at the crack of dawn," he said. "That's the best thing for you."

"Frankly, Doc," the patient answered, "I don't deserve the best. What's second best?"

—"Our Town" in White Plains, N.Y., *Reporter Dispatch*

AT THE DOCTOR'S for an after-baby checkup, I was being given a lecture for not getting enough rest. But with a new baby to keep me up at night and a two-year-old to chase all day, I didn't see what I could do about it.

"You've *got* to rest," the doctor said sternly, "both for your own good and for the welfare of your family."

Knowing his wife had a new baby, I blurted out, "Does *your* wife?"

"No," he replied blandly, "but she's not my patient." —K. E. C.

THE DOCTOR diagnosed the Anglo-Indian colonel's illness as hydropsy. What was that? Too much water in the body, the doctor explained. The whiskey-drinking Briton was indignant. "But I've never drunk a drop of water in all my life, Doctor!" He paused. Then, sadly, he concluded, "Must have been the ice." —NANA

Icecapades

I WAS TRUDGING up the steep and snowy driveway of the Portland Hospital. Suddenly WHOOSH!—something shot by me like a streak. It was a nurse, sitting up straight as a dart, her dark-blue cape streaming out behind her. Then another figure zipped by, and another. There wasn't a sled in sight, and I was completely baffled about what carried them so smoothly over the snow. But as I watched, one of the nurses landed in a snowbank halfway down the hill. Getting to her feet she gaily brushed herself off, reached down to retrieve a white enameled bedpan, settled herself on it and whizzed on down the hill. —Jean Wells Jerabeck

ON A WINTER morning when the streets of New York were slick with ice, I saw a man sitting in the middle of the sidewalk. Thinking he must be hurt I asked, "May I help you up?"

"No, thank you," he laughed. "I'm just sitting here to melt the ice on this particular spot." He moved aside for a moment. There under the ice was a five-dollar bill which he was hatching.

—R. M. Geis

ON ONE OF Portland's iciest days a little woman was seen walking uphill gripping what looked like a walking stick. Actually it was a plumber's helper. She'd thrust the suction cup down in front of her at arm's length and walk up to it. Then she'd yank it up with a wet squoosh and shove it ahead of her again for another leg of her treacherous journey. —William Moyes in Portland *Oregonian*

No Business Like Snow Business

By Jesse L. Lasky

To make the picture *The Alaskan,* I sent the company on location in northern California. We could have built the sets at the studio and covered them with salt, but salt and faces sweating from klieg lights couldn't evoke the spell of the Yukon as well as real snow and breath clouds. So an Alaskan mining camp was erected at Lake Tahoe, and the whole company moved there to be ready to start the picture the minute there was a heavy snowfall.

It didn't snow for weeks, but nobody complained. Lake Tahoe is a gorgeous setting for an extended vacation. They were all careful not to let any weather reports seep back to the studio. It was a gold-digging operation, all right. Every week shipments of gold bullion, or a reasonable facsimile, arrived from the studio to grubstake the gold-bricking gold-miners. Finally I called studio manager Charles Eyton into my office and demanded he do something about the situation right away. He did, too. He had several carloads of salt trucked in and poured it over our synthetic mining camp, and strung roof eaves with fake icicles. A pall of gloom settled over the company. Their idyll had come to an end. Tomorrow they had to work.

That night it snowed—generously and photogenically. The next morning there was snow everywhere—except on our expensively duplicated gold-rush town. For there the salt had melted the snow and the water had washed the salt away, leaving a naked eyesore thrust up through the white-blanketed countryside.

—As told to Don Weldon, *I Blow My Own Horn* (Doubleday)

Toward More Picturesque Speech

SHELLEY WINTERS on location at Lake Tahoe: "It was so cold I almost got married" (Erskine Johnson)

Word Games: An easy government job in the swivel service (Walter Matson) . . . Henny Youngman's comment on a movie starlet: "She moves in the best triangles" (Erskine Johnson) . . . They get along like two peeves in a pod (*Everybody's* London) . . . A women's bridge club going at it hammer and tongues (B. Zeigler)

THERE'S one thing to be said about the opposite sex—boy, can they be opposite! (Al Lafayette, quoted by Earl Wilson) . . . Maybe it's a good thing men don't understand women. Women understand women and don't like them (*Industrial News Review*)

Home Sweet Home: The one time modern man's home really feels like a castle is when the furnace goes out (Paul McElaney in *The Saturday Evening Post*) . . . All that keeps some families from having a home of their own is a teen-age daughter . . . The handwriting on the wall usually means there's a child in the family (Franklin P. Jones in *The Saturday Evening Post*) . . . Give the neighbors' kids an inch and they'll take a yard (Helen Castle in *The Saturday Evening Post*) . . . Rainy days are when Mother's little jewels are only semiprecious (Floyd R. Miller in *Look*)

IF YOU think a woman driving a car can snarl up traffic, you ought to see a man pushing a cart in the supermarket (Bill Vaughan)

PSYCHOLOGISTS say people with hobbies are not likely to go crazy —but this doesn't apply to the people they live with (*The Wall Street Journal*)

Type Casting: The type of woman who manages to produce the effect of a majority (Ellen Glasgow) . . . The type who wouldn't listen to you talk if he didn't know it was his turn next (Edgar Watson Howe) . . . The sort of chap who follows you into a revolving door and comes out first (William Hickey in London *Daily Express*) . . . One of those people of whom it takes all kinds to make a world (Walter Stewart)

ANYBODY who asks for advice nowadays just hasn't been listening (*Changing Times, The Kiplinger Magazine*) . . . Anyone who has time to look for a four-leaf clover needs to find one (Mary C. Dorsey)

Well-Known Human Race

Seeing ourselves as others see us wouldn't do much good. We wouldn't believe it anyway.
—M. Walthall Jackson in *The Saturday Evening Post*

A FRIEND of mine whose husband and children have a healthy respect for our spring tornadoes always complained bitterly each time she was forced into the storm cellar by her anxious family. Year after year the storms missed them and with each trip to the cellar she became more embittered in her remarks as they trudged back to the house. One spring, however, they emerged to find the house rubble and their possessions scattered to the four winds. Her husband patted her shoulder, searching for words of comfort.

He was stunned to hear her say in tones of great satisfaction, "Now, *that's* the way I like to see things when I come up out of a storm cellar!" —Mrs. C. Farris

FROM A column in the Landrum, S. C., *Leader* giving news of employes at Bommer Spring Hinge Co.: "Anyone interested in joining our bowling team will please give his name to Mr. Frank Phillips. He is trying to organize a Bommer bowling team. Anyone knowing where bowling alleys are located will please come forth with that information also."

AN ECCENTRIC old lady confided to her neighbor that she kept her money at home, hidden in a coffee can. "But," reminded the neighbor, "you're losing interest."

"Oh, no, I'm not," the old lady insisted serenely. "I'm putting away a little extra, just for that."
—Minnie Johnson Schachner in Chicago *Tribune*

BEFORE boarding a Chicago-to-Cleveland plane a sales executive had bought a New York paper. His seat partner was a pleasant-looking middle-aged woman, so when he had read the paper he turned to her and asked, "Care to see a copy of the New York *Times?*"

"No, thank you," said the lady cheerfully. "I don't know anybody there." —Kenneth Nichols in Akron *Beacon Journal*

SAUNTERING along the streets of our home town of Lander, Wyo., one summer evening my husband and I passed two men, evidently tourists, who were admiring the gorgeous sunset which lighted the mountainous horizon. "Do you often have such beautiful sunsets?" one of them asked.

"Very often," I replied.

"Well, Lander certainly should be proud. It's really wonderful for such a small town!"

—Ruth H. Abbott

ALTHOUGH our daughter had finished college and was teaching, my husband still thought of her as his little girl and, when she announced her intention of marrying, he was thoroughly upset. Setting out to dissuade her suitor my husband told him, "You don't know what you're getting into. My daughter isn't ready for marriage. She can't cook or sew. She doesn't even keep her own room in order. She's always losing things and she has *no* idea of the value of money."

"Oh," replied the young man, "I know her faults, sir. But I want to marry her anyway."

My husband glared at him. "*What* faults?" he roared.

—Mrs. G. C. Kirkpatrick

A WOMAN telephoned postal authorities in Dallas and complained about the substitute mail carrier on her route. "The regular carrier gets along with our dog," she explained angrily, "but every time the substitute makes the route it upsets the dog."

"Where is the dog now?" a postal authority asked.

"Oh, he's under our mimosa tree."

"And where's the mail carrier?"

"He's up in the tree. It's upsetting my dog and making him bark."

—AP

IN DOWNTOWN Los Angeles I watched a woman driver make a left turn into a busy one-way street, the wrong way. Instantly the traffic knotted to a standstill. Finally a policeman appeared and hustled over to the spot where the woman sat helplessly enmeshed in her incriminating position. But she beat him to the draw.

As he approached she stuck her head out the window and demanded angrily, "And where were *you?*"

—John P. Wagner

On Parade

A LONDON bobby on duty during a parade was forced to push a very pregnant woman back into the line of spectators several times. "Listen, lidey," he pleaded finally, "why don't ye tyke the little feller 'ome? 'E cawn't see nothin'."

"I know 'e cawn't see nothin'," said the woman huffily, "but there ain't no 'arm in 'is 'earin' a bit o' music, is there?"

—Edward Streeter, *Merry Christmas, Mr. Baxter* (Harper)

BACK IN the days when Indonesia was a colony, the Dutch Resident was paying an official visit to a village in Bali. For his reception the road was lined with village belles in their native dress, a batik sarong fastened at the waist—and nothing else. And then at the last minute word came that the Resident would be accompanied by his wife, a strait-laced woman who sternly disapproved of native "immodesty." It was too late to send the girls home for shawls or jackets, but word was passed that they should do their best to hide their bare breasts when the good lady rode by.

As the Resident's carriage drew level with each section, the girls, with one accord, stooped down, caught hold of the hems of their sarongs and raised them to their necks. Since few, if any, of the Balinese wear anything beneath their sarongs, one can imagine the horror of the Resident's wife—and the enjoyment of her more appreciative spouse.

—Lim Chong Hum

DURING A Shriners' convention in Los Angeles one of the downtown boulevards was roped off for a parade. Only official cars with large signs such as *Potentate* and *Past Potentate* were allowed there; all other traffic was halted or rerouted. But one ingenious Californian got by the police blockade and drove nonchalantly down the street. His placard read: *Past Participle!* —Milford P. Johnson

AT AN American Legion convention in Chicago, banners all through the parade displayed the Legion Post numbers of each group. But a small boxer puppy stole the show as he marched along between the columns bearing a sign: "ANY OLD POST WILL DO." —Claude H. Asbell

WHEN NEW port facilities were inaugurated at Aarhus, Denmark, King Christian X honored the occasion with his presence. All along the route of the royal car school children waved banners and shouted. The sidewalks were swarming with them.

"My goodness," the King cried in wonder, "where do all these children come from?"

"Your Majesty," said the mayor, "we have been preparing for this great day for years."

—New York *Times Magazine*

RADIO announcer on southern newscast: "Our neighbors over in Columbia, Tenn., largest outdoor mule market in the world, held a jackass parade yesterday, headed by the governor."

—Kermit Schafer, "Pardon My Blooper" (Jay-Gee Record Co.)

The Jackasses and I

By Arch Oboler

IN MY LATE 20's, happily married and out of the arroyos of the city for the first time, I looked at and then bought 400 acres of California mountain and meadow. One day, impressed by my acreage, I decided that now I would become a horse owner.

As if fated, that very evening I noticed a classified ad in the two-sheet local weekly: "Two brrs. Chp. Eves. Rcky. Rnch."

That eve I phoned the Rcky. Rnch. "About those burros you advertised. Are they healthy animals?"

"Yep!"

"Burros run around in the open and don't need any exercise boy or stables, do they? And they forage off the country?"

"Yep!"

"$25 for the pair?"

"Nope!"

"$30?"

"Nope!"

At $45 I got into the "Yep" dialogue again, and the following day a trailer tailgate clanged on the road and the burros came into my startled view. Instead of the small burros I had expected, within the trailer sat (both animals were definitely sitting) one small-horse-sized gray individual with huge rabbit ears and one long-eared brown creature the size of a big dog and covered with the unmistakable fuzz of animal infancy.

Mr. Rcky. Rnch. informed me, as he pocketed my check, that the gray animal was named Peter, he was between eight and ten years old, and the Great Dane with the skyscraper ears was Peter's two-month-old son, Tony. The seller also reassured me that I needn't worry, them animals would stay put.

This was a true statement: we had no trouble with the critters staying at home. Papa Peter, trailed by his fuzzy papoose, conducted a tour of inspection of the house worthy of an appraiser for a second-mortgage loan. After a few hours Tony got bored with his father's route and chased Jeanie, our sedate cocker spaniel, until she hid in a closet. Then he found his own reflection in the swimming pool and spent a fascinating three hours looking at himself, until he fell in.

Having been evicted from the kitchen for the tenth time, Papa Peter stationed himself at the living-room window. There he critically contemplated our evening activities until we turned off the lights. After that, it developed the following morning, he had moved in among my fledgling orange trees, decapitating and digesting about $150 worth.

He announced this fact proudly at sunrise with his opening concert—the first of many years of such sun salutes. Boy and man, I have heard most of the loud sounds of our time, but I say unequivocally that the bray of a full-grown jackass outside one's bedroom window is a sound that ranks high among the psychological weapons of all time. Son Tony joined in that first paean to the Oboler arising—on a more youthful note than father, of course, but with a fullness of tonality that foreshadowed future greatness.

This pair of vocalizing equines followed us around like dogs, they gamboled like lambs and, above all, they ate like goats. Everything on the place was Three Star Duncan Hines on their menu. I consulted Mr. Rcky. Rnch. by phone. He told me that any blamed fool knew that an old car axle was the only kind of tie-out stake to use on jackasses. I drove to the closest junk yard and returned with a pair of old axles and chains which cost enough to have been silver-plated.

First I staked out Junior, and then Papa. Papa put his weight against the chain. A link unfolded like an earthworm stretching out in a rain puddle, and with one triumphant kick of his heels Papa was off to the fruit trees, while his son squealed in frustration.

It took me a week to find the right combination of massive logging chain, forged-steel truck axle and case-hardened lock before Papa was safely moored. Meanwhile our landscaping had attained a naturalistic look—back to the original sagebrush, ribbonwood and manzanita, all our expensive plantings having gone by way of Peter's insatiable gullet.

"You're not going to keep those animals chained up all the time!" said Mrs. O.

I told her it was my intention to restrain the jackass family until Papa learned the difference between hay and orange trees.

My wife said, "What are you going to do, give him botany lessons?"

The following morning I summoned a local contractor and crew to build a corral, a king-sized enclosure worthy of my wife's insistence on Freedom for Jackasses. Between munches of rolled oats and Danish pastry left over from our breakfast, Peter and Tony watched every detail of the process as the hand-hewn redwood poles were nestled into pools of concrete and coils of barbed wire whipped around the landscape.

By noon the new enclosure was done and I managed to herd the animals into their open-air Alcatraz. As I began to show them the details of their expensive suite Peter, with a wild flail of heels, began racing around the block-long corral, son Tony squealing in close pursuit. I said, "They're looking for an escape route," and then laughed, because hadn't the expert said it was jackass-proof?

That night two mournful heads gazed into our bedroom window. The morning light revealed that somehow they had managed to paw a couple of strands of wire loose and climb through.

Next I consulted our mail-order catalogue. There I discovered an apparatus which, by charging the fence wire with a jolting flow of electricity, would keep even the most amorous bull in docile containment.

Operation Shocking, including the high-voltage injectors and the waterproof extension to the closest AC line, cost me well over the original price of the beasts, but no matter—we had to have it because Tony was munching on the laundry and Papa Peter was pruning the flowering eucalyptus.

The fence completed, I plugged in the current. Mrs. O. said, "You ought to test it."

I said, "How?"

She said, "You're not afraid of a little shock, are you?"

Tony guffawed and headed for the shreds of the lemon trees.

I said, "The instructions say it's not harmful to man or beast, but you'll find my will in the cookie jar." I lightly touched the wire and picked myself up off the ground six feet away.

The electric fence was a triumph for 48 hours. But on the next morning there were brays outside our bedroom window, and father and son did a merry pirouette as I gaped in unbelief. Suddenly I knew—the fuse must have blown and the current was off. I tore out to the corral, grabbed the wire—and landed on my back.

For three nights those donkeys got out of the electrified corral. The gate and wires were intact, and the jolt was strong enough to smelt one's gold fillings, yet those animals got out.

The mystery was solved one frosty 4 a.m. when I came out just in time to see Peter get down on his forelegs and squirm under the charged wire. Junior then went through the same maneuver, his small rump wriggling well out of reach of that possible shock.

Fifteen years and many coils of rusted barbed wire have gone by, and my jackasses and I have long since established a truce in the matter of containment. Our agreement is this: as long as they get sufficient alfalfa and oat hay by eight in the morning with enough left over to snack on through the day, and as long as someone goes to the corral before nightfall to talk to them man to burro and scratch their ears, Peter and Son stay put.

But should we forget that ear-stroking routine, or should the pitchfork fail to deliver a sufficiently elevated pile of plant life, away they go, homing unerringly to the laundry line.

As the children arrived and began to grow, the jackasses took on new stature—as combination jungle-gyms, rollercoasters and king-sized kiddy-cars. The sight of one small boy sliding off Peter's broad derrière, to land within inches of those massive hoofs, while another youngster was busily examining Tony's jagged teeth, was definitely not covered by the book on children's care, but I was calm. I had found out that, intertwined with that fence-breaking perseverance, patience and common sense were also heraldic devices on the jackass escutcheon.

My jackasses have only one pet hate—the jeep. Every fender of this inoffensive ranch vehicle has felt the impact of their dislike; they decapitated the original canvas top and ever since have been working on the aluminum enclosure that I substituted.

I have puzzled over this feud and have come to the conclusion that in the jeep Peter and Son see the terror of the Mechanical Age, which sets a pattern of work all day, leaving no time to heehaw or raise one's head to watch a hawk gliding above, a peculiar cloud formation, the fall of rain, a branch swaying in the wind—all the things around them that are head-lifting wonders to my jackasses in this remarkable world of theirs.

They prefer to live each day for the day; when trouble comes along they simply become immovable objects. Sometimes, listening closely, I fancy I hear them mutter to themselves the credo of all jackasses since jackasses began: "This, too, shall pass."

Rustic Tales

YEARS AGO Grandpa Taubeneck bought a Missouri mule for his farm. It was a sad deal. He couldn't make the critter gee-haw, whoa or anything. So he hired a professional mule trainer. The first thing the trainer did was whap the mule over the head with a two-by-four plank. The mule didn't budge. The trainer whacked him again with his murderous bludgeon.

"Hey," protested Grandpa, "are you aimin' to kill off my mule?"

"Guess you don't know nuthin' about these here animules," said the trainer. "First off, you gotta get their attention."

—George Taubeneck in Detroit Sigma Delta Chi newsletter

DRIVING TO town one morning a farmer and his wife passed a lake. The wife, conscious of their frequent quarrels and spats, said, "Pa, look over yonder at that goose and gander a-gliding along the water so nice and peaceful. Wouldn't it be wonderful if people could live so peaceable?"

Long-married Pa drove on in silence.

Just before sunset the couple passed the same lake on their way home. There, silhouetted by the setting sun, were a goose and gander gliding along the water. "Pa," said the wife, "look at the goose and gander, still real peaceable. Wouldn't it be wonderful if people could live like that?"

"Ma," said the farmer, "if you look a little closer, you'll notice that ain't the same gander!"

—Quoted by Howard White in Burlington, N. C., *Times-News*

MY UNCLE, helping a farmer prepare his tax return, examined his ledger. There were no debit or credit columns, but instead the entries read: "Sold eggs $2.68" or "Bought feed $16.92." Most of the items were easy to interpret, but one reading simply

"Horse $10" stumped my uncle. "Did you buy the horse for ten dollars or sell him?" he asked.

"Well," said the farmer, "it's like this: I bought that ornery animal for ten dollars. He right away kicked down two stalls, and that cost ten dollars. Then I used him to pull a car out of a mud rut, and got paid ten dollars. Once I sold him for ten dollars, but he caused such a peck of trouble that I bought him back for ten dollars. I used him to take some kids for a ride, and they gave me ten dollars. Finally the fool horse wandered into the road, and a guy hit him and killed him. He paid me ten dollars, but I had to turn around and pay ten dollars to have the carcass hauled away. And you know," said the farmer, "I must of lost track somewhere, 'cause I can't figure whether that durn horse ended up owing me or me owing him."

—Helen T. Morrison

ALLAN M. TROUT, columnist of the Louisville *Courier-Journal*, tells the story of Uncle Gran Philpott, who long ago came down from the mountains for a spell in the Kentucky legislature. He was a giant of a man with a peg leg and a positive personality. He was much courted by politicians, who knew he held his section of the state in the hollow of his huge hand. They gave a banquet to welcome him to Frankfort.

The first course was consommé. Uncle Gran looked puzzled but consumed it. Someone passed him a bunch of celery. He ate it. Then a waiter put a broiled lobster in front of him. Uncle Gran arose, stomped his peg leg for attention and said, "Gent'men, I drunk the dishwater and I et the bouquet. But I'll be durned if I eat this bug. Take 'er away."

—Beverly Smith in *The Saturday Evening Post*

IN FORT WORTH I met a two-fisted, speculative oil driller who had hit it rich in the east Texas fields. The day "Big Jim" took me up to see his prize well, a wire was waiting for him at the site—he was to return at once to the hospital where his wife was a patient.

Back in Fort Worth Jim located the doctor and demanded, "What's the matter with the little woman, Doc?"

"Everything's going to be all right," the specialist assured him. "We just wanted your consent to perform an exploratory operation."

Jim's answer was immediate and final: "No, you don't! Ain't nobody going to wildcat on my wife!"

—B. C. Baker

Literal Interpretations

A WESTERN sheriff confiscated a group of slot machines on the basis of a law banning the use of steel traps for catching dumb animals.

—*The Pure Globe*

A PUBLISHER'S secretary incurred his ire by presuming to make some necessary grammatical changes in a letter he had dictated. "I want my letters typed exactly as I dictate them!" he stormed. "Is that *quite* clear? Now take this."

That afternoon the secretary planked this letter on his desk:

"Dear Smythe: The idiot spells it with an 'e.' Thinks it's aristocratic. His old man was a janitor. With regard to your letter of—look it up. Anybody who can read that handwriting deserves a medal. You ask the best discount we can allow on 5000 juveniles, assorted titles. In order to make any profit at all we cannot go above—hey, Lew, what do you think Smythe will stand for on that juvenile deal? Forty-five percent? Hm-m-m—our accountants figure that 43 percent is the furthest we dare go. The extra two percent is for that damn 'e' he sticks on his name. Trusting to receive your esteemed order, etc., etc., etc."

—Bennett Cerf in *The Saturday Review*

A SEATTLE woman was in the midst of preparations for a dinner for 16 when Penelope, a neighbor's cat, wandered in and kept getting underfoot. Annoyed, the hostess finally burst out, "Oh, go catch a mouse!" and shooed the cat out of the house.

The dinner was a success, and the guests were contentedly

sipping their coffee when Penelope appeared in a dining-room window, leaped lightly to the table and carefully placed a dead mouse beside the hostess's cup. —"Strolling Around" in Seattle *Times*

THE OFFICER of engineers in charge of constructing a road through a swampy section ordered a lieutenant to take 15 men and get on with the job. "Colonel," the lieutenant reported later, "the mud is over the men's heads. We can't get through."

"Nonsense!" roared the officer. "Make out a requisition slip for anything you need and I'll see that you get it."

A few minutes later, the lieutenant laid this memorandum on the colonel's desk: "NEED 15 MEN 18 FEET TALL TO CROSS A SWAMP 15 FEET DEEP." —Frances Rodman

NEEDING some clothes cleaned in a hurry I searched the small Georgia town in which I was visiting until I found a sign which read: "Cleaning and Pressing, 24-Hour Service." After explaining my needs I said, "I'll be back for my suit tomorrow."

"Won't be ready till Satiddy," replied the proprietor. "But I thought you had 24-hour service," I protested. "We do, son," he said reproachfully. "But we only work eight hours a day. Today's Thursday—eight hours today, eight hours Friday, eight on Satiddy. *That's* 24-hour service." —Frank D. McSherry, Jr.

ONE BLISTERING hot day when we had guests for dinner, I asked my four-year-old to say the blessing. Embarrassed, she protested that she didn't know what to say. "Oh, just say what you've heard me say," I told her. Obediently she bowed her head and said, "Oh, Lord, why did I invite these people here this hot day?"
—Mrs. E. C. James

IN THE Hartford office of the Connecticut State Motor Vehicles Department a woman was wandering around holding her operator's license in her hand. An inspector, trying to be helpful, told her, "Stand in that line."

"I can't. I'm married," she replied, pointing to a sign that read, "Single Line Only." —AP

DURING MY first week of medical practice in a country town there was a knock on my door about 4:30 a.m. I rushed downstairs ready to cope with an emergency. "My wife's in the car," the farmer on the porch told me. Hurrying after him, I found a cheerful young woman sitting calmly in the car. When I asked what I could do for her, she looked surprised.

"Why," she said, "you told me to come in for a blood test before breakfast." —Paul E. Weathers, M.D., in *Medical Economics*

WILLIAM FRITH, the English painter, was chatting backstage in a theater with a scene-shifter who said he himself had been a player in the provinces. In fact, he had played the part of " 'Amlet."

"Very interesting," said Mr. Frith. "Tell me—what is your conception of Hamlet's relation to Ophelia? Did he, so to speak, love her not wisely but too well?"

"I don't know, sir, if 'Amlet did," was the unblushing answer, "but *I* did." —Walter Sichel, *The Sands of Time* (Doran)

"This Is Groucho . . ."

GROUCHO MARX asked a lovely young tennis star appearing on his program about her training for future tournaments. "I need to improve my form and speed," she replied.

"If your form improves," said Groucho slyly, "you are going to need all the speed you can muster." —NBC

GROUCHO, I'm told, resigned from the Friars Club with the simple explanation: "I don't want to belong to any club that would accept me as one of its members."

—John Crosby in New York *Herald Tribune*

WHEN TOLD he could smoke if he didn't annoy the lady airplane passengers, Groucho said, "You mean there's a choice! Then I'll annoy the ladies."

—Larry Wolters, Chicago Tribune-New York News Syndicate

"I FIND television very educating," says Groucho. "Every time somebody turns on the set I go into the other room and read a book."

WHEN AN actress arrived at a Hollywood party in a very revealing, tight-fitting gown, Groucho appraised her and said, "One false move—and I'll appreciate it." —Leonard Lyons

TALKING about a girl, Groucho said, "I don't like her and judging from all the things I've said about her, I'm sure I never will."

—Erskine Johnson, NEA

INTRODUCING a film at a Hollywood première Groucho announced: "Every once in a while Hollywood makes a great picture, a distinguished film, a movie which is a work of art. Unfortunately, this isn't the picture we are about to see."

—Sidney Skolsky in New York *Post*

GROUCHO IS an avid reader. His son Arthur relates in his book, *Life With Groucho:* "He was even interested in the children's books that he bought for me which he hadn't had the opportunity to read when he was a child. After he read the first chapter of *Swiss Family Robinson* to me one night, he sent me to bed and stayed up until dawn finishing the book. The next night I brought out *Swiss Family Robinson* again, but Father returned it to the shelf and selected another book.

"When I protested he said, 'I've already finished that book. I'll tell you how it comes out. You wouldn't like the middle part anyway. It's too good for children.' " —Published by Simon and Schuster

File Under S for Sentiment

Condensed from Today's Living

Cynthia Lindsay

MY HUSBAND was on the attic floor, covered by myriads of pieces of colored paper. As I dug him out, he growled, "What in God's name is all this junk? I was reaching up on the top shelf and suddenly a whole box of stuff fell on me, and this thing hit me on the head. What *is* it anyway?"

He held out a large ceramic blob glazed a bilious green.

"A horse," I said. "Mike made it in kindergarten."

My husband looked at me. "Michael is now 18 and in the Army, and you still *have* this thing?"

"Well, yes," I answered. "I just can't seem to throw away the things they make."

"Well," he said, "sentiment or no sentiment, we're going to start right now. What about this old post card? You certainly don't want that."

One side of the card pictured a squirrel. Under the squirrel was printed, "Greetings from a little friend." On the reverse side, beneath the name of a summer camp our son had attended at the age of seven, was written: "Dear Mom, I hope you are feeling well because I am not. I caught my hand in the washing machine and got all my teeth bashed in. Love, Mike."

My husband laughed and said, "Better file that." He sat down in the middle of the debris and started sorting. "We'll make a series of piles. Keep them as chronological as possible. Then, if there are a few things from each pile that you just can't part with, we'll file them away."

Five nights later the piles had spread out into the upstairs hall and a few scattered specimens made their way into the living room. Meg, aged six, with a delighted cry of recognition, had retrieved a soft powdery clay Easter basket, one of her first nursery-school efforts, and was playing with it on the floor, where it was working its colorful way deep into the nap of the rug. Michael, home on leave, was mending a cedar chest he had made in the fifth grade. The sawdust and

Today's Living (March 16, '58),

glue combined with the clay dust to make a lovely pattern.

"I think you might have consulted me before throwing this chest out," our son said reproachfully. "After all, I may have a son myself some day, and I'd like to have *something* to pass on to him."

"Let's get some boxes," said my husband. "You may all take one or two precious items from each pile, put them in the boxes for saving, and we'll get rid of the rest." We filed upstairs, boxes in hand.

"I won't need these any more," said Michael, tossing aside a set of Exacto knives he formerly used in the creation of model airplanes.

My husband cried, "Don't throw those away—I can use them in my tool kit."

Father now supervised while we filled the "Save" boxes with hammered copper plaques depicting tired Mexicans leaning on cacti, woven leather lanyards for wearing a whistle about the neck, Indian beadwork complete with fringe, a dried toad (previously run over and very flat), a champagne cork from our wedding supper and one small white sugar dove from same, nursery-school gold stars, and then all these finger paintings. They were the worst.

I sent Meg downstairs on a false errand, and like thieves in the night we grabbed a bunch of the pictures and stuffed them into a wastebasket. But we weren't quick enough. She returned, caught us in the act and screamed, "My paintings!" Then she dragged them out of the basket. "All day long in school nothing but cut and paste, cut and paste, and then you throw them away—that certainly isn't very nice, I'm never going to make anything for anybody ever again, I may not even live here any more! I may go in the Army like Mike!"

By this time she had both men on their knees, saying, "Don't cry, Baby, we won't throw them away, we'll keep them, we'll frame them!"

Well, it went on that way, really quite an emotional experience, and then suddenly we were through. The "Save" boxes were filled to the brim, the "Throw Away" box remained empty except for a Christmas tree ornament I had made when I was a child—a plastic wood Santa Claus with a cotton beard. However, nobody seemed to care about that, which seemed to me rather mean.

My husband surveyed the fruits of our labors. "Marvelous," he said. "We have accomplished a great deal. Everything has been shifted from one box to another. I'm going to call a carpenter and have a proper cupboard made for this stuff."

As he walked toward the stairs I retrieved the Santa Claus from the "Throw Away" box. Without turning around he said, "Put that back."

I put it back, but sneaked it later from the incinerator, and now it's safely in a drawer of this marvelous cupboard we have. Deep drawers for ceramic and copper work, small drawers for high-jump medals and baby teeth, middle-sized drawers for lanyards and raffia objects (which never seem to fit in any drawer) and a huge flat drawer for finger paintings. Of course we don't have to have a lot of space for finger paintings because so many of them have been framed.

The cupboard was worth every cent it cost—and not a minute too soon. Michael has just mailed home a sharpshooter's medal, and some subversive element in Meg's school is teaching her to *sew.*

Labeled With Care

A filing cabinet is a place where you can lose things systematically.
—T. Harry Thompson in *Sales Management*

A BACHELOR friend was showing me through his new house, and when I complimented him on how orderly everything was so soon after moving he commented, "Yes, I'm a believer in that old saw, 'A place for everything and everything in its place.'"

A few minutes later I appreciated how great a believer he was when I paused by the book-lined wall in his study. Not only were the books carefully arranged in three sections, but each section was labeled with a neat, hand-lettered sign. The first and smallest group of volumes was labeled: BOOKS I HAVE READ. The sign on the second, somewhat larger group, read: BOOKS I INTEND TO READ. And the third section, by far the largest, carried this notation: BOOKS I DON'T THINK I'LL EVER READ. —Ted Harrison

SHE WAS sick in bed, and her husband, who was fixing her a cup of tea, called out that he couldn't find the tea. "I don't know what could be easier to find," she answered. "It's right in front on the pantry shelf in a cocoa tin marked 'Matches'!" —Alfred L. Prosser

FORMER Secretary of State Dean Acheson has one of those "work organizers" with compartments labeled "To Dictate," "To File," etc. The last compartment of Acheson's is labeled: "Too Hard." —Bill Gold in Washington *Post and Times Herald*

THE MEMBERS of a church in my former home town were exceedingly proud of their new minister and went all out to include him in every civic activity. But the Rotary Club had them stopped for a while. In this organization each type of business may have only one representative; and for years the churches' member had been an Episcopal bishop.

However, the young minister soon turned up as a Rotarian in good standing. He was classified as "Religion, retail" and the bishop as "Religion, wholesale."

—Mrs. C. T. Coughlin

MY FRIEND, a true daughter of the State of Maine, was closing her summer cottage. On the shady side of 60, she believed in preparing for emergencies. Methodically she tied up a bundle of summer things, which she neatly labeled: "If I die these are rags; if I live they're clothes."

—Mrs. B. K. Fisk

Eager Beavers

GRANDMA'S never content unless she's doing two or three things at once. But when she had a bad cold and we persuaded her to use her steam kettle with camphor, we were sure this was one time she'd have to sit still for a while. When we came back from town though, she wasn't sitting by the kettle. We found her in the sewing room, ironing in a cloud of scented steam from her big steam iron.

"I just poured some camphor in the iron with the water," she explained. "No sense in wasting all that time just breathing."

—Beatrice La Force

SHE WAS a college graduate trained in thoroughness, accuracy and efficiency. When she applied for a job to a wholesale grocer, he was impressed and engaged her. As her first task she was told to make a complete inventory of his stock, beginning with the goods in the cellar.

Three days passed. The merchant saw her come and go each day, and finally, wondering what she was doing all that time down in the cellar, he went to find out. She was working at his stock of peanuts, pretty, flushed and energetic. Asked how she was getting along, she wiped her dewy forehead and said, "I've had time to count only a few sacks, but I'm sure my figures are exact. So far, there are precisely 26,657,871 peanuts." —Gelett Burgess

As a Navy bride I was warned about moving day: "Never sit still while they're packing, or you'll get crated!" It wasn't long before I learned what was meant. In Honolulu the movers packed and crated our gear and shipped it to Florida. At our new post we found one medium-sized crate that neither my husband nor I could identify. Inside was a carefully packed memento of our last day in the islands—a large bag of garbage! —Cissy Adams

My mother once visited a friend's farm and was startled to see a full-grown rooster setting on a nest. Noticing Mother's astonishment, the thrifty farm woman explained, "He broke his leg, and I'm not going to have him sitting around all day doing nothing. So I gave him some eggs to hatch to earn his keep." —Mrs. I. V. Reeder

A manufacturer of electrical appliances had gone with his wife and friends to a night club. They were watching a very active rumba dancer when his wife exclaimed, "Why, look at Jack! He's positively enraptured!"

"Quiet!" growled the magnate, never taking his gaze off the shapely hip-twister. "I've got an idea for a new agitator in our washing machines."

—*The Wall Street Journal*

Driving through Mathis, Texas, early one morning, Charles A. Schnable, Jr., a part-time salesman of vitamin pills, banged into another auto. Damage to the other car was just over $100, and Schnable settled the debt on the spot by giving the driver a six-months' supply of his vitamins. While waiting for the local justice of the peace to awaken and rule on possible traffic violations, the zealous Mr. Schnable sold the arresting policeman some more pills. The judge fined Schnable $5, but bought a supply of his product. And the judge and his daughter are now dealers for Mr. Schnable's pills.

—*The Wall Street Journal*

They Got the Job

THERE WERE some star writers working for the Denver *Post* when Damon Runyon applied there for a job. Like aspiring youngsters the world over, he sat in an outer office twirling a hat in his hand, completely at the mercy of an office boy who carried his vital request to the busy editor. The kid, not even getting the name right, told his boss, "It's a fellow named Ranyan, or somethin' like that."

The boss took a dim view. "Well, tell him to send in his card," he growled.

The boy came back with the message. Runyon had no cards, but he was resourceful right from the start. He reached into a pocket and pulled out a deck of cards, carefully extracted an ace and said, "Give him that!"

He got in—and he got his job!

—Tom O'Reilly in New York *Telegraph*

THE PEERLESS Weighing and Vending Machine Corp. of Long Island, N. Y., whose scales dispense the date, your weight and character for one cent, advertised for a sales executive to head its East Coast staff. One applicant stated in his letter: "I am clever, intelligent, diplomatic, tactful, loyal, enterprising, persevering, resourceful, trustworthy and ambitious." He clinched the job by attaching ten Peerless cards attesting to these virtues as his evidence.

—Mort Weisinger in *This Week Magazine*

EAGER TO work for TV manager Ted Cott, Dick Firestone once rented a homing pigeon, attached a capsule to one of its legs, had it delivered to Cott by messenger. In the capsule Cott found a note from Firestone asking for a job, and an application blank with two choices: "(1) I would like to interview you on __________ at __________ o'clock" and "(2) I think you are inane, presumptuous and completely odious and will not interview you under any circumstances." Firestone got his interview—and the job.

—James A. Linen in *Time*

Deft Definitions

Propaganda: Baloney disguised as food for thought.

—Cincinnati *Enquirer*

Four-year-old's definition of nursery school: A place where they try to teach children who hit, not to hit; and children who don't hit, to hit back. —Mrs. M. S. N. in *Parents' Magazine*

Gentleman: A man who is always as nice as he sometimes is.

—Evan Esar, Register and Tribune Syndicate

America: The wonderful land where it's trashy to sit on the back stoop in your undershirt but gracious living if you've got nothing on but your shorts.

—Bill Vaughan, Bell Syndicate

Political economy: Two words that should be divorced on grounds of incompatibility.

—*The Wall Street Journal*

Confidence: The cocky feeling you have just before you know better. —Galen Drake, CBS

Science: An orderly arrangement of what at the moment seem to be facts.

—Quoted in *Research Viewpoint*

Die-hard: A man who worships the very ground his head's in.

—Bill Sterm in *Ladies' Home Journal*

Husband: A man who, if you give him enough rope, will be tied up at the office. —Earl Wilson, Hall Syndicate

Flashlight: A case in which to carry dead batteries.

—David H. Robbins

Committee: A group of the unfit, appointed by the unwilling to do the unnecessary.

—Victor Riesel, Hall Syndicate

Optimist: A woman who leaves the dinner dishes because she will feel more like washing them in the morning. —*Pipe Dreams*

Ulcers: The result of mountain-climbing over molehills.

—*The Wall Street Journal*

Philosophical: A cheerful attitude assumed by everybody not directly involved in the trouble.

—Ford A. Grimm

Vacation: A period during which people find out where to stay away from next year.

—Paul H. Gilbert, General Features Corp.

Vacation Time

Best place to spend your vacation is just inside your income.
—Wilf Bennett in Vancouver, B. C., *Province*

SIGN IN Miami Beach: "Keep Florida Green—Bring Money."
—Portland *Oregonian*

OFFICE GIRL leaving on vacation to substitute: "While I'm gone you'll continue what I was working on—but that doesn't include Mr. Haynes!"
—d'Alessio cartoon, Publishers Syndicate

ASKED HOW he enjoyed his vacation, a chap just back from a family motor trip to Florida replied, "Have you ever spent four days in a small Studebaker with those you love best?"
—Bill Roos, quoted by John G. Fuller in *The Saturday Review*

WHILE MY husband was having a fitting in a Hollywood costume-rental shop, a man came in and asked to see a space helmet. He was shown a clear plastic helmet about 18 inches in diameter. "That's exactly what I want," he told the clerk. "I'll take it for a week." The clerk pointed out that he could rent it for just the day of the party if he liked.

"I need it for a week. You see," he explained, "my family and I are leaving tomorrow on a vacation trip. We all like to drive with the top down except my mother-in-law, who always fusses about the breeze. The space helmet is for her." —Betty Barbour

SIGN IN a Kingston, Ont., repair shop:

Closed July 1 to July 15
Open July 21 for sure.
—*Maclean's Magazine*

THE GUIDE on a sight-seeing bus in Milwaukee informed his passengers that at that moment they were passing the largest brewery in the world. A bored man in the back suddenly came to life. "Why?" he demanded, rising to his feet.
—Walter Davenport in *Collier's*

VACATIONIST in drugstore: "Have you anything good for mosquito bites on top of poison ivy over sunburn?" —UP

ONE GIRL to another on cruise ship: "Everything's just as I imagined it would be—soft breezes, tropical moon, romantic music and no men!"

—Mary Gibson cartoon in *The Saturday Evening Post*

MY HUSBAND owns a gaudy sport shirt splashed with photographs of scenes like the Eiffel Tower, Hawaiian hula girls by the surf, Rio's mosaic walks, a Japanese pagoda, the Taj Mahal. One day when he went into a drugstore wearing this wonderful creation, a salesgirl looked at him for a moment. Then she came out from behind the counter and without a word walked slowly all around him. This completed, she went back behind the counter and announced, "Well, I've had *my* vacation!" —Ruth M. Cordell

HUSBAND painting house to neighbor washing windows: "You're lucky only getting a two-week vacation. I get *three!*"

—Don Tobin cartoon in *Look*

TWO MATRONLY ladies to travel agent: "We'd like to get completely away from civilization, near some nice shopping district."

—Franklin Folger cartoon, Chicago Sun-Times Syndicate

Mix Masters

The difference between the right word and the almost-right word is the difference between lightning and the lightning bug.

—Mark Twain, quoted by Donald Day

A MINNEAPOLIS hospital official was startled to receive a telephone call from a woman who wanted to know when she could come in for a post-mortem examination.

—"Almanac" in Minneapolis *Tribune*

THE ROMANTIC proposal was once put before the New York Board of Estimate to purchase six Venetian gondolas for the lake in Central Park. A Tammany member of the board, with an eye toward pleasing his constituents with his economy, made this suggestion to his colleagues: "I heartily approve of enhancing the beauty of our park with these Venetian gondolas, but I think six is an excessive expense. Why don't we simply buy two—a male and a female—and let nature take its course?"

—W. A. Powers in *Town & Country*

An elderly woman who worked for me spent everything she made on doctor bills. She was convinced she was suffering from liver trouble, though the doctor could find nothing wrong. One day, however, she arrived in a good mood and with a relieved expression on her face. It developed that she and the doctor had figured out her trouble. "The doctor was kinda stumped," she explained. "But when he finally asked me what *I* thought I had, I told him, and he said I was so right!"

"What was it?"

"Psychosis of the liver!" she announced, beaming triumphantly. —Blanche Cronk

The squire had attained his 80th birthday and his gardener was offering respectful congratulations. "I never thought, sir," he declared with fervor, "that I should live to be working for an octogeranium."—Janus in *Spectator*

Flustered woman's-club speaker after overeffusive introduction: "Gracious, I'm not that good—just take it with a dose of salts." —Quoted by Charles P. Taft

In the Army they have an arrangement called "compassionate transfer," to take care of special cases such as a soldier who wants to be near a dying wife or mother. Representative William Beck Widnall of New Jersey received a letter from a soldier who said he had a wife in England, then added, "I want one of those passionate transfers."

—George Dixon, King Features

Our maid, who aspires to culture, scorns words of less than three syllables. One morning I heard her tell a telephone caller, "Unfortunately Mrs. G. is decomposed." —Helen Gellert

On completing the study of *Ivanhoe* a high-school class was asked to submit compositions on the outstanding virtue of any character in the novel. One youngster, impressed by Rebecca's courage in resisting Bois-Guilbert's advances, wrote: "The Knight Templar leered as he asked Rebecca to be his mistress, but the brave girl reclined to do so." —Loring Raines

Capsule Wisdom

AN INDIANA University coed on kissing: "The important thing in saying good night is to keep your feet on the ground."

—Quoted by Sexson Humphreys in Indianapolis *News*

GEN. Ben Chidlaw, former Air Defense Commander, talking about the need for increased air defense quoted an old Cheyenne chief: "It is better to have less thunder in the mouth and more lightning in the hand." —*Time*

OLIVER HERFORD's respect for the lower forms of life accounted for the oft-quoted maxim: "The crab, more than any of God's creatures, has formulated the perfect philosophy of life. Whenever he is confronted by a great moral crisis in life, he first makes up his mind what is right, and then goes sideways as fast as he can."

—Quoted by Julian Street in *The Saturday Review*

ROBERT FROST: The best way out is always through.

LOUIS ADAMIC: My grandfather always said that living is like licking honey off a thorn.

A PIOUS fraud was telling a Quaker of the misfortunes suffered by a poor relation. "I certainly did feel sorry for him," said the man sadly.

"Yes, friend," replied the Quaker, "but did thee feel in the right place—in thy pocket?"

—Ethel Edsall in *True*

SPEAK when you're angry and you'll make the best speech you'll ever regret. —Anonymous

WHY NOT go out on a limb? Isn't that where the fruit is?

—Frank Scully, quoted by Walter Winchell

ALWAYS behave like a duck—keep calm and unruffled on the surface but paddle like the devil underneath.—London *Daily Express*

A MAN becomes wise by watching what happens to him when he isn't. —*Dublin Opinion*

FORMER Defense Secretary Charles E. Wilson prefers not to rehash old troubles. "It's too much like trying to make birth control retroactive," he says.

—Homer Bigart in New York *Herald Tribune*

A WISE matron was asked if she had as yet made the long trip to California to pay a visit to her son and his new wife. "No, I've been waiting until they have that first baby," she replied. "You see, I have a theory that grandmas are more welcome than mothers-in-law." —*The Wall Street Journal*

ALL WORK and no play makes Jack a dull boy and Jill a well-to-do widow. —Raymond Duncan in Ellaville, Ga., *Sun*

IT ISN'T the people who tell all they know that cause most of the trouble in this world, it's the ones who tell more.
—Quoted in *Management Digest*

Exit Line

AT A BUSINESSMEN'S convention four old cronies, all pillars of the same community, got together in a hotel room and before long they were discussing their shortcomings. "Well," said one, a leading businessman known as a teetotaler, "I confess I have a little weakness. I like to drink. But I never let it interfere with my work. Every now and then I go off to another town, have a little binge and come back home again, none the worse for wear."

"I have to confess my weakness is women," said another. "Now and then—a lonesome widow—very discreet, you know, and nobody's the wiser . . . ."

"Mine is betting," said the leading banker. "Not much—but when I get a chance, I put a little on the horses."

They all looked expectantly at the fourth man, who didn't seem inclined to volunteer anything. "Come on, now," they said, "how about you?"

"I—I—just don't want to tell . . . " he stalled.

They all looked askance. What sinister vice was he covering up? They coaxed and coaxed and finally told him he was damned unfair since they had all been so frank.

"All right," he said reluctantly. "If you must know it's gossip. And I just *can't* wait to get out of this room!"

—Louis Untermeyer

The Second Mrs. Ellenoy

Condensed from "Life Among the Savages"

Shirley Jackson

One morning I glanced out the kitchen window and saw my older daughter up to her knees in a mud puddle. Drying my hands on the dishtowel, I made for the back door. "Joanne," I said sharply, "what are you doing in that mud?"

My daughter looked at me, amused. "This is Mrs. Ellenoy," she said. "I'm over there." And she pointed.

Joanne was almost five, and it was very difficult to remember sometimes whether you were addressing Janey Ellenoy or a small girl with seven daughters named Martha. But since there is always confusion in our house anyway, no one worried excessively when Joanne began calling herself, variously, Jane, Anne, Linda, Barbara, Sally, Margaret, Marilyn and—imposingly—Mrs. Ellenoy. The *second* Mrs. Ellenoy.

The former Mrs. Ellenoy—I had this straight from Joanne—was a lovely woman, mother of seven daughters all named Martha, and she and Mr. Ellenoy used to be very angry with one another, until one day they grew so *very* angry that they up and killed each other with swords. As a result my daughter became the new Mrs. Ellenoy and inherited all the Marthas as stepdaughters. When she was not named Jean, Linda, Barbara, Sally, and so on, but was being Mrs. Ellenoy, her daughters were allowed to assume these names, so that there was a constant bewildering shifting of names among them. Since my second daughter is Sally, we got into difficulty with Sally Ellenoy. So we called the one Baby and the other Sallyellenoy.

One trouble about all this was that it was extraordinarily easy to be taken in by my older daughter's statements. That morning on the back step I found myself addressing the empty air where she was pointing. "Joanne," I said, "get out of that mud puddle this minute."

"Get out at once," Mrs. Ellenoy added emphatically. She turned to me. "I don't know what we're going to do with her," she said. "Joanne," she added again, "you heard your mother. Get out of that mud puddle right now." She nodded reassuringly. "She'll be right in," she said. "I'll stay out here and wait for her."

I went back inside, talking to myself, and after a minute Mrs. Ellenoy poked her head in the kitchen door. "Martha's out here," she said, "and she won't stop crying till you give her a cookie."

"I'm not giving a cookie to any little girl covered with mud," I said.

"Martha's not covered with mud," Mrs. Ellenoy said reasonably. "That was bad Anne. Martha's been playing quietly under the apple tree all this time."

My husband is a man easily thrown off balance. And one touching incident really marked him. I glanced into the study one day and saw Joanne settling herself on the couch next to her father. She had *The Wizard of Oz* and, smiling fondly, asked her father, "Will you read to me?" In my subsequent wandering through the house I frequently passed the study door and heard the drone of my husband's voice plowing his way toward the Emerald City. Finally, looking in and seeing him still reading aloud, but alone, I said in surprise, "Still reading?"

"I'm reading to Marilyn till Joanne gets back," he said, not looking up from the book.

I went outdoors to where my daughter was sitting drawing pictures under the apple tree and said conversationally, "Dad's still reading to Marilyn."

"I know," said my daughter. "I got too restless so I left."

We played a game of croquet and picked some flowers and ordered the groceries and my husband was still reading. After a while my daughter went back into the study, said softly, "Move over, Marilyn," and settled down to hear the rest of the book.

"Dad was reading out loud to himself all morning," my son Laurie observed at dinner.

"No, I wasn't," said my husband. "I was reading to Marilyn."

We never knew when the Ellenoys would turn up, or where. One memorable day I took Joanne and Laurie shopping in a department store. We all looked very nice. Joanne was wearing her best red coat; Laurie was wearing his suit which is a little too small, his spurs and two pearl-handled revolvers. As we stepped on the escalator I said, "Careful, children, please."

"Linda," Joanne repeated anxiously, "watch your step getting off the escalator. Susan, be careful. Linda, jump now; Barbara, help Linda; Marilyn, wait for your turn; Margaret . . ."

"Joanne," I said, "please stop.

They can get off by themselves." I was beginning to be aware of a familiar and dreadful feeling: that of being stared at by hordes of people—salesladies, floorwalkers, mothers, immaculate children and perhaps truant officers. "Come on," I said nervously, and added just in time, "my dears."

By this time I was carrying Joanne's doll carriage under my arm. When I put it down Joanne settled herself behind it. "Linda," she said softly, "all girls, get in line behind me, please." A man who had been watching us looked long at Laurie, long at Joanne and, inscrutably, at me. But it was in the restaurant that the frightful moment occurred.

Just as the waitress was putting down a plate of soup all seven Ellenoy girls tried to climb onto Mrs. Ellenoy's lap. "You *can't* get into my lap now, can't you see I'm having my lunch?" Mrs. Ellenoy said crossly, and the waitress gave me a startled look and retreated—backing directly into Laurie's spurs.

With the opening of school the Ellenoys went away. All Joanne's girls, it was reliably reported, retired to a ranch in Texas from which, very rarely, they wrote illegible letters to their mother.

But before they left there was the black morning the census taker spent at our house. (She arrived before I was dressed and Joanne entertained her until I came down.) And they were responsible for the uncomfortable incident when my daughter trotted in to me and said, "There's a lady outside named Mrs. Harper and she wants to know will you give her a dollar?" I replied absently, "Tell Mrs. Harper she may take the penny off my desk and not to bother me any more." My daughter told Mrs. Harper and Mrs. Harper went away furious and a little frightened, and I was entered on the PTA books as refusing to pay my dues.

Door Ways

A FELLOW in our office told us about a household incident of which he had been an innocent but perplexed spectator. Our friend had called a Venetian-blind repairman to come pick up a faulty blind, and the next morning, while the family was seated at the breakfast table, the doorbell rang. Our friend's wife went to the door, and the man outside said, "I'm here for the Venetian blind." Excusing herself in a preoccupied way the wife went to the kitchen, fished a dollar from the food money, pressed it into the repairman's hand, then gently closed the door and returned to the table. "Somebody collecting," she explained, pouring the coffee.

—Caskie Stinnett in *Speaking of Holiday*

HUSBAND to wife as he announces unexpected callers: "Here—in spite of snow, sleet, frost and biting winds—are the Thompsons." —Cartoon in *Punch*

ONE CHILLY night I was awakened by persistent knocking on the landing outside my apartment. Knowing that my neighbor could sleep through anything, I got up to investigate and found a Western Union boy pounding at his door. I offered my heavier hand and the two of us rained blows on the door until both my neighbor and his wife were roused.

When, sleepy, shivering and annoyed by this midnight intrusion, they opened the door the boy handed in his message. "Telegram for Norman Hummon," he said.

I shall never forget my neighbors' glare. The message was for me. —Norman Hummon

DOING MY Christmas shopping when I was stationed at one of our continental Marine Corps Air Stations, I ran across a toy bagpipe. It seemed an ideal present for the young son of one of my brother officers on the base; so I sent it to him with a card: "Love to Peter from Uncle Jock."

About ten o'clock on Christmas morning I was awakened by a knock on my door at Bachelor Officers Quarters. There stood my young friend, dressed in his Sunday best, with suitcase and bagpipe. From his neck hung a card: "To Uncle Jock with love from Peter's Parents."

—Col. John T. L. D. Gabbert

A WOMAN in Fort Wayne, Ind., had just stepped from the shower when the doorbell rang. Since she was expecting a visit from her sister she grabbed a towel and, holding it modestly in front of her, sprinted for the door. To her horror, when she threw open the door there stood a delivery man waiting for her to sign for a package. There was nothing to do but clutch her towel firmly and sign.

As she stood there she was conscious that the delivery man was glancing intently at something behind her. But it wasn't until after he'd left that she remembered the full-length mirror on the living-room wall! —Simon M. Schwartz

Shutter Bugs

A NEWLY organized camera club had dreamed of the day when it could have a live model for some nude photographic studies. But the members didn't have much money and it took some time for the club treasury to get enough. Finally the big night came. The model arrived, the cameras were ready.

But it seemed the model had been wearing tight garters and her legs were deeply imprinted. For half an hour she and various volunteers tried to rub away the garter marks so they wouldn't show in the pictures. Finally it was decided that she would wait in another room for an hour while they had their business meeting. An hour later when they went in to get her, she got up—and she'd been sitting for an hour on a cane-bottomed chair.

—Vance Spencer, quoted by Ollie James in Cincinnati *Enquirer*

WHEN our ship tied up for a few days at a small Pacific island the comely females, who wore a saronglike affair around the hips and nothing above, evoked the undivided interest of the entire crew. One young seaman spent most of his time posing the undraped natives, singly and in groups, meanwhile happily snapping away with his small box camera.

Finally my curiosity got the better of me and I asked him, "Just when and where do you expect to get all those films developed?"

"Films?" he repeated, grinning. "Who's got films?" —E. M. Sims

CAMERA salesman showing equipment to customer: "With it you get everything you need to show your pictures to friends—projector, screen, film splicer, bars for windows and padlocks for all doors." —Charles Skiles cartoon in *The Rotarian*

FOR A camera bug's 50th birthday a White Plains woman decided to present him with 50 flash bulbs. She knew little about cameras, but she purchased a box camera with a flash attachment for herself at the same time she bought the bulbs. And before wrapping each bulb in gold paper she carefully tested it in the attachment. She was delighted that every bulb "worked," and happily sent them off to her friend—who hadn't the heart to tell her the facts of life about flash bulbs.

—"Our Town" in White Plains, N. Y., *Reporter Dispatch*

Osmond Borradaile, chief cameraman for *Royal Journey,* the record of Elizabeth and Philip's tour of Canada, tells this anecdote:

In Washington the royal visitors had been exposed for the first time to the fantastic informality of big-time American press photographers, who are awed by nobody. Back at Ste. Agathe in the Laurentians a few days later the future Queen strolled out of the lodge, holding her own little movie camera. She spotted her husband standing at the other side of the courtyard, whipped the camera up to her eye and shouted in a voice of stunning nasality and volume:

"Hey—you, Dook! Look dis way a sec! Dat's it! *Tanks a lot!*"

—Clyde Gilmour in *Maclean's Magazine*

Art Buchwald, Paris correspondent of the New York *Herald Tribune,* has a story about two camera addicts who were draped over a bar in Paris, one telling the other of an experience that morning. In the Bois de Boulogne he had noticed an old crone huddled beneath a bundle of rags. Hungry and homeless, she told him the heartbreaking story of her life. Once a countess, and beautiful, she had been the toast of the Continent. But step by step she lost everything and was now a wretched old woman with nothing to live for.

"The poor thing," said the other photographer. "What did you give her?"

"Well, it was sunny," said the first photographer, "so I gave her f/11 at 1/100." —*Newsweek*

Perfectionists

"One of my favorite golfing yarns," relates Bing Crosby in his book *Call Me Lucky,* "is the story of Lou Thomas, a fine putter, but a man so meticulous on the greens, so insistent on silence, that playing with him was sometimes a trial. One day he had a 12-footer to sink on the 14th green. Lou surveyed his putt from the upper and lower angles, tested the wind, spent five minutes reading the contours, the grass, even the roots. He picked up some loose blades of grass, some lint, tiny bits of sand, then turned to his caddy and asked, 'Was this green cut this morning?'

" 'Yes,' the caddy replied. Whereupon Lou putted and missed.

"His opponent, who had spent this long interlude impatiently leaning on his putter, stepped up to his ball and stood over it waggling his club. But suddenly he stopped and, turning to Lou's caddy, inquired: 'What time?' "

—As told to Pete Martin, © 1953 by Bing Crosby and published by Simon and Schuster

IN KANSAS a mail sack, bulging with letters, fell under the wheels of a train and was cut to shreds. The scraps and tatters were collected and the whole jumble dropped into the Post Office's lap to be pieced together. The Post Office was equal to the task. The job was done so thoroughly that one man received a letter he'd read, torn up and thrown away while waiting for his train on that fateful day. —*This Week Magazine*

IN THE South Pole region U. S. Navy scientists and personnel dubiously eyed the one cracked egg included in the crated supplies dropped by Air Force parachute, then discovered a penciled message: "This egg cracked before we dropped it. Air Force."

—*Time*

A CHARWOMAN in a New York bank was telling of her prowess in polishing floors. "When I started to work here the floors was in bad shape. But since I've been doing them," she said with quiet pride, "three ladies has fell down."

—*Treasury of Modern Humor*, edited by Martha Lupton (Droke)

Wolf Calls

A wolf is a man who believes in Life, Liberty and the Happiness of Pursuit.

A FELLOW I always thought of as quite shy and reserved with girls was driving me to the movies when he suddenly went around a sharp corner and I slid over to his side of the car. I commented on what slippery seat covers he had.

He answered with a frank grin, "I wax them."

—Mary Kay Brown

MIDDLE-AGED diner to blonde seated alone in restaurant: "Would you care to join my expense account?"

—Wilkinson cartoon in *The Saturday Evening Post*

A FERRY-BOAT captain shouted down to the crew's quarters below decks, "Is there a macintosh down there big enough to keep two young ladies warm?"

"No," came the booming answer, "but there's a MacPherson here who's willin' to try!" —*Bell Telephone News*

A STRAIT-LACED old lady annoyed by the amorous couple in front of her at the movies tapped the youth on the shoulder and asked, "Must you behave like this in public? Have you no place of your own you can go to?"

The ardent swain turned to her eagerly. "Oh, madam," he said, "if only you could persuade her!" —*Tatler and Bystander*

A POPULAR young bachelor whom I was seeing off at the airport had a $5 bill changed into quarters. Then as I watched in astonishment, he fed all the quarters into one of those machines that sell life insurance on your flight—a $5000 policy for a quarter. "Heavens," I exclaimed, looking at the fistful of policies, "you must have a dreadful premonition about this flight!"

"Oh, no," he answered. "I always do this when I fly; I send a policy to each of my girls. You'd be surprised how it cements relations."

—Fred Clisson

IT HAD BEEN a long, boring evening, but the young man finally succeeded in stealing a good-night kiss from the young lady. "That's your reward for being a gentleman," the girl murmured.

"Reward?" scowled the young man. "That's just workman's compensation."

—Helen Rich

DURING A food service demonstration at the Naval School of Hospital Administration a shapely young lady handed out samples of foodstuffs. At the end of the lecture each student officer was requested to turn in a list of questions concerning the dishes in which he was most interested.

One enterprising young officer requested, "More information about the dish in the white sweater!" —Alyce W. Edwards

A YOUNG man-about-town took a glamorous girl out on a date. They were driving down a moonlit country lane when the engine suddenly coughed and the car came to a halt.

"That's funny," said the young man. "I wonder what that knocking was?"

"Well, I can tell you one thing for sure," the girl answered icily. "It wasn't opportunity." —E. E. Kenyon in *The American Weekly*

A BLONDE had just told a wolfish GI she wouldn't go out with a perfect stranger. "Don't worry, Babe," the GI grinned. "I'm not perfect." —Earl Wilson, Hall Syndicate

WOMEN ARE wonderful, especially if you haven't seen one for a year. During World War II our LST had been in the New Guinea area for about that long when we learned there were three Red Cross girls on the beach at Hollandia. Our skipper invited them aboard for dinner and sent a young ensign ashore to bring them out. When the ensign returned he rushed over to where I was standing with the supply officer and said breathlessly, "One of those girls slipped while she was getting out of the boat and I caught her! I had her right in my arms!"

The supply officer nodded. "I touched one once," he said, his eyes fogged with memory. "Soft, ain't they?"

—Charles E. Parker, Jr., in *The Saturday Evening Post*

The Incomparable Buzz-Saw

By H. L. Mencken

THE ALLUREMENT that women hold out to men is precisely the allurement that Cape Hatteras holds out to sailors: they are enormously dangerous and hence enormously fascinating. To the average man, doomed to some banal drudgery all his life long, they offer the only grand hazard that he ever encounters. Take them away and his existence would be as flat and secure as that of a moo-cow. Even to the unusual man, the adventurous man, the imaginative and romantic man, they offer the adventure of adventures. Civilization tends to dilute and cheapen all other hazards, but civilization has not made women a bit more safe than they were in Solomon's time; they are still inordinately menacing, and hence inordinately provocative, and hence inordinately charming.

The most disgusting cad in the world is the man who, on grounds of decorum and morality, avoids the game of love. He is one who puts his own ease and security above the most laudable of philanthropies. Women have a hard time of it in this world. They are oppressed by man-made laws, man-made social customs, masculine egoism, the delusion of masculine superiority. Their one comfort is the assurance that, even though it may be impossible to prevail against man, it is always possible to enslave and torture a man. This feeling is fostered when one makes love to them. One need not be a great beau, a seductive catch, to do it effectively. Any man is better than none. To shrink from giving so much happiness at such small expense, to evade the business on the ground that it has hazards—this is the act of a puling and tacky fellow.

—*A Mencken Chrestomathy* **(Knopf)**

Papa's Not a Knucklehead *or* Now I Understand Women

Condensed from "20,000 Leagues Behind the 8 Ball"

David Dodge

I WAS SOAKING in the bathtub one afternoon in a Buenos Aires hotel when I received a revelation. It came to me when I overheard my wife, Elva, telling my nine-year-old daughter, Kendal, some of the facts of life, the most cold-blooded conversation I ever listened to.

They didn't know I was there, having just returned from a shopping spree loaded with new clothes. While Elva, humming contentedly to herself, was storing the loot away in a suitcase, Kendal said, "Mama, is Papa really as poor as he says he is all the time?"

"Of course not. He just likes us to think he has to work hard to keep us happy."

"Doesn't he?"

"Not so hard that it's killing him." I was going to put my rebuttal in then, but Elva went on before I could open my mouth.

"It's a kind of a game, honey. You'll play it yourself when you grow up. All men are the same.

You have to flatter them. They like to think they are big and strong and clever and hard-working, and that we couldn't get along without them. Have you ever noticed that when your papa is around I can never open a suitcase without breaking my fingernails?"

"Yes."

"I can open them all right when he isn't here. But men don't like women who are efficient. You want to remember that when you have a husband of your own. They prefer wives who are helpless and a little bit stupid, so they can feel superior. What you have to start learning about right now is to be helpless at the right time. And never let a man see that you know more than he does. He'll never forgive you."

Kendal thought it over. I waited, just my nose and ears out of the water, like a hippopotamus. I wanted to get it all.

Kendal said, "Don't you love Papa?"

"Of course I love him. That's why I keep him contented by letting him break *his* fingernails on suitcases. He's happy because he's strong and clever and can open suitcases, while I'm too dumb to buy a railroad ticket for myself without help and can't get the top off a tube of toothpaste." After a moment she added, with what sounded like a choke in her throat, "Or get up to get myself a glass of water on a cold night."

I pretended to be asleep in the bathtub when they found me there, so they wouldn't know I had eavesdropped on this bloodcurdling dialogue. I wanted to see how soon Kendal would try to put the philosophy into action, and then I planned to whale it out of her with a hairbrush. Elva was too far gone down the path of deception to be worth the trouble, but Kendal could still be saved.

Her approach, when it came, wasn't what I expected. That evening she came to stand by my chair while I was reading. I thought, here it comes. First the build-up, then the request for an increased allowance, finally the hairbrush.

She said, "Papa."

"Yes?"

"You know what?"

"No. What?"

"Mama thinks you're a knucklehead."

"What makes you say that?"

"She said so. She said you aren't as smart as you think you are."

"That wasn't what she said — I mean, when was all this?"

"Today. She said all men are dumb, and that if you oil them right you can make them do practically anything for you."

"What do *you* think?" I asked.

Her essential honesty was clearly coming to the fore. I didn't have to worry about *her*. Not Kendal. I felt a great surge of affection for my daughter.

She said, "I don't think *you're* dumb. You wouldn't fall for that kind of business. Maybe other men would, but not my papa. No, sir. I'll bet"— she slid her arm around my neck —"nobody is as clever as you are. Nobody can make kites as good as you can." She climbed into my lap. "Or tell such good stories." She put her head under my chin. "Or throw a ball as high as you can." She put both arms around my neck and squeezed. "I *like* you. I'll bet you're the smartest man in the whole world. I don't care what Mama says."

Twenty-five cents a week is hardly a decent allowance for a nine-year-old girl, after all. So right then and there I raised her to 50 cents.

Caught in Passing

THE PULLMAN porter had just roused me and, still half-asleep, I was sitting on the edge of my lower berth, unshaven and tousled. A mother and daughter passed by on their way to the diner and I got up and followed toward the men's lounge.

"Don't worry, dear," I heard the older woman say encouragingly, "they *all* look like that in the morning." —H. F. Stern

THE SAILOR and his girl had been having a disagreement; she was crying and he was trying to comfort her. As I got closer I heard him say, "Honest, honey, you gotta believe me—I ain't got a sweetheart in ev'ry port!" As I moved on I heard his closing argument: "I ain't *been* in ev'ry port!" —Roy L. Nicholson

ONE HOT summer day a little boy was walking along behind a very large woman, so closely in her footsteps as to be annoying. Finally she turned on him, demanding why and threatening to call the police.

"Please don't do that," the child pleaded. "It's just that you're the only real shady spot on the street."

—Chub de Wolfe in Toledo *Blade*

I WAS VISITING the exhibition of Austrian Art Treasures at the Metropolitan Museum in New York and had stopped to admire Correggio's painting of a nude Venus being caressed by Adonis, when I overheard feminine voices beside me. "That's just the way we do at home," one said, "and the whole family loves it."

As the two women moved on to the adjoining picture I heard the second say earnestly, "Next time, Helen, you might even try it with honey instead of sugar." —F. C. M. Jahn

AFTER CHURCH service in a neighboring town I overheard a member and a visitor discussing the new minister. "Why did you let the other pastor go?" the visitor asked.

"Oh, he always preached that if we didn't mend our ways we would go straight to hell."

"But that's just what this minister said today!"

"Yes," replied the member, "but the other one acted as if he was *glad!*" —E. V. J.

OVERHEARD IN a San Francisco bar: "She's mad at me for drinking, and I'm mad at her for never sewing buttons on my shirts. So I reach into the icebox last night—and she's frozen a button in every ice cube!" —Herb Caen in San Francisco *Examiner*

TWO DIGNIFIED, well-dressed gentlemen were gazing in silent absorption at a construction crew wielding its Gargantuan machinery. A heavy length of pipe was being lifted by a large derrick which was badly in need of lubrication, and the process was accompanied by screeches and banshee wails.

"That reminds me, Harry," one of the men said to the other, "I have a dental appointment at two!" —Verna M. Lombard

Signs of the Times

CROWD watches steam shovel at work, on its side this sign: "NOW OPERATING, EDDIE BRIGGS—FORMERLY SEEN IN SUCH HITS AS: 'MID-TOWN TUNNEL'—'CITY BANK BUILDING'—'8TH STREET BRIDGE.' "
—Dave Hirsch cartoon in *The Saturday Evening Post*

SEEN IN a French antique shop in New York: "English and French Spoken—Cash Understood."
—Jack Sterling, CBS

IN BIRMINGHAM, Mich., there's a swanky strip of shops with such signs as "Furs by Robert" and "Coiffures by Charles." At the end of the block a gas station says: "Petrol by Murphy."
—Elsie Devine, quoted by Eleanor Clarage in Cleveland *Plain Dealer*

ON a used-car lot in Pontiac, Mich.: "Quiet, timid salesman now on duty."
—Mrs. R. W. Hodge

CHILDISH SCRAWL chalked on a New York City wall: "Robert Smith Is a Boron Isotope."
—Carol Feldman

IN A HOLLYWOOD photo lab: "All orders for delivery yesterday must be placed before noon tomorrow."
—Bill Kennedy in Los Angeles *Herald and Express*

IN A PSYCHIATRIST'S office: "Five couches—no waiting."
—David E. Green

ADJACENT highway posters near Baltimore: "Are You Prepared to Meet Your Maker?" "Use Unguentine for Burns."
—*The Lutheran*

IN A LOS ANGELES maternity shop: "We Provide the Accessories After the Fact."
—David Deutsch

The Writing Public

A Hollywood maternity shop received this note: "Dear Sir: You have not yet delivered that maternity dress I ordered. Please cancel the order. My delivery was faster than yours."

—Bill Kennedy in Los Angeles *Herald and Express*

A U. S. Navy destroyer received a letter from one of the big book clubs notifying the wardroom mess that its subscription was about to run out. The letter, addressed to "Mr. Wardroom Mess," began, "Dear Mr. Mess." —Bennett Cerf

Unconscious humor frequently appeared in the correspondence the late Dorothy Dix's advice column elicited from its readers. One letter read: "I had a date with my boy friend and on the way home he said let's get married or something. But I read your column, Miss Dix, and I said let's get married or nothing."

—Ella Bentley Arthur and Harnett T. Kane, *My Husband Keeps Telling Me to Go to Hell* (Hanover)

Letter received by the Cleveland Museum of Natural History after a school field trip to the museum: "Thank you for making the tripe so interesting."

A radio program hitting the air at 7 a.m. each day received this note from a feminine fan: "Before I tuned in your program, I could never get my husband out of bed in the morning. Now he can't get out of the house fast enough."

—Neal O'Hara, McNaught Syndicate

Letter to *The Christian Science Monitor:* "Dear Sir: When I subscribed a year ago you stated that if I was not satisfied at the end of the year I could have my money back. Well, I would like to have it back.

"On second thought, to save you trouble, you may apply it on my next year's subscription."

In Wichita, Kan., the siren on Deputy Sheriff Charles Baxter's car was fixed after he left this note for the mechanic: "The syreen on car No. 7 ain't a-workin'. It will sigh, but it won't reen."

—UP

To Walter Davenport's column in *Collier's* came this letter:

"Some time ago you had an item that was 100 percent wrong. I clipped it out and was going to send it to you but lost it. I been so busy I forget what it was but if you will look back a few weeks you will find it. You can't miss it because it was 100 percent wrong."

My husband has had some amusing notes left in the milk boxes on his route, but this one tops them all: "Dear Milkman: Starting today leave 1 homo on Mondays and Thursdays but none on Saturday—then leave 1 heavy cream on Tuesdays and 1 sour cream on Wednesdays with 1 quart of homo. Then leave 1 quart of homo on Friday with the heavy cream, for the weekends leave 2 homo and 1 sour cream on a Saturday and 1 heavy cream on a Sunday. Please alternate this for me. If the heavy cream falls on a Saturday leave 1 homo with it then. Empty bottles are in the garage. Climb through side window. Garage is locked."

—Shirley Glick

When my son came bounding into the house carrying a football he had won in a box-top contest, I was amazed. The rules had stated that prizes would be awarded to the youngsters who wrote the best sentences on why they liked the product. The judges must have had a sense of humor because my prodigy's contribution was: "I like your cereal because it doesn't snap, crackle or pop—it just lays there quietly and sogs."

—Samm S. Baker

SENATOR Spessard L. Holland of Florida received a letter from a private stationed in Germany asking, "Is there anything in Army regulations that says a private can't go out with a major's daughter?" The Senator referred the problem to the Pentagon and was able to write back to the private that there was nothing in regulations to stop him from dating a major's daughter.

Soon the Senator received a thank-you note from the GI with this postscript: "Now if you'll just tell the major about it, too, everything will be all right." —UP

Maid's Eye View

My maid was a jewel, but she left me for a better setting.
—Mildred I. Wicks

A FRIEND gave Dorothy Parker a young alligator some three feet long. Not knowing what else to do with it the author put it in her bathtub. She went out shopping, and when she returned she found this note from her maid, who had come in during her absence: "I have resigned. I refuse to work in a house where there is an alligator in the bathtub. I would have told you this before, but I did not think the matter would ever come up."
—J. Y. Henderson and Richard Taplinger, *Circus Doctor* (Little, Brown)

MY FRIEND Ruth, packing for an extended trip, was seized with misgivings about leaving her husband. "Mamie," she said to the maid who had been with the family for years, "promise you'll write me at once should Mr. Harper become blue or lonesome or ill. I'll come right straight home."

" 'Deed I will, Miss Ruth," said Mamie. Then after a thoughtful moment she added, "I'll write you if he seems too happy, too."
—Mrs. R. Stanley Piland

OUR MAID looked unusually tired one morning, and I asked what the matter was. "I've been buying things on the lay-awake plan," she told me.

"Don't you mean lay-away plan?" I asked.

"No," she said, "I mean what I said. You buy things you can't afford and then you lay awake worrying how you're going to pay for them." —Alfred Steinberg

I HAD EXPLAINED to Marie, our new maid, how the call-box in the kitchen would register the name of the room from which I was buzzing if I wanted her to come to me in another part of the house. She was still studying the box when I turned to leave the kitchen. As I reached the door she asked, "Mrs. Horner, where is the buzzer I push when I want you?" —Lucy R. Horner

A WEALTHY society lady had just engaged a new maid and was instructing her. "At dinner, Mary," she explained, "you must remember always to serve from the left and take the plates from the right. Is that clear?"

"Yes, ma'am," answered the girl condescendingly. "What's the matter, superstitious or something?" —New York *Telegraph*

MATRON discussing new cleaning woman: "She's expert at putting everything back where she didn't find it." —Mary Pressly

A PROMINENT D.A.R. of Chattanooga from time to time had helped her cook in the preparation of speeches for her church society. One time, however, she was out of the city when needed, and on her return asked the cook how she had got along. "Lawsy," she answered. "I jus' found one of yo' old speeches and put Gawd's name where you had D.A.R. and it went fine." —Frank A. Nelson

THOUGH SHE considers herself lucky my friend is not entirely satisfied with her maid-of-all-work. When she saw an announcement in the newspaper that a two-day course in housekeeping was going to be given locally, she decided to give her maid time off to attend. But Mary balked. "Ma'am," she said, "I don't think I want to go. I already know how to do more than I want to do."

—Jerome B. Pillow

Labor Pains

A BROADWAY play, *Mid-Summer,* which featured a slatternly maid who flipped a duster casually around a hotel room and went out, was picketed until the management agreed to run the following program note: "The character Rosie is intended to bear no resemblance to actual hotel maids of the present day. The producers recognize the fact that the 7000 maids who are members of the Hotel and Club Employes Union, Local 6, New York, are industrious and able."

DAVID DUBINSKY tells about the labor leader who went to a matrimonial agency. "Is this a union shop?" he inquired. Assured that it was he picked out a picture of a luscious 25-year-old and said, "I'll take her."

"No, you have to take this lady," said the manager showing a picture of a gray-haired woman of 60.

"Why do I have to take her?" thundered the labor leader.

"She," said the manager, "has seniority."

—Earl Wilson, Hall Syndicate

AUSTRALIAN dock workers once demanded what they called Temptation Money. If they loaded or unloaded anything which they might be tempted to steal, such as tobacco, whiskey, wine or perfume, they considered that they should be fortified by extra payment against the temptation to steal.

—"Brutus" in *The Recorder* (London)

CONSTERNATION reigned at Transfilm Inc., because the holes in a slice of Swiss cheese to be used on a television food commercial weren't photogenic enough. A union jurisdictional problem arose when it became necessary to use a brace and bit to drill more holes, with both Local 52 of the prop men's union and Local 608 of the carpenter's union clamoring for the job. The prop department finally won out. —Leslie Lieber in *This Week Magazine*

ONE CHORUS GIRL to another: "He's only a tycoon, but he spends money like it was out of a union welfare fund!"

—Pearson cartoon in New York *Herald Tribune*

IN ST. LOUIS, MO., a contractor who held up a $500,000 building job until a robin that had built a nest on the site could hatch her eggs explained: "I'm no bird lover. I just respect a fellow contractor."

—Arthur Lansing in *The American Magazine*

A MOVIE HOUSE showing a popular thriller-diller was being picketed, but crowds continued to throng into the movie. Union officials decided a drastic step was necessary.

The next day a lone picket stood silently by the box office. His sign read: "The hero's uncle did it."

—Jim Lowe, CBS

ASSISTANT reporting to corporation president: "A guaranteed annual wage, a guaranteed annual bonus, a guaranteed pension plan is fine with the employes, Chief. Except they would like a guarantee you won't go broke."

—Lichty cartoon, Chicago Sun-Times Syndicate

THE INTERNATIONAL Brotherhood of Teamsters requested a separate union unit at a New England plant. According to a union man at a National Labor Relations Board hearing, some employes mow the lawn.

"We consider that truck driving," he said. "Anything on wheels we consider truck driving."

—New York *Times*

IT WAS a heated discussion of election procedures in the labor unions, and the group was evenly divided as to their honesty until one young man said, "I know the elections are crooked. In our last election I ran for shop steward of our local and voted for myself three times, but when the returns were completed, I never got a vote!"

—Charles Wesdell

It's Human Nature

WALDICK, N. J., was in a state of considerable confusion after a referendum on Election Day. The voters in the Bergen County borough voted 1078 to 808 in favor of establishing a full-time system of police protection, then voted against spending the additional $10,000 yearly it would cost and, finally, voted 956 to 905 in favor of retaining the present part-time system.

—Don Ross in New York *Herald Tribune*

AT A "HOME SHOW" in Kansas City, Mo., the Federal Housing Administration and the Department of Commerce distributed the same pamphlet at different booths. FHA, which gave them away, had few takers. Commerce sold them at 15 cents apiece, could hardly keep up with the demand. —*This Week Magazine*

AFTER SEVERAL practice fire drills the employes of the Veterans Administration regional office in Montgomery, Ala., invited the fire chief and his staff to watch them go through a drill. With the ringing of the fire alarm the 600 employes evacuated the four-story building in three minutes and ten seconds. Everyone was proud and pleased—until the buzzer sounded for quitting time that afternoon and someone timed that evacuation.

This time the building was cleared in two minutes flat.

—Quoted by Jerry Kluttz in Washington *Post*

AN ASSIGNMENT in my sociology class called for getting some firsthand information on neighborhoods. To do this I went from door to door interviewing people. I put my first question to one man: "What do you especially like about living in this neighborhood?"

The man answered slowly. "It's nice and friendly," he said. "Folks are always coming to visit us, and we visit them. And there are lots of kids around."

"And what are the things you don't like about it?" I asked next.

The man thought a moment and then said, "Same things, I guess." —Ingrid Hilke

Answer Men

A YOUNG contestant on Arthur Godfrey's "Talent Scouts" was asked if he was married. "No," replied the youth, "but I've been thinking about it."

Godfrey then asked what kind of girl he was considering. "Well," said the contestant, "I want the kind of girl who wouldn't be interested in a man like me!" —Donna Mae Sutton

CONFRONTED BY that time-honored query, "If you were marooned on a desert island, what would you like to have for reading matter?" a Broadway chorus babe gave the answer to end all others: "A tattooed sailor." —Bennett Cerf

WHEN A QUIZMASTER asked a contestant to "name something beginning with the letter M which you will need to make mayonnaise," the girl answered, "Mother."

—John Crosby in New York *Herald Tribune*

APPEARING ON TV during a visit to Florida at the time he was governor of Georgia, Herman Talmadge was being needled by the interviewer, who pointed out that thousands of Georgians had migrated to Florida. "Governor," the interviewer rattled on, "can you tell us how you feel about so many of Georgia's native sons leaving your state for the better life in Florida?"

Talmadge smiled. "I think," he said, "that it raises the level of intelligence in both states."

—Richard Powell Carter in *The Saturday Evening Post*

AN MC was discussing feminine styles with an elderly male contestant on his quiz show. "I suppose," he said, "you remember the wasplike waists?"

"Remember!" snorted the man. "That's when I got stung!"

—*Capper's Weekly*

ON A "Strike It Rich" broadcast the quizmaster asked a contestant, the father of 17 children, why he wanted to "strike it rich." The answer—"So I can buy my wife some laborsaving devices"—brought down the house and won him $800.

WHEN A QUIZ contestant was asked whether he could name a product in which the supply exceeds the demand, he replied, "Trouble." —Larry Wolters, Chicago Tribune-New York News Syndicate

"WHAT MADE you decide to be a parachute jumper?" Garry Moore asked a contestant on "I've Got a Secret."

"A plane with three dead engines." —Anthony J. Pettito

Pardon, Your Slip Is Showing®

FROM A Pioneer Air Lines ad in the Waco, Texas, *Times-Herald:* "Two Frights Daily . . ."

FROM THE Lansing, Mich., *Catholic Weekly:* "The second unit in the parish building program is being completed on a yap-as-you-go basis at an estimated cost of $22,500."

FROM THE Monterey, Calif., *Peninsula Herald:* "Miss Roberta Ford was injured while driving a car near this city yesterday. The area in which Miss Ford was injured is spectacularly scenic."

—Quoted by Kenneth Nichols in Akron *Beacon Journal*

FROM THE Akron, Ohio, *Beacon Journal:* "The free dental clinic will be for indignant children of the city."

FROM THE Honolulu *Star-Bulletin:* "A well-known beauty expert says that beauty is not a question of age. It is making the best of one's good paints."

AD IN Tampa, Fla., *Sunday Tribune:* "GENUINE DIAMOND, 1¼ carats, from our loan dept. $365. Lay-it-away. You'll thrill owing so much for so little."

FROM THE Kingsport, Tenn., *Times:* "The All-Girl Orchestra was rather weak in the bras section."

—Quoted in Charlotte, N. C., *News*

FROM THE Kenton, Ohio, *Times:* "Dinner was served at a table beautifully decorated with evergreens and Christmas bills."

SOCIETY NOTE in the Fort Lauderdale, Fla., *Daily News:* "Mr. and Mrs. Thomas A. Hodges entertained friends at cocktails followed by a buffet suffer."

FROM A note to parents sent by Onekama, Mich., Consolidated School: "Please examine, sigh, and have your children return their report cards promptly."

FROM THE Quincy, Mass., *Patriot Ledger:* "Reverend David B. Matthews presided and opened and opened and opened and opened the meeting with prayer."

FROM THE Lake Andes, S. D., *Wave:* "Mrs. George Padrnos' name was intentionally omitted from the list of guests attending Mrs. Frey's birthday party last week."

FROM A wedding announcement in the Houston, Texas, *Press:* "She got worried over the weekend and left on a honeymoon."

—Quoted by Roger Allen in Grand Rapids, Mich., *Press*

PICTURE caption in *The Kiwanis Magazine:* "There is a picnic during the two-day outing which practically doubles the population of the town each year."

FROM THE Lynchburg, Va., *Daily Advance:* " 'I's very happy,' said Olga, a medical student, in perfect English . . ."

—Quoted in *Editor & Publisher*

The French Touch

WHILE TEACHING navigation to a class of aviation cadets—some of them foreign students under the Mutual Defense Assistance Program—I used the word "rendezvous" in describing a meeting of fighters and bombers. A French student raised his hand and asked the meaning of the word.

Surprised, I replied that certainly a Frenchman ought to know the meaning. It was a French word.

"I know what means rendezvous," he answered, "but this with fighters and bombers is not it."

—Capt. David R. Nelson

"AM I in favor of the preservation of the gallant French habit of kissing ladies' hands?" mused French playwright-actor Sacha Guitry. "Definitely. After all, one must start somewhere."

—Quoted by Wallace Reyburn in Toronto *Telegram*

WHILE WE were living in Paris our bell rang one morning and my husband opened the door and found himself confronted by a policeman, who presented him with a ticket for illegal parking. It happened that on the date of the ticket we had been in Arles, and we even had our hotel bill to prove it. But the policeman brushed the explanation aside.

My husband decided to try another approach. Asking the policeman to step outside with him, he whispered, "You're right. I was in Paris on that date, but my wife thinks I was in Arles."

"Mais, alors!" said the officer, smiling broadly—and tore up the ticket. —Mrs. Eugene English

TELEVISION STATIONS in the United States send out geometric designs as test patterns before starting the day's program. Back in the '40's France's lone TV station had more sense. Its test pattern was a picture of a beautiful girl from the Folies Bergère, a different one each day of the week.

—John Crosby in New York *Herald Tribune*

YOUNG AND starry-eyed, I was window-shopping in Geneva when I realized that a very dapper-looking man was following me. I moved on, but he came up beside me, doffed his hat and with a charming smile addressed me with a volley of French. I shook my head uncomprehendingly. A try at German was no more helpful. Then English: "How to put it delicately, so as not to offend? I very much want to know you."

With what I considered great presence of mind I invoked a mythical protector. "But," I said, "my husband wouldn't like that a bit."

"Ah-h, you have the husband?" Then, with a shrug, *"Mais, madame*—that is a condition, not an excuse!"

—L. R. P.

IF A WOMAN and two men are shipwrecked on a desert island for a month, what would happen?

If they're Spanish, one of the men would kill the other.

If they're Italian, the woman would kill one of the men.

If they're English, nothing would happen, because they hadn't been introduced.

If they're American, nothing would happen because the men would be too busy talking business to join the lady.

And if they are French—there is no problem.

—Andre Visson

Zoo's Who

IT WAS feeding time at the Paris Vincennes Zoo when a shapely Parisian miss in a fur coat stopped at the gorilla's cage to watch him eat. The gorilla, instead of eating, went into all sorts of acrobatics to keep the girl's attention. Finally a keeper approached. "Mademoiselle," he pleaded, "will you please move on— you are tiring the gorilla."

—George Révay

ONE FINE spring morning I took my three-year-old daughter and her small boy friend to the zoo to view the wonders of the animal kingdom. We went first to the monkey cage, where several of the young were nursing. The little boy asked what they were doing and I told him that was the way the babies got the milk for their supper.

Thereafter, as we moved from cage to cage, his first question was whether that animal gave milk, too. At the camel's pen, however, my little girl answered before I could. "Of course not, silly," she said scornfully. "Everybody knows that camels give soup."

—MacKenzie G. Frey

A GROUP of children who were taken to the Philadelphia zoo were keenly disappointed to find no monkeys visible at either the monkey house or on monkey island. "Where *are* all the monkeys?" the young lady chaperoning the party asked an attendant.

"This is their mating season," he replied. "They are all back in the cages."

"Oh," said the lady, then after a moment's thought, "The children are terribly disappointed. Do you think if they threw peanuts into the cages the monkeys would come out?"

"I don't know, lady," the attendant replied laconically. "Would you?"

—Helen F. Lees

Spellbinders

I'm sorry for any man who has not the imagination to spell a word two ways.

—Mark Twain, quoted by Donald Day

AN INDEPENDENT five-year-old, given to keeping his own counsel, wanted to write his uncle in California. Although he had already mastered "Uncle Jack," he had no idea how to spell the necessary "Dear." But his frequent visits to the zoo offered a solution. He searched the dictionary until he found a certain picture, with the delightful result that his letter started: "Caribou Uncle Jack."

—Virginia S. Leist

RIDING IN a radio cab we heard the dispatcher tell another driver to go to an address and pick up a passenger in apartment Q. "Apartment Q," the dispatcher repeated. "Q like in cucumber."

—"All Things Considered" in Milwaukee *Journal*

YEARS AGO Chuck Egan told us the following yarn: Once upon a time there was a football player named Bumpkin, who worked for Vandy, or Tinnissee, or some such college. He was what the broadcasters in the area called "a tahr of straint on the deefense," but he was also decidedly weak-brained. The professors, therefore, sometimes had difficulty with their consciences, giving Bumpkin a passing mark. Finally a long-suffering professor of English Lit flunked Bumpkin. What with three big games coming up, the coach was frantic. He ran to Prexy, who had the professor up on the carpet. "Ah'd pass him if he could only spell one word," said Professor.

"He kin so spell a woid," said Coach. "Trouble is you want him to spell big woids."

"He cain't even spell 'coffee,' " said Professor. "If he'd get jest even one little letter rah't in it, Ah'd pass him."

"Prexy, I'll buy that," said Coach. "I garntee he kin git one letter right." So they called Bumpkin in and explained the academic crisis, how the glory of Old Vandy depended on the muscles of his bony head. "So now, Bumpkin," said Coach, "git in there and spell 'coffee,' and if you git just one little letter okay, you kin keep on playing."

So Bumpkin braced his feet, concentrated hard and spelled slowly, "K . . . A . . . U . . . P . . . H . . . Y."

—From a Washington *Daily News* editorial

ASKED IF she could spell banana, a little girl said, "I know how to spell banana but I never know when to stop."

—Quoted by Charles Poore in New York *Times*

IN ENGLAND a young man wanting to talk to a friend in Ealing went to the telephone and said to the operator, "Ealing 6000, please."

"What number did you say, sir?"

"I said, 'Ealing 6000.' "

"Spell it, please."

"All right. E for 'erbert, A for what 'orses heat, L for where you are going, I for me, N for what lays the heggs, and G for jeep."

He was promptly connected with the right number.

—Lincoln MacVeagh

WHEN ACTOR Dan Duryea's son Dickie was four, he answered the phone one day while Dan was sleeping. Trying to be grown-up he asked the caller, "Would you like to leave a message?"

"Yes," said the caller. "Tell him Mr. Brown called." Dickie got a pencil and paper and said, "Mr. Brown? How do you spell it?" "B-R-O-W-N." A moment of silence, then a very small voice asked plaintively, "How do you make a 'B'?"

—Irving Hoffman in *The Hollywood Reporter*

A YOUNG PROFESSOR and his wife were meticulous about the language used in their children's hearing. After one of those hectic days which befall every mother of small fry, the father greeted his family with a cheery, "Well, how is everything?"

"Oh, John," wailed his wife, "I've had a hell of a d-a-y!"

—Gertrude M. Pomeroy

SOME YEARS AGO a fresh busher was making his debut with the Cleveland Indians. Tough George Moriarty was the umpire behind the plate. The rookie took one called strike without protest. Then another. Then he turned to the umpire and politely asked, "I beg your pardon, sir, but how do you spell your name?" Surprised, Umpire Moriarty obliged as he spelled out his name letter by letter. The rookie sighed, stepped back in the box and said gently, "Just as I thought, sir, only one 'i.' "

—Mac Davis, *Great American Sports Humor* (Pocket Books)

ONE OF THE most frustrating conversations in theatrical history is recorded by *Theatre Arts* magazine: A subscriber dialed "Information" for the magazine's number. "Sorry," drawled the lady, "but there is nobody listed by the name of 'Theodore Arts.' "

"It's not a person; it's a publication," insisted the subscriber. "I want *Theatre Arts.*"

The operator's voice rose a few decibels. "I told you," she repeated, "we have no listing for Theodore Arts."

"Confound it," hollered the subscriber, "the word is Theatre—T-H-E-A-T-R-E."

"That," said the operator with crushing finality, "is not the way to spell Theodore."

—Bennett Cerf in *The Saturday Review*

Stage Business

THE LATE Fanny Brice was always somewhat absent-minded, except about certain matters. On one occasion when Jesse Block, an old-time vaudeville acquaintance, was visiting her in Hollywood, he mentioned having been on the same bill with her at the Oriental Theater in Chicago.

"I never played the Oriental," said Miss Brice.

"You did," said Block, "and after the show we went to the College Inn."

"I never went to the College Inn with you."

"Don't you remember?" said Block. "I pointed out Al Capone to you."

"Who's Al Capone?" asked Fanny.

"Fanny," said Block, "that was the week at the Oriental you got $7500."

"I did not," said Miss Brice. "I got $8000." —Leonard Lyons

ASKED IF he considered himself successful, Walt Disney replied, "Well, I must be—I owe eight million dollars!"

—Tom O'Malley and Bob Cunniff, Newspaper Features

PERRY COMO asked Pearl Bailey, guest star on his TV show, whether she ever sang for the pleasure of singing. She replied, "Well, if you'll examine that musical scale, you'll find it begins and ends with 'dough.' " —Minneapolis *Star*

THEATRICAL PRODUCER Max Reinhardt, a man of grandiose ideas, was the despair of his business adviser. One day a friend overheard the two discussing a new production. He listened while the adviser vetoed each of the producer's suggestions. When the adviser had gone the friend said, "I wish I had someone like that working with me. He must save you a lot of money. Do you always listen to him?"

"Almost always," replied Reinhardt. "Ninety-nine percent of the time he is right and I am wrong. But one percent of the time he is wrong and I am right. On that one percent we make a living."

—E. E. Edgar

THE POPULAR and successful actor Rex Harrison, who cannot keep track of his money, once promised to jot down every penny he spent, returned home with a scrap of paper on which he had noted: "Taxi $1.50, tip $.50; misc. items $83." —*Time*

NOBODY KNEW why, but for years Alfred Lunt and Lynn Fontanne had laid an egg in Pittsburgh. It exasperated Lunt, and the night before they were to open in *The Taming of the Shrew* he took Larry Farrell, their company manager, aside. "Larry, I don't mean to be critical," he began, "but I think the reason we don't make a profit in Pittsburgh is that the company isn't managed properly."

"Would you like to take over while we are here?" asked Farrell. The actor agreed and Farrell handed him the books. On Saturday night when they closed, Lunt was brimming with good news. "We made $4000," he told the manager proudly. "Here are the books."

The manager glanced over the ledger. "One thing, Alfred," he pointed out, "you forgot to pay the Lunts." —Jean Meegan in *Esquire*

AN ACTOR down on his luck once asked comedian W. C. Fields for a loan. "I'd be glad to help you, my good man," Fields replied, "but all my money's tied up in currency." —Earl Wilson, Hall Syndicate

IN HER BOOK, *Family Circle,* Cornelia Otis Skinner, daughter of the famous actor, tells about the time during World War I when it was customary for the star of every show to appear between acts and sell Liberty Bonds. "Father's current New York play was a complete flop," she relates, "and the bottom of the family till was plainly visible. But he planned one evening to enliven his public salesmanship by offering to purchase for himself ten $50 bonds for every ten people in the audience who would match his bid.

"Mother, sitting in a box that night, was filled with pride. Father had already committed himself for a thousand dollars when a young officer, his right arm off at the shoulder, rose and said, 'Mr. Skinner, I haven't the money to buy more, but I'll take a $50 bond.' Mother, carried away with emotion, sprang to her feet and in the tones of Barbara Frietchie cried out, 'I'll take a $50 bond for every uniformed man in the house!' A little stunned, Father ordered the house lights turned on. Mother, who previously had seen only a few uniforms about the orchestra floor, now found her eyes being drawn in horror to the balcony—a solid blue and khaki. Business being bad, the company manager had filled all unsold seats with sailors and doughboys!"

—Published by Houghton Mifflin

Mother's Bills

Condensed from "Life With Father"

Clarence Day

FATHER WAS always trying to make Mother keep track of the household expenses. He had a full set of account books at home in addition to those in his office, and his ledger showed at a glance exactly how much a month or a year his clothes or his club or his cigar bills amounted to. Before he got married these books had apparently given him great satisfaction, but he said they were never the same after that. He still knew what his personal expenses were, but they were microscopic compared to his household expenses, and of these he knew no details, only the horrible total.

Every once in so often he tried to explain his system to Mother. But Mother didn't feel that women should have anything to do with accounts, any more than men should have to see that the parlor was dusted. Every time Father showed her his ledger she was unsympathetic. She had to do the mending and marketing and take care of the children, and she told Father she had no time to learn to be a bookkeeper, too.

Father knew where some of the

money went, for part of the expenses were charged. But looking at the bills he said that many of the details were not clear to him, and most of the rest were incredible. He tried to go over the bills regularly with Mother, demanding information about items he did not understand. But every now and then there were items she didn't understand either. She behaved as though the bill were a total stranger to her. This was one of the features that enraged Father most.

Mother was one of those persons for whom charge accounts were invented. When she bought something and charged it, the first of the next month seemed far away, and she hoped that Father might be nice about it for once. She was a different woman entirely when she had to pay cash. It was hard to get cash out of Father, and she thought twice before she could bear to part with the money. But shopping on a charge account was fun.

Father did his level best to take the fun out of it. Once every month he held court and sat as judge and required her to explain her crimes and misdemeanors. When she cried, he said at the top of his voice that he wished to be reasonable but that he couldn't afford to spend money that way and they would have to do better. What made household expenses jump up and down so? "Anyone would suppose that there would be some regularity after a while which would let a man try to make plans, but I never know from one month to the next what to expect."

Mother said she didn't either. All she knew was that when the bills mounted up it didn't mean that she had been extravagant.

"Well, it certainly means that you've spent a devil of a lot of money," said Father.

There were times when every month the totals went up and up; and then, just as Father had resigned himself to this awful outgo, the expenses, to his utter amazement, would take a sharp drop.

Mother didn't keep track of these totals; she was too busy watching small details, and Father never knew whether to tell her the good news or not. He always did tell her, because he couldn't keep things to himself. But he always had cause to regret it. He told her in as disciplinary a manner as possible. He appeared at her door waving the bills at her with a threatening scowl, and said, "I've told you again and again that you could keep expenses down if you tried, and this shows I was right."

Mother was always startled at these attacks, but she didn't lose her presence of mind. She asked how much the amount was and said it was all due to her good management, and that Father ought to give her the difference.

At this point Father suddenly found himself on the defensive and the entire moral lecture he had intended to deliver was wrecked. The more they talked, the clearer it seemed to Mother that he owed her that money. Only when he was lucky could he get out of her room without paying it. He said this was one of the things about her that was enough to drive a man mad.

The other thing was her lack of system, which was always cropping up in new ways. Father at last invented what seemed a perfect method of recording expenses. Whenever he gave any money to Mother he asked her what it was for and made a note of it. His idea was that these items, added to those in the itemized bills, would show him exactly where every dollar had gone.

But they didn't.

He consulted his notebook. "I gave you six dollars on the 25th of last month," he said, "to buy a new coffeepot."

"Yes," Mother said, "because you broke your old one. You threw it right on the floor."

Father frowned. "I'm not talking about that," he answered. "I am simply endeavoring to find out from you, if I can—"

"But it's so silly to break a nice coffeepot, Clare, and there was nothing the matter with the coffee that morning; it was made just the same as it always is."

"It wasn't," said Father. "It was made in a damned barbaric manner."

"And I couldn't get another French one," Mother continued, "because that little shop had stopped selling them."

"But I gave you six dollars to buy a new pot," Father firmly repeated, "and now I find that you apparently got one at Lewis & Conger's and charged it. Here's their bill: 'one brown earthenware drip coffeepot, $5.' "

"So I saved you a dollar," Mother said triumphantly, "and you can hand it right over to me."

"Bah! What nonsense you talk!" Father cried. "Is there no way to get this thing straightened out? What did you do with the six dollars?"

"Why, Clare! I can't tell you now, dear. Why didn't you ask at the time?"

"Oh, my God!" Father groaned.

"Wait a moment," said Mother. "I spent four dollars and a half for that nice new umbrella I told you I wanted, and you said I didn't need a new one, but I did, very much."

Father wrote, "New Umbrella for Vinnie" in his notebook.

"And that must have been the week," Mother went on, "that I paid for two extra days' washing, so that was two dollars more out of it, which makes it six-fifty. There's another fifty cents you owe me."

"I don't owe you anything," Father said. "You have managed to turn a coffeepot for me into an umbrella for you. No matter what I give you money for, you buy something else with it, and if this is to keep on I might as well not keep account books at all. I'm not made of money. You seem to think I have only to put my hand in my pocket to get some."

Mother not only thought this, she knew it. His wallet always was full. That was the provoking part —she knew he had the money, but she had to argue it out of him. "Well, you can put your hand in your pockets and give me that dollar-fifty this minute," she said.

Father said he didn't have a dollar-fifty to spare and tried to get back to his desk, but Mother wouldn't let him go till he paid her. She said she wouldn't put up with injustice.

Boston Bred

A STORY in Cleveland Amory's *Proper Bostonians* tells about a breakfast at the home of Judge John Lowell. The Judge's face was hidden behind his morning paper when a frightened maid tiptoed into the room and whispered something in Mrs. Lowell's ear. Mrs. Lowell squared her shoulders resolutely and said, "John, the cook has burned the oatmeal and there is no more in the house. I am afraid that this morning, for the first time in 17 years, you will have to go without your oatmeal." The Judge, without putting down his paper, answered, "It's all right, my dear. Frankly, I never cared for it anyhow."

—Bennett Cerf, *Shake Well Before Using* (Simon and Schuster)

ONE DAY an erect, spry, determined Bostonian fell into conversation with John P. Marquand. "I've read all your books, Mr. Marquand," he said, "but let me tell you this—you've never written anything better than the first, *Sorrel and Son.*"

"Thank you, sir, but that wasn't mine. It was Warwick Deeping's."

"Nonsense," said the other, stalking off, an erect, spry, determined Bostonian. —Lewis Nichols in New York *Times Book Review*

IN THE MIDST of conversation a prideful proper Bostonian admitted that he was born in Seattle. After this horrible confession he hastily added, "But I was conceived in Boston!"

—Allison V. MacCullough

AT BAR HARBOR a woman who was in mourning debated the propriety of attending a party, came to this decision: "I shall go," she said, "but I shan't mingle."

—Cleveland Amory, *The Last Resorts* (Harper)

A VIVACIOUS young Clevelander shocked her Boston-reared beau by drawing on her gloves as they started down the street on their first date. "Where I come from," chided the young man stuffily, "people would as soon see a woman put on her stockings in public, as her gloves."

"Where I come from," retorted the young lady, "they'd rather!"

—Eleanor Clarage in Cleveland *Plain Dealer*

A WELL-FILLED bus was proceeding down a Boston thoroughfare when a truck cut sharply into its path, and only the bus driver's quick wits and action prevented disaster. Pale and shaken he voiced his estimate of the vanishing truck driver's character, origin and mode of life in words appallingly stark. Then, remembering the audience at his back, he turned to face them.

A white-haired woman whose demeanor and dress bespoke her Beacon Hill lineage forestalled his apology. "My congratulations," she said, "upon an admirable presentation of what we may reasonably assume to be the facts." —Thomas C. Higgins

SHORTLY AFTER Robert Cutler, the Boston banker, returned to Washington as a special Presidential aide on national security affairs, a group of proper Bostonians were discussing him one day in a proper Bostonian club. One noted cautiously that Mr. Cutler was making something of a name for himself. Another responded cautiously, "Yes, that's true, but only nationally." —New York *Times*

IN PREPARATION for its 25th reunion, Harvard '26 mailed a confidential Kinsey-like questionnaire to its members. One budding George Apley returned his promptly, blank, save for this marginal comment:

"In my opinion sex is a subject to be discussed with women, not with an International Business Machine."

—Bennett Cerf in *This Week Magazine*

BOSTONIAN commenting on his plain sister who, true to her Boston heritage, wore straight hair, flat shoes and a shiny nose: "She's the kind of girl who thinks it's insincere to look anything but her worst." —Margaret French Cresson

Thumbnail Sketches

SHE WAS the type whose mind is bounded on the north by her servants, on the east by her children, on the south by her ailments and on the west by her clothes.

—Cleveland Amory, *The Proper Bostonians* (Dutton)

HAROLD ICKES describing another New Dealer: "He was an infant prodigy. The trouble was that he kept on being an infant long after he ceased being a prodigy."

—Sydney J. Harris, General Features Corp.

AFTER A trip to Washington some years ago Lewis Douglas, former ambassador to Great Britain, was asked how a member of the Democratic administration was handling a particularly vexing problem.

"You don't have to worry a bit," said Douglas. "He's got the situation right in the hollow of his head." —Jim Hart

DESCRIPTION OF a bubbly woman whose veracity had come into question: "Well, she doesn't exactly tell the truth all the time. There just isn't that much truth."

—Chicago *Tribune,* quoted in Charlotte, N. C., *News*

FORMER Representative Clifton Young of Nevada, on a quick-tempered member of the Cabinet: "The trouble with him is he picks a quarrel before it's ripe." —Leonard Lyons

SIR WINSTON CHURCHILL, about a Parliamentary opponent: "He has a genius for compressing a minimum of thought into a maximum of words." —Leo Cherne in New York *Times Magazine*

Oh, Say, Can You Ski?

By Corey Ford

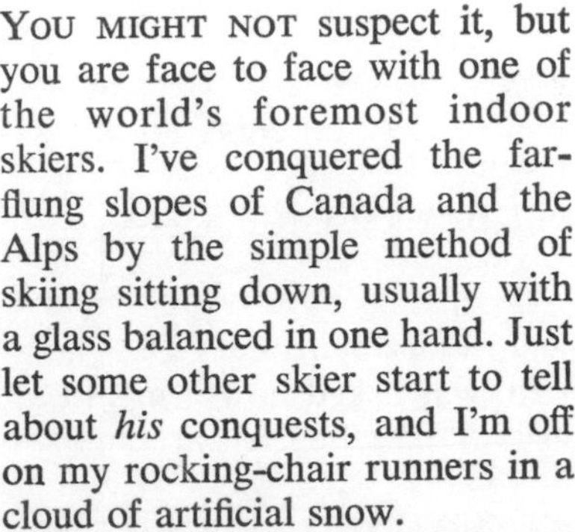

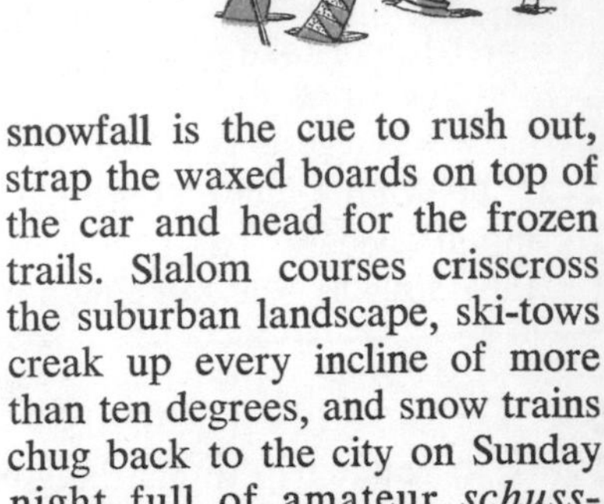

YOU MIGHT NOT suspect it, but you are face to face with one of the world's foremost indoor skiers. I've conquered the far-flung slopes of Canada and the Alps by the simple method of skiing sitting down, usually with a glass balanced in one hand. Just let some other skier start to tell about *his* conquests, and I'm off on my rocking-chair runners in a cloud of artificial snow.

My breath-taking triumphs on the hickories (as we old pros call them) are all the more remarkable because I don't know a *sitzmark* from a hole in the ground. Frankly, winter sports leave me cold. Why climb a mountain at 20 below zero when you can fall downstairs in a nice warm house?

It's my idea that winter is a good time to catch up on your sleep. Nobody went outdoors in the old days. People used to board up the windows and sit around the fire playing parcheesi or doing card tricks until spring. That is probably why they lived longer then. At least it seemed longer.

Not any more, though. The first snowfall is the cue to rush out, strap the waxed boards on top of the car and head for the frozen trails. Slalom courses crisscross the suburban landscape, ski-tows creak up every incline of more than ten degrees, and snow trains chug back to the city on Sunday night full of amateur *schussboomers* with bloodshot eyes, a pair of frostbitten ears and one arm in a sling.

Not that I have any objection to people who ski, provided they shut the door behind them when they go out. What I object to is the social stigma which attaches these days to people who don't. Winter is hard enough without facing the taunts of those enthusiasts who insist on dragging you off for a robust weekend upside down in six feet of snow. "Come on, you old fogy," they jeer. "Get some red roses in those cheeks. Put on the barrel staves and let's try a few *gelandesprungs.*"

Travel posters add their seductive siren-songs. "Visit our winter wonderland at beautiful Mount Traction," they urge, "complete with emergency first-aid stations, 24-hour stretcher service and a fully equipped modern hospital conveniently located at the bottom of the hill." Even the family joins in the assault. "Why don't you let Junior take you out to the children's slope this afternoon?" your wife suggests pointedly. "He can hold your hand in case you get going too fast."

There's only one way to maintain your self-respect as a red-blooded male, and still avoid getting snow down your neck—take up indoor skiing. All you need is a few hours under a sun lamp, the names of several prominent mountain ranges and a smattering of German phrases like *"Ski heil!"* and *"Prosit!"* It also helps if you can yodel.

The first step is to purchase a pair of skis. This involves a trip to a sporting-goods store, but you can avoid undue exertion by taking a taxi, and the clerk will be glad to stoop over and fasten the bindings for you if you can't reach them. Walk up and down the floor a couple of times, just to make sure the skis fit. If they are the right length, the curved points of the tips will just coincide with your forehead as you fall forward. When you have made your selection break them across your knee, carry the pieces home and hang the shattered ends over your mantel with a small sign reading: "Splint's Ledge, Feb. 22, 1958." The rest of the skis can be used to start a fire.

Next you'll need a complete ski outfit. Naturally your clothing should be imported, so you can drape your jacket carelessly across a chair with the foreign manufacturer's name exposed. In case nobody notices it, pick up somebody else's jacket and remark apologetically, "Say, I guess I got hold of the wrong one—mine has an Innsbruck label."

Now for the real snow job. Armed with dark glasses, sun-tan lotion and a plaster cast on one leg (just in case somebody asks you to ski), hie yourself north to a popular resort. Take a chairlift to the top of the mountain and stretch out on a chaise longue in the glass-enclosed sun deck. This is one of the best places to practice indoor skiing, for the chances are that nobody else knows any more about it than you do.

The trick is to break in on another skier's story. Let us say that an expert is expounding his pet theory on how to take the downhill slalom. Interrupt with some lighthearted quip like: "Speaking of slalom, I took one in Newfoundland that went 20 pounds." (I admit this isn't very good, but anything to throw him off stride for a moment.)

Expert *(recovering):* As I was saying, it's all in distributing your weight properly. You should lean slightly forward—

You: Except in Chile. Everybody leans backward down there because it's on the other side of the equator. I suppose you're familiar with the big jump at Satan's Sacroiliac?

Expert: Well, no, I've never been in South America.

You: Oh, that's not in South America, that's in the Alps. *(Craftily.)* Personally I think the Alps have it all over Switzerland, don't you?

Expert *(walking right into it):* I thought that Switzerland was *in* the Alps.

You: I mean the Himalayan Alps, of course. *(This is what I mean about keeping him off balance.)* You haven't been skiing until you've gone down Old Nick's Adam's Apple. Have you ever run the Apple?

Expert *(weakly):* I'm not exactly sure where—

You: Never forget the time I took it blindfolded on a dare. Glare ice, you know, and what made it even harder was the fact that I lost one ski when I hit a mountain goat. Fortunately I caught up with a snowslide going in the same direction and rode it the rest of the way down... Wait a minute, please don't go. I want to tell you about doing Hell's Handbasket with both feet tied behind me.... Do you really have to leave?

By this time all the other skiers will have departed as well, and you can ride the chairlift back to the bottom of the mountain, full of the buoyant spirits and ruddy glow of health that an afternoon of indoor skiing gives.

An even simpler solution to the winter-sports problem, of course, is to take a plane to Florida or California, and stay there until the snow melts. But watch out. There's always the danger that someone will ask you to go water-skiing.

ATTENDANT AT hotel desk to couple checking into ski resort: "Could I have name, address and next of kin?" —Cartoon in *Punch*

SOON AFTER a New York fashion expert checked into a Minneapolis hotel one hot day, she phoned the desk and asked them to send up a glass of lemonade. "Sorry," came the reply, "our bellboys are all busy." With a glint in her eyes she telephoned another hotel several blocks away. In a few minutes a bellboy from the rival establishment paraded past the wide-eyed desk clerks, toting a giant lemonade.

From then on she got service with a capital "S."

—Kenny Ruble, quoted by George Grim in Minneapolis *Tribune*

WHY ARE hotel-room walls so thin when you sleep and so thick when you listen?

—Arthur Godfrey, quoted in *Coronet*

THE HOTEL KIMBALL in Springfield, Mass., received the following letter from a Mr. Thompson:

"With regard to my reservation, Mrs. Thompson would like a room on the third or fourth floor and away from the elevators, and not near any room assigned to folks who speak above a whisper or otherwise tend to disturb the peace. Mrs. Thompson wants to sleep. Will you see what you can do for her? If everything is quiet —including Mrs. Thompson— maybe I can sleep too."

—Beatrice Merrick

A HOTEL IN Jackson, Miss., advertises: "Convenient to everything, including better hotels."

—Neal O'Hara, McNaught Syndicate

IN THE early hours of the morning during a stay at the Waldorf I left a friend's room and rang for the elevator. Then I realized that I was going down only one floor. At that hour I could well imagine what the elevator man would say when I told him I had only one floor to go—and down, too! When he arrived I apologized, saying that I should have walked down.

The elevator man bowed from the waist and in his most dignified manner said, "Madam, one does not walk in the Waldorf!"

—Mrs. Oscar A. Ahlgren in *General Federation Clubwoman*

A NEW YORKER arriving in Miami Beach at the height of the season was told not a room was available. "There must be a room. There always is," the man said.

"No," the desk clerk insisted.

"Look," said the man, "if you heard that Eisenhower was coming, you'd find a room. Right?"

"Right, for Eisenhower," said the clerk.

"Well, the President can't come," said the man, "so let me have his room." —Leonard Lyons

BASIL RATHBONE was visiting in Victor Borge's hotel room, and the Dane was telling the actor of the versatility of the piano. He told Rathbone that he could even tell time by the piano. The actor was skeptical; so Borge sat down and crashed out a few bars from a Sousa march. Immediately there was a pounding on the wall and a sleepy voice rumbled angrily, "Stop that noise, you idiot! Don't you know it's 1:30 in the morning?" —Victor Borge as told to Dean Jennings in *The Saturday Evening Post*

ON HER REGULAR visits to Oslo a prominent Norwegian woman from the provinces stays at one of the best hotels. Active in society and in charities she usually spends a lot of time telephoning, especially before getting up. This particular morning she first telephoned room service and ordered breakfast, then decided to make some calls. Not wanting to disturb the people in the neighboring rooms she retreated with the telephone under the covers to muffle the conversation. She was so absorbed in her various calls that she never heard the waiter come in with her breakfast.

He had quietly laid the table for two.

—*Farmand,* quoted by Stephen King-Hall in *National News-Letter*

First Nighters

ON THEIR wedding night a young lieutenant's bride was taken ill and fainted. Frantic, the groom called the night clerk and said excitedly, "Send up the house doctor. A young lady has just fainted in my room."

The bride, who had by then regained consciousness, corrected, "Honey, tell him I'm your wife."

"She says to tell you she's my wife," the rattled lieutenant blurted into the receiver.

—Mrs. J. W. Wester

PLACARD ON back of newlyweds' car: "Amateur Night."

DRIVING NORTH through Alabama one summer my mother and I picked up a young man carrying a worn valise and all slicked up to a shine. We were surprised to learn that his destination was New York City.

"You see, ma'am," he confided, "I just got married today. I always promised Sue we'd go to New York for our honeymoon—but there wasn't enough money for both of us to ride the bus. So here I am, ma'am. I sure hope I get there before Sue does."

—Patricia Harris

A MAN WROTE to the Credit Bureau of Salem, Mass.: "Sorry this bill has remained unpaid for so long. I've been married and have been on my honeymoon. As soon as I get on my feet, I'll be in to make a payment."

—Tom Tucker

IN QUITO, Ecuador, a young teacher substituted for a friend who was taking a week's honeymoon. A month later at a party someone started to introduce the groom to her.

"Oh," he answered brightly, "I know Miss R__ very well indeed. She substituted for my wife on our honeymoon!"

—Katherine MacGregor Wallis

WHEN FRIENDS commented on how tired she looked, an Austin, Texas, woman said that her 17-year-old daughter had gotten married and she had just returned from driving the newlyweds to San Antonio for their honeymoon. "They were just too young to drive," she explained. —AP

New at the Game

WHEN A young bride asked for oysters in a sea-food store the dealer said, "Large or small, madam?"

"Well, I'm not quite sure," hesitated the bride. "But they're for a man with a size 15 collar."

—*West Lynn Works News*

A COLLEGE graduate applying for a position on the editorial staff of the New York *Times* explained to the editor that he had a burning desire to be a newspaperman. He simply wanted a job, a job of any kind for a start.

The editor explained the high degree of specialization on a newspaper like the *Times*. You did not apply for a job, he went on, you applied for some definite kind of work. He outlined many different kinds, then asked the young man, "What would you like to do on the *Times?*"

"If it's all the same to you," responded the young hopeful, "I should like to write the editorials."

—Neil MacNeil (New York *Times*)

AFTER A few weeks' training at a football announcers' school a neophyte sports announcer was doing fine in his first test—Northwestern vs. Illinois—until he saw the referee pick up the ball and start walking.

"There's a penalty against Northwestern," the young man said confidently. "Let's see—it's 5, 10, 15, 20, 30, 40, 50, 60, 70, 80, 90 yards! I don't know what the foul could be to get a 90-yard penalty. I'll have to check."

Just then an assistant nudged the broadcaster and whispered briefly in his ear. "Folks," the broadcaster said courageously, "that wasn't a penalty at all. It was the end of the quarter, and the referee was moving the ball to the other end of the field. If anybody has a job for an ex-sports announcer, just let me know!"

—Bob Addie in Washington *Post and Times Herald*

MORE IN bewilderment than in anger an Army sergeant wrote an acquaintance of his efforts to arouse a group of draftees after their first night in the barracks. The sergeant bellowed out the information that it was four o'clock, and one draftee raised himself on an elbow: "Four o'clock!" he gasped. "Man, you better get to bed. We got a big day tomorrow."

—Caskie Stinnett in *Speaking of Holiday*

SWEET YOUNG thing at her first baseball game to escort: "Is that all you meant by wanting to get to first base?"

—Bill Wenzel cartoon in *Saga*

DURING OUR take-off on a training flight, as I was tightening a loose hydraulic connection, I suddenly saw that an engine was on fire. Wrench in hand I turned, touched the pilot calmly on the shoulder with it and told him, "We're on fire."

He soon had us safely back on the ground, and a short time later I was modestly explaining my great presence of mind in a trying situation to an admiring audience. Just then two medics passed, carrying our pilot on a stretcher. Startled, I called, "What's the matter with him?"

"Broken shoulder," came the laconic answer. —Les Black

ONE GIRL explaining bowling to another: "Be careful not to knock down all the pins with the first ball, because if you do you get cheated out of a second throw."

—Des Moines *Sunday Register*

A YOUNG MAN came into a bookstore in San Francisco where a friend of mine works and asked if they sold medical books.

"Yes," she replied. "What branch of medicine are you interested in?"

After some embarrassed shuffling the young man said, "S-something on birth control."

"Have you any particular author or title in mind?"

"No, miss," said the young man rather desperately. "I don't care what, so long as it's for beginners." —Susan Alberti

S. O. S.

REPRESENTATIVE Ross Bass (Tenn.) broke his rule against sending more than ten government publications to any one person at one time. He sent 76 of the do-it-yourself pamphlets to a Tennessee man who pleaded: "Recently married, expecting, just moved into new home and broke. I do not know anything about anything. Neither does my wife. Thanks." —AP

FROM THE Portland *Oregon Journal:* "Will lady who saved $130 on automatic washer I advertised in last week's *Journal* please call me—it was the *drier* that my wife wanted me to sell!"

NOVELIST Arnot Robinson once received this query: "Please tell me the facts of life before next Friday—I have never wanted to know before."

Miss Robinson replied: "If you have never wanted to know before, you are obviously not ready for next Friday."
—London *Evening Standard*

BACK WHEN the Middle East situation was so confusing and frightening—Israel invading Egypt, England and France charging into the mess, Russia muttering threats—the Pentagon, I have it on excellent authority, sent a top-secret wire to the Mediterranean Fleet. The message told the fleet to be alert and prepared to move at a moment's notice. Back came the reply: "We are ready and prepared. Who's the enemy?" —Terry Turner in Akron *Beacon Journal*

FROM *Your Weekly Guide to Cape Cod:* "I have male and female hamsters. Will trade the whole lot of them for anything . . . anything!"

A CHICAGO youngster, burdened by his duties of keeping his room tidy at Phillips Exeter Academy, sent an emergency airmail letter to his parents. "Please send me a rug right away quick," read the brief missive. "I need something to sweep under."
—Judith Cass in Chicago *Tribune*

Christmas Preview

Excerpt from the book "Merry Christmas, Mr. Baxter"

Edward Streeter

THIS YEAR Mr. and Mrs. Baxter had decided to cut down their Christmas expenditures. But along about November the inevitable subject of Christmas cards came up. "I thought we had decided to eliminate them and save money," said Mrs. Baxter.

"Okay with me," said Mr. Baxter. "That means, of course, that we lose touch with a lot of old friends."

"Who, for instance?"

"Well, Joe and Annie. Christmas cards are about our only contact with them since they moved out West."

"I wouldn't think of not sending a card to Joe and Annie," Mrs. Baxter said indignantly. "We'll send cards to all our good friends who live a long way off. What I object to is sending cards to every Tom, Dick and Harry that we see all the time."

"You mean," said Mr. Baxter, "that you wouldn't send Sam and Helen a card just because they live two blocks away?"

"Darling, of course we would. They're our best friends."

"I see," said Mr. Baxter.

"I'll get my book," said Mrs. Baxter, who was a born record keeper and now brought out a black leather book containing their Christmas-card transactions for years back. She turned its pages thoughtfully. "Last year," she said, "we sent out 247 cards."

"Utterly absurd," said Mr. Baxter. "We don't know 247 people. You must buy a mailing list or something."

"I'll tell you one group we can cut out," said Mrs. Baxter. "That's young marrieds like the Cassels. I don't see why we should take on our *children's* friends."

"It's good for old crocks like us to keep up our contacts with youth," mused Mr. Baxter. "No, let's cut somewhere else."

"Here's certainly a pair you can throw out," said Mrs. Baxter. "Mr. and Mrs. Joel de Sanchez. I never even heard of them."

Mr. Baxter looked pained. "Sometimes I think you don't listen when I tell you things. Joel de Sanchez has been one of my best customers for 15 years."

"Business!" cried Mrs. Baxter somewhat overdramatically. "Does it have to take over Christmas as well as everything else?"

"Listen, dear," said Mr. Baxter using his patient voice, "one gets to know certain people in the business world in a very intimate way. I regard Joel de Sanchez as a personal friend. . . . Now, here's one that can go. The James Wenickes. Who in the world are the James Wenickes? What a *name!*"

"They're my *cousins*. They live in Peoria and I wouldn't *think* of not sending them a card," said Mrs. Baxter, and turned the page. "Who's Henry Snell?" she asked.

"Must be another of your cousins," said Mr. Baxter.

"Never heard of him," said Mrs. Baxter. She drew a heavy line through the Henry Snells. "*Now* we're getting somewhere."

When they reached the end of the list they had eliminated 14 names. "There's another section over here," said Mrs. Baxter. "These are the people who sent *us* cards last year and we didn't send one to *them*. Now personally I think we ought to send these people who sent us last year."

Mr. Baxter agreed. He disliked being under obligations. He also disliked the idea of people sitting around all over the country saying, "Here's one we can cut—the Baxters. They never send *us* a card." "Yes, of course. Never cared much for them anyway."

Two hours later Mrs. Baxter added up the revised list. It was increased by 35 names. "We started by not sending *any,*" she wailed. "Now we have to order more than we ever have." Mr. Baxter shrugged. "I know," he said, "but, after all, it's *Christmas.*"

Noël! Noël!

WHEN HE served in the Agricultural Administration Adlai Stevenson wrote a marketing agreement for the walnut industry. "Christmas of that year," he recalls, "I received an enormous gunnysack full of Christmas packages of walnuts. It solved our Christmas-shopping problem, because we took out the packages and sent them to everybody around Washington. And then I discovered, to my chagrin, that in each package was a little card saying, 'Merry Christmas from the walnut industry to Adlai Stevenson.' "

—*Adlai's Almanac,* edited by Bessie R. James and Mary Waterstreet (Schuman)

ONE CHRISTMAS a man in Tulsa received a gaily wrapped flat envelope from his wife. Inside was a gift certificate. He read it, and read it again. Then he nearly fell over backward. The card said: "Gift certificate—to be delivered on or about August 24—a baby boy or girl." —Roger V. Devlin in Tulsa *Tribune*

A HUSBAND gave his wife a bathrobe for Christmas because, he told her as she unwrapped it, "the moment the salesgirl pulled it out, I could see you in it." With an affectionate hug his wife explained why: She had been wearing one just like it for two years.
—Neil Morgan in San Diego *Tribune*

THE CRY of the Army nurses who came into the hospital wards to give hypo injections was "Bottoms up." One popular nurse's patients chipped in at Christmastime to buy her a present, which they tagged: "To the best rear gunner in the outfit." —A. Hannah

WEALTHY Detroit matron to friend: "I gave my husband a Cadillac for Christmas so I wouldn't have anything to wrap."
—Marie Michau

SOON AFTER Christmas Macy's in New York had a visit from a boy returning a large doll, which he traded for an arsenal of water pistols. "Who on earth would give you a doll?" he was asked.

"My uncle," he said patiently. "He always does. He thinks I'm a niece." —Robert M. Yoder in *Woman's Day*

WHEN THE TIME came for the Christmas pageant, a fifth-grade teacher who encourages her class to undertake projects on its own had no idea of what she was about to see. Songs had been practiced, costumes contrived and rehearsals conducted in solemn secrecy.

The pageant fully justified her hands-off policy. First came a group of slowly marching angels—little girls dressed in white party dresses and aluminum-wrap wings. Next came Joseph, leading a donkey, played by a sturdy little girl crawling on all fours. Astride the donkey was Mary, looking radiant in her bathrobe. But next came a little girl named Helen, whose role was not clear to the teacher. She was wearing an ordinary dress and carrying a doll partly concealed under her arm. She placed the doll in the manger and quietly withdrew while the pageant continued.

When it was over the teacher, genuinely touched, hastened to congratulate the cast. She gave special praise to the girl who had directed the performance. "It was wonderful," she said, "but tell me—what role was Helen playing?"

"Helen?" said the director, a little surprised that the teacher hadn't understood. "Why, Helen was the stork."

—Charles McDowell, Jr., in Richmond *Times-Dispatch*

FACED WITH the problem of what to give her fiancé for Christmas, a friend of mine decided on an identification bracelet. On the outside she had engraved his name, rank and serial number—Lt. Lawrence J. Bishop, 0-404-9017—and, on the inside, Cathryn Miller, 36-24-36. —Kay Duplichan

DURING THE Christmas season when I went to the clinic for a checkup, there was an air of gay excitement as doctors and nurses, carrying beribboned packages, hurried by me toward a certain room. Finally my curiosity got the better of me and I asked my nurse if there was something special going on. "No," she explained laughing. "It's just that when anyone on the staff gets a 'Do Not Open Until Christmas' present, they bring it down here to the fluoroscope machine so they can see what's in it." —Rita R. Irwin

Applied Science

RECUPERATING FROM an operation I began to wonder if the young doctor who was looking after me was competent. He always had such a dreamy, faraway look in his eyes. But when the day came for him to remove my stitches he attacked the job with unusual concentration. And as each stitch came out he whispered something under his breath. When he got to the last one he held it up and beamed at me. "She loves me!" he confided gleefully.

—G. F. Krupp

WHEN HIS COMPLAINTS about the inadequate heat in his top-floor Brooklyn apartment had no effect, electronic engineer Melvin A. Carter rigged up an ingenious gadget. Attached to the thermostat, it consisted of a record player with an amplifying system arranged so that the sound was beamed down the dumb-waiter shaft to the landlord's first-floor apartment. Whenever the temperature dropped below 65 degrees, Carter's recorded voice automatically intoned, "Mr. Cadogan: Under section 225 of the Sanitary Code, a landlord who does not provide 65 degrees of heat when the outdoor temperature falls below 55 degrees is liable to a $500 fine and/or a year in jail. The temperature in this apartment is now below 65 degrees." —New York *Herald Tribune*

I WAS IN a small tavern in northern Michigan one night when the lights went off for an instant. People around me chuckled, and someone called out, "Go on home, Tom."

From a far corner an old fellow rose and stalked out, grumbling. The man on my left explained: "Tom and his wife own the dynamo up the river, and when she figures he's been here long enough she just turns off the power. Us townsfolk always see to it that he leaves right away, because the next time the lights go off they don't come back on."

—Eddie Edwards

A NEIGHBOR of ours who has three cherished orange trees had often bemoaned the fact that such devices as smudge pots and wind machines, used by the large citrus growers to combat frosts, were impractical for him. When we visited him one evening, however, we found he had solved his problem. Snug against the approaching frost nestled the three trees—each in its own electric blanket.

—Mrs. Paul C. Smith

LATE FOR AN appointment and creeping along through the heavy traffic at a snail's pace, a radio director wondered desperately how he could extricate himself. Suddenly he recalled that a certain "crime doesn't pay" program, which opened with the sound of wailing police sirens, was about to start. He turned on his car radio full blast, and the air was rent with a crescendo of shrieking sirens. Motorists ahead pulled to the curb, and the ingenious gentleman of the air waves hastened away to his appointment.

—*The Wall Street Journal*

MY 12-YEAR-OLD son had not displayed any interest in the opposite sex. Then one day he came to me and indignantly thrust a calendar-girl picture in front of me. "Isn't this just terrible?" he sputtered.

It was one of those drawings of an alluring girl provocatively leaning out of a bathtub to answer the telephone while she held an artfully draped towel across her. "Oh, oh," I thought to myself, "he's really growing up." But I wasn't sure how he expected me to react, and I hedged for time. "Why do you think it's so terrible?" I asked.

He looked at me scornfully. "Don't you see how wrong the picture is?" he exclaimed. "That girl shouldn't answer a telephone while she's in the tub. Water conducts electricity, and she could be electrocuted!"

—Florence Saltz

Cartoon Quips

FRANTIC chemist to boss: "We can't conform to these specifications. We've combined trillium, chlorophyll, irium, phosphate and X29, but there's no room left for toothpaste!"

—Bernhardt in *The Christian Science Monitor*

GIRL TO suitor: "There's no one else, Don. It's just that I'm determined there *will* be."

—Kirk in *Collier's*

DRESSMAKER measuring stout matron dictates to assistant: "Bust 32, waist 24, hips 35; scale 1½ inches to one inch." —*Punch*

ONE SENATOR to another, leaving Capitol: "I'd hate to have to go out and make a living under those laws we just passed."
—Currier in *The Coffee Break,* edited by Charles Preston (Dutton)

GUEST ON beach of Florida hotel, holding conch shell to his ear, to wife: "All *I* hear is a voice saying, '$40 a day.' "
—W. F. Brown in *The Saturday Evening Post*

TEACHER TO colleague: "Not only is he the worst behaved child in school, he has a perfect attendance record!" —Dick Turner, NEA

ONE MATRON of bridge foursome to another: "I wish you'd pay attention to the game, Adele! We're discussing Irene's new fur coat—*not* Helen's divorce suit!" —Lichty, Chicago Sun-Times Syndicate

CHAIRMAN at advertising agency meeting: "Madison Avenue! Madison Avenue! Why don't they go back to picking on Wall Street?"
—Mirachi in *The Wall Street Journal*

HUSBAND TO wife at dinner: "I think what I liked most about my mother's cooking was it didn't cost me anything."
—Bob Barnes in *The Saturday Evening Post*

MOONING teen-age daughter to mother: "Mother, were you ever in love?" —Muriel Jacobs in *The Saturday Evening Post*

ONE CHORUS girl to another: "And when I threatened to tell his wife you should have seen the furs fly."
—Reamer Keller, King Features

MAN TO family climbing out of car: "Well, we finally found a parking space. Does anybody remember why we're here?"
—George Clark, Chicago Tribune-New York News Syndicate

ONE WEDDING guest to another: "Her 'something borrowed' is my boy friend." —Charles Skiles, King Features

HOUSEWIFE hanging out huge wash to neighbor: "One advantage our mothers had—not everything in the house was washable!" —George Clark, Chicago Tribune-New York News Syndicate

Changing Times

REMEMBER WHEN your mother used to say, "Go to your room—" This was a terrible penalty. Now when a mother says the same thing, a kid goes to his room. There he's got an air-conditioner, a TV set, an inter-com, a short-wave radio—he's better off than he was in the first place.

—Sam Levenson, quoted by Tom O'Malley and Bob Cunniff, Newspaper Features

AN ANN ARBOR professor realized how old he was getting when he asked his young daughter what she was studying. "Oh," she replied, "all about some jerk named Hitler."

—Bennett Cerf in *The Saturday Review*

WHERE ARE the days when men used to admire the entire woman? If current trends continue we may have to breed women the way they breed chickens—either all bosom or all leg.

—Grace Downs in *Look*

WHEN I WAS an undergraduate a middle-aged widow who taught at a mountain school was working for her degree at a summer session. In gym class where we clumsily attempted the Virginia reel, she volunteered to set us straight. Soon we were doing it perfectly. She brushed off our grateful thanks. "Shucks," she said, "I learned to dance when it was a sin." —Wileta Mathes

AN OLD FRIEND was living in solitary grandeur in her three-story mansard-roofed mansion which was all that was left of the family estate. Her ancestral acres had been sold for building lots and hundreds of one-story houses had mushroomed up around the mansion. When her grandchildren from the West Coast came to visit her she decided to give a party and invite the children from the development. The next day I asked her how the party had gone. I knew she had planned it in the grand manner with a magician and ventriloquist.

"Times have changed even more than I ever dreamed," she said. "The children said they were sick of looking at magicians and ventriloquists on television. All they wanted to do all afternoon was slide down my banisters!" —Margaret B. Link

REMEMBER WHEN the only difficult thing about parking a car was getting the girl to agree to it?

—Randy Merriman, quoted in Milwaukee *Journal*

ONCE YOU COULD fix a broken chair with a length of wire. Today the chair *is* a length of wire. —Marjorie Murch Stanley in *Quote*

BARGING IN next door one afternoon to borrow a cup of sugar I found my neighbor sitting in her darkened living room watching a movie on television.

"Come in," she said—and burst out laughing. "I was just thinking how little things change. Here I am playing hooky from my housework to watch the same movie I played hooky from school to see!"

—Joy Gallagher

THE WORLD started going to smash about the time it abandoned the hand-cranked ice-cream freezer, the finest device ever invented for teaching youth that work has its rewards. —Cleveland *News*

"WHEN I WAS your age, young lady," her mother said sternly, "a nice girl didn't think of holding a man's hand."

"But, Mother," the daughter protested, "nowadays a nice girl *has* to hold a man's hand."

—*Expanding Circle,* quoted in *Woodmen of the World Magazine*

MAN gazing into liquor-store window to companion: "Remember the fun it was fighting a cold before the antihistamines?"

—Fritz Wilkinson cartoon in *Collier's*

For the Health of It

Speaking of ailments—don't.—Hot Springs, Ark., *Sentinel-Record*

HUSBAND TO wife trying on fur coat: "For heaven's sake, Ruth, there are other ways to fight a cold!"

—Franklin Folger cartoon, Chicago Sun-Times Syndicate

A WALKING virus case blaming vitamins and the new drugs for his uncertain status: "I've been sick on my feet now for two months. I'm too strong to get sick and too weak to get well."

—Hugh Park in Atlanta *Journal*

WHEN HIS doctor advised a change of climate the eastern city-dweller went looking for a healthful place to live in the Southwest. In one small Arizona town he approached an old-timer sitting on the steps of the general store.

Preventive Medicine

MY GREAT AUNT had raised nine children on a Michigan farm, fed them and the farm hands, done all her own housework and helped with the outdoor chores. And she had never been ill in her life. Finally her family doctor asked her secret. "I constantly see young women," he said, "who have only one or two children and whose homes are full of gadgets to lighten work, but who suffer from nervous exhaustion or psychosomatic aches and pains. How is it that you managed never to have a nervous breakdown?"

"You know, Doctor," she replied, "I've always *wanted* to have a nervous breakdown. But every time I was about to get around to it, it was time to fix somebody a meal." —Beach Conger

"Say," he asked, "what's the death rate around here?"

"Same as it is back east, bub," came the answer. "One to a person."

The Crucible

MATRON TO greeting-card clerk: "Do you have a get-well card that hints she's not as sick as she thinks she is?"

—Corka cartoon in *Farm Journal*

ANYBODY WHO can swallow a pill at a drinking fountain deserves to get well. —Richard Armour

OVERHEARD ON a Madison Avenue bus: "He's been quite sick. He has that disease—I've forgotten the name—where the red popsicles eat up all the white popsicles." —Mrs. W. K. Rienecke

HUSBAND TO wife opening envelope as he serves her breakfast in bed: "It's a get-well-quick card—from me!"

—Don Tobin cartoon, King Features

EPITAPH ON the grave of a hypochondriac: "I *told* you I was sick!" —Phil Stone in Toronto *Telegram*

Jalopies I Cursed and Loved

Condensed from Holiday

John Steinbeck

ONE SUNDAY afternoon I drove from Garrison-on-Hudson to New York, one unit in a creeping parade of metal, inching along bumper to bumper. Every so often we passed a car pulled off the road with motor trouble, its driver and passengers waiting patiently for a tow car or a mechanic. Not one of the drivers seemed even to consider fixing the difficulty himself.

I began to think of old times and old cars. Understand, I don't want to go back to those old dogs. I love the fine efficient car I have. But in those days you fixed your own car or you didn't go anyplace.

The first car I remember in the little town where I was born was, I think, a Reo with a chain drive and a steering bar. It was owned by a veterinary who got himself a bad name for owning it. He seemed disloyal to horses. We didn't like that car. We shouted insults at it as it splashed by. Then, gradually, more automobiles came into town. We didn't have a car for many years. My parents never accepted the time-payment plan. To them it was a debt like any other debt, and to them debt was a sin.

Now it took a long time for a car to get in a condition where I could afford it—roughly about 15 years. My first two cars were Model T's. They never got so beat up that you couldn't somehow make them run. The first one was a touring car. The steering wheel was cracked so that if you put any weight on it, it pinched your fingers when you let up. The back seat was for tools, wire and spare tires. I still confuse that car with my first love affair. The two were inextricably involved.

I had it a long time. I remember how it used to shudder and sigh when I cranked it and how its crank would kick back viciously. It was a mean car. It loved no one. It ran in spurts and seemed to be as much influenced by magic as by mechanics.

My second Model T was a sedan. The back seat had a high ceiling and was designed to look like a small drawing room. It had lace curtains and cut-glass vases for flowers. It needed only a coal grate to make it a perfect Victorian living room. And sometimes it served as a boudoir. There were gray silk roller shades you could pull down to make it cozy and private.

But ladylike as this car was, it had also the indestructibility of ladies. Once I stalled in a snowstorm a quarter of a mile from my mountain cabin; I drained the water from the radiator and abandoned the car for the winter. From my window I could see it hub-deep in the snow. In the spring I dug it out. A kettle of hot water in the radiator, and that rolling parlor started right off. It ran all summer.

The Model T's cooling system was based on the law that warm water rises and cool water sinks. It doesn't do this very fast, but then Model T's didn't run very fast. When a Model T sprung a radiator leak the remedy was a handful of corn meal. The hot water cooked the meal to mush and it plugged the leak. A little bag of meal was standard equipment in the tool kit.

In time I bought an open Chevrolet which looked like a black bathtub on wheels, a noble car full of innovations. I was living in Los Angeles at the time and my mother was coming to visit me. Before I went to meet her at the station I washed the car, and noticed that the radiator was leaking. We had no corn meal in the kitchen, but there was oatmeal, which is even better because it is more gooey. I put a cup of it in the radiator.

Now that Chevrolet had a water pump to circulate the water faster. I had forgotten. The trip to the station must have cooked the oatmeal thoroughly.

My mother arrived wearing a hat with many flowers. She sat proudly beside me in the front seat as we started home. Suddenly there was an explosion. A wall of oatmeal rose into the air, cleared the windshield, splashed on my mother's hat and ran down her face. And it didn't stop there. We went through Los Angeles traffic exploding oatmeal in short bursts. We arrived home practically in flames because the water system was clogged and the limping car gave off clouds of smoke that smelled like burned oatmeal, and was. It took a long time to scrape my mother. She had never really believed in automobiles and this didn't help.

About this time the Depression came along and increased the complications. Gasoline was hard to come by. One of my friends, wishing to impress his date, would drive into a filling station, extend two fingers out the window, out of the girl's sight, and say, "Fill her up." Then with two gallons in the tank he would drive grandly away.

In the days of my nonsensical youth there were all kinds of practices which were normal then but now seem just plain nuts. A friend of mine had a Model T coupé which rested in a lot behind his house and after a while he became convinced someone was stealing his gasoline. The tank was under the front seat and could ordinarily be protected by locking the doors. But this car had no locks. First he left notes on the seat begging people not to steal his gasoline, and when this didn't work he rigged an elaborate trap. He designed his snare so that if anyone opened the car door the horn would blow and a shotgun would fire.

Now, how it happened we don't know. Perhaps a drop of water, perhaps a slight earthquake. Anyway, in the middle of the night the horn went off. My friend leaped from bed, put on a bathrobe and a hat, I don't know why, raced out the back door shouting, "Got you!"—yanked open the car door and the shotgun blew his hat to bits. It was his best hat, too.

With the Depression came an era of automotive nonsense. It was no longer possible to buy a small car cheaply, but big cars could be had for a song because they cost so much to run. At that time I had an old, four-cylinder Dodge. It was a very desirable car —supposed to run forever, no matter how much oil it pumped. But gradually I detected symptoms of demise. We had developed an instinct for this. The trick was to trade your car in just before it exploded.

I wanted something small, but that I couldn't have. For my Dodge and $10 I got a Marmon, a great, low, racy car with aluminum body and aluminum crankcase—a lovely thing with a deep purring roar and a top speed of nearly 100 miles an hour. It was the best car I had ever owned. The only trouble was that it got about eight miles to the gallon of gasoline.

One day while I was driving, there was a disturbing click in the rear end and then a crash. With a hand jack I gradually raised the rear end onto concrete blocks, until it stuck up in the air like an anopheles mosquito. Then I drained the rear end, removed the covers. The ring gear had sheared three teeth. A new gear and pinions installed would come to $95.

I walked to a wrecking yard three miles away. They had no Marmons. It took a week to find one of my vintage. After two days of bargaining I finally got the price down to $6. I had to remove the ring gear and pinions myself, but the yard generously loaned tools. This took two days. Then, with my treasures back at my house, I spent several days more lying on my back fitting the new parts. I don't ever remember being dirtier or more uncomfortable. Kids from as far as six blocks away gathered to give satiric advice.

Finally all was in place. I had to make new gaskets out of cardboard and tighten everything all around. I put in new grease, let the rear end gently down. There was a large and friendly delegation to see the trial run—neighbors, kids, dogs, skeptics, well-wishers. A parrot next door kept saying "Nuts!" in a loud, squawking voice.

I started the engine. It sounded wonderful. I put the car in gear and crept out to the street. I got half a block before the rear end disintegrated with a crash like the unloading of a gravel car. Even the housing of the rear end was shattered. I don't know what I did wrong, but what I did was final. I sold the Marmon as it stood for $12.

It's all different now. Everything is chrome and shiny paint. A car used to be as close and known and troublesome and dear as a wife. Now we drive about in strangers. It's more comfortable, sure, but something has been lost. I hope I never get it back.

Clouded Crystal Ball, Inc.

FROM THE July 1899 *Scientific American:* "The improvement in city conditions by the general adoption of the motorcar can hardly be overestimated. Streets —clean, dustless and odorless— with light rubber-tired vehicles moving swiftly and noiselessly over their smooth expanse would eliminate a greater part of the nervousness, distraction and strain of modern metropolitan life."

—Reprinted in *Scientific American*

DURING A 1906 debate on expenditures for the Air Force, an unidentified Congressman demanded, "Why all the fuss about airplanes—the Army has one, hasn't it?"

—Quoted by Maj. Gen. Clements McMullen in *Quote*

SORTING A collection of books left to me by my grandfather, I came across a dictionary printed in 1901. I leafed through it, and my eyes fell upon "uranium." The definition read: "A worthless white metal, not found in the United States." —Owen W. Stout

LEWIS L. STRAUSS, Chairman of the Atomic Energy Commission, likes to illustrate with this story that invention has not come to the end of its tether:

In the 1870's a bishop who had charge of a small denominational college made his annual visit and stayed with the president. The bishop boasted a firm belief that everything that could be invented had been invented. The college president thought otherwise. "In 50 years," he said, "men will learn how to fly like birds."

The bishop, shocked, replied, "Flight is reserved for angels and you have been guilty of blasphemy."

The name of the bishop was Milton Wright and back home he had two small sons—Orville and Wilbur. —New York *Times*

OVER Fred Astaire's fireplace in Beverly Hills is a yellowed MGM interoffice studio memo—souvenir of the dancer's first screen test. Dated 1933 and sent by the testing director to his superior, it reads: "Fred Astaire. Can't act. Slightly bald. Can dance a little." —J. Z. in *Cue*

Critics at Large

FANNY BRICE, watching swimmer Esther Williams do a scene in an MGM movie, was asked if she thought Miss Williams was a star. "Wet, she's a star. Dry, she ain't," Miss Brice replied.

—Leonard Lyons in *Argosy*

JAMES MELTON summed up a Broadway flop: "A cast of 50, buried in one plot."

—Earl Wilson, Hall Syndicate

HUSBAND TO wife as they leave movie: "Well, if you *must* know, it's given me a colossal, sensational, stupendous, terrific, breathtaking headache!"

—Robyn cartoon in *London Opinion*

PRODUCER Alfred de Liagre took his small son and daughter to a Broadway musical. Just before the curtain went up he cautioned, "Remember now, no talk, no coughing, no fidgeting."

"But, Papa," persisted five-year-old Christine, "if I get sick, may I vomit?"

De Liagre leaned over to the man in front of him, predicted ruefully, "She'll grow up to be a critic!"

—John Mason Brown, quoted by Bennett Cerf in *The Saturday Review*

CLIFTON FADIMAN, reviewing an autobiography: "As far as I can see, the book has only one defect: poor choice of subject matter."

ASKED HIS opinion of a movie which had received a tremendous build-up, George S. Kaufman said, "Frankly, I was underwhelmed." —Leonard Lyons

MAN, reading novel, to wife: "If there's a hero in this book, he should kill the author!"

—Reamer Keller cartoon in Chicago *Tribune*

"Parsifal is the kind of opera that starts at six o'clock," wrote music critic David Randolph, "and after it has been going three hours you look at your watch and it says 6:20." —Clifton Fadiman in *The American Treasury* (Harper)

WHEN THE Kinsey Report on sexual behavior came out a few years ago an executive at RCA, after skimming its pages, observed tartly, "I think the good doctor is more interested in High Frequency than he is in High Fidelity."

—Bennett Cerf in *The Saturday Review*

DIRECTOR Lloyd Bacon, after seeing one of those swash-buckling movies, remarked, "It buckled where it should have swashed."

—Erskine Johnson in *Photoplay*

HEYWOOD BROUN, while serving the New York *Tribune* as drama critic, was once sued for libel by an actor whose performance, he wrote, was the worst he'd ever seen. The actor lost his suit. Shortly Broun sat in judgment on the unfortunate again. His comment? "Mr. Doe's performance was not up to his usual standard."

—Richard Maney, *Fanfare, The Confessions of a Press Agent* (Harper)

THE LATE Professor Barrett Wendell, after seeing a performance of the opera *L'Enfant Prodigue:* "The only signs of a Biblical source were the fatted calves."

—Robert Withington

Sunday-School Lessons

ASKED WHAT he'd learned at Sunday school, the ten-year-old began, "Well, our teacher told us about when God sent Moses behind the enemy lines to rescue the Israelites from the Egyptians. When they came to the Red Sea Moses called for the engineers to build a pontoon bridge. After they had all crossed they looked back and saw the Egyptian tanks coming. Quick as a flash Moses radioed headquarters on his walkie-talkie to send bombers to blow up the bridge and saved the Israelites."

"Bobby," exclaimed his startled mother, "is that really the way your teacher told that story?"

"Well, not exactly. But if I told it her way, you'd never believe it!"

—Dr. John F. Anderson in Dallas *News*

IN DENVER the members of a Sunday-school class were asked to set down their favorite Biblical truths. One youngster laboriously printed, "Do one to others as others do one to you."

—Lee Olson in Denver *Post*

THE first-graders at an Episcopal Sunday school in San Diego were told to draw their conceptions of the Flight into Egypt. One little girl turned in a picture of an airplane with three people in the back, all with halos, and a fourth up front without one. Perplexed about the fourth person, the teacher asked who it was. "Oh," replied the youngster, "that's Pontius, the pilot." —Mary L. Fisher

LOOKING at a Sunday-school picture of the Christians being thrown to the lions, the child pointed and sobbed out, "That poor little lion ain't got no Christian!"

THE Lord's Prayer has had to withstand considerable abuse, especially from children trying to learn it from poor enunciators or from mumbling congregations.

One little boy was heard to pray, "Harold be Thy name." Another begged, "Give us this day our jelly bread." A New York child petitioned, "Lead us not into Penn station."

—St. Louis Cathedral *Bulletin*

Innocents Abroad

A YOUNG California couple took a visiting aunt for a drive, and pointed out a fig tree as one of the sights. "Fig tree!" exclaimed the elderly woman. "That can't be a fig tree."

"Certainly is," said her niece. "What makes you think different?"

"Well," said the aunt, subsiding a little, "I just thought . . . surely . . . the leaves must be bigger than that!"

—Sherry North, quoted in Toledo *Blade*

MY SISTER-IN-LAW from the backwoods of North Carolina was seeing the sights in Washington, D.C. At one street corner she paid no attention at all to a large square light which read, DON'T WALK. She was halfway across the street when a policeman came running and demanded, "What's the matter, lady, can't you read?"

"Why, yes," she said, and he continued, "Well, then, why on earth are you deliberately walking across this street when that light up there says DON'T WALK?"

Much surprised, she replied in all seriousness, "Why, my goodness, I thought that was an advertisement for buses!"

—Gloria Vitello Tyson

IT HAPPENED during June 1944, when the press camp of General Patton's army was pinned down in a Normandy hayfield. Before dawn I was awakened by excited gabble of the patrol policing the camp. Their topic was a pungent, mysterious aroma which had flooded the area and which none of them could identify. Perhaps Hitler, maddened by reverses in the West, was starting a poison-gas attack? An alert had been telephoned to an outfit trained for such emergencies.

As day broke, there came the sound of an arriving vehicle. After a quick investigation, a new voice, disgusted and weary, snapped, "So this is why we have to stumble out in the middle of the night, load a truck with gas masks, chemicals and impregnated garments—just because a dumb bunch of city wise guys don't recognize the smell of new-mown hay!"

—Richard L. Stokes

AN ACCOUNT executive of a Cincinnati stock-and-bond firm telephoned a woman client who had purchased her first stock, ten shares of Proctor & Gamble, and excitedly told her that Proctor & Gamble just announced they were going to split.

"Oh, what a shame!" replied the woman. "They've been together so long!" —Edwin Tessel

STOPPED BY a motorcycle policeman for driving too fast, I didn't try to argue with the law. But from the back seat my aunt piped up helpfully in my defense, "Why, officer, she wasn't driving any faster than she always does."

—Nancy M. Sherman

A SPORTSMAN had plans drawn for a residential camp in Wisconsin's north woods. He sent the plans to a local carpenter with instructions to begin construction immediately. A few days later the client received a post card stating: "The plans are all wrong. I can do nothing until you get them straightened out. If I was to build that house the way it's planned, you'd have two bathrooms!"

—*National Architect*

The Hunting Season

GUIDE, who has lost way, to disgruntled hunters: "I *am* the best guide in Maine, only I think we're in Canada now."

—Rodrigues cartoon in *Sports Illustrated*

MY SISTER wanted her new husband to take her deer hunting with him. A serious-minded hunter, he said she could go along if she obeyed the rules. "But none of that feminine-intuition stuff," he warned. "Use your head. Be logical."

They had just walked over the first hill when a deer charged through the brush ahead of them. As they paused, along came another one in hot pursuit. My sister raised her gun and brought down the second deer. With sweat on his brow my brother-in-law ran to the fallen animal. "Say, how did you know this was a legal buck?" he asked. "*I* couldn't see him through the brush."

"Using my head, like you said, I figured the one doing the chasing was the buck," she explained. "And then, logically, I figured if he was old enough to chase a doe he was old enough to shoot. So I shot him." —Darleen Harader

A FORMER Fifth Avenue mansion now houses a school for models. Mounted heads of moose and lions no longer fill the trophy room—instead it contains pictures of wealthy and famous husbands captured by school graduates.

—Robert Sylvester, Chicago Tribune-New York News Syndicate

WOMAN hunter, about to fire, to husband: "Of course I heard it moo—why shouldn't a moose moo?" —Al Ross cartoon in *The American Legion Magazine*

WITH MY brother, a war veteran, I was visiting the National Gallery in Washington. Both of us admired Renoir's beautiful painting of the nude Diana and the deer which she has just slain. I moved on, but my brother continued to stand meditatively in front of Diana. A little embarrassed, I wondered if people would notice how long he had been staring at the nude. At last he turned from it to say thoughtfully, "You know, that arrow would never have killed that deer." —Loris Troup

IN A Texas hunting lodge the sportsmen burn their names into the wall, along with the description of what they've bagged. Beside one name is written: "Killed: One case of Scotch." —AP

AN ENGLISHMAN once went out shooting with a pointer he had borrowed from a friend who was a crack shot. He himself was a very poor shot and missed again and again, the pointer each time looking at him in bewilderment.

Finally the dog set a pheasant right out in an open field, and glanced back at the approaching man as much as to say, "Now, here's a perfectly good shot. For pity's sake, see if you can do anything this time."

The pheasant rose and flew off;

the man missed twice. Whereupon the pointer sat down on his haunches, raised his nose to high heaven and howled long and dolorously. Then, with never another look at the amateur huntsman, he turned and trotted home.

—Samuel A. Derieux, *Animal Personalities* (Doubleday)

WOMAN talking on phone: "Harry had good luck on his hunting trip—he got back alive."

—Mel Millar cartoon in *National Safety News*

A FARMER in Craig County, Okla., which pays a bounty for every wolf killed, made no attempt—despite frequent opportunities—to kill a wolf that lived on his property and constantly raided local chicken coops. Finally his neighbors demanded to know why.

"Well," he explained, "I got bounties off her nine pups this spring and bounties off her seven last year. Guess I'm just too softhearted, thinking of a mother and her young."

—Homer M. Stivers in *True*

Individual Approach

TWO MIDDLE-AGED schoolteachers who rented sight-unseen a camp in New Hampshire were dismayed by its isolation. After a few frightening nights they offered the old fellow who supplied them with ice and firewood a small sum weekly if he would sleep on a cot on their screened porch every night. He agreed, and my friends enjoyed the summer so much that they took the camp the following summer. They immediately looked up old Joe, but were stopped in their tracks by the sign above his door:

JOE JIMPSON
ICE WOOD BAIT ODD JOBS
NARVUS WIMMEN SLEPT WITH
25 CENTS A NITE

—Agnes R. McCarthy

WHEN THE musical *South Pacific* was a Broadway smash hit, a Greenwich, Conn., teacher, after a long wait, managed to get matinee tickets for her class and triumphantly conducted them to the theater for the big experience.

During intermission, to make sure everything was all right, she counted heads. Sure enough, there were 21 heads—but the 21st one was bald! It developed, upon her alarmed questioning, that one of the brighter boys had sold his ticket to the middle-aged gent for $20 as the class was on its way into the theater; then he hiked off to a movie.

—Dorothy Kilgallen, King Features

DURING World War II an especially good-looking WAC, scheduled for a minor operation at an Army camp hospital, found herself covered with only a sheet on a wheeltable parked in the corridor. Presently a man clothed in white came briskly along, raised the sheet, examined her, then walked on. Immediately behind him came another white-clad man, who repeated the examination and moved on. Then a third figure hove in sight. "For heaven's sake," cried the young lady, "when are you going to operate?"

The white-coated lad paused with the sheet upraised and replied cheerfully, "Darned if I know, baby—I just gave the orderly three bucks for this outfit, like the rest of those guys."

—C. M. Voorhees in *True*

AD IN THE Yuma, Ariz., *Daily Sun:* "WANTED: Part-time job for 11-year-old boy for the summer. Necessary to build his $elf-e$teem. Capable geologist from spending much time in desert hunting valuable rocks to decorate mother's house. Experienced as a carpenter's helper. Guaranteed to put 100 nails in each board. Experienced as a painter and can be relied on to let paint dry thoroughly in brush before second coat. Has unspoken agreement with lawn mower. If mower is too tired, he won't push it. Has experience as a designer and inventor. Can give intricate details on how to build a rocket to fly to the moon. For appointment call SU 3-7649."

A CUSTOMER in a Copenhagen department store complained to the management about the attendant in the ladies' rest room, who had given her a frosty stare when she failed to leave a generous tip.

"Why, we have no attendant in the ladies' room," said the manager. And a check revealed that the "attendant" was a woman who had wandered in for a rest a year ago. While relaxing with her knitting the woman had received coins from patrons who thought she was the attendant. Recognizing opportunity when it knocked, the woman had come in regularly ever since, netting while she knitted.

—Walter Kiernan, WJZ

Artistic Touches

A FEW YEARS ago Grandma Moses got a hurry call from a New York gallery for two paintings at $100. But her pictures had been selling so rapidly that she was down to one, a snowy farm scene. So what did the dear, sweet, naive old lady do? She cut the canvas in two, framed both ends and sold them without batting an eye.

—Jimmy Savage in Chicago *Tribune*

SHE WAS five feet tall, weighed about 180 pounds. Day after day she waddled in to see the Vienna Collections at the National Gallery in Washington. Always she came out smiling. "I love art," she told the receptionist one day. "Beside those big Rubens nudes I don't even feel fat."

—*Pathfinder*

AMERICAN matron in the Louvre to her companions: "Now I'll read the guidebook and you look. We'll get through much faster that way."

—Emily Kimbrough, *So Near and Yet So Far* (Harper)

WHEN A certain well-known artist arrived at his studio one day, his model, who had been posing for his unfinished study of a nude, started toward the screen to disrobe. "Don't undress," the artist told her. "I shan't be painting today. I have a bad headache, and I'm just going to make myself a cup of tea and go home."

"Oh, please let me make it for you," the model said. The artist thanked her and told her to make one for herself, too. Just as they began to drink, however, the artist heard familiar footsteps in the hall.

"Good heavens!" he exclaimed. "Here comes my wife! Get those clothes off—quick!"

—G.B.

A WEALTHY New Yorker in quest of an even wealthier widow consulted a marriage broker. A candidate described as "a girl who looks like a picture" took the client's fancy, and the broker arranged for them to meet her at a corner table in a certain Broadway night spot. But the client winced as he spotted the woman, conspicuous by her cauliflower ears, a nose that resembled a bent fender and a hank of hair that fell over her forehead like a dangling participle. "I thought," he scolded the go-between, "that you said she looked like a picture."

The broker shrugged. "Either you like Picasso or you don't!"

—Hy Gardner in New York *Herald Tribune*

AN ACQUAINTANCE of my husband had monopolized the conversation with a monologue on modern art. When he departed I asked my husband why he hadn't warned me Mr. Bibbs was an artist. "Oh, he isn't," Jim replied. "He just babbles in art."

—Camille Madden Stewart

ASKED HOW he achieved such natural, delicate flesh tints on his nudes, the painter Renoir is said to have replied, "I just keep painting and painting until I feel like pinching—then I know it's right."

—*This Week Magazine*

MARNE EAMES, who was with the New York Museum of Modern Art at the time, tells of noticing a nice-looking little old man one day hunting carefully through the prints on sale. After long consideration he picked out a picture called "Whistle Stop"—a rather stark painting of a cluster of shacks on a hillside and, small in the distance, a train.

The little man paid for the picture, waited patiently for it to be wrapped and walked briskly through the revolving door leading to the street. But instead of going out he made the complete revolution and popped back in to confront Marne sternly. "I don't want you to think I like modern art," he said. "I just like trains!"

—Claire MacMurray in Cleveland *Plain Dealer*

In Transit

WHEN A young man in uniform and a girl boarded our train holding hands, it occasioned little interest on the part of the other passengers. It was not long, however, before they were the center of attention. Oblivious to the rest of us, they put on a love scene to rival the best Hollywood has to offer. As the train reached the young lady's destination and she rose to depart, we all waited for what we were sure would be a cataclysmic farewell kiss. But the girl sent the entire car into peals of laughter when she gravely shook the young man's hand and said, "I'm very glad to have met you!" —Mrs. Roy M. Matthews, Jr.

FROM THE Holland, Mich., *Evening Sentinel:* "WANTED—Man with car and controversial nature to share car pool to downtown Grand Rapids. Must be willing to take opposite side in all discussions."

EXCHANGE between two homeward-bound commuters:

"And can you imagine," one sighed, "we're having company for dinner tonight!"

"Ye gods!" said the other. "I hope it isn't us!" —Paul Norton

IT WAS rush hour on the New York subway, but I had managed to get a seat and was absorbed in conversation with my boy friend, who stood in front of me. Suddenly the woman beside me cut in, "Miss, would you mind changing the subject and talk about the weather or some other uninteresting topic?" I stared at her with amazement, but before I could say anything she continued, "You see, I get up early, stand up all day, rush home to cook dinner and then do the dishes. The only chance I get for a nap is on the way home, and your conversation is so interesting it's keeping me awake." I changed the subject. —Christine Camardella

On a Los Angeles bus a lady seated herself in the only vacant place, next to a rather tipsy gentleman. Opening her purse she took out a map of Hawaii, unfolded it and started to peruse it intently. She hadn't noticed her seat partner studying the map, too, until he tapped her on the shoulder and said solicitously, "Madam, you're on the wrong bus!" —*Script*

The subway shuttle from New York City's Times Square to Grand Central Station was packed, and since I had baggage—and plenty of time—I stepped back to wait for an empty train. "When does the next train get in?" I asked a guard.

"Why didn't you take the one that just pulled out?" he asked reproachfully. "There won't be another one for three minutes!" —Helene C. Safford

Man on bus to fellow straphanger: "The long tiresome ride to work doesn't bother me at all. It's *getting* there that I don't like." —Bernhardt cartoon in *Pipe Dreams*

On a business trip to Boston a government executive was looking forward to reading a book on the train. But the girl sharing the seat had other ideas, kept advancing conversational feelers. After her fifth attempt he turned to her and asked, "Do you like to read?"

"Oh, yes. I love it," she replied eagerly, hoping he'd start a discussion of his book.

Instead he tore out the first three chapters and handed them to her. "I've finished these," he said, "so you start on them."

For the rest of their trip he ripped out the pages as he read them and handed them to his silenced companion. —Joe Harrington in Boston *Post*

Quotable Quotes

Robert Benchley: Probably the most common of all antagonisms arises from a man's taking a seat beside you on a train, a seat to which he is completely entitled.

Anonymous: No woman ever takes another woman's advice about frocks. Naturally you don't ask the enemy how to win the war. —New York *Times*

Dr. Konrad Lorenz, zoologist: I believe I've found the missing link between animal and civilized man. It is us. —Woodrow Wirsig in *Woman's Home Companion*

Oscar Wilde: In America the young are always ready to give those who are older than themselves the full benefit of their inexperience.

Mark Twain: When some men discharge an obligation you can hear the report for miles around. —Quoted by Donald Day

Dan Bennett: The reason why the Ten Commandments are short and clear is that they were handed down direct, not through several committees. —*The Saturday Evening Post*

Luke Neely: The way blood flows in them these days, it's easy to see why they're called traffic arteries. —*Quote*

Portuguese proverb: Visits always give pleasure—if not the coming, then the going.

Frank Lloyd Wright: A doctor can bury his mistakes, but an architect can only advise his client to plant vines. —Quoted in Boston *Daily Globe*

Herbert V. Prochnow: What the world needs is a good loudspeaker for the still, small voice. —*The Saturday Evening Post*

Hartwell, Ga., *Sun*: There is one thing to be said about ignorance —it sure causes a lot of interesting arguments.

Marcelene Cox: No man knows his true character until he has run out of gas, purchased something on the instalment plan and raised an adolescent. —*Ladies' Home Journal*

Abe Martin: A good listener is usually thinkin' about somethin' else. —John F. Dille Syndicate

I Keep Hearing Voices

By Cornelia Otis Skinner

IT COMES as a shock suddenly to discover in oneself some eccentricity of behavior which one may have had for years without ever before being aware of it. Take voices, for instance. I find, to my fascination, that many persons, myself in particular, have a curious collection of varying voices.

I don't mean accents picked up during exposure to regional pronunciation. (I return from a trip through the South with an accent of Georgia peach-fuzz, while 24 hours in London finds me as British as a Trafalgar lion given the power of speech.) I refer to the tone and manner of delivery we use on specific occasions.

For example, the ways in which people address the elderly. It seems to be a universal conclusion that to be advanced in years means *ipso facto* to be advanced in deafness. Whoever is presented to, say, a venerable old gentleman starts conversing in a deferential bellow. The opposite approach is the hospital voice of mute concern coupled with a note of awe indicating that to grow old automatically means to grow holy.

I have a cousin who is a chipper 89 and when I've introduced people to her I have watched them shake her hand as if it might be a fragile bluebell and speak with the solemn reverence of addressing a saint not long for this world. Actually the old girl is about as fragile as a sturdy oak, has probably just downed a double whiskey-sour and is rarin' to get to the Canasta table.

Certain variations in voices seem to be peculiar to male behavior—as the looking-forward-to-breakfast halloo, particularly on Pullman trains at an early hour when you're trying to sleep. But women are not without their own peculiar noises of enthusiasm. Take, for example, the chance meeting of former schoolmates after the hiatus of years. All of a sudden the staggering fact dawns that the one is . . . not surely *Mary Smith!!!* and the other . . . it isn't possible, *Sally Jones!!!* The emotion of recognition is expressed in the mounting melodics of slightly hysterical sirens—and I don't refer to the sort who sat on rocks and lured mariners with dulcet sounds.

Then there is the delivery the female uses when talking to her own child in the presence of company. Plunging into a dewy-eyed motherhood act, she lilts out sweet suggestions such as, "Isn't it time we went to beddy-bye?" while what she'd like to shrill out is, "You little pain-in-the-neck, get the hell up to bed!" Even when the child grows older the mother employs a parlance suggestive of a Victorian elocution mistress giving the proper reading of "Birds in their little nests agree." As my own son once rudely summed it up, "For Pete's sake, Mom, when you're talking about me do you have to *sing?*"

Of the barnyard imitations and birdcalls women employ when addressing household pets, it is almost too embarrassing to speak. A shameless weakness for dogs releases from me a flow of baby talk and babbling asininities. My dogs don't seem to mind, but my family does. My parakeet voice is also pretty dreadful, being a stream of baby jargon in a falsetto soprano similar to a leaking steam valve. In fact, all domestic animals appear to reduce me to a state of infantilism, and I have even heard myself addressing a police horse as though it were swaddled in diapers and cooing in a bassinet.

I am aware that I have a voice of cheer, full of ersatz sunshine that makes its nauseating appearance when I am suddenly confronted by the children of my friends—young creatures on whom I've not set eyes for years. This voice with hypocritical eagerness utters banalities like, "How's the new math teacher?" or, "Your dad says you're coming along just fine with your surfboard!"

Only a week ago I shared a train seat with an attractive young woman who turned out to be the daughter of former neighbors. I didn't recognize her until she introduced herself saying that she was Penelope E. I immediately came out with a loud "Why Penny *Pen!*" and pumping her hand with splendid vigor exclaimed, "Last time I saw you, you were covered with poison ivy!" What she was covered with then was discomfort. Obviously she hadn't been called the distressing nickname in years. However, she smiled indulgently and replied politely to my elephantine inquiries as to how was the family, did she enjoy school and mercy it wasn't possible that she had graduated from *college!* Shortly Penny Pen, under pretext of smoking a cigarette, sought refuge in another car.

Another locution I have discovered is my doctor voice. Not the confiding mutter used in situations of illness or consultation, but the one I catch myself using when I meet one of the medical profession socially. Possibly out of a desire to give the impression that I have no need for his professional services, I talk with great animation in tones vibrant with radiant health. If he happens to be a psychiatrist also, I have the disquieting feeling that the chair I am sitting on is about to let down into a couch and that my every gesture is indicative of deep-rooted neuroses. The result is a careful enunciation to show how frightfully normal I am.

However, there is nothing to equal my talking-with-a-foreigner delivery. And I do not refer to someone who speaks only a foreign tongue, with whom one decides the only means of communication is through a bellow of English. I mean the cultured linguist who speaks my language with far greater elegance than I. If through the perfection of his Oxford verbiage there comes the slightest hint of foreign accent, I slow down to LP speed, mouthing each syllable with meticulous deliberation and using the basic words of a *First Primer*. It is the form of painstaking peroration William Penn must have used when explaining his treaty to the Indians.

Then there is my chatting-with-clergymen parlance. The sight of a clerical collar, and I go right into my voice of piety: a combination of the hostess of a Cape Cod tea shoppe and Beth in *Little Women,* hushed and hallowed, as though we were about to step into the next room and view the remains. It is somewhat reassuring to note that others converse with parsons in the same funereal manner. It must be one of the more doleful exactions of the dedicated life.

Finally there is my losing-interest voice, which is less a voice than a fade-out. This creeps slowly upon me during some interminable tete-à-tete with, say, a golf enthusiast or someone just back from Europe and determined to present an unillustrated travelogue. What issues from my mouth is quite mechanical; in fact, I usually have no idea what I am saying. This is disturbing for it creates that eerie sensation of standing outside yourself and listening to a complete stranger.

This listening to myself is making me uncomfortably self-conscious. Perhaps I had better stop enumerating all my varying forms of speech. Perhaps, as a matter of fact, in certain situations it might be best for me to stop speaking altogether.

Battle of the Sexes

Neal O'Hara: You never realize how the human voice can change until a woman quits scolding her husband and answers the phone.
—McNaught Syndicate

Arthur Godfrey: It always puzzles me to hear of professional women—are there any amateurs?

George Jean Nathan: Whenever a man encounters a woman in a mood he does not understand, he wants to know if she is tired.
—King Features Syndicate

Tulsa *World*: Most men need two women in their lives—a secretary to take everything down and a wife to pick everything up.

Jack Seaman: You can't kiss a girl unexpectedly—only sooner than she thought you would. —*The Saturday Evening Post*

Ralph E. Johnston: My wife says that when I take a notion to empty the ash trays I always convey the impression that I'm having to do most of the housework. —*Better Homes & Gardens*

Hy Sheridan: There are two kinds of women—one who wants to correct a man's mistakes and the other who wants to be one.
—*Aviation Week*

Helen Rowland: The hardest problem of a girl's life is to find out why a man seems bored if she doesn't respond to him and frightened if she does. —*Reflections of a Bachelor Girl* (McBride)

H. L. Mencken: In the duel of sex woman fights from a dreadnaught and man from an open raft.
—*A Mencken Chrestomathy* (Knopf)

Reason Enough

ASKED WHAT kind of woman his wife was, a Detroit man suing for divorce told the judge, "If you were to say to her that a lot of water went under the bridge since we first met, she'd say, 'What bridge?' " —Frances Rodman in New York *Times Magazine*

A DETACHMENT of Marines in Korea, writes Sergeant Frank Creasy, was engaged in the usual evening bull session, and the subject, also as usual, got around to the girls who had been left behind. Were they faithful or were they not?

"My girl's not doing any playing around," a blond young corporal from Hoboken announced with absolute conviction.

"How can you be so sure?" asked a friend.

"Well, for one thing," said the corporal, "she's got three more years to serve in reform school." —Bennett Cerf in *This Week Magazine*

AFTER HIS teacher told me that my fourth-grade son had saved one of his classmates from drowning at the school picnic, I asked him why he hadn't said anything about it. "Ah, gee, Ma," he stammered sheepishly, "I had to save him. I pushed him in."

—Mrs. C. Hammerly

IT WAS AN attractive coed's first big fraternity dance, and she and her mother were awaiting her escort. "Are you sure he's a good, safe driver?" the mother asked anxiously.

"Oh, yes, Mother," the girl quickly assured her. "He has to be. He can only have one more arrest before his driver's license is revoked!" —Margo Marks

A YOUNG GOB phoned his station and requested an extension of his pass, but was told to return immediately. "But I can't," he protested. "There are ten of us at this party, and we're having too much fun for me to break it up."

"How come your leaving the party will break it up?" snapped the petty officer at the station.

"Well, you see, Chief," said the gob, "nine of us are girls!"

—Maurice Peacock, Jr.

CARL C. LINDSAY of the General Services Bureau likes the story of the westerner who was celebrating his 100th birthday. Asked by reporters to what he attributed his longevity, he answered, "Remember the shooting of Pancho Veretto? Well, sir, I attribute my old age mostly to the fact that the police never did find out who killed Pancho."

—Bill Gold in Washington *Post and Times Herald*

THE MEMBERS of a crew on a submarine were about to take battle stations, and the ship's captain was worried about a young seaman second class whose job it was to close the water-tight doors between certain compartments. The boy didn't seem to realize his responsibility and the captain undertook to impress him.

He told him that if he failed in his job the ship might be lost, and it had cost around eight million dollars. Not only that, some of the men aboard were specialists and it cost Uncle Sam thousands to train each of them; these men might be drowned. "So you see how important it is that you do your job right. This very expensive ship, these important men—" the captain concluded.

"Yes, sir, and then there's me, too," replied the lad.

The captain stopped worrying. —Ruth Rossiter

AS PERSONNEL technician for a large government agency I was asked to find a stenographer for the engineering division. I picked a well-stacked blonde with a Marilyn Monroe walk and sent her along to the chief engineer for an interview.

The next day the girl's application came back to my desk—she didn't get the job. Affixed to it was this note: "She'd be dangerous to have around—too many moving parts." —Felix J. Cuervo

"HOW TO Get and Keep Better Teachers" was the problem under discussion by a group at a Texas State Conference on Education. When one delegate quietly remarked that there wasn't a shortage of teachers in his town—in fact they had a waiting list—the others began bombarding him with questions.

"Do you pay high salaries?"

"No, the state minimum."

"Do you offer lots of special privileges?"

"No."

Similar questions were equally unrewarding, and finally the delegate ended their suspense. "It could be," he drawled, "because our little town has 17 bachelor millionaires." —Fleta Burke

State of Superiority

AT A FILLING station in a small Texas town my husband and I were refreshing ourselves with a cold drink. "Everything looks very dry," I remarked to an elderly gentleman who sat dejectedly watching the cars go by.

"Yep."

"When did it rain last?"

" 'Bout three years ago, I reckon."

"That must be very hard on the ranchers around here," my husband said sympathetically.

The man slowly and sadly shook his head. "Don't know what's to become of us. We've spent thousands drilling for water, and what comes up? *Oil!*" —Helen Gillingham

A KENTUCKIAN was bragging about the wonders of his state to a Texan: "Why, we've got the most beautiful women in the world, and the finest horses, and the best pasture. And we've got so much gold at Fort Knox that we could build a gold wall four feet high and a foot thick all around the state of Texas."

"Well," said the Texan, "you go ahead and build it, and if I like it I'll buy it." —Duncan Emrich in *Holiday*

A TEXAN who saw Niagara Falls described it to a friend: "Man, the water was flowing like champagne!"

—Bob Downey, quoted by Earl Wilson, Hall Syndicate

HAVING RECEIVED a marriage proposal from a handsome Texan, a New York fashion model wanted to find out how wealthy he was. "I suppose you own a lot of oil wells," she said.

"Nope," said the Texan. "Not a one."

"You go in for cattle?"

The Texan shook his head.

"How much land do you have, then?" she persisted.

"About 35 acres, I reckon."

The model was plainly disappointed. "That's not much of a ranch," she said, "but what do you call it?"

"Well, ma'am," the Texan replied, "last time I saw it they called it downtown Dallas."

—Mac Laddon, quoted by Frank Rhoades in San Diego *Union*

IT WAS A little boy from Texas who marched up to Santa Claus and asked, "What can I do for you?"

—Gene Sherman in Los Angeles *Times*

WHEN A woman having dinner in a Dallas restaurant gave the waiter a $500 bill to pay for her check, the manager suggested, "See if she doesn't have something smaller."

"Yes, sir," said the waiter, "but I don't think she do, boss. She had to rummage around in her money to find this."

—Paul Crume in Dallas *Morning News*

WHEN *Quo Vadis* opened in a Texas town, the picture was advertised thus: "QUO VADIS (Where Y'All Goin'?)"

—Betty Hensler

TWO TEXAS oilmen walked into a Cadillac showroom in Dallas and one of them asked a salesman, "How much is that de luxe model?"

"Ten thousand dollars."

"I'll take it," the Texan said, and began to peel thousand-dollar notes from a bulky roll. His friend whipped out his wallet. "Oh, no you don't," he said. "After all, you bought *lunch!*"

—Peter Lind Hayes

ONE OF THE richest and most remarkable of all Texas oilmen was the late Everette Lee DeGolyer, who was raised in Oklahoma. Whenever he grew tired of pompous Texas talk he liked to tell the "true" history of the settling of Texas. The pioneers, he claimed, traveled westward via Tennessee and Arkansas to the Red River. There they saw a sign pointing northwest. "To Oklahoma," it said.

"And," DeGolyer would conclude, "those who could read turned off."

—Cleveland Amory in *Holiday*

Garden Digs

One of the nicest things about gardening is that if you put it off long enough it eventually is too late. —Bill Vaughan, Bell Syndicate

A WONDERFUL old lady, who is a proper Bostonian and a pillar of the North Shore Garden Club, told me this true story.

It seems the garden clubs went to Texas on a tour. All the gardens were in true Texas style, everything twice as big as life and as spectacular as color television.

One exhibitor had a group of azaleas so remarkable that my friend was overcome and asked the owner how she had managed to grow them to such a state of perfection. To which the Texan replied simply, "Mink manure."

And it was, too, because she had, among her other vast possessions, a mink farm.

—Avis DeVoto, quoted by Helen Ferril in Denver *Rocky Mountain Herald*

MAN OVER back fence to neighbor toiling in garden: "I had phenomenal luck with my garden this year—not a thing came up."

—Bill Yates cartoon in *The Saturday Evening Post*

THE BEST WAY to get real enjoyment out of a garden is to put on a wide straw hat, dress in thin, loose-fitting clothes, hold a trowel in one hand and a cool drink in the other and tell the man where to dig.

—Charles Barr, quoted by Frances Rodman in New York *Times Magazine*

A FARMER who sent for a book, *How to Grow Tomatoes,* wrote the publisher: "The man who writ the ad shoulda writ the book."

—*The Mining Journal*

NOTE IN A Surrey, England, seedsman's catalogue: "If your neighbor has a flower he is very proud of, let us know and we will supply seeds of one larger or in an entirely new color. We specialize in this work."

—Wallace Reyburn in Toronto *Telegram*

BUYING SOME plants at a local nursery my sister-in-law consulted the nurseryman about a particular spot where nothing seemed to grow. "What do you suggest," she asked, "for a spot that gets very little rain because of overhanging eaves, that has too much hot afternoon sun, that has clay soil and that's on a rocky ledge?"

"Lady," he said, "how about a nice flagpole?"

—Ethel E. Jackson

A PARK AVENUE matron was being complimented on the magnificent cactus display in her apartment window.

"They do well because we take care of them according to nature's plan," she explained. "The important thing is to water them at exactly the right intervals. These plants are from western Texas, and when my husband brought them home we subscribed to a Texas newspaper. We always read it carefully and when the paper says it has just rained in west Texas"—she smiled happily—"*that's* when we water the cactus."

—Dora Davis

When Ladies Meet

FROM THE Van Wert, Ohio, *Times-Bulletin:* "The Garden Study Club will meet Thursday. The study topic, 'My Potted Friends,' will be given by Mrs. Gene Kintz."

FROM THE Marshfield, Mo., *Mail:* "The Women's Birthday Club met to help celebrate Mrs. Eliza Beach's birthday. As the club had been organized a year and practically all members had had birthdays this past year and there would be too few having birthdays the next few years, it was decided to discontinue the club." —Quoted by Dale Freeman in Springfield, Mo., *News and Leader*

FROM THE Drexel, Mo., *Star:* "The Sunny Hour Club met at the home of Mrs. Florence Long. The meeting was called to order by the reading of the 23rd Psalm and roll call was answered by Septic Tank Problems."

FROM AN account of a women's club meeting in the Yerington, Nev., *Mason Valley News:* "Josephine Farias, who spoke on 'Nature,' narrowed her topic down to astronomy, biology, geology, heavenly bodies, living things and earth formations. It was a very informative speech and enjoyed by all."

FROM THE society page of the Clifton Forge, Va., *Daily Review:* "A surprise pink and blue shower was given to Mrs. F. L. Jones Thursday evening. After Mrs. Jones opened the gifts, the big surprise came when she told those present she was not expecting."

FROM THE Bedford, England, *Bedfordshire Times and Standard:* "At the Pleasant Wednesday Afternoon meeting held in the

Congregational Church schoolroom, Miss E. Boucher recited her poem of 206 verses, entitled 'Mother's Last Words.' "

—Quoted by Minneapolis *Tribune*

FROM THE Tuscola, Ill., *Review:* "The Home Bureau held its annual picnic last Thursday. No program was planned so the group talked about members who were not present."

Malice With Forethought

THE RAF PILOT'S decorations demonstrated his courage. But, though he was invaluable as a fighter, as a person he was quite obnoxious. When he was transferred to another post, his new commander received this report: "Splendid officer at 6000 feet. Should never come any lower."

—P. V. Russel

FROM A will: "And to my Communist nephew, Oswald, I leave the sum of 10,000 pounds—to be shared equally with his fellow Britishers."

—John Carpenter

A SCOTSMAN about to leave India was asked by his highly unsatisfactory manservant for a letter of recommendation. He pondered a moment, then wrote: "To Whom It May Concern. The bearer of this note, Raju Ram, has served me during the last two years to his complete satisfaction. If you are thinking of giving him a berth, be sure to make it a wide one."

—Clifford A. Scotton

AN EMPLOYMENT office was checking on an applicant's list of references. "How long did this man work for you?" a former employer was asked.

"About four hours," was the quick reply.

"Why, he told us he'd been there a long time," said the astonished caller.

"Oh, yes," answered the ex-employer, "he's been here two years."

—*The Wall Street Journal*

Easy Does It

As a gardener who was shared by several neighbors passed her house, Miss Susie called to him to come in and finish a job he had begun for her.

"No'm, Miss Susie, I can't come today."

"Why not?"

"Well, Miss Susie, Miss Lucy paid me a dollar she owed me and I ain't spent it. And Mr. Jones, he give me a check for two dollars and I got it right here in my pocket. And I jus' don't believe in oversupporting myself." —Mrs. Sam Cox

One of my associates, a young lawyer, had been watching the construction of a building across the street. Suddenly he turned to me. "See that fellow over there, Art? I've been watching that loafer for the last two hours and he hasn't done a stroke of work."

—*City Lawyer,* © 1942 by Arthur Garfield Hays and published by Simon and Schuster

Our ten-year-old was going on his first real visit away from home, and I wanted to be sure we'd hear from him. So I addressed a postal for each day that he would be gone and told him, "All you need to do is write 'O.K., Marvin.' "

"All right," said Marvin. "But you put the O.K. on—and if I'm not, I'll scratch it out." —Mary E. Cornette

I had moved into a backwoods community in Arkansas and, because I was considered an outsider, I tried to avoid doing anything to offend.

When my tool house was finished I added a bright new lock to it. Next morning a neighbor came over, and then several more strolled in. After quite a bit of polite talk one of them said, "Mr. Hicks, we are sorry you don't trust us."

"Of course I do," I replied. "What makes you say that?"

"You keep your tool house locked. Don't you know that nobody in Arkansas never stole nothing to work with?" —C. E. Hicks

DURING THE 1957 World Series a writer asked the Milwaukee Braves' Bob Buhl what he was going to do after it was over. "I'm going to Saginaw to help my father," said Buhl.

"And what does he do?"

"Nothing," replied Buhl. —Bob Cooke in New York *Herald Tribune*

A GROUP OF Cub Scouts were talking over plans for a hike. The leader suggested meeting at ten in the morning because it was about a two-hour hike to the destination. One of the boys, a newcomer, paled visibly. "You mean we're going to *walk?*" he asked.

—Pleasantville, N. Y., *Townsman*

A SUMMER visitor at a Maine fishing village went down to the wharf to buy some lobsters. The dealer sat on an upturned bait barrel mending a lobster trap. During their conversation the visitor asked what he did in winter.

"Well," said the lobsterman, "I paint my boat, mend her if she needs it, fix up my lobsterin' gear, maybe chop a little wood. Rest of the time I mostly bottom chairs."

"You *do?* You're just the man I'm looking for! I have three chairs that need repairing. Would you come over to the cottage and—"

"Hold on a mite, ma'am!" the old fellow interrupted. "I wasn't talkin' about *mendin'* chairs—don't know a thing about it. I meant I just *set*." —Mary E. Johnston

A CITY BANKER who had spent his youth on a farm persuaded an old neighbor to take on his son for the summer. When the father called to ask how the boy was making out, the farmer declared, "I ain't the one to bandy words with you. If that boy of yours had one more hand, he'd need a third pocket to put it in."

—Bennett Cerf

Added Attractions

AD IN the Oak Ridge, Tenn., *Oak Ridger:* "Lawn mower, push type. Used very little and, when used, pushed very slow."

A DETROIT theater reviving Douglas Fairbanks, Sr.'s, 25-year-old silent film, *The Man in the Iron Mask,* ran this advertisement: "No reason to stay home. There is none older on television."
—UP

AD IN Springfield *Illinois State Register:* "WANTED. A secretary who—looks like a girl—thinks like a man—acts like a lady—and works like a dog."

THIS AD IN the Princeton, N. J., *Town Topics* caused much speculation: "ATTENTION UNDERGRADS —Handsome Princeton Alumnus wishes to go with the girls again, in excellent shape, have all my hair, large size. Best offer takes me."

It turned out that a raccoon coat was being offered.

FROM *Your Weekly Guide to Boston:* "Widow with two spoiled children taking auto trip to West Coast. Wants someone to accompany her to share expenses. If you long for children of your own or a trip to the Coast—here is your chance to get over it."

PERSONAL IN *The Saturday Review:* "Male, old enough to know better, wishes correspondence with female not quite that old."

AD IN Salinas *Californian:* "For your NEW YEAR'S EVE PARTY it's Gallatin's of course! Halfway between the Hospital and the Jail, Monterey, Calif."

AD IN the Long Beach, Calif., *Tri-Shopper:* "JOINTER-PLANE—used once to cut off thumb. Will sell cheap."

AD IN Rome, N. Y., *Daily Sentinel:* "PIANO MOVING. If you have a piano to move, take advantage of our expert service and careful handling. Kindling wood for sale."

AD IN *Trade-A-Plane Service:* "Your choice, 1941 Piper J-5 three-place, $600, or 1919 model full-blooded Norwegian wife, very hot tempered, $6,000,000. Can't keep both."

"Want the Wig?"

Condensed from The Rotarian

J. P. McEvoy

YEARS AGO out in Hollywood they were shooting a swashbuckling costume movie. The hero had to do a douglasfairbanks from the castle wall, grab a rope, swing out over the moat and land on a flight of stone steps. Too dangerous for the star to attempt, so the top stunt man in Hollywood was called in. He measured the distances, calculated his chances of survival and told the director, "No dice." The director sneered, "Scared, eh?" The stunt man said, "No—just careful," and then went on to explain that anybody who tried this stunt would find when he swung over the stone steps he'd be a good 25 feet up in the air, and when he let go and landed he'd break his neck.

The director was a hairy-chested graduate of the rough, tough old silent-movie school. "Okay, sucker," he said. "You're just yellow. *Give me the wig,* and I'll do it myself!"

He got into costume, hollered to the cameraman, *"Get* this!," leaped off the wall, swung out over the moat and let go. When he landed he broke his back, both legs, and was in the hospital for six months.

Now when I find myself offering my wife some mighty sensible advice about running the house or raising the children, instead of a snappy "Mind your own business!" she merely purrs, "Want the wig?"—and I get going right out of there. On the other hand, when she starts that wifely back-seat driving, whether I'm running the car or answering the phone, or doing any of the things which a man does better, I just smirk tolerantly, "Want the wig?" Wonderful to relate, it cools her off.

There are two kinds of people in the world: the aggravating kind who get up early in the morning and fade out early in the evening, and the others who just can't wake up until late afternoon and then can't be dragged off to bed before the following dawn. These two have a fatal attraction for each other. Early-rising husbands marry late-rising wives, and vice versa. Result: about 11 o'clock in the evening the one who got up

The Rotarian (January, '48), © 1947 by Rotary International, 1600 Ridge Ave., Evanston, Ill.

early is falling on his face, while the other is going strong and wants to stay up all night.

Often such a couple will find themselves trapped with friends around midnight—friends who believe they are that ideal man and wife, perfectly mated and adjusted. How can the Weary One signal the Cheery One that he has a long day tomorrow and wants to get the hell home?

"Has the balloon gone up?" is publisher Richard Simon's code for resolving this perpetual problem, meaning, "We're going home—and no fooling." It is the tag of an old chestnut about a farmer who took his grandson to the county fair. The old man couldn't see very well and constantly pestered the boy with, "Has the balloon gone up?" "No," said the boy, and "No" again a dozen times. Finally, collapsing with fatigue and boredom, the old man croaked, "Has the balloon gone up?" and the lad said, "Yes." The old man straightened up with a sigh of relief and said, "Good! Let's go home!"

Mrs. Arthur Garfield Hays had a maid who was an old sourpuss. One morning Hays said to his wife, "If only that maid would smile—just once!" And in she came, as if on cue, with a smile from ear to ear, and greeted them with, "Guess what we have for breakfast—no coffee!" Ever since then the Hayses use this when faced with situations that defy solution. And I might add, as do the McEvoys, who know a good thing when they seize it.

"Pay the two dollars" has saved us many a headache, heartache—and bankache. It's an old stage classic played for years by the Howard Brothers. Willie was the little fellow who was riding on the subway with his lawyer. The little fellow spit on the floor, and was immediately arrested. The police magistrate said, "The fine is two dollars." The lawyer retorted, "This is an outrage! My client won't pay it." "He'll pay it or go to jail," said the magistrate. The little fellow pleaded with his lawyer, "Pay the two dollars!" "No!" said the lawyer. "This is a matter of principle." So they hauled the little fellow off to jail.

The following day the lawyer said, "I've asked for a jury trial. The case comes up in three months. We'll show 'em. Meanwhile I should have a $500 retainer." The little fellow clung to the bars of his cell and bleated, "Pay the two dollars!" But the lawyer was a man of character.

The trial came up and the little fellow lost. On the way home in the subway the lawyer said, "It's true we didn't win, but we gave them a fight."

"So what happened?" said the little fellow. "In the end I had to pay the two dollars. But before you let me do it I was in jail for months—I lost my business—my wife left me—you got all my money. Fine lawyer you are. Phooey!" And with that the little fellow spat in derision on the floor. Instantly a heavy hand fell on his shoulder and the Voice of the Law boomed, "Come with me. That will cost you two dollars!"

"Don't pay it!" cried the lawyer majestically. "We'll fight it!" Once more the little fellow was dragged off to jail, wailing piteously, *"Pay the two dollars!"*

Probably all of us have been victimized at some time by greedy tradesmen or workmen. But peace of mind, we've found, is better than giving them "a piece of our mind." So our motto is: "Pay the two dollars."

Many married couples have learned that a joke can be the shortest distance between two points of view. "Want the wig?" stops me cold when I go into a smug-husband routine—or puts my wife in her place without the danger of sitting her down so hard she will bounce right back at me.

But maybe *you* have some better ones?

Marriage Counselors

When one thinks how many people there are that one does not in the least want to marry, and how many there are that do not in the least want to marry one, and how small one's social circle really is, any marriage at all seems a miracle. —Barry Pain, quoted in *McCall's*

ON HIS 50th wedding anniversary an old gentleman gave his recipe for marital happiness: "I've always tried to treat Ma in such a fashion that if I died it would take more than a hot water bottle to replace me."

—*Industrial News Review*, quoted in Altoona, Pa., *Mirror*

"HOW COME you never married?" I once asked our middle-aged hired man. "A woman won't bite you."

"No," he retorted, "but they kin sure gnaw." —John Bobula

NOT LONG after Mr. and Mrs. Blank's only daughter and her family had moved to a distant state, their only son left for the Army. As he drove away Mrs. Blank turned to her husband and said tearfully, "You are all I have left now."

"Darling," he replied consolingly, "I'm all you had to start with."

AGATHA CHRISTIE, the detective-story writer, lives most of the time in Bagdad, where her archeologist husband is working on important excavations. "An archeologist," she says with conviction, "is the best husband any woman can have. The older she gets, the more he is interested in her."

—*Gothenburg Trade and Shipping Journal,* quoted by Alec de Montmorency, NANA

YOU NEED a background of at least ten years of happy marriage before you can laugh at the story of the couple who, on their golden-wedding anniversary, were interviewed by a reporter. "And tell me," he asked, pencil poised, "in all this time together, did you ever consider divorce?"

"Oh, no, not divorce," the little old lady said, "but sometimes"—she paused and winked at her husband—"murder!"

—Helen Papashvily in *Good Housekeeping*

STOPPING TO chat with an old friend while shopping one day, I was astonished to note from the labels of the boxes he carried that he had bought flowers, perfume and lingerie. "Whatever are you buying such things for?" I asked impulsively. Then, horrified at myself, I started to babble apologies.

"It's all right," he said smiling. "Some men when they get to middle age start looking for greener pastures, but I . . . well, I thought I'd just fertilize the one I have." —Mrs. M. E. Jensen

A REAL-ESTATE agent was showing an old farmhouse to a woman prospect who made a few sketches on a pad and admitted, "I could do a lot with that house." But then she added wistfully, "On the other hand, I believe I said the same thing the first time I looked at my husband."

—Bennett Cerf in *This Week Magazine*

THE IDEAL wife is one who knows when her husband wants to be forced to do something against his will.

—Sydney J. Harris, General Features

THE TROUBLE with a lot of marriages is that the husband is so busy bringing home the bacon that he forgets the applesauce.

—Dan Bennett

ON THE tombstone of her husband's grave a southern mountain woman chiseled in rough and uneven letters this epitaph: "He always appreciated."

—Albert Edward Wiggam, *New Techniques of Happiness* (Funk)

Earmarked

THE WOMEN at the next table were deep in a discussion on food when one asked, "What is the opposite of 'gourmet'?"

Replied another, "Anybody who's had to live with one for years." —Eleanor Clarage in Cleveland *Plain Dealer*

WIFE SETTING out with husband: "Now if it's a dull party, just leave it that way." —Quin Ryan in Chicago *Tribune*

WOMAN TO friend: "The worst thing about living in a trailer is that there's no place to put anything except where it belongs." —Nancy Barnhisel

DELEGATE AT the closing session of an Oregon PTA convention: "The thing that gave me the greatest impression during this convention was the folding chairs." —Mrs. John Alto

OVERHEARD IN the lobby of a Johannesburg hotel: "My wife is an hour late. She's either been kidnaped, hit by a motorcar or she's shopping. I hope she hasn't been shopping." —Johannesburg *Sunday Times*

WOMAN ON bus to seatmate: "They're starting out with just what they have to have—bed, stove and television set." —Clyde Moore in Columbus *Ohio State Journal*

OVERHEARD IN Chicago's Pump Room: "Some people grow old gracefully. But *you*, you've got to *samba!*" —E. E. Kenyon in *The American Weekly*

OVERHEARD IN Washington, D. C.: "I'm getting so accustomed to being tense that when I'm calm I get nervous." —Bill Gold in Washington *Post*

FATHER'S comment: "I just want to live long enough to be as much of a nuisance to my children as they have been to me." —Walter Davenport in *Collier's*

Parents vs. Children

WOMAN looking at child-care books to clerk: "Don't you have any that stick up for the parents?"

—Franklin Folger cartoon, Chicago Sun-Times Syndicate

SMALL BOY to librarian: "Do you have anything on the parent from 30 to 35?"

—J. Monahan cartoon in *Family Circle*

A YOUNG mother of four confessed: "When I had my first baby I phoned the doctor every time he sneezed. My youngest swallowed a nickel the other day. I just looked at him and said, 'Young man, that money comes out of your allowance!' "

—Laura Bergquist in *Look*

A CHILD's comment on piggy banks: "They teach children to become misers, and parents to become bank robbers."

—*The Wall Street Journal*

BOSS TO secretary: "I've got to call up my wife. Send my daughter a telegram to get off the phone."

—Kirk Stiles cartoon in *Collier's*

ASTOUNDED teen-ager at the telephone: "Of all the crazy things! It's for *you,* Father!"

—d'Alessio cartoon, Publishers Syndicate

FATHER spanking small son with hairbrush to mother: "I'm going through a phase myself."

—Goldstein cartoon in *Ladies' Home Journal*

A YOUNGSTER being called down for a poor report card asked: "What do you think the trouble with me is, Dad—heredity or environment?" —H. J. Ohms

MAN IS probably the only animal which even attempts to have anything to do with his half-grown young. —George Ross Wells, *The Art of Being a Person* (Appleton-Century-Crofts)

CHILD ABOUT school play: "We're going to have real people there—not just mothers and fathers." —Sidney Skolsky in *Quick*

ON MY LIST of New Year's resolutions was: "Be more patient with my daughter, Janet. No matter how irritating she is, remember that, after all, she is only 15 and is going through the exasperating period of adolescence."

Imagine then my feeling when, quite by accident, I came across Janet's New Year's resolutions and saw at the head of her list: "Try and be more patient with Mother." —Mrs. C. R. Knowles

Pot Luck

ON AN NBC program Sam Levenson told one of his favorite stories:

My mother was of the old school, and she always had a hot pot on the stove with chicken legs in case unexpected company came in. We never had a whole chicken, but chicken legs by the million. Then one night Uncle Louis and Aunt Lena and 11 kids suddenly dropped in. Now here's the problem. Mama is always ready. Her prestige, her honor is at stake, because she's always been able to feed anybody who comes in. But now she hasn't got enough to go around.

She calls us children into the bedroom and says, "Children, do me a favor. Say you don't like chicken."

Well, what can you do? We understood. All right, so we don't like chicken. So we went in, and we ate, and of course the relatives offered to share their chicken. We said, "No, we don't like chicken."

And I sit there watching the invaders eating my food. So we go through this. Then we get around to the dessert. Mama turns to all her kids. "Now," she says, "all the children who refused the chicken don't get any dessert!"

Grand Finale

A potpourri of all-time favorites from the Digest pages which might now be termed "classics."

A FRIEND of mine with three children in college was badly upset when her physician told her she was going to have another child. "I simply can't go through it again, Doctor!" she wailed.

"Did you have complications with your other pregnancies?" he asked sympathetically.

"Heavens, no! Having babies never bothered me a bit, physically. It's the PTA that gets me down!" —Marie Hamel

A YOUNG Cleveland matron stalled her car at a traffic light one winter day. She stamped on the starter, tried again, choked her engine, while behind her an impatient citizen honked his horn steadily. Finally she got out and walked back. "I'm awfully sorry, but I don't seem to be able to start my car," she told the driver of the other car. "If you'll go up there and start it for me, I'll stay here and lean on your horn." —Harriet L. Clark

ONE DAY my elderly and unmarried aunt told me that her Pomeranian dog Peggy had been behaving most peculiarly. As I was a medical student at the time, she expected me to examine her pet and prescribe treatment. With some embarrassment I explained that it was spring, that animals—well, that Peggy needed a mate. Aunt Fanny ordered me to find Peggy a suitable one immediately.

After locating a fine Pomeranian at a nearby kennel, I described the dog to my aunt: its long pedigree, good coloring, record of healthy litters, all its fine qualifications. The fee, I added, would be $25.

Aunt Fanny told me to attend to the matter right away. Before starting off with Peggy I explained that the kennel owner would probably require his fee in advance, and since I was broke asked her to give me the $25. Aunt Fanny was obviously startled. "Do you mean *Peggy* has to pay?" she gasped. —Capt. H. L. Finsten

A FARMER hired a hand and set him to chopping wood. In the middle of the morning the farmer went down to see how the hand was coming along. To his astonishment he found the wood all chopped. Next day the farmer told the man to stack the wood in the shed. This involved a lot of toting and the farmer figured the job would keep the man busy. But by noon he had it done.

On the third day the farmer, thinking he'd give the man a light job for a change, told him to sort out the potatoes in the bin. "Put the good ones in one pile, the doubtful in another and throw out the rotten ones," said the farmer.

An hour or so later he went back to see how the job was coming. He found the hired man passed out cold, with virtually nothing done. After throwing water in the man's face and bringing him around, the farmer demanded an explanation.

"Hell," the man said wearily, "it's making them decisions that's killing me."

GUESTS IN a Cairo hotel, hearing a scream in the corridor, discovered a damsel in negligee being pursued by a gentleman who was, to put it bluntly, nude. Later it developed that the impetuous Romeo was an English major, who was promptly court-martialed. His lawyer won him an acquittal, however, by virtue of the following paragraph in the army manual: "It is not compulsory for an officer to wear a uniform at all times, as long as he is suitably garbed for the sport in which he is engaged."

—Mabel Dana Lyon, quoted by Bennett Cerf in *The Saturday Review*

THEN 80, and a member of an old Boston family, she still lived on Beacon Hill and carried on the family traditions. She was entertaining a guest from the Middle West to whom she presented her small but select circle of friends. Shortly before leaving, the guest remarked, "Emily, your friends are wonderful women, but tell me, where *do* they get their hats?"

"Oh, my dear," the Bostonian said with pained surprise, "we don't *get* our hats. We *have* our hats." —Mrs. Paul W. Alexander

AT A WEDDING not long after World War II the groom, only recently back from overseas, had hardly glimpsed his bride before the ceremony. Therefore when time came for the kiss it was a long one, lasting on and on until a child's voice rang out in the silence of the church:

"Mummy, is he spreading the pollen on her now?"

—E. P. Goodnow

LITTLE CLAUDE's mother had reluctantly allowed her precious child to attend public school. She gave the teacher a long list of instructions. "My Claude is so sensitive," she explained. "Don't ever punish him. Just slap the boy next to him. That will frighten Claude." —Philadelphia *Bulletin*

A GI RETURNED to camp exhausted after a weekend of wine, women and song. On the bunk that held his recumbent form, his buddies hung a sign: "Temporarily Out of Ardor."

—James T. Shaw

WE ONCE had a very capable Negro woman working for us. Her husband, however, was a happy-go-lucky fellow who, although very likable, never seemed able to keep a job and seldom bothered to try. One day I asked her why she put up with him. Without hesitating she said, "It's like this, Mis'. I makes de livin' and he makes de livin' worth while." —Alvada Pope

I HAD BEEN sitting in the doctor's waiting room a long time. Every chair was filled and some patients were standing. There was desultory conversation, but after a while a silence fell and we sat waiting—waiting—waiting. Finally an old man stood up wearily and remarked, "Well, guess I'll go home and die a natural death." —Mrs. Paul B. Davis

IN THE DAZZLING white armor of Lohengrin, Lauritz Melchior once sang his sad farewell to Elsa, moving step by step with the surging music toward the swan boat which would carry him away. But something happened off stage, and the mechanics pulled the swan into the wings before Melchior could step into it. Finishing his song, in a *sotto voce* plainly audible in the fifth row he asked, "What time does the next swan leave?"

—Mona Gardner in *The Saturday Evening Post*

RUDOLPH HAD heard a great deal about his little cousin Peter, but had never met him. So when he learned Peter was coming for a visit the youngster was overjoyed. But when his cousin arrived, he took one look at him and burst into tears. "I thought," he wailed, "that Peter was a rabbit!"

—Mary C. Thomson in *Today's Woman*

A YOUNG LADY with a touch of hay fever took with her to a dinner party two handkerchiefs, one of which she stuck in her bosom. At dinner she began rummaging to right and left in her bosom for the fresh handkerchief. Engrossed in her search she suddenly realized that conversation had ceased and people were watching her, fascinated.

In her confusion she murmured, "I *know* I had two when I came."

—John Erskine

UPON THEIR return from Europe a movie producer and his wife were telling about a painting of Adam and Eve and the serpent they saw in the Louvre. "You see," gushed the lady, "we found it especially interesting because we knew the anecdote!"

—Irving Hoffman in *The Hollywood Reporter*

Index

A Subject-matter Guide to Groups
(Italicized page numbers indicate single stories within other groups related to the subject)

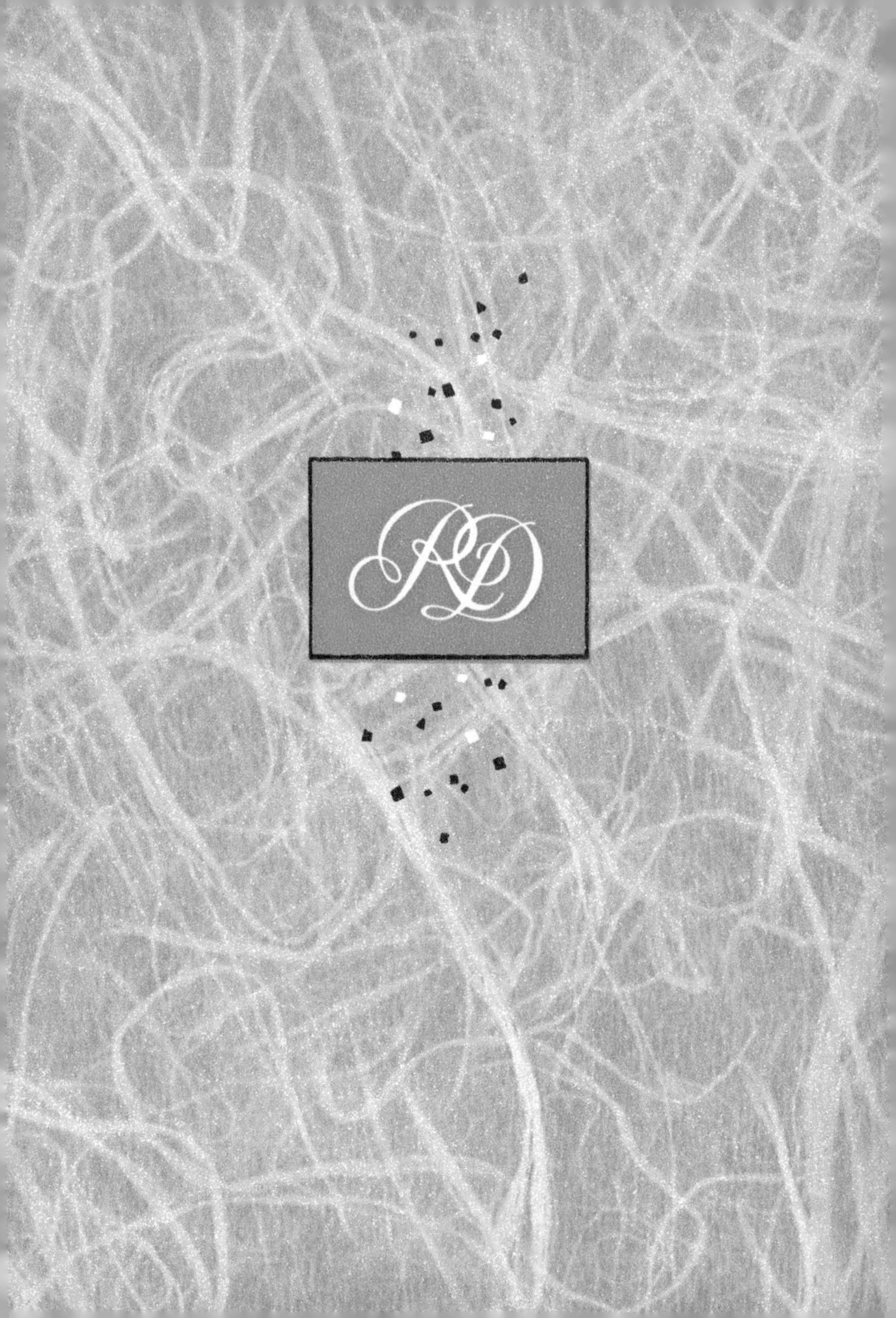